The Treaty of Nice

Designed to succeed previous books on the Maastricht and Amsterdam treaties, this new work includes contributions from leading EU lawyers assessing the Nice Treaty and the Post-Nice process, which is rapidly developing in the lead-up to the next Intergovernmental conference. The book's central theme is the discussion of a European Constitution and European Constitutionalism. The new constitutional balance after institutional reform, the Luxembourg courts after Nice, the future of the three-pillar Treaty structure and the Human Rights charter are the other main topics.

THE TREATY
OF NICE AND BEYOND

Enlargement and Constitutional Reform

EDITED BY
MADS ANDENAS

Director, British Institute of International and Comparative
Law, London; Senior Teaching Fellow, Institute of European
and Comparative Law, University of Oxford

and

JOHN A USHER

Salvesen Professor of European Institutions and Director of
the Europa Institute, University of Edinburgh

·HART·
PUBLISHING

HART PUBLISHING
OXFORD AND PORTLAND, OREGON
2003

Published in North America (US and Canada) by
Hart Publishing
c/o International Specialized Book Services
5804 NE Hassalo Street
Portland, Oregon
97213-3644
USA

Hart Publishing is a specialist legal publisher based in Oxford, England.
To order further copies of this book or to request a list of other
publications please write to:

Hart Publishing, Salters Boatyard, Folly Bridge, Abingdon Rd, Oxford,
OX1 4LB Telephone: +44 (0)1865 245533 Fax: +44 (0) 1865 794882
email: mail@hartpub.co.uk
WEBSITE: http//:www.hartpub.co.uk

British Library Cataloguing in Publication Data
Data Available

ISBN 1-84113-339-6 (hardback)

Typeset by Olympus Infotech, India, in Sabon 10/12 pt.
Printed and bound in Great Britain by
MPG Books Ltd, Bodmin, Cornwall (www.mpg-books.com)

Preface

This edited collection explores legal issues raised by the Treaty of Nice, enlargement of the Union and the constitutional reform process leading up to the Intergovernmental Conference in 2004. Most of the papers have been presented at different seminars and conferences at the British Institute of International and Comparative Law in London. A number of them were presented at two events organised with the Europa Institute of the University of Edinburgh, the first on the Treaty of Nice (in 2001), and the second on the Constitutional Convention (in 2002). The cooperation between the two institutes has been very fruitful and we hope it can continue and develop over the years. A major contribution to the different events has also been made by the Institute of European and Comparative Law, University of Oxford and its members. Other institutions involved in the cooperation with the British Institute and the Europa Institute reflected in this book include the UK Association of European Law (UKAEL) and the International Federation of European Law (FIDE). Chapter 1 is based on Peter Oliver's report at the XX FIDE Congress, and Chapter 2 on the report by Jacqueline Dutheil de la Rochère and Ingolf Pernice to this Congress which was organised at the British Institute in October and November 2002. Chapter 3 is based on a paper that Professor Di Fabio, a judge of the German Constitutional Court, delivered at the London-Leiden Meeting in June 2002, and is one outcome of a more than forty years old cooperation between the British Institute and the University of Leiden.

The book falls in four parts. The first, Chapters 1 to 5, is concerned with issues relating to the constitutional reform process and the European Convention on the future of the Union. One recurring theme in this part is the relationships between national constitutions and European Union Law. Part II, Chapters 6 to 10, focuses on the Nice Treaty. The way is now open for Treaty ratification after the positive outcome of the popular referendum in the Republic of Ireland. In Part III, Chapters 11 to 14 dealing with the European Courts are placed together. Finally Part IV, the three final chapters, provides different perspectives on the EU Human Rights Charter.

Mads Andenas
London

John Usher
Edinburgh

Contents

Part III—The European Courts

Part IV—The Human Rights Charter

Part I

The European Constitution

1

The Convention on the Future of Europe: the Issues and Prospects

PETER OLIVER*

L'Europe ne se fera pas d'un coup, ni dans une construction d'ensemble: elle se fera par des réalisations concrètes créant d'abord une solidarité de fait.
Schuman Declaration 9 May 1950

Es stellte sich ... als richtig heraus, 'pragmatisch' vorzugehen.... Wir mußten das große Ziel lebendig halten. Zugleich aber setzten wir uns begrenzte, konkrete Ziele, die unmittelbar einleuchteten.
Walter Hallstein, *Der unvollendete Bundestaat* (1969) 249

I. INTRODUCTION

A. General

AT THE PRESENT juncture, an attempt to describe proposals for reform of the European Union must be regarded as an uncertain venture. The work of the European Convention on the future of the Union ('the Convention') is still under way and will not be completed for several months. Meanwhile, a question mark hangs over the future of the Treaty of Nice: following its rejection by the people of Ireland in a referendum in June 2001, a fresh referendum is due to be held in October 2002; and the opinion polls by no means predict a clear outcome.[1] Third, negotiations for further enlargement of the Union, which is a key factor in

---

* Legal Adviser, European Commission. This article was completed in September 2002. First and foremost, the author wishes to thank his wife, Philippa Watson, for her help and support. His thanks also go to Andrew Duff MEP, Clemens Ladenburger, Charles Reich, Dimitris Triantafyllou, Pieter van Nuffel and Alain van Solinge for giving up their valuable time to assist him. However, the views expressed in this article, which was presented as the Community Report to Topic 1 *EU Law and National Constitutions* at the 2002 FIDE Congress, remains the responsibility of the author acting in a wholly personal capacity.
[1] In the event, and before this book went to press, the referendum went in favour of ratification of the Treaty. The Treaty (2002 OJ C325/1) came into force on 1 February 2003.

its reform, are still under way. The European Council meeting in Seville on 21 and 22 June 2002 re-affirmed its determination to conclude the negotiations with ten candidate countries by the end of 2002, provided that the present rate of progress in the negotiations is maintained and that those countries are ready; and it indicated that in that event the Treaty of Accession will be signed in the spring of 2003.[2] Many significant developments can therefore be expected to occur in the immediate future.

In a short article such as this, it is plainly quite impossible to cover exhaustively all the aspects of reform of the Treaties currently under consideration, let alone all the proposals and ideas in circulation. Of necessity, therefore, this article will focus primarily on the work which has been undertaken so far within the Convention.

First of all, the Treaty of Nice will be briefly considered. Next, Part II will set out developments on the reform of the Treaties, beginning with the Laeken Declaration of December 2001. While Part II is concerned exclusively with proposals for reform, Parts III and IV will examine in greater depth two important areas, both from the point of view of current law and with an eye to reform: fundamental rights, and the role of the regions. Finally, Part V contains a succinct conclusion.

B.   The Treaty of Nice

The Treaty of Nice[3] was signed on 26 February 2001. On 7 June 2001, the people of Ireland rejected that Treaty in a referendum. No other Member State held a referendum on the issue. Virtually all the others have now formally lodged their instruments of ratification.[4] As already mentioned, a further referendum is expected to be held in Ireland in October 2002.[5] According to Article 48 of the Treaty of European Union ('TEU'), amendments to the Treaties can only enter into force after 'being ratified by all the Member States in accordance with their respective constitutional requirements'.

Together with its various protocols, the Treaty of Nice is designed to effect a number of major changes to the European institutions[6]. While many

---

[2] In the event, the Accession Treaty was signed on 16 April 2003 in Athens; it is set to come into force on 1 May 2004. See also the Commission's website on enlargement: http://europa.eu.int/comm/enlargement, in particular the scoreboard and the document entitled 'Enlargement of the European Union: Guide to the Negotiations Chapter by Chapter'.
[3] 2001 OJ C80/1.
[4] http://europa.eu.int/comm/nice_treaty/ratiftable_en.pdf.
[5] See note 1 above.
[6] A summary of its provisions is to be found in Commission document SEC(2001)99. See also K Bradley 'Institutional Design in the Treaty of Nice' 2001 *Common Market Law Review* 1095, A Dashwood 'The Constitution of the European Union after the Treaty of Nice' 2001 *European Law Review* 215, F Dehousse 'Le traité de Nice : un tournant fondamental dans l'histoire de l'intégration européenne' 2001 *Journal des tribunaux* 409, J-M Favret 'Le traité de Nice du 26 février 2001 : vers un affaiblissement irréversible de la capacité d'action de l'Union européenne?'

of these changes are linked to the prospect of further enlargement of the Union, others are not.[7] For instance, the provisions on the Court of Justice are to be amended with a view to the adoption of the proposed Regulation on the Community patent.[8]

In the unfortunate event of that Treaty being rejected a second time by the Irish people, its provisions could be incorporated into the next round of reform currently being considered by the Convention, in so far as they are still relevant.[9] Alternatively, it is sometimes suggested that those provisions of the Treaty of Nice which relate to enlargement might be incorporated into the Act of Accession with the candidate countries to be concluded pursuant to Article 49 TEU. At all events, the Union institutions and the Convention itself are continuing to work on the optimistic assumption that the outcome of the second Irish referendum will be positive, and this article is based on the same hypothesis.

II.   THE CONVENTION

A.   The Plan of this Part

This part of the article is divided up as follows: sections B and C deal with the background to the establishment of the Convention; section D very briefly describes the Convention's work so far; sections E and F cover the positions of the European Parliament and the Commission respectively; sections G to K concern certain pivotal themes; and section L considers the work of the first six working groups.

2001 *Revue trimestrielle de droit européen* 343, Fischer 'Der Vertrag von Nizza' 2001, D Galloway 'The Treaty of Nice and Beyond: Realities and Illusions of Power in the EU' (Sheffield Academic Press, 2001), A Johnston 'Judicial Reform and the Treaty of Nice' 2001 *Common Market Law Review* 499, J-V Louis 'Le traité de Nice' 2001 *Journal des Tribunaux droit européen* 25, Pieter van Nuffel 'Le traité de Nice : un commentaire' 2001 RDUE 11, S van Raepenbusch 'Le traité de Nice: entre espoirs et déceptions' 2001 Actualités du Droit 77, Advocate General D Ruiz-Jarabo 'La réforme de la Cour de justice opérée par le traité de Nice et sa mise en oeuvre future' 2001 *Revue trimestrielle de droit européen* 705, J Temple Lang 'How Much Do the Smaller Member States Need the European Commission? The Role of the Commission in a Changing Europe' 2002 *Common Market Law Review* 315, J Wouters 'Institutional and Constitutional Challenges for the European Union – Some Reflections in the Light of the Treaty of Nice' 2001 *European Law Review* 342, X Yataganas 'The Treaty of Nice: the Sharing of Power and the Institutional Balance in the European Union – A Continental Perspective' Jean Monnet Workshop 2001 http://www.jeanmonnetprogram.org.

[7] The Treaty of Nice is in part the sequel to the Protocol on the institutions with the prospect of enlargement of the European Union, which was agreed at Amsterdam (1997 OJ C340/111). That Protocol only contains two provisions, which can scarcely be regarded as clear or unconditional. Clearly, that protocol was no substitute for the Treaty of Nice.
[8] 2000 OJ C337E/278.
[9] On the supposition that it would enter into force before the ECSC Treaty lapsed on 23 July 2002, the Treaty of Nice is expressed to effect certain amendments to the latter Treaty. In the event, the ECSC Treaty has already lapsed and the Treaty of Nice has yet to come into effect.

B.   The Declaration Made at Nice

Amongst the various declarations appended to the Treaty of Nice and adopted by the Intergovernmental Conference (IGC) is Declaration number 23 on the future of the European Union. In that document, the IGC called for a 'deeper and wider debate' about the future of the Union. 'Wide-ranging discussions' were envisaged with 'all interested parties', including 'representatives of national parliaments and those reflecting public opinion, namely political, economic and university circles' and 'representatives of civil society'. The candidate countries were also to be 'associated in this process in ways to be defined'. In particular point 5 stated that the process should address, *inter alia*, the following questions:

"–   how to establish and monitor a more precise delimitation of powers between the European Union and the Member States, reflecting the principle of subsidiarity;
–   the status of the Charter of Fundamental Rights of the European Union, proclaimed in Nice, in accordance with the conclusions of the European Council in Cologne;
–   a simplification of the Treaties with a view to making them clearer and better understood without changing their meaning;
–   the role of national parliaments in the European architecture."

The IGC expressly recognised the need to 'improve and monitor the democratic legitimacy and transparency of the Union and its institutions, in order to bring them closer to the citizens of the Member States'.

This process is to culminate in a new IGC to be called in 2004, it being understood that the procedure for amending the Treaties enshrined in Article 48 TEU is then to be followed. Finally, the Declaration makes it clear that this IGC is not to constitute any form of obstacle or pre-condition to the further enlargement of the Union.

C.   The Laeken Declaration

As specifically envisaged in the Declaration appended to the Treaty of Nice, the European Council meeting at Laeken on 14 and 15 December 2001 adopted a further Declaration on the future of the European Union.[10] This document listed four main themes, namely: a better division and

---

[10] http://ue.eu.int/Newsroom; see K Lenaerts 'La déclaration de Laeken : premier jalon d'une Constitution européenne' 2002 *Journal des Tribunaux droit européen* 29, I Pernice 'Die Erklärung von Laeken zur Zukunft der EU' editorial 2002 *Europaische Zeitschrift für Wirtschaftsrecht* 65.

definition of competence in the European Union; simplification of the Union's instruments; more democracy, transparency and efficiency; and the need for a 'Constitution for European citizens'. In so doing, it touched on a number of the specific topics which will be discussed below, including the possibility of a merger of the Treaties, the incorporation of the Charter of Fundamental Rights[11] ('the Charter') into those Treaties in some form and the possibility of accession to the European Convention on Human Rights ('ECHR').

The Laeken Declaration also posed a number of bold and poignant questions, such as:

> How can the authority and efficiency of the European Commission be enhanced? How should the President of the Commission be appointed: by the European Council, by the European Parliament or should he be directly elected by the citizens? Should the role of the European Parliament be strengthened? Should we extend the right of co-decision or not? Should the way in which we elect the Members of the European Parliament be reviewed? Should a European electoral constituency be created, or should constituencies be continued to be determined nationally? ...

In addition, the Laeken Declaration announced the establishment of a Convention, under the Chairmanship of Mr Valéry Giscard d'Estaing, former President of France, to pave the way for the IGC which is due to be convened in 2004. Messrs. Giuliano Amato and Jean-Luc Dehaene, former Prime Ministers of Italy and Belgium respectively, were appointed Vice-Chairmen.

D.   The Work of the Convention: the Current State of Play

The Convention is composed of 105 members, as follows: the Chairman and two Vice-Chairmen; one representative of the Head of State or of Government of each Member State; two representatives of each national Parliament; 16 Members of the European Parliament (MEPs); two representatives of the Commission (Commissioners António Vitorino and Michel Barnier); a representative of the Government of each of the 13 candidate countries; and two representatives of the national Parliaments of the latter group of countries.[12] Should any member of the Convention be unable

---

[11] 2000 OJ C364/1.

[12] For a full list of the members and their alternates, as well as the observers, see the website of the Convention: http://european-convention.eu.int. Initially, Mr Pierre Moscovici, a member of the former Socialist led Government of France, has maintained his seat in the Convention, although that Government was ousted in the Parliamentary elections of June 2002 (Le Monde, 30 July 2002, http://www.lemonde.fr/). However, in November 2002 he withdrew in favour of Mr Dominique de Villepin, the French Foreign Minister.

to attend, then he is replaced by his alternate, who is appointed in the same way; only the Chairman and two Vice-Chairmen have no alternates.

The Praesidium, which provides the impetus for the work of the Convention, consists of 12 members: the Chairman and two Vice-Chairmen, one representative of the Governments of each of the three Member States holding the Council Presidency over the period of operation of the Convention (Spain, Denmark and Greece in that chronological order), two representatives of national Parliaments, two representatives of the European Parliament and the two Commission representatives. In addition, one 'invitee' representing the candidate countries is also a member. All the members of the Praesidium are simultaneously members of the Convention.

The Committee of the Regions, the Economic and Social Committee and the European Social Partners have all nominated observers; the European Ombudsman also enjoys the status of observer.

All the proceedings of the Convention are held in public and its documents, including contributions from third parties, are available on its website.[13] What is more, submissions from civil society are encouraged.[14] This highly transparent procedure—indeed the very concept of the Convention—is closely modelled on that followed successfully for drawing up the Charter;[15] it represents a conscious break with past negotiations for the amendment of the Treaties, which were held behind closed doors.[16]

The Convention held its first meeting on 28 February 2002. The Laeken Declaration envisaged that the Convention would conclude its work within a year, but it now seems clear that this deadline will not be met.[17] According to the Laeken Declaration, the final document must reflect the consensus of the participants in so far as possible. While members of the Convention from the candidate countries are not mere observers, they have no power to prevent any consensus which may emerge amongst the Member States.

Since its first meeting, the Convention has met in plenary once a month except in August.[18] Until June, it was in a 'listening phase' involving general

---

[13] See previous footnote.

[14] See http://european-convention.eu.int/forum and http://european-convention.eu.int/forum; also CONV 120/02 and CONV 167/02.

[15] One difference is that candidate countries were not represented in the Convention on the Charter. For the composition of that body, see the Commission's website on the Charter: http://europa.eu.int/comm/justice_home/unit/*charte/en/charter01.html*.

[16] Having said that, a number of important documents relating to the negotiations leading up to the Treaty of Nice have been posted on a dedicated website: http://europa.eu.int/comm/archives/igc2000/index_en.htm.

[17] According to the timetable set out in CONV 262/02 of 12 September 2002, the Convention's proceedings will continue until June 2003.

[18] The minutes of these meetings are contained in documents CONV 7/02, 14/02 40/02, 60/02, 97/02, 167/0 and 200/02, all available of the website of the Convention.

debates in plenary session. Cynics might suggest that four months were lost in this process, but they would be wrong: given the variety of institutions represented by the speakers as well as their different backgrounds and the complete openness of the entire work of the Convention, this broad airing of views served an important political purpose in terms of breaching the gap with public opinion.[19] In addition, the 'listening phase' enabled the Convention to complete a good deal of important groundwork and to determine which issues required the most immediate attention.

In May 2002, the Praesidium announced the establishment of 6 Working Groups with the following mandates:[20]

- Group I: How can verification of compliance with the principle of subsidiarity be ensured? Should a verification mechanism be introduced? Should such a procedure be political and/or judicial in character?
- Group II: If it is decided to include the Charter in the Treaty, how should this be done and what would be the consequences thereof? What would be the consequences of accession by the Community/ Union to the European Convention of Human Rights?
- Group III: What would be the consequences of an explicit recognition of the legal personality of the EU, and of a fusion of the legal personalities of the EU and the European Community? Might they contribute to simplification of the Treaties?
- Group IV: How is the role of national parliaments carried out in the present architecture of the European Union? What are the national arrangements which function best? Should new mechanisms/procedures be envisaged at national or European level?
- Group V: How should 'complementary' competence be treated in future? Should Member States be accorded full competence for matters in which the Union at present has complementary competence, or should the limits of the Union's complementary competence be spelled out?
- Group VI: The introduction of the single currency implies closer economic and financial co-operation. What forms might such co-operation take?

These groups, which first met in July, are required to submit their conclusions to the plenary session at various dates between September and November 2002. Their work will be discussed in detail below.

---

[19] Giscard d'Estaing 'Les dernières nouvelles de la Convention européenne' Le Monde 23 July 2002: '*La phase d'écoute à laquelle nous avons procédé pendant quatre mois était importante pour réduire l'écart entre les Conventionnels et les attentes des citoyens*', available on http://www.lemonde.fr and on the website of the Convention (see n 12 above).
[20] CONV 52/02 of 17 May 2002.

In July 2002, a further four working groups were set up to examine the following issues:[21]

- justice and home affairs;
- external relations;
- defence; and
- the simplification of decision-making procedures.

These new working groups are set to hold their first meetings during the course of September 2002. At the time of writing, it is impossible to consider the work of those groups in this article.[22] However, positions taken by the European Parliament and the Commission on these issues will be touched on very briefly below.

It will be noted that some of the themes addressed by the Laeken Declaration—such as whether the President of the Commission should be directly elected—are not covered by any of the working groups.

In law, the Convention will have no means of forcing the IGC to accept its blueprint, when the latter body is convened in 2004. Manifestly, then, the higher the degree of consensus reached within the Convention, the greater will be its influence on the IGC.

E.   The Position of the European Parliament

On 29 November 2001, even before the Laeken Declaration, the European Parliament had adopted a resolution on the constitutional process and the future of the Union,[23] on the basis of the report of its Committee on Constitutional Affairs.[24] The preamble to that resolution criticises the 'current drift towards intergovernmental methods and the consequent weakening of the Community method'. Consequently, that resolution calls for the Common Foreign and Security Policy (CFSP) to be incorporated

---

[21] CONV 206/02. This document sets out the precise mandate of each of these 4 groups.

[22] However, these matters have been discussed in plenary sessions of the Convention and have been the subject of notes from the Praesidium: on justice and home affairs, see CONV 69/02 (note from the Praesidium) and CONV 97/02 (report on plenary session of 6 and 7 June); on EU external action, see CONV 161/02 (note from the Praesidium) and CONV 200/02 (report on plenary session of 11 and 12 July); and on legislative procedures, see CONV 60/02 (report of plenary session of 23 and 24 May) and CONV 216/02 (note from the Praesidium). On the latter point, the Parliament has called for qualified voting in the Council and co-decision involving the Parliament to be the 'general principle' (resolution of 29 November 2001, 2001/2180(INI)), point 4c); this is available on the Parliament's website, http://www.europarl.eu.int/. In its Communication of 22 May entitled 'A Project for the European Union' (COM(2002) 247 final), the Commission states: 'Qualified majority voting must become the single procedural rule for decision-making in the Council'; and it advocates a greater degree of involvement by the European Parliament in legislative procedures, with its exact role 'depending on the instruments being considered'.

[23] See the previous footnote.

[24] Leinen and Méndez de Vigo report of 23 October 2001 (A5–0368/2001).

into the Community pillar and for all or most aspects of freedom, security and justice to be merged within the Community framework, with the Court of Justice being granted full jurisdiction of the later field. Frequent reference will be made to that resolution in the course of this article. The Parliament has also adopted a series of other resolutions on specific issues, which will be considered in relation to each one.

F. The Commission's Stance

On 22 May 2002, the Commission issued a Communication on the work of the Convention in the shape of a report entitled 'A Project for the European Union'.[25] The parts of that document which are of the greatest interest in the present context will be considered below. For completeness, however, some of the other points contained in this Communication should also be touched on here.

The Communication calls for an end to the exceptions granted to individual Member States, which it regards as detracting from the equality of citizens of Europe. What is more, reinforced co-operation is said to be valid only for 'one-off actions not linked to the Union's main policy thrusts and which might justify adjustments to the common institutional framework'. This Communication also makes a range of other proposals such as the incorporation in the Treaties of legal bases for facilitating the adoption of rules on criminal proceedings in cases of cross-border fraud.

What is more, the Communication also calls for: enhanced coordination of economic policies, with the Commission's own role being strengthened; a reinforcement of measures relating to freedom, security and justice, including common measures of control and surveillance of external borders and genuine common policies on immigration and asylum; and an improved CFSP, with decisions being taken by a majority outside the fields of security and defence, and the gradual transfer of the functions of the High Representative for CFSP to a member of the Commission.

The Commission has also issued papers on specific issues, which will be discussed below at the appropriate juncture. In addition, it is due to issue a further document on the architecture of the institutions in the autumn.

G. Constitution, Treaty or Constitutional Treaty?

As long ago as 1986, the Court of Justice described the EC Treaty as the 'basic constitutional charter' of the Community.[26] This statement is tantamount to

---

[25] N 22 above.
[26] Case 294/83 *Les Verts v Parliament* [1986] ECR 1339 at 1365, confirmed in Opinion 1/91 [1991] ECR 6079 at 6102.

saying that that Treaty is to be construed and applied like the Constitution of a State, even though it is couched in the language of an instrument of international law. Whether the same applies to the Treaty on European Union is a matter on which the Court has not had occasion to rule.[27]

As already mentioned, the Laeken Declaration spoke of the need for a 'Constitution for European citizens'. In its Communication of May 2002 on the work of the Convention,[28] the Commission has spoken of the need to establish a 'constitutional treaty', while the European Parliament has referred to the need to draft a 'Constitution for the European Union'.[29] Equally, in his renowned speech delivered at the Humboldt University in May 2000,[30] German Foreign Minister Joschka Fischer referred variously to the drafting of a Constitution and of a constitutional treaty, as did President Giscard d'Estaing in his recent article in Le Monde on the progress of the Convention.[31]

Accordingly, at the conclusion of its work, the Convention is likely to opt for one of these two terms in preference to the less integrationist title 'treaty'.[32] Needless to say, even if the Convention chose not to do so, that would not reverse the Court's long-standing case law.

H.   The Division of Powers

As indicated by the very first indent of the Nice Declaration, the division of powers (also known as 'competences' or 'competencies') between the Union and the Member States, including the principle of subsidiarity, is one of the major themes—if not *the* major theme—of the Convention. It is also one of the most delicate.[33] Not surprisingly, then, no less than two of the Working Groups (numbers I and V) are devoted to this issue.

---

[27] On these hotly debated questions, see generally P. Craig 'Constitutions, Constitutionalism and the European Union' 2001 *European Law Journal* 125, I Pernice 'Multilevel Constitutionalism and the Treaty of Amsterdam: European Constitution-making Revisited?' 1999 *Common Market Law Review* 703; J-C Piris 'L'Union européenne a-t-elle une constitution? Lui en faut-il une?' 1999 *Revue trimestrielle de droit européen* 599 (also published in English as 'Does the European Union have a Constitution? Does it Need One?' Jean Monnet Working Papers 5/00 http://www.jeanmonnetprogram.org/papers/00/000501.html), J H H Weiler 'The Constitution of Europe: Do the Clothes have a New Emperor? and Other Essays on European Integration' (1999), especially ch 6 'The Reformation of European Constitutionalism'.

[28] N 22 above.

[29] Resolution of 29 November 2001 (n 22 above), point 1.

[30] Speech of 12 May 2000 (htpp://www.rewi.hu-berlin.de and http://www.auswaertiges-amt.de).

[31] Art of 23 July 2002, n 19 above.

[32] That outcome now seems more likely in the light of the speech delivered in Edinburgh on 27 August 2002 Jack Straw MP, United Kingdom Foreign Secretary, spoke out in favour of a written constitution for the EU (http://www.fco.gov.uk).

[33] See A Bogdandy and J Bast 'The European Union's Vertical Order of Competences: the Current Law and Proposals for its Reform' (2002) *Common Market Law Review* 227; V Constantinesco 'Repenser les méthodes de partage et de contrôle des compétences de l'Union

What is more, this topic is also intimately linked to the role of the regions and local authorities, which will be considered at the end of this article. Indeed, the regions of a number of federal Member States, not least the German *Länder*, which have become increasingly concerned at what they regard as encroachments by the Union on their preserve, have played a key role in bringing the whole issue of the division of powers to the top of the Convention's agenda.[34]

I. Simplifying the Treaties

As we noticed earlier, one of the issues to be addressed in accordance with the Declaration of Nice is the simplification of the Treaties 'without changing their meaning', the avowed purpose being to make them more easily understood by the public; and that simplification is also one of the four main themes of the Laeken Declaration, on the basis that it is essential if greater transparency is to be achieved.[35]

Official concern at the complexity of the Treaties predates the Treaty of Nice. Indeed, Articles 9 to 12 of the Treaty of Amsterdam took the first step in the process of simplification, notably by removing obsolete articles and protocols. Furthermore, one of the Declarations made by the IGC at Amsterdam expresses the wish of all the Member States that:

> the technical work begun during the course of this Intergovernmental Conference shall continue as speedily as possible with the aim of drafting a consolidation of all the relevant Treaties, including the Treaty on European Union.

it was understood that 'this technical work ... shall have no legal value'.[36]

---

européenne' in 'L'Europe 2004 – Le Grand Débat' http://europa.eu.int/comm/dg10/university; A Dashwood 'The Limits of European Community Powers' (1996) 21 *European Law Review* 113; B de Witte 'Clarifying the Delimitation of Powers: A Proposal with Comments'; I Pernice 'Rethinking the Methods of Dividing and Controlling the Competencies of the Union' in 'L'Europe 2004 ...'; and Piris, n 27 above at pp 615 ff.

[34] See Opinion of the Committee of the Regions of 11 March 1999 (CdR 302/98); and the Declaration on subsidiarity by Austria, Belgium and Germany, which was annexed to the Treaty of Amsterdam and which stated that that principle not only concerns the Member States, but also their regional entities 'to the extent that they have their own law-making powers conferred on them under national constitutional law' (1997 OJ C340/143). As to the *Länder* in particular, see J Schwarze 'Constitutional Perspectives of the European Union with Regard to the Next Intergovernmental Conference in 2004' 2002 European Public Law 241 at p 242.

[35] The issue of simplification has been considered in an unpublished paper by B de Witte entitled 'Reorganisation of the Treaties: Merger, Splitting or Mutation?' delivered at the EUI conference on 'The Emerging Constitution of the European Union' held on 19–20 April 2002. See also the note devoted to this subject by the secretariat of the Convention, CONV 250/02 of 10 September 2002.

[36] Declaration no 42 (1997 OJ C340/140). In consequence, a consolidated version of the EU and EC Treaties was prepared within the Council (SN 1845/00 and SN 1846/00).

In May 2000, the European University Institute (EUI) in Florence submitted to the Commission a draft 'Basic Treaty of the European Union',[37] which contained 95 articles covering the most important aspects of the TEU and EC Treaties and which would have been supplemented *inter alia* by a shortened version of the EC Treaty.[38] In its Communication of July 2000,[39] the Commission broadly welcomed the approach followed in this draft, but refrained from taking a position on the details of the text. It confirmed this approach in its Communication of May 2002 on the work of the Convention.[40] Consequently, the EUI draft is likely to constitute a valuable point of reference for the Convention.

In the same document, the Commission advocated restructuring the EU and EC Treaties, inserting the fundamental provisions into the Basic Treaty and the others into an annexed Treaty which could be amended according to a simplified procedure. Again, in its Communication of May 2002 the Commission reiterated this idea, which is also mooted in the Laeken Declaration.

Although the Declarations annexed to the Treaties of Amsterdam and Nice spoke of simplifying the Treaties without altering their substance, this process would of necessity require some minor changes of substance, if it is to be effective.[41] Quite apart from that, it is clear that the Treaties are about to undergo a number of fundamental changes as a result of the Convention itself, so that it will rather be a question of simplifying the Treaties *as amended.*

At the political level, it is manifestly of the utmost importance that the process of negotiating and ratifying a simplified version of the Treaties should not in any way undermine the *acquis communautaire*. In the past, some Member States have been unwilling to engage in this process for fear that the *acquis communautaire* might be questioned in the course of ratification.[42]

In addition, a number of more technical issues will have to be faced. First, account must be taken not only of the TEU and the EC Treaty, but also of the Euratom Treaty and of the myriad protocols annexed to the various Treaties. Second, sensitive value judgements will have to be made as to which provisions are so important that they must be incorporated into the Basic Treaty. Third, consideration might be given to incorporating some of the case law of the Court of Justice into the Treaties.[43] Indeed, the Laeken

---

[37] COM(2000) 434 final of 12 July 2000.
[38] Another model entitled 'Ein Grundvertrag für die Europäische Union' was drafted by the Bertelsmann Forschungsgruppe für Politik, Centrum für angewandte Politikforschung http://www.cap.uni-muenchen.de
[39] 'A Basic Treaty for the European Union', Commission Communication of 12 July 2000 (COM(2000) 434).
[40] N 22 above.
[41] This point is stressed in the Commission's Communication of July 2000 (n 37 above) at p 6.
[42] Piris, n 27 above at p 623.
[43] The simplified version of the EC Treaty drafted by the Cambridge Centre for European Legal Studies (CELS) incorporates large swathes of case law, including that relating to remedies for enforcing Community law rights before national courts (1997 *European Law Review* 395).

Declaration specifically raises the question as to whether Articles 95 and 308 EC should be reworded by incorporating the relevant case law.[44] This process has already occurred with respect to the principle of proportionality, which was initially developed by the Court and is now set out in the final paragraph of Article 5 EC as well as in the Protocol on the application of the principles of subsidiarity and proportionality.[45] It is a moot point whether such a step would be appropriate in every case, since it might stifle further development of the case law.[46,47]

Despite these problems, it is generally agreed that this nettle must be grasped, if greater transparency and legal certainty are to be ensured. Simplification of the Treaties is therefore set to become one of the major themes of the Convention. In keeping with this, two of the Working Groups (Group III on legal personality of the Union and the merger of the Treaties, and the Group examining the simplification of decision-making procedures) are directly concerned with this matter. In the same spirit, consideration is being given to simplifying the catalogue of legal instruments available to the Union, as the proliferation of different types of instrument available to the Union is the butt of much criticism.[48] Plainly, one of the ideas examined

---

[44] Judge K Lenaerts and M Desomer 'Bricks for a Constitutional Treaty of the European Union: values, objectives and means' 2002 *European Law Review* 377 at pp 395–7 maintain that this would create greater legal certainty.

[45] 1997 OJ C340/105.

[46] For example, this might be true of the case law relating to the 'mandatory requirements' which constitute an exception to Art 28 of the EC (see Case 120/78 *Rewe-Zentral v Bundesmonopolverwaltung für Branntwein* ('Cassis de Dijon') [1979] E C R 649). The Court has frequently recognised new 'mandatory requirements' and the list is still not closed; for a recent case recognising a new 'mandatory requirement', see C–368/95 *Vereinigte Familiapress v Heinrich Bauer Verlag* [1997] E C R I–3689 (maintenance of press diversity). See P Oliver assisted by M Jarvis 'Free Movement of Goods in the European Community' (4th edn), ch 8 at p 203.

[47] Thought might also be given to withdrawing some of the Declarations appended to the various Treaties. Although they are not binding, the Court may have regard to them. In view of their non-binding nature, they cannot be formally repealed. Nevertheless, the IGC could issue a fresh Declaration renouncing certain named Declarations. On the other hand, it is questionable whether any purpose would be served by replacing existing Declarations by new, consolidated Declarations.

[48] See the report of the meeting of the Convention of 23 and 24 May 2002 (CONV 60/02) and the note of the Praesidium on this subject (CONV 162/02); and point 14 the Parliament's resolution of 16 May 2002 (P5-TA(2002)0247) adopting the Lamassoure Report dated 24 April 2002 of its Committee on Constitutional Affairs on the division of competences between the Union and the Member States (A5–0133/2002), which resolution calls for Art 249 EC to be amended so as to contain an exhaustive list of all the 'legal acts and other forms of action' which may be taken by the Union. See also Lenaerts and Desomer, n 44 above, at pp 398 ff.

What is more, in point 4f) of its resolution of 29 November 2001 (n 22 above), the Parliament has called for a hierarchy of acts to be established; the same proposal has been made at earlier IGCs. Indeed, it harks back to the draft Treaty establishing the European Union adopted by the European Parliament in 1984 (the Spinelli Report), 1984 OJ C77/24; see F Capotorti, M Hilf, F Jacobs and J-P Jacqué 'Le Traité d'Union européenne' (1985). That draft Treaty made a distinction between 'laws', which would be adopted by the Parliament and the Council as joint legislative authority, and Commission acts ('regulations' and 'decisions').

by Group III—the merger of the Treaties—would result in the most radical simplification, provided that it is carried out effectively.[49]

J.   Amending the Procedure for Revising the Treaties

Whatever the Irish people decide in their second referendum on the Treaty of Nice, one point is now clear: following the first referendum and following the difficulties experienced by Denmark in ratifying the Treaty of Maastricht, serious thought must be given to modifying Article 48 TEU so as to remove the requirement of unanimous ratification of treaty amendments, possibly with an alternative solution for non-participating Member States. Naturally, this problem will become even more acute when the number of Member States is substantially increased as a result of further enlargement. Although the Convention has yet to consider this highly important question, it seems likely to do so in the coming months.

In July 2000, the EUI submitted a report to the Commission on this subject.[50] Amongst the ideas set out in that report, which could be adopted either on an alternative or on a cumulative basis, are the following:

(a)   transferring certain provisions of the Treaties to protocols which could be amended according to an alleviated procedure (a 'super-qualified majority');

(b)   requiring the prior approval of the Court of Justice, as in the simplified treaty amendment procedure in the fourth paragraph of Article 95 of the (now defunct) ECSC Treaty; and

(c)   recourse to a Convention along the lines of that currently under way *instead of* the IGC procedure.

As explained above under the previous heading, suggestion (a) has already been endorsed by the Commission. As to (b), despite the precedent set by the ECSC Treaty, one might wonder whether such a reform would be opportune, unless the Court is given a clear yardstick by which to judge the lawfulness of proposed amendments to the Treaties. Alternatively, if this task is intended to be non-judicial in nature, then the value of this procedure will be questionable. As to (c), this appears set to appeal to many members of the current Convention. Clearly, the precise composition of such constitutional Conventions would have to be laid down in the Treaties themselves.

In addition, the EUI report points out that, to ensure greater flexibility, two alternative amendment procedures might be laid down, as is the case

---

[49] See document WGIII/16 of 18 September 2002, which is specifically devoted to this issue.
[50] Second report on the reorganisation of the Treaties on 31 July 2000, entitled 'Reforming the Treaties' Amendment Procedure' http://europa.eu.int/comm/archives/igc2000/offdoc/repoflo_en2.pdf.

under Article 89 of the French Constitution and Article V of the US Constitution.

Finally, as to the position of Member States placed in a minority, it seems clear that 'opt-outs' can only be envisaged in relation to specific sectors, as is presently the case.[51] Institutional changes applying across the board (eg any alteration of the number, or method of designation, of Commissioners) would by definition have to apply *erga omnes*.

K.   Dual Legitimacy—a Union of States and of Peoples

Radical though his speech of May 2000[52] may have been, Joschka Fischer took great care to stress that his vision of the future of the Union as a European federation would not undermine the nation State.[53] Similarly, in a recent resolution the European Parliament has spoken of the Union's 'dual legitimacy' resulting from its being a Union of States and of peoples.[54] Whether this elegant formulation might find its way into (the preamble to) the future Constitution or constitutional treaty must be a matter for speculation at this early stage.

L.   The Working Groups

1.   *Group I: Subsidiarity*

As indicated earlier, the principle of subsidiarity goes to the heart of the debate about the division of powers. Hence the considerable quantity of ink which has flowed over it.[55]

That principle was first introduced into the Treaties by the Treaty of Maastricht. Today it is enshrined in the second paragraph of Article 5 EC,

---

[51] Eg Protocol on the application of certain aspects of Art 14 EC to the United Kingdom (1997 OJ C340/97) (free movement of persons); and the Protocols agreed at Maastricht on certain provisions relating to the United Kingdom and on certain provisions relating to Denmark (economic and monetary union).

[52] N 30 above.

[53] Whether this idea is already expressed by Art 6(3) TEU, as is sometimes suggested, is open to doubt. That paragraph reads as follows: 'The Union shall respect the national identities of its Member States'. Most probably, this provision is to be construed as referring to the *cultural* identity of the Member States, in which case it is to be read with Art 151 EC. However, A Dashwood ('The Limits ...') n 33 above, implies that Art 6(3) refers to the political identity of the Member States.

[54] Resolution of 7 February 2002 (P5–TA(2002)0058) adopting the Napolitano Report of its Committee on Constitutional Affairs A5–0023/2002 of 23 January 2002; see also R Toulemon 'Quelle constitution pour quelle Europe?' 2001 *Revue des Market unique européen* 293 at p 300.

[55] See eg the proceedings of the colloquium entitled 'Subsidiarité, défi du changement' held at the European Institute of Public Administration in Maastricht in 1991 (contributions of President Delors and others), the 1994 FIDE reports on subsidiarity; N Bernard, 'The Future of European Economic Law in the light of the Principle of Subsidiarity' (1996) 33 *Common*

where it is expressed to apply 'in areas which do not fall within the exclusive competence of the Community'; it is also referred to in Article 2 TEU.[56] What is more, since the Treaty of Amsterdam, this principle has been the subject of a special protocol to the EC Treaty, which also covers the principle of proportionality.[57] That Protocol sets out in considerable detail the issues to be weighed up, as well as the steps which should be taken in this regard by the Community institutions.[58]

Any lingering doubts as to whether the principle of subsidiarity is justiciable were dispelled by the judgment in *United Kingdom v Council* ('working time Directive').[59] Moreover, Article 13 of the Protocol now states that 'compliance with the principle of subsidiarity shall be reviewed in accordance with the rules laid down by the Treaty'. Having said that, the Court's task in reviewing the observance of this principle is by no means easy, given its vague nature; the Court has never quashed an act on these grounds.[60]

Within the Working Group, there is a clear desire to strengthen the principle of subsidiarity or at the very least the monitoring or review of

---

Market Law Review 633; L Besselink 'Entrapped by the Maximum Standard: on Fundamental Rights, Pluralism and Subsidiarity in the European Union' (1998) *Common Market Law Review* 629; R von Borries, 'Das Subsidiaritätsprinzip im Recht der Europäischen Union' (1994) *Europarecht* 263; C Calliess 'Subsidiaritäts- und Solidaritätsprinzip in der Europäischen Union' (1999); K Lenaerts and P van Ypersele, 'Le principe de la subsidiarité et son contexte: étude de l'article 3B du Traité' (1994) *Cahiers de droit européen* 3; Rohe 'Binnenmarkt oder Interessenverband? Zum Verhältnis von Binnenmarktziel und Subsidiaritätsprinzip nach dem Maastricht-Vertrag' 1997, RabelsZ. 1; M Soares, 'Pre-Emption, Conflicts of Powers and Subsidiarity' (1998) 23 European Law Review 132; D Wyatt 'Subsidiarity and Judicial Review' in Liber Amicorum in Honour of Lord Slynn of Hadley (2000), vol. 1 'Judicial Review in European Union Law' at 505. For a comparison with the United States see G Bermann, 'Taking Subsidiarity Seriously: Federalism in the European Community and the United States' (1994) *Columbia Law Review* 331.

[56] See the statement of the European Council held at Edinburgh in December 1992 (Bull E C 12–1992 p 13); the Interinstitutional Agreement between the Parliament, the Council and the Commission ([1993] O J C 329/132); and annual Commission communications since 1992 (SEC(92) 1990, COM(93) 545, COM(94) 553, SEC(95) 580, SEC(96) 7, COM(97) 626, COM(98) 715, COM(99) 562 and COM(2000) 772 and COM(2001)728). As the Commission reports show, the principle of subsidiarity has enabled the Community institutions to weed out some inappropriate suggestions for legislation. Since the entry into force of the Treaty of Amsterdam, the Commission has been required to submit these reports under Art 9 of the Protocol on the application of the principles of subsidiarity and proportionality (n 43 above).

[57] N 45 above.

[58] See the more recent materials referred to in n 55 above; also Constantinesco, 'Le protocole sur l'application des principes de subsidiarité et de proportionalité' (1997) 33 *Revue trimestrielle de droit européen* 765.

[59] Case C–84/94 [1996] E C R I–5755, paras 46–47.

[60] Arguments based on this principle have been dismissed in Cases 84/94 (see previous footnote) and C–377/98 *Netherlands v Parliament and Council* ('biotechnology Directive') [2001] E C R I–7079. In addition, as regards the reasoning of legislative acts, the Court has held that an express reference to the principle of subsidiarity cannot be required: Case C–233/94 *Germany v Parliament and Council* ('Directive on deposit-guarantee schemes') [1997] E C R I–2405, paras 22–29 (especially para 28).

proposals for compliance with that principle,[61] despite the general realisation that the very concept of subsidiarity is essentially political and subjective.[62] The majority has taken the view that *ex ante* monitoring of legislation should continue to be of an essentially political nature.[63] It therefore envisages strengthening such monitoring, notably by enhancing the involvement of national parliaments.[64]

Nevertheless, the majority of the Group maintains that *ex post* monitoring of subsidiarity should be of a judicial nature and advocates a broadening of the procedures for bringing such matters before the Court of Justice.[65] One suggestion is to create a special Chamber within the Court devoted to questions of subsidiarity.[66] Another is to confer on national parliaments (individually or collectively), and possibly the Committee of the Regions, the right to seise the Court of such questions.[67]

No formal position has yet been taken by the Court itself on any of these ideas. In any event, it seems clear that, while the Court is well equipped to ensure that the prescribed procedure is followed prior to the adoption of legislation, substantive judicial review of compliance with the principle of subsidiarity is always likely to be fraught with difficulty, in view of the subjective character of that principle.

The work of this Group is closely linked to that of Groups IV and V and to the role of the regions and local authorities, all of which are discussed below.

2.   Group II: Fundamental Rights

This topic will be considered in Part III below.

---

[61] See also the resolution of the European Parliament of 16 May 2002 adopting the Lamassoure Report (n 48 above).

[62] This was stressed in the speech delivered to this Working Group on 25 June 2002 by Jean-Claude Piris, Director-General of the Legal Service of the Council (document WG I/4). As he pointed out, the word 'better' at the end of the second paragraph of Art 5 EC necessarily implies a value judgement; ('... the Community shall take action ... only in so far as the objectives of the proposed action ... can ... be *better* achieved by the Community'; emphasis added). The subjective nature of this principle is clearly illustrated by Council Directive 1999/22 relating to the keeping of wild animals in zoos (1999 OJ L94/24): in view of the principle of subsidiarity, the Commission proposed a mere recommendation, but the Council and the Parliament opted for a legislative instrument instead (see the speech delivered on 17 June 2002 by Michel Petite, Director-General of the Legal Service of the Commission (document WGI/3)).

[63] Document WGI/9 of 29 July 2002 setting out the Group's 'initial proposals for conclusions'.

[64] *Ibid.*

[65] *Ibid.*

[66] *Ibid.* See also point 39 of the Lamassoure Report (n 48 above).

[67] Summary of the joint meeting of 22 July 2002 between Working Groups I and IV (CONV 210/02 of 30 July 2002). This document suggests in particular that such a right of action might be granted to the Conference of European Affairs Committees of national parliaments (COSAC), a body discussed further below in relation to Group IV.

3.   *Group III: The Legal Personality of the Union; Merger of the Treaties*

Articles 281 EC and 184 Euratom expressly confer legal personality on their respective Communities, which enjoy broad treaty-making powers by virtue of express provisions (eg in the case of the EC, Article 133 EC). In contrast, the TEU contains no such provision, although Article 24 of that Treaty does confer certain treaty-making powers on the Union.[68] Accordingly, it is debatable whether the Union possesses legal personality.[69]

The Byzantine complexity of these arrangements can give rise to unwarranted and embarrassing difficulties in international negotiations.[70]

At the same time, as the reader will be well aware, the provisions of the first pillar (the EC Treaty) entail a far greater degree of integration than those on the second pillar (the CFSP laid down in Title V TEU) and the third (justice and home affairs, Title VI of the TEU). For instance, while the Court of Justice enjoys full jurisdiction under the EC and Euratom Treaties (with the exception of Article 68 EC), it has none whatever under the CFSP (Articles 41 and 46 TEU) and only limited jurisdiction under the provisions on justice and home affairs (Articles 35 and 46 TEU). Under Article 68 EC, which is closely linked to the third pillar, the Court's jurisdiction is also limited.

In its Communication of 22 May on the Convention,[71] the Commission unequivocally proposed that legal personality be conferred on the Union and that the Treaties be merged. The European Parliament had already adopted various resolutions to the same effect.[72]

---

[68] Agreements have been concluded on the basis of Art 24 TEU with the Former Republic of Yugoslavia on the activities of the European Monitoring Mission (2001 OJ L125/1) and with the Former Yugoslav Republic of Macedonia with respect to the same matter (2001 OJ L241/1).

[69] See O De Schutter and Y Lejeune 'L'adhésion de la Communauté à la Convention européenne des droits de l'homme – A propos de l'avis 2/94 de la Cour de justice des Communautés' 1996 CDE 555 at 600, J-V Louis 'Le traité d'Amsterdam: une occasion perdue?' 1997 2 *Revue dis Marché unique européen* 5 at p 9; and M Pechstein 'Die Justitiabilität des Unionsrechts' 1999 Europarecht 1 at 2. S van Raepenbusch argues that the Union possesses external legal personality ('L'émergence de l'Union européenne dans l'ordre juridique international' in 'Mélanges en hommage à Michel Waelbroeck' 1999). Also, A von Bogdandy, relying *inter alia* on the ruling in Case C–170/96 *Commission v Council* (transit visas) [1998] ECR I–2673, argues that the Union and the Community are already to be treated as a single entity with a single legal system ('The Legal Case for Unity: the European Union as a Single Organisation with a Single Legal System' 1999 *Common Market Law Review* 887). In his speech of 26 June 2002 to the Working Group, J-C Piris also espoused the view that the Union already enjoys a degree of legal personality (document WG III/6).

[70] See the speech given by Pieter Jan Kuijper, Director of the Legal Service of the Commission, delivered to the Working Group on 26 June 2002 (document WG III/3).

[71] N 22 above.

[72] Resolution of 29 November 2001 (n 22 above), point 3; resolution of 14 March 2002 (P5–TA(2002)0126) adopting the Carnero González Report of the Committee of Constitutional Affairs (A5–0409/2001); and resolution of 16 May 2002 adopting the Lamassoure Report (n 48 above), point 3.

A broad consensus appears to have built up within the Convention on the following points: legal personality should be expressly conferred on the Union; the legal personality of the Union should be merged with that of the EC (and conceivably Euratom); and, if that step were taken, the rationale for a TEU separate from the EC Treaty would fall away, so that it would then be logical to merge those two Treaties.[73]

Equally, it is generally agreed that this reform would not necessarily entail merging the powers and procedures of the three pillars.[74] Having said that, some of the experts who addressed the Group advocated certain amendments to the provisions relating to the first and third pillars. For instance, Mr Gregorio Garzón Clariana, Jurisconsult of the European Parliament, advised the Group that, following Opinion 2/94,[75] it would be necessary to incorporate into the Treaties a provision empowering the Union to accede to the ECHR.[76] Also, Professor Jean-Victor Louis criticised the undemocratic nature of the procedure for concluding international agreements under Article 24 TEU, which did not involve the intervention of any parliament unless a Member State chose to make its consent subject to the completion of its own constitutional procedures; and he proposed that this unsatisfactory situation be altered as part of the forthcoming reform.[77] This idea has now been accepted by a majority of the group, which has recommended that the constitutional Treaty should provide for the European Parliament to be consulted on all treaties concluded under the second and third pillars, and indeed under Article 133 EC.[78]

In addition, a majority of the group has recommended that the Court of Justice be granted jurisdiction over treaties concluded under the second pillar.[79]

4.   Group IV: The Role of National Parliaments

At Amsterdam, a Protocol on the role of national parliaments in the European Union was annexed to the TEU, as well as the EC, ECSC and Euratom Treaties.[80] That Protocol provides in particular that all the Commission's legislative proposals be made available to those parliaments

---

[73] See documents WGIII/6 of 15 July 2002 and WG III/15 of 17 September 2002.
[74] *Ibid.*
[75] [1996] ECR I–1759.
[76] Speech of 26 June 2002 (document WG III/6); see further point 4.4 below.
[77] Speech delivered to the Group on 10 July 2002 (document WG III/8, CONV 201/02).
[78] Above-mentioned document WG III/15.
[79] *Ibid.*
[80] 1997 OJ C340/113. For a general discussion of this Protocol and other aspects of the involvement of national parliaments in the work of the Union, see A Maurer's paper for the Working Group entitled 'National Parliaments in the European Architecture: Elements for Establishing a Best Practice Mechanism' (document WG IV/8 of 9 July 2002) and M Schröder 'Die Parlamente im europäischen Entscheidungsgefüge' 2002 *Europarecht* 301.

in good time, the purpose of this provision being to enable them to scrutinise these proposals in accordance with their own procedures. The Protocol also gives formal status to the Conference of European Affairs Committees of national parliaments (COSAC), which was established in November 1989, and entitles it to make any 'contributions which it deems appropriate' on the legislative activities of the Union.

It appears to be generally agreed that national parliaments could and should play much more of a role in the work of the Union. In this regard, the fact that those parliaments were represented in the Convention which drew up the Charter and in the current Convention must in itself be regarded as a historic breakthrough.

One idea which has gained ground is that representatives of national parliaments should meet in a third legislative Chamber in addition to the European Parliament and the Council—or, as Joschka Fischer put it, representatives of national parliaments should sit in a second Chamber of the European Parliament.[81] However, the European Parliament has recently rejected this suggestion on the grounds that it would merely serve to prolong the legislative procedure to the detriment of democracy and transparency.[82] At the same time, the Parliament pointed out that 'dual legitimacy—a Union of States and peoples—already finds expression at European level in the legislative sphere through the participation of the Council and the Parliament'.

On the other hand, the European Parliament determined in its resolution that its cooperation with national parliaments, and more particularly between the respective sectoral committees, should be stepped up. It also called for membership of the European Parliament to be made incompatible with holding a seat in a national or regional parliament.

Another suggestion, put forward by Andrew Duff MEP, a member of the Convention, is to require a third reading of a proposal by the Conciliation Committee of the European Parliament and the Council, where a specified majority of national parliaments object to the proposal and formulate a reasoned amendment.[83]

More specifically, various ideas have been floated to the effect that national parliaments have a role to play in particular types of legislative or pre-legislative procedure. As mentioned earlier, it has been suggested that national parliaments, possibly through the medium of COSAC, should take part in vetting the compatibility of proposed legislation with the principle of subsidiarity. Another proposal is to involve national parliaments in the adoption of legislation under Article 308 EC.[84]

---

[81] N 30 above.
[82] Resolution of 7 February 2002 (n 54 above).
[83] Document WG IV/4 of 5 July 2002.
[84] *Ibid.*

Furthermore, it has been argued that greater openness in the conduct of the Council's proceedings would enable each national parliament to scrutinise the work of its government more effectively.[85] Plainly, this would not require any change in the Treaties.

Other suggestions relate to non-legislative functions: national parliaments might participate in drawing up the work programme of the Union;[86] or be represented in a congress in an equal number with the European Parliament for the election of the President of the Commission, along the lines of the *Bundesversammlung* which elects the German Federal President pursuant to Article 54 of the Basic Law. [87]

In short, whilst a wealth of ideas has been submitted for enhancing the role of national parliaments, there is as yet no consensus on how this might be achieved in the procedure for adopting individual legislative instruments without rendering that procedure more cumbersome.

5.   Group V: Complementary Powers

A more precise delimitation of powers between the Union and the Member States is the first of the four main themes of the Laeken Declaration, of which the question of complementary powers is merely one aspect.

As is well known, the Union only possesses the powers conferred on it: Article 5 TEU and Articles 5 and 7(1) EC. In particular, the first paragraph of Article 5 EC provides: 'The Community shall act within the limits of the powers conferred upon it by this Treaty and of the objectives assigned to it thereunder.' However, such powers need not be expressly set out in the Treaties; they may be implied, where this is necessary to supplement express powers.[88]

Such powers as are conferred on the Union are frequently divided into three categories:[89] those which are *exclusive* to the Union and which therefore collectively constitute its 'exclusive competence' within the meaning of Articles 5 (second paragraph) and 11(1)(a) EC; those which it enjoys concurrently with the Member States (*concurrent or shared powers*); and *complementary powers* under which action by the Union is limited to supplementing, supporting or coordinating the action of Member States. These three categories may be described as follows:

[85] Contribution of Messrs Andrew Duff and Alain Lamassoure and others entitled 'Issues of competence and subsidiarity, and confusion arising therefrom' CONV 178/02, CONTRIB 60.
[86] *Ibid.*
[87] *Ibid.*
[88] Cases 281/85 *Germany and others v Commission* [1987] ECR 3203, C–295/90 *Parliament v Council* (Directive on residence of students) [1992] ECR I–4193, Opinion 1/94 [1994] ECR I–5267, paras 72 ff. See Dashwood 'The Limits ...' at p 124, Lenaerts and Desomer n 44 above, at p 385.
[89] See generally CONV 47/02 and the Parliament's resolution of 16 May 2002 adopting the Lamassoure Report (n 46 above); also Lenaerts and Desomer n 44 above, at pp 385ff.

- very few matters fall within the *exclusive powers* of the Union. Amongst the very rare examples are: certain aspects of the common commercial policy (Article 133 EC);[90] and fishing conditions designed to ensure the protection of fishing grounds and the conservation of the biological resources of the sea (Article 102 of the 1972 Act of Accession).[91] Action by the Member States in these areas is possible only where the Union has duly empowered them to act;
- most of the Union's powers are subsumed within the second category (eg agriculture, competition, internal market and transport). To the extent that the Union exercises its *concurrent powers*, action by the Member States is pre-empted. In reality, Union legislation in such areas is often so extensive that little room is left for the Member States; agricultural policy is a case in point;
- examples of *complementary powers* include: employment (Article 125 EC), education (Article 149 EC), vocational training (Article 150 EC) and, in most respects, public health (Article 152 EC). As explained in the next paragraph, harmonising legislation is expressly excluded by the Treaty in each of these areas.

Over certain matters, the Union holds no powers at all, either because none are attributed to it or because the Treaties expressly exclude them. Thus the EC Treaty expressly excludes harmonisation in relation to employment (Article 129), education (Article 149(4)), vocational training (Article 150(4)), culture (Article 151(5)) and most aspects of public health (Article 152(4)(c)).[92] Equally, once it is amended by the Treaty of Nice, Article 137(4) EC will preclude legislation under that article affecting the 'right of Member States to define the fundamental provisions of their social security systems' and legislation 'significantly' affecting the 'fundamental equilibrium' thereof. Having said that, in each case there is nothing to preclude the adoption of harmonising legislation based on other provisions of the EC Treaty, which have an impact on these matters.[93]

---

[90] Opinion 1/75 [1975] ECR 1355 at pp 1363–5; Case 41/76 *Donckerwolcke v Procureur de la République* [1976] ECR 1921, para 32; Opinion 1/78 [1978] ECR 2871, paras 52–60.

[91] Cases 3–4/76 *Krämer* [1976] ECR 1279 and 804/79 *Commission v United Kingdom* [1981] ECR 1045.

[92] For a detailed account of measures which have been adopted in these fields, see the Commission's note of 4 July to Group V (WGV/1).

[93] Case C–376/98 *Germany v Parliament and Council* ('tobacco advertising') [2000] E C R I–8419, paras 78, 79 and 88; Opinion of Advocate General Geelhoed dated 10 September 2002 in Case C–491/01 *The Queen v Secretary of State for Health ex parte British American Tobacco*, para 114.

With respect to many areas, there is considerable debate as to which of the three categories is applicable.[94] Moreover, there is no unanimous view on the consequences of a given power falling within the category of complementary competences.[95] In these circumstances, the debate within the Group on how to clarify these powers is not yet very advanced.

While there is a clear wish on all sides to clarify the powers of the Union, the Commission has expressed its opposition to drawing up either a positive or a negative catalogue of the Union's powers, on the grounds that that would not lead to any significant clarification and would act as a straightjacket on the Union;[96] and a majority of members of the Convention have endorsed that view.[97] However, at the time of writing, this idea has not been definitively abandoned.[98]

The Commission is advocating an alternative approach.[99] In its view, clarification will be achieved by incorporating into the Treaties definitions of the various scales of action, the possibility of specifying the extent of European action desirable for certain areas, and the obligation to give reasons in each case for opting for a given course of action.

As to Article 308 EC, that provision does not confer *Kompetenz-Kompetenz* (ie the power to extend one's own competences) on the Union.[100] Rather, it merely empowers the Union to expand the range of attributed competences in order to meet some presumed necessity for action stemming from existing Treaty objectives. On this basis, the Commission has argued forcefully against the removal of this provision from the Treaties on the grounds that this would deprive the Union of the flexibility necessary to enable it to meet challenges in the future.[101] At the same time, the Commission has stated that, in order to circumscribe more effectively what should remain very limited use of this provision, it would be preferable to begin by reviewing the common objectives set out *inter alia* in Article 3 EC and, if necessary, to set out expressly the powers to act needed to attain those objectives.[102]

On the same provision, the European Parliament has stated:

... it would be useful to maintain a mechanism similar to the current Article 308 of the EC Treaty which could be applied only in exceptional circumstances and

---

[94] See eg the Commission's note to Group V entitled 'Delimitation of powers: a matter of scale of intervention' (WGV/4) of 10 July 2002.
[95] See the Commission's note to Group V entitled 'The European Union's complementary powers: scope and limits' (WGV/7) of 29 July 2002.
[96] Communication of May 2002 (n 22 above).
[97] CONV 60/02 (report of plenary session of 23 and 24 May), point 9.
[98] See the contribution by Mr Peter Altmeier (WGV/9) of 15 July 2002 and the summary of the Group's meeting of 17 July 2002 (WV/7, CONV 209/02, of 19 July 2002).
[99] WGV/4 (n 94 above).
[100] Opinion 2/94 (n 75 above), paras 29 and 30.
[101] Communication of May 2002, p 21; Commission note of 10 July 2002 entitled 'Delimitation of competences: a matter of scale of intervention' (WG V/4), p 11.
[102] Communication of May 2002, p 21.

which works in both directions by enabling competences to be returned to the Member States when the need for Community intervention has ceased ....[103]

The Working Group broadly accepts that Article 308 should be retained.[104]

6.   Group VI: Economic Governance

The theme of this Group differs from those already considered in one obvious respect: it concerns one specific sector, namely the monetary policy of the Euro. What is more, at present discussions within the Group have revealed that its members in general have little appetite for altering the status quo, except that they have agreed that 'efforts should be made to increase the effectiveness of the external representation of the Eurozone'.[105]

III.   FUNDAMENTAL RIGHTS

A.   General

The case law of the Court of Justice on fundamental rights is too well known to be examined here.[106] Suffice it then to make two general points.

First, the Union is bound to respect the body of fundamental rights recognised by the Court, as are the Member States, when they implement Union law or act within its scope.[107] However, it is not the task of the Union to ensure respect for human rights by the Member States beyond those confines. Articles 6(1) and 7 TEU, which constitute the only exception to that rule, will be discussed below.

---

[103] Resolution of 16 May 2002 (n 48 above), point 35.

[104] Summary of meeting of 6 September, CONV 251/02, WG V/9 of 9 September 2002.

[105] Documents WG VI/5, VI/6, VI/8, VI/9, VI/10 and VI/12. In its Communication of May 2002 (n 22 above), the Commission proposed that economic policy coordination be strengthened in various ways.

[106] See eg Cases 11/70 *Internationale Handelsgesellschaft v EVGF* [1970] ECR 1125 at p 1134, 4/73 *Nold v Commission* [1974] ECR 491 at p 507, 222/84 *Johnston v Chief Constable of the RUC* [1986] ECR 1651, C–13/94 *P v S and Cornwall County Council* [1996] ECR I–2143, point 16, C–129/95 *Criminal Proceedings v X* [1996] ECR I–6609, point 25, C–368/95 *Familiapress* (note 46 above), point 26 and C–17/98 *Emesa Sugar (Free Zone) NV v Aruba* [2000] ECR I–665 (the latter case is noted by Lawson, 2000 *Common Marker Law Review* 983 and discussed by Spielmann, 2000 585). Recent publications include: P Alston (ed) 'The EU and Human Rights' (1999), L Besselink, n 55 above. M Colvin and P Noorlander 'Human Rights and Accountability after the Treaty of Amsterdam' 1998 191, P Gallagher 'The Treaty of Amsterdam and Fundamental Rights' 1998 21, Judge K. Lenaerts 'Fundamental Rights in the European Union' 2000 *European Law Review* 575, J-V Louis n 69 above, P Oliver 'Fundamental Rights in European Union Law after the Treaty of Amsterdam' in Liber Amicorum in Honour of Lord Slynn of Hadley, n 55 above at 319, P Wachsmann 'Le traité d'Amsterdam: les droits de l'homme' 1997 *Revue trimestrielle de droit européen* 883.

[107] Cases 5/88 *Wachauf v Germany* [1989] ECR 2609, point 19, C–260/89 *ERT v Dimotiki Etaira* [1991] ECR I–2925 and *Familiapress* (note 46 above).

Second, the case law of the Court is to some extent enshrined in Article 6(2) TEU, which provides:

> The Union shall respect fundamental rights, as guaranteed by the European Convention for the Protection of Human Rights and Fundamental Freedoms signed in Rome on 4 November 1950 and as they result from the constitutional traditions common to the Member States, as general principles of Community law.[108]

It is now appropriate to consider in some depth three topical issues relating to fundamental rights, namely: Articles 6(1) and 7 TEU, the Charter and finally the possibility of the Union acceding to the ECHR. The latter two issues are currently being considered by Working Group II of the Convention.

B.   Articles 6(1) and 7 TEU

The Treaty of Amsterdam amended what is now Article 6(1) TEU to read as follows:

> The Union is founded on the principles of liberty, democracy, respect for human rights and fundamental freedoms, and the rule of law, principles which are common to the Member States.[109]

According to Article 49 TEU, only those European States which respect the principles enshrined in Article 6(1) may accede to the Union.[110]

Moreover, the Treaty of Amsterdam also inserted a wholly new provision into the TEU in the shape of Article 7, which empowers the Council,

> meeting in the composition of the Heads of State or Government and acting by unanimity on a proposal by one third of the Member States or by the Commission and after obtaining the assent of the European Parliament,

---

[108] This provision (formerly Article F(2) TEU) had not been altered by the Treaty of Amsterdam (1997 OJ C340), which entered into force on 1 May 1999 (1999 OJ L114/56).

Art 46(d) TEU confers jurisdiction on the Court over Art 6(2) TEU, but only with respect to acts of the European institutions. Given that the Court developed its case law on fundamental rights long before Art 6(2) TEU was adopted (as Art F(2) of the original TEU signed at Maastricht), this has not deterred the Court from continuing to develop its case law concerning fundamental rights and the Member States (see eg Cases C–309/96 *Annibaldi v Lazio* [1997] ECR I–7493, para 13, C–292/97 *Karlsson* [2000] ECR I–2737, para 37 and Case C–313/99 *Mulligan v Attorney-General* [2002] ECR I–5719, para 36).

[109] On the Treaty of Amsterdam, see the previous footnote.

[110] M Nowak 'Human Rights "Conditionality" in Relation to Entry to, and Full Participation in, the EU' in Alston, n 106 above, at p 697 has pointed to the anomaly whereby, under Art 46 TEU, Art 6(1) TEU falls outside the Court's jurisdiction but Art 49 TEU falls within it. Having said that, in Case 93/78 *Mattheus v Doego* [1978] ECR 2203 the Court declined to rule on whether Greece, Portugal and Spain fulfilled the conditions for accession set out in the EC Treaty as it was worded at the time.

to

> determine the existence of a serious and persistent breach by a Member State
> of principles mentioned in Article 6(1), after inviting the government of the
> Member State in question to submit its observations.

Plainly, great weight will be attached to such a determination in view of the onerous nature of the procedure. Since Article 7 speaks of a breach of 'principles mentioned in Article 6(1)' without the definite article, there is clearly no need to show a simultaneous infringement of all the principles enshrined in Article 6(1).

Where it makes such a determination, the Council may suspend some of the rights of that State, including its right to vote in the Council; if such a decision is taken, then by virtue of Article 309(1) EC, that State's voting rights in the same institution will also be suspended automatically in relation to European Community matters. Article 309(2) EC goes further in that it empowers the Council to suspend other 'rights deriving from the application of this Treaty to the Member State in question', although that institution is required to 'take into account the possible consequences of such a suspension on the rights and obligations of natural and legal persons'.

What is more, the Protocol on asylum for nationals of Member States agreed at Amsterdam[111] specifies that, where proceedings have been initiated under Article 7(1) or a determination has been made under that provision with respect to a particular Member State, the latter does not qualify as a 'safe country of origin'.

This procedure has yet to be applied.

The Treaty of Nice is set to strengthen Article 7 TEU by expressly empowering the Council, after following a specified procedure, to take preventative action where there is a 'clear risk' of a serious breach of principles mentioned in Article 6(1). In that event, the Council will be empowered to 'address appropriate recommendations to that State'. While it seems clear that the Council can already take such action even without the Treaty of Nice, the amended Article 7 is no doubt designed to confer a particularly solemn character on the envisaged recommendations.

Moreover, Article 46 TEU, which concerns the jurisdiction of the Court of Justice, is also set to be amended by the Treaty of Nice: whereas at present the Court may not review action taken under Article 7 TEU, in future it will have jurisdiction to review the observance of 'the purely procedural stipulations in Article 7'.

In contrast, the Treaty of Nice is not expressed to effect any substantive change to Article 309 EC. The Court of Justice already has jurisdiction with respect to that provision. Arguably, however, Article 309(1) merely lays

---

[111] 1997 OJ C340/103.

down the automatic consequence of a decision being taken by the Council pursuant to Article 7 TEU without providing for the adoption of a separate act which could be quashed by the Court. On the other hand, Article 309(2) clearly provides for the Council to take separate decisions that could be the subject of actions for annulment.

C.   The Charter

1.   Introduction

The Charter of Fundamental Rights of the European Union was 'solemnly proclaimed' by the European Parliament, the Council and the Commission at Nice on 7 December 2000.[112]

The Charter had been drafted by a Convention called into being by the European Council meeting in Cologne in June 1999 and composed on similar lines to the current Convention on the future of the Union. That body met under the Chairmanship of Roman Herzog, former President of Germany and former President of the German Constitutional Court.[113] No decision was taken beforehand as to whether or not the Charter would be binding, as this was to be decided afterwards at the European Council in Nice; but the Convention on the Charter nevertheless decided to draft the text on the basis that it would have binding effect. In the event, the European Council did not decide to render the Charter binding.

In consequence of this procedure, the Charter contains no statement as to whether it is binding. Nevertheless, its preamble merits particular attention in this regard. Following the third recital, which sets out a range of common values and principles, the fourth recital states:

> To this end, it is necessary to *strengthen* the protection of the fundamental rights in the light of changes in society, social progress and scientific and technological developments by making those rights *visible* in a Charter. (emphasis added)

The seventh and final recital reads as follows:

> The Union therefore *recognises* the rights, freedoms and principles set out hereafter. (emphasis added)

---

[112] N 9 above. After the Convention on the Charter had finished drafting that document but prior to its official proclamation, the Praesidium of that Convention issued a commentary on the text (CHARTE 4473/00, CONVENT 49 of 11 October 2000); that commentary is expressed to have no legal value.

[113] See G de Búrca 'The Drafting of the European Union Charter of Fundamental Rights' 2001 *European Law Review* 126 and the various authorities referred to in fn 115 below.

The general provisions at the end of the Charter also deserve particular attention. Article 51 is worded as follows:

1.   The provisions of this Charter are addressed to the institutions and bodies of the Union with due regard for the principle of subsidiarity and to the Member States only when they are implementing Union law. They shall therefore respect the rights, observe the principles and promote the application thereof in accordance with their respective powers.
2.   This Charter does not establish any new power or task for the Community or the Union, or modify the powers and tasks defined by the Treaties.

Article 52(1) contains a general exception clause which purports to apply to all the rights set out in the Charter.[114] According to Article 52(3), in so far as rights in the Charter correspond to those in the ECHR, 'the meaning and the scope of those rights shall be the same as those laid down by the said Convention'; but this 'shall not prevent Union law providing more extensive protection'. Finally, Article 53 states that nothing in the Charter shall restrict or adversely affect existing rights in national law, Union law or international law.

Not surprisingly, this document has spawned a vast body of learned literature,[115] which cannot all be summarised here. What is more, considerations of space do not allow for a discussion of the various substantive rights apparently enshrined in the Charter. Rather, it is preferable to concentrate, albeit very briefly, on the views of a few authors on the status of the Charter and its added value.

---

[114] In reality some of these rights, such as freedom from torture (Art 4) and slavery (Art 5), would appear to be absolute: Triantafyllou 'The European Charter of Fundamental Rights and the "Rule of Law": Restricting Fundamental Rights by Reference' 2002 *Common Market Law Review* 53 at p 55.

[115] Apart from the articles referred to in the following footnotes, see in particular: Advocate General S Alber 'Die EU-Charta der Grundrechte und ihre Auswirkungen auf die Rechtsprechung' 2000 EuGRZ 497; R Alonso García 'The General Provisions of the Charter of Fundamental Rights of the European Union' Jean Monnet Working Paper 4/02 http://www.jeanmonnetprogram.org; D Curtin 'The 'EU Human Rights' Charter and the Union Legal Order: the "Banns" before the Marriage' in Liber Amicorum in Honour of Lord Slynn of Hadley, n 55 above, at 303; J Dutheil de la Rochère 'La Charte des droits fondamentaux de l'Union européenne : quelle valeur ajoutée, quel avenir?' 2000 *Revue du Marche Unique européen* 674 ; C Engel 'The European Charter of Fundamental Rights' 2001 *European Law Journal* 151; E Hirsch Ballin '"Een wezenlijke maatstaf voor alle actoren in de Gemeenschap"—De voorlopige juridische status van het Handvest van de Grondrechten van de Europese Unie' 2001 *Social Economische Wetgeving* 330; G de Kerchove and C Ladenburger 'Le point de vue d'acteurs de la Convention' in 'La Charte des droits fondamentaux de l'Union européenne – Hommage à Silvio Marcus Helmons' ed. J-Y Carlier and O de Schutter (eds Brussels, 2002); C Ladenburger 'L'apport de la Charte dans le domaine des droits civils et politiques' in 'Hommage à S M Helmons'; J B Liisberg 'Does the EU Charter of Fundamental Rights Threaten the Supremacy of Community Law' 2001 *Common Market*

For Judge Wathelet,[116] it is plain beyond peradventure that the Charter is not binding, but it has some legal value as a 'soft law' instrument, which might in some instances reflect rights referred to in Article 6(2) TEU. He also regards it as an inter-institutional agreement which must be observed by the three institutions that proclaimed it. Subject to certain differences of emphasis, this appears to be the prevailing view.[117] As Schwarze points out,[118] an inter-institutional agreement may not alter the Treaties, as that can only be achieved according to the procedure laid down in Article 48 TEU.[119]

A slightly different view is expressed by Lord Goldsmith, who represented the Government of the United Kingdom at the Convention on the Charter. He welcomes the Charter as a 'political declaration' lacking 'the precision of language necessary to allow it legal force', while acknowledging that the Court of Justice might choose to refer to it and interpret it.[120]

In contrast, Ladenburger sees the Charter as an authoritative declaration of the existing fundamental rights already guaranteed by the ECHR and the 'constitutional traditions common to the Member States' within the meaning of Article 6(2) TEU.[121]

None of these authors goes so far as to suggest that the Charter is a *definitive* statement of the rights referred to in Article 6(2) TEU and that it is therefore binding *de facto*.

Whilst it is generally agreed that the Charter recasts pre-existing provisions in different language, a clear divergence of views exists as to whether such an exercise is valuable at all. Thus Lord Goldsmith writes: '... the exercise was not about minting new rights but rather an exercise in increasing the visibility of existing rights'. Judge Lenaerts and De Smijter make much the same point, but in a negative light, when they say that the Charter 'essentially contains new descriptions of existing fundamental rights'

Law Review 1171; and editorial comments 'The EU Charter of Fundamental Rights Still under Discussion' 2001 *Common Market Law Review* 1.

[116]'La Charte des droits fondamentaux : un bon pas dans une course qui reste longue' 2000 *Cahiers de droit européen* 585.
[117]C Callies 'Die Charta der Grundrechte der Europäischen Union — Fragen der Konzeption, Kompetenz und Verbindlichkeit' 2001 *Europaische Zeitscheift fiis Wirtschaftsrechts* 261; J Dutheil de la Rochère 'Droits de l'homme : la Charte des droits fondamentaux et au-delà' Jean Monnet Paper 2001 http://www.jeanmonnetprogram.org; J Schwarze 'Der Grundrechtsschutz für Unternehmen in der Europäischen Grundrechtecharta' 2001 *Europaische Zeitscheift fiis Wirtschaftsrechts* 517.
[118]N 117 above.
[119]In support of this view, one might also refer to Declaration no 3 by the IGC on Art 10 EC, which is appended to the Treaty of Nice (2001 OJ C80/77). That Declaration states *inter alia* that interinstitutional agreements concluded between the European Parliament, the Council and the Commission 'may not amend or supplement' the provisions of the EC Treaty.
[120]'A Charter of Rights, Freedoms and Principles' 2001 *Common Market Law Review* 1201 at p 1215.
[121]'L'application pratique de la Charte des droits fondamentaux par la Commission européenne' European Review of Public Law (forthcoming).

and dub it no more than 'a handy catalogue of the fundamental rights recognised at present'.[122]

What is more, Lenaerts and De Smijter repeatedly complain that, because of this redrafting, certain provisions of the Charter are at variance with existing provisions and case law. In addition, Judge Wathelet[123] has voiced his surprise at the fact that, according to Article 51(1), the Charter applies to the Member States only when they 'implement Union law', whereas the Court has held that the Member States are bound by the body of fundamental rights recognised by the Court whenever they act within its scope.[124]

Finally, the draftsmen of the Charter are also berated for failing to clarify adequately its relationship to the Treaties and to the ECHR (Article 52(2) and (3) respectively).[125]

In short, the Charter has generated a good deal of interest, but has not met with universal acclaim. Possibly the prize for the most outspoken comment should go to Weiler who, writing before the Charter was completed, described the prospect of the proclamation of a non-binding instrument as a 'symbol of European impotence and refusal to take rights seriously'.[126] No doubt, he is not alone in this view. However, if, as is widely hoped, the Charter turns out to have been the first step towards the insertion of a catalogue of rights into the Treaties themselves, then it will undoubtedly have proved its worth.

2.   Application by the Institutions of the Union

a)   The Commission, the Council and the Parliament   On 11 October 2000, before the Charter had been proclaimed, the Commission issued a Communication on its legal nature.[127] In that Communication, the Commission expressed the view that the Charter would produce legal effects, not least because it was highly likely that the Court would draw inspiration from it. Indeed, the Commission ventured to express its expectation that the Charter would become mandatory through the Court's interpretation of it as belonging to the general principles of Community law. At all events, it would be difficult, the Commission stated, for itself and the Council in their legislative function to ignore the Charter, after having solemnly proclaimed it.

---

[122] p 281.
[123] N 116 above.
[124] N 107 above.
[125] Lenaerts and De Smijter, at pp 292–4. On Art 52(3) specifically, see Dutheil 'Droits de l'homme ...' and C. McCrudden 'The Future of the EU Charter of Fundamental Rights' Jean Monnet Paper 2001 http://www.jeanmonnetprogram.org.
[126] 'Editorial: Does the European Union Truly Need a Charter of Rights?' 2000 *European Law Journal* 95 at p 96.
[127] COM(2000) 644 final.

Next, in March 2001, the Commission adopted a Communication on the application of the Charter,[128] which stated *inter alia* that the Commission must 'make compliance with the rights contained in the Charter the touchstone for its action'. The Communication also announced that any proposal for legislation and any draft instrument to be adopted by the Commission would be scrutinised for compatibility with the Charter as part of the normal decision-making procedures. Moreover, the preamble to legislative proposals which 'have a specific link with fundamental rights' would contain a special recital as a formal statement of compatibility with the Charter. A number of legislative Acts adopted since then contain such a recital,[129] so that the two branches of the legislature—the European Parliament and the Council—may thus be said to have given their blessing to the Commission's approach.

b) The Court of Justice The case law of the CFI contains frequent references to the Charter, as do numerous Opinions of the Advocates General.[130]

The CFI's initial venture into this field occurred in *Mannesmannröhren-Werke v Commission*,[131] where it dismissed an argument based on the Charter. The CFI's reasoning was that that document had not been proclaimed when the Commission adopted the contested Decision and that it therefore had no bearing on the case. That would appear to suggest that the Charter has constitutive, not declaratory effect. In contrast, in *max.mobil v Commission*,[132] the CFI described the Charter as 'confirmation' of the constitutional traditions common to the Member States—a clear reference to Article 6(2) TEU. The judgment in *Jégo-Quéré v Commission*[133] was circumspect on this point (though not on others). In that case, the CFI simply referred to the Charter, without in any way indicating its perception of its status.

As to the Advocates General, no less than seven of them have referred to the Charter in their Opinions, albeit sometimes only in passing.[134] Where they have discussed its status, they have consistently declared it not

---

[128] SEC(2001) 380/3. See Ladenburger 'L'application pratique ...'.
[129] Eg Reg 1049/2001 of the European Parliament and the Council regarding public access to European Parliament, Council and Commission documents (2001 OJ L145/43) (recital 2); Decision 1247/2002 of the European Parliament, the Council and the Commission on the European Data-Protection Supervisor (2002 L183/1) (recital 2); Council Framework Decision 2002/584/JHA on the European arrest warrant (2002 L190/1) (recital 12); and Directive 2002/58 of the European Parliament and the Council on privacy and electronic communications (2002 OJ L201/37) (recital 2).
[130] For an overview of this case law and of important pending cases, see Ladenburger 'L'application pratique ...'.
[131] Case T–112/98 [2001] ECR II–729.
[132] Case T–54/99 [2002] ECR II–313, paras 48 and 57.
[133] Case T–177/01 [2002] ECR II–2365, paras 42 and 47; that ruling is currently under appeal (Case C–263/02P).
[134] AG Alber in Case C–340/99 *TNT v Poste Italiane* [2001] ECR I–4109, para 94; AG Geelhoed in Mulligan (n 108 above), para 28, C–413/99 *Baumbast v Secretary of State for the Home Department* (pending), para 59 and Case C–491/01 *The Queen v Secretary of State for*

to be binding.[135] Nevertheless, in certain instances they have stated that the Charter 'includes statements which appear in large measure to reaffirm rights which are enshrined in other instruments'[136] or that certain Articles of the Charter proclaim generally recognised principles.[137] One of the fullest accounts of the status of the Charter is that of Advocate General Mischo in *Booker v The Scottish Ministers*, where he said:

> the Charter is not legally binding, but it is worthwhile referring to it given that it constitutes the expression, at the highest level, of a democratically established political consensus on what must today be considered as the catalogue of fundamental rights guaranteed by the Community legal order.[138]

Moreover, in *Council v Hautala* Advocate General Léger expressed the following view:

> Naturally, the clearly expressed wish of the authors of the Charter not to endow it with binding legal force should not be overlooked. However, aside from any consideration regarding its legislative scope, the nature of the rights set down in the Charter of Fundamental Rights precludes it from being regarded as a mere list of purely moral principles without any consequences. It should be noted that those values have in common the fact of being unanimously shared by the Member States, which have chosen to make them more visible by placing them in a charter in order to increase their protection. The Charter has undeniably placed the rights which form its subject-matter at the highest level of values common to the Member States.[139]

For its part, the Court of Justice itself has so far refrained from referring to the Charter at all, even in cases where the Advocate General's Opinion had

---

Health ex parte BAT (pending), paras 47 and 259; AG Jacobs in Cases C–377/98 *Netherlands v Parliament and Council* (biotechnology Directive) (n 60 above), paras 97 and 210, C–270/99P *Z v Parliament* [2001] ECR I–9197, para 40, and C–50/00P *Unión de Pequeños Agricoltores v Council* [2002] ECR I–667, para 39; AG Léger in Cases C–353/99P *Council v Hautala* (judgment of 6 December 2001), paras 51, 73 and 78–80, and C–309/99 *Wouters v Nederlandse Orde van Advocaten* (judgment of 19 February 2002), paras 173 and 175; AG Mischo in Cases C–122 and 125/99 *D v Council* [2001] ECR I–4319, para 97, and C–20/00 and 64/00 *Booker Aquaculture v The Scottish Ministers* (pending), para 126; AG Stix-Hackl in Case C–49/00 *Commission v Italy*, para 57, and C–459/99 *MRAX v Belgium* [2002] ECR I–6591, para 64; and AG Tizzano in Case C–173/99 *The Queen v Secretary of State for Trade and Industry ex parte BECTU* [2001] ECR I–4881, para 27. Paragraph references are to the Opinions of the Advocates General, not the judgements.

[135] *Baumbast* para 59, *BECTU* para 27, *Council v Hautala* para 80, *Mulligan* para 28, *Unión de Pequeños Agricoltores* para 39, *Z*, para 40.
[136] *BECTU*, para 27.
[137] *Unión de Pequeños Agricoltores*, para 39; *Z*, para 40. Both these Opinions were delivered by Advocate General Jacobs.
[138] Para 126.
[139] Para 80.

done so. Should this coyness be taken as a sign that the Court is ambivalent about the legal status of the Charter?

3.   *Possible Incorporation into the Treaties*

Beyond any doubt, the force of the Charter would be greatly enhanced if it were incorporated in some form into the future constitutional Treaty. As already mentioned, one of the tasks of the Convention's Working Group II is to examine whether and, if so, how this should to be done.

In the 21st century, a modern Western Constitution *without* so much as a reference to a catalogue of fundamental rights scarcely seems conceivable; and the limited terms of Article 6(2) TEU can hardly be deemed sufficient. Not surprisingly, then, discussions within the Group have revealed that a majority is in favour of incorporating the Charter into the Treaties.[140]

A note from the Secretariat of the Convention sets out the various forms which this could take.[141] Moving from the minimalist to the most far-reaching solution, these options are as follows:

(a)   The Charter could simply be attached to the Treaties in the form of a solemn declaration;

(b)   A reference to the Charter could be inserted into Article 6(2) TEU. In that case, it would merely be a source of 'general principles' of Union law;

(c)   A provision could be inserted into the Treaties to the effect that the Union respects the rights, freedoms and principles enshrined in the Charter;

(d)   The preamble to the new constitutional Treaty could contain a reference to the Charter;

(e)   The Charter could be transformed into a new Protocol to the Treaties; and

(f)   The full body of the Charter could be incorporated into the Treaties.

Manifestly, the first two options would not render the Charter fully binding, but merely give it greater force than it has today. The note points out that various combinations of options (a) to (e) could also be envisaged; for example, options (a) and (b) could be combined.

As to option (f), this is favoured by the majority of the Group, since it gives the greatest visibility to the fundamental rights of the Union.[142]

---

[140] Summary of the Group's meeting of 12 July 2002 (document CONV 203/02, WG II/7 of 18 July 2002).

[141] Note of 18 June 2002, CONV 116/02, WG II/1. See also Dutheil 'Droits de l'homme ...'.

[142] CONV 203/02 (n 140 above).

However, the Charter could not be incorporated into the Treaties without certain amendments.[143] Within the confines of this report, it is only possible to give two examples of the various drafting problems which would have to be addressed. One question is: what would become of the preamble to the Charter, which would of necessity have to be detached from the body of that document? The preamble to the Charter could no doubt be inserted, in whole or in part, into the preamble to the constitutional Treaty, if this were desired. Second, what of those articles of the Charter which reproduce the substance of provisions of the Treaties, such as those relating to citizens' rights (most of the provisions contained in Articles 39 to 46)? Should they appear twice in the Treaty? Third, a number of more technical changes would be necessary.[144,145]

D.   Possible Accession to the ECHR

The other task of Working Group II is to reflect on the consequences of the Community's accession to the ECHR. It is now widely recognised that the proclamation of the Charter and its incorporation into the Treaties are no substitute for the Union's accession to the ECHR—and *vice versa*.[146]

As the reader will be aware, in 1979 the Commission first proposed that the Community should accede to the Convention,[147] and renewed that

---

[143] See the above-mentioned note of the Secretariat of 18 June and notes from Commissioner Vitorino dated 5 July 2002 (WG II/3) and 18 July 2002 (document WG II/9).

[144] For instance, Art 51(1) reads as follows: 'This Charter does not establish any new power or task for the Community or the Union, or modify powers and tasks defined by the Treaties'. Art 52(2) provides: 'Rights recognised by this Charter which are based on Community Treaties or the Treaty on European Union shall be exercised under the conditions and within the limits defined by those Treaties.' The words 'this Charter' would obviously be out of place in the basic Treaty; but naturally that problem will arise with a number of provisions. More specifically, 'the Treaties' and 'those Treaties' in Art 51(1) and 52(1) respectively would need to be replaced by other terms such as 'other provisions of this Treaty'.

[145] Moreover, if option (f) were chosen, then some thought would need to be given as to how the current version of the Charter would be extinguished. Probably, it would not be strictly necessary to do this at all, but it would be preferable for the avoidance of doubt.

According to the theory known as '*parallélisme des formes*', legal acts should in general be modified or 'repealed' by following the procedure used for their adoption. On that view, the appropriate course would be for the Commission, the Council and the European Parliament to adopt a 'solemn proclamation', at the time of the signature of the new constitutional Treaty, to the effect that, on its entry into force, the latter will replace the current Charter. Arguably, however, the theory of '*parallélisme des formes*' is not applicable in any event, because the Charter is not a formal legal Act. Thus a declaration by the IGC appended to the constitutional Treaty might suffice.

[146] See Commission's Communication of 11 October 2000 (n 127 above), para 9; also the speeches given on 31 January 2002 by Mr Gil Carlos Rodríguez Iglesias, President of the Court of Justice, and by Mr Luzius Wildhaber, President of the ECtHR http://www.echr.coe.int/ Bilingual/documents; and Lenaerts and De Smijter, at p 292.

[147] Supplement 2/79 to the Bulletin of the European Communities.

suggestion in 1990.[148] The European Parliament has made the same proposal on more than one occasion.[149] Both institutions continue to hold to that view.

In Opinion 2/94,[150] the Court held that no provision in the Treaties conferred any power on the Community to accede to the ECHR and that a Treaty amendment would therefore be required. Interestingly, in a speech delivered in January 2002 to the European Court of Human Rights ('EctHR'), Mr Gil Carlos Rodríguez Iglesias, President of the Court of Justice, emphasised that:

> that Opinion did not in any way constitute the expression of a negative attitude on the part of the Court of Justice towards the principle of such accession, still less the manifestation of any reluctance to occupy a position subordinate to the Strasbourg Court.[151]

He added:

> ... the Opinion was delivered on the eve of an intergovernmental conference which could easily have created the constitutional basis for the conferment of the competence needed for accession, had the political will needed to do so existed.[152]

The backdrop to this long-standing debate may change significantly in the light of the recent judgment of the ECtHR in *Matthews v United Kingdom*,[153] which arguably raises the prospect of all the Member States of the Union being held collectively liable for its acts before that Court. This prospect appears to be looming nearer now that just such an action has

[148] SEC(90)2087 final.
[149] Resolutions of 18 January 1994 (1994 OJ C44/32) and 16 March 2000 (A5–0064/2000).
[150] N 75 above.
[151] N 146 above.
[152] These remarks are no doubt a response to the hostile comments of numerous learned authors to Opinion 2/94. See O De Schutter and Y Lejeune 'L'adhésion de la Communauté à la Convention européenne des droits de l'homme – A propos de l'avis 2/94 de la Cour de justice des Communautés' 1996 CDE 555, G Gaja casenote 1996 *Common Market Law Review* 973, P Wachsmann 'L'avis 2/94 de la Cour de justice relatif à l'adhésion de la Communauté européenne à la Convention de sauvegarde des droits de l'homme et des libertés fondamentales' 1996 *Revue trimestrielle de droit européen* 467, M Waelbroeck 'La Cour de justice et la Convention européenne des droits de l'homme' 1996 *Cahiers de droit européen* 549. Even R Errera ('La fin d'un songe: l'avis de la Cour de justice des Communautés sur l'adhésion de la Communauté à la Convention européenne des droits de l'homme' 1996 Gazette du Palais III p 1467) and C Vedder (casenote, 1996 *Eusapasecht* 309), who consider the Opinion to be unquestionably correct in its result, criticise its reasoning.
[153] Application 24833/94, judgment of 18 February 1999, noted by H Schermers 1999 *Common Market Law Review* 673 and by O De Schutter and O L'Hoest 2000 *Cahiers de droit européen* 141. To some extent, the approach taken in that judgment was heralded by that *Cantoni v France*, application 17862/91, judgment of 15 November 1996 (reports 1996–V), noted by D Spielmann 1997 Rev. Trim. Dr. H. 689 and S Winkler 1999 EuGRZ 181.

been brought against the 15 Member States with respect to a Commission Decision on competition, which was upheld by the Court of Justice.[154]

If the ECtHR does make EU law subject to its *de facto* control, then there will be no room left for opponents of accession to argue that this step would undermine the autonomy of EU law. Equally, there will be less force in the counter-argument that the Union should accede to the ECHR so as to 'set a good example' in the eyes of the countries of Central and Eastern Europe; but that counter-argument will still retain some force, because in such eminently political matters appearances clearly count.

In that event, the principle argument for accession will be that it is unsatisfactory for the Union to be an outsider in such proceedings. The shortcomings of a system in which parties are constrained to attack 'men of straw' in the form of the Member States in respect of acts of the Community institutions are plain: the States concerned will find themselves in the invidious position of having to defend measures which they did not take; the Union will be reliant on the Member States to present argument on their behalf, since it will at best be entitled to appear as a third party intervenor; and the Union will not even enjoy the advantage of having its own judge on the ECtHR.[155] Such a convoluted scheme would scarcely be in the interests of justice.

A further serious drawback would be that, in view of their liability before the latter court, the Member States would be tempted to scrutinise draft Union measures for their compatibility with the ECHR.

Recently, the climate of informed opinion has shifted markedly in favour of accession to the ECHR. This is perhaps best illustrated by the House of Lords Select Committee on the European Communities, which has now advocated accession[156] after rejecting it twice on the grounds that the complexities outweighed the advantages.[157] At the same time, the Council of Europe itself has recently made various overtures to the Union actively inviting it to accede to the ECHR as part of a coherent approach to the effective protection of human rights in Europe.[158]

If the Working Group finds that accession is desirable, it will presumably propose that an appropriate legal basis be inserted into the basic Treaty. The most suitable position for such a provision might be either the Title on

---

[154] Action brought by DSR Senator Lines against the 15 Member States (application 56672/00).
[155] Speech given on 23 July 2002 by Mr Michel Petite, Director-General of the Commission Legal Service (document WG II/3 at p. 52). For the same reason, Mr Petite rejected the suggestion then in circulation that the Union might be subjected by means of a treaty to the jurisdiction of the ECtHR without becoming party to the ECHR.
[156] Report entitled 'EU Charter of Fundamental Rights' 1999–2000.
[157] Report entitled 'Human Rights' 1979–80, and report entitled 'Human Rights Re-examined' 1992–3.
[158] Contributions to the Convention from Mr Walter Schwimmer, Secretary-General of the Council of Europe, and from the Parliamentary Assembly of the same organisation (CONV 157/02 and CONV 193/02).

fundamental rights (ie the adapted Charter) or what is now Article 303 EC. That Article reads as follows: 'The Community shall establish all appropriate forms of cooperation with the Council of Europe'.

However, that would by no means be the end of the matter, since a number of complex issues would have to be addressed prior to such accession.[159] Various amendments to Council of Europe instruments would be required,[160] and no doubt numerous provisions of Union law would also require revision.

The principal issues to be addressed are as follows:

–   First, either Article 59 ECHR or Articles 2 and 4 of the Statute of the Council of Europe would need revision: the first of these provisions restricts the right to sign the ECHR to members of the Council of Europe, while Articles 2 and 4 of the Statute limit membership of that organisation to European 'States';[161]

–   Second, some solution would have to be devised so as to ensure that the ECtHR did not become involved in questions relating to the division of powers between the Union and its Member States;

–   Third, the Member States have not ratified all the Protocols to the ECHR.[162] They have also entered a variety of reservations to the Conventions and the Protocols thereto. Given the need for the uniform application of the law of the Union, it seems hard to imagine how, even today, the body of fundamental rights recognised by the Court of Justice and referred to in Article 6(2) TEU can vary as between Member States. Having said that, the Court has not yet had occasion to rule on this specific issue. At all events, accession to the ECHR must surely entail its uniform application in all the Member States, although the Union need not accede to

---

[159] See *inter alia* the note of 18 June (fn 141 above).

[160] For a detailed account of the requisite amendments, see the study carried out within the Council of Europe of technical and legal issues of a possible EC/EU accession to the ECHR (document WG II/8).

[161] In its submissions to the ECJ prior to Opinion 2/94, the Council stated that only the ECHR should be amended, since it was not intended that the Community should become a member of the Council of Europe.

[162] All the Member States are party to Protocols 1, 6 and 11; in any event, the latter instrument is applicable *erga omnes*. On the other hand, Greece, Spain and the United Kingdom have not ratified Protocol 4; and Belgium, Germany, the Netherlands, Portugal, Spain and the United Kingdom have yet to ratify Protocol 7. The other Protocols have lapsed with the entry into force of Protocol 11. G. Cohen-Jonathan 'L'adhésion de la Communauté européenne à la Convention européenne des droits de l'homme' (1995 *Journal des Tribunaux droit européen* 49) maintains that the Community should only ratify those Protocols to which all its Member States are party, while at the same time advocating a coordinated approach by those States to the ratification of the Protocols.

The position is much more straightforward with respect to Protocol 12 to the Convention, since no Member State has yet ratified it. This is scarcely surprising, as it has only been open for signature since 4 November 2000.

all the Protocols and could enter its own reservations at the time of signature or ratification;[163]

–   Fourth, a mechanism would need to be established for the appointment of the Union's judge on the ECtHR;

–   Fifth, thought should be given to amending Article 292 EC, which provides: 'Member States undertake not to submit a dispute concerning the interpretation or application of this Treaty to any method of settlement other than those provided for therein'. At present, it would be contrary to Article 10 EC for the Community institutions and the Member States to litigate against one another before the ECtHR. The language of Article 55 ECHR is similar to that of Article 292 EC, except that Article 55 permits parties to opt for other fora by 'special agreement'; and

–   Sixth, it is sometimes suggested that a special procedure should be laid down whereby the acts of the Union would be brought before the ECtHR. One possibility would be for the Court of Justice to be empowered to refer a case to the ECtHR, but this could be expected to result in considerable delay. The most appropriate option might simply be to allow the existing procedures to be applied so that actions could be brought against the Union before the ECtHR, once remedies within the Union are exhausted.

Finally, it is important to dispel one widespread misconception: contrary to what is often suggested, accession to the ECHR would not confer general powers on the Union with regard to fundamental rights. As we noticed earlier, beyond the limited exceptions in Articles 6(1) and 7 TEU, it is not the task of the Union to ensure respect for human rights by Member States when they act outside the scope of the Treaties. Accession to the ECHR would not change that.[164]

IV.   THE ROLE OF THE REGIONS AND LOCAL AUTHORITIES

A.   The Current Situation

Decentralisation has been a general trend throughout Western Europe since 1957 when the original Treaty of Rome was signed, to the point where a

---

[163] Reservations are governed by Art 57 (ex 64) of the Convention, and similar provisions in each of the Protocols thereto; see generally S Spiliopoulou Åkermark 'Reservations: breaking new ground in the Council of Europe' 1999 *European Law Review* 499. In its submissions to the Court of Justice prior to Opinion 2/94, the Council maintained that the continued application of national reservations would not be tolerated within the scope of Community law.

Fortunately, the Member States have exercised considerable restraint in entering reservations, unlike some other Contracting Parties such as Russia and Switzerland.

[164] See the above-mentioned speech of 23 July 2002 by Mr Michel Petite.

large number of Member States now have regions with legislative powers (eg the autonomous regions of Spain, the German Länder, Flanders and Wallonia, and Scotland).

In keeping with that development, the position of the regions and local authorities first in the EEC and then the EU has evolved considerably since the Treaty of Rome first came into force. Whereas they initially had no particular place in the EEC at all, their importance has now been recognised in various ways. This may be demonstrated by the following examples:

- the creation of the Regional Fund, which is now enshrined in Article 159 EC along with the other Structural Funds;[165]
- the amendment at Maastricht of what is now Article 203 EC so as to allow each Member State to be represented by regional ministers, provided that they are 'authorised to commit the government of that Member State';
- the establishment of the Committee of the Regions by the Treaty of Maastricht (now Articles 263 to 265 EC);
- the introduction by the Treaty of Maastricht of electoral rights at municipal elections for citizens of the Union (now Article 19(1) EC);[166] and
- Article 151(1) EC which speaks rather poetically of the Community contributing to the 'flowering of the cultures of the Member States, while respecting their national and *regional* diversity ...' (emphasis added). Similarly, the third recital in the preamble to the Charter states: 'The Union ... respect[s] ... the national identities of the Member States and the organisation of their public authorities at national, regional and local levels'.

Moreover, it is no accident that many of the areas in which harmonisation by the Union is expressly ruled out by amendments effected by the Treaties of Maastricht and Amsterdam are frequently vested in regional authorities; this is especially true of education (Article 149(4) EC), vocational training (Article 150(4) EC), and culture (Article 151(5) EC).

Nevertheless, it is clear that the regional and local authorities do not currently enjoy the same status as the central governments of the Member States, which are the privileged partners of the European institutions. Equally, it is plainly inappropriate for the Community institutions to become embroiled in disputes between the Member States and the authorities responsible for their various territorial units.

[165] The Regional Fund was established initially by Council Regulation 724/75 (1975 OJ L73/1).
[166] That provision was implemented by Council Directive 94/80 (1994 OJ L368/38), as amended by Council Directive 96/30 (1996 OJ L122/14); see P Oliver 'Electoral Rights under Article 8B of the Treaty of Rome' 1996 *Common Market Law Review* 473.

Both these propositions are most poignantly illustrated by the Order of the Court of Justice in *Région wallonne v Commission*.[167] In that case, the applicant claimed that it should be regarded as a 'Member State' so that its action for annulment brought pursuant to Article 33 ECSC (the equivalent of Article 230 EC) could be heard by that Court rather than the CFI. The Court rejected this argument in the most forthright terms, which deserve to be quoted in full:

> ... it is apparent from the general scheme of the Treaties that the term 'Member State', for the purposes of the institutional provisions and, in particular, those relating to proceedings before the courts, refers only to government authorities of the Member States of the European Communities and cannot include the governments of regions and autonomous communities, irrespective of the powers they may have. If the contrary were true, it would undermine the institutional balance provided for by the Treaties, which govern the conditions under which the Member States, that is to say, the States parties to the Treaties establishing the Communities and Accession Treaties, participate in the functioning of the Community institutions. It is not possible for the European Communities to comprise a greater number of Member States than the number of States between which they were established.
>
> According to settled case law, although it is for all the authorities of the Member States, whether it be the central authorities of the State or the authorities of a federal State, or other territorial authorities, to ensure observance of the rules of Community law within the sphere of their competence, it is not the task of the Community institutions to rule on the division of powers by the institutional rules proper to each Member State, or on the obligations which may be imposed on federal State authorities and the federal State (see, *inter alia*, Case C-8/88 *Germany v Commission* [1990] ECR I–2321, paragraph 13). Thus an action whereby the Commission, under Article [226] of the EC Treaty, or a Member State, under Article [227], can seek a ruling from the Court of Justice that another Member State has failed to fulfil one of its obligations can only be brought against the government of the Member State in question, even if the failure to act is the result of the action or omission of the authorities of a federal State, a region or an autonomous community (see, in particular, precisely in relation to Belgium, Cases 227/85, 228/85, 229/85 and 230/85 *Commission v Belgium* [1988] ECR 1 and Case C–211/91 *Commission v Belgium* [1992] ECR I–6757).
>
> As the action by the Walloon Region cannot be treated as an action by a Member State ... the Court clearly has no jurisdiction to take cognisance of the action.[168, 169]

---

[167] Case C–95/97 [1997] ECR I–1787, noted by J Scott 1999 *Common Market Law Review* 227.
[168] See also Case C–180/97 *Regione Toscana v Commission* [1997] ECR I–5245.
[169] A further illustration of the principle that the Member States are the privileged partners of the Union's institutions is to be found in Art 8 of Council Regulation 1260/1999 laying down general provisions on the Structural Funds (1999 OJ L161/1). According to that provision, certain action is to be taken in close consultation ('partnership') between 'the Commission and

From this ruling it necessarily follows that a region does not constitute a 'Member State' for the purposes of the second paragraph of Article 230 EC. Consequently, it can only commence proceedings pursuant to that provision where it is 'directly and individually concerned' by the act in question within the meaning of the fourth paragraph of that provision. According to well established case law, a region fulfils this requirement where it is defending the legality of a State aid which it has granted, but not where it is merely seeking to defend the economic interests of its residents.[170]

According to one suggestion designed to overcome this case law, each Member State should be entitled to delegate its right of action under the first paragraph of Article 230—as *presently* worded.[171] With respect, that view is not easy to reconcile with the particularly strong language of the Court in *Région wallonne*, which would suggest that the privileges of the Member States are inalienable and thus cannot be assigned or delegated. Moreover, Member States would then be entitled to delegate this right even to the smallest local authority or, for that matter, to other public bodies. By the same token, this would open the door to the European institutions similarly delegating their rights of action to other bodies such as the Economic and Social Committee or the Committee of Regions itself. Would this really be acceptable?[172]

the Member State, together with the authorities and bodies designated by the Member State within the framework of its national rules and current practices, namely regional and local authorities ...'.

In addition, it should be pointed out that point 4 of the Lamassoure Report (n 48 above) states: 'It is important that there should be no ambiguity about the fact that each Member State is entirely and exclusively competent to define the level, geographical scope, powers and status of its regional and local authorities. Each national Constitution devotes considerable space to this matter ... These provisions lie at the very heart of national identity and sovereignty.'

[170] See generally Cases T–214/95 *Vlaams Gewest v Commission* [1998] ECR II–717, T–238/97 *Comunidad Autónoma de Cantabria v Council* [1998] ECR II–2271, T–609/97 *Regione Puglia v Commission* [1998] ECR II–4051, and T–132 and 143/96 *Freistaat Sachsen v Commission* [1999] ECR II–3663; C–452/98 *Netherlands Antilles v Council* [2001] ECR I–8973; (the applicant in the latter case was not a region within the Community, but one of the Overseas Countries and Territories governed by Art 182 to 188 European Communities; yet nothing turned on this distinction.) See, however, the ruling in Cases T–32 and 41/98 *Netherlands Antilles v Commission* [2000] ECR II–201, currently the subject of an appeal (Case C–142/00P *Commission v Netherlands Antilles*), which Advocate General Léger urged the Court to reject (Opinion of 12 September 2002). Also see Piet van Nuffel 'What's in a Member State? Central and Decentralized Authorities before the Community Courts?' 2001 *Common Market Law Review* 871.

Naturally, this case law must be seen in the broader context of the continuing controversy as to the concept of 'direct and individual concern' under Art 230 EC: see most recently Cases C–50/00 *Unión de Pequeños Agricoltores* (n 134 above) and T–177/01 *Jégo-Quéré v Commission* (n 133 above).

[171] van Nuffel (see previous fn) at p 880.

[172] In contrast, there would appear to be no objection to a Member State being represented in court by an official of a regional or local authority, provided that he fulfils the conditions laid down in Art 17 of the Statute of the Court of the EC.

B.   Proposals for Reform

As mentioned earlier, considerable pressure for reform of the status of the regions and local authorities has come from the regions of certain federal Member States, notably the German *Länder*.

Recently, both the Commission and the European Parliament have called for regional and local authorities to be more fully involved in the decision-making process and in the implementation of Union law, in accordance with the constitutional rules of each Member State.[173] At the same time, they have stressed that the responsibility for ensuring this lies primarily with the Member States themselves. Also, the Commission suggested that certain policies such as environmental protection be implemented by tripartite contracts between the Commission, the central government of the Member State concerned and a regional or local authority.[174]

In its submissions to the Convention,[175] the Committee of the Regions has proposed that, as the body which represents the levels of government closest to the public, it should have a specific role in monitoring compliance with the principle of subsidiarity. It also requests that it be granted the status of an institution of the Union as well as the right to bring actions before the Court of Justice, at least in defence of its prerogatives and of the subsidiarity principle (ie where an act is adopted in breach of an obligation to consult that Committee). Furthermore, it maintains that mandatory consultation should be extended to 'all areas relating to the powers of the local and regional authorities, such as, for example, agriculture and research and technological development'.

Another possibility would be to confer on the regions, or at least on those with special powers, a privileged right of action on the same basis as the Member States, thereby reversing the case law just considered. At the IGC which led to the Treaty of Nice, both Belgium and the Committee of

---

[173] As to the Commission, see not only its Communication of May 2002 (n 22 above), but also its White Paper on Governance (COM(2001) 428 final, also published in 2001 OJ C287/1 and on the Commission's dedicated website: http://europa.eu.int/comm/governance. The White Paper was the subject of a resolution of the European Parliament dated 29 November 2001 (A5–0399/2001). See also the Commission's Communication of 5 June 2002 entitled 'European Governance: Better Lawmaking' (COM(2002) 275 final), also available on the Commission's website on governance. In addition, see 'Mountain or Molehill? A Critical Appraisal of the Commission White Paper on Governance' published under the auspices of the European University Institute and the New York University School of Law (htpp://www.jeanmonnetprogram.org/papers/01) with contributions by *inter alios* D Curtin, C Joerges, N MacCormick, N Walker, and J H H Weiler; also C Joerges '"Good Governance" im Europäischen Binnenmarkt: Über die Spannung zwischen zwei rechtswissenschaftlichen Integrationskonzepten und deren Aufhebung' 2002 *Europasecht* 17 and 'The Commission's White Paper on Governance in the EU – a Symptom of Crisis?' Guest Editorial 2002 *Common Market Law Review* 441.
As to the Parliament, see recitals Q and R to, and points 38–40, of the resolution of 16 May 2002 (n 48 above).
[174] *Ibid.*
[175] CONV 195/02, CONTRIB 68.

the Regions submitted a proposal to that effect with respect to 'regions with legislative powers'.[176] Yet, apart from any purely political considerations, any proposal to confer such rights on territorial units within Member States poses an inherent difficulty, given the considerable variations in the powers of the regions across the Union. Surely, it would be anomalous to confer broader rights of action on any region than it enjoys before its national courts or to grant it rights of action over matters for which it is not competent in national law. On the other hand, as we already noticed, the Court of Justice would be reluctant to be drawn into internal disputes between the central government and a region of a Member State as to the extent of the powers of that region. Confining such rights of action to 'regions with legislative powers' would require the Court to do just that.

By way of compromise, thought might be given to widening the rights of intervention of regional and local authorities. The Court has been relatively liberal as regards requests to intervene by regional and local authorities seeking to defend the economic interests of their territories, by interpreting widely the concept of 'interest' under Article 37 of the Statute of the Court of the EC.[177] However, in direct actions to which only Member States and/or institutions are party that provision expressly precludes interventions by persons not falling within either category. It follows, for example, that in infringement proceedings against a Member State under Article 226 EC involving the legislation enacted by a region, intervention by that region is precluded. What is more, Article 40 of the new Statute, which will replace Article 37 of the current Statute on the entry into force of the Treaty of Nice, is drafted in the same terms. This change could be effected without amending the Treaties: by virtue of Article 245 EC, Article 40 could be amended by unanimous vote of the Council. Once again, it will be essential to ensure that the language of the amendment is not such as to embroil the Court in domestic disputes between the central government of a Member State and its regional or local authorities.

---

[176] As to Belgium, see CONFER 4742/00 of 12 May 2000 http://europa.eu.int/comm/archives/igc2000/; as to the Committee of the Regions, see point 5.13 of its Opinion on the IGC (2000 OJ C156/6). This idea was taken up by Professor Neil MacCormick, MEP for the Scottish National Party, in his 'A Comment on the Governance Paper' in 'Mountain or Molehill? ...' (n 173 above) at p 205 (' ... The governments and parliaments of constitutional regions should, for obvious reasons, have an independent right of recourse to such a constitutional court. In the meantime (and in any event) it would also be desirable for constitutional regions to have access directly to the European Court of Justice in case of controversies concerning the lawfulness or validity of governmental or legislative action at the level of the internal nation.')

[177] Cases T–194/95 *Area Cova v Council* [1996] ECR II–591 and T–138/98 *ACAV v Council* [1999] ECR II–1797 and the unpublished Orders referred to there. In *Area Cova* and *ACAV*, the CFI did not have regard to the powers of the authorities concerned.

V.   CONCLUSION

As indicated by the two quotations set out at the beginning of this article, it was envisaged from the outset that the process of European integration would follow an incremental and pragmatic approach—and what could be more quintessentially British?! Clearly, this approach has borne fruit. Nevertheless, the time has now come to recast, streamline and simplify the Treaties, in view of the perceived need for greater transparency and democratic legitimacy and with an eye to the further enlargement of the Union. Alain Lamassoure MEP, a member of the Convention, has expressed this point in the following terms:

> ... Europe is finally glimpsing the possibility of escaping from the provisional status that has been characteristic of its long process of growing up, from deepening to enlargement, at an average rate of one treaty every three years! The time has come to conclude the final treaty or to embark upon a different process: the process of producing the Constitution of the European Union....[178]

This is a daunting task, which involves tackling a series of sensitive issues. Yet, it seems safe to say that a surprising degree of consensus has already built up within the Convention on a number of matters which have proved problematic in the recent past, including: the use of the term 'Constitution', or at least 'Constitutional Treaty', rather than the less integrationist 'Treaty'; conferring legal personality on the Union; and the incorporation of the Charter into the Union's 'Constitution' in some form. However, that is by no means to deny that an arduous road lies ahead.

---

[178] 'The European Union: Four Possible Models' note of 3 September 2002, CONV 235/02, CONTRIB 83.

2

European Union Law and National Constitutions

JACQUELINE DUTHEIL DE LA ROCHÈRE AND
INGOLF PERNICE*

I.   INTRODUCTION: FOUNDATIONS OF EUROPEAN CONSTITUTIONALISM

T HE CONSTITUTIONAL PROCESS in the European Union has reached a new stage: Following the Nice Declaration on the Future of the Union and the Laeken Summit's call for 'a Constitution for European citizens',[1] the European Convention is currently discussing the structure and the contents of a new constitutional settlement,[2] first drafts of which are being circulated.[3] In the academic community, a broad doctrinal debate has begun on what is called the 'Europeanization' of the national constitutions and which focuses on the implications of European integration on the normative reality of national constitutional law.[4] Our discourse

* Professor Jacqueline Dutheil de la Rochère, Professor of European Law, Director of the Centre of European Law at the University of Paris II (Panthéon-Assas); Professor Dr Ingolf Pernice, Professor of Public, International and European Law, Managing Director of the Walter Hallstein Institute for European Constitutional Law at the Humboldt-University of Berlin (www.whi-berlin.de). Quotations of national constitutions are taken from www.ecln.net, subsection on constitutional discourse. The authors are grateful to Daniel Thym, assistant at the Walter Hallstein Institute, for his critical review of the draft, and his valuable suggestions and his technical assistance. This chapter was written in October 2001.

[1] Laeken Declaration on the Future of the European Union, Annex I to the Presidency Conclusions, Laeken European Council, 15 December 2001 \ue.eu.int/en/info/eurocouncil, s II.

[2] For a picture of the state of discussion in the Convention see P Oliver in ch 2 of this book.

[3] See the 'Proposal of a Constitution' of the Swedish Liberal Party of March 2002, referred to in: G Schäder/M. Melin, 'European Union Law and National Constitutions: Sweden', in Lord Slynn of Hadley and M Andenas (eds), *FIDE XX. Congress London 2002, Volume 1, National Reports* (London, British Institute of International and Comparative Law, 2002), p 387 at 395 and the references at \www.whi-berlin.de (subsection 'draft constitutions'), which will be constantly updated.

[4] See the references and various national reports submitted and more generally I Pernice, The Impact of European Integration on Member State's Constitutional Systems, lecture given at the

on 'European Union Law and National Constitutions' covers both the developments in the academic world and the political arena, which go hand in hand and are two complementary faces of European constitutionalism.

The questionnaire submitted to the national rapporteurs to the 2002 Congress of the International Federation of European Law (FIDE) reflected this. As a guideline it concentrated on two aspects: (1) the interrelationship and interdependence of the national concepts of constitution and the provisions of the constitutions of the Member States allowing and conditioning the constitution-making process at the European level, and (2) the repercussions of this process on the constitutional autonomy (or sovereignty) of the Member States, their legal system and the functions of their respective institutions. Ideally, our undertaking results in a better understanding of what European constitutionalism is about among the scientific community as well as the politicians and citizens. On this basis, we may be able to draw some practical conclusions for the ongoing constitutional debate in the European Convention. A comparative constitutional discourse is the more important, the more it becomes apparent that European constitutionalism is not a matter of states only, but involves and concerns directly the peoples and citizens who have defined themselves in the EC Treaty as the citizens of the Union. In the same way as our national constitutions and the concept of constitutionalism are, in each Member State, the expression of a specific (political) culture[5] and can only be understood and interpreted in the context of its history, religion, philosophy and the economic conditions of the particular country,[6] the constitutional process in Europe must also be conceptualised as a process forming a common political culture and a European identity of the citizens of the Union.[7]

Many excellent reports were submitted,[8] while reports from Denmark, France and Belgium did not arrive, at least not in time, and there is also no report from a candidate country of central and eastern Europe. The exercise of producing a 'general report' as reproduced in this chapter, had to be partial and incomplete. The general report draws from the national reports and generally follows the structure of the questionnaire. With a view to preparing a fruitful discussion at the FIDE Congress, specific focus is given,

International Meeting 'The European Political System', Naples, 26–27 September 2002 forthcoming on \www.whi-berlin.de, subsection WHI Papers 2002.

[5] For this approach see P Häberle, *Verfassungslehre als Kulturwissenschaft*, 1982, 2nd edn (1998).

[6] P Häberle, 'Die Verfassung im Kontext', in: D Thürer, J-F Aubert and J P Müller (eds), *Verfassungsrecht der Schweiz* (2001) p 17 *et seq*.

[7] On the question of a identity-building function of the constitution see M Nettesheim, 'EU-Recht und nationales Verfassungsrecht: Deutscher Bericht', in Lord Slynn of Hadley and M Andenas (eds), *FIDE XX*, above n 3, p 81 at 95 *et seq*.

[8] For a comprehensive overview see \www.FIDE2000.org.

as far as possible, to the five items on the agenda of the congress workshop which were envisaged:

— Constitutionalism Revisited: What Does 'Constitution' Mean for the EU?
— Supremacy and Pre-emption: Constitutional Principles and National Safeguards
— The European Charter of Fundamental Rights: Legal Status and Judicial Review
— The Reorganisation of the European Executive: Giving the Union a Face?
— European and National Parliaments: Enhancing Democratic Legitimacy and Control

A. The Concept of a Constitution in the Member States

'There exists a common theoretical basis of European constitutionalism, viz. the doctrine of social contract and the idea of basic human rights and fundamental freedoms ...' This statement in the Austrian Report is qualified by a reference to quite different practical developments in the various European countries.[9] Indeed, the comparison of the national reports shows the existence of very different constitutional traditions and broad conceptual variations (a) which may explain why a meaningful revision of the EU/EC architecture under the heading of 'constitutionalism' will be a difficult undertaking (b), even if the use of the term 'constitution' cannot be regarded as a taboo any more after the Laeken Declaration.

a. What is a Constitution: Theoretical Concepts and Basic Notions

The Dutch report clearly states that 'Dutch constitutional law is not based— either in positive law, or in the doctrine—on the idea of popular sovereignty'.[10] Talking about a 'social contract' will also be difficult for countries like Luxembourg and Cyprus: Luxembourg has been created, as an independent state by an international treaty, the Final Act of the Congress of Vienna of 9 June 1815, and confirmed by the Treaties of London of 1839 and 1867. The function of its first constitution in 1841 was, thus, not to constitute or found the state, but rather to organise the already existing state and,

[9] F Köck, 'EU Law and National Constitutions: The Austrian Case', in Lord Slynn of Hadley and M Andenas (eds), *FIDE XX*, above n 3, p 5 at 7.
[10] C A J M Kortmann, 'European Union Law and National Constitutions: The Netherlands', in Lord Slynn of Hadley and M Andenas (eds), *FIDE XX*, above n 3, p 299 at p 301.

in particular, its legal system.[11] Even more striking is the example of Cyprus: its Constitution has been imposed upon the people by the Zurich Treaty of 1959 between Greece and Turkey and the London Treaty which was concluded a week later on the initiative of the colonial powers. There was no question of consent of the people or their representatives, so the Constitution as well as the (partial) independence and integrity are based on international law rather than on a 'social contract'.[12]

Do these statements and facts, however, exclude the idea or, as the Dutch report says, 'ideology'[13] of popular sovereignty and social contract as a principle? In Germany the elaboration and adoption of the German Fundamental Law ('Grundgesetz') after the second world war (1949) was not an act of a sovereign German people. Its Fundamental Law was formally adopted by a qualified majority of the German *Länder* which had been established between 1945 and 1949 and it is nevertheless argued that it was legitimised by the subsequent democratic elections, by its recognition in practice[14] and, finally, by its confirmation following German unification in 1990.[15] The idea of a social contract, therefore, is more a normative *petitum* than a description of the origin of the constitution in Germany.

Moreover, the concept of popular sovereignty is explicitly mentioned as a general principle in Article 20 (2) of the German Constitution and similar explicit references can be found in the Constitutions of Sweden,[16] France, Finland (since 1919)[17] and Austria. The latter's Article 1 may be cited as an example: 'Austria is a democratic republic. Her legal order originates in the people'. And the Austrian report explains that:

> all legislative acts applicable in Austria would require, as their ultimate basis, the will of the *Austrian* people, and that they would therefore have to be

---

[11] G Wivenes, 'Le droit européen et les constitutions nationales: Luxembourg, in Lord Slynn of Hadley and M Andenas (eds), *FIDE XX*, above n 3, p 267 at p 270 *et seq.*

[12] C Josephides, 'L'ordre juridique communautaire et les constitutions nationales: la constitution de Chypre face au débat constitutionnel dans l'Union européenne', in Lord Slynn of Hadley and M Andenas (eds), *FIDE XX*, above n 3, p 57 at p 64 *et seq* under reference to the Treaty of Guarantee and the Treaty of Alliance.

[13] Kortmann, above n 10, p 299.

[14] Regarding the (re-)establishment of the German Länder: M Stolleis, '§ 5 Besatzungsherrschaft und Wiederaufbau deutscher Staatlichkeit 1945–1949', in J Isensee and P Kirchhof (eds), *Handbuch des Staatsrechts der Bundesrepublik Deutschlands, Volume I Grundlagen von Staat und Verfassung* (1987), p 173 at 195 *et seq*; regarding the subsequent legitimisation of the Constitution see R Mußgnug, '§ 6 Zustandekommen des Grundgesetzes und Entstehen der Bundesrepublik Deutschland', in *ibid* p 219 at 255 *et seq.*

[15] For details see J Isensee and P Kirchhof (eds), *Handbuch des Staatsrechts der Bundesrepublik Deutschlands, Volume VIII Die Einheit Deutschlands - Entwicklung und Grundlagen* (1995), and in particular the contribution of M Heckel, '§ 197 Die Legitimation des Grundgesetzes durch das deutsche Volk', *ibid* 489 *et seq.*

[16] Schäder and Melin, above n 3, p 388.

[17] Z Sundström, Boedeker and K Kauppi, 'EU Law and National Constitutions: Finland', FIDE XX. Congress London 2002 (published on \www.fide2002.org), at p 6.

enacted by a legislature elected, not just by a democratically constituted people, but by, and only by, the *Austrian* people.[18]

Is it possible to combine the concept of popular sovereignty as the main source of legitimacy of European public authority with opposite traditions in other Member States, such as the Netherlands referred to earlier, or the United Kingdom,[19] where not only the sequence of historical developments, but general constitutional law doctrine does not accept the concept? One aspect, which may be taken into account in this context, is the concept of 'political sovereignty' of the people in a system of 'representative democracy', which underlies the Constitution of the Netherlands,[20] the United Kingdom and Luxembourg,[21] although they do not refer to the people as the constituent power. At least in this respect, the legitimacy of public authority is based upon the will of the citizens of the country. Moreover, the report from Cyprus stresses that, even if the concept did not apply domestically, it could nonetheless be applied at least to the European Constitution,[22] which has a different conceptual basis than the national constitution.

Generally, one may talk about a social contract in cases in which it is 'the will of the people represented in the constitution that is regarded as truly sovereign'.[23] Switzerland is another example: it considers itself as a nation of will ('Willensnation'), and the prominent function of its constitutional law, according to the Swiss report, is to keep this nation of will together by means of federalism.[24] The idea of a social contract is common to countries where it is, like in France, the joint will for political association under well determined principles of a constitution—shortly, the constitution—by which the individuals have defined themselves as a 'nation'.[25] Accordingly *Abbé Sieyès* said that the nation is 'un corps d'associés vivant

---

[18] Köck, above n 9, p 12.

[19] For the United Kingdom, see the general remarks in P Craig, 'European Union Law and National Constitutions: The United Kingdom', FIDE XX. Congress London 2002 (published on www.fide2002.org), p 1 *et seq* and, more specifically on the absence of popular sovereignty and perspectives of its adoption for European public authority also from a British perspective, D Thym, 'European Constitutional Theory and the Post-Nice Process', ch 8 of this book.

[20] Köck, above n 9, p 5, see nevertheless p 6, where 'popular sovereignty' is opposed to 'representative democracy, although an abrogating consultative referendum is possible since 1 January 2002'.

[21] Ch IV to VI of the Constitution, see Wivenes, above n 11, p 270.

[22] Josephides, above n 12, p 60, 65.

[23] With these terms the distinction drawn in Köck, above n 9, p 9, to constitutions which are no more than a programmatic guideline for a parliament which is, itself, 'regarded the collective representation of people's sovereignty, and thus sovereign itself'.

[24] M Freiermuth Abt and R Mosters, 'EU-Recht und nationale Verfassungen: Schweiz', in Lord Slynn of Hadley and M Andenas (eds), *FIDE XX*, above n 3, p 405 at p 410 *et seq.*

[25] See also H Hofmann, 'Von der Staatssoziologie zu einer Soziologie der Verfassung', 1999 *Juristenzeitung* 1065 at 1069 *et seq.*

sous une loi commune et représentés par la même législature'.[26] In the tradition of the French revolution this law cannot be anything else than the expression of the will of the associated individuals. Talking about the will, therefore, seems to refer to the origin of legitimacy of public authority and legislation or to what the Finish report calls 'the rule of recognition':[27] the Constitution is the expression of this will on who has such authority and how the relevant rules may be changed.

The term 'constitution' does not necessarily refer to a unique legal instrument or even a written text at all. The latter is the case with the United Kingdom,[28] the former the case with Sweden and Austria. Sweden has 'four laws of superior nature, together forming the Constitution', the most important being the 'Instrument of Government', which qualifies the other three — the Act of Succession (1810), the Freedom of the Press Act (1949) and the Freedom of Expression Act (1991) as 'the fundamental laws of the Realm'.[29] In Austria, the central Federal Constitution ('Bundesverfassungsgesetz') is complemented by numerous federal constitutional laws which have the same authority and protection against revision, but to some extent of less importance and even 'forgotten'.[30] While in other Member States the term 'Constitution' seems to be reserved to one formal written legal instrument which ranges at the top of the hierarchy of norms and the revision of which is subject to a specific procedure,[31] the term 'constitutional law' is broader and used, as in the Netherlands, to cover the 'Charter of the Kingdom', organic regulations, judge-made law, constitutional conventions and, what is important, 'parts of international and supranational law, especially Community law and the European Convention on Human Rights'.[32]

On the basis of the distinction between the formal and the material meaning of the term constitution[33] the latter areas would certainly be excluded from the body of formal constitutional law, while they are part of

---

[26] E Sieyès, *Qu'est-ce que le Tiers Etat?* (1789), edition R Zapperi 1970, p 126 at 204 et suiv.; see also the explanations given by P Allott, 'The Crisis of European Constitutionalism: Reflections on the Revolution in Europe', 34 *Common Market Law Review* (1997) 452 et seq.
[27] Sundström, Boedeker and Kauppi, above n 17, p 1, with a reference to N McCormick, 'Questioning Sovereignty', in *ibid*, *Law, State and Nation in the European Commonwealth* (1999), p 80–83.
[28] See Craig, above n 19, p 3.
[29] Schäder and Melin, above n 3, p 387, pointing out that the 'Instrument of Government' of 1974 is the most important of these fundamental laws and
[30] Köck, above n 9, p 10.
[31] See also the comparative analysis by I Pernice, 'Bestandssicherung der Verfassungen: Verfassungsrechtliche Mechanismen zur Wahrung der Verfassungsordnung', in R Bieber and P Widmer (eds), *L'espace constitutionnel européen. Der Europäische Verfassungsraum. The European Constitutional Area* (1995) p 225.
[32] Kortmann, above n 10, p 299.
[33] Eg in Freiermuth Abt and Mosters, above n 24, p 409 et seq; J Iliopoulos-Strangas and E Prevedourou, 'Le droit de l'Union europénne et les Constitutions nationales. Rapport hellénique', FIDE XX. Congress London 2002 (published on www.fide2002.org), at p 5 et seq;

and determine the rules on constitutional matters in substance. They would also be outside the term, as the concept of 'constitution' relates to states only. Many reports contain such a definition: eg 'Constitution' is defined in the

— Austrian report,[34] as 'legal rules which provide for a state's basic organisation by setting up the necessary institutions, endowing them with the necessary powers, and regulating the procedures by which they may fulfil their legislative, administrative, and judicial functions';
— Finnish report,[35] as 'the legal rules and norms in force within a state that regulate pro primo the competencies, functioning and mutual relations of the highest state organs as well as how they are appointed and elected, and pro secundo the legal status of the citizens in relation to the state power';
— Spanish report,[36] calling 'constitutional' the provisions which govern the fundamental legal positions of the citizens towards the state, aiming at granting the liberty of the individual in an organised political community, as well as the distribution of the powers between the institutions thereof, provisions which, due to their fundamental and determining character for the legal system, are generally superior in the hierarchy of norms and regarding their obligatory force.
— Luxembourg report,[37] in relation to the state, pointing out that the constitutional law in Luxembourg understands the 'constitution comme loi organique fondamentale de l'Etat';
— Greek report,[38] to be an act, qualified as fundamental law, given supreme legal force and containing the fundamental rules and principles for the organisation and exercise of state power as well as the relations of the state to individuals, other states and the international community;
— Italian report,[39] pointing out that 'the very essence of the Constitution relies on the fact that it synthesises in a single legal act the unity of the state as a politically organised entity';

---

[34] Köck, above n 9, p 8.
[35] Sundström, Boedeker and Kauppi, above n 17, p 1
[36] J Martín y Pérez de Nanclares and M López Castillo, 'Droit de l'UE et constitutions nationales: Espagne', in Lord Slynn of Hadley and M Andenas (eds), *FIDE XX*, above n 3, p 313 at p 315.
[37] Wivenes, above n 11, p 270.
[38] Iliopoulos-Strangas and Prevedourou, above n 33, p 7 (my translation).
[39] E Cannizzano, 'EU Law and National Constitution: A Pluralist Constitution for a Pluralist Legal Order? National Report Italy', in Lord Slynn of Hadley and M Andenas (eds), *FIDE XX*, above n 3, p 243 at p 243 *et seq*.

— German report,[40] as the fundamental liberal political order of the state, the very essence of the supreme rules of law, normally laid down in a constitutional document, which determine the organisation of the state regarding the institutions, form and structure as well as the fundamental relationship to its citizens and other issues with a view to giving them greates protection against abrogation or revision.

This 'traditional' concept has, however, been questioned with regard to the recent developments within the European Union. In this respect, the Italian report develops a 'pluralistic conception of Constitution, which rejects the idea of a unitary source of state sovereignty and admits the existence of diverse legal perspectives in which the exercise of political power can be framed'.[41] The German report emphasises that the state-centred view has lost ground and the prevailing view today is an 'abstract' or 'post national' concept of the constitution.[42] It points to the central criterion of the constitution which is the principle of democracy, the idea of 'self-legislation',[43] and refers to the French Declaration of Human Rights of 1789: 'Toute société dans laquelle la garantie des droits n'est pas assurée, ni la séparation des pouvoirs déterminée, n'a point de constitution'.[44] Likewise, the Austrian report stresses that to reserve the term

> constitution ... to the fundamental law of an (albeit federal) state that disposes of unlimited powers, at least in principle ..., such terminological purity is neither generally accepted in doctrine nor necessary in practice, and is, as was already shown, alien also to everyday legal terminology.[45]

The definitions cited above are quite similar in substance, and the question may be put whether the definition could be extended to cover the primary law of the European Union by replacing the word 'state' in each of them by the term 'community' or 'public authority'. Though the relation to the state may be explained by the mere fact that historically there was no other kind of political organisation with a similar interaction between the individual and public authority, there is some reluctance in the debate—and hence the

---

[40] Nettesheim, above n 7, p 93.

[41] Cannizzano, above n 39, p 245 *et seq*.

[42] Nettesheim, above n 7, p 90, 91.

[43] Nettesheim, above n 7, p 94, with reference to W Kägi, *Die Verfassung als rechtliche Grundordnung des Staates* (1945; new print 1971), p 49: 'Selbstgesetzgebung'

[44] Nettesheim, above n 7, p 94. For the value of this principle in Greece, see Iliopoulos-Strangas and Prevedourou, above n 33, p 4 *et seq*.

[45] Köck, above n 9, p 27; for more detail see I Pernice, 'Europäisches und nationales Verfassungsrecht', 60 *Veröffentlichungen der Vereinigung der Deutschen Staatsrechtslehrer* (2001) 148 at 155 *et seq* developing the 'postnational' concept of constitution. See also the recent study of A Peters, *Elemente einer Theorie der europäischen Verfassung* (2001), p 93–166.

national reports—to use the term 'constitution' to describe the primary law of the Union. There is a strong connection, in particular, with the idea of state sovereignty or, as the Italian report stresses, (popular) sovereignty which belongs 'only to the citizens, considered as a comprehensive and unitary body'.[46] Its proposed 'pluralistic conception of Constitution' assumes the co-existence of 'a plurality of legal perspectives, each claiming autonomy and possessing its own source of legitimacy and its own sets of values and principles'.[47] But can the citizens—or people—be considered as a unitary body, if the same citizens legitimise both the national and European level of government? It is the Swiss report which concludes from the integration clauses of the national constitutions that public authority can be divided and vested with national and European institutions: divided sovereignty, as can be drawn from the Swiss Constitution of 2000, Article 3 of which declares the Cantons 'sovereign', though Switzerland is a sovereign state as well.[48] The American tradition reflected in the Federalist Papers may explain the concept of a democratically divided power system in which powers are entrusted, by the citizens, to the national and federal level of government. James Madison wrote in the Federalist No. 46:

> The Federal and State Governments are in fact but different agents and trustees of the people, instituted with different powers, and designated for different purposes.

Where, like in France, Portugal or Luxembourg, sovereignty cannot be divided[49] it is the exercise of sovereign rights which is considered to be shared or, as the British debate says, in part pooled at the European level. More clearly than in other Member States, there seems to be little openness in Portugal for a conception of divided sovereignty and a reluctance to see the European power as original or constitutional.[50] Yet, whatever the construction may be, it is essential to see that the instrument by which the European level of government is created and sovereignty is pooled has the same function as a national constitution: it establishes institutions, provides them with limited competencies and powers, organises the political process, including the election of the representatives in the institutions and the

---

[46] Cannizzano, above n 39, 245 *et seq*.
[47] *Ibid*.
[48] Freiermuth Abt and Mosters, above n 24, p 409, 415, 416.
[49] Wivenes, above n 11, p 272 *et seq*; M Poiares Maduro, 'EU Law and National Constitutions: Portugal. The State of the Portuguese European Constitutional Discourse', FIDE XX. Congress London 2002 (published on www.fide2002.org), text following notes 64 and 73, with a reference to Art 3 § 1 of the Constitution. Maduro points out, however, the direct relationship between EC law and the peoples of the Member States, and proposes a 'notion of competing sovereignties' (*ibid* last four lines). For France, see Art 3 of the Constitution.
[50] Poiares Maduro, above n 49, near footnote 61–62.

decision-making procedures, and defines the status and rights of the individual as a citizen of this community.

The differences between the concept of a constitution as 'self-contained'[51] and building a complete picture of the establishment, distribution and limitation of powers of a state, and the European set of fundamental rules laid down in the European Treaties are nevertheless obvious. While, in accordance with the jurisprudence of the Court of Justice,[52] the constitutional character of European primary law is largely recognised, it is complementary to and depends on, the existence of democratic constitutions in the Member States. Many authors therefore prefer to talk of a 'de facto' constitution or a 'basic order of the Union' (Unionsgrundordnung[53]) with a view to taking account of existing 'deficits' and differences.[54]

b. The EU/EC Architecture and National Constitutional Traditions

What is the European Union, thus, in terms of the constitutional traditions of the Member States? There is considerable consensus, as the Greek report stresses, that at present to qualify the European Union as a federal state is excluded.[55] Is it a 'state in the making' or still an international organisation,[56] possibly of a particular nature?[57] Assuming that its contractual foundation—even in the form of an international treaty—does not necessarily exclude the suggestion of a constitution,[58] would it be a (federal) state just because the basis of its legitimacy is found in the will of the European citizens?[59] The Swedish report seems to see it this way, when it says that:

> it would not be in conformity with the initial provision of the Constitution to let the co-operation develop into the creation of a federal state, the powers of

---

[51] This expression used in Köck, above n 9, p 12.

[52] Case 294/83, *Les Verts*, [1986] ECR 1339 at 1365; see also Oliver, above n 2, p 10

[53] See D Tsatsos, 'Die europäische Unionsgrundordnung', 22 *Europäische Grundrechte-Zeitschrift* (1995) 287.

[54] See eg the conclusions in Nettesheim, above n 7, p 96.

[55] Iliopoulos-Strangas and Prevedourou, above n 33, p 9.

[56] Clearly in this sense: Wivenes, above n 11, p 274; this qualification seems to be without any difficulty adequate also to the Dutch (monistic) system, where international law prevails over national law in any event, see Kortmann, above n 10, p 300, 305; much emphasis is put on the quality as international treaties in Schäder and Melin, above n 3, p 392 against this qualification: Martín y Pérez de Nanclares and López Castillo, above n 36, p 319; see also I Pernice, 'Multilevel Constitutionalism in the European Union', 27 *European Law Review* (2002) 511, 517 *et seq.*

[57] See the questions in Nettesheim, above n 7, p 101 *et seq*, and p 103 *et seq* with many references. Nettesheim seems to support the thesis of a 'state in the making' *ibid*, p 25. For a list of arguments for and against each concept see Martín y Pérez de Nanclares and López Castillo, above n 36, p 318 *et seq.*

[58] Peters, above n 45, at p 220–43, where the 'contractual constitution' is considered as a specific form of international law; *ibid* 239 *et seq.*

[59] See Nettesheim, above n 7, p 104 *et seq*, where my approach is so qualified.

which derive their legitimacy from a mandate given by a European people in common elections.[60]

Given the specific multilevel structure of the Union[61] and the aim of its founding fathers to develop a new form of supranational political organisation with a view to overcoming the nineteenth century-system of sovereign nation states, which, in the light of the horrible experience of the two world wars, had failed, as Walter Hallstein pointed out, its test of utility as an instrument to preserve peace in Europe,[62] it seems, indeed, to be safe to conceptualise and develop further the European Union and its Member States as a system *sui generis*.[63] The system thus created may be called, as Ingolf Pernice proposed in 1995, a 'composed constitutional system' (Verfassungsverbund)[64] or, as the German report suggests in more political terms, a 'consociative federation' (konsoziative Föderation), thereby stressing the fact that the members remain sovereign states.[65] Also, in the view of the Finish report:

> EU law should hence be regarded as an independent legal system, in the sense that it is not derived from any national legal system and not dependent on decisions of the national legal systems. It is a system that is affecting the national legal systems and, therefore, intertwined with national legal systems.[66]

For Member States of the European Union it is not, any more, just the will of the national people who, in the European Union, can be considered as the ultimate basis of all legislative acts applicable to them. The specific nature of the Union implies that where the minister of the country has been outvoted in the Council, such acts are legitimised only by the people of other Member states and by membership of the Union as such. This implication of the accession to the Union has been considered in Austria as a 'fundamental change of the Austrian Constitution' which required a referendum.[67]

---

[60] Schäder and Melin, above n 3, p 390.
[61] Most recently Pernice, above n 56, at p 511 *et seq*.
[62] W Hallstein, *Der unvollendete Bundesstaat* (1969), at p 16; see also H Steinberger, 'Die Europäische Union im Lichte der Entscheidung des Bundesverfassungsgerichts vom 12 Okt 1993', in *Festschrift Bernhardt* (1995), p 1313, 1326: 'Das System der Nationalstaaten hat den wichtigsten Test des 20. Jahrhunderts nicht bestanden: es hat sich in zwei Weltkriegen als unfähig erwiesen, den Frieden zu bewahren'. G Hirsch, 'Nizza: Ende einer Etappe, Beginn einer Epoche?', *Neue Juristische Wochenschrift* (2001) 2677 at 2678.
[63] In this sense: Sundström, Boedeker and Kauppi, above n 17, p 4; Martín y Pérez de Nanclares and López Castillo, above n 36, p 319; Wivenes, above n 11, p 277; Iliopoulos-Strangas and Prevedourou, above n 33, p 9.
[64] Pernice, above n 31, at 261 *et seq*. One might also translate the term 'Verfassungsverbund' as 'constitutional federation', thereby deliberately avoiding the term 'federal constitution'—so proposed by Thym, above n 19, in s I.C.4.
[65] Nettesheim, above n 7, p 106 *et seq*, 109 *et seq*.
[66] Sundström, Boedeker and Kauppi, above n 17, p 4.
[67] Köck, above n 9, p 12.

The direct impact of the EU membership on the basic concepts and principles of the national constitutions becomes more evident when, with the accession of a new Member State its internal law changes fundamentally from one day to the other. This also appears from the Finish report which states that 'the Constitution was actually more profoundly changed when Finland became a member of the European Union than it was with the adoption of the Constitution 2000'.[68] In Greece, the adoption of the Treaty of Maastricht without any express amendment of the Constitution finds its only explanation in the power, given under Article 28(2) and (3), to a 'tacit quasi-revision' of the Constitution.[69] The new Article 23(1) of the German Constitution requires that the procedural conditions of a constitutional revision are respected for the ratification in case the revision of the EU Treaties has the effect of a material revision of the Constitution. The Spanish report, finally, describes clearly this modulation of the public powers in the Member States caused by European integration:[70]

> Dans le processus d'intégration communautaire, il se produit en effet un réaménagement du pouvoir public dans un espace politique et dans un cadre juridique différencié, auquel participent les Etats et les citoyens.

It becomes clear that the EU Treaties and their revision have a constitutional character. It is also clear that they are not the same as what we usually call a constitution of a state: one of the main features which distinguishes the Union from a state is, in the view of a number of national reports, its double basis of legitimacy: the citizens and the Member States.[71] It is, as the Cyprus' report puts it, a union of peoples and states, whose constitution is addressed to the Member States as well as to the citizens of the Union or the future European people.[72] Up to now, the Spanish report has stressed—as did the German Constitutional Court in its *Maastricht* decision[73]—that the Member States are the 'masters of the Treaties', but, it continues 'from tomorrow on it will be the "European people"'.[74] This double basis of legitimacy is qualified, in parts of the Greek doctrine, as the specific character of

---

[68] Sundström, Boedeker and Kauppi, above n 17, p 6.

[69] Iliopoulos-Strangas and Prevedourou, above n 33, p 14.

[70] Martín y Pérez de Nanclares and López Castillo, above n 36, p 316.

[71] See Martín y Pérez de Nanclares and López Castillo, above n 36, p 318, 325 *et seq*; Wivenes, above n 11, p 277; Iliopoulos-Strangas and Prevedourou, above n 33, p 10, with reference to Tsatsos.

[72] Josephides, above n 12, p 60 *et seq*; see also Martín y Pérez de Nanclares and López Castillo, above n 36, p 325.

[73] Bundesverfassungsgericht, Cases 2 BvR 2134/92 & 2159/92 *Maastricht*, 89 BVerfGE 155; reported in English as *Manfred Brunner and Others v The European Union Treaty*, [1994] 1 *Common Market Law Review* 57 at para 49.

[74] Martín y Pérez de Nanclares and López Castillo, above n 36, p 325/326, see also *ibid*, p 14: 'En définitive, la 'Constitution de l'Europe' doit donc attendre la naissance du peuple

the 'postfederal' construction of the Union, incompatible with the federal approach and respectful of national and popular sovereignty as well as of the 'institutional equality' of the Member States. Another doctrinal stream, however, sees the process of constitutionalisation of the Union as based upon the Member States which will remain necessary and important, though pointing to the progressive increase of powers at the Union level which is compensated by the enhanced introduction of hitherto state-style constitutional principles such as democracy, the rule of law and the protection of human rights.[75]

The question remains whether states are able to provide legitimacy by themselves, in which case the construction of double legitimacy may give the Union a specific character which may differ from a federal structure, or whether they have to be considered, ultimately, as representing their respective peoples or citizens the will of whom they are deemed to express. In this latter case double legitimacy would, in reality, have its origin in the same citizens but be provided through two different channels: one is the direct relationship between the individual citizens and the Union, the other is the state through the actors of which the citizens in their respective national identity are represented collectively at the European level. If the will of a democratic state cannot be legitimised other than by the will of its citizens, it is difficult to construe a double legitimacy of the Union and its legislation otherwise.

B. National Provisions for the Adoption of a 'Constitution' of the European Union

There is no provision in any constitution of the Member States explicitly providing for the adoption of a Constitution of the European Union. Some national reports, on the contrary, point out that the adoption of a Constitution directly by the citizens or through a body of representatives would require substantial changes of the constitution[76] or would even be excluded.[77] Very carefully, the Italian report points out: 'Art. 11 and Art. 117 of the Italian Constitution may constitute a sufficient legal basis for the establishment of a constitutional order of a new type, not aimed at embedding the existing national constitutions into a monistic perspective, but based on the respect for the constitutional autonomy of the Member States'.[78] The Luxembourg report goes further: 'Giving up the international character of

européen, comme conséquence d'une solidarité de fait plus étendue, ou même généralisée, et comme résultat d'un processus qu'il serait insencé de trop accélerer'.
[75] Iliopoulos-Strangas and Prevedourou, above n 33, p 11, referring to Tsatsos on the one hand and Papadimitriou on the other.
[76] Sundström, Boedeker and Kauppi, above n 17, p 6, 7 *et seq.*
[77] More open Köck, above n 9, p 17 *et seq.*
[78] Cannizzano, above n 39, p 250.

the Union in favour of a constitutional system which would be adopted by the European peoples or their representatives, may not be covered by Article 49bis of the Luxembourg Constitution'.[79] Our contention is that this has been the position of the European Community from the outset, as was made clear by the Court of Justice in *Van Gend & Loos*: it is a legal order of a new kind, different from international law.[80] However, making a European Constitution, comparable to that of a federal state would, indeed, be an act of revolution and outside the procedures both of Article 48 TEU and the integration clauses of the national constitutions. The question, instead, focuses on the conditions laid down in the national constitutions, of a substantial revision of the primary law of the Union with a view to, as the Convention is undertaking, simplifying it in order to achieve greates transparency, democracy and efficiency in a revised and consolidated text which may correspond more than the actual Treaties to what citizens understand as a constitution.

a.   Constitutional Conditions for and Limits to Further Steps of Integration (Substance)

Two national constitutions, the Greek and the German stipulate the aim to complete European integration: a new interpretative declaration (2001) on Article 28 of the Greek Constitution,[81] and the new Article 23(1) of the German Grundgesetz (1993). Article 28(3) of the Greek Constitution provides that limiting the exercise of national sovereignty shall 'not infringe upon the rights of man and the foundations of democratic government and is given effect on the basis of the principles of equality and under the condition of reciprocity'. The Greek report indicates that the principle of equality could limit the power to design a Constitution which provides for a 'two speed Europe', and also that the provision on reciprocity could act as a limit in the event that under the future Constitution of the Union violations of reciprocity occur generally and systematically.[82] It also stresses that, at least in the light of the 'clauses of eternity' like for the republican form of the state, common also to Germany (Article 79(3)), France (Article 89(5)) and Italy (Article 139), the national constitution could not form the basis for the construction of a European Union which would question the substance of statehood of its members.[83]

---

[79] Wivenes, above n 11, p 275.

[80] Case 26/62, *van Gend and Loos*, (1963) ECR 1 at paras 9 and 10; see also Poiares Maduro, above n 49, near fn 72 and I Pernice, 'Multilevel Constitutionalism and the Treaty of Amsterdam: European Constitution-Making Revisited?' 36 *Common Market Law Review* (1999) 703 at 707 *et seq*.

[81] The Declaration reads: Art 28 constitutes the foundation for the participation of the Country in the European integration process. See also Iliopoulos-Strangas and Prevedourou, above n 33, p 16.

[82] Iliopoulos-Strangas and Prevedourou, above n 33, p 18.

[83] Iliopoulos-Strangas and Prevedourou, above n 33, p 20. See also Sundström,Boedeker and Kauppi, above n 17, p 7, where a similar limit is drawn from S 1 of the Constitution, stating that Finland is a sovereign republic.

This may also be intended in the reference to 'federal principles' in the German Constitution. It even goes a step further in Article 23(1) in qualifying which principles shall govern the European Union,:

> With a view to establishing a united Europe, the Federal Republic of Germany shall participate in the development of the European Union that is committed to democratic, social, and federal principles, to the rule of law, and to the principle of subsidiarity, and that guarantees a level of protection of basic rights essentially comparable to that afforded by this Basic Law ....

It is clear that the European integration process will bring about a specific European translation of these requirements, the vagueness of which leaves enough room for solutions which are no copy of the respective German model.[84] A real limit on the possible extent and form of European integration, however, is laid down in Article 23(3) referring to the 'eternity clause' of Article 79(3) of the German Constitution. It is the constitutional identity of Germany which is protected in that provision. Yet, taking account of the preamble and the ongoing 'mutation' even of this 'identity'—contrary to some doctrinal submission—even this clause cannot be interpreted as a substantial guaranty of the sovereign statehood of the country[85]. This may be different in the case of Luxembourg, where, under Article 49bis of the Constitution, 'the exercise of the powers reserved by the Constitution to the legislature, executive, and judiciary may be temporarily (!) vested by treaty in institutions governed by international law'. Thus, the Luxembourg report states that the devolution is considered temporary and non-definitive,[86] while in fact, Luxembourg has consented to Article 51 TEU and Article 312 TEC which provide that the Treaties are concluded 'for an unlimited period'.

The protection of human rights is an important condition also for Sweden: according to Chapter 10, Article 5 of the Instrument of Government, the Swedish report says,

> the Riksdag may transfer decision-making rights to the European Communities 'long as' the Communities have a system of protection of fundamental rights and freedoms 'corresponding to' that provided for by the Instrument of Government and by the European Convention on Human Rights.[87]

Though the Spanish Constitution, in Article 93, is silent in this regard, the Spanish report refers to similar conditions discussed in the doctrine,

---

[84] For more details see Nettesheim, above n 7, p 111 *et seq.*
[85] Nettesheim, above n 7, p 112 *et seq.*
[86] Wivenes, above n 11, p 273
[87] Schäder and Melin, above n 3, p 390.

adding the respect for the principles of the democratic and the regional state.[88] Accordingly, Section 94 of the Finish Constitution states that an international obligation must not endanger the democratic foundations of the Constitution.[89] The Swiss report stresses, though the Constitution does not provide for express limitations of its revision, that in case of the accession of Switzerland the essential characteristics of the Swiss Constitution, its federal structure and neutrality as elements of the national identity, would have to be respected.[90]

In contrast to this, the Austrian report qualifies the Austrian constitutional order as a 'strictly positive one' which 'does not know any principles which could not be abrogated, or at least changed in its scope, by a decision of the sovereign, i.e. the people'. Talking about 'a substantive core, and if so, whether it is therefore, to that extent, inalienable and resistant to integration', would not be more than an 'academic question'.[91] Whatever the contents of the revised Treaty would be, even if it were to be called 'Constitution of the European Union', Austrian constitutional law could not, legally, be opposed to its ratification.[92]

b.   *Procedural Requirements under National Constitutional Provisions*

Given the constitutional character and impact on national constitutions of the attribution of sovereign rights to the European Union, it is important to see how the constitutions organise the conclusion of the European Treaties or the accession to the Union. While in most Member States, this question is regarded as a case of international action,[93] it is the subject of a specific constitutional provision in others.[94] Accession was made possible in Austria under Article 50(3) of the Federal Constitutional Law by qualified majority of the National Council, and was treated as a fundamental change of the Constitution requiring a referendum, while the Austrian report suggests that further integration is already covered by the Accession Enabling Act of 1994 and 'with regard to future enlargement and consolidation Treaties ... the alleviated conditions of article 50(1) B-VG' would be sufficient.[95] The Finnish Constitution requires, in Section 95 at least, the 'simplified procedure for

---

[88] Martín y Pérez de Nanclares and López Castillo, above n 36, p 321.

[89] Sundström, Boedeker and Kauppi, above n 17, p 7 *et seq*.

[90] Freiermuth Abt and Mosters, above n 24, p 419 with examples in fn 77, 420–22.

[91] Köck, above n 9, p 14 *et seq*.

[92] Köck, above n 9, p 15–18.

[93] Wivenes, above n 11, p 271 *et seq*; Martín y Pérez de Nanclares and López Castillo, above n 36, p 322 *et seq*; Kortmann, above n 10, p 300.

[94] See the abovementioned Art 23 § 1 of the German Constitution, Art 28 of the Greek Constitution, Ch 10 Art 5 of the Swedish Instrument of Government. See for more details I Pernice, 'Fondements de droit constitutionnel européen', WHI Paper 5/00, www.whiberlin.de/pernice-fondements.htm, § 3.

[95] Köck, above n 9, p 12 *et seq*, 15 *et seq*.

adopting constitutional amendments', but the adoption of 'a state-dependent constitution of the EU' would—because of its impact on the democratic foundations of the national constitution—be subject to the very complicated procedure of Section 73 for the adoption of constitutional amendments.[96] According to the Finnish report 'the accession act was on several points in conflict with the Constitution. Therefore it had to be adopted by the same procedure as an international treaty amending the Constitution'.[97] Also in Luxembourg, the devolution of the exercise of attributions reserved by the Constitution to the legislative, executive and judiciary to an international institution needs the qualified majority required for constitutional amendments.[98] In Germany, the procedure provided for constitutional amendments is applicable under Article 23(1) of the Constitution, whenever accession to the Union or revision of the Treaties, as regularly, implies a material modification of the Fundamental Law.[99] This was the case at least with the Treaties of Maastricht, Amsterdam and Nice. The Greek Constitution is not clear on the applicable procedures, but according to the Greek report the combination of Article 28(2) and (3) of the Constitution is the appropriate solution. This would mean that authorisation is given by a majority of three fifths of the total number of deputies of the Parliament, and were a European Constitution to be adopted, a referendum under Article 44(2) would be appropriate.[100] Even more exacting requirements are called for in Sweden, where, under Chapter 10 Article 5 of the Instrument of Government a majority of three fourths of the Riksdag is necessary if the demanding procedure for constitutional amendment is not followed.[101]

The Spanish Constitution is less demanding, requiring, in Article 93, a simple organic law adopted by the *Cortes Generales* with an absolute majority at the Congress (Article 81 § 2). Though the ratification of an international agreement which would be contrary to the Constitution is subject to prior constitutional amendment, according to the Spanish report all the steps of European integration have been authorised, so far, by organic law and the demanding procedure of Article 95 not used.[102] The Constitution of the Netherlands even allows for authorisation of the ratification of treaties by an ordinary majority, even in the case—to be established by an ordinary majority as well—of deviation from the Constitution, where in principle a two thirds majority is necessary.[103] The least demanding requirements are found in Italy, where a simple majority of the Parliament

---

[96] Sundström, Boedeker and Kauppi, above n 17, p 7 *et seq.*
[97] Sundström, Boedeker and Kauppi, above n 17, p 7.
[98] Wivenes, above n 11, p 272.
[99] Nettesheim, above n 7, p 114 *et seq.*
[100] Iliopoulos-Strangas and Prevedourou, above n 33, p 24 *et seq.*
[101] Schäder and Melin, above n 3, p 392.
[102] Martín y Pérez de Nanclares and López Castillo, above n 36, p 322–325, though the majorities required for a constitutional amendment under Art 168 have been achieved (*ibid* p 12).
[103] Kortmann, above n 10, p 301.

is necessary to authorise the consent, to be given by the Government, to any revision of the treaties including a European Constitution.[104]

The Irish Constitution is a special case. Following the 'Crotty' jurisprudence of the Irish Supreme Court, the Irish report explains why accession to the European Union, but also each of the subsequent revision Treaties required an amendment of the Constitution with a majority of the two Houses of the Oireachtas, and a majority of the voters at a referendum: the exclusive law-making powers of the Oireachtas under Article 15(2)(1) of the Irish Constitution was 'plainly inconsistent with the provisions of the Treaty conferring law-making powers on the Community'. But also the inclusion of the Charter of Fundamental Rights into the primary law of the Union would be subject to this procedure. The new provisions of the Constitution gave, and will give, on the other hand, full supremacy to European law and empower the state to ratify the Treaties and exercise the options or discretions they provide for.

c. The Role of the Citizens: International Treaty or European
Social Contract?

Is there room, on the basis of these provisions, for considering the revised (constitutional) Treaty as a renewed European social contract between the citizens of the Union? Most of the national reports are reluctant, some expressly opposed to such a perspective. They stress that the Union is based on international treaties,[105] that the question of a constituent power or of a real European Constitution adopted by representatives of the peoples is not put,[106] that the Member States are the masters of the Treaties and that the Constitution of Europe needs to wait for the birthday of the European people,[107] that the idea of a social contract is even outside the scope of the national constitution[108] or contrary to the constitutional tradition of the country, according to which the nation has been constituted by the revolution, an act of collective entity.[109] There 'has not been any exercise of original constitutional power (*pouvoir constituant*) at the EU level', the Portuguese report says and continues 'European constitutionalism may not even have the necessary conditions (a *demos* for example) to promote such exercise of *pouvoir constituant* at the EU level'.[110] A European social contract, the Italian report states,

> to be concluded among European citizens considered by themselves as
> autonomous political subjects, and not regrouped in social and political

---

[104] Cannizzano, above n 39, p 250. Note that up to 1993 the German Constitution also required not more than a simple law of ratification under Art 24 § 1 and 59(2).
[105] Schäder and Melin, above n 3, p 392.
[106] Wivenes, above n 11, p 277.
[107] Martín y Pérez de Nanclares and López Castillo, above n 36, p 325, 326.
[108] Kortmann, above n 10, p 301.
[109] Iliopoulos-Strangas and Prevedourou, above n 33, p 25.
[110] Poiares Maduro, above n 49, near fn 61.

communities such as the Member States, is inconsistent with the positive grant of the Italian Constitution.[111]

The assimilation of an original constitutional power to an assembly,

> which will derive from a revolutionary act by which the people, or its repre-
> sentatives, or those who have the power to effectively claim that they speak
> for the people, create a new fundamental legal order that has no direct con-
> nection with the former one,

leads the Austrian report also to reject the idea.[112]

Some reports, however, hesitantly concede that a referendum on the European Constitution could support the argument for the concept of a social contract.[113] But this is not the point. The idea is to see the process of European integration from another perspective, that of the citizen for whom political organisation, be it at the regional, national or European level, is not more than an instrument for meeting specific needs and challenges: safety, peace, freedom, welfare etc. At the European level of government, citizens should be considered as acting through the respective representational bodies of their Member State in order to reach an agreement with citizens of other Member States on the 'constitution' of European institutions. There is no contradiction, ultimately, in conceiving the European Treaties thus established as international treaties from a legal perspective and regarding the Member States as the masters of these Treaties, if 'Member States' means the peoples or citizens of each country organised in and represented by the state.[114] But it may lead to greater awareness among the citizens that the European construction is their own matter.

C.   The Constitution-Making Process: Preparing the IGC 2004 in Practice

Both, the Nice Declaration and the Declaration of Laeken on the Future of the European Union state the need for a broad European-wide debate, involving all citizens, to inform and guide the work of the Convention, and the success of this work will depend on the extent to which the citizens and civil society, finally, will have had the opportunity for active participation.

---

[111] Cannizzano, above n 39, p 250.
[112] Köck, above n 9, p 17.
[113] Iliopoulos-Strangas and Prevedourou, above n 33, p 26; Nettesheim, above n 7, p 120 *et seq*; Cannizzano, above n 39, p 250.
[114] For more details see I Pernice, F Mayer and S Wernicke, 'Renewing the European Social Contract. The Challenge of Institutional Reform and Enlargement in the Light of Multilevel Constitutionalism' 12 *King's College Law Journal* Special Editors: J Gardner and M Andenas (2001) 60 *et seq*.

Without repeating the national and European reports in detail, it seems appropriate, nevertheless, to summarise and evaluate briefly the way this debate is organised and which are the main issues raised.

a.   How Is the Internal Debate on the Future of the European Union Organised?

In a number of Member States the debate has been actively organised by the government or the European affairs committees of the parliaments.[115] Speeches[116] and articles in newspapers by political leaders and public hearings at the parliamentary committees[117] are on the agenda in order to open and promote the public discourse. Austria has already organised a high level 'Round Table on Europe' twice with representatives of all politically relevant institutions as well as experts on European affairs.[118] Finland has, since September 2001, established an active 'Civil Forum on the Future of the European Union', which has organised meetings with around 90 organisations under the chairmanship of the prime minister or other ministers. A special web-site 'Mr Europe' hosts three discussion groups and contains a database with relevant materials on the Laeken process.[119] In Spain, a Royal Decree (779/2001) has established a specific institution, the 'Council for the Debate on the Future of the European Union' which leads a general and simplified two-tier discussion for all citizens on the basis of Internet and for specialised representatives of civil society on the basis of a questionnaire which comprises 59 questions the answers to which are evaluated by the University of Oviedo.[120] Similarly, a special committee has been created in Sweden to organise public seminars and hearings, to initiate and sponsor scientific reports and to develop a special web-site.[121] Moreover, chambers of commerce and trade unions participate in debates which are broadcast[122]

---

[115] Josephides, above n 12, p 65.

[116] See the series of the 'Forum Constitutionis Europae', in the frame of which the German minister for foreign affairs, Joschka Fischer gave his 'Humboldt-speech' in May 2000, 'From Confederacy to Federation-Thoughts on the Finality of European Integration', FCE Special 2/00, www.whi-berlin.de, subsection speeches.

[117] Martín y Pérez de Nanclares and López Castillo, above n 36, p 328; for Germany see references in Nettesheim, above n 7, p 122 *et seq*, as well as Deutscher Bundestag, Ausschuß für die Angelegenheiten der Europäischen Union, 'Der Europäische Verfassungskonvent. Gemeinsame öffentliche Anhörung der Europaausschüsse von Bundestag und Bundesrat am 26. Juni 2002', Texte und Materialien, Volume 26 (2002), including the protocol of the 101st meeting of this committee.

[118] Köck, above n 9, 21 *et seq*.

[119] Sundström, Boedeker and Kauppi, above n 17, p 8.

[120] Martín y Pérez de Nanclares and López Castillo, above n 36, p 328.

[121] Schäder and Melin, above n 3, p 393, stating that a budget of 15 million SEK has been allocated to this Committee.

[122] Josephides, above n 12, p 65.

and we should also mention that universities and academic institutions—like FIDE—are very active in the field as well.[123]

Other reports, however, are silent on this question or state that interest among the citizens is low and the information incomplete.[124] But it is fair to add that the European institutions contribute to the organisation of a public debate, such as the Brussels Congress 'Europe 2004: Le grand debat: Setting the Agenda and Outlining the Options', organised by the Commission in October 2001[125] or the public hearing by the Convention itself in June 2002.[126] In July 2002, a Youth Convention was successfully organised giving young people from all Member States an opportunity to develop their ideas on the future of Europe.[127] An Internet discussion with the President of the Convention, Valéry Giscard d'Estaing, is being organised to takes place on 28 October 2002[128] following the example of individual members of the Convention. All these initiatives, however, do not seem to reach the public sufficiently, let alone initiate a broad European discourse as would be appropriate for a 'constitutional moment' in Europe. As in Greece and Sweden, there seems to be only minimal interest in constitutional and institutional issues as in almost all Member States and candidate countries.[129]

b.   What Are the Key Issues and Proposals of the Leading Political Groups?

The governments of the Member States and the leading political groups have quite diverse ideas about how the future European primary law should look. The work of the Convention and its working groups, summarised in the EU report, reflects many points reported from the debate in the Member States.[130] Nevertheless, it seems possible to group the European and national debates on the reform of the Treaties under the following headings:

— European Constitution or a Mere Simplification of the Constitutional Treaties?

The (former) Dutch government opted for a 'European Constitution for an effective and democratic Union'.[131] Also in Germany, the need for a simple

---

[123] Josephides, above n 12, p 65, Iliopoulos-Strangas and Prevedourou, above n 33, p 27 *et seq.*
[124] Iliopoulos-Strangas and Prevedourou, above n 33, p 27.
[125] European Commission, 'Europe 2004: le grand débat' (2002).
[126] Plenary meeting of the Convention of 24 and 25 June 2002, Summary in CONV 167/02.
[127] http://european-convention.eu.int/youth.asp?lang = EN&content = intro.
[128] Announcement on: www.europa.eu.int/comm/chat/vge/index_en.htm.
[129] Schäder/Melin, above n 3, p 395; Iliopoulos-Strangas and Prevedourou, above n 33, p 27.
[130] Oliver, above n 2, p 6 *et seq*, 15 *et seq.*
[131] Kortmann, above n 10, p 303.

and clarified constitutional Treaty seems to be accepted quasi unanimously. In September 2000 the German Chancellor underlined the right of European citizens to a Constitution which is precise and comprehensible for everybody. The Christian democrats also opt for a constitutional Treaty which contains rules on the distribution of competencies, financial provisions, institutions and decision-making procedures as well as the Charter of Fundamental Rights. The German report says, however, that there is no great expectation that the Convention will produce a draft Treaty and that a Constitution will be adopted.[132] But the more recent reports on the work of the Convention support a less sceptical view.[133] Also, the Austrian government is reported to 'favour a Constitution as compared to a mere simplification of the constitutional Treaties'.[134] Luxembourg is not opposed to a future Constitution, but the discussion concentrates rather on specific issues like a better delimitation of competencies, the incorporation of the Charter of Fundamental Rights or the role of national parliaments. There seems also to be a claim for a better anchorage of the European construction in the national constitutions.[135] According to the Austrian Social Democrat Party and the Green Party, a Constitution would, in particular, mean strengthening or 're-establishing' democracy at the transnational level.[136]

A rather 'minimalist' approach seems to prevail in Italy and consists

in simplifying the decision-making process, merging the three pillars, preserving the competence of the MS from a too invasive activity of the Union, specifying and embodying in the constitutional text the bill of rights of the Union.[137]

The Finish Foreign Affairs Committee supports the simplification of the Treaties, but there is no discourse on a Constitution.[138] The Greek socialist party as well as the Prime Minister would accept a Constitution but do not see a need for abstract discussions. They rather support an enhanced social and humanist profile of the Union by strengthening the provisions on employment, labour relations and the combat of poverty as well as stronger cohesion policies and integrated economic policies.[139] Also, the Swedish Prime Minister Göran Persson said that the question of a Constitution is less important; the existing Treaties may well be 'seen as a constitution' with the important question being 'what kind of constitution we want'.[140] He stressed, however, that he 'would not be prepared to accept any transfer of competence from the national to the European level … without ratification by national parliaments'.[141] This will be important for the question whether a splitting of the Treaties with

---

[132] Nettesheim, above n 7, p 123 *et seq.*
[133] Oliver, above n 2, p 10,
[134] Köck, above n 9, p 24.
[135] Wivenes, above n 11, p 277 *et seq.*
[136] Köck, above n 9, p 23 *et seq.*
[137] Cannizzano, above n 39, p 251.
[138] Sundström, Boedeker and Kauppi, above n 17, p 9.
[139] Iliopoulos-Strangas and Prevedourou, above n 33, p 28 *et seq.*
[140] Schäder and Melin, above n 3, p 394.
[141] Schäder and Melin, above n 3, p 394.

a view to allowing a simplified revision procedure for the 'less important' technical part is a realistic option.

— A Clearer Division and Delimitation of Competencies

The need for clearer definitions of the European competencies was originally emphasised by the German *Länder*, and this claim was the historic origin of the entire Post-Nice process. While the idea of a 'Kompetenzkatalog' (catalogue of competencies) is not really supported any more, a more systematic and better defined attribution of limited competencies continues to feature strongly in the discussion.[142] Indeed, the Commission and most of the members of the Convention seem to be opposed to the idea of a positive or a negative catalogue of the Union's powers.[143] A clarification of the distribution of competencies is supported also by the Dutch Labour Party and Christian Democrats,[144] as well as by the Austrian Freedom Party,[145] the Swedish Prime Minister[146] and all political actors in Finland. The latter keep to the existing attribution of competencies, which should always be specified in the Treaties, while the 'competence-competence' should remain with the Member States.[147] In any event there is no reported voice opting for a change in this regard. Also, the Austrian political debate supports a better delimitation of the competencies of the European Union and stresses the importance of the principle of subsidiarity.[148] This seems to be the position in Cyprus as well,[149] while in Luxembourg there seems to be some hesitation regarding the rigid delimitation of competencies despite the general acceptance of the importance of the principle. Instead, there is a preference for a 'progressive and gradual determination' of the Union's competencies, which would continue to include the present Article 308 TEC.

— Integration of the Charter of Fundamental Rights as Binding Law

The integration of the European Charter of Fundamental Rights into the constituent texts of the Union is strongly supported by the Greek government and the Socialist Party[150]—a view shared by the (former) Dutch government

---

[142] Nettesheim, above n 7, p 124 *et seq*: this is reported as the view of Wolfgang Clement (Social Democrat), as well as of Joschka Fischer (Greens) and Schäuble and Bocklet (Christian Democrats).

[143] Oliver, above n 2, p 22.

[144] Kortmann, above n 10, p 303, while the Volkspartij is 'clearly opposed to fixing a distribution of competences between the EU and the Member States'.

[145] Köck, above n 9, p 23.

[146] Schäder and Melin, above n 3, p 394, but he emphasises that this shall not lead to a 'dismantling of what the EU has achieved over the years'.

[147] Sundström, Boedeker and Kauppi, above n 17, p 9.

[148] Köck, above n 9, p 23, referring to the hope of the Austrian Freedom Party, that 'a Constitution would stop the ongoing discussion about the correct division of powers and what it considers the inherent threat of curtailing Member States competencies at each Council meeting'.

[149] Josephides, above n 12, p 65 *et seq*.

[150] Iliopoulos-Strangas and Prevedourou, above n 33, p 28

and all political actors in Germany.[151] How the Charter could be incorporated has yet to be seen.[152] Although the Finish Foreign Affairs Committee emphasises the need for protection of human rights, it opts for an adhesion of the European Union to the European Convention on Human Rights.[153] This seems also to be the view of the Swedish Prime Minister Göran Persson who regards the Charter as being insufficiently precise.[154]

— Democracy: Strengthening the Role of the European and the National Parliaments

In the view of the German Social Democrats as well as the (former) Dutch government and the Labour Party, the Commission should be strengthened and its President be elected by the European Parliament;[155] the European Parliament should be one of the legislative chambers, the other being the Council.[156] This is also the view of the chairman of the European Affairs Committee of the Bundestag (Christian Democrat).[157] The (former) chairman of the Christian Democrat fraction of the Bundestag, Friedrich Merz, adds the need for a general co-decision power of the European Parliament,[158] which finds the support of the Dutch Christian Democrats[159] and the Luxembourg government.[160] In the view of the Dutch Labour Party, the European Parliament should also have the right to dismiss individual Commissioners, while the Commission should be able to dissolve the European Parliament.[161] Clearly, further powers for the Parliament was the claim made by Joschka Fischer in his Humboldt speech of May 2000.[162]

The Austrian People's Party, however, does not see strengthening the national parliaments as a matter for the European Constitution, but rather as one lying within the competence of each national constitution. Instead, it favours a transformation of the European Parliament into a Parliament with full competencies, in particular in the legislative (initiative) and budgetary fields.[163]

— The European Union at the International Scene: Securing Efficient Action in the CFSP

The extension of the attributions to the Union in the area of CFSP as well as in home affairs—and even their communitarianism—is favoured by the political

---

[151] Kortmann, above n 10, p 303; Nettesheim, above n 7, p 123 *et seq.*
[152] For the problems and options see Oliver, above n 2, p 32 *et seq.*
[153] Sundström, Boedeker and Kauppi, above n 17, p 9.
[154] Schäder and Melin, above n 3, p 394.
[155] Nettesheim, above n 7, p 124 *et seq.* Kortmann, above n 10, p 303.
[156] Nettesheim, above n 7, p 124 *et seq.*
[157] Nettesheim, above n 7, p 126 *et seq.*
[158] Nettesheim, above n 7, p 126/127.
[159] Kortmann, above n 10, p 303.
[160] Wivenes, above n 11, p 276.
[161] Kortmann, above n 10, p 303.
[162] Nettesheim, above n 7, p 125.
[163] Köck, above n 9, p 23.

leaders in Luxembourg, including external representation in EMU matters.[164] Also, the report from Cyprus underlines the need for a strong Common Foreign and Security Policy and a strong Europe on the international scene in order to contribute efficiently to the problems of Palestine, Cyprus and other parts of the world.[165] This also seems to be one of the issues strongly supported by the Greek New Democracy Party which emphasises this with a view to the absence of security at the Greek borders.[166]

— A European Government and a President of the European Union?

For Göran Persson the European Council and the Council of Minister will continue 'to play the central role in the governing of Europe', no fundamental change would be the wish of the Member States.[167] The other reports do not take a position on this question.

— How Should the European Union Look After 2004?

There seems to be a broad consensus that the Laeken process should lead to a revision of the existing Treaties with a view to consolidating, simplifying and clarifying the primary law of the Union in a text which may be called Constitution or constitutional Treaty. Valéry Giscard d'Estaing also seems to favour one of these titles.[168] The name, however, is less important than a content and structure that citizens can understand and accept as the legal foundation of the Union. Nobody in the political arena seems to call for a European federal state and it was Tony Blair who expressed this in his speech in Warsaw: 'A superpower, not a superstate'.

The question is, however, how this 'superpower' should look. While Joschka Fischer talked about a 'federation'—thereby excluding, at least implicitly, the option of a 'federal state'—the Finish Foreign Affairs Committee seems to opt for developing the European Union as a close cooperation of independent states and the peoples of Europe.[169] Little has been reported of the views of other Member States concerning the 'finality' of the process. A quite original position was taken in 2001 by the (former) Prime Minister of Saxonia, Kurt Biedenkopf, who opted for a 'Europe of Regions' instead of a Europe of nation states, but there was little support for this vision.[170] As in Germany, the position and rights of the regions appears to be an important issue in the debate in Spain.[171] But this does not concern, so much, the *sui generis* character of the European Union in the future.

---

[164] Wivenes, above n 11, p 276.
[165] Josephides, above n 12, p 65 *et seq.*
[166] Iliopoulos-Strangas and Prevedourou, above n 33, p 29.
[167] Schäder and Melin, above n 3, p 394.
[168] Oliver, above n 2, p 10, referring to Giscard d'Estaing, 'Les dernières nouvelles de la Convention européenne', *Le Monde* of 23 July 2002 www.lemonde.fr.
[169] Sundström, Boedeker and Kauppi, above n 17, p 9.
[170] Nettesheim, above n 7, p 127 *et seq.*
[171] Martín y Pérez de Nanclares and López Castillo, above n 36, p 328 *et seq.*

One question will be how to react, if one or some of the Member States do not ratify a possible constitutional Treaty of the European Union. Joschka Fischer's vision, in this case, was a centre of gravity, being built by some Member States ready to agree upon a Constitution as a nucleus for the Federation.[172] This seems to parallel the avant-garde concept defended by Jacques Delors. But do the existing Treaties make room for such a solution?

II.   RELATIONSHIP AND INTERACTION OF EC/EU LAW AND NATIONAL CONSTITUTIONS

One key issue, not only in legal terms, will be the relationship of the future Treaty to national constitutions and the interaction between these two levels of law within the European system. Whatever may be the general qualification (be it regarded as two autonomous and separate bodies of law[173] or be it qualified as two elements in a multilevel constitutional system), there is no doubt that European and national law are distinct[174] and have each their own source of legitimacy. But they are closely interwoven, related and complementary to each other and the same citizens are, ultimately, the basis for their legitimacy and the people to which they are addressed; the system is meant to produce one single legal answer in each case, be it developed from provisions of European or from national law. This, in our view, is the very consequence of the divided sovereignty in Europe referred to in the Swedish report[175] and it is important to examine what this means in practice. There may be implications for Member States' constitutional autonomy (below section 1.), for the question whether there are and, eventually, which are the common values of the Union (below section 2.), for the ongoing discussion on the supremacy of European law (below section 3.) and for the new functions of national institutions (below section 4.).

A.   Member States' Constitutional Autonomy under European Constraints

There seems to be a safeguard in the EU Treaty, for the identity of the Member States, but the question, recently debated at the annual meeting of

---

[172] Nettesheim, above n 7, p 126.

[173] This is the approach of the Court of Justice in Case 26/62, *Van Gend & Loos*, [1963] ECR 1; this is also the position of all those who qualify European law as international law, see Peters, above n 45, at p 248 *et seq.*

[174] The critical remarks in Nettesheim, above n 7, p 106 with footnotes 63 and 64, are easily accepted, but Ingolf Pernice did not intend to say that no distinction may be drawn between the European Constitution and national Constitutions.

[175] Schäder and Melin, above n 3, p 390, 397, 399; see also above, at the end of point I.1.a.

the Association of the German Professors of Public Law,[176] was to know what is meant by national as well as European identity. It could well limit the extension of the EC/EU competencies and thereby protect the constitutional autonomy of the Member States (below section 1.), while, on the other hand, the provisions of Article 6(1) and Article 7 TEU may impose limits on the liberty of Member States to determine independently their internal structure and political system, thereby putting constraints on the constitutional autonomy of the Member States (below section 2.).

a. National Identities of the Member States and the Extension of the EC/EU Competencies

The views of the national reports on the meaning of Article 6(3) TEU are divergent: it is seen, by the Austrian report, as an 'accessory principle'—national identity cannot be regarded as a limit to the full exercise of the powers given to the EC including under Article 308 ECT, and it is 'no impediment for changes in the area of primary law and does not prevent any revision of the constitutional Treaties that the Member states should see fit'.[177] The prevalence in the institutions of certain languages, it says,

> and the emergence, or perhaps, even ordainment, of a kind of *lingua franca* for the EU/EC, is a much more serious threat to the national identities of Member States than some minor issue of competence.[178]

Other reports regard the language as an important element of identity too,[179] whereas in the view of the Luxembourg report, shared by a number of reports,[180] Article 6(3) TEU is rather a programmatic principle than a legal rule limiting the extension of competencies[181] and giving guidance to the interpretation of the rules governing European competencies.[182]

> A limit is, however, drawn from Article 6(3) TEU by the Swedish report: It would not be in conformity with the initial provision of the Constitution to

---

[176] See for the meeting of 3–5 October 2002 in St Gallen and the reports of Armin von Bogdandy and, 'Europäische und nationale Identität', 60 *Veröffentlichungen der Vereinigung der Deutschen Staatsrechtslehrer* (2003, forthcoming); see also E Pache, 'Europäische und nationale Identität: Integration durch Verfassungsrecht', *Deutsche Verwaltungsblätter* (2002), 1157.

[177] Köck, above n 9, p 26, 27.

[178] Köck, above n 9, p 27.

[179] Nettesheim, above n 7, p 130, Iliopoulos-Strangas and Prevedourou, above n 33, 32.

[180] See Craig, above n 19, p 6; Kortmann, above n 10, p 304; Josephides, above n 12, p 67: '... la disposition de l'article 6.3 n'apparait pas nécessaire'.

[181] Wivenes, above n 11, p 279. *Et seq*, referring to case C–473/93, Commission/Luxembourg, 1996 ECR I–3207.

[182] Nettesheim, above n 7, p 130, which, however, is going a step further in saying that, consequently, it must be understood as limiting the exercise and use of existing competencies.

let the co-operation develop into the creation of a federal state, the powers of which derive their legitimacy from a mandate given by a European people in common elections.

Hence, the creation of a European federal state would not be in conformity with Article 6(3) TEU.[183] This reflects a broad, though not unanimous,[184] feeling expressed by other reports as well.[185] Nonetheless, the Swedish report emphasises that the position of the Swedish Parliament 'as the principle organ of the state must not be substantially undermined through the transfer of legislative powers' and already at the time of accession it was understood in Sweden that the free formation of opinion, public access to documents and the right of local self determination are values of great importance which could not be affected by the EU competencies.[186] In defining what is meant by national identity, the reports often refer to the constitutional provisions which have already been quoted as limits to further integration.[187]

The Greek report adds that culture—language, cultural heritage, relation between the state and the church—is an element of national identity and could be an implicit limit to the extension of European competencies as well.[188] Indeed stresses that Article 6(3) TEU also obliges the Union to take affirmative action with a view to preserving the national identity of the Member States.[189] On the other hand, the principles laid down in Article 6(1) TEU are seen as an implicit limit on the autonomy of the Member States to determine their own national identity, and the values which determine national identity are subject to the evolution of the multinational and poly-centric frame constituted by the Union.[190] The German report follows the same line in emphasising that the normative construction of Article 6(3) TEU should realise that European and national identities are not conflicting, antag-onistic or even competing, but complementary, multi-referential and multi-layered.[191] Only such elements of a national identity would benefit from the protection under this provision which are not contrary to the concept of the multilevel structure of complementary national and European identities.[192]

---

[183] Schäder and Melin, above n 3, p 390, 395.

[184] For the opposite view, saying that even a federal state would not be contrary to this provision: Kortmann, above n 10, p 304.

[185] Martín y Pérez de Nanclares and López Castillo, above n 36, p 330: '... tout autant que le principe de l'Etat de Droit que le principe démocratique, ainsi que la protection des droits fon-damentaux et la survivance de l'Espagne comme un Etat souverain et indépendant, sont des éléments minimums et indispensables de l'identité nationale espagnole'. See also Cannizzano, above n 39, p 252.

[186] Schäder and Melin, above n 3, p 396.

[187] Above point I.2.a.; see in particular Iliopoulos-Strangas and Prevedourou, above n 33, p 32; Nettesheim, above n 7, p 130.

[188] Iliopoulos-Strangas and Prevedourou, above n 33, p 31, 32 *et seq.*

[189] Iliopoulos-Strangas and Prevedourou, above n 33, p 31

[190] Iliopoulos-Strangas and Prevedourou, above n 33, p 31 *et seq.*

[191] Nettesheim, above n 7, p 131.

[192] Nettesheim, above n 7, p 132. See also Pache, above n 176.

b. *Articles 6(1) and 7 TEU as Limits to the Constitutional*
   Autonomy of the Member States

There is a close relationship between Article 6(1) and (3) TEU with the latter conditioning the former. The Union—including respect for the identity of the Member States—is based upon the common values and principles referred to in Article 6(1) TEU. This provision together with Article 7 TEU, as is stated in the Swedish report, 'quite naturally puts limits to the constitutional autonomy of the Member States. That is their purpose'.[193] They express, in the view of the German report, the very core of the common constitutional heritage in Europe[194] and establish, together with the corresponding conditions in the national integration clauses,[195] a collective system of reciprocal constitutional stabilisation.[196] The Italian report emphasises the importance of Article 6(1)

> in the process of emerging of shared principles and values through reciprocal influence by the MS and the EU Institutions ... Given the fact that the institutional dimension of the EU is also based on procedures of decision-making that take place within the legal orders of the MS, the conclusion can be drawn that the fully realisation of democracy in the EU context requires that democracy is fully realised within each MS legal order.[197]

Indeed, the same seems to be true for the rule of law and the respect of fundamental rights as well as for the decision-making processes at the European level.

It is, consequently, the predominant view in the national reports that through these provisions the basic principles of Article 6(1) TEU act of limits on the autonomy of the Member States, though—as the Austrian report points out—'in only a very formal way'.[198] The Dutch report points to the existing internal system which end uses that such limits are only theoretical ones[199] a 'hypothèse d'école' as the Luxembourg report says.[200] Be it as it may, it is worth quoting from the Austrian report the practical insight that:

> it is detrimental for the development of the European Union, with or without a 'constitution', if Articles 6 and 7, or even the idea behind them, are abused

---

[193] Schäder and Melin, above n 3, p 397.
[194] Nettesheim, above n 7, p 134: 'Kerngehalt 'gemeineuropäischen Verfassungsrechts'.
[195] See point I.2.a.
[196] Nettesheim, above n 7, p 133.
[197] Cannizzano, above n 39, p 253.
[198] Köck, above n 9, p 28.
[199] Kortmann, above n 10, p 304. See also Iliopoulos-Strangas and Prevedourou, above n 33, p 34.
[200] Wivenes, above n 11, p 281.

for political reason in order to illegitimately intervene in the internal affairs of a Member State.[201]

Appropriate sanctions under Article 7, the Greek report points out, are on the other hand welcomed under Greek constitutional law as an assurance of the constitutional requirement of reciprocity of rights and obligations of the Member States that have joined the Union.[202]

B.   Common Values: the Charter of Fundamental Rights of the European Union

It is clear that talking about common values and the principles of Article 6(1) TEU immediately leads to the Charter of Fundamental Rights of the European Union (hereafter CFR), which was proclaimed at the Nice Summit and which is on the agenda of the Laeken Convention for its legal status to be determined. The questions on the Charter have provoked diverse answers in length and in substance, developments which in part go far beyond the reach of the questions put and which are recommended, as such, for intense study and discussion. The first question to be dealt with hereafter relates to the content of the Charter as compared to the human rights standards guaranteed in the Member States and aims to establish whether or not it will provide sufficient protection for fundamental rights at the European level (below section a.). The second is of a more practical nature and focuses on the possible use of the Charter in national courts, which are—as partners in the judicial dialogue with the Court of Justice— the basic element of the existing European system for the judicial protection of fundamental rights (below section b.). The third question leads us back to Article 6(1) TEU and aims to establish the extent to which the Charter can contribute to clarifying the common principles referred to in this provision (below section c.). Some other important aspects have been raised by the national reports, one of which is the question of the scope of the Charter and its relation to the European Convention on Human Rights (ECHR; below section d).

a.   The CFR and the Basic Human Rights Standards of National Law?

There is an important reference in the Swiss report to a famous saying by Rudolf Smend, which should be born in mind by everybody engaged in

---

[201] Köck, above n 9, p 28. See, on the other hand, Cannizzano, above n 39, p 253, where the right of the other Member States is seen, even 'to adopt, outside the institutionalised frame set out by Art 7 TUE, some means of constraints in order to induce the breaching State to revert its course and to assure full respect of these principles'.

[202] Iliopoulos-Strangas and Prevedourou, above n 33, p 34.

comparative constitutional law, which the report relates to the many similarities between the Charter and the provisions of the Swiss Federal Constitution of 2000: 'If two constitutions say the same, this may not (necessarily) mean the same'.[203] Most of the national reports contain a broad concordance between their national guarantees and the rights laid down in the Charter,[204] though, in particular, the vagueness of the provision on possible limitations in Article 52(1) CFR raises uncertainties regarding the level of protection guaranteed by the specific provisions of the Charter.[205] The Luxembourg report states that it goes far beyond the rights recognised by the national constitution.[206]

Accordingly, the German report, first, points out the similarity between the protection established by the Charter and the German Constitution in general terms. With a view to the German initiative for the process, it states: 'Without this concordance, there would be no Charter'.[207] A number of 'deficits', however, demonstrate that the actual text of the Charter is the result of compromises: many of the rights it criticises, eg the references to the freedom to conduct a business or the right of collective bargaining and action (Articles 16 and 28), are recognised only 'in accordance with Community law and national laws and practices'. Even if legally binding, this would not provide the individual with any right which could be enforced in the context of such 'laws and practices'.[208] The general provision on limitations would not give more assurance and legal certainty and the absence of differentiation between rights such as the prohibition of reproductive cloning, on the one hand, and the right to paid maternity leave, on the other hand, signalled that almost everything was left to the Court of Justice.[209] The Italian report finds a regrettable omission in Article 52 CFR, which does 'not enumerate the public interests that can legitimately restrict the individual rights'.[210] Given the uncertainties raised by the Charter, the Swedish report concludes that it is 'difficult to assess the importance of it'.[211]

---

[203] Freiermuth Abt and Mosters, above n 24, p 422, quoted from Häberle, above n 6, at p 17.
[204] Iliopoulos-Strangas and Prevedourou, above n 33, p 36, with a detailed comparison of the Charter with several national constitutions, *ibid*, p 37 *et seq*; see also Sundström, Boedeker and Kauppi, above n 17, p 9; Köck, above n 9, p 29; see also the following fn.
[205] Kortmann, above n 10, p 305: 'significant correlation'; Craig, above n 19, p 7, with questions, however, regarding the social rights; Martín y Pérez de Nanclares and López Castillo, above n 36, p 332: 'correspondance ... relative'; see also the comparison with Article 36 of the Swiss constitution in Freiermuth Abt and Mosters, above n 24, p 425 *et seq*.
[206] Wivenes, above n 11, p 281.
[207] Nettesheim, above n 7, p 136.
[208] Nettesheim, above n 7, p 137 *et seq*; criticism to this effect also in Martín y Pérez de Nanclares and López Castillo, above n 36, p 334.
[209] Nettesheim, above n 7, p 139 *et seq*.
[210] Cannizzano, above n 39, pp 254 *et seq*; Martín y Pérez de Nanclares and López Castillo, above n 36, p 334.
[211] Schäder and Melin, above n 3, p 398.

Serious doubts as to the practical use of some rights of the Charter follow for the Irish report from the definition of its scope in Article 51 CFR. While the rights are 'guaranteed in accordance with the national laws governing the exercise of these rights' or 'under the conditions established by national laws and practices', the areas concerned are those where the Union has no competence to act and, thus, even national implementing measures for European acts would not be conceivable. The report finds all these guarantees meaningless and legally paradoxical.[212] It may not be very satisfactory to say that at least the values are expressed in such provisions of fundamental rights and the legal impact for the European Union is rather to stop it from any action which would affect the standards of protection achieved within the Member States.

In general terms, the comparative analysis given in the Greek report, between the Charter and several national constitutions, however, leads to its conclusion, that in spite of differences as to the subject matter of guarantees and their actual scope and binding force, there is a good balance of social rights in the Charter; it reflects the standards of protection contained in the national constitutions.[213]

b.   The Charter as a Reference for Fundamental Rights Protection in National Courts

The Charter has been referred to in a number of cases already by the Court of First Instance and by advocates general of the Court of Justice.[214] For the Commission 'compliance with the rights contained in the Charter' are to become a 'touchstone for its action'[215] and the EU report says that 'the two branches of the legislature—the European Parliament and the Council—may thus be said to have given their blessing to the Commission's approach.[216] It will be, as the Swiss report states, an important source of inspiration for national courts and will contribute to the evolution of European *ius commune* in that it promotes the Europeanisation and approximation of the national law and its interpretation.[217]

The Finish report rightly states that, as long as the Charter has no binding effect, reference to it can only made as a 'politically agreed indication of existing rights'[218] making them more 'visible'. Yet, it follows from the

---

[212] G Hogan, 'European Union Law and National Constitutions: Ireland', *FIDE XX*. Congress London 2002 (published on www.fide2002.org), pp 15–18.
[213] Iliopoulos-Strangas and Prevedourou, above n 33, p 42 *et seq.*
[214] References in Oliver, above n 2, p 30 at fns 129–32; Iliopoulos-Strangas and Prevedourou, above n 33, p 46 at fn 173.
[215] Oliver, above n 2, p 29, with reference to the Communication of the Commission on the application of the Charter, SEC (2001) 380/3.
[216] Oliver, above n 2, p 29 *et seq.*
[217] Freiermuth Abt and Mosters, above n 24, p 426.
[218] Sundström, Boedeker and Kauppi, above n 17, p 11.

national reports that the Charter may be[219] and has already been quoted by national judges a few times. The first example is the Spanish Constitutional Court, which has referred to Article 8 of the Charter even before it was proclaimed in Nice,[220] and also after that event the Constitutional Court referred to it (Article 18) with a view to making an argument relating to a national measure.[221] The Corte d'Appello di Roma has also given consideration to the Charter (Article 47) in a case regarding labour law.[222] The Luxembourg report, however, states that as long as the Charter is not binding, there is no room for references to it by national courts.[223]

Though the Charter may give national courts like to the Court of Justice an orientation on what are the fundamental rights *in concreto*, there is one case from Austria only, in which a national court has requested from the Court of Justice a preliminary ruling on the compatibility of a measure with the fundamental rights contained in the Charter.[224] The ruling of the Court has yet to be given, and it will be interesting to see whether it takes a position on the Charter or continues to avoid referring to it in keeping with the decision of the Nice Summit not yet to give it legally binding effect.

c.   The Impact of the Charter on the Standards Referred to in Article 6.1 TEU

There is a clear statement in several national reports that the Charter will influence the standards which are set out in Article 6(1) TEU.[225] It will serve, as the Austrian report says, 'as a source of reference for the better understanding of, and substantial consequences deriving from, these principles'[226] and in view of others like the Luxembourg, Greek, Swedish and the United Kingdom's reports it could help to explain more precisely what is meant by Article 6(1) TEU.[227] The German report, finally, emphasises that there is no doubt that the Charter will have effects both on the principle of democracy and the protection of fundamental rights as provided for in Article 6(1) and (2) TEU.[228]

---

[219] See also Köck, above n 9, p 29 *et seq*; Craig, above n 19, p 7; Kortmann, above n 10, p 305; Cannizzano, above n 39, p 255; Nettesheim, above n 7, p 141 *et seq*.
[220] Martín y Pérez de Nanclares and López Castillo, above n 36, p 335.
[221] Martín y Pérez de Nanclares and López Castillo, above n 36, p 335 *et seq*.
[222] Iliopoulos-Strangas and Prevedourou, above n 33, p 43.
[223] Wivenes, above n 11, p 282.
[224] Nettesheim, above n 7, p 142, with reference to case C–248/01, *Pfanner Getränke* (pending).
[225] Martín y Pérez de Nanclares and López Castillo, above n 36, p 336.
[226] Köck, above n 9, p 30.
[227] Wivenes, above n 11, p 283; Iliopoulos-Strangas and Prevedourou, above n 33, p 45. See also Schäder and Melin, above n 3, p 398: The Charter will ... certainly set the standards for the references in article 6.1'; Craig, above n 19, p 10: 'The answer is surely that the Charter would be regarded as 'fleshing out' the meaning of the 'human rights and fundamental freedoms' mentioned in that Article'.
[228] Nettesheim, above n 7, p 142 *et seq*.

d.   The Scope of the Charter and Its Relation to the ECHR

It is the Italian report which stresses that Article 53 CFR should be understood
to give an assurance that in each case the highest standard of protection should
be achieved:

> In case that the Charter does not reproduce exactly the balance between individ-
> ual liberties and public interests established in the ECHR, the Courts must apply
> the standard of protection that grants greater consideration for the former.[229]

The United Kingdom's report draws attention to the conflicts which may
arise due to the fact that national constitutional courts like the German and
the Italian, do not accept, as a principle, that the 'respective sphere of application', according to Article 53 CFR, of the national fundamental rights is
limited to national measures only. Moreover, a Charter right may be applied
so as to comply with the fundamental rights standards of one Member
State, but would not satisfy the requirements of another fundamental
rights guarantee of another Member State.[230] The Swedish report, finally,
states that there is 'a risk that the importance of the Convention would be
deteriorated', should the Charter become a binding instrument.[231]

The EU-report finds many reasons for the Union to accede to the ECHR,
and states that 'the climate of informed opinion has shifted markedly in
favour of accession'.[232] The adoption of the Charter as legally binding
would not challenge, but underline the value of human rights, for the
protection of which the ECHR and the complaint to Strasbourg would be a
'last remedy' for the citizen against the EU—as it is against the Member
States today. By the way, is it conceivable that the interpretation of the
Charter, indeed, 'affects' human rights as recognised in other instruments,
national constitutions or the ECHR? What may affect or violate such
human rights is always the European or national measure under review. In
case the protection of fundamental rights provided by the Charter should
prove insufficient, as compared to the protection which would be given
under national or ECHR standards, the real question seems to be whether
or not the measure may be challenged before national courts or the
Strasbourg Court. The answer to this question is not given in Article 53
CFR nor in the Charter.[233] As long as the EU is not, itself, party to the ECHR,

---

[229] Cannizzano, above n 39, p 255.
[230] Craig, above n 19, p 7 *et seq.*
[231] Schäder and Melin, above n 3, p 398.
[232] Oliver, above n 2, p 34 *et seq.*
[233] For the relationship to the European Convention of Human Rights see Ingolf Pernice, The
European Constitution, in Sinclair House Debates 16, Europe's Constitution-a framework for
the future of the Union (2001), p 18, at 30 *et seq* and D Thym, 'Charter of Fundamental
Rights: Competition or Consistency of Human Rights Protection in Europe?', XI *Finnish
Yearbook of International Law* (2002/3 forthcoming).

it is a question of the supremacy of European law, to which we shall now turn.

C.   The Question of the Supremacy of EC/EU law and Its Constitutional Effects

Although the established jurisprudence of the Court of Justice since 1964 leaves doubt as to the supremacy of European law over national law,[234] the position of Member States and their supreme courts is much less clear, if not opposed.[235] This is the key question regarding the relation between European Union law and national constitutions and the functioning of the European construction. The approach chosen seems to depend very much on the various concepts of constitution, discussed above, and how the foundations of European law are conceptualised: where they are found in the national constitutions and regarded as international law, the supremacy of European law will be conditioned by the provisions of the national constitution and their interpretation by national (constitutional) courts— yet, the supremacy may be recognised as a consequence of the monistic approach of the respective Member State. Where the Union and its law is conceptualised, ultimately, as a social contract to which the people or citizens of the Member States are parties, acting through their respective national institutions, supremacy would follow from their common desire to establish a working system the law of which applies equally throughout the Union.

Except for Portugal, the national reports do not draw a meaningful distinction between the primary and the secondary law of the Union, so that the question of supremacy is dealt with in general (below section a.) before the impact of it for implicit modifications of the national constitutions are discussed in brief (below section b.).

a.   Supremacy of Community Law and National Constitutions

In some 'monistic' Member States the supremacy of European law is recognised without reservation: this seems to be the case for the Austrian legal order, which unconditionally recognises the autonomous force of EU/EC law as elaborated in the case law of the Court of Justice: 'Any norm of Community law', the Austrian report says, 'whether contained in the constitutional Treaties or in the legislative acts of Community institutions, has primacy over any norm of national law, whether contained in the

---

[234] See Case 6/64, *Costa v ENEL*, [1964] ECR 1251; Case C–213/89, *Factortame (No. 2)*, [1990] ECR I–2243; Case 106/77, *Simmenthal*, [1978] ECR 629.
[235] See for an exhaustive analysis of the attitudes of national courts: F C Mayer, *Kompetenzüberschreitung und Letztentscheidung* (2000), at p 87–273.

Constitution or in "simple" law'.[236] The same is true, according to the Dutch report, in the Netherlands: According to Article 94 of the Dutch constitution and without distinction between primary and secondary law, 'all Community law is superior to national (constitutional) law'.[237] Also the Spanish situation is clear. According to Article 93 of the Spanish Constitution, direct effect and supremacy even over constitutional law is recognised, though the Constitution provides for a previous control of the constitutionality of international treaties and, in case of a variance, the amendment of the Constitution.[238] Similar rules also seem to apply in France.[239] Though the Constitutional Court of Luxembourg has not yet pronounced on the matter, the Luxembourg report finds that, due to the clear monistic approach of its country, international law including Community law always prevails over national law. This was recognised, recently, by the Constitutional Court for the European Convention on Human Rights and would be valid, *a fortiori* for Community law.[240]

The situation is less clear in countries where the 'dualistic' approach has been chosen. The *Maastricht* judgment of the German Constitutional Court,[241] based on the 'international' approach has confirmed its right to exercise ultimate control over the application of European Acts in Germany and seems to have been a 'leading' case also for other Member States.[242] Yet, the German report rightly states that the more recent judgment of the same Court in the *Bananas* case[243] clearly shows that, at present, the control of a European Act by this Court is practically excluded.[244] The German report finds the reason for the supremacy in the fact that, as opposed to classical international law, Community law does not leave the question of its relation to national law to the contracting parties, but has taken the decision by itself. Whether or not this decision is recognised within a Member State, is a different question and may be ruled upon by the national constitution.[245] The question, however, whether or not such recognition is part of the deal, is left open in the report. Instead, it

---

[236] Köck, above n 9, p 32.
[237] Kortmann, above n 10, p 305 *et seq*.
[238] Martín y Pérez de Nanclares and López Castillo, above n 36, p 337 *et seq*.
[239] See the references in Pernice, above n 94.
[240] 283 *et seq*.
[241] Bundesverfassungsgericht, above n 73.
[242] See the reference to it in Schäder and Melin, above n 3, p 399; Poiares Maduro, above n 49, near fns 26–29; Sundström, Boedeker and Kauppi, above n 17, p 12; Hogan, above n 212, p 23 with fn 52.
[243] Bundesverfassungsgericht, Decision of 7 June 2000, *Bananenmarktordnung*, BVerfGE 102, 147; see for comments I Pernice, 'Les bananes et les droits fondamentaux: La Cour constitutionelle allemande fait le point', Ca de Cahiers de Dioit European (2001) 427 at 439.
[244] Nettesheim, above n 7, p 145 *et seq*.
[245] Nettesheim, above n 7, p 146. For the opposite view in Portugal see Poiares Maduro, above n 49, near fn 20, while other views are quoted *ibid*, in fn 21. See, however, the approach developed by Maduro, *ibid* near fn 42–54, and after fn 71.

discusses—and rejects—the idea that notwithstanding the supremacy rule, the relationship between European and national law would have to be seen as non-hierarchical.[246]

Though the conditions are very different, a similar solution seems to be found in the United Kingdom. With reference to the *Factortame* case and the statements of Lord Bridge, the British report finds supremacy of Community law founded, for the UK, in three 'aspects': a *contractarian*, an *a priori* and *functional*, and in the *European Communities Act 1972*.[247] Though there is no question about the recognition of supremacy rule by British courts, a limit, however, would still be the sovereignty of Parliament. How national courts would react in a case of a clash between a European rule and an Act of the British Parliament derogating expressly and unequivocally, however, is a question which has not been solved. The British report finds that there is a way to construct a right for national courts to give priority to the European rule, on the basis of 'normative arguments of legal principle the content of which can and will vary across time': Due to the 'UK's membership of the EC, as exemplified by the contractarian and functional elements' of the arguments in *Factortame*, the Parliament would not be regarded any more as legally omnipotent.[248]

The Irish case is different from all other Member States in so far as Article 29(4)(3) of the Irish Constitution gives priority to all Community measures as well as national measures necessitated by the obligations of membership of the Communities. As the Irish Supreme Court has stated in the *Crotty* case in 1987, any 'essential alteration in the scope and objectives of the Communities' would require an express amendment of the Constitution.[249] Consequently, the Irish courts are reported to have, save in the special case of abortion, 'unhesitatingly acknowledged the supremacy of Community law.[250] One case, however, where the Supreme Court has, consequently, given priority also to a national measure implementing a Council Regulation on milk quotas because it did not more than give effect to the Regulation, has been criticised by the 'anti-Nice campaigners' and has motivated the Government 'to bring about greater domestic scrutiny of EU legislative proposals in advance of the referendum'.[251]

Other Member States seem to envisage, more generally control of European Acts by national courts where these is a clash with national constitutions. The Italian Constitutional Court is reported to maintain the 'idea of the supremacy of the National Constitution over EC law, without however

---

[246] Nettesheim, above n 7, p 146–149.
[247] Craig, above n 19, p 11 *et seq.*
[248] Craig, above n 19, p 14–16.
[249] Hogan, above n 212, p 4–6, referring to *Crotty v An Taoiseach*, (1987) IR 713, with more references.
[250] Hogan, above n 212, p 19 *et seq.*
[251] Hogan, above n 212, p 24 *et seq.*

limiting to a heavily the autonomy of the EC legal system', in requiring only 'a certain structural conformity of the supranational legal order to the national Constitution' and limiting its judicial review to cases of 'grave and persistent breach of fundamental human rights, not duly repaired by the judicial institutions of the Union'.[252] The new Article 117 of the Italian Constitution is said, however, to contain some basic rules concerning the supremacy of EC law over ordinary Italian legislation: 'Legislative powers shall be vested in the State and the Regions in compliance with the Constitution and with the constraints deriving from EU legislation and international obligations'.[253] Yet, there is no sign of a general recognition of the supremacy of such law over the provisions of the Italian Constitution.

On the same lines, the Portuguese report states, with regard to Article 8 of the Portuguese Constitution that 'the Portuguese Constitution is generally interpreted so as to guarantee the supremacy of EU law with regard to infra-constitutional norms but it is also seen as conditioning that supremacy and in holding to itself the ultimate power of authority'.[254] The way to avoid clashes with EC law, therefore, is the prior amendment of the Constitution.[255] The prevalent idea is that of a clear supremacy of the Constitution, based on a classical concept of sovereignty.[256] In Greece also, the primacy of European law is disputed both in jurisprudence and doctrine[257]; there are judgments recognising the principle of supremacy and others rejecting it. The autonomy of the European legal order is seen to be based on Community, constitutional and international law. Yet, as long as the sovereign nation states exist in the Union, the Greek report says, the national institutions will give priority to national constitutions.[258]

Though there is no constitutional court in Finland, a move is signalled in the Finish report towards control of constitutionality of Acts by national courts under Article 106 of the Finish Constitution.[259] A subsidiary control of the constitutionality of European Acts by the Federal Court would, in spite of the monistic tradition of the country, not be excluded by the Swiss report.[260] Finally, without an amendment to the Constitution (Article 169(3)), the Cyprus report states that the EU Treaty or the future Constitution would be subordinate to the Constitution of Cyprus, but superior to the national legislation.

---

[252] Cannizzano, above n 39, p 256 *et seq.*
[253] Cannizzano, above n 39, p 249 *et seq.*
[254] Poiares Maduro, above n 49, after fn 4, near fn 20.
[255] Poiares Maduro, above n 49, near fn 7.
[256] Poiares Maduro, above n 49, near fns 58–61: 'States are the only true sovereign powers and they can always revoke their acceptance of supremacy'.
[257] Iliopoulos-Strangas and Prevedourou, above n 33, p 48 *et seq.*
[258] Iliopoulos-Strangas and Prevedourou, above n 33, p 51 *et seq.*
[259] Sundström, Boedeker and Kauppi, above n 17, p 12.
[260] Freiermuth Abt and Mosters, above n 24, p 427 *et seq.*

b. Implicit Modification of National Constitutions by the Revision and Application of the TEU

The conclusion or revision of or adhesion to the European Treaties have made necessary, in a number of Member States, express amendments of constitutions. Such amendments are necessary, as already mentioned in the cases of Spain, France and Portugal, in any case of a conflict between the new Treaty provisions and the constitution. Austria has introduced new provisions into its constitution to enable it to adapt to the requirements of EU membership, thereby opening up the Austrian legal order to European law, but also ensuring the participation of Austrian representatives in the EU system.[261] The Cyprus report sets out the need for a profound revision of the Cyprus Constitution before accession to the European Union, in order to prevent conflicts with the European Treaties.[262] In Germany too, several amendments to the constitution (the integration-clause, local elections, central bank), have been provoked by the Maastricht Treaty.[263] A further amendment was felt necessary after a surprising interpretation by the Court of Justice of the directive on equal treatment of men and woman in the army. These would not have been necessary and were strongly criticised for other reasons, but the German report finds such amendments useful—for reasons of 'constitutional aesthetics'.[264] Other sensitive areas having a strong impact on existing constitutional provisions in Germany are the asylum and the anti-discrimination legislation enacted since the Treaty of Amsterdam.[265]

'Implicit modification of national constitutions by the revision and application of the Maastricht Treaty are immanent to the system', the Austrian report says, and adaptations are 'a matter to be decided by domestic law' and useful for the sake of clarity.[266] The Spanish report also sets out this requirement and the constitutional basis for the acceptance of such implicit modifications is seen in Article 93 of the Constitution. The report stresses that it is for this reason that an 'organic law' is required to give effect to a Treaty revising the EU Treaty.[267] In Greece, there has been no amendment of the Constitution at all—neither when Greece acceded to the European Union nor at a later time. With diverging dogmatic constructions, all consequential changes to constitutional law are considered as tacit or quasi-tacit alterations of the Constitution and the procedure for the revision of the Constitution (Article 110) is not applied.[268] The Dutch report

---

[261] Köck, above n 9, p 13 *et seq.*
[262] Josephides, above n 12, p 17.
[263] Nettesheim, above n 7, p 148.
[264] Nettesheim, above n 7, p 150 *et seq.*
[265] Nettesheim, above n 7, p 151.
[266] Köck, above n 9, p 32.
[267] Martín y Pérez de Nanclares and López Castillo, above n 36, p 341 *et seq.*
[268] Iliopoulos-Strangas and Prevedourou, above n 33, p 52.

not only recognises that 'constitutional law has surely been modified by community law in an implicit way', but also gives striking examples: the *Costa/ENEL* judgment, which exceeded what is provided by Article 94 of the Constitution in giving priority to all EC law over Dutch law, the monetary competence of the ECB being contrary to Article 106 of the Constitution, which states that the monetary system shall be regulated by an Act of Parliament and the dominant position of the Prime Minister in EU policies, which is contrary to the constitutional role of the Prime Minister as 'first among equals'.[269]

While other reports, like the ones from Finland, Sweden and the United Kingdom, are silent on this point, the Swiss report stresses the impact of possible accession to the European Union on the principle of direct democracy in Switzerland. This may not, however, stop the country's accession, and in fact Swiss legislation is already following the Union model 'autonomously' to a great extent.[270]

D.   Institutional Interdependence: European Functions of National Institutions

Among the, regularly- implicit, alterations of national constitutions are the new or different functions of national authorities in view of their participation in the making and the implementation and application of European decisions. The Spanish report draws attention to the fact that this influence has an impact on the constitutional autonomy of Member States. It points out that the 'dédoublement fonctionnel' does not transform national authorities into European ones,[271] and, as the Finnish report reminds us, the national authorities implementing European law are still appointed by national governments.[272] Yet, there is, as the German report notes, a fundamental change in the exercise of political power which affects the core of national sovereignty.[273] The European functions of national authorities are generally recognised, though most of them are not explained or even reflected in the texts of the national constitutions.[274] The Swiss report states that important modification of the Constitution would be needed to adapt it to these new tasks.[275] Without such express provisions, it is merely

---

[269] Kortmann, above n 10, p 306.

[270] Freiermuth Abt and Mosters, above n 24, p 428 *et seq.*

[271] Martín y Pérez de Nanclares and López Castillo, above n 36, p 342, 346. See also Nettesheim, above n 7, p 151.

[272] Sundström, Boedeker and Kauppi, above n 17, p 14.

[273] Nettesheim, above n 7, p 152.

[274] See, however, Article 93 of the Spanish Constitution regarding the obligation of the Cortes Generales and the Government to implement European law—Martín y Pérez de Nanclares and López Castillo, above n 36, p 343. See also Art 70(8) of the Greek Constitution.

[275] Freiermuth Abt and Mosters, above n 24, p 429 *et seq.*

through knowledge of European law and procedures that they can be identified and by the implicit alterations of the constitutions, due to membership to the European Union, that they are legitimised. The national reports explain how this looks in terms of the practice of Member States regarding their national parliaments, governmental and administrative functions and the judiciary.

a. *The National Parliaments in the European Legislative Process*

As to the national and, where applicable, regional parliaments, their European role is described by mainly three functions:

— In transposing Community directives and providing for implementing measures regulations they implement European legislation and are part of the legislative machinery of the European Union, though partly in a very formal sense[276]—at least in so far as internal decision-making powers have not delegated implementation to the executive.[277] In Spain, a certain cooperation with the autonomous regions has settled the controversy on eventual coercive measures by the government in case a region, in the field of its competencies, does not implement European law.[278] The implication of national parliaments in the transposition and implementation of Community law is seen, by the German report, as another instrument for providing European legislation with more democratic legitimacy.[279] The very fact, finally, that they are bound, in the frame of the 'two-tier' legislative process, to implement the directives which ministers have agreed in the council-though progressively by joint decision making with the European Parliament—may induce national parliaments, as was reported from Ireland, to watch more closely the positions taken by ministers in the Council.[280]

— The Dutch like the Spanish report, in addition, emphasises the fundamental role of national parliaments in the constitutional process:[281] ratification of the Treaties, and, in the Netherlands, the consent of the Dutch representative to certain decisions of the

---

[276] Wivenes, above n 11, p 286
[277] Kortmann, above n 10, p 307; see also Art 43 of the Greek Constitution, and Iliopoulos-Strangas and Prevedourou, above n 33, p 59.
[278] Martín y Pérez de Nanclares and López Castillo, above n 36, p 344, referring to Art 155.1 of the Spanish Constitution.
[279] Nettesheim, above n 7, p 155. Similarly: Schäder and Melin, above n 3, p 400.
[280] See also Schäder and Melin, above n 3, p 400: '... it also makes the national implementation easier if the parliamentarians have had a finger in the pie'.
[281] Kortmann, above n 10, p 306; Martín y Pérez de Nanclares and López Castillo, above n 36, p 344.

European Council need prior approval of the Houses of Parliament.[282] Attention is also drawn to the fact that according to the EU/EC Treaties national parliaments have to approve certain Acts decided by the Council. The Finnish report emphasis that since the Convention method has been introduced, national parliaments participate actively in the preparation of new treaties.[283]

— Above all, national parliaments have to legitimise and control national ministers acting in the Council, this being the decisive stage of the European legislature.[284] They have a very important role to play in the European legislative process, the Swedish report states, since the legitimacy afforded by the European Parliament is not sufficient.[285] This control may be quite limited, as reported by Italy[286] and by the Netherlands, where the Dutch Parliament can 'only exercise political pressure on the minister'.[287] It is not strong in the United Kingdom either, where the scrutiny of European draft legislation is exercised—on the initiative of a 'Select Committee on European Scrutiny'—by two 'standing committees' of the House of Commons. Though the interest in their opinions, which may well differ from that of the ministers, may not be great, the British report qualifies as 'undoubtedly beneficial' that there is 'another body within the UK looking at such issues'.[288] In addition, the House of Lords Select Committee on European Union exercises, through its investigations and reports, considerable control over European policies. Much more emphasis is given to control exercised by the national Parliament over European policies by ministers in Finland, where the Eduskunta has to give an opinion on all matters within its field of competence, 'i.e. matters concerning national laws'.[289] In Spain, the practice is, as in Denmark, that the Parliament sometimes gives clear instructions for negotiations to the government or seeks a postponement of a Council's decision in order to allow for prior parliamentary consideration.[290] A special 'Mixed Commission for the European Union',

---

[282] Kortmann, above n 10, p 307.
[283] Sundström, Boedeker and Kauppi, above n 17, p 14.
[284] Wivenes, above n 11, p 286:
[285] Schäder and Melin, above n 3, p 400.
[286] Cannizzano, above n 39, p 257 *et seq*: the contribution of the Italian Parliament to the shaping of the EC/EU politics appears in practice meaningless'.
[287] Kortmann, above n 10, p 307.
[288] Craig, above n 19, p 17.
[289] Sundström, Boedeker and Kauppi, above n 17, p 13.
[290] Martín y Pérez de Nanclares and López Castillo, above n 36, p 345. Similarly, a 'Comité permanent des affaires européennes' has been created in 2001 in Greece, Iliopoulos-Strangas and Prevedourou, above n 33, p 56.

composed of members of the Congress and of the Senate has been created by a simple law with a view to enhancing parliamentary control of the Government acting in the Council.[291] The procedure for the participation of the national Parliament in European matters has been formalised in Greece by a revision of the Constitution in 2001, through new provisions in Article 70(8) to the effect that the government is bound to forward drafts of European regulating Acts to the President of the Parliament, the Parliament may after an opinion and the government is obliged to inform the Parliament of the outcome.[292] There are similar provisions, since the accession to the European Union, in the Austrian Constitution (Article 23e),[293] and also Article 23(3) of the German Constitution, introduced as a result of the ratification of the Treaty of Maastricht, which provide for the Parliament to be heard before the minister takes a position in the Council. The German report suggests, idealistically, that this consultation procedure expresses the cooperative character of this joint responsibility of the government and the Parliament,[294] though it acknowledges that in substance the participation of the Bundestag is extremely weak in providing sufficient democratic legitimacy to the legislation of the Union.[295]

Given the practical difficulties for a national parliament to effectively control European legislation, the Italian report suggests a general division of responsibilities: the European Parliament 'should contribute to the adoption of Acts of supranational character, while the national Parliament should rather focus on Acts having intrinsically an intergovernmental nature'.[296]

b. European Functions of National Administrations: A Double Mandate for the Executive

Also the national executives are involved both, in the legislative process of the European Union and, in particular, in the implementation of European law. Regarding involvement in the legislative process, the Luxembourg report criticises national administrations, double function as being hardly compatible with the traditional principle of the separation of powers—they

---

[291] Martín y Pérez de Nanclares and López Castillo, above n 36, p 345.
[292] Iliopoulos-Strangas and Prevedourou, above n 33, p 55 *et seq.*
[293] See for the procedure in detail Köck, above n 9, p 35 *et seq.*
[294] Nettesheim, above n 7, p 153: 'kooperativer Prozeß ... danach steht das Recht zur Bestimmung dieser Positionen Parlament und Regierung 'zur gesamten Hand' zu'.
[295] Nettesheim, above n 7, p 154.
[296] Cannizzano, above n 39, p 259.

are co-legislators at the European level and executive at the national.[297] This seems not to be a problem for other reports. As with the German report,[298] the Dutch report recognises this double role as a given: it is 'obvious that the Dutch government and especially the ministers act as Dutch and EU officers'.[299]

As to the role of national administrations as implementing bodies for the European legislation the Austrian report says, 'when applying EU/EC law, these institutions may also be regarded as exercising a function within the EU/EC system, and thus having the character of decentralised EU/EC institutions', this is one aspect of what Georges Scelle had termed '*dédoublement fonctionnel*'.[300] European law provokes substantial changes in the function of national administrations as well as of the material administrative law—discussed in Germany under the heading 'Europeanization of administrative law'.[301] The Spanish and the German reports explain this in detail and give examples, including the new development of transnational cooperation between decentralised national administrations.[302]

On the other hand, the Greek report underlines the fact that national administrations in do not, in practice, give the same priority to European matters as to national ones, a problem which is only in part remedied by the cooperation between the European Commission's services and the national 'Service Spécial du Contentieux Communautaire'.[303] The Spanish report points to the harmonising effect which this common function of national authorities has on the institutional organisation of the administrative instruments within the Member States; the Ministry for Environment was created in Spain to conform to European policies, like new autonomous agencies such as for energy or telecommunications, and the statute of the Spanish Central Bank, of course, was changed for the same reason.

c.   *Judicial protection in the European Union through National Judges*

Regarding the judiciary, national reports describe the important role judges play in the application and, in case of conflicts, in the enforcement of Community law.[304] The 'double loyalty' resulting from the role of the

---

[297] Wivenes, above n 11, p 287.
[298] Nettesheim, above n 7, p 151 *et seq*.
[299] Kortmann, above n 10, p 307.
[300] Köck, above n 9, p 37.
[301] Nettesheim, above n 7, p 155.
[302] Martín y Pérez de Nanclares and López Castillo, above n 36, p 347; Nettesheim, above n 7, 155 *et seq*, with many more references.
[303] Iliopoulos-Strangas and Prevedourou, above n 33, p 56 *et seq*.
[304] See Craig, above n 19, p 18 *et seq*; Martín y Pérez de Nanclares and López Castillo, above n 36, p 348 *et seq*; excellent and exhaustive: Iliopoulos-Strangas and Prevedourou, above n 33, p 62–72; Köck, above n 9, p 38 *et seq*.

national judge to apply both European and national law, as the Spanish report notes, poses considerable problems.[305] Also in Germany, problems arise where the Court of Justice and the German Constitutional Court take positions in subsequent preliminary rulings on the same matter, even if, as in the *Alcan* case, they do not diverge.[306] In Austria, as in Germany, 'the Court of Justice is … regarded, for the purpose of giving preliminary rulings, as part of the Austrian judicial system'. This means, as the Constitutional Courts have confirmed, that an arbitrary refusal to refer to the Court of Justice under Article 234 TEC would be a violation of the constitutional guarantee of access to the 'judge established by law'.[307] The report from Cyprus announces that the national courts will become courts of the Union, meaning that they will have the responsibility of applying the law of the Union in the national sphere.[308]

Regarding the procedures, the Spanish report emphasises the positive repercussions of the Court of Justice's jurisprudence on interim measures on the constitutional standards of judicial protection in Spain.[309] In Germany, a fundamental re-orientation of the procedural law for administrative courts is reported.[310] Though procedural autonomy of the judiciary is generally recognised as an important value, some reports find 'the harmonisation of the different procedural systems of the Member States … ineluctable'[311] with a view to equal protection for the citizens of the Union. The Italian report stresses the need for a European remedy, at least in cases in which a national court refuses to comply with its obligation to refer a case to the Court of Justice and suggests giving individuals the possibility of lodge an appeal with the Court of Justice.[312] It is interesting to note that in the case of an alleged violation of European fundamental rights, the German Constitutional Court has found that the refusal of the competent court to refer the case to the Court of Justice under Article 234 TEC is generally—and not only in the case of arbitrariness—a violation of the right of access to the 'judge established by law' as it is guaranteed in Article 101(1)(2) of the German Constitution.[313] If all national constitutional or supreme courts followed this line, there would not only be no need for harmonisation, but this would result in a system of decentralised judicial protection of fundamental rights in the European Union which might be preferable to a system of direct access to the Court of Justice.

---

[305] Martín y Pérez de Nanclares and López Castillo, above n 36, p 348.
[306] Nettesheim, above n 7, p 157 *et seq*.
[307] Köck, above n 9, p 38.
[308] Josephides, above n 12, p 73.
[309] Martín y Pérez de Nanclares and López Castillo, above n 36, p 352.
[310] Nettesheim, above n 7, p 158.
[311] Kortmann, above n 10, p 308.
[312] Cannizzano, above n 39, p 260.
[313] Bundesverfassungsgericht, Judgment of 9 January 2001, *Teilzeitarbeit*, reported in *Europäische Zeitschrift für Wirtschaftsrecht* (2001), 255.

III.   THE ROLE OF THE REGIONS AND LOCAL AUTHORITIES IN A EU CONSTITUTION

Regionalisation has become a strong trend in the past decades of constitutional developments in the Member States. Although European constitutional law does not interfere with the internal structure of the Member States, the EU report shows that regions and local authorities have found recognition in the European Treaties in many respects.[314] A number of proposals are already on the table to give the regions and, in particular, the 'regions with legislative powers' more influence over European policies, for example by giving the Committee of the Regions a special role in monitoring subsidiarity and the status of an institution of the Union and by granting it—or the regions—privileged access to the Court of Justice.[315] Indeed, the German report also sees a need for the recognition of territorial sub-divisions of the Member States: the Union shall not be 'blind' in this regard, as would be the traditional attitude for an international organisation. European policies are part of the internal—and not 'foreign'—policies[316] of the Member States, but this fact is not reflected in the institutional and procedural law of the Union.[317]

The national reports give an excellent picture of not only the role of the *Länder*, regions or other territorial subdivisions—if any—of the Member States, but also of the differences in their respective status and rights regarding participation in the definition of the national position at the Council. What was the role of the EU law in this development (below section 1.) and what are the consequences for EU law of the respective regionalisation or decentralisation processes in the Member States (below section 2.)?

A.   EU Law and the Constitutional Settlement in Relation to Regions and Local Authorities

Apart from recent developments in Belgium, it seems that throughout the Union the role and status of the *Länder* in Germany is the strongest of all regions. They have the status as original states and are granted broad constitutional autonomy. Their fundamental role in the German federal structure may not be changed, it is immune—according to the 'eternity clause' of Article 79(3) of the German Grundgesetz—even against constitutional revisions. The effect of German membership of the European Union,

---

[314] Oliver, above n 2, p 37 *et seq.*
[315] See Oliver, above n 2, p 40 *et seq.*
[316] For this important view see also the Spanish Constitutional Court in its judgment of 26 May 1994, ATC 165/94, reported in Martín y Pérez de Nanclares and López Castillo, above n 36, p 353 *et seq.*
[317] Nettesheim, above n 7, p 159 *et seq.*

the German report explains, is that their status as autonomous sub-national entities is drawn down to third level—or class—actors; their competencies, their room for political action and, thus, their statehood and very existence are progressively eroded.[318] New rights provided by Article 23(4) and (7) of the Grundgesetz concerning the participation of the *Länder* through the Federal Chamber in the determination of the German position at the Council are not regarded a satisfactory compensation—even though the opinions of the Federal Chamber are binding in matters where the *Länder* have exclusive legislative competence. Furthermore, the parliaments of the *Länder* are of marginal importance and the functioning of the internal parliamentary system is open to question. Therefore, a revitalisation of German federalism is deemed urgent.[319] Another new problem arising in Germany from the EU constitutional developments since Maastricht is the financial responsibility of the Federal Republic in cases where an infringement (Article 226, 228 TEC) or a failure to comply with the stability requirements under Article 104 TEC is the consequence of irregularities of one ore more *Länder*: no solution has, so far, been found for such situations.[320]

The situation of the component 'states' in Austria is similar. They lost competencies, and the 'states have only a limited constitutional compensation through the establishment, by article 23 B-VG, of the so-called procedure for participation of the states'.[321] The position of the states may be given as 'general comments' individually or made up within a special body, the Integration Conference, and are binding on the representatives of the country at the Council insofar as the matter falls within the legislative competence of the states.[322] Similar rights and procedures would need to be introduced for the Swiss Cantons were Switzerland to join the European Union: The new Swiss Constitution recognises, in Article 3, the sovereignty of the Cantons and other provisions guarantee their autonomy and their right to conduct foreign policies in the areas of their competence (Articles 47 and 56).[323] There would be a need for a revision of the division of powers between the Federation and the Cantons as well as of the financial provisions in the Constitution.[324]

Cyprus seems to intend, in the framework of its accession to the European Union, introducing a regional level in dividing the country in two new regions which would have elected councils and participate in the EU Committee of the Regions.[325] A positive effect of EU law on decentralisation of the country is also reported from Greece. It was for being able to

---

[318] Nettesheim, above n 7, p 160 *et seq.*
[319] Nettesheim, above n 7, p 162.
[320] Nettesheim, above n 7, p 162 *et seq.*
[321] Köck, above n 9, p 40.
[322] Köck, above n 9, p 40 *et seq.*
[323] Freiermuth Abt and Mosters, above n 24, p 431 *et seq*, 433 *et seq.*
[324] Freiermuth Abt and Mosters, above n 24, p 434.
[325] Josephides, above n 12, p 74.

send elected representatives of regions—which previously could not takes place—to the EU Committee of the Regions that according to Article 102(1) of the Greek Constitution the 'decentralisation of second degree' has been undertaken by legislation, with the result that the 'departments' have been accorded legal capacity, more administrative authority and elected representatives.[326] Similarly, local communities have been merged in order to strengthen them and they have been accorded more administrative tasks.[327] More radical seem to be the reforms in Italy concerning the role of the regions in 2001, which are said to have changed the centralised state into one which is similar to a federal state.[328] However, even where the regions have exclusive legislative competence, they do not have greater rights of participation than to be informed and heard on the relevant drafts discussed at the Council. Regarding the implementation of European legislation, the State has the power to legislate in matters falling within the competence of the regions, though the regions may substitute state legislation with their own legislation.[329] The Autonomous Regions of Spain have gradually been given increased competencies in the field of European matters after the initial exclusion from any participation in foreign policies, including European affairs. In particular, the Spanish report points to the famous case of the Basque country establishing a permanent office in Brussels, which was found compatible with the Constitution by the Constitutional Court—given that the European integration process has led to a new legal system which, for all the Member States, can be considered to a certain degree 'internal'.[330] The coordination of the policies of the Regions and the central government in Spain is organised within Sectorial Conferences or the Conference for European Community Matters. A representative of the Regions' 'Consejero Antonómico' exercises the function of an observer in the Permanent Representation of Spain in Brussels, but the Autonomous Regions are not represented in the Council, although its representatives may participate in the work of its working groups.[331]

Other national reports do not refer to the implications of the European constitutional process on their country with regard to regionalisation or decentralisation. This is true for the United Kingdom, where—apart from the statement that Scotland is responsible for implementation of EU law in the devolved areas—only the question of an 'impact of the EU on separatist tendencies' are dealt with: though, for Scotland, it may be attractive to have its own seat in the Council, the British report says that in a Union with 27 Member States 'the prospects of a small state, with few votes in the Council,

---

[326] Iliopoulos-Strangas and Prevedourou, above n 33, p 76 *et seq.*
[327] Iliopoulos-Strangas and Prevedourou, above n 33, p 77 *et seq.*
[328] Cannizzano, above n 39, p 261.
[329] Cannizzano, above n 39, p 261.
[330] Martín y Pérez de Nanclares and López Castillo, above n 36, p 353 *et seq.*
[331] Martín y Pérez de Nanclares and López Castillo, above n 36, p 354 *et seq.*

winning significant concessions are not great'.[332] The Swedish report notes that the decentralised—'but certainly not federal'—structure of a country, in which the municipalities as local administrative authorities have a strong role, is not affected by the constitutional developments in the European Union and that their existence has no consequences for EU law and decision-making either.[333] The situation in Finland and the Netherlands seems to be the same.[334] The Luxembourg report stresses that the role of local communities, cities and communes, is given insufficient attention in the European debate on regionalism and decentralisation.[335]

B.   Regionalisation and Decentralisation in the Member States and EU law

The Italian report stresses that 'one should recall that the constitutional autonomy of local entities must be now considered as among the fundamental principles concerning the constitutional organisation of some of the MS'.[336] The development of the Autonomous Regions in Spain has led to a claim for a *ius standi* in the Court of Justice as well as for more powers of the Committee of the Regions, in which they are represented with 17 members.[337] The Swiss report, finally, stresses the advantages of its federal concept for the maintenance of cultural diversity, subsidiarity, efficiency and the better participation of its citizens in the political process. It has a strong identity—building effect and could contribute to a 'Europe of citizens', in which a European people could evolve, being based on an identity composed of different peoples and cultures.[338]

IV.   CONCLUSIONS AND RECOMMENDATIONS FOR 2004

What can be drawn from these developments regarding the constitutions of, and the positions taken by the Member States and candidate countries? It is clear that the conclusions and recommendations of each report are a result of national law and political culture of the respective states and it is difficult to deduce from them any kind of consensus or general

---

[332] Craig, above n 19, p 19 *et seq.*
[333] Schäder and Melin, above n 3, p 389, 401.
[334] Sundström, Boedeker and Kauppi, above n 17, p 14; Kortmann, above n 10, p 308, where, however, the autonomy of the 12 decentralised bodies implies that they cannot be compelled by government order to implement European legislation, but only by an Act of Parliament.
[335] Wivenes, above n 11, p 288 *et seq.*
[336] Cannizzano, above n 39, p 262.
[337] Martín y Pérez de Nanclares and López Castillo, above n 36, p 357 *et seq.*
[338] Freiermuth Abt and Mosters, above n 24, p 437.

recommendation for the Convention and the Intergovernmental Conference of 2004. It is worth, nevertheless, identifying some common or prevailing views and some original ideas which have been developed in the reports. On that basis, recommendations are formulated with a view to stimulating discussion.[339]

A.   A New Architecture: How Should an EU Constitution or EU Basic Treaty Look?

Given the constitutional character of the European Treaties, the German report notes that the question is not whether Europe needs a Constitution but rather 'what kind of constitution Europe needs'.[340] There seems to be, indeed, a broad consensus on the need for what the Swedish report says: 'the fundamental Treaties should be subject to an operation of "legal cleansing"'. It calls for an

> EU Constitution containing the basic objectives of the Union and the fundamental rules on general principles of law to be respected, on citizenship of the Union, identifying the areas of common policy and giving the basic norms governing the institutions of the Union and the division of competencies between them would undoubtedly make the structure and legislation of the Union more clear, understandable and easy to apply for all its subjects.[341]

The Austrian report is not far from this, when it favours a European Constitution which contains only provisions 'establishing the main institutions and defining their powers as well as the procedures by which these competencies would have to be exercised'.[342] The 'communitarisation' of the second and the third pillars considered necessary by the Luxembourg report in the medium-term.[343] The British report considers important the inclusion of 'the norms dealing with the relationship between national law and Community law and the norms dealing with the relationship between the citizen and the Community'.[344] As it appears from the EU report, the merger of the Treaties with a view to simplifying the structure of the Union as well as to giving it an explicit and single legal personality is not only supported

---

[339] For these recommendations Ingolf Pernice alone is responsible. There was no time for the coordination of divergent views as they may exist.

[340] Nettesheim, above n 7, p 165.

[341] Schäder and Melin, above n 3, p 402; Craig, above n 19, p 21. For a simplification of the Treaties also: Nettesheim, above n 7, p 169.

[342] Köck, above n 9, p 41 *et seq.*

[343] Wivenes, above n 11, p 290.

[344] Craig, above n 19, p 21.

by the Commission, but finds a broad consensus within the working group of the Convention.[345]

Yet, there are different views on particular points and a number of specific suggestions on what the Laeken process should aim at:

a.   A 'Constitutional Treaty' for the European Union: Concepts and Supremacy

While, for the Swedish report, there is no problem with the use of the term 'Constitution' for the European Union, even if a limited approach were to be chosen of 'just sorting out the rules of a fundamental character from the present Treaties and arranging them in a separate document'.[346] the Luxembourg report could accept this only in 'a vision of constitutional pluralism' which considers as a constitution any infra-state, para-state or supra-state structure.[347] On the same line, the Italian report favours 'the establishment of a legal frame in which a plurality of entities endowed with partial sovereign powers may co-exist ... What the European legal order needs is a pluralist Constitution governing a pluralist legal order'.[348]

It is interesting to note that the Cyprus' report stresses the establishment of the Convention as a development which demonstrates that the Member States are, no longer, the only 'masters on board' and that this is a welcome development in the process of transformation.[349] The Constitution would certainly be complementary to those of the Member States and, following a step-by-step approach, there will be, the report says, in 2004 a constitutional Treaty rather than a Constitution in the classical sense.[350] While for the contents the Dutch report does not diverge much from the above-mentioned lines, it also stresses that 'a real European Constitution' would be rather unlikely and that 'a basic European Treaty seems feasible'.[351] This is the solution favoured by the Spanish report as well.[352]

The Dutch report also underlines the need for splitting the Treaties: 'The tasks of policy of the institutions of the European Union should not be covered by the basic Treaty, but laid down in one or more substantive Treaties'.[353] This is what the European University Institute in Florence has

---

[345] Oliver, above n 2, p 17 *et seq* (near fn 70).
[346] Schäder and Melin, above n 3, p 402.
[347] Wivenes, above n 11, p 289, with a reference to the former Judge of the ECJ, Pierre Pescatore.
[348] Cannizzano, above n 39, p 262.
[349] Josephides, above n 12, p 20.
[350] Josephides, above n 12, p 20 *et seq.*
[351] Kortmann, above n 10, p 309.
[352] Martín y Pérez de Nanclares and López Castillo, above n 36, p 364.
[353] Kortmann, above n 10, p 309.

tried to work out and what the Commission seems to support as well.[354] Yet, the Luxembourg report takes a more cautious position: it finds it difficult to distinguish between fundamental questions to be dealt with in a constitutional Treaty and more technical provisions the revision of which might be subject to a simplified procedure in which unanimity is abandoned.[355] Though the Swedish report opts for preserving the 'present complicated and time-consuming amendment procedures for rules of a fundamental character', thereby allowing a simplified procedure 'not necessarily involving national parliaments in their legislative capacity',[356] the statement of the Swedish Prime Minister, in which he said that he would 'not be prepared' to accept that a transfer of competence from the national to the European level could be made without ratification by national parliaments, should be born in mind.[357]

The first recommendation for 2004 is:

The European treaties should be merged and streamlined into one single European Constitutional Treaty which lays down the objectives and principles of the Union, among which the primacy of European law over conflicting national law, includes the fundamental rights as laid down in the Charter, the rights of the citizen, the attribution of the competences of the Union in a clear and systematic order, provisions on institutions and legislative procedures, financial provisions, an appropriate procedure for the amendment of the Treaty as well as for a simplified amendment of Protocols in which the existing EC and Euratom Treaties remain in force insofar as they are not replaced by or contrary to the Constitutional Treaty.

b. Common Values: Giving Teeth to the Charter of Fundamental Rights

While the Luxembourg report sees it rather as a question of political philosophy,[358] the integration of the Charter of Fundamental Rights as binding law into the Treaties is a suggestion common to the majority of national reports.[359] The Cyprus' report makes it clear that this would indeed introduce a new dimension to the future of the Union which is not a simple economic union but more and more a union of states and peoples based on the common values of democracy, human rights and the rule of law.[360]

---

[354] Oliver, above n 2, p 12.
[355] Wivenes, above n 11, p 290.
[356] Schäder and Melin, above n 3, p 403.
[357] Schäder and Melin, above n 3, p 394.
[358] Wivenes, above n 11, p 290.
[359] See for example: Kortmann, above n 10, p 309; Nettesheim, above n 7, p 166.
[360] Josephides, above n 12, p 74 *et seq.*

The Austrian report, however, like the German report,[361] sees no problem in keeping the Charter as a separate instrument 'if only it were binding on the institutions',[362] and, similarly, the Spanish report also considers such a solution to be realistic and perhaps even more adequate for maintaining the equilibrium of the established European system for the protection of fundamental rights.[363]

It is worth noting that the Commission, the Council and the European Parliament have already taken action with a view to ensuring compliance with the Charter,[364] that the Court of First Instance and the Advocates General of the Court of Justice refer to it, while the Court of Justice as such abstains from doing so[365]—a practice which is probably meant to respect the decision of the governments not (yet) to make it a legally binding instrument. The EU report lists the options under discussion for making it legally binding and finds that the majority of the working group on the Charter favours the incorporation of the full body of the Charter into the Treaties.[366] There are, nevertheless, open questions, it points out, as to the preamble of the Charter and some overlapping—eg for citizens' rights—with more or less identical provisions in the existing Treaties.[367]

The second recommendation for 2004 is:

> The European Charter of Fundamental Rights should become part of the European Constitutional Treaty, as its second chapter, and the Preamble should be adapted and merged with the Preambles of the EU/EC-Treaties, the provisions on the citizens' rights should form a separate Title and substitute similar provisions of the EC-Treaty, and more objective guarantees including access to services of general economic interest, environment and consumer protection, should be incorporated into the chapter on objectives and principles; in addition, provisions should be included for the accession of the Union to the ECHR.

c. Who Does What in Europe: Towards a Clearer System of Attributions

'The future European Constitution cannot be construed as curtailing existing powers of the EU/EC', the Austrian report says and, like the Charter of Fundamental Rights, the distribution of powers between the EC/EU and the

---

[361] Nettesheim, above n 7, p 166.
[362] Köck, above n 9, p 42.
[363] Martín y Pérez de Nanclares and López Castillo, above n 36, p 360 *et seq.*
[364] Oliver, above n 2, p 29 *et seq.*
[365] See Hogan, above n 212, p 30 *et seq.*
[366] Oliver, above n 2, p 32.
[367] Oliver, above n 2, p 32.

Member States may come into it 'useful, although the latter may also be deduced from the powers given to the EU/EC institutions.[368] A number of national reports, indeed, see no absolute necessity for a new system—or even a catalogue[369]—of competences, though more clarity and flexibility of the distribution of powers is a general demand.[370] The Commission, like others, is said to be absolutely opposed to the idea of a catalogue, whilst all sides in the Convention agree on the need for clarification.[371] What is needed, the Spanish report says, is better identification of the titles of competence and a simplification and clarification of the structure of normative attributions, which differ from norms on procedure or directives—a solution which would not give all the power to those who ultimately interpret the relevant provisions.[372] The report also suggests consolidating the political control of the application of the principle of subsidiarity[373] and the German report discusses the option for a specific 'Mediation Committee' as it is proposed in the German doctrine.[374]

The third recommendation for 2004 is:

> The chapter on competences in the European Constitutional Treaty should be structured so as to distinguish clearly exclusive and shared legislative competences, powers for encouraging and coordinating national policies and executive powers including responsibilities in the areas of budget and control for each category containing clear and simplified attributions, while for monitoring adhesence to the principles of subsidiarity and proportionality and the limits of the respective attributions, a special body should be instituted, in which the political actors should be represented who have the most immediate interest in the adhesence to these principles.

d. Strengthening the European Executive: Institutional Reform of the European Union

The question of a European government is discussed in the Spanish report. But it does not make a specific proposal, just drawing attention to the risks of a parliamentary system based on simple majorities, in which a 'permanent minority' of Member States might evolve. It points out that safeguards are necessary in case majority rule is introduced generally, to protect against

---

[368] Köck, above n 9, p 42.
[369] For references regarding this proposal see Nettesheim, above n 7, p 166 *et seq* with fn 433.
[370] See Kortmann, above n 10, p 309; Martín y Pérez de Nanclares and López Castillo, above n 36, p 363 *et seq*.
[371] Oliver, above n 2, p 22.
[372] Martín y Pérez de Nanclares and López Castillo, above n 36, p 364.
[373] Martín y Pérez de Nanclares and López Castillo, above n 36, p 363.
[374] Nettesheim, above n 7, p 167 *et seq*; see also the proposals discussed by V Constantinesco and I Pernice, 'La Question des Compétences Communautaires: Vues d'Allemagne et de France', WHI-Paper 6/02 www.whi-berlin.de.

violation of the very real interests of a Member State.[375] According to the Austrian report, 'transforming the Commission into *the* executive organ of the EU/EC and thus to a kind of European government, might also make the Union, and the Community, respectively, more comprehensible, and thus emotionally more acceptable, to the man in the street'.[376] The Italian report notes that the process of European integration is leading to the co-existence of a plurality of international actors, each disposing of some competence, but none disposing of full sovereignty'.[377] This problem for international partners will probably continue to exist for a while, but a European government—or President—giving the Union a visible and reliable 'face' towards the outside world would provide for more clarity and enhance the effectiveness of its foreign policies.[378]

The fourth recommendation for 2004 is:

> The executive function of the Union should be reorganised in the European Constitutional Treaty so as to ensure that the Union has a 'face' and is represented by one person—a European President—to its international partners as well as vis-à-vis its citizens, and it is the original function of the Commission's President to take this responsibility; the Council should, in its legislative function, act as a Second Chamber while, in its executive function regarding economic, employment and financial, foreign and security policies it should be the forum of coordination deciding on the policies to be implemented by the Commission or the national governments.

e. Enhancing Democracy in Europe: European and National Parliaments

The role of the European Parliament would be confirmed, the Luxembourg report says, the extension of the joint decision-making regime with the democratic deficit being remedied by associating national parliaments more closely with the decision-making process of the Union.[379] The Dutch report calls for a bicameral parliament, based on a parliamentary system as it is—broadly speaking—present in some Member States.[380] The Spanish report

---

[375] Martín y Pérez de Nanclares and López Castillo, above n 36, p 361 *et seq.*
[376] Köck, above n 9, p 20.
[377] Cannizzano, above n 39, p 264.
[378] For different options to reform and streamline the institutional arrangements for CFSP decision-making procedures and the external representation of the positions thus agreed upon see I Pernice and D Thym, 'A New Institutional Balance for European Foreign Policy?', 7 *European Foreign Affairs Review* (2002) issue 4 forthcoming. See also I Pernice, 'Reform der Aufgabenverteilung und der Entscheidungsverfahren in der GASP/ESVP', WHI-Paper 8/02 and *ibid*, 'Neuordnung der Exekutive in der EU', WHI-Paper 10/02 both www.whi-berlin.de.
[379] Wivenes, above n 11, p 290.
[380] Kortmann, above n 10, p 309.

also considers the possibility of creating a second chamber, but does not take a definitive position. It signals, however, the consequence of such a debate on a possible claim by regional parliaments to a greater stake in European policies.[381] The Italian report is most critical of 'direct involvement of the National Parliaments in the European decision-making process', as they 'express a fragmented democratic legitimacy' and since it is appropriate to 'assign to the National Parliaments a role subsidiary to that of the European Parliament' in view of the asymmetric character of European integration.[382] This is in line with the German report which, against the many options discussed in Germany, favours enhancing parliamentary democracy in the Union not by a vertical parliamentary mix but rather by a horizontal strengthening of the powers of the European Parliament.[383] There is a broad feeling in the Convention that the role of national parliaments should be enhanced, but given the 'wealth of ideas' submitted, there is not yet a consensus.[384]

The fifth recommendation for 2004 is:

> Democratic legitimacy and accountability should be strengthened in the European Constitutional Treaty by giving, on the one hand, the European Parliament the right to elect and, if necessary, to dismiss the European President, the right of joint decision-making in all areas of legislation and the to right to adopt a budget for the Union, while, on the other hand, the National Parliaments should be given direct control over national ministers acting in the Council, the right to evaluate and comment on the annual legislative programme of the Union and a role in monitoring adhesence to the principle of subsidiarity.

f.   Specific Suggestions for Consideration

Other suggestions for consideration are the extension of the jurisdiction of the Court of Justice as a 'Constitutional Court' to all matters related to the EC and the EU Treaty,[385] to anchor more clearly the European construction and their implication in national constitutions,[386] to introduce a more precise provision for citizens' access to documents held by the institutions and, in particular, an enumeration of the 'general grounds on which a document may be kept secret',[387] and to provide for the possibility of a

---

[381] Martín y Pérez de Nanclares and López Castillo, above n 36, p 362 *et seq* 12.
[382] Cannizzano, above n 39, p 263.
[383] Nettesheim, above n 7, p 165 *et seq.*
[384] Oliver, above n 2, p 20.
[385] Köck, above n 9, p 42.
[386] Wivenes, above n 11, p 290.
[387] Schäder and Melin, above n 3, p 402.

Member State withdrawing from the system, even if this would be cause for a great deal of practical uncertainty:

> In an enlarged Europe, the possibility, albeit theoretical, that a State can recess and pursue its own way outside the frame of the integration would strengthen rather than weaken the stability of the system,

the Italian report says.[388]

B.   A Constitution for the European Union: Conditions of Adoption and Amendment

According to the Swedish report, the adoption of a Constitution of the European Union in the classical sense, which is:

> adding new fundamental rules to those existing in the present Treaties, for example (by) introducing a formal Bill of Rights, would—in order to possess the legitimacy for the future of such a document—require a broad general debate and a specific form of adoption involving the peoples, if not the people, of the Union.

Thus, it opts for a more limited approach consisting in the adoption of the Constitution 'in the same way as are the fundamental Treaties at the present'; in such an approach 'no new competencies would be transferred from the Member States to the Union'.[389]

More openness is shown in the Austrian report: a future European Constitution should be based on a Treaty concluded and ratified by the Member States according to Article 48 TEU, whether it 'contains itself the Constitution or empowers a particular body (eg a 'convent') to adopt a Constitution with binding effect for all Member States'.[390] Similarly, the German report confirms that there is no objection to creating a Constitution for the Union by means of an international agreement. The Grundgesetz would allow such an option as long as ratification is provided for by a national legislative Act. Even a European referendum is said not to be excluded, but it would not replace the ratification required by Article 23(1) of the German Constitution.[391] The Spanish report takes the view that whatever the reform will produce, ratification under Article 93 of the Constitution would be necessary, following modification of the Spanish constitution. Nevertheless, in case

---

[388] Cannizzano, above n 39, p 264 *et seq.*
[389] Schäder and Melin, above n 3, p 402 *et seq.*
[390] Köck, above n 9, p 42.
[391] Nettesheim, above n 7, p 172 *et seq.*

of a real split of opinion in Spain concerning the new Treaty, a prior referendum under Article 92 might be appropriate. The modification of Article 48 TEU with a view to including the preparatory work and recommendations of future conventions to future intergovernmental conferences would, finally, not be objectionable, but rather enhance the legitimacy of the process.[392]

The Dutch report is even more radical in considering a modification of the procedure provided for in Article 48 TEU: not all Member States would need to agree to amendments of the Treaty. The chapter on fundamental rights, for example, could be 'amended by a referendum of the citizens of the European Union, on a joint proposal of the Council of the European Union and the European Parliament'.[393] Accordingly, the Cyprus report considers generally abandoning the principle of unanimity and instead envisages adoption or amendment of the Constitution with a very large majority of Member States and peoples. A long-term perspective could even be the adoption by a direct referendum, an option which would, however, presuppose a strong feeling of belongingness which may evolve within the European political system and would draw its legitimacy from a European *demos*.[394]

The sixth recommendation for 2004 is:

> The European Constitutional Treaty should be adopted in accordance with the procedure laid down in Article 48 TEC, though a European referendum should be added after ratification by all the Member States so as to involve the citizens more directly and to enhance its democratic legitimacy; the procedure of Article 48 TEC should be completed by the formal involvement of the Constitutional Convention which prepares and submits to the IGC a draft for discussion and adoption and which shall be represented at the IGC by the President and the two vice-Presidents for explanation and mediation purposes.

C.   Merging the Constitutional Process and Enlargement: How to Involve the Candidates?

The question how to ensure the fair participation of candidate countries in the debate on the European Constitution within the Convention has been appropriately solved by the Laeken Declaration as well as by the Presidency of the Convention: they are equally represented and have an 'invitee' in the Presidium; although they have full rights of participation in the debates, they may not block a compromise arising among the representatives of the

---

[392] Martín y Pérez de Nanclares and López Castillo, above n 36, p 365 *et seq.*
[393] Kortmann, above n 10, p 310.
[394] Josephides, above n 12, p 21.

European institutions and the Member States.[395] The comments of the national reports—if any—on this arrangement are generally positive.[396] The Spanish report raises some doubts, however, concerning the positive effects of the inclusion of the candidate countries in the evaluation of the work of the Convention by the subsequent Intergovernmental Conference.[397] In contrast, the only report from a candidate country, Cyprus, emphasises that the candidate countries' effective participation in the process will concentrate minds and will help to develop the feeling among the citizens of these countries that they belong to a European people, a feeling which it considers being the basis for the adoption of a Constitution of the Union.

The seventh recommendation for 2004 is:

The full participation of the candidate countries in the Convention as well as in the IGC 2004 should be ensured, including their representation in the Presidium, so as to include them—as well as the civil society of their respective countries—closely in the discourse on, and the preparation of a draft of the European Constitutional Treaty, which should be for the citizens of the candidate countries as much as for the citizens of the Union, the expression of their common values, common objectives and a democratic and fair instrument to meet their common goals and challenges internally and in the international arena.

[395] Oliver, above n 2, p 6 *et seq*.
[396] See eg Köck, above n 9, p 43; Martín y Pérez de Nanclares and López Castillo, above n 36, p 366; Kortmann, above n 10, p 310 *et seq*; Schäder and Melin, above n 3, p 404; Cannizzano, above n 39, p 265: 'politically wise'.
[397] Martín y Pérez de Nanclares and López Castillo, above n 36, p 366 *et seq*.

3

The Allocation of Competences Between the European Union and its Member States

UDO DI FABIO*

I. INTRODUCTION

T HE EUROPEAN UNION and its Member States are struggling to achieve a balance of power. The Charter of Fundamental Rights of the European Union is supposed to limit the power of the Union; it directly serves the freedom of the citizens of Europe.[1] It is relatively easy to formulate fundamental rights; in the context of the Charter, this means making the citizens' liberty rights binding on the European institutions. One only had, and still has, to take care not to promise too much, and to respect the Member States' constitutional sovereignty, *that is,* not to indirectly bind them too strongly. More is at issue now, however, namely: (1) how to organise the distribution of power; and (2) the role of the Council, the Commission and the Parliament, but also: (3) the allocation of competences itself.[2] Who is supposed to exercise legislative competences and administrative powers: the European Union or its Member States? This issue makes the matter exciting and difficult. But it is exactly for this reason that one should not set one's expectations too high, because the interests that are involved here are complex. Some Member States want to keep certain competences, or want such competences back. Other states, however,

---

* Judge of the German Federal Constitutional Court, Karlsruhe and Professor of Law, University of Munich. This Chapter was written in October 2001.
[1] On the Charter of Fundamental Rights, see S Alber and U Widmaier, 'Die EU-Charta der Grundrechte und Ihre Auswirkungen auf die Rechtsprechung – Zu den Beziehungen zwischen EuGH und EGMR' in Europäische Grundrechtszeitung (EuGRZ) 2000, 497; A von Bogdandy, 'Grundrechtsgemeinschaft als Integrationsziel?' in JuristenZeitung (JZ) 2001, 157.
[2] Some relevant literature: E Steindorff *Grenzen der EG-Kompetenzen* (Heidelberg, 1990); I Boeck *Die Abgrenzung der Rechtssetzungskompetenzen von Gemeinschaft und Mitgliedstaaten in der Europäischen Union: zur Notwendigkeit und zu den Vorteilen bzw.*

want to prevent the reallocation of competences because they fear burdens, conflict and cost. The Union level is somewhat more homogeneous. Parliament and Commission speak about the reallocation of competences only in terms of a defensive formula, the *acquis communautaire,* or Community patrimony, whereas the pro-active formula of greater competences for the Union is: continuation and safeguarding of integration in an enlarged Union.

I. Are there Normative Precepts for the Development of the Future Allocation of Competences Between the European Union and its Member States?

This controversy is a political one, which, in the first place and ultimately, must be settled by the 'masters of the Treaties', *that is,* in the framework of intergovernmental conferences. Those, however, who want to give such regulations the aura of a constitutional treaty also claim by doing so, that such a treaty is theoretically consistent, that it has a systematic structure and that it is free of contradictions. I would like to apply these criteria and would like to look for answers with their help.

In essence, the allocation of competences between the European Union and its Member States results from a pragmatic decision that is not predetermined by law. The decision is taken freely by the Member States as the masters of the Treaties. The beginning of integration was marked by the powers that the States entrusted to a High Authority, an intergovernmental institution, in order to exercise it jointly.[3] The competences and areas of policies that have successively been delegated to the Communities in vigorous waves or in small, individual steps have shaped the image of a Europe that has embarked on unification. It started as an economic community, *that is,* with a limited range of subjects; through extensions of its competences, however, it has developed in such a way that its image now comes near to that of a universally competent state.[4]

The statement that the allocation of competences is the result of pragmatic negotiations between the Member States must, however, be qualified in its two aspects. It is true that the allocation of competences is performed

---

Nachteilen der Aufstellung eines Kompetenzkatalogs in den Gemeinschaftsverträgen (Baden-Baden, 2000); F Mayer, 'Die drei Dimensionen der europäischen Kompetenzdebatte' in *Zeitschrift für ausländisches öffentliches Recht und Völkerrecht* (ZaöRV) 61 [2001], 577; A von Bogdandy and J Bast, 'Die vertikale Kompetenzordnung der Europäischen Union – Rechtsdogmatischer Bestand und verfassungspolitische Reformperspektiven' in *Europäische Grundrechtszeitung* (EuGRZ) 2001, 441; I Pernice, 'Kompetenzabgrenzung im Europäischen Verfassungsverbund' in *JuristenZeitung (JZ)* 2000, 866.
[3] This is the terminology that is used in the Basic Law, *eg,* in Art 23, sub-section 1, sentences 1 and 2, and Art 24, sub-section 1.
[4] T Oppermann *Europarecht: Ein Studienbuch* 2nd edn (Munich 1999) 334 *et seq.*

through primary law, that is, the Treaties, into which a constitutional treaty must integrate. In the meantime, however, the Treaties, and their practical implementation, have given the European institutions a strong weight of their own. Parliament and Commission self-confidently take the floor and address their opinions to the heads of State and Government, which take action. The contributions that are made by Parliament and Commission carry considerable weight. This also applies to bodies that have been specially established, like, for instance, the Constitutional Convention for the reform of the European Union that was convened on the basis of the Laeken Declaration. Thus, the Member States decide on the allocation of competences also under the influence of Community institutions and of the political bodies that act at the European Union level.

Today, however, the allocation of competences can no longer be understood as a decision that is free of legal constraints. The logic of the Treaties, and the Union's interest, which is inherent in the Treaties, in continuing and maintaining its own existence, at any rate, do not admit an allocation of competences that evidently endangers the Union's functions; this would create law in European Treaties that is contrary to the Treaties themselves. If, for instance, at the state of integration that has been achieved today, the decision were taken to completely deprive the Community of its competences under Articles 94 to 97 of the EC Treaty that concern the Internal Market, and if such deprivation resulted in a de-harmonisation of the Internal Market, this would strike at the root of European integration.[5] Here, one could possibly, identify a borderline, which is also drawn by law, against an amendment of the Treaties, as long as it is assumed that the Member States and the peoples that are organised within the Member States continue to be in favour of integration. Moreover, German participation in evident acts of de-integration would constitute a violation of German constitutional law because the Basic Law expressly provides for the development of the European Union as an aim of the state (Article 23, sub-section 1 of the Basic Law in conjunction with the Preamble); in this context, the Basic Law sets limits on development and, at the same time, establishes an obligation of development.

Such functional criteria are normative although they are not expressly laid down as positive Community law; nor can they be positive Community law exactly because they deal with the creation of new, and highest-ranking, law in European Treaties. Such normative obligations of development follow nevertheless from the overall concept of European integration and from the

---

[5] Whether this would already happen if Art 95 of the EC Treaty were repealed, following the proposals of Mr Clement, the minister-president of North Rhine-Westphalia, is doubtful. This view, however, is put forward by A von Bogdandy and J Bast 'Die vertikale Kompetenzordnung der Europäischen Union – Rechtsdogmatischer Bestand und verfassungspolitische Reformperspektiven' in *Europäische Grundrechtszeitung (EuGRZ)* 2001, 441 at 453.

corresponding content of the constitutional systems of the Member States, which have, in the meantime, opened up to European integration and to integration under international law. There are, in fact, specific ways of developing the existing basic order of a political community that violate this very existing basic order. At the nation state level, we call this unconstitutional constitutional law; in European Community law, it can, possibly, be referred to as law in European Treaties that is contrary to the Treaties.[6]

Apart from such legal constraints that come into being either when law is laid down in international treaties, or, on the domestic level, when a constitution is created, and which are strictly limited to evident exceptions, there are precepts of consistency; as a general rule, such precepts of consistency are only theoretically substantiated but can establish indirect legal obligations of consistency that are 'soft' in their effect. Such demands for consistency can result from models of state philosophy on which the law is based, or from the supranational rule that is confirmed time and again. Indeed, the Union follows a logic of its own. One can debate the details of its content; the idea of integration, however, has an impressive power of persuasion by now. The formation, by the free peoples of Europe, of an efficient and firm political community that serves peace and freedom is a new model for political rule beyond closed nation states. A characteristic feature of this model is its *complementary* structure: on their own initiative, states open up to a joint exercise of public authority. They complement their claim to shaping the polity on the domestic level by an external form of cooperation; thus, the borders between States become more open without losing their function as legal borders and borders of responsibility. The more visible the shape of this model becomes, the more important will it be to ensure that the architecture of the institutions and the allocation of competences is consistent and free of contradictions. However, in order to make statements about a *consistent* allocation of competences on this basis, there must be an agreement about the essential aspects of how to describe the model.

II.   The Balance of Functional Interests in the System of European States

The model of the European Union provides that the institutions of the Union are strong, that they meet democratic requirements, and that they are bound, in the citizens' interest, to the fundamental rights and to the rule of law. Their strength, however, also results from the fact that everyday practice of cooperation forces the institutions to act. It also stems from the requirements of economic and monetary union and from the constraints of

---

[6] This equivalent of the legal concept of unconstitutional constitutional law can be substantiated very well, see, for instance BVerfGE [Decisions of the Federal Constitutional Court] 94, 49 at 102; cf also C Schmitt *Verfassungslehre* (Berlin 1928, reprint 8th edn Berlin 1993) at 62 *et seq*.

successful integration. This, however, does not at all mean that the European Union must have the competence to determine the allocation of competences. The European Union lacks the *Kompetenz-Kompetenz*, that is, the power of self-organisation, which, in principle, is unrestricted;[7] this means that it lacks the power to give itself a constitution. It is dependent on the member states determining, in negotiations and contracts that result from the negotiations, (1) the structure of the Union's institutions; and (2) its competences. Also in legal relations under international law, the European Union lacks the relevant legal sovereignty. The European Union represents the will of the peoples but it does not act in its own right but on the basis of a right that was conferred on it by treaties; the European Community, for instance, is authorised, pursuant to Article 300 of the EC Treaty, to conclude agreements under international law that are also binding upon the Member States without any further act being required (Article 300, paragraph 7 of the EC Treaty).[8] Because of the strong position of the Council as an institution, and because of their position as the masters of the Treaties, the Member States therefore remain in a strong position as a counteracting force to the tendency towards centralisation that is due to technical constraints; at any rate, their position is stronger than that of the constituent states of a federative state.

Today, it has become evident in many areas, and an overall consideration will possibly come to the same result, that an approximate balance of power between the Union and the Member States has been achieved,[9] a kind of vertical separation of powers in the European system of States.[10] From this it follows, as a general insight regarding the allocation of competences, that not only the capability of the Communities to function, and of the Union, draws the ultimate limit to a new allocation of competences, but that the Member States' interest in their own continued existence and in their functioning must be taken into account in the same way.

Indeed, the secret of the European Union lies in its *dual identity*: what is essential is to maintain and promote the identity of the European Union as

[7] T Schmitz *Integration in der Supranationalen Union: das europäische Organisationsmodell einer prozeßhaften geo-regionalen Integration und seine rechtlichen und staatstheoretischen Implikationen* (Baden-Baden, 2001) at 244–45.
[8] C Busse *Die völkerrechtliche Einordnung der Europäischen Union* (Köln, 1999) deals in greater detail with the participation of the European Union and its Communities in legal relations under international law.
[9] On the legal aspects of such a balance, see P Kirchhof JZ 1998, pp 244–45.
[10] P Kirchhof, 'Gewaltenbalance zwischen europäischen und mitgliedstaatlichen Organen' in J Isensee (ed) *Gewaltenteilung heute, Symposium aus Anlass der Vollendung des 65. Lebensjahres von Fritz Ossenbühl* at 99 *et seq*; T Apolte, 'Vertikale Kompetenzverteilung in der Union' in M E Streit and S Voigt (eds) *Europa reformieren. Ökonomen und Juristen zur zukünftigen Verfaßtheit Europas* (Baden-Baden, 1996) at 13 *et seq*; A von Bogdandy and J Bast, 'Die vertikale Kompetenzordnung der Europäischen Union – Rechtsdogmatischer Bestand und verfassungspolitische Reformperspektiven' in *Europäische Grundrechtszeitung (EuGRZ)* 2001, 441 *et seq*; U Di Fabio, 'Gewaltenteilung' in J Isensee and P Kirchhof (eds) *Handbuch des Staatsrechts, Volume I*, 3rd edn (Heidelberg, forthcoming).

an active community of states and, at the same time, to maintain and promote the Member States' identity as the living foundation of freedom and democracy. The European Union must therefore strive, within, for a minimum of coherence and solidarity between the member states and their peoples (Article 1, sub-paragraph 3, sentence 2 of the Treaty on European Union). Outwards, it must assert its identity on the international scene and safeguard this identity (Article 2, sub-paragraph 1, 2nd part of the Treaty on European Union). At the same time, the European Union is to preserve the national identities of its Member States (Article 6, paragraph 3 of the Treaty on European Union). This does not only mean that national folklore is respected. National identity can only be preserved if the Member States remain intact as political communities and if their leeway for responsible decisions is sufficiently great.

Besides the claims for identity that have been laid down in the Treaties, other general principles of applicable European Union law and Community law correspond to the balance of functional interests of the Union and of the Member States. The principle that the powers of the Community are limited to those specifically conferred on it makes it clear[11] that competences may not be conferred in the shape of a tangled bundle, and that the institutions of the European Communities may, in principle, not expand the scope of their competences by interpreting the relevant documents to the detriment of the Member States.[12] The principle of subsidiarity[13] (Article 5 of the EC Treaty) not only limits the use of non-exclusive Community competence but it is also a rule the idea behind which shows which way to go in the further development of the Treaties, and it particularly takes the problem of dual identity into account.

III.   Are There Competences That are Peculiar to a Specific Level?

If one tries to draw conclusions for an adequate allocation of competences from this general insight and from the above-mentioned principles of law, an intermediate stage needs to be introduced. One could say that some competences are just as typical of a supranational system as other competences

---

[11] As regards the principle that the powers of the Community are limited to those specifically conferred on it: Judgment of the Court of Justice of 5 October 2000, Case C–376/98 (*Federal Republic of Germany v European Parliament and Council of the European Union*) European Court Reports 2000, Page I–08419, marginal nos 83 and 107.

[12] The principle of implied powers under international law is therefore to be applied in a restrictive manner; see A von Bogdandy and J Bast 'Die vertikale Kompetenzordnung der Europäischen Union – Rechtsdogmatischer Bestand und verfassungspolitische Reformperspektiven' in *Europäische Grundrechtszeitung (EuGRZ)* 2001, 441 at 444.

[13] As concerns the foundations of the principle of subsidiarity in intellectual history: A Waschkuhn *Was ist Subsidiarität? Ein sozialphilosophisches Ordnungsprinzip: von Thomas von Aquin bis zur 'Civil Society'* (Opladen, 1995).

are for a nation state. The competences that concern the Internal Market, the harmonisation of the flows of goods, services and capital are typical Community competences. This also applies to the development of trans-European networks and to the formulation and implementation of a common commercial policy. Compared to that, the state is a national association that is close to the citizens' life; the members of such an association share a common fate and are united in solidarity. The state is the holder of administrative power. Moreover, the Member States must remain capable of acting as social states. In essence, the competence of taking the classical fundamental decisions on freedom and property still rests with them. The following conclusions could be drawn from this: when looking at the distinctive features of the respective community, the decision on the burden of charges, tax policy and the responsibility concerning income and expenses must remain with the national parliaments.

Such a classification made according to special competences that correspond to the particularities of the respective levels must, however, explain in greater detail the reasons for which certain competences must rest with the State and others with the Union. To do so, one would have to define the typical, the specific features of the Community and the States, and one would have to be able to allocate, on the basis of this categorisation, specific legislative and administrative competences to either the Community or the Member States. In this context, the principle of democracy is an obvious basis on which to proceed. When applying the principle of democracy, one asks: what do the citizens expect of the respective political level, where do their primary loyalties lie, what do they regard as the power of last resort when everything else fails?

IV. An Open System of Competences

At the present state of integration, such a categorisation has a certain prospect of being plausible; it must, however, not be aimed at preserving a specific situation. The object of primary loyalty may change. Someone who today, above all, regards himself or herself as an English or a Spanish citizen may tomorrow define himself or herself primarily as a European citizen and expect the solution of existential problems from Brussels. In that respect, the European nation states have entered political competition on the institutional level. Rivalry and the struggle for power among themselves has turned into peaceful competition.[14] Direct dispute among Member States has been subdued; it has, basically, been transferred to the Community level.

[14] P Bernholz *Der internationale Wettbewerb von Staaten als Ursache der Entwicklung von Rechtsordnung, freien Märkten und Innovationsfreudigkeit: das Beispiel des frühen Altertums* (Jena 1996); H Siebert and M J Koop 'Institutional Competition versus Centralisation: Quo vadis Europe?' in *Oxford Review of Economic Policy*, 9 [1993] at 15 *et seq*; L Gerken *Der Wettbewerb der Staaten* (Tübingen 1999).

The member states no longer engage in direct disputes with each other but settle their disputes within the European institutions, and with the European institutions. Thus, the struggle among the Member States is transformed into a cultivated competition among them, and into a mediated competition of the states with the European Union, *that is*, a competition with a political community that has been jointly created by them.

In order for the institutional competition to function, competences for legislation and administration must be weighed and determined anew from time to time. No one wants the system of competences to depend on the ups and downs of public opinion research. However, there is much to be said for keeping the system of competences permanently open and elastic. Only thus can the factual conditions of solidarity and loyalty be successfully brought to bear when dealing with disparate interests—and only thus will democracy keep a chance of developing further in a system that consists of several levels.

V.   Interlacement and Unitarisation as Antagonists of a Clear System of Competences

If one takes a closer look at the present allocation of competences, doubts grow, however, as to whether a clear delimitation of competences is at all possible. Federative units in a broad sense, irrespective of whether they are federative states or supranational communities on the pattern of the European Union, show two tendencies: a tendency towards an uninterrupted centralisation and unitarisation, but also a tendency towards cooperation on different levels to compensate the loss of importance that is suffered by the losers in the process of centralisation. This, on the one hand, results in a division of competences that works according to the following pattern: fundamental decisions are taken on the higher level, practical details that directly concern the citizens' daily life are dealt with on the lower level. On the other hand, the losers in the process of centralisation insist on compensation and on the right to participate at the higher level and thus reinforce the process of unitarisation. Judging from the experiences in federative states, we should expect three developments:

1. The centralist argument that a specific subject matter needs to be regulated in Brussels, will, on an average, have greater prospects of success than arguments that invoke diversity or nation-state identity. In the case of grievances or scandals, there are, regularly, calls for drastic measures to be taken at the higher level.
2. It is to be expected that a division of competences that cuts across subject matters (framework regulations at the Union level)

will have greater prospects of success than a clear-cut division according to exclusive competences.

3. Finally, it is to be expected that the Member States will be offered rights of political participation and financial transfers, or that the Member States will demand them, if they, for their part, give in to the demand of centralisation.

The conventional effects of interlacement and unitarisation that exist in a federative state do not permit too much optimism, in the context of a political union of the European states, as concerns a clear division of competences that the citizens can understand. My subsequent remarks, in which I will ask, in a kind of naive manner, how competences can be allocated between the Union and its Member States in a well-founded way, will intensify this mpresssion.

VI. The Fundamental Competences of the State are Core Competences of the Member States

The experiences that have been made in federative states are not, from the outset, an impediment to the search for systematic solutions to an allocation of competences that is in line with the state of integration. Let us start by looking at the Member States: what is their minimum stock of own rights? To prevent the gap between sovereignty under international law and tangible competences widening too much, the Member States need at least two core competences of a modern state system: (1) the competence to guarantee the security of their citizens; and (2) the competence that concerns the state's own income, above all, the power to tax. It was the modern state that started to guarantee internal security and to pacify its territory; the modern state could only fulfil this task by claiming the monopoly on the right to exercise force and by endowing itself with financial means. For this reason, the transfer of competences for internal security or for judicial policy happens as slowly as the transfer of competences for Community taxation.

To these original competences, other competences are added that are traditionally associated with the nation state as a community with a common culture that is united in solidarity. The competence for fundamental decisions in the cultural sphere is, now as before, attributed to the Member States because the states are still regarded as sovereign systems that unite those who belong together culturally, or because this concept of the state is, at any rate, presupposed without explicitly mentioning it. Regulations that concern family life, schools, vocational training and the universities concern the cultural identity of every nation, of every member state. Article 6, paragraph 3 of the Treaty on European Union refers to the Member States' 'national identity', which, however, requires as an essential precondition that the fundamental decisions in the cultural sphere are taken by the Member States. Some of these fundamental decisions are, for instance, the competence for the organisation of the media, of the press and of broadcasting. Another powerful pillar of member-state competence, which, however, is not always pleasant for politicians, is social politics, social security, medical care, old age pension schemes, the care of the elderly and the needy.

If specific supranational core competences could also be identified, like, for instance, a single economic and monetary policy, global trade policy, or the achievement of coherence among the member states, this would make it possible to outline an allocation of competences that is materially substantiated. In most cases, however, it would hardly be possible to formulate mutually exclusive spheres of competences in accordance with this approach because this would contradict the complementary character of the European system of states. At any rate, there is a third level that asserts functional interests; this is the level of vertical and horizontal cooperation. Only in very few cases is it possible to proceed according to the clear and simple pattern of allocating exclusive, non-overlapping competences.

VII.   The Formation of the Community in the Spirit of Cooperation

The European Communities and their institutions regard themselves as guarantors of a European regulatory policy. They fight against too narrow particularisms on the side of the Member States, they also fight national networks that have grown too large. The European Communities' primary aim is, and has been, to facilitate a convergence of the economies and thus, a convergence of the European citizens' general living conditions. The strongest weapon in this context is free competition; the subjective lever is the fundamental freedoms. What is required in order to ensure competition are competences for the harmonisation of market conditions and a control of competition on the European level. The first competence is directed against the Member States, the second competence is directed against powerful private actors, like, for instance, enterprises that are subject to the European ban on cartels (Article 81 of the EC Treaty) and to the ban on the abuse of a dominant position in the common market (Article 82 of the EC Treaty).

In their initial phases, the European Community and the European Union fought, particularly against the diversity of regulations in the Member States that was an obstacle to the free market, and were successful in doing so. It is true, however, that when the general climate is characterised by a free trade policy, market liberalisation and a decrease of direct market intervention by the state, the aims and the adversaries change. What is essential now is to supervise the international concentration of enterprises and to focus attention on the conditions for the take-over of joint-stock companies. What must be done now is to formulate the outlines of a unified civil law and to put the subject of European broadcasting rules in a prominent position on the agenda. Market liberalisation leads to an increased need for public regulation; this need must be met Union-wide at first, and then it must be expressed with Europe speaking with one voice in the global concert.

Many regard such a mandate as necessary to ensure that politics keep a chance of actively influencing the dynamism of world economy. This, however, creates a dilemma for the entire approach of allocating competences in a way that does justice to functional aspects as well as to democracy. Those who want a clear-cut and mutually exclusive allocation of competences and want to strengthen politics as a power that influences the economy, would, in many cases, have to transfer even more competences to Brussels and would have to do without many established forms of cooperation between the administrations of the Member States and the Commission. They could not make an exception for cultural and social politics. This, however, would call opposing forces into action, would possibly place the will to show solidarity under too much of a strain, and would, gradually, reduce the Member States to secondary administrative entities; this way of acting would not be in line with the present standard of democratic legitimisation.

It would be less risky to continue following the approach of divided and competing competences, also at the price of having to live with not very transparent situations of *interlacement*. A way of achieving coherence is to formulate binding aims for the member states, as has been done, for instance, in Article 104 of the EC Treaty as regards budgetary discipline; in this case, however, intervention only takes place if serious undesirable developments have occurred. This does not diminish the Member States' responsibility, but the Union moderates and limits the Member States' control over their budgets in the interest of the economic stability of the common currency and of the European Economic Area. In the opposite direction, one could also imagine that the Communities further develop their system of own funds in a way that increases the European Parliament's freedom in decision-making but preserves the Member States' overall responsibility. In principle, it would be possible to vest the European Community with the right to levy its own taxes; the limits of such right, however, would have to be drawn so narrowly that it would not very convincingly represent the intended European responsibility. Were the limits of such a right not drawn very narrowly as regards the type and amount of taxes, this would greatly endanger Member States' responsibility for their own budgets. It is therefore obvious that the European Union is better advised not to levy its own taxes and to reduce, instead, negative competition between different locations by moderate harmonisation and by a ban on tax concessions that have a distinct cross-border effect.

In the case of parallel or competing competences, it is less important to engage in lengthy discussions about a 'correct' allocation of competences that will take place sometime in the future; what is important instead is to consistently apply the principle of subsidiarity. In this respect, discipline in law-making must be demanded of all European institutions, also of the Council as a law-making body. Reservation clauses in the pattern of Article 16 of the EC Treaty provide further protection of the Member States' functions that are threatened by the process of unitarisation. This clause draws limits to the control of monopolies and subsidies so that services of general economic interest are kept viable. Further protective effects and a strengthening of the principle that the powers of the Community are limited to those specifically conferred on it can be achieved by establishing in the Treaty a priority of powers that are specifically conferred on the Community as against the general internal market competence that is laid down in Articles 94 and 95 of the EC Treaty.

VII.   Outlook: New Competences for the European Union?

The list of the rights the retransfer of which is desired, especially, inter alia, by the German *Bundesländer* (Federal States), is not very long.[15] The German *Länder* are interested in keeping or recovering the freedom to take their own decisions eg in the areas of regional structural planning and the promotion of regional economic development. Such demands are legitimate because in the past, the Commission has frequently shown a certain euphoria as regards planning and a tendency to concentrate on details that can hardly be reconciled with the principle of subsidiarity. What is more important in this context is to orient secondary legislation towards the functional core competences of the Union. This means, for instance, that bans on discrimination under labour law must not become a lever for making Community law prevail even though individual competences in special subject areas are allocated to other levels of government; and even though reserved domains exist. This includes decisions that were issued by the Commission under the law of competition in cases that lack an important cross-border effect on the internal market. All in all, the principle that the powers of the Community are limited to those specifically conferred on it must be taken more seriously. This also applies, and particularly so, to the interpretation of the scope of application of secondary legislation. In this context, not everything can be left to the chances of everyday political business and also not to the good intention of the Court of Justice; such good intention certainly exists, but must be made clear by indications in primary law and by indications in the text of the Treaty.

---

[15] Decision of the (Council of State Governments) of 20 December 2001, *Bundesratsdrucksache* (BRDrs, Records of the *Bundesrat*) 1081/01.

What would seem even more exciting than a cutback of secondary legislation, which has expanded too much in some respects, in a manner that corresponds to the functions of secondary legislation is the discussion about new Community competences. Foreign policy needs a new stage that goes beyond mere intergovernmental concertation but also beyond a immediate transfer of competences to the Community. Here, a representative who is elected by the Council for a prolonged period of time, and who can also be voted out of office, should be best suited to keep the balance between a single foreign policy of the Union and the Member States' continued will to act on the scene of foreign policy. The competences for immigration and for the cross-border fight against crime need to be shifted more to the European level, but if this is to happen, the respective competences of Europol must be more clearly delimited. The cooperative foundations of the European Police Office should, however, not be abandoned; also in this context, complementary co-operation is essential. European asylum and immigration policy should become more visible through considerate steering regulations and framework regulations, which, however, must have a calculable effect. However, the framework should be so wide that Member States can continue to effectively assume responsibility for the flow of immigrants to their territory. Too simple solutions, however, must be warned of. Those who think that they can solve any problem by creating a central Community competence are wrong, just like those who indulge in the romanticism of far-ranging re-nationalisation. Both approaches are dangerous and squander the institutional possibilities that are provided by a form of government that is situated *beyond* the nation states but is performed, at the same time, *together with* open nation states as indispensable democratic environments.

Ladies and gentlemen! The discussion about the allocation of competences will continue even after the end of the Convention's work. Politicians will make their decisions according to their interests of how to shape politics. It would be a good thing, however, if scholarship provided more impulses in this context. We still lack a convincing theory of the European Union from which we could infer where competences belong and how their allocation can be performed in a transparent and effective manner.

4

Rethinking the Methods of Dividing and Controlling the Competencies of the Union

INGOLF PERNICE*

I. INTRODUCTION

T ALKING ABOUT 'WHO does what in the EU', at first sight, concerns the system of power sharing between the national and the European level of government.[1] The German Länder initiated the debate with a view to preserving some meaningful freedom of action and political discretion for those democratically elected bodies in the Union that are closest to the citizens. But it also concerns the horizontal division of powers among the institutions, the degree of democratic legitimacy of the decision-making process and, in particular, the extent of qualified majority voting in the Council. What kind of powers may be entrusted to the European institutions and within which limits very much depends both on the efficiency of the procedures and the effectiveness of democratic control— be it direct by the European Parliament or indirect, controlling the ministers in the Council. Finally, the issue is closely connected to the protection of fundamental rights and freedoms of those citizens who could not consent to the transfer of public authority to institutions which are not strictly bound to respect fundamental rights and to follow, in framing their policies, the orientations and values expressed by the fundamental rights. Consequently, 'rethinking the methods of dividing and controlling the competencies of the

* Professor of Public Law, International and European Law at Humboldt University (Berlin), Managing Director of the Walter Hallstein Institute for European Constitutional Law at Humboldt University (Berlin), www.whi-berlin.de. This contribution was completed in October 2001, as a contribution to the Brussels symposium on 'Europe 2004—le grand debat'. The author expresses his gratitude to Ralf Kanitz and Daniel Thym for their valuable contributions.
[1] For a detailed analysis of the debate see Mayer, 'Die drei Dimensionen der europäischen Kompetenzdebatte', (2001) 61 *Zeitschrift für ausländisches öffentliches Recht und Völkerrecht*, 577.

Union' must be understood as an exercise which is interdependent with the progress of the institutional debate aiming at more transparency, democratic accountability and efficiency—on the one hand—and with the readiness to give the European Charter of Fundamental Rights binding effect so that it can be enforced by individuals against any use of European power by which he or she might be affected,[2] on the other.

Talking about the division of powers does not imply that all these powers have always existed, at the national (regional) or the European level. Given that eg legislative power for the harmonisation of legislation throughout the European Union didn't exist before the foundation of the European Communities, this perspective would be too narrow. Therefore, the process of integration does indeed entail the progressive creation of new powers as well as the reorganisation of existing powers at both levels of governance, in accordance with new challenges and political aspirations of the citizens. Competencies in the area of the environment, for example, have been created at national and European level long after the Treaty of Rome; European powers to combat international terrorism may well be the next to be extended. Therefore, the question we face is not the division of powers in a static structure, but in an evolving, dynamic multilevel system of governance. The aim of achieving legal certainty by detailed definitions must be balanced by securing the degree of openness and flexibility necessary for the effective functioning of the system. Given the political character of the use of competencies in practice as well as the dynamics of interpretation and necessary limits to legal certainty, any attempt to improve the existing situation would fail, if the work on constitutional texts was not coupled with procedural arrangements.

A third preliminary remark concerns the adequacy of possible procedures for the definition and delimitation of European competencies: a number of political and academic actors have already expressed their support for a new catalogue of competencies[3] or even a new constitution for the European Union comprising a solution for the question of competencies.[4] Though it is laudable to engage in such exercises with a view to designing models as to how a revised treaty or constitution could be structured and

---

[2] See the general considerations and proposals made by Pernice, 'Kompetenzabgrenzung im Europäischen Verfassungsverbund', (2000) *Juristenzeitung*, 866 et seq. (also published in: www.whi-berlin.de/pernice3.htm); for other contributions to the subject see the speech of Prime Minister Wolfgang Clement, *Europa gestalten - nicht verwalten*, FCE 10/2000, http://www.whi-berlin.de/Clement.htm.

[3] See the early draft of the Berlin Chancellery of State Franßen-de la Cerda, *Verbesserte Kompetenzabgrenzung zwischen der Europäischen Gemeinschaft und den Mitgliedstaaten*, Skzl EB 4 of 21 January 1999; Fischer/Schley, *Organizing a Federal Structure for Europe. An EU Catalogue of Competencies* (2000).

[4] Economist 28 October 3 November 2000, 21 *et seq*; Juppé/Toubon/Gaymard, *Esquisse d'une Constitution Européenne*, presented 28 June 2000 at the Colloque: 'Quelle constitution pour quelle Europe' in the Sénat—Palais du Luxembourg; Union pour la Démocratie Française, *Projet pour une Constitution de l'Union européenne* (2000).

might look, the final solution to the problems we face is a political one and can only be the result of the political process. This political and 'constitutional' character of the exercise should be reflected in the procedure chosen. It should, in the first stage, be organised following the 'Convention' model. The proposals and options of the Convention should then be submitted, in a second phase, to an IGC and a final summit for discussion and adoption. A European referendum should be held on the 'European Constitutional Treaty' so elaborated, to underline its character as a new European social contract.[5] After it has become definitively clear in Nice that the traditional procedure under Article 48 EU is neither efficient nor democratic, adaptation of the procedure for 'constitution-making' in Europe is inevitable.

If this exercise is a political one, there is, on the other hand, no reason to re-invent the wheel. Most of the problems which were at the origin of the debate do not indeed concern the attribution of competencies and their limits, but the excessive exercise of given Community competencies which are, in principle, not disputed: the application of the state aid regime, the structural policies and certain measures in the field of environment.[6] My conclusions and recommendations, will therefore try to find some pragmatic improvements of the existing system (D) and are based on a brief oversight of the existing catalogue of competencies in the European Treaties and the constitutions of other federal systems (B) as well as on some remarks on the characteristics of the European multilevel constitutional system which requires solutions different to those found in federal states (C).

II.   MODELS FOR A NEW ORDER OF COMPETENCIES IN THE EUROPEAN UNION

Before examining new systems or structures for the division and control of the competencies of the European Union, it is necessary to understand the existing system and the difficulties it creates (I). The comparison with other federal systems allows the experience of countries around the world to be built upon without ignoring the fundamental differences between the European system and federal states (II). Existing proposals for a revised European system of competencies will be examined against this background (III).

---

[5] See Pernice, 'The European Constitution', in Herbert Quandt Foundation (ed), *Europe's constitution—a framework for the future of the Union*, Sinclair House Debates (2001), p 18 (37). See also Pernice/Mayer/Wernicke, 'Renewing the European Social Contract. The Challenge of Institutional Reform and Enlargement in the Light of Multilevel Constitutionalism', in Andenas/Gardener (eds), *Can Europe Have a Constitution?* Kings College London, February 2000, 12 *King's College Law Journal* (2001), 61–74.
[6] See in particular Clement, above n 2. For an overview of the issues raised by the German Länder see Mayer, above n 1, at II.

I.   The Catalogue of Competencies in the European Treaties

The European Treaties include a very detailed and differentiated—and therefore complex—catalogue of competencies and means for their control. Without going into too much detail, it is possible to describe the system with the following five characteristics:

1.   The principle of limited, attributed competence: Article 5 EC provides that 'the Community shall act within the limits of the powers conferred upon it by this Treaty and of the objectives assigned to it therein'. Accordingly, Articles 1(2) and (5) EU state that the objectives of the Union shall be achieved 'as provided in this Treaty ...' and that the institutions 'shall exercise their powers under the conditions and for the purposes' provided for by the provisions of the EC Treaty and the Treaty on European Union. Thus, the European institutions have no power unless expressly provided for by the Treaties. This presumption of Member State competence is underlined by the principle of subsidiarity as defined in Article 5(2) EC and specified by the Amsterdam Protocol (no 30) and Declaration (no 43) on the Application of the Principles of Subsidiarity and Proportionality.

2.   Though there is no systematic distinction, most of the competencies conferred on the European level of government by the Treaties are competencies for legislative action. As opposed to the American approach of 'dual federalism', implementation and financing of European policies is left largely to the Member States. Article 175(4) EC declares this expressly in the case of the environment and the Amsterdam Declaration on the Application of the Principles of Subsidiarity and Proportionality clearly confirms it. In its *Milchkontor* judgment, the Court of Justice has established that the Member States are bound, under Article 10 EC, to implement European policies in accordance with their respective national administrative law in an effective, non-discriminatory and loyal way.[7] The implementing powers referred to in Article 202, last indent, and Article 211, last indent, EC concern either legislative acts specifying Community legislation or, exceptionally, administrative powers of the Commission which need to be exercised at the European level, such as competition and state aids or the administration of the structural funds. These exceptions, however, confirm the rule of national implementation, a rule which is important for the vertical division of

[7] [1983] ECR 2633.

powers, for the political coherence of the system and for ensuring that measures which directly affect the citizens are put into effect at a point which is as near them as possible.

3. While Article 3 EC contains a general list of areas in which the European Community may act, four categories of provisions dealing with legislative competencies can be distinguished in the Treaties:

— *Competencies defined by areas*, for the conduct of concrete Community policies, such as customs (Articles 26, 27 and 135 EC), agriculture (Articles 32 to 38 EC), visas, asylum, immigration etc (Article 61 to 69 EC), transport (Articles 70 to 80 EC), competition and state aids (Articles 81 to 89 EC), the coordination of economic policies (Articles 98 to 104), monetary policy (Articles 105 to 111 EC), employment (Articles 125 to 130 EC), commercial policy (Articles 131 to 134 EC), social policy (Articles 136 to 148 EC), research (Articles 163 to 173 EC), environment (Articles 174 to 176 EC) etc. Specific powers for coordination and common action are, in addition, conferred on the European Union by the provisions on common foreign and security policy and on the police and judicial cooperation in criminal matters in the EU Treaty. All these competencies are each of very different reach and intensity, and defined by areas of action, by the indication of specific objectives, by the means of action and by the procedures to be followed.

— *Competencies defined by objectives* for the achievement of specific goals of horizontal character and, in particular, of the internal market, such as the general provision of Article 94 EC and the specific provisions of Article 95 EC for goods, Articles 40, 42 and 47 EC for the free circulation and social security of workers, the freedom of establishment, and the freedom to provide services. Even broader is the revision clause of Article 308 EC, under which any measure may be taken, in case of the absence of a specific competence, if deemed necessary to meet an objective of the Treaty in the framework of the common market. These provisions are not related to specific policy areas, and measures taken to achieve the objectives defined therein may extend to any other policy area, including those for which the Union has (expressly) no specific power to legislate or to act otherwise. Only where legislative powers eg for harmonisation are expressly excluded (eg Articles 149 to 152 EC on education, culture, public health), such general provisions may not be used.

— *Negative competencies*, ie provisions which expressly exclude certain kinds of action by the Union in specific areas. The most important clauses of this kind are the provisions just mentioned in the areas of education, culture, public health etc which exclude any kind of harmonisation of legislation. Article 152(5) EC goes further in securing that Community action 'shall fully respect the responsibilities of the Member States for the organisation and delivery of health services and medical care'. Article 137(6) EC states that Community competence in social matters 'shall not apply to pay, the right of association, the right to strike or the right to impose lock-outs', Articles 64(1) and 68(2) EC as well as Articles 33 and 35(5) EU make sure that 'the exercise of the responsibilities incumbent on Member States with regard to the maintenance of law and order and the safeguarding of internal security' is not affected by European provisions, and under Article 135 EC the European measures on customs cooperation 'shall not concern the application of national criminal law or the national administration of justice'.

— *'Abolished' competencies*, ie prohibitions on action, both for the Member States and for the Union,[8] such as the prohibition on establishing customs duties or other barriers to trade between Member States (Articles 23, 25, 28 to 31 EC), barriers to the free movement of persons (Articles 43 and 49 EC) and capital (Article 56 EC) or the prohibition on tax discrimination (Articles 90 to 92 EC). The prohibition, under Articles 10, 81, 82 and 86 EC on establishing or promoting restrictions on competition and the prohibition on state aids contrary to the common market may also be added to this category. These provisions do not confer any competence on the European institutions, except the power of the Commission to control the p rohibition and to take action in the case of violation, and the powers conferred on the Court of Justice to rule on cases brought to it in relation to such infringements.

A mix of the above-mentioned powers can be observed in the provisions on economic and social cohesion (Articles 158 to 162 EC). The policies of the structural funds are closely linked, in practice, to the application of the rules on state-aids, with the result that Member

---

[8] See the category of 'compétences abolies', developed by Simon, *Le système juridique communautaire* 2nd edn (1998), 83 *et seq*, on the basis of considerations made by Constantinesco, *Compétences et pouvoirs dans les Communautés européennes* (1974), 231 *et seq*, at 248.

States' freedom of action in their regional policies is heavily restricted.[9]

4.   The decision whether or not the Treaties provide for a European competence in a given case, and to what extent the principle of subsidiarity is respected is entrusted to the hands of the institutions. Each institution is bound to respect the limits of competencies conferred on it, and political practice shows that the cases where such limits have been exceeded are very rare. It is, in particular, the 'in-built' control by ministers in the Council, by which the interest of the Member States in safeguarding their respective competencies and preserving their freedom of political action and discretion is secured. However, in practice, governments sometimes tend to use the 'European channel' to implement policies which—for political reasons—they are unable to achieve at the national level.[10]

5.   It is up to the Court of Justice to decide cases submitted to it, to examine and judge in any case the legality of the European measures and legislation in question. The *Tobacco* case, in which it was found that the Directive on the prohibition on advertising for tobacco products was ill-founded and, therefore, void, has already become a famous example.[11] An increasing tendency of the Court to find balanced solutions between the objectives of integration and the interest of the Member States to preserve their freedom of action, now expressed by Article 6(3) EU and the principle of subsidiarity, can already be found in its opinion on the power of the Community to adhere to the European Convention on Human Rights.[12] Although the question of limits on competencies under the Treaties and the principle of subsidiarity is largely political, the Court could become a reliable arbiter between the national and European institutions in such questions.

II.   Comparative Analysis: The Division of Competencies in Federal States

Although there is a great variety of ways in which competencies are divided and delimited in federal states, it seems to be possible to distinguish broadly three categories or models. As the debate in the European Union basically relates to the legislative competencies and the above-mentioned principle,

---

[9] See the remarks made by Clement, above n 2.
[10] Kohl, 'Europa auf dem Weg zur politischen Union' in Konrad Adenauer Stiftung (ed), *Europa auf dem Weg zur politischen Union. Documentation of a congress of the Konrad Adenauer Foundation*, 1993, 11 *et seq*, 14 *et seq*; cf also Pernice, above n 2, at 874.
[11] [2000] ECR I–2247.
[12] [1996] ECR I–1759.

that implementation and financing of European policies are a matter for the Member States, shall not be questioned, it is appropriate to focus on how legislative competencies are assigned to the different levels of governance in other federal systems.

1. *Special Assignment of Federal Competencies*

Most common is a system—comparable to the European approach—of explicit assignment of legislative competencies to the federal level with residuary legislative power on the state or regional level. Thus, whenever there is no responsibility assigned to the federal level, the state level is competent to legislate on the matter. This model is open for exclusive as well as concurrent or other legislative competencies on the federal level, with concurrent competencies understood as legislative powers that the state level may use as long as the federal level has not passed any legislation in a particular policy area. A good example is the German Grundgesetz: it provides for catalogues of exclusive, concurrent and framework legislative competencies assigned to the federal level (Articles 71 *et seq*), whereas the Länder have residuary legislative power (Articles 30 and 70). This model—with minor deviations—can also be found in the constitutions of the United States,[13] Brazil,[14] Australia[15] and Austria.[16]

2. *Residuary Powers of the Federal Level*

In a second model explicit legislative powers are assigned to the state or regional level while residuary legislative competence remains at the federal level. This model is basically one that is followed by the constitution

---

[13] Legislative competency assignment to the federal level (Art I Section 8 Constitution of the United States), residuary competence on state level (Amendment X), exclusive and concurrent ('Dormant Commerce Clause') competencies (see Brugger, *Einführung in das öffentliche Recht der USA* (1993), at 56 *et seq*), supremacy of federal law in case of inconsistency (Art VI clause 2 Constitution of the United States).

[14] Catalogue of exclusive legislative competencies assigned to the federal level (Art 22 Constitution of the Federative Republic of Brazil), catalogue of concurrent legislative competencies (Art 24 Constitution of the Federative Republic of Brazil).

[15] Enumeration of exclusive (Art 52 Constitution of Australia) and parallel (Art 51 Constitution of Australia) legislative competencies assigned to the federal level, residuary competence on state level (Art 107 Constitution of Australia), in case of inconsistency federal law shall prevail over state law (Art 109 Constitution of Australia).

[16] Catalogue of exclusive legislative competencies assigned to the federal level (Art 10, 11 Federal Constitutional Law of Austria), enumeration of basic/framework legislative competencies assigned to the federal level (Art 12 Federal Constitutional Law of Austria), detailed bipolar listing of legislative competencies in educational matters (Art 14, 14a Federal Constitutional Law of Austria), residuary legislative power (Art 15 (1) Federal Constitutional Law of Austria) on state level.

of Canada.[17] The process of devolution in the United Kingdom[18] seems to follow the same line, although the UK is far from being a federal system.

3. Bipolar Assignment of Competencies

A third model takes its bearings from a bipolar or dual structure of competency assignment: explicit legislative competencies assigned to both the federal and the state level. However, a distinction shall be made between a strict and an open bipolar system. In the strict bipolar system, only exclusive competencies are dealt with. The federal constitution confers exclusive competencies on the different levels of governance and the responsibility for a specific policy belongs either to the states or to the federation. This system can be found in Belgium. In the open bipolar system, the federal constitution not only refers to exclusive competencies on both levels but also to concurrent or parallel legislative powers, and distributes such powers (partly including even powers for the administrative implementation and financing) by very detailed and specific rules (Switzerland,[19] India[20]).

4. Modalities of Assignment and Control

A general overview also allows two further distinctions to be made with respect to the delimitation of competencies in federal systems:

— Attributed powers may be described in terms of specific tasks or may be delimited on the basis of policy areas. Most common among competency catalogues is a mix of both forms. The assignment of general competencies just for the attainment of certain objectives, such as the establishment or functioning of the internal market, however, seems to be reserved to the European Union.

---

[17] Catalogue of exclusive legislative competencies assigned to the state/provincial level (Art 92 Constitution Act, 1867), residuary legislative power on federal level, though enumeration 'for greater certainty' (Art 91 Constitution Act, 1867).

[18] See Bogdanor, 'Devolution: The Constitutional Aspects', in The University of Cambridge Centre for Public Law (ed), *Constitutional Reform in the United Kingdom: Practice and Principles* (1998) 9 *et seq*; Pahl, '"Devolution" und Europa - Die neuen Regelungen zur Mitwirkung der Regionen des Vereinigten Königreichs in EU-Angelegenheiten', (2000) 23 *Integration*, at 245.

[19] Very detailed catalogue of exclusive, concurrent and supplementary competencies for both the federal and cantonal levels (Art 54 *et seq* Federal Constitution of the Swiss Confederation), residuary competence at cantonal level (Art 3, 42 Federal Constitution of the Swiss Confederation, 1998).

[20] Catalogues of exclusive state (State List), exclusive federal (Union list), and concurrent legislative competencies (Concurrent list) in the Seventh Schedule of the Constitution of India, federal level has residuary legislative competencies if the relevant matter is not enumerated in the state or concurrent list (Art 248 (1) Constitution of India).

—   In all analysed systems competency delimitation conflicts are decided by supreme courts or federal constitutional courts.[21] The alternative of a rather political control has been chosen in Belgium, where a special Court of Arbitration (Article 142 Constitution of Belgium) decides on competency conflicts between Regions, Communities and the Federal State.[22]

III.   Proposals Under Discussion in the European Debate

A number of draft constitutions or at least proposals for drafting a new catalogue of competencies exist already. One, similar to the bipolar Swiss model, provides for the full assignment and distribution of powers between the two levels of government (1), others take over the existing system of assigned competencies, while splitting the Treaties into two parts (2) and two French proposals plead for the special assignment of European competencies by the treaty or by organic laws adopted under the treaty (3). The Economist opts for specially assigned competencies to the Union in the framework of a European Constitution which shall co-exist with the revised Treaties (4) and the German Länder are still searching for a compromise in view of a more systematic order of competencies combined with some procedural safeguards (5).

1.   *The Bipolar or Dual System Developed by Fischer and Schley*

The proposal of *Fischer* and *Schley*[23] merely follows the strict bipolar approach.[24] However, the model goes beyond the dual listing of responsibilities which belong exclusively to the Member States and the European level by introducing the additional distinction between primary and partial competencies on both the national and the supranational level. Primary competencies cover cases in which the powers of the Member States and the European level are normally exercised in a given policy area, whereas the partial competencies state the exceptions to this rule with regard to the other level.

Developing a model for the Treaty-based reorganisation of the division of competencies between the European Union and its Member States,

---

[21] See eg Art 93 (1) no 3 of the German Grundgesetz or Art III Section 2 Constitution of the United States.
[22] For more details see Alen, *Treatise on Belgian Constitutional Law* (1992), 117 *et seq* and at 145 *et seq*.
[23] Fischer/Schley, above n 3.
[24] A model which was already proposed by the 'Commission on European Structures' in 1994, see Weidenfels (ed), *Europe' 96. Reforming the European Union* (1994), 18 *et seq*.

Fischer and *Schley* propose the use of the subsidiarity principle of the Treaties with its 'necessity' (insufficient) and 'effectiveness' (better) clause for the compilation of a 'competency test' to determine the distribution of competencies between the European Union and the Member States. The principle of subsidiarity is thereby mutated from a rule on the use of competencies into a rule governing their distribution. For this purpose, they propose a set of criteria for scrutinising and reorganising European responsibilities in a *dual catalogue of competencies*. Applying these criteria, they eventually give a short description of each competence. They suggest, in addition, a new procedure for the transfer of competencies in order to make sure that the integration process—despite the precise delimitation of responsibilities—can develop in a dynamic way.

Though the approach looks very attractive and promises both a high degree of legal certainty and dynamism, it is questionable whether it can accommodate the special features of the European Union. Could a European Treaty define the competencies of the Member States without interfering too much with their constitutional autonomy? If additional competencies could be conferred on the Union under a simplified procedure with a view to more flexibility, another crucial difference between the Union and a federal state, the principle of consent, ie the veto on basic constitutional questions, would disappear. As long as the specific features of the EU are to be maintained, it is preferable, therefore, to be content with the assignment and definition of European competencies and its institutions and not to interfere more than necessary with the autonomy of the Member States. This does not exclude, however, a broader use of 'negative competencies' mentioned above, by which certain kinds of action are excluded from the scope of European competencies with a view to protecting national freedom of action.

2.   Simplification by Splitting - the EUI and Bertelsmann Proposals

The drafts for a of the *EUI*[25] and the *Bertelsmann Group for Policy Research*[26] propose a reorganisation of the presentation and form of the Treaties, while largely respecting the present legal situation. It is clear,

---

[25] European University Institute, Robert Schuman Centre for Advanced Studies, *A Basic Treaty for the European Union. A study of the reorganisation of the Treaties. Report submitted on 15 May 2000 to Mr Romano Prodi, President of the European Commission*, http://europa.eu.int/comm/archives/igc2000/offdoc/repoflo_en.pdf.

[26] Bertelsmann Group for Policy Research at the Center for Applied Policy Research, *A Basic Treaty for the European Union. Draft Version for the Reorganisation of the Treaties* (May 2000) http://www.cap.unimuenchen.de/download/treaty.pdf; a synthesis of all the attempts at consolidating the founding Treaties in a single document is given by Schmid, 'Konsolidierung und Vereinfachung des europäischen Primärrechts — wissenschaftliche Modelle, aktueller Stand und Perspektiven', in v Bogdandy/Ehlermann, *Konsoldierung und Kohäränz des Primärrechts nach Amsterdam* (1998) Europarecht, Beiheft 2.

therefore, that these proposals cannot produce substantial changes to the existing system of competencies in the European Union.

Yet, it is worth mentioning that both the EUI and the Bertelsmann Group for Policy Research propose that the Treaties should be divided into two parts, with a Basic Treaty and a separate Treaty containing more specific regulations. In the Basic Treaty, they restructure the whole primary law in a consistent way and set out the fundamental features of the European Union. The main purpose of this exercise is clarification and simplification. An enormous body of complex rules is reduced to a short, clearly structured text for the benefit of the citizens of the Union. This basic treaty would have the advantage of enhancing legal certainty and respect for the primary law, while endowing the Union with a symbolic and identity-creating document with effect similar to the Charter of Fundamental Rights. The more readable document might eventually lead to more transparency and acceptance of the European Union.

It is questionable, however, whether the complexity of the 'European constitution' would be reduced and legal certainty regarding the division of competencies between the Union and its Member States would be enhanced. To really understand who does what, people and experts would have to read the Basic Treaty *and* the continuing provisions of the European Treaties, establish which of both has prevalence over the other in case of conflict or open questions, and eventually would have to refer to the different provisions to make a specific argument. The exercise would therefore result in more complexity instead of reducing it. To achieve a clearer delimitation of competencies was neither the task nor the purpose of the authors, anyway.

3.   *Flexible Mechanisms in a European Constitution: the Juppé and UDF Proposals*

A draft paper by a group of French politicians around *Alain Juppé*[27] seems to be close to the first model of attributed competencies mentioned above (B.II.1). It distinguishes three categories of legislative competencies: exclusive competencies assigned to the European Union level in the Treaties, shared competencies (compétences partagées) enumerated in an organic law—'loi organique', which can be altered more easily than Treaty provisions, which would still require a more formal procedure than ordinary secondary legislation, and residuary legislative powers of the Member States. Within the framework of a wider approach including institutional reforms, it is proposed to introduce a special political control for the exercise of powers conferred on the Union in particular with regard to the principle of subsidiarity, by a new 'second chamber' which shall be composed of

---

[27] Juppé / Toubon/Gaymard, above n 4.

representatives of national parliaments ('Chambre des Nations'). It takes up, in this respect, an idea of the French Senate, which has apparently been calling for such a Second Chamber for a long time.[28]

The draft-constitution of the UDF[29] is another French proposal based on the model of assigned competencies. It distinguishes between exclusive legislative competencies (compétences fédérales) and shared European competencies (compétences partagées), both to be determined in and exercised according to the conditions laid down in organic laws as well as the principles of subsidiarity and proportionality (Articles 9, 6, 1). The principle of subsidiarity is applied not only to the exercise of existing competencies, but also as a rule governing the assignment of competencies to the Union (Article 6). A residuary legislative competence rests with the Member States (Article 7) which they may exercise collectively outside the Treaty framework. The exercise of competencies is subject to control by the Court of Justice (Article 19).

Both French proposals seem to rely on a 'hierarchy of norms'—an approach by which the flexibility of the assignment and the division of competencies is found in the special procedure designed for such decisions of a constitutional character. The aim does not seem to be more legal certainty or the effective preservation of the freedom of action of the Member States. Though the system would be simpler and more transparent, and both proposals consider, by a 'Chamber of nations' or by the Court of Justice, a control which respects the limits of competencies including subsidiarity, their main purpose is drafting as simple a constitution as possible, replacing the existing Treaties and setting the Union on a new basis.

4. A British Proposal for a European Constitution: the Economist

A different path is taken with the proposal for a European Constitution submitted by The Economist.[30] The European Constitution is proposed to be a basic document that is, like the Basic Treaty of the EUI, designed to co-exist with the Treaty of Rome and with the other Treaties of the Union. However, these would be amended substantially. The proposal includes an enumeration of legislative competencies for the European Union in the Constitution (Article 13 *et seq*) or in the Treaties (Article 1) and residuary competencies for the Member States (Article 1). It does not distinguish between different types of competencies. Powers can also be returned to Member States, if all Member States agree (Article 17). The proposal provides for a new chamber of representatives of national parliaments,

---

[28] See Hoeffel, *Rapport d'information fait au nom de la délégation du Sénat pour l'Union européenne sur une deuxième chambre européenne*, No. 381 Sénat session ordinaire de 2000–2001.
[29] Union pour la Démocratie Française, above n 4.
[30] Economist, above n 4.

the 'Council of Nations', and charges this body with the task of constitutional oversight (Article 6). The Council will even have the power to overrule the Court of Justice (Article 6 and Article 9) in constitutional matters.

Compared to the ideas Tony Blair expressed in Warsaw last year,[31] this proposal seems to be more courageous in so far as it suggests a European Constitution. It does, however, neither add much to reducing the complexity of the system nor clarifying the delimitation of competencies. Tony Blair suggested a political charter of competencies which would serve as a guideline for the institutions in applying the provisions of the Treaties, and—like Juppé and the French Senate, and followed so by the Danish minister of foreign affairs, Lykketoft—a parliamentary chamber for the political control of subsidiarity and the limits of European competencies.[32]

5.   The German Debate on a Catalogue of Competencies

After almost two years of discussion in Germany, a first important conclusion seems to be that the original idea of a catalogue of competencies 'a la tedesca' is dead. This is not because such a catalogue would transform the Union into a federal state, as was stated recently by Andrew Duff.[33] But it has become clear that the system of the German constitution, including catalogues of exclusive, concurrent and framework competencies, criteria for their exercise and control by the Constitutional Court did not prevent a continuous process of centralisation eroding the competencies of the Länder. The debate is still going on. While the Länder are close to find a compromise among themselves[34] and the foreign office is making up its mind, the think tank of the Christian democrat party under the guidance of *Wolfgang Schäuble* is preparing a comprehensive paper in which the general approach for the European competencies in the framework of a European Constitutional Treaty will be outlined and proposals for a clearer and more balanced attribution of powers in each policy area of the Union will be made. Fianally, a working group of the Social Democrat Party has worked out and published, in mid-October, some thoughts on a concept for the division of competencies, pointing out that the key question is that of the exercise, not of an excessive attribution of competencies to the Union.[35]

---

[31] Blair, *Europe's Political Future*, Speech by the Prime Minister to the Polish Stock Exchange, Warsaw, Friday 6 October 2000, http://www.fco.gov.uk.

[32] Blair, above n 32; Lykketoft, Speech of 26 August 2001 at the Außenpolitische Gesellschaft, reported in *Frankfurter Rundschau* No 198 of 27 August 2001, 2: 'Die Suche nach Gegengewichten'.

[33] Duff, ELDR Task Force Paper on the Future of Europe, *Towards a Liberal Laeken* (2001), www.andrewduffmep.org, at point 11.7.

[34] At their meeting of 11/12 October 2001 in Goslar they seem to have agreed a first paper on a common position.

[35] SPD working group European Integration, paper no 10 (September 2001) on Kompetenzausübung, nicht Kompetenzverteilung ist das eigentliche europäische 'Kompetenzproblem', http://www.fes.de/indexipa.html.

What can be said so far, is that:

— the German Länder and the Schäuble group will insist on a more systematic and transparent approach. This does not only mean to distinguish more systematically different categories of competencies, such as exclusive, basic/framework and competencies for complementary action. But it also includes the idea of determining different forms and categories of European action: direct regulation, harmonisation, mutual recognition, measures of coordination, (financial) support and administrative action;

— there is a discussion on a more precise drafting of Article 95 EC, namely with a view to conditioning any measure of harmonisation more strictly by the proper functioning of the internal market, the introduction, in addition, of more specific powers for harmonisation in technical standards etc and the abolition of Article 308 EC which is considered superfluous at this advanced stage of integration;

— serious thought is given to the question to what extent agriculture policies and certain competencies in other areas such as transport and research can be re-transferred to the Member States, in order to secure them more freedom of action;

— there is a strong questioning also whether the system and operations of the structural funds: if more than 50percent of the national contribution finds its way back to the funding Member State, would it not be safer, more transparent and cheaper to limit financial transactions to the amount which represents a real transfer? Thought is given to substitute the structural funds on these lines by a 'fund of solidarity';

— a more precise drafting of certain provisions of the Treaties is proposed to enhance legal certainty and to give the Court of Justice—or a special Court for Competencies to be created— more ground for strict legal control;

— a number of procedural safeguards are discussed, such as provisions for earlier participation by Member States in the legislative process, the internal control of subsidiarity in the Commission by a 'subsidiarity officer', independent control of subsidiarity and respect for the limits of European competencies during the lawmaking process by an expert committee or a 'Parliamentary Subsidiarity Committee';

— it is finally suggested that a right be established for the regions to seize the European Court of Justice of matters of competence and subsidiarity.

A number of the proposals mentioned above need further consideration. To abolish Article 308 EC, however, would put at serious risk the dynamic development of the Union and would be in nobody's interest. The revision of the Treaties is too heavy an instrument for creating legal basis in a specific case of need. Touching the rules on agriculture policies would bring into question a basic agreement between Germany and France, but the question is, to what extent it would also be in the interest of France and other Member States to reconsider the pros and cons of the present situation, namely with a view to enlargement. Neither the rules on economic and social cohesion, nor structural funds, finally, will be sufficient to solve the social and economic problems eventually linked to the internal market under the conditions of Economic and Monetary Union. It will be necessary, therefore, to consider new ways for a system of horizontal financial transfer within the framework of a new financial constitution for the European Union.

The German debate, therefore, has left the 'catalogue' issue far behind and seems to move rather towards proposals which bring the call for clarification and delimitation in balance with a clear demand for concentration on certain core policies, including new and enhanced supranational powers in areas where the EU so far remains ineffective:

— international trade policy and the establishment of a legal framework of the global order,
— foreign and security policy, including a common defence and action for the solution of regional conflicts,
— a common policy in matters of immigration, visas, refugees and asylum, including the question of a balanced burden-sharing,
— the creation of a real European legal area through enhanced judicial cooperation,
— combat of organised international crime and terrorism, a matter that has acquired a new dimension since the events of 11 September 2001.

With these important changes in mind, it is clear that the option of Nice simplifying the Treaties 'with a view to making them clearer and better understood without changing their meaning' cannot be the guideline for preparation for the Intergovernmental Conference of 2004. What the post-Nice process is about, is instead the reorganisation of the Treaties including the assignment of new and the delimitation of old competencies, based on the common values as expressed by the objectives and the Charter of fundamental rights, which, understood as a catalogue of 'negative competencies' with regard of the protection of citizens' rights[36] and existing social institutions at the national level.[37]

---

[36] In this sense: Ehmke, *Wirtschaft und Verfassung* (1961) at 29 *et seq*; Häberle, *Öffentliches Interesse als juristisches Problem* (1970) at 666; Alexy, *Theorie der Grundrechte* (1985) at 223 *et seq*; more generally: Mayer, above n 1, at I.1.b), and applied to the EC: *ibid*, I.1.d).
[37] Pernice, Editorial: 'Europäische Grundrechte-Charta und Abgrenzung der Kompetenzen', (2001) *EuZW* 673.

III. EU-POWER SHARING IN THE LIGHT OF MULTILEVEL
CONSTITUTIONALISM

Evaluating the numerous proposals discussed and considering concrete
steps to clarify and, if necessary, complete the European system of competencies in a revised Constitutional Treaty should be based on a common
understanding of the very nature of the Union. My view is, that it is not an
international organisation the 'masters' of which are the Member States
and the acts of which reach their citizens as a result of a validating act of
each Member State. I suggest conceptualising it as a multilevel constitutional system, composed of—as the case may be—local, regional, national
and European levels of political integration and action, and, thus, a system
of (multi-)layered competencies established to meet the needs of the citizens
most effectively at the appropriate level. Let me first give some elements of
the theoretical approach on which my considerations are based (I), and then
draw in some conclusions for the criteria and methods for dividing and controlling the Competencies of the Union (2).

I. **Elements of Multilevel Constitutionalism**

Multilevel constitutionalism[38] is the legal 'pendant' to the political theory
of multilevel governance in Europe.[39] To describe what it means in our context, the following five elements are crucial:

1. In the process of globalisation, states are increasingly unable to
   meet the challenges and serve effectively the needs of their
   citizens regarding peace, security, welfare etc. The 'postnational
   constellation' described by J Habermas[40] requires supra- and

---

[38] For the concept see Pernice, 'Constitutional Law Implications for a State Participating in a
Process of Regional Integration. German Constitution and 'Multilevel Constitutionalism'', in
Riedel (ed), *German Reports on Public Law Presented to the XV International Congress on
Comparative Law*, Bristol, 26 July to 1 August 1998 (1998), 40 *et seq*; further developed in
Pernice, 'Multilevel Constitutionalism and the Treaty of Amsterdam: European Constitution-
Making Revisited?', (1999) 36 *Common Market Law Review.*, 703 *et seq*; Pernice/Mayer, 'De la
constitution *composée de l'Europe*', (2000) 36 *Review Trimstrick de droit european*, 623 *et seq*
at 631 *et seq*; cf also: Schuppert, 'Anforderungen an eine europäische Verfassung' in
Klingemann/Neidhardt (eds), *Zur Zukunft der Demokratie. Herausforderungen im Zeitalter der
Globalisierung* (2000) 237 *et seq* at 256 *et seq*; v Bogdandy, 'A Bird's Eye View on the Science of
European Law: Structures, Debates and Development Prospects of Basic Research on the Law of
the European Union in a German Perspective', (2000) 6 *European Law Journal* 208 et seq. at
226 *et seq*; Bauer, 'Europäisierung des Verfassungsrechts', (2000) *JBl.*, 749 *et seq* at 751.
[39] See Marks/Hooghe/Blank, *European Integration and the State* at 7; Mayer,
Kompetenzüberschreitung und Letztentscheidung (2000) at 36.
[40] Habermas, 'Die postnationale Konstellation und die Zukunft der Demokratie', in *ibid, Die
postnationale Konstellation. Politische Essays* (1998) 91 *et seq*; Zürn, *The State in the Post-
National Constellation - Societal Denationalization and Multi-Level Governance,*

international structures serving as complementary instruments to fill this growing lacuna. On the basis of a functional—or as I would call it 'postnational'—concept of constitutionalism,[41] it does not seem necessary to assume that only states can have a constitution. But generally, the term means rather the legal instrument by which the people of a certain territory agree to create institutions vested with public authority, ie powers to achieve certain objectives in their common or general interest, and define their respective rights with regard to such institutions and their status as citizens of the organisation, 'community' or polity so created.[42]

2.   There are many ways, historically, that constitutions have been created. One, if not the most appropriate and attractive, is to empower representatives of the groups of people concerned to negotiate a draft that is later submitted for ratification. This is exactly how, on the basis of the integration clauses, conditions and procedures set out in the constitutions of the Member States, the European Treaties have been adopted and developed: as an expression of the common will, as an instrument for pursuing certain common goals, the citizens of the Member States—through their respective governments and constitutional processes have agreed to create supranational institutions, entrust them with certain competencies to be exercised according to the procedures laid down in the Treaties, and have defined their own common status as citizens of this Union, their rights and freedoms. The statehood of the Member States and national citizenship are not called into question, but a new constitutional layer establishing a complementary public authority has been added for matters of common interest, drawing its legitimacy from the people who are subject to its policies.

3.   This process has significant impact on the realities of national constitutions, the powers and the functions of the institutions of the Member States and on the national legal systems. Every revision of the European Treaties, which the Court so rightly calls the 'constitutional charter of a legal community',[43] entails an

ARENA Working Papers WP 99/35, www.arena.uio.no; Schuppert, 'Demokratische Legitimation jenseits des Nationalstaates. Einige Bemerkungen zum Legitimationsproblem der Europäischen Union', in Heyde/ Schaber (eds), *Demokratisches Regieren in Europa? Zur Legitimation einer Europäischen Rechtsordnung* (2000) 65 *et seq* at 76 *et seq*: 'Die postnationale Konstellation oder die EU als dynamisches Mehrebenensystem'.

[41] See Pernice, 'Europäisches und nationales Verfassungsrecht', (2001) 60 *VVDStRL* 148 at 155 *et seq*.

[42] For the application of this concept to the constitutional tradition of the United Kingdom see Thym, 'European Constitutional Theory and the Post-Nice Process' in Andenas/ Usher (eds), *The Treaty of Nice, Enlargement and Constitutional Reform*, this volume ch 5.

[43] [1991] ECR I–6079 at 6102; and already [1986] ECR 1339 at 1365 *et seq*; more recently [1996] ECR I–1759 at 1789.

implicit or explicit modification of the national constitutions: it may 'destitute' powers at the national level and constitute them at the European level. Although 'autonomous' in their origin, both constitutional levels strongly depend on each other: the European authority could not function without the national institutions and legal systems on which it is based, and the national authorities have to rely on and operate through the European institutions if they want to achieve the results which on their own, they would not be able to reach.

4.   As a result of European integration, the citizens of the Member States have adopted multiple identities—local, regional, national, European—which correspond to the various levels of political community they are citizens of. Rules of conflict make sure that, at whatever level decisions are taken, the system produces for each case only one legal solution. In applying European law which prevails over conflicting national law, national authorities act as European agencies, while on the other hand, national authorities are strongly involved in the process of European policy-making, so that the European functions of the national governments and parliaments more and more outweigh their national responsibilities.[44]

5.   To conceptualise the process of European integration as a process of 'multilevel constitutionalism', by which the allocation of powers shared by the national and European levels of government is continuously reorganised and re-shifted, while all public authority—national or European—draws its legitimacy from the same citizens, therefore, means to raise awareness of the fact that the European Union is as much our own instrument of political action as are the Member States and their regions, and not a foreign, nameless power. The 'European constitution' therefore already exists and it is to be understood as a composed multilevel constitutional system comprising two or more constitutional levels which are closely interwoven, interdependent and connected to each other. It is the multilevel character of this system which allows and the complexity of the system which requires a revision of its structure, procedures and constitutional texts, if possible resulting in a consolidated Constitutional Treaty of the European Union.

---

[44] For the qualification of national parliaments as European parliaments see Pernice, 'The Role of National Parliaments in the European Union' in Melissas/Pernice (eds), *Perspectives of the Nice Treaty and the Intergovernmental in 2004* (2002) p 73.

II. Consequences: Criteria for a Revised System of Power Sharing in the EU

A first important consequence of this approach is that the discussion as to whether or not the post-Nice process shall aim at a European constitution is futile. A constitution, at least in a 'postnational' sense, already exists and the question we face is how to improve and simplify it and, perhaps, bring it closer to the traditional perception of formal constitutions. It was Jacques Chirac who demonstrated this perspective in his speech to the German parliament in June 2000.[45] A second consequence would be to realise that reconsidering the competence-order of the Union also means reconsidering the distribution of powers under the national constitutions. A third consequence is that it is the perspective and the interest of the citizen which matters, not the preferences of national administrations and ministers who might find it odd to leave certain powers to the European level, which they may prefer to exercise autonomously. The case law of the Court of Justice shows how heavily national governments rely upon national prerogatives and a restrictive interpretation of the Treaties, namely provisions concerning the four freedoms and non-discrimination, contrary to the interests of citizens who invoke these provisions as individual rights. The decisive criterion therefore is what the citizens want to be considered at the European level, even if their relative democratic influence and control is minimised. This, again, is by and large a political consideration.

Though there is little doubt about the justification for all the powers the European Union disposes of at present, it is a common view that the Treaties are so complex that nobody really understands who is responsible for what. The multilevel structure of the European political system, as such, implies a high degree of complexity. This complexity is multiplied by the mere fact that those who take a stake in the policy-making at European level are not only European politicians—elected members of the European Parliament or Commissioners appointed by the Member States—but to a large degree representatives of national institutions. Democracy, however, is based on transparency and on the accountability of those who take decisions. The more the Treaty provisions on competencies are differentiated and set out in detail with regard to their objectives, conditions and the manner of their functioning, the more difficult it is to establish clear responsibilities. Simplification means transparency, but contrary to what is suggested in Declaration no 23 of the Nice summit, simplification implies modification in substance following some logic and system.

---

[45] Chirac, *Notre Europe*, Discours prononcé par Monsieur Jacques Chirac, Président de la République Française, devant le Bundestag', 27.6.2000, www.botschaft-frankreich.de, at 12.

IV. CONCLUSIONS AND RECOMMENDATIONS FOR THE DIVISION OF POWERS IN THE EU

What is at issue, therefore, is to simplify and clarify the attribution of competencies to the European Union, to concentrate on core responsibilities which have to be assumed at the European level and to enhance the capacities of the system for political monitoring and control of the limits of the competencies assigned to the European Union and of the principle of subsidiarity. Against this background, the following measures are recommended for further consideration:

I. Consolidation of the Treaties into one European Constitutional Treaty

Declaration (no 42) to the Treaty of Amsterdam stresses the need for a consolidation of the Treaties. Contrary to what the three 'wise man' have suggested[46] and what the EUI has elaborated in its careful study,[47] this need not lead to another splitting of the European primary law but to one consolidated 'Constitutional' Treaty in which people can find the objectives of the Union, the Charter of Fundamental Rights, provisions defining the competencies and policies of the Union, the institutions including the appointment procedures and the procedure(s) for decision-making. Though it is clear that the objectives already give guidelines for the use of the assigned competencies, and fundamental rights, in addition, limit their use in favour of the individual and as a safeguard for social standards and regimes achieved in the Member States, the core of this Constitutional Treaty would have to be a system of competence attributions including the powers of coordination and common action provided for, so far, in the second and third pillar of the EU Treaty.

II. A General Clause on the Division of Functions and Mutual Loyalty

The principle, mentioned above, that policies and legislation in a given area shall be a matter for the Union to the extent that common action or rules applying equally to all the citizens of the Union is deemed necessary, and implementation should be a matter for the Member States and their regions whose administrations are closer to the citizens, know more about the specific conditions on the spot and are therefore able to achieve more adequate and better results, this principle of a functional separation of powers between

---

[46] Cf v Weizsäcker/Dehaene/Simon, 'Die institutionellen Auswirkungen der Erweiterung. Report to the European Commission', 18 October 1999, *FAZ* no 244, 20 October 1999, 9 *et seq.*
[47] European University Institute, above n 26.

the two levels of action should be spelled out more clearly in the new Treaty. Article 5(1) EC is not sufficient in this respect. Implementation means the transposition of Community directives by national legislators, but also the administrative execution and control of application of European law. Article 5 EC and, in particular, its paragraph 3 reserve for national authorities a maximum of political discretion, freedom for creativity and autonomy.

This responsibility of national and regional authorities is a major element in the functioning of the Union and a condition for effective government in a multilevel system. It requires *mutual* respect and loyalties, not only discipline from the Member States. Therefore, Article 10 EC should be amended by a provision addressed to the institutions of the Union requiring them expressly to have regard and consideration for particular national and regional interests and difficulties. While Article 6(3) EU requires the respect of the national identities of the Member States, this provision would underline a specific feature of European identity, which is—in the light of multilevel constitutionalism—based on mutual respect and cooperation of the institutions at two levels of government which are not in a hierarchical order but equal instruments of the citizens in pursuing common goals.

If powers for administrative implementation and execution at the European level are the exception, they should be reduced to a strict minimum and conferred on the Commission by express provisions of the Treaty or secondary law.

III.   System and Categories of European Competencies

A more systematic approach to the attribution of competencies to the Union is needed. Areas and matters of exclusive competence (customs, trade policies, monetary policy) must be distinguished from areas in which competencies are shared between the Union and the Member States (agriculture, transport, environment, social, regional, consumer, health, research, immigration, asylum policies etc) and areas where the Union just provides the framework for the coordination of national policies or intergovernmental cooperation and no legislative powers (economic and employment, foreign, security and defence policies, home affairs, criminal justice etc). Simplification would be achieved, if the existing differentiation between the various forms of action, decision-making procedures, voting-methods in the Council and participation of other institutions could be abolished in favour of one common procedure, which should be joint decision-making by the Council and the European Parliament after consultation with the relevant committees. Though the catalogue of possible forms of action in Article 249 EC (regulation, directive, decision, recommendation) may be completed by framework directives, common strategies, joint actions and common positions, the choice of the appropriate instrument should be left to the political process and the institutions, with due regard to the principles of subsidiarity and proportionality.

It is clear that this exercise would not only imply a new order of competencies, but also major changes in substance. The complexity of the present Treaty is a result of difficult and long negotiations resulting in detailed exceptions and qualifications, specific conditions and procedures coupled with protocols and declarations annexed to the Treaties. But the compromises negotiated between diplomats, ministers and Heads of State or Government are unreadable and, in part, impracticable—such as the new provisions in Article 133(5)–(7) EC amended by the Treaty of Nice – and in any event did not produce the desired effect of making clear who does what. It is time to reduce the rhetoric of international diplomacy to the very essence of powers attributed to the Union, and to give it responsibility for meeting the expectations of the citizens.

IV. Definition of Competencies and 'Negative Competence Clauses'

Some of the provisions of the present Treaties need stricter definition, some others a broader scope. While Article 133 EC regarding the common commercial policy should clearly state that services including transport are covered by this policy, Article 95 EC would need to be redrafted in order to reduce its scope to measures directly preventing restrictions of trade or serious distortions of competition. Likewise, Article 308 EC should refer to the internal market and its functioning, and not allow for such schemes as food aid or programmes such as PHARE and TACIS.[48] The Parliamentary Subsidiarity Committee, proposed below, may play a special role in the context of these provisions.

To secure room for national action in certain areas or matters, related to subjects for which competence is given to the Union, the existing practice of including 'negative competence clauses' may be extended to other areas. It should be clear, however, that there is no policy area where the need for limited action at the European level can totally be excluded. The negative clauses, therefore, could refer to a revised Article 308 EC, to allow such exceptional limited action subject to its specific procedural requirements.

V. Procedural Safeguards: a Parliamentary Subsidiarity Committee

What degree of specificity provisions on competencies in the Treaty may have and their interpretation and application in practice will always be a matter of political and hermeneutic discretion. Though it is—and should

---

[48] Crit. also Dashwood, 'The Limits of European Community Powers', (1996) 21 *European Law Review* 113 at 120 *et seq* relating to Art 100a EC, and at 123 *et seq* on Art 235 EC.

always be—the task of the European Court of Justice to exercise final control[49], those who really have an interest in maintaining a place for national legislation should have a stake in the decision-making process: the national parliaments. Some way in line with the ideas for a Second Chamber developed by the French Senate, Juppé/Tourbon and Tony Blair, it seems appropriate to underline the European function of national parliaments by giving them a consultative role to ensure respect, from the European institutions, for the principle of subsidiarity and limits on European competencies.

This would—and should—however, not be a Second Chamber stricto sensu, since the Council in its legislative capacity already functions as the second chamber of the Union. Instead, it might be a second branch—or a special committee[50]—of the Council and might even be present during its deliberations. In full knowledge of the various positions of the ministers, it could be consulted where there was any doubt as to matters of subsidiarity and competence, before the Council takes any final decision. Its (reasoned) opinion would not be binding, but might well compel the ministers to re-examine their position and provide reasoned arguments as to why they consider to be competent and respectful of subsidiarity in any given case. All the arguments exchanged in this open and public discourse could be submitted to the Court of Justice, should a Member State or another privileged complainant bring an action before the Court.

Such a 'Parliamentary Subsidiarity Committee' (PSC) should be composed of at least two representatives of each national parliament, one representing the party or parties supporting the government and one from the opposition. The presence of the opposition would contribute to the political neutrality of the Committee and secure some divergence of the Committee's view from the position of the ministers. It might also include representatives of regional parliaments, in so far as they have autonomous legislative competencies they may wish to preserve.

To enhance the role of national parliaments in this context, the PSC might, in addition, be involved more directly in the decision-making process, where specific political control is needed because of the vagueness of the competencies entrusted to the Union. This would be the case, in particular, for competencies defined by purpose and not by area, such as Articles 95 and 308 EC. In these cases, the Committee could have a veto or a right to ask for the postponement of the decision to be taken by the Council. It should, furthermore, be the task of the PSC to prepare regular reports on the extent to which the legislation during the previous year has

---

[49] For the discussion of alternative proposals, including a 'Court of Review' (European Constitutional Group), a 'Common Constitutional Court' (Di Fabio) or a 'Constitutional Council' (Weiler), see Mayer, above n 1, at I.2.
[50] For the concept of a parliamentary subsidiarity committee see Pernice, above n 2.

shown sufficient respect for subsidiarity and the limits of the competencies of the Union.[51]

VI.   Political Guidelines For the Use of European Competencies

Given the remaining uncertainties as to whether, in a given area of European competence defined by the Treaty, the Union should act or leave the legislation to the Member States, it seems to be useful to complete the more or less vague attribution in the provisions of the Treaty by a political declaration setting out all necessary differentiation. This could be the 'Charter of competencies' proposed by Tony Blair. In the framework of environmental policies, for example, it seems obvious that combating climate change with all its international and internal implications, including burden-sharing between the Member States, should be a matter for the Union. On the other hand, individual Member States can themselves deal with the preservation of soil or the quality of inland water. The same would apply to transport, agriculture, health, education and other policies, even to the application of competition and state aid rules in sectors which are, in certain Member States, regarded as matters of public service.

Such political guidelines might be established by either the PSC or by the PSC together with the Council and the European Parliament. Although they would not be mandatory in any respect, concrete measures for the Union could be checked against them and specific arguments would have to be made to justify any deviation from its provisions. The guidelines themselves would be subject to regular revision following the procedure of their enactment, they would be a flexible criterion for monitoring the delimitation of competencies between the European Union and its Member States and would not inadequately block the dynamics of European integration.

---

[51] For a system of regular reports see Mayer, above n 1, at I.2.c.bb.

5

European Constitutional Theory and the Post-Nice Process

DANIEL THYM*

T HE ACADEMIC COMMUNITY and the general public—not only in Ireland—may still be digesting the Treaty of Nice, but the European train has already continued its journey. This time, not the technical necessities of institutional reform but the very 'future of the European Union' has been set as the destination. According to a joint declaration annexed to the Treaty of Nice, the European Union will revisit its constitutional foundations by discussing, *inter alia*, the delimitation of competence, the status of the Charter of Fundamental Rights, a simplification of the Treaties, the role of national parliaments and the democratic legitimacy and transparency of the institutions.[1] The debate on these issues shall be referred to as the 'post-Nice process'.

This article explores the extent to which European constitutional theory can provide a theoretical foundation and orientation for the political choices Europe faces post-Nice. Against this background, the first part of the article discusses different aspects of European constitutional theory, which in a complementary fashion, make up a broader picture of the constitutional foundation of European integration (I). Based on the first political post-Nice contributions, the second part then examines possible answers to the specific items on the post-Nice agenda in the light of European constitutional theory. We can see that the silhouette of the final post-Nice destination is already looming on the horizon (II).

* Research Assistant, Walter Hallstein Institute for European Constitutional Law, Humboldt-University Berlin (www.whi-berlin.de). I would like to thank Professor Mads Andenas, Professor Piet Eeckhout, Päivi Leino, Theo Gavrielides and Luther Weate for their assistance and critical remarks on an earlier version of this article. The usual disclaimer applies. The manuscript for this contribution was written in summer/autumn 2001.
[1] Declaration on the Future of the European Union (Nice) recitals 5 and 6 (OJ 2001 C 80/85).

I.   EUROPEAN CONSTITUTIONAL THEORY

Although being a relatively new subject of academic research, European constitutional theory can build upon the experience and insights of more than 200 years in which constitutionalism has been the ultimate point of reference of (continental) European and American public law. Space obviously precludes a comprehensive discussion of all or even the majority of substantive issues dominating constitutional law discourse in some or all legal systems. It is rather necessary to concentrate on selected aspects which can arguably build a solid foundation for European constitutional theory, since they either express an original European tradition stemming from the development of the Treaties in the past 50 years or reflect a constitutional tradition common to most or all Member States.

As the post-Nice process will draw a lot of inspiration from the constitutional traditions of the Member States, this article examines the extent to which European constitutional theory can be harmoniously combined with the constitutional traditions of the United Kingdom and Germany. The selective focus on these two Member States is of particular interest, since the constitutional traditions of the United Kingdom and Germany differ greatly and British and German politicians seem to position themselves at opposing ends of the political post-Nice spectrum. Despite my German legal background and the focus on the British and German perspective, the European constitutional theory outlined on the following pages attempts not simply to transplant national constitutional features on the European level. The limited space available, however, requires a streamlined presentation, which ignores many valuable ideas and alternatives which explain or contest the argument of this article.

Whenever this contribution refers to 'European constitutional theory' it is to be understood as a reference to the four complementary topics being the focus of this first part. They may prove to be the four essential elements of a more comprehensive European constitutional theory which remains to be written: after a functional approach (A), the article looks at the legal dimension of European constitutional theory. It will be argued that the case law of the Court of Justice already fulfils the requirements of legal constitutionalism, which consequently will not feature prominently on the post-Nice agenda (B). The survey continues with a more abstract examination of non-statal constitutionalism. The arguments put forward will serve as a foundation upon which a non-hierarchical relationship between national and European constitutions can be built (C). The first part of this article concludes by identifying the enhancement of democratic constitutionalism as the main theme underlying the post-Nice process (D).

A.   Functional Approach

Leaving aside the problems arising from the non-statal character of European integration for the moment, a focus on constitutional core functions allows an arguably uncomplicated first approach to European constitutional theory. Although each constitutional settlement depends on the historical environment and political choices in favour of a specific model, some functions may be identified as common to all constitutions. De Vattel, the author of a widely used 18th century monograph on public international law, defines the nature of a constitution as:

> ... the fundamental rules governing the exercise of public authority. It lays down the form in which the people act politically, how and by whom they are governed and their rights and duties. The constitution is basically the act establishing the framework within which a people intends to work together in order to realize the goals, which to achieve the political society was established.[2]

In the European context of the early 21st century, one should probably add that the exercise of legislative, executive and judicial power in accordance with the constitution should be democratically legitimised and subject to some form of restraint guaranteeing fundamental rights and freedoms of the citizens.

Every lawyer familiar with the basic structures of the European Union's institutional and constitutional law is aware that the Treaties do, at least from a formal point of view, fulfil these functions in principle: they establish and limit European public authority exercised by the institutions, which do at least claim to have direct or indirect democratic legitimacy and interact on the basis of the institutional balance established by the Treaties. The doctrine of direct effect creates a direct legal link between the citizens and European public authority, which is limited by the general principles of Community law, including fundamental rights. In so doing, the Treaties 'perform, in fact, the same functions as the Constitution of a federal State'.[3]

The functional approach certainly does not provide a satisfactory answer to theoretical challenges stemming from the non-statal character of European integration and the democratic deficit, but it may serve as a common denominator from which we can embark on our journey. Whenever faced with what seems to be an irreconcilable constitutional dilemma, it might help to remember that from a rather unsophisticated (and maybe simplistic) point of view the European Treaties fulfil basic constitutional functions. The rules governing the exercise of these functions have been changed in Maastricht, Amsterdam and Nice and will be altered again post-Nice, but the functional substratum underlying the European treaties will persist in the foreseeable future.

---

[2] M de Vattel, *Le droit des gens, tomé I* (Paris, Videco ed 1853) in Chapter III § 27 (own translation).
[3] So the former President of the Court of Justice Ole Due, 'A Constitutional Court for the European Communities', in D Curtin/D O'Keeffe (eds), *Constitutional Adjudication in European Community and National Law* (Dublin, Butterworth 1992) 3 at 4.

B.   The Court's Legal Constitutionalism

Walter Hallstein[4] has highlighted the importance of law for the process of integration in his memoirs:

> The Community is created by the law, it is an original legal source and it is a new legal order .... That is the decisive difference from earlier attempts to unite Europe. Neither force nor hegemony is used as a method but a moral, a cultural power: the law.[5]

This perception of European integration as a legal project is a good starting point for a closer look at the Court of Justice's approach to European constitutionalism, which I shall hereafter call 'legal constitutionalism'. It has so far symbolically culminated in the Court's opinion 1/91 on the European Economic Area: '[T]he EEC Treaty, albeit concluded in the form of an international agreement, nonetheless constitutes the constitutional charter of a Community based on the rule of law'.[6]

The most basic assumption of legal constitutionalism is the hierarchical relationship between constitutional and sub-constitutional law in a self-reflective legal system based on a *Grundnorm* as the highest level of legal *Stufenbau* (if one is a Kelsenian)[7] or the 'ultimate rule of recognition' (if one is Hartian).[8] While the theoretical concept of a legal constitution as a set of hierarchically supreme procedural and substantive norms governing the exercise of public authority may as such be shared by the constitutional doctrine of all Member States,[9] the degree to and procedures under which (constitutional) courts can review the compatibility of executive and possibly even legislative decisions with constitutional principles varies between the individual constitutional settlements. In the case of the European Union the interpretation of the Treaties by the Court of Justice provides for far-reaching judicial remedies in the case of non-compliance with the hierarchically supreme European Treaties.

All three cases in which the Court has so far explicitly referred to the 'constitutional' nature of primary law concerned the effectiveness

---

[4] Law professor, German chief negotiator for the European Coal and Steel Community and first President of the Commission.

[5] W Hallstein, *Der unvollendete Bundesstaat* (Düsseldorf, Econ, 1969) at 33 (own translation).

[6] Opinion 1/91 *(European Economic Area)*, [1991] ECR 6079 at para 21.

[7] H Kelsen, *Allgemeine Staatslehre* (Wien, Staatsdruckerei reprint 1993) at 248 *et seq*.

[8] HLA Hart, The *Concept of Law* (Oxford, Clarendon, 1961) at 145. Space precludes any theoretical discussion of similarities and differences of the Hartian and the Kelsenian approach.

[9] Leaving aside the specific case of the United Kingdom as the only Member State without a written constitution whose constitutional lawyers may nonetheless agree to supremacy as a characteristic of (written or unwritten) constitutional law, which in the British case may be limited to the single rule of Parliamentary sovereignty. See also the common law perspective of the present Lord Justice of Appeal Sir Stephen S Sedley, 'The Sound of Silence: Constitutional Law without a Constitution', (1994) 110 *Law Quarterly Review* 270.

and independence of its role as a 'guardian of the constitution'.[10] The 'constitutional argument' is used to support an extension of judicial review or to protect the Court's independence against influences by a proposed Court of the European Economic Area or the European Court of Human Rights.[11] The argument in the *Les Verts* case, in which the constitutional argument serves as a theoretical foundation for possible annulment actions not foreseen by the wording of Art. 230 EC, is particularly clear:

> [The EEC] is a Community based on the rule of law, inasmuch as neither its Member States nor its institutions can avoid a review of the question whether the measures adopted by them are in conformity with the basic constitutional charter, the Treaty.[12]

More generally, the Court's case law on the direct effect and supremacy of Community law can be identified as the 'big bang' of legal constitutionalism on the European level. Its assumption of European law as 'an independent source of law'[13] first established the autonomy of the European legal order as a necessary precondition for the Treaties enjoying supreme normative effect over sub-constitutional law. Leaving aside the issue of supremacy and direct effect for the moment (see below 4), the Court's subsequent 'constitutional' jurisprudence established and fine-tuned other well-known substantive constitutional principles. Three of them are revisited post-Nice and shall therefore be mentioned explicitly: the European Union has to comply with fundamental rights,[14] the institutional balance established by the Treaties has to be respected[15] and after many years of criticism of its integrationist jurisprudence the Court finally seems to have accepted its role as an independent arbiter of the limits of Community competence.[16]

The jurisprudence on direct effect, supremacy and fundamental rights, which built legal constitutionalism on 'the spirit' and 'general scheme'[17] rather than the wording of the Treaties, is a prime example of European

[10] On the ECJ as a constitutional Court, *inter alia*, Due, above n 3; FG Jacobs, 'Is the Court of Justice of the European Communities a Constitutional Court?', in D Curtin/D O'Keeffe (eds), *Constitutional Adjudication in European Community and National Law* (1992) 25; GC Rodríguez Iglesias, 'Gedanken zum Entstehen der Europäischen Rechtsordnung', 1999 1; P Eeckhout, 'The European Court of Justice and the Legislator', (1998) 18 *Yearbook of European Law* 1.

[11] See opinion 1/91, above n 6, and opinion 2/94, above n 16, which officially deals with the 'constitutional argument' in the context of competences and not the protection of its independence, which may nonetheless be regarded as the 'politically' underlying issue.

[12] Case 294/83 *Parti écologiste 'Les Verts' v European Parliament,* [1986] ECR 1339 at para 23.

[13] Case 6/64 *Costa v ENEL,* [1964] ECR 1251 at page 1269. In Case 26/62 *van Gend en Loos,* [1963] ECR 1 at page 25 the Court had still argued that 'the Community constitutes a new legal order *of international law*' (own emphasis).

[14] See now Art 6(2), 46(d) EU.

[15] See, *inter alia*, the Les Verts case, above n 12.

[16] Case C–376/98 *Germany v Parliament and Council* [2000] ECR I–2247.

[17] Case 26/62 *van Gend en Loos,* [1963] ECR 1 at page 4.

legal constitutionalism being largely the Court's own creation. Assuming that post-Nice will not revisit the very foundations of the Court's legal constitutionalism, the existing jurisprudence has to be accepted as the constitutional *status quo* despite the criticism the Court has come under for its activism. Given that the Court's legal constitutionalism provides a legally more or less satisfactory answer to three basic features of the post-Nice agenda (competences, fundamental rights and institutional balance), one might well ask what the post-Nice debate may add to the existing system. A comparison of the German and British constitutional tradition and emerging political post-Nice position, provides first possible answers, which will be discussed in detail in the second part of this article.

The German constitution provides for one of the strongest models of legal constitutionalism among the Member States—with the proactive *Bundesverfassungsgericht*[18] as its engine. It is therefore not surprising that most German politicians favour a binding Charter of Fundamental Rights and believe that the issue of competences should be resolved by judicial instruments.[19] They are regarded as a means of filling alleged loopholes in the Court's design of legal constitutionalism and are therefore motivated by the desire to reinforce legal constitutionalism on the European level. The opinion of the *Bundesverfassungsgericht's* President Limbach may be representative:

> (T)here is need of a constitution to confirm and delimit the power of Brussels. A constitution could at long last provide clarity, and not just about the rights of Union citizens. It should set bounds on Europe, and once and for all settle the tension between European and national law .... For it is a prime task of a modern constitution to set bounds on political rule, in order to guarantee the freedom of the citizens.[20]

On the background of the British constitutional model and in characteristic contrast to his German colleagues, Prime Minister Blair has pleaded the case for a political solution to the issue of competences.[21] In fact, the British experience with non-legal mechanisms of constitutional conflict resolution might be an important post-Nice contribution, even if recent domestic experiences within the context of European integration,[22] devolution,[23]

---

[18] The German federal constitutional Court; abbreviation: BVerfG.

[19] See the references below parts B and C.

[20] J Limbach, 'The Concept of the Supremacy of the Constitution', (2001) 64 *Modern Law Review* 1 at 10.

[21] See below II B.

[22] Cf P Craig, 'Britain in the European Union', in J Jowell/D Oliver (eds), *The Changing Constitution* (2000) 61 at 75–9. See also below part 3.

[23] On devolution and judicial review by the Privy Council see, for example, P Craig/M Walters, 'The Courts, Devolution and Judicial Review', 1999 *Public law* 274.

human rights protection[24] and the common law[25] might generally help the United Kingdom to accommodate itself to the existing model of European legal constitutionalism established by the Treaties and the Court.

Retrospectively, one should not forget that until the 1990s European political union and a real democratisation of European governance appeared as a remote project of the future. In the absence of democratic constitutionalism, the path of legal constitutionalism followed by the Court was a crucial tool for achieving European integration by depoliticising conflicts between the Member States.[26] If the development of democratic constitutionalism is the main post-Nice challenge, as will be argued later, the Court will in future no longer play the pivotal part it has played in the history of European integration hitherto. While it will continue to ensure that the achievements of its earlier jurisprudence are observed within the post-Nice framework, the development of democratic constitutionalism and other post-Nice issues will be left to the political actors.

C.   The Non-Statal European Constitution

Can there be a European constitution without a European state or is the political and academic debate on European constitutionalism an attempt to distract from the real development: the creation of a European 'superstate' replacing the Member States? It seems to be a common feature of the British and the German debate that constitutionalism is often linked to the concept of sovereignty and all-embracing statal competence. From this perspective, there are either sovereign Member States delegating some powers to the European Union or a new European 'superstate' replacing the Member States. Or, as Baroness Thatcher put it during the 2001 election campaign:

> The greatest issue in this election, indeed the greatest issue before our country, is whether Britain is to remain a free, independent nation state or whether we are to be dissolved in a federal Europe. There are no half-measures, no third ways and no second chances.[27]

---

[24] Cf on s 3(1) of the Human Rights Act 1998 eg D Feldman, 'The Human Rights Act 1998 and Constitutional Principles', 1999 *Legal Studies* 165 and N Bamforth, 'Parliamentary Sovereignty and the Human Rights Act 1998', 1998 *Public Law* 572.

[25] See for example the articles by T Allan, 'The Rule of Law as The Rule of Reason: Consent and Constitutionalism', (1999) 115 *Law Quarterly Review* 221 and J Jowell, 'Beyond the Rule of Law: Towards Constitutional Judicial Review', 2000 *Public Law* 671.

[26] Theoretical foundations of 'integration through law' are discussed, *inter alia*, by JHH Weiler, 'We Will Hearken ...', in *ibid* (ed), *The Constitution of Europe* (Cambridge, CUP, 1999) 221 and K Armstrong, 'Legal Integration: Theorizing the Legal Dimension of European Integration', (1998) 36 *Journal of Common Market Studies* 155.

[27] Cited after E MacAskill, 'Thatcher says never to single currency', The Guardian 23 May 2001, p 1.

Based on different ideas developed by various authors, this section outlines a theoretical concept of a non-statal but nonetheless original European constitution. It goes beyond the specific issues on the post-Nice agenda, for which it might nevertheless provide a theoretical foundation and orientation. After a brief look at the question of all-embracing sovereignty (a), the article presents the idea of a European *contrat social* as the theoretical basis of European public authority (b). On this basis, it will be possible to evaluate how far such a model can be reconciled with the British constitutional tradition (c). Finally, the article will consider how the national and the European constitutions inter-relate (d). In this section, in particular, space requires a concentration on one line of argument leaving aside many alternative arguments and views.

1.   *All-Embracing Sovereignty?*

The uncompromising confrontation of national independence and a European superstate in Baroness Thatcher's speech cited above, is based on the historical concept of post-Westphalian sovereignty as an all-embracing competence to regulate whatever happens within the territory of a state. In this traditional shape, sovereignty does not allow for a middle course, an adaptation to the 'postnational constellation'.[28] In order not to enter the debate on what sovereignty means in contemporary terms and whether the concept should be abandoned altogether,[29] this presentation may limit itself to reminding the reader that, despite the legal claim to abstract normative existence, the very foundations of law and constitutional theory depend on the social realities creating and supporting them. If the social realities change, law and constitutional theory have to take these changes into account.

Social scientists and economists have long argued that the increasing 'globalisation' of trade, investment, financial markets, transport, communication, migration and environmental challenges undermines the actual ability of states to act as 'sovereign' entities.[30] If public authority wants to avoid a loss of ability to influence social and economic developments, decisions have to be transferred to supranational levels creating a system of 'multi-level governance' as it has been described and analysed by political science.[31]

---

[28] J Habermas, *Die postnationale Konstellation* (Frankfurt, Suhrkamp, 1998) at 91.

[29] The work of Neil MacCormick continues to be an inspiring source for this debate, cf N MacCormick, *Questioning Sovereignty* 2nd edn, (Oxford, OUP, 1999).

[30] Cf, *inter alia*, Habermas, above n 28, A Giddens, *The Consequences of Modernity* (Cambridge, Polity, 1990), U Beck (ed), *Die Politik der Globalisierung* (Frankfurt, Suhrkamp, 1998). See also CMG Himsworth, 'In a State No Longer: The End of Constitutionalism', 1996 *Public Law* 639 at 643–8.

[31] See, eg, F Scharpf, 'The Problems Solving Capacity of Multi-Level Governance', (1997) 4 520 and the book edited by G Marks/F Scharpf/P Schmitter/W Streek (eds), *Governance in the European Union* (1996). Additionally, the pluralisation of modern societies challenges the

Thus, in a time in which most states have lost the real power to control many important developments affecting their territory, the traditional state-centred model of all-embracing sovereignty has become a judicial construction.[32] A non-statal, postnational constitutional theory tries to bridge the resulting gap. Based on the idea that public authority may be split between different levels of public governance, it is not an attempt to revisit sovereign statehood at the European level.[33] As long as several of these multiple tiers of governance qualify as a constitution—which will be discussed for Europe in the next section—there is a coexistence of two or more constitutional orders within a given territory. If all these constitutions are constitutions in their own right, none has a claim for all-embracing competence or sovereignty: they are non-statal constitutions.

2. European *Contrat Social*

If post-national constitutional theory may qualify a non-statal level of public governance as a constitution, this does not necessarily mean that every supra- or infranational level of governance actually has a constitutional nature. Besides the functional approach and the idea of legal and democratic constitutionalism, the democratic European context suggests another precondition for the existence of an original constitution in its own right: the concept of popular sovereignty and the idea of a *contrat social* as the theoretical foundation of society and public authority.[34] Popular sovereignty is a concept common to most Member States.[35]

---

concept of state sovereignty from within by dissolving its (mythical) foundation of national homogeneity, cf D Thym, *Die verfassungsgebende Gewalt in demokratischen Gesellschaften*, WHI Paper 1/97, online www.whi-berlin.de/thym.htm esp at paras 74–5.

[32] See also J Straw, *A Europe for its Citizens*, Lecture at the Royal Institute of International Affairs, London, 27 July 2001, online www.fco.gov.uk: 'In today's interdependent world, pooling sovereignty, when we choose to, is the way to strengthen sovereignty, not lose it.'

[33] One might, on the contrary, argue that a postnational constitutional theory tries to secure the achievements and values of national constitutionalism, eg by emphasising the necessity of democratic constitutionalism also on the European level.

[34] See for the contribution of English political philosophy Thomas Hobbes, *Leviathan* (London, Dent ed, 1994) and John Locke, *Two Treatises of Government* (London, Everyman ed, 1993). For an alternative model based on the concept of 'cosmopolitan ideas' as it has been developed, *inter alia*, by Immanuel Kant see P Eleftheriadis, 'The European Constitution and Cosmopolitan Ideals', (2001) 7 21 esp at 35–39.

[35] See the explicit references to popular sovereignty in the constitutions of all Republican Member States: Austria Art 1, Finlands 2(1), France Art 3(1), Germany Art 20 (1), Greece Art 1(2), Ireland Art 1, Italy Art 1(2) and Portugal Art 3(1). Even the constitutions of four monarchies explicitly refer to the concept: Belgium Art 33(1), Luxembourg Art 32, Spain Art 1(2) and Sweden Art 1(1): 'All public power in Sweden proceeds from the people.' Only the constitutions of Denmark and the Netherlands contain no explicit reference to popular sovereignty. On the United Kingdom see the following section.

Based on the assumption 'that the *contrat social*, the concept developed by Rousseau, does not necessarily create one unitary state',[36] Ingolf Pernice has repeatedly described and developed the idea that the European Treaties are already the expression of a European *contrat social*:

> The national ratification expresses the democratic choice of the citizens to create and develop the Union together with the citizens of the other Member States. In accordance with the conditions and procedures of national constitutional law the citizens of the Member States constitute supranational public authority through successive Treatie .... The European Treaties are therefore, much less fictitious than normal constitutions, the expression of a *contrat social européen*. They constitute a reciprocal arrangement, document the will of the citizens of the Member States to agree, again and again, on the common good and organise the process of the ever closer Union, i.e. integration. The Treaties are a 'constitutional contract' .... They constitute public authority in the same original way as the constitution of a state does.[37]

Even if one argued that Pernice's view was too optimistic and that at the current stage of European integration the original nature of the European constitution was not yet fully achieved, but continued to be—at least partially[38]—derived from the national constitutions,[39] the idea can serve as a point of orientation and alternative model of explanation at a time when the post-Nice process may be about to take a historic step towards the formal constitutionalisation of the Treaties.

The concept of a European constitution based on popular sovereignty and co-existing beside the national constitutions certainly implies that the latter no longer cover the competences in so far as public authority has been delegated to the European level. But it should be emphasised that even on the basis of this theoretical construction a withdrawal from the European Union would, not only for the United Kingdom, still be possible: either through a European constitutional resettlement in which the Union as a whole allows a Member

---

[36] I Pernice, Multilevel Constitutionalism and the Treaty of Amsterdam: European Constitution-making Revisited?, (1999) 36 *Common Market Law Review* 703 at 709.

[37] I Pernice, 'Europäisches und nationales Verfassungsrecht', 2001 *Veröffentlichungen des Vereins Deutscher Staatsrechtslehrer* (60) 148 at 166–7 (own translation, references omitted).

[38] W Hertel, *Supranationalität als Verfassungsprinzip* (Berlin, Duncker & Humboldt, 1998) esp 148–151 bases European constitutionalism on the citizens *and* the Member States. See also Case 26/62 *van Gend en Loos*, [1963] ECR 1: '[T]he Community constitutes a new legal order ... the subjects of which comprise not only Member States but also their nationals.'

[39] A substantial section of prominent German academics stick to the idea that a constitution—also within a European context—necessarily requires the framework of a state. Cf, for example, J Isensee, 'Staat und Verfassung', in J Isensee/P Kirchhof (eds), *Handbuch des Staatsrechts der Bundesrepublik Deutschland*, Volume 1 (Heidelberg, Müller 1987) § 13 at 87; P Kirchhof, 'Die Identität der Verfassung in ihren unabänderlichen Inhalten', in *ibid* § 19 at 18; E-W Böckenförde, *Staat, Nation, Europa* (Frankfurt, Suhrkamp, 1999) at 133 *et seq*; D Grimm, 'Die Zukunft der Verfassung', in UK Preuß (ed), *Zum Begriff der Verfassung* (Frankfurt, Fischer, 1994) 277 at 291.

State to leave the European Union (as happened with Greenland in 1983) or by means of a 'constitutional secession' in which the citizens of a Member State unilaterally take back the public authority they once delegated to Europe. Such a 'constitutional secession' could be expressed in an *actus contrarius* to the participation in the European *contrat social*: in the case of Britain through an Act of Parliament, possibly accompanied by a referendum.[40]

Generally, the concept of a European *contrat social* arguably has two main advantages: (1) it transcends the perspective of legal constitutionalism, which concentrates on the effects of European law in the Member States, by bringing in the idea that European law does not only apply directly to the citizens, but is also constituted by them. Thereby, it lays the theoretical foundation for the development of democratic constitutionalism. (2) If the European constitution has the same theoretical legitimacy as (most) national constitutions, you may construe their relationship on a non-hierarchical basis. Before the article turns to this crucial issue of European constitutional theory, it shall examine how far the concept of a European *contrat social* can be harmoniously combined with the very foundations of British constitutionalism, whose specificities in comparison to other Member States raise particular difficulties for an harmonious combination with European constitutional theory.[41]

3. The British Tradition

In the United Kingdom, the idea of an original, non-statal European constitution based on a direct delegation of public authority from the people is more difficult to combine with domestic constitutional theory. In the absence of any post-1689 dissent, which could not be resolved or at least defused within the existing constitutional framework,[42] it has seemed unnecessary to formally base British constitutional theory on the concept of popular sovereignty. In the classical Diceyan conception, the electors may well be 'the predominant part of the politically sovereign power',[43] but legal sovereignty is vested in the omnipotent Parliament. If Parliament can 'make or unmake any law whatever'[44] and does theoretically not depend

---

[40] The same procedure would have to be followed for an overall withdrawal in accordance with the prevailing British constitutional theory.

[41] An overview of more Member States is given by Pernice, above n 37, at 156–8.

[42] The main motivation behind the German adoption of the concept of popular sovereignty and the related concept that 'there is no more state than established by the constitution' (P Häberle, *Verfassungslehre als Kulturwissenschaft* 2nd edn (Baden-Baden, Nomos, 1998) at 620; own translation) after 1919 and the World War II was to accommodate the existing German constitutional theory to the new democratic environment.

[43] AV Dicey, *Introduction to the Study of the Law of the Constitution* 9th edn (London, MacMillan, 1945) at 76.

[44] *Ibid* 39–40.

on the delegation of public authority from the people, the co-existence of classic British constitutional theory and the idea of a European *contrat social* is difficult to convey.

Whereas the German federal tradition[45] certainly facilitates the acceptance of a complementary European constitution, co-existing besides the *Grundgesetz*[46] and the constitutions of the *Länder*,[47] the British debate about constitutional aspects of European integration still focuses on the domestic perspective and the pivotal question of parliamentary sovereignty. Not only the prevailing 'construction view'[48] but also Wade's 'technical revolution',[49] the revived discussion of 'fundamental laws'[50] and the changing interpretation of Parliamentary sovereignty within a common law context[51] discuss possible limitations of Parliamentary sovereignty on the basis of British constitutional law and are not based on the idea of an original European constitution.

Even if the United Kingdom continues to base its constitutional settlement on the legal sovereignty of Parliament and not on the legal concept of popular sovereignty, there seems to be no irreconcilable theoretical contradiction to assume that within the limited area of public authority conferred on the European Union a new constitution-based popular sovereignty has been established. Classic British constitutional doctrine would continue to apply domestically. While the British remain, in constitutional theory, 'subjects' within their national constitutional systems, they have constituted the European constitution as 'citizens'.[52] In 1980, long

---

[45] The concepts of federalism and popular sovereignty are combined in amendment X to the Constitution of the United States: 'The powers not delegated to the United States by the Constitution, nor prohibited by the States, are reserved to the States respectively, or to the people'.

[46] The constitution of the Federal Republic of Germany from 23 May 1949.

[47] The *Länder* are the German constitutional regions.

[48] Eg J Laws, 'Law and Democracy', 1995 *Public Law* 72 at 89 and T Hartley, 'The Constitutional Foundations of the European Union', (2001) 117 *Law Quarterly Review* 225.

[49] H Wade, 'Sovereignty—Revolution or Evolution?', (1996) 112 *Law Quarterly Review* 568 at 574.

[50] The revived discussion of whether there are 'fundamental laws', which have a higher constitutional value and are not subject to unconditional Parliamentary sovereignty, may be a prelude to this traditional argument being applied to the devolution Acts, the Human Rights Act and the European Communities Act. Cf lately N Walker, 'Beyond the Unitary Conception of the United Kingdom Constitution?', 2000 *Public Law* 384, E Wicks, 'A New Constitution for a New State? The 1707 Union of England and Scotland', (2001) 117 *Law Quarterly Review* 109 who both refuse the argument, which had been put forward prominently by P Allott, 'The Courts and Parliament: Who Whom?', (1979) 38 *Cambridge Law Journal* 79.

[51] Craig, above n 22, at 79: sovereignty of Parliament and constraints on its omnipotence 'must be justified by arguments of principle, which are normatively convincing.... These arguments would moreover be convincing and have force even if section 2(4) had never been included in the 1972 Act.' See also T Allan, 'Parliamentary Sovereignty: Law, Politics, and Revolution', (1997) 113 *Law Quarterly Review* 443.

[52] For T Allan, *ibid*, at 445 the 1975 popular consent is an important argument in his common law reasoning on the restriction of parliamentary sovereignty: 'A judge's ... belief that

before *Factortame*[53] and the current debate on European constitutionalism, Mitchell put forward a related argument:

> The change, which resulted from the exercise of a larger sovereignty and in which Parliament played its appropriate (but not legislative) role was an exercise of residual constituent power. The limitations upon Parliament result not from any exercise of self-limitation on its part, but from a constitutional re-arrangement among the Member States .... It can indeed be said that two constitutional systems co-exist on the territory of each Member State.[54]

4. Constitutional Federation v Federal Constitution

Probably the most important building block of European constitutional theory is the definition of the relationship between the European and national constitutions.[55] Building partly upon the work of Pernice, this section proposes to construe the relationship on the basis of a non-hierarchical 'constitutional federation' which may serve as an alternative model to avoid, unless politically desired, an orientation of the post-Nice discourse towards a proper 'federal constitution' of the European Union repeating the federalising development in the United States or Germany. After a presentation of the conceptual foundation of a non-hierarchical constitutional federation its practical difference to a federal constitution shall be put in concrete terms by proposing guidelines for several core post-Nice issues.

The concept of a non-hierarchical constitutional federation takes the idea of popular sovereignty as its starting-point: assuming that, at least in continental Europe, national and European constitutionalism are based on popular sovereignty and do therefore have the same theoretical legitimacy, the different constitutional orders co-exist on an equal footing. From a theoretical perspective, European constitutional theory may therefore construe their relationship, contrary to most federal constitutions,[56] on a non-hierarchical basis without an unconditional supremacy of European law over national law—and *vice versa*.

Parliament *and the people* had chosen to join such a supranational entity, understanding and accepting the legal and political consequences, would certainly be pertinent, if not necessarily conclusive' (emphasis added).

[53] *R v Secretary of State for Transport, exp. Factortame (No 2)* [1991] AC 603.
[54] J Mitchell, 'What Happened to the Constitution on 1st January 1973?', (1980) 11 *Cumbria Law Review* 69 at 82–3, last sentence 81. This view may have the additional attraction of not focusing on the judicial *Factortame* decision but the 1973 accession and the 1975 referendum as the moment of possible constitutional change. Although in contrast to strict Hartian thinking, the political decision characterising the possible adaptation of Parliamentary sovereignty is thereby not vested in the courts, but the citizens and Parliament.
[55] Again, space precludes even the most general discussion of the existing views.
[56] The supremacy of federal law is explicitly enshrined in most federal constitutions; cf Art 31 *Grundgesetz* and Art 6 of the US Constitution.

Since the human rights dispute between the *Bundesverfassungsgericht* and the Court of Justice seems to be settled at last even before the possible integration of the Charter of Fundamental Rights post-Nice,[57] the delimitation of Community competences remains the main potential reason for a clash between national constitutional orders and the European constitution—not only in Germany.[58] Assuming there was such a clash, the Court of Justice would certainly argue that it is the ultimate umpire of Community law and it would be right to say so solely from the point of view of the European constitution. But if the European and national constitutions are both based on popular sovereignty and are therefore equally legitimised and if, consequently, the relationship between the constitutional orders is non-hierarchical, the position of a national (constitutional) court arguing that the national constitution prevailed under specific circumstances would be equally correct.[59]

What seems to be a constitutional dilemma at first glance, may actually turn into a great strength of European constitutional theory: a non-hierarchical co-existence of national and European constitutions provides a theoretical explanation, which allows—and even requires—us to leave the question whether European or national law ultimately prevails, unresolved. Based on a principle of mutual respect between the constitutional orders in Europe, the rule of the game of judicial practice would be 'problem avoidance' instead of 'problem resolution.' The rather cooperative practice of the Court of Justice[60] might be regarded as an expression thereof as well as the 'relationship of cooperation' postulated by the German *Bundesverfassungsgericht*.[61]

Although neither the Court of Justice nor the German *Bundesverfassungsgericht* have so far explicitly recognised the argument outlined in this section, their case law on the relationship between national and European law contains elements of such a non-hierarchical relationship. The Court of

---

[57] See the contribution by Jürgen Schwarze in ch 20 of this book.

[58] For Germany see the following footnote. For the British perspective see P Craig, 'Report on the United Kingdom', in A-M Slaughter/A Stone Sweet/J Weiler (eds), *The European Courts and National Courts, Doctrine and Jurisprudence* (Oxford, Hart, 1998) ch 7 at p 206–9 who refers to Lord Bridge in *Factortame* (No 2), above n 53 at 659: 'Thus there is nothing in any way novel in according supremacy to rules of Community law *in those areas to which they apply* ...' (emphasis added). A comprehensive analysis of the situation in all Member States is given by FC Mayer, *Kompetenzüberschreitung und Letztentscheidung* (München, C H Beck, 2000).

[59] Cf eg Bundesverfassungsgericht, Cases 2 BvR 2134/92 & 2159/92 *Maastricht*, 89 BVerfGE 155 at 184; reported in English as *Manfred Brunner and Others v The European Union Treaty*, [1994] 1 *Common Market Law Review* 57 at para 49: if a Community measure was *ultra vires*, the 'German state organs would be prevented for constitutional reasons from applying them in Germany. Accordingly the Federal Constitutional Court will review legal instruments of European institutions and agencies to see whether they remain within the limits of the sovereign rights conferred on them or transgress them.'

[60] See above part B for its jurisprudence on human rights and competences, which was at least partly motivated by national constitutional caveats.

[61] BVerfG *Maastricht*, above n 59 at para 13.

Justice's doctrine of 'disapplication' in the case of conflict[62] avoids a claim to unconditional legal hierarchy as carefully as the constitutional caveats which the *Bundesverfassungsgericht* has postulated. In the case of an irreconcilable conflict between the hard core of the German constitution and European law, the latter may, similarly to the doctrine of disapplication, 'not be applied' within the German legal order.[63]

Building upon these ideas, Pernice has developed the concept of a European *Verfassungsverbund*, which might be translated as 'multilevel constitutionalism'[64] or 'constitutional federation'.[65] Although the constitutional federation builds upon the formal separation of the constitutional orders, Pernice emphasises various legal inter-connections and dependencies. He conceives the European Treaties and the national constitutions as complementary partial constitutional orders, which together form the constitutional federation:

> The term European *Verfassungsverbund* comprises the Member States and their supranational integration in its entirety. From the citizen's perspective the European constitution is a multilevel system, constituted and structured according to the different challenges in a system of 'multilevel constitutionalism'. Their inter-dependence forges the national and the European constitutional level into a single system, European and national constitutional law form a substantive legal unit.[66]

Apart from providing a conceptual foundation for a non-hierarchical relationship of European and national law, the idea of the national constitutions and their European counterpart co-existing on an equal footing can serve as an orientation for some political choices Europe faces in the post-Nice process. Unless politically desired otherwise, post-Nice should, in particular, preserve what you might call national constitutional autonomy.[67]

---

[62] Case C–213/89 *Factortame (No 2)*, [1990] ECR I–2243 at para 52: '[I]t was sufficient for the two rules concerning the presumption of compatibility and Crown immunity to be disapplied'.
[63] Explicitly Bundesverfassungsgericht, BvL 52/71 *Solange I*, 37 BVerfGE 271 at 281: 'The *Bundesverfassungsgericht* never rules on the validity or invalidity of Community law. It could only come to the conclusion that such a rule may not be applied by the authorities and courts of the Federal Republic of Germany' (own translation).
[64] Cf Pernice, above n 36.
[65] Cf WT Eijsbouts, 'Classical and baroque constitutionalism in the face of change (Review essay)', (2000) 37 *Common Market Law Review* 213 at 218. This English terminology reflects the German linguistic contrast between *Verfassungsverbund* (constitutional federation) and *Staatenverbund* (federation of states), which the *Bundesverfassungsgericht* has put forward in the *Maastricht* decision, above n 59 at para 39.
[66] Pernice, above n 37, at 173–4 (own translation; references omitted). He later combines the theoretical concept with answers to various questions of European law, including the European function of national authorities and the common responsibility for European core values, cf *ibid* at 176–86.
[67] See also recital 3 of the preamble of the Charter of Fundamental Rights: The Union respects 'the national identities of the Member States *and the organisation of their public authorities at national, regional and local levels*' (emphasis added).

Three issues on the post-Nice agenda are particularly liable for a limitation of this autonomy. If Europe wants to avoid a federalising avenue turning away from the non-hierarchical constitutional federation towards a federal constitution, post-Nice should: (1) not determine the powers of the regions in the European constitution, (2) not apply the Charter of Fundamental Rights to wholly internal situations in the Member States, and (3) not regulate the relations between the national parliaments and governments on the European level. We shall see later how this theoretical postulation is being translated into specific proposals.

D.   *The Challenge: Democratic Constitutionalism*

It has already been indicated and is well-known to every reader that there is another aspect of European constitutionalism besides the functional approach, the Court's legal constitutionalism and the European constitutional theory discussed hitherto: the democratic deficit. Contrary to the already existing legal constitutionalism (see above B), democratic constitutionalism within the framework of the Treaties[68] is largely no *status quo* but a project for the future. It will be argued that the post-Nice process can be seen as an agenda for the enhancement of democratic constitutionalism in the European Union. The view of Prime Minister Blair might be a good starting-point:

> There are issues of democratic accountability in Europe—the so-called demo-cratic deficit. But we can spend hours on end, trying to devise a perfect form of European democracy and get nowhere. The truth is, the primary sources of democratic accountability in Europe are the directly elected and representative institutions of the nations of Europe: national parliaments and governments. That is not to say Europe will not in future generations develop its own strong demos or polity, but it hasn't yet.[69]

Again, space precludes even a general outline of the academic reflections on European democracy—an issue which has been dealt with by many prominent authors.[70] This article instead focuses on the relevance of the

---

[68] The concept of 'democratic constitutionalism' does not build on the idea of a 'political con-stitution' in which the legal rules are neglected in favour of real power relations; cf for the British context J Griffith, 'The Political Constitution', (1979) 42 *Modern Law Review* 1. For a general critique of formal-legal constitutionalism in the European Union see G de Búrca, 'The Institutional Development of the EU: A Constitutional Analysis', in P Craig/G de Búrca (eds), *The Evolution of EU Law* (Oxford, OUP, 1999) 55 esp at 61–3.

[69] T Blair, *A Larger, Stronger, more Democratic Europe*, Speech to the Polish Stock Exchange, Warsaw, 6 October 2000, online www.number-10.gov.uk.

[70] The analytical overview by P Craig, 'The Nature of the Community: Integration, Democracy and Legitimacy', in *ibid*/G de Búrca (eds), above n 68, at 1–51 and the work of JHH Weiler, 'To Be a European Citizen: Eros and Civilization', in *ibid* (ed), *The Constitution of Europe*

academic discussion for the post-Nice process. If post-Nice is indeed mainly about the creation of European democratic constitutionalism, two connected aspects can be identified as underlying the emerging post-Nice discourse on this issue: the idea of two parallel sources of democratic legitimacy (a) and the desire to strengthen the truly European line of legitimacy by building a stronger European identity (b).

1. Two Sources of Democratic Legitimacy   Since the early days of European integration, observers and commentators have tended to portray a black and white picture of the forces behind European integration: you were either a federalist or a functionalist, supported either supranationalism or intergovernmentalism. Translated into the context of democratic constitutionalism, this dichotomy continues with those who support a democratisation of the European Union via the European Parliament holding the Commission accountable, whereas others favour the national parliaments controlling the (European) Council. Like all generalisations, this one has a damaging effect, once it prevents what seems to be a reasonable and pragmatic compromise.

So far, all actors in the post-Nice debate have paid at least lip-service to the ideal of a more democratic European Union. But as we shall see later when we look at the specific post-Nice proposals, most contributions have aligned themselves with either the European Parliament/Commission or the national parliaments/Council camp. A mutually reinforcing combination of the two sources of democratic legitimacy might not only be a compromise but indeed the best solution. A European constitutional theory understanding European integration as a *contrat social* between its citizens co-existing besides the *contrat social* upon which the national constitutions of the Member States are built, may serve as a theoretical foundation for a double source of democratic legitimacy confining the expression of the democratic will of the people to neither the national nor the European arena.[71]

The idea underlying complementary sources of democratic legitimacy is the concept of 'multiple *demoi*'. Weiler has argued forcefully in favour of multiple identity, which 'invites individuals to see themselves as belonging simultaneously to two *demoi*, based, critically, on different subjective factors of identification'.[72] This concept can arguably be based on the political, social and cultural inhomogeneity guaranteed by the protection of fundamental rights within our pluralistic democratic societies. If even within the nation state the common identity of the people is nowadays only

---

(Cambridge, CUP, 1999) 324–357 and, lately, I Ward, 'Beyond Constitutionalism: The Search for a European Political Imagination', (2001) 7 *European Law Journal* 24–40 should be highlighted.

[71] A combination of the two sources of legitimacy is examined by Hertel, above n 38, esp 151–183.
[72] Weiler, above n 70, 324 at 346.

a partial one qualified by legally protected pluralism, each citizen may find it easier to identify itself with variosus forms of regional, national and European belongingness supplementing his or her unique identity as an individual.[73]

Again, the German and British experiences with multiple identity vary. Whereas almost all Germans do already have a strong multiple identity as local, regional and national citizens on the basis of which they might accept an additional European level more pragmatically, the United Kingdom's experiences with quasi-federal forms of government are relatively recent and asymmetrically limited to some regions. The idea of a multiple public identity nourishing various sources of democratic legitimacy within a European constitutional federation is therefore more difficult to combine with the hitherto centralised British tradition. It may also explain the position of the British government on various post-Nice topics, rejecting the idea of an original European democracy co-existing with the national one.[74]

Before the article attempts to identify possible post-Nice answers to the challenge of democratic constitutionalism, the following citation from the *Maastricht* decision of the *Bundesverfassungsgericht* provides an apt summary of the concept of two complementary sources of democratic legitimacy for European public authority:

> If the Union carries out sovereign tasks and exercises sovereign powers for those purposes, it is first and foremost the national peoples of the member-States who, through their national parliaments, have to provide the democratic legitimation for its so doing. At the same time, with the building-up of the functions and powers of the Community, it becomes increasingly necessary to allow the democratic legitimation and influence provided by way of the national parliaments to be accompanied by a representation of the peoples of the member-States through a European Parliament as the source of a supplementary democratic support for the policies of the European Union. With the establishment of union citizenship by the Maastricht Treaty, a legal bond is formed between the nationals of the individual member-States which is intended to be lasting and which, although it does not have a tightness comparable to the common nationality of a single state, provides a legally binding expression of the degree of de facto community already in existence.[75]

2. Identity Building   To assume that a European *demos* may co-exist with the national one and establish a complementary source of democratic legitimacy for the European Union does not necessarily imply that it already exists. One may, on the contrary, argue that there is no more than a

---

[73] See in detail Thym, above n 31, esp paras 67–75.
[74] Eg by preferring democratic legitimacy through national governments in the Council to the control of the Commission by the European Parliament; cf below part II E 2.
[75] BVerfG *Maastricht*, above n 33 at para s 39–40.

rudimentary beginning of European identity. Leaving the empirical evaluation of its degree to social scientists,[76] the post-Nice process can, as indicated earlier, from a point of view of European constitutional theory be widely understood as a means of enhancing European identity and democratic constitutionalism.

Academic opinions on the nature of the identity, upon which the cohesion of a democratic *demos* depends, reach from the postulation of cultural homogeneity to the simple requirement of public awareness that European law collectively affects all citizens of the Union and that they can democratically influence the policy orientation. They also include the demand for a common vision of the organisation of society (*modèle social européen*), shared political values of democracy, human rights and the rule of law and the participatory approach in the field of economic regulation.[77] In the context of the post-Nice process, an intergovernmental conference or a constitutional convention can certainly not create common values or even a common cultural heritage, but the outcome, and maybe even the discourse as such, may enhance awareness among the citizens of the Union of belonging to a European polity, which at least aspires to be democratic. Several topics on the post-Nice agenda can be identified as such 'identity building' measures.[78]

The Charter of Fundamental Rights is certainly the prime example.[79] While it largely confirms the Court's jurisprudence from the perspective of legal constitutionalism, its symbolic significance in 'making those rights more visible'[80] is rather obvious. Also the simplification of the Treaties shall be achieved 'with a view to making them clearer and better understood'[81] and even the delimitation of competences may by means of intelligibility contribute to European identity building. Besides, an increased role for national parliaments might restrain the growing political apathy in many Member States, while a possible legal change in the electoral system for the European Parliament or an increased political importance of the European elections would strengthen the European source of democratic legitimacy.[82] Finally, the citizens might be more interested in electing a Parliament which passes 'laws' and 'framework laws' instead of directives and regulations and would more easily find their way around a Treaty, whose articles have an official title.

---

[76] See eg the analysis of J Schild, '*National v European* Identities? French and Germans in the European Multi-Level System', (2001) 39 *Journal of Common Market Studies* 331.

[77] Generally, see the articles above n 70, which all include extensive further references.

[78] *Inter alia*, R Smend, 'Verfassung und Verfassungsrecht' (1928), in *ibid* (ed), *Staatsrechtliche Abhandlungen* 3rd edn (1994) 128 at 136–70 has analysed the importance of various means of social 'integration' within the context of constitutional theory.

[79] But see critically as to a common European human rights conception P Leino, 'A European Approach to Human Rights? Universality Explored', (forthcoming).

[80] Charter of Fundamental Rights, recital 4 of the preamble.

[81] Declaration on the Future of the European Union (Nice) recital 5.

[82] For details see above part 1.

The formal adoption of a 'Constitution of the European Union' could certainly be the single most important identity building measure of the post-Nice process. Again, it would have little legal significance, if the substantive contents of this capital-C Constitution were largely identical to the current Treaties, which are already a constitution within the meaning of the European constitutional theory presented earlier. But not only if the adoption was accompanied by a European referendum, the existence of a 'Constitution of the European Union' would strengthen the feeling that 'we Europeans' are the source and object of a European public authority.

Given that the extension of Community competences does not feature on the post-Nice agenda and assuming that its impact on legal constitutionalism will be limited, the enhancement of democratic constitutionalism examined in this section is the prime motivation and objective of the post-Nice process. But even if post-Nice should agree on an ambitious package of identity building measures, the development of democratic constitutionalism in a constitutional federation remains a unique historical experiment whose outcome is uncertain and ultimately depends on its acceptance by the citizens.

II.   THE POST-NICE PROCESS

The second part of this article examines the agenda of the post-Nice process in the light of the European constitutional theory described hitherto. The term 'post-Nice process' originated in the ignorance of the geographical venue of the intergovernmental conference planned for 2004. Although this abstract terminology, whose meaning many citizens may not understand immediately, could impede the democratic transparency of the debate, it does adequately describe its substantive openness: contrary to Nice, post-Nice is not determined by any 'left overs'; the European Union has rather embarked on a journey, whose final destination 'post-Nice' has yet to be defined.

The official post-Nice agenda is set by the declaration on the future of the European Union annexed to the Treaty of Nice, which states rather vaguely:

The process should address, *inter alia*, the following questions:

— how to establish and monitor a more precise delimitation of powers between the European Union and the Member States, reflecting the principle of subsidiarity;

— the status of the Charter of Fundamental Rights of the European Union , proclaimed in Nice, in accordance with the conclusions of the European Council in Cologne;

— a simplification of the Treaties with a view to making them
clearer and better understood without changing their meaning;
— the role of national parliaments in the European architecture.[83]

But the Belgian Presidency, which will play a pivotal part in launching the
next stage of the process, has already indicated that it intends to extend the
post-Nice agenda to:

> the financing of the European Union, the decision-making procedures, the
> institutional architecture and the inter-institutional balance, the role of
> the regions, the treaty structure, a modernised *méthode communautaire* and
> the role of social dialogue and of civil society.[84]

Assuming that the original four topics agreed on by all Member States in Nice
will nonetheless be the focus of attention, this article concentrates on them and
refers to other aspects only in passing. After a look at the process itself (A), the
article shall therefore examine the future status of the Charter of Fundamental
Rights (B) and the delimitation of competences (C) before turning to the role
of national parliaments (D)—an issue which cannot be adequately discussed
outside the broader perspective of the general institutional balance in the
European Union (E). Finally, the simplification of the Treaties is addressed
within the context of their possible formal constitutionalisation (F).

When this contribution was finalised in autumn 2001, a remarkable
number of European politicians, including Prime Minister Blair, had
already expressed their view on the emerging debate.[85] Given the variety of
proposals and the prospect of an ever wider spectrum and number of
contributions in the near future, it is impossible to offer a detailed analysis
of all developments and proposals here. Instead, this analysis concentrates
on those proposals relating to the main post-Nice issues, which have a connection to European constitutional theory and may arguably have a good
prospect of being finally adopted.

---

[83] Declaration on the Future of the European Union (Nice) recital 5.
[84] The Belgian Presidency of the European Union (ed), *Priority Notes*, June 2001, online
www.eu2001.be at 8.
[85] See Blair, above n 69, and the German foreign minister Joschka Fischer, *Vom Staatenverbund
zur Föderation*, FCE special 2/2000, online www.whi-berlib.de/fischer.htm, the French president
Jacques Chirac, *Notre Europe*, Speech to the German *Bundestag*, 26 June 2000, online
www.elysee.fr, the Belgian prime minister Guy Verhofstadt, *A Vision for Europe*, Speech to the
European Policy Centre, Brussels, 21 September 2001, online www.premier.fgov.be, the German
president Johannes Rau, *Plea for a European Constitution*, Speech to the European Parliament,
March 2001, online www.bundespraesident.de, the Finnish prime minister Paavo Lipponen,
Speech to the College of Europe, Bruge, 10 November 2000, online www.vn.fi/vnk, the governing
German social democrats SPD (ed), *Leitantrag: Verantwortung für Europa*, online www.spd.de,
the Luxembourgian prime minister Jean-Claude Juncker, *Mes convictions pour l'Europe*, Speech
in the *Maison du Grand Duché de Luxembourg*, 15 May 2001, www.gouvernement.lu, the
Portuguese prime minister António Guterres, *The European Treaties revisited: What role for
Europe in the globalised world*, FCE 5/2001, online www.whi-berlin.de/guterres.htm, the French

A.   The Process

The post-Nice process will have three main stages: (1) a public debate in the Member States and on the European level, (2) an 'appropriate initiative for the continuation of this process'[86] to be agreed on by the European Council meeting in Brussels-Laken in December 2001 and (3) an intergovernmental conference to be convened in 2004.[87]

The public debate, which is to be launched in every Member State and on the European level, shall encourage 'wide-ranging discussions with all interested parties: representatives of national parliaments and all those reflecting public opinion, namely political, economic and university circles, representatives of civil society, etc'.[88] The encouragement of a truly open discourse during the post-Nice process is certainly a remarkable break with the intergovernmental past of earlier Treaty revisions, although it remains to be seen how far the actors of civil society will actually participate in the debate and whether the political actors will take their views into account.

At the time of writing, there were strong signs that the European Council meeting in Brussels-Laken in December 2001 would build upon the predominantly positive experience with the Convention, which had drafted the Charter of Fundamental Rights,[89] and launch another 'post-Nice convention' comprising members of national parliaments, the European Parliament, the Commission and national governments.[90] If the European Council in Brussels-Laken opts for a new convention—a model first used in England in the 17th century[91]—its influence will largely depend on its

prime minister Lionel Jospin, *L'avenir de l'Europe élargie*, Speech from 28 May 2001, online www.premier-ministre.gouv.fr, the President of the European Commission Romani Prodi, *For a Strong Europe, with a Grand Design and the Means of Action*, Speech to the Institut d'Etudes Politiques, Paris, 29 May 2001, online www.europa.eu.int/futurum; the Spanish socialist party PSOE (ed), *El futuro de Europa*, 5 June 2001, online www.europa.eu.int/futurum and the British Foreign Minister Jack Straw, above n 32.

[86] Declaration on the Future of the European Union (Nice) recital 4.
[87] *Ibid* recital 7.
[88] *Ibid* recital 3.
[89] On the drafting of the Charter of Fundamental Rights cf G de Búrca, 'The Drafting of the European Charter of Fundamental Rights', (2001) 26 *European Law Review* 126–38.
[90] The Benelux countries, including the incoming Belgian Presidency, seem to favour the term 'forum', cf Benelux (ed), *Benelux Memorandum on the Future of Europe*, June 2001, online www.europa.eu.int/futurum. Moreover, a convention/forum was supported, *inter alia*, by the European Parliament (ed), *Report on the Treaty of Nice and the Future of the European Union*, 31 May 2001, Doc. A5-0168/2001 at 38 and, after long discussions, by a majority of 10 out of 15 delegations in the Conference of National Parliaments COSAC (ed), Contribution from the XXIVth COSAC in Stockholm to the European Council, 22 May 2001, online www.europa.eu.int/futurum, conclusion 3. The German chancellor Gerhard Schröder has already indicated that the German government might be represented at the convention by Wolfgang Schäuble, the former leader of the Christian democrats.
[91] According to C Schmitt, *Verfassungslehre* 8th edn (Berlin, Duncker & Humboldt, 1993) at 85–6 the British conventions of 1660 and 1689 were the first in history and later adopted, *inter alia*, during the American war of independence and the French revolution.

working method: will it only discuss the constitutional development of the European Union in general terms or draft specific proposals for the intergovernmental conference? If proposals are drafted, will there be one draft Treaty or different alternatives among which the intergovernmental conference can pick and choose? Will there be formal votes or adoptions of proposals drafted by an influential presidium by consensus?[92]

The candidate countries from Central and Eastern Europe and the Mediterranean will be closely associated with the process. Any country whose accession treaty will have been signed—but not necessarily ratified—in 2004 will participate in the final intergovernmental conference with equal rights.[93] This is first of all a democratic necessity, but will also clarify that the accession is not the end but rather a beginning: post-Nice may answer many questions about the future of Europe, but the Union will remain an 'ever closer union,' in whose development the new Member States will participate. Thus, the active involvement of the candidate countries will help to bridge the often lamented dichotomy between enlargement and the possibility of further constitutional change post-Nice.

As mentioned at the outset, the final post-Nice choices will, again, be left to an intergovernmental conference. It remains to be seen whether the expected transparency and democratic aspirations of the public debate and the possible convention will create a momentum, which actually involves civil society as well as the general public and which could hardly be disregarded by Nice-style power politics of an intergovernmental conference gathering behind closed doors. If this was the case, the post-Nice process itself would be a remarkable step forward in enhancing the European identity among the citizens and an important building block for democratic constitutionalism. The final ratification by the citizens through their national parliaments or referenda would then only be a last democratic involvement in a process, which everybody could accept as a reformulation of the European *contrat social*.

B.   Charter of Fundamental Rights

The future status of the Charter of Fundamental Rights may turn out to be an uncontroversial post-Nice issue. Since there is already a new text, which the post-Nice process will probably not revisit, there is only one question left to answer: will the Charter of Fundamental Rights be formally integrated in the new Treaty? From the point of view of legal constitutionalism, the consequences of a full integration would be limited, as the Court of Justice already

---

[92] One hears that the forum/convention may be chaired by the former Finnish President Martti Ahtisaari.
[93] Declaration on the Future of the European Union (Nice) recital 8.

protects fundamental rights *de lege lata* (see above IB) and has started referring to the Charter as a declaratory confirmation of its jurisprudence.

Democratic constitutionalism could nonetheless be strengthened through the formal integration of the Charter of Fundamental Rights. The Charter would develop its identity-building potential, identified earlier, to the full, if it became an integral part of new Treaty/Constitution. The European identity of the citizens could be considerably reinforced, if the Charter symbolically expressed that the Union 'places the individual at the heart of its activities'.[94]

It has been elaborated earlier that a limitation of the fundamental rights of the European constitution on the exercise of European public authority prevents a federalisation of the European constitution (see above 4). Against this background, Article 51 of the Charter of Fundamental Rights should be scrutinised carefully. Although the limitation of the scope of the Charter to the European institutions and the 'Member States only when they are implementing Union law' laid down in this article largely reflects the case law of the Court of Justice,[95] the latter formulation may nonetheless be the gateway for a reversed European *Barron* decision, in which the Court of Justice follows the argument rejected by the US Supreme Court and applies the Charter of Fundamental Rights to wholly internal situations in the Member States, ie also to situations so far exclusively covered by national fundamental rights and the European Convention on Human Rights but not by the fundamental rights of EC law.[96] A clarification of Article 51 could avoid possible misinterpretations and preserve the European constitutional federation in the future.[97]

C.   Delimitation of Competences

During the intergovernmental conference, which finally agreed on the Treaty of Nice, the German *Länder* repeatedly urged the German government to press for a clearer delimitation of competences between the

---

[94] Charter of Fundamental Rights, recital 2 of the preamble.

[95] See, *inter alia*, Case 222/84 *Johnston v Royal Ulster Constabulary* [1986] ECR 1651; Case 5/88 *Wachauf v Germany* [1989] ECR 2609 and Case C–260/89 *Elliniki Radiophonia AE v Dimotki Etairia Plifoforissis and Sotirios Kouvelas* [1991] ECR I–2925 and L Besselink, 'The Member States, the National Constitutions and the Scope of the Charter', (2001) 8 *Maastricht Journal* 68 at 76–9.

[96] Cf *Barron v Mayor and the City Council of Baltimore*, 32 US 243, 8 L Ed 672 (1833). The pragmatism expressed by the President of the Bundesverfassungsgericht Jutta Limbach, who looks forward to a 'human rights competition' between the Bundesverfassungsgericht, the European Court of Human Rights and the Court of Justice, may be surprising to many British readers. Cf the contribution by Jürgen Schwarze in chapter 17 of this book. For more detail, D Thym, 'Charter of Fundamental Rights: Competition or Consistency of Human Rights Protection in Europe', (2001) XI *Finnish Yearbook of International Law* 11.

[97] One may add the sentence: 'Under no circumstances does the Charter apply to wholly internal situations in the Member States.'

European Union, the Member States and the regions in order to prevent what they regard as a steady limitation of their freedom to act. The idea of defining the powers of the regions in the European Treaties has already been rejected as a potential threat to the constitutional autonomy of the Member States, which should, unless politically desired otherwise, be preserved within a European constitutional federation and be protected against federalist tendencies (see above I.C. 4)—and it seems as if the German *Länder* do now support this view.[98] But even if the original starting point of the post-Nice process, the definition of the powers of the regions, is taken off the agenda, the remaining task of creating 'a more precise delimitation of powers *between the European Union and the Member States*, reflecting the principle of subsidiarity',[99] is by no means easy to achieve.

Generally, the delimitation of competences could turn into the most disputed item on the post-Nice agenda, if the different proposals are not limited to a clarification of the existing rules, but do include both a renationalisation and an extension of Community competences. It should be noted that European constitutional theory cannot provide any substantial guidance on this question, since any change in the extent of Community competences has to be decided on political grounds and is therefore outside the ambit of this contribution.

The challenge of democratic constitutionalism might be met by simply renaming Community competences, since a new terminology would render the scope and importance of European law more visible and enhance a feeling of 'shared destiny' upon which democratic constitutionalism can be built (see above I.D. 2). Thus, the wording of Article 3 EC and the specific Treaty articles could be replaced by a more systematic categorisation following *topoi* such as: exclusive, shared or supplementary powers and the coordination of national policies.[100] This attempt to clarify the existing competences would not affect their legal scope. Without legal side-effects, regulations could be called 'European laws,' whereas directives would become 'framework laws.'

Any political attempt to clarify the delimitation of competences should not forget that the existing system does, in principle, already fulfil the requirements of legal constitutionalism—even if the Court may be criticised for interpreting the extent of Community competences too generously (see above I.B). Given the German tradition of legal constitutionalism, it is

---

[98] W Clement, *Europa gestalten—nicht verwalten: Die Kompetenzordnung der Europäischen Union nach Nizza*, FCE 1/2001, online www.whi-berlin.de/Clement.htm at para 14. Given the asymmetry of the powers of the regions between and within some Member States, it would have been almost impossible to define the powers of all European regions in the European Treaties.
[99] Declaration on the Future of the European Union (Nice) recital 5 (emphasis added).
[100] The Common Commercial Policy is an example for exclusive competences, whereas environmental and transport policies could be officially called a shared competence and Art 151 EC on culture a supplementary power. Economic and employment policies are only coordinated on the European level.

not surprising that the prime minister of the largest German *Land,* Clement, has proposed to give the Committee of Regions the power to bring actions of annulment to the Court of Justice.[101] Like a new European Constitutional Council for the resolution of conflicts on competences, proposed by Weiler,[102] this would strengthen the procedural aspect of the present system of legal constitutionalism.

Prime Minister Blair has proposed a different model, which non-British observers might better understand against the background of the British constitutional tradition mentioned earlier:

> What I think is both desirable and realistic is to draw up a statement of the principles according to which we should decide what is best done at the European level and what should be done at the national level, a kind of charter of competences .... This Statement of Principles would be a political, not a legal document.[103]

If this charter of competences were to replace the current system of competences, which are legally defined and limited by the objectives of the various Community policies[104] and supplemented by the principle of subsidiarity and explicit limitations in certain areas,[105] this would constitute a radical brake with the present Treaties' legal constitutionalism and I personally doubt whether post-Nice could and should agree on such a constitutional about-turn.[106] It might be worth remembering that depoliticising European policy-making by a system of legal constitutionalism was originally a deliberate choice to ease political tensions among the European nation states.[107]

Nonetheless, Blair's proposal to delimit competences within the political process might be a solid foundation for an acceptable post-Nice compromise. As the experience of various federal States—including Germany—indicates that instruments of legal constitutionalism are hardly effective in limiting a process of centralisation in the field of shared competences, a procedural innovation might be a golden solution.[108] A 'subsidiarity

---

[101] Clement, n 98 above, at para 29.

[102] See now Weiler, above n 70, 353.

[103] Blair, above n 69. See also Straw, above n 32: '(W)e should have a political not a legal document .... We cannot sweep the Treaties aside and replace them with something new. Nor do we wish to. What, however, we can do is simplify the language in which they are written so that people can understand them.'

[104] The *tobacco advertisement* decision was based on the argument that the directive does not contribute to achieving the main objective of Art 95 EC: the establishment and functioning of the single market; cf above n 16.

[105] Cf eg Art 151(5) EC: 'excluding any harmonisation of the laws and regulations of the Member States.'

[106] See below part F on the question, whether the simplification of the Treaties might lead to a 'political' and a 'legal' part.

[107] See above part I.B.

[108] See also the Declaration on the Future of the European Union (Nice) recital 5, which calls upon post-Nice to '*establish and monitor* a more precise delimitation of powers' (emphasis added).

committee' (Pernice)[109] or a second parliamentary chamber composed of national parliamentarians (Blair and Fischer),[110] could render the legally rather toothless principle of subsidiarity political effective. Thereby, the alleged centripetal force might be countered within the current system of legal constitutionalism and without opening the Pandora's box of changing existing Community competences, which could easily become a political stumbling block for the whole post-Nice process.

D.   Role of National Parliaments

The prominent role national parliaments enjoy on the official post-Nice agenda is apparently the result of a direct intervention by Prime Minister Blair at the final stages of the Nice summit. The passage of his Warsaw speech cited earlier shows that he regards this initiative as a means of countering the alleged democratic deficit of the European Union.[111] Again, the various existing political proposals shall be examined in the light of European constitutional theory.

The most far-reaching involvement of national parliaments would be the creation of a second chamber of the European Parliament composed of national Parliamentarians.[112] Although this proposal may be rather convincing at first sight, a second guess advises caution. Apart from the complexity of a triangular co-decision procedure, the underlying assumption that the pooling of national parliamentarians in a second chamber would be accompanied by a transfer of the achievements of national democracy may be 'simplistic'. In fact, nothing guarantees that the media would cover the work of a second chamber as thoroughly as the developments in national parliaments. Moreover, the double workload as a national and European parliamentarian may simply exceed the capacity of its members and alienate them from their colleagues in the national parliaments and their constituencies.[113] Thus, a second chamber would not necessarily enhance democratic constitutionalism in the European Union.

If the post-Nice actors wanted to increase the role of national parliaments on the European level without going as far as creating a second

---

[109] I Pernice, 'Kompetenzabgrenzung im Europäischen Verfassungsverbund', 2000 866 at 876. On the limited importance of the principle of subsidiarity in the case law of the Court of Justice cf Case C–85/94 *United Kingdom v Council* [1996] ECR I–5755 and Case 233/94 *Germany v European Parliament and Council* [1997] ECR I–2405.

[110] Blair, above n 69, and Fischer, above n 85, para 35. See also the next section.

[111] Cf the citation above part I.D.

[112] See above n 110.

[113] This is emphasised by the President of the Committee on EU Affairs of the German Bundestag, who explicitly rejects the idea of a greater involvement of national parliaments on the European level, cf F Pflüger, *Die Beteiligung der Parlamente in der Europäischen Verfassungsentwicklung*, FCE 4/2001, online www.whi-berlin.de/Pflueger.htm esp at paras 67–8.

chamber of the European Parliament, they might opt for the model proposed by the French prime minister Jospin. In May 2001, he proposed transforming the existing Conference of European Affairs Committees (COSAC)[114] in to a 'European Congress,' which would meet regularly to discuss 'the state of the Union' and secure the respect of the principle of subsidiarity. Furthermore, such a Congress could vote for 'non-constitutional' amendments of the Treaties.[115]

From the point of view of European constitutional theory, it is important to remember that national parliaments are only one of two sources of democratic legitimacy in the European Union (see above I.D. 1). Rather than confusing the indirect legitimacy through national parliaments with the potential of European democracy expressed through the European Parliament by creating a second chamber, the system as a whole may be much more effective, if the role of national parliaments and the European Parliament was considerably strengthened within the present system. National parliaments should concentrate on scrutinising their national minister in the Council of Ministers, whereas the European Parliament should be primarily responsible for direct democratic control on the European level (see below II.E. 1).

Following this argument, the best solution might actually be to do almost nothing about national parliaments, since the relationship between national parliaments and the executives should remain the autonomous constitutional choice of each Member State,[116] within which the absence of a uniform European format encourages the development of new models and the adoption of best practices by other Member States. Of course, the existing safeguard measures for effective control by national parliaments of the European may be reinforced post-Nice, eg by extending the 'grace period' of six weeks between Community proposals and their final adoption, which the Treaty of Amsterdam introduced for the third pillar, to other areas[117] or by establishing a more efficient information exchange network, which ensures timely information for national parliaments.[118] Other forms of cooperation, such as joint sessions of specialised committees, may be realised without a formal provision in the new Treaty.[119]

---

[114] See part II of the Protocol on the Role of National Parliaments in the European Union (Amsterdam).

[115] Cf Jospin, above n 85. He does not elaborate on the procedure for securing the respect of the principle of subsidiarity, which might be modelled on the 'subsidiarity committee' proposed by Pernice, above n 109.

[116] See above part I.B. 4.

[117] Cf part I.3 of the Protocol on the Role of National Parliaments in the European Union (Amsterdam). In other areas the national parliaments are only informed (part I.1–2).

[118] In its post-Nice contribution the Conference of national parliaments established under part II of the said protocol points out that presently some national parliaments are not informed in time, cf COSAC, above n 90, conclusion 8.

[119] This and other proposals have been put forward by R Hazell, 'Westminster: Squeezed from Above and Below', in *ibid* (ed), *Constitutional Futures* (Oxford, OUP, 1999) 111 at 129–30.

Finally, it should be emphasised that national parliaments will be among the key actors of the post-Nice process itself. First, in a possible convention and later following the intergovernmental conference, when the final outcome of the post-Nice process will have to be ratified by national referenda or the national parliaments.

E.   Institutional Balance

Although the institutional balance between the existing institutions does not feature explicitly on the post-Nice agenda, the working programme of the incoming Belgian Presidency and the speeches by various European politicians on the post-Nice process suggest that the post-Nice debate will embrace the European institutions as well.[120] After some remarks on the future role of the European Parliament (1) this article discusses whether the Commission or the Council (or both) should be regarded as the foundation of a future 'European government' (2). Generally, the issues of institutional balance, which will be discussed post-Nice, will probably not revisit the Treaty of Nice. Whereas the latter concerned mainly the intra-institutional balance, the post-Nice process will discuss the inter-institutional balance.

1.   European Parliament

The European Parliament has rightly been identified as the main 'winner' of the past Treaty revisions, when the co-decision procedure was constantly extended to an ever wider area of Community policy. Moreover, the European Parliament's right to confirm or reject a new Commission and the possibility of a motion of censure have increased its influence over the European Commission. But as the turnout in the European Parliament elections has nonetheless decreased in 1999, these increased powers have apparently not enhanced the connection the citizens of the Union feel with the Parliament. This might partially originate in the technical abstractness of the Parliament's powers. Identity building measures making the powers of the Parliament more visible may therefore be an important post-Nice contribution to democratic constitutionalism in the European Union.

The elections of the European Parliament could be further 'politicised,' if the voters felt that they made a real political choice. This could for example be achieved, if the European political party or coalition of parties, which

---

[120] See also the Declaration on the Future of the European Union (Nice) recital 6: '[T]he Conference recognises the need to improve and to monitor the democratic legitimacy and transparency of the Union and its institutions, in order to bring them closer to the citizens of the Member States.'

won the European elections,[121] pro-actively nominated a candidate as the future President of the Commission instead of simply confirming or rejecting the choice of the national governments.[122] Possibly in combination with a uniform election procedure—either through European lists[123] or regional constituencies enhancing the connection of Parliamentarians with the citizens[124]—this would entail a personification of the European elections, which seems to be a prerequisite of modern democracies. By giving them the possibility of voting for or against the proposed Commission, the citizens of the Union would finally feel that their vote does really matter.

Given the almost certain opposition by some Member States, it seems futile to elaborate any further on a European tax replacing the current national contributions to the EU budget,[125] even if one might rather convincingly argue that a European tax could be an effective building block for democratic constitutionalism. Assuming that a European tax would not be higher than the current national contributions and that any change would require unanimity in the Council and ratification by the Member States,[126] a European tax would not change much in practice; but it could create a European 'taxpayer identity' upon which a European public discourse could be built. Turning an historic slogan upside down, one might say: 'no representation without taxation'.

2.   *Commission v Council?*

A certain tension between the Commission and the (European) Council has been noticed by many observers. The underlying tension between the two institutions may be the competing aspiration to become the 'European government' which takes policy initiatives and is in charge of policy orientation. The media hype following the recent proposal of the German social democrats

> to create a European system with a balance of power ... by reforming the Commission to become a strong European executive instance ... and by

---

[121] The contribution of political parties at European level 'to forming a European awareness' is explicitly recognised by Art 191 EC.
[122] Cf Jospin, above n 85. The Benelux countries propose a direct election, cf Benelux, above n 90, s IV. The German Christian democrats have already considered nominating the current Luxembourgian prime minister Jean-Claude Juncker as a possible President of the Commission after the 2004 elections, cf Pflüger, above n 113, at para 97.
[123] As proposed by the Spanish socialists PSOE, above n 85. Cf also R Toulemon, 'Quelle constitution pour quelle Europe', 2001, 293 at 300, proposing to elect 5 or 10% of all MEPs on the basis of pan-European lists.
[124] Cf Jospin, above n 85.
[125] As proposed by Prodi, above n 85.
[126] Cf the current procedure under Art 269 EC.

expanding the Council to become a [parliamentary] Chamber of European Nations[127]

shows that the debate is highly sensitive.

The debate seems to originate in the ambivalence of the current institutional balance according to which executive functions are vested in the Commission in the first pillar, whereas the Council has created its own administrative foundation in the second and third pillar.[128] As long as this attribution of executive powers is not changed fundamentally post-Nice, a lawyer may wonder what the German social democrats mean when they contrast the 'executive' functions of the Commission with the 'legislative' future of the Council.[129] First indications show that some larger Member States like the United Kingdom will reject any plan to strengthen the Commission substantially, whereas smaller Member States, especially the Benelux who fear a *directoire* of big Member States in the Council, will resist attempts to build a European government upon the (European) Council. Faced with such a deadlock, Jospin's position might turn out to be the post-Nice orientation: 'Although each of the institutions shall be reinforced in order to make European decision-making more efficient, the triangular institutional equilibrium shall be maintained'.[130]

The previous section has already outlined the proposal to strengthen the Commission by linking its composition more directly to the European elections. If the post-Nice process were to come to the conclusion that the role of the (European) Council should be strengthened, they could contemplate a permanent Council of Ministers[131] and sanction the currently largely unofficial role of the European Council in all pillars. Jospin has already taken up the idea, originally proposed by Blair, of the European Council adopting a legislative agenda for the European Union.[132] Finally, the position of the High Representative for the Common Foreign and Security Policy, currently held by Javier Solana, will certainly be discussed post-Nice, within the broader context of streamlining the external representation of the European Union, whose present division between the Commission,

---

[127] SPD, above n 85, ss 9 and 10.
[128] Cf the bodies of the Common Foreign and Security Policy and the new Common Security and Defence Policy in the second and Europol, the future Eurojust and the former Schengen Secretariat, which is now integrated in the Council Secretariat, in the third pillar.
[129] The specific proposals of the German social democrats for the second and third pillar do not propose a transfer of administrative functions to the Commission, which is arguably the only legal manifestation of a more executive Commission and a legislative Council. Cf SPD, above n 85, ss 4 and 6.
[130] Jospin, above n 85, section III.3 (own translation).
[131] Jospin, above n 85.
[132] *Ibid* favours a pluri-annual programme initiated by the Commission or the European Parliament, whereas Blair, above n 69, had simply proposed 'an annual agenda for Europe, set by the European Council' (apparently without major involvement of the Commission, as is already the case with common strategies under Art 13 EU).

the High Representative and the Council Presidency is widely regarded as being inefficient.[133]

Most changes outlined in this section would leave the current institutional balance largely untouched. Therefore, the development of a more clear separation of powers, as it exists in the Member States, will probably have to be left to future constitutional changes. From the point of view of European constitutional theory, it is worth remembering that all changes in the institutional balance will, in principle, not affect the theoretical conclusion that the interaction of the various institutions fulfils constitutional functions.[134]

F.   Simplification of the Treaties

Two years after the entry into force of the re-numeration of the EC Treaty, lawyers should prepare themselves for another memory training exercise, since post-Nice has been given the official task of considering 'a simplification of the Treaties with a view to making them clearer and better understood without changing their meaning'.[135] Any simplification will certainly entail some form of re-numeration, especially if the present multi-Treaty structure is to be overcome, the complexity of which undermines the intelligibility of Community law for non-specialised lawyers, let alone for citizens without a legal background.

The creation of a single Treaty will be facilitated by the phasing out of the European Steel and Coal Community Treaty in 2002. But a merger of the present three pillars is impeded by the intergovernmental character of the second and third pillar. In this context, the largely intergovernmental cooperation of economic and employments policies[136] is certainly a precedence that the intergovernmental and the Community method can co-exist in a single Treaty document. But several problems do nonetheless persist: if the substance of the new single Treaty shall not differ from the present situation, Article 35 EU on the Court's jurisdiction in the present third pillar will have to be integrated in the new single Treaty alongside the 'normal' rules on the Court's jurisdiction and the existing *lex specialis* in Article 68 EC. The three pillar structure may well be eliminated thereby, but the persisting substantive differences would undermine the aim of making the new Treaty 'clearer and better understood'.[137]

---

[133] For more detail, see I Pernice, D Thym, 'A New Institutional Balance for European Foreign Policy?', (2002) 7 *EFA Rev* 369–400.

[134] Cf above part I.A.

[135] Declaration on the Future of the European Union (Nice) recital 5.

[136] Cf Art 98–104 and 125–30 EC.

[137] Besides the rules on the Court's jurisdiction, the integration of the second and the third pillar would require special rules on instruments and procedures (cf Art 249–52 EC; Art 12 *et seq*, 34 EU) and raise difficult issues concerning the institutional balance (the administrative

The post-Nice process might therefore decide to build upon the proposal of the European University Institute for a simplified 'Basic Treaty of the European Union',[138] whose 95 articles would be legally specified by the EC Treaty and two protocols on the present second and third pillar annexed to the Basic Treaty. Assuming that it would not derogate from the legal norms contained in the more specific instruments,[139] the Basic Treaty could indeed be a rather intelligble instrument, which does not change the legal *status quo*.

As mentioned earlier, the most important identity-building measure enhancing democratic constitutionalism could be the creation of a single Treaty called the 'Constitution of the European Union.' Its mere existence could strengthen the feeling that 'we Europeans' are the source and object of European public authority[140] and might therefore contribute to European identity building much more than a truly intelligible Treaty, which most citizens would read as rarely as their national constitutional documents, whose integrative force is arguably based on the abstract knowledge that they exist. Although the formal constitutionalisation does not feature officially on the post-Nice agenda, there is already strong support for this idea in many Member States.[141] But even if the legal substance of the Constitution were identical with the current Treaties, some Member States might have strong political objections to formal constitutionalisation.[142] Maybe the adoption of a simplified 'Constitutional Treaty of the European Union' could be a compromise, on which all post-Nice actors could finally agree.

III.   PERSPECTIVES

The article has identified various inter-connections between European constitutional theory and the post-Nice agenda, which might serve as a

---

sub-structure the Council has established outside the EC Treaty may arguably be contrary to the Commission's executive function in the first pillar, cf above n 135). Moreover, legal issues, such as the application of the *ERTA*-principles on external competences to the present third pillar, would have to be resolved.

[138] Robert Schuman Centre for Advanced Legal Studies at the European University Institute, *Draft Basic Treaty of the European Union* (2000).

[139] Cf clause 88 of the EUI-proposal.

[140] See above part I.D. 2.

[141] Support is particularly strong in Germany, cf Fischer, Rau, SPD, all above n 85. But in favour also Chirac, Verhofstadt and PSOE, all above n 85, and the European Parliament, above n 90, at 6.

[142] Lipponen, Juncker and Jospin, all above n 85, are sceptical and point to the necessary support of the public. Blair, above n 69, has argued: 'I suspect that, given the sheer diversity and complexity of the EU, *its constitution*, like the British constitution, will continue to be found in a number of different treaties, laws and precedents' (emphasis added). Pragmatically, Straw, above n 32: 'We should not reject other people's ideas simply because of the words they use. As Samuel Johnson said, "words are but the signs of ideas". So let us not get hung up on labels, and look instead at the ideas behind them.'

foundation and orientation for the discussion. In particular, European constitutional theory provides a conceptual basis for a non-statal European constitution co-existing with the national constitutions on a non-hierarchical basis. Based on the concept of popular sovereignty, it furthermore supports the enhancement of democratic constitutionalism, which appears as the main post-Nice challenge. The analysis of the debate on the specific post-Nice topics shows various proposals, which could actively contribute to achieving this goal. It remains to be seen whether the envisaged transparency and public involvement in the post-Nice process actually develops a momentum, which is in itself an important building block for democratic constitutionalism.

It cannot be ruled out that the final outcome of the post-Nice process will ultimately depend on items beyond the official post-Nice agenda—such as the result of a possible British euro-referendum or attempts to link the constitutional post-Nice process to the envisaged reform of the Common Agricultural Policy and the structural funds. A possible convention will play a crucial part in preventing such a development and in preparing a draft Treaty, which contains more than a lowest common denominator, but to which all Member States can nonetheless agree at the final intergovernmental conference. Given the limited legal significance of most post-Nice topics in comparison with the paramount challenge of democratic constitutionalism, the historical significance of the post-Nice process will ultimately depend on whether it has strengthened the bond between the European constitution and the constitutional sovereign: the people.

Part II

The Treaty of Nice

6

Assessment of the Treaty of Nice—Goals of Institutional Reform

JOHN A USHER*

I. BACKGROUND

THE ENTRY INTO force of the Treaty of Nice and the signature of the Treaty of Accession in 2003 confirm that enlargement and the Treaty of Nice are in reality necessary companions. Both the legal requirement for the Intergovernmental Conference which led to the Treaty of Nice, and its parameters, flow from the 'Protocol on the institutions with the prospect of enlargement of the European Union' agreed at Amsterdam.

The requirement was in the second paragraph of that Protocol which provided that:

> at least one year before the membership of the European Union exceeds twenty, a conference of representatives of the governments of Member States shall be convened in order to carry out a comprehensive review of the provisions of the Treaties on the composition and functioning of the institutions.

The basic parameters were laid down in the first paragraph:

> at the date of entry into force of the first enlargement of the Union, notwith-standing [Article 213(1)] of the TEC, the Commission shall comprise one national of each of the Member States, provided that, by that date, the weighting of the votes in the Council has been modified, whether by reweighting of the votes or by dual majority, in a manner acceptable to all Member States, taking into account all relevant elements, notably compensating those Member States which give up the possibility of nominating a second member of the Commission.

* Salvesen Professor of European Institutions and Director of the Europa Institute, University of Edinburgh.

From this it is clear that:

— The problems at issue were known, but not resolved, at Amsterdam,
— The problems arise from the prospect of enlargement,
— A linkage is made between voting rights in the Council and the size of the Commission which might seem inappropriate given that the Council comprises representatives of the Member States whereas the Commissioners have a legal duty to be independent and not to take instructions from Member States, *but*
— The Protocol effectively requires an overview to be taken of the institutional structure of the EU before enlargement.

The mandate and agenda for the IGC in 2000 were set by the European Council meetings in Cologne (3–4 June 1999) and Helsinki (10–11 December 1999) and further matters were added by the Feira European Council (19 and 20 June 2000). While the Treaty of Nice has received a rather negative press, it has to be accepted that the matters left unresolved at Amsterdam have now been resolved in a new Protocol on the Enlargement of the EU setting out the rules applying from 1 January 2005 with regard to the Council and Commission and from 1 January 2004 with regard to the European Parliament, accompanied by a Declaration on the Enlargement of the EU setting out the common position to be adopted by Member States at the accession conferences. There are however other important reforms, relating in particular to the European courts, and to the use of enhanced cooperation.

II.   THE MAIN ISSUES

a.   Council

The basic rule laid down by Article 148(1) of the EC Treaty has always been that 'save as otherwise provided in this Treaty, the Council shall act by a majority of its members'. There were however relatively few provisions in the Treaty which did not provide otherwise, thus allowing the Council to act by a simple majority, and their number has been reduced further by the Single European Act and the Maastricht Treaty. Critics of the Single European Act would in fact count it as a retrograde step that whereas the old Article 49 of the EC Treaty, dealing with legislation on the free movement for workers, allowed the Council to act by a simple majority, albeit without being expressly required to consult the European Parliament, the version introduced by Article 6(3) of the Single European Act required the Council to act by a qualified majority, even if it was in cooperation with the European Parliament (and further amendment by the Maastricht Treaty introduced the co-decision procedure to this provision).

On the other hand, simple majority voting remained possible in the area of vocational training under Article 128 of the original version of the EEC Treaty, a provision held to be wide enough to cover the second phase of the programme on cooperation between universities and industry regarding training in the field of technology (COMETT II) in Cases C–51, 90 and 94/89 *United Kingdom, France and Germany v Council*,[1] until its replacement by the more specific provisions on education introduced by the Maastricht Treaty. It may however be observed that whereas the current Article 126 on education allows the Council to act in codecision with the Parliament, Article 127 on vocational training requires it to use the cooperation procedure.

These procedures, introduced by the Single European Act and the Maastricht Treaty, and simplified by the Treaty of Amsterdam, have led to a greatly increased use of qualified majority voting, since both procedures involve the use of that system in the Council. The original version of the EC Treaty did, of course, contain a number of provisions allowing for a qualified majority to be used, but the opportunity was very rarely taken to make use of it. This, to a large extent, is usually attributed to the influence of the so-called Luxembourg Accords of 1966. In anticipation of the introduction of qualified majority voting in the Council of Ministers with regard to agricultural legislation under Article 43(2) and (3) of the EC Treaty, at the end of the second stage of the original transitional period (ie 1 January 1966), the French government pursued its 'empty chair' policy in the second half of 1965, refusing to send a Minister to attend Council meetings. The Accords, which in reality appeared to be no more than a press release recording the terms of the settlement under which France agreed to end its 'empty chair' policy, record the agreement of the Member States that even where decisions could be taken by a majority vote, where very important interests of a Member State were at stake, the members of the Council would endeavour to reach solutions which could be adopted by all the members of the Council, and a second paragraph added that the French delegation considered that where very important interests were at stake, the discussion must be continued until unanimous agreement was reached. Whatever may be the precise legal status of this agreement to disagree, it has been of considerable political importance. It gave rise to what was effectively a convention that policy-making legislation would only be adopted in the Council when a consensus had been achieved; so, for example, it took 17 years to reach agreement on a Directive concerning the activities of architects. However, on one of the few occasions on which the United Kingdom formally invoked the Luxembourg accords, in relation to the 1982 agricultural prices, a vote was still taken and the United Kingdom was out-voted. It may nevertheless be doubted whether all the participants

---

[1] [1991] ECR I–2757.

intended simply to override the Luxembourg Accords: it would appear that France (which voted with the majority) took the view that the agricultural prices as such were not 'very important interests' for the UK, whose real argument was over contributions to the EC budget.

That the use of unanimity, albeit with abstentions, was really a matter of political will, rather than legal obligation, is illustrated by the fact that although until 1986 the number of decisions taken by the Council on a majority basis barely reached double figures in any one year, in 1986, even though the Single European Act was not yet in force, during the first half of the year under the Dutch Presidency, some 43 items of legislation were adopted on a majority basis, and in the second half of the year, under the United Kingdom presidency, no less than 55 legislative acts were adopted on a majority basis. Subsequently, qualified majority voting has become the norm in most areas of Community policy-making (with the notable exception of taxation).

Qualified majorities involve a system of weighted voting, approximately related to the size of the Member State, so that the four big Member States, the United Kingdom, France, Germany and Italy, each have 10 votes, whereas at the other end of the scale, Luxembourg has two votes.[2] Until the accession of Spain and Portugal in 1986, the system was designed to ensure that no more than one big Member State could be out-voted, but that the big Member States could not by themselves out-vote the smaller Member States. However, from 1986 onwards, it has in fact been possible for two of the large Member States to be out-voted on a qualified majority vote; in other words, France and the United Kingdom, for example, could vote against a proposal and it could still become Community law. This trend has been continued following the accession of Sweden, Austria and Finland (though it is still not possible for three big states to be outvoted), and gave rise to UK resistance, which led to the so-called 'Ioannina compromise'. While in principle following the 1995 accessions a qualified majority requires 62 of the total of 87 votes distributed between the Member States, under that political compromise,

> if members of the Council representing a total of 23 to 25 votes indicate their intention to oppose the adoption by the Council of a decision by qualified majority, the Council will do all within its power to reach, within a reasonable time and without prejudicing the obligatory time limits laid down by the Treaties and by secondary legislation, such as those in Articles [251] and [252] of the Treaty establishing the European Community, a satisfactory solution that can be adopted by at least 65 votes. During this period, and with full regard for the Rules of Procedure of the Council, the President, with the assistance of the Commission, will undertake any initiatives necessary to facilitate

[2] EC Treaty Art 205.

a wider basis of agreement in the Council. The members of the Council will lend him their assistance.

This appears to be an attempt (albeit limited in scope) politically to preserve the rights of what would have been a blocking minority before the 1995 accessions (when a qualified majority was 54 out of 76 votes). Its status would however appear to have been enhanced by a Declaration to the Final Act introduced by the Treaty of Amsterdam to the effect that 'until the entry into force of the first enlargement it is agreed that the decision of the Council of 29 March 1994 ("the Ioannina Compromise") will be reconducted'.

Indeed, the Council Secretariat calculated that if the previous trend in the development of qualified majorities continued unaltered, in a Community of 28 (including East European and Mediterranean countries) a group of States representing less than half of the total population could constitute a qualified majority.

While the problem was left unresolved at Amsterdam, the solution adopted in the Treaty of Nice involves reweighting in favour of larger Member States (which for these purposes include Spain, since Spain is a Member State from which two Commissioners are currently appointed) and the imposition of a population requirement. Article 3 of the Protocol on the Enlargement of the EU provides that as from 1 January 2005, where the Council is required to act by a qualified majority, the votes of its members shall be weighted as follows:

Belgium 12
Denmark 7
Germany 29
Greece 12
Spain 27
France 29
Ireland 7
Italy 29
Luxembourg 4
Netherlands 13
Austria 10
Portugal 12
Finland 7
Sweden 10
United Kingdom 29

It is further provided that acts of the Council shall require for their adoption at least 169 votes in favour (out of 237) cast by a majority of the members where the Treaty requires them to be adopted on a proposal from the Commission, and that in other cases, for their adoption acts of the Council shall require at least 169 votes in favour, cast by at least two-thirds of the members. In practical terms this continues however to mean that two big States may be outvoted, though the position of the bigger States is reinforced from 2005 by the population requirement in Article 205(4), which declares that when a decision is to be adopted by the Council by a qualified majority, a member of the Council may request verification that the Member States constituting the qualified majority represent at least 62 percent of the total population of the Union. If that condition is shown not to have been met, the decision in question shall not be adopted.

This Protocol must be read with the Declaration on the enlargement of the European Union also adopted at the Nice IGC. This Declaration sets out 'the common position to be adopted by the Member States at the accession conferences', as regards the distribution of seats at the European Parliament, the weighting of votes in the Council, the composition of the Economic and Social Committee and the composition of the Committee of the Regions.

With regard to the weighting of votes in the Council, it sets out figures for the Member States and for all those States with which negotiations have begun:

Germany 29
United Kingdom 29
France 29
Italy 29
Spain 27
Poland 27
Romania 14
Netherlands 13
Greece 12
Czech Republic 12
Belgium 12
Hungary 12
Portugal 12
Sweden 10
Bulgaria 10
Austria 10
Slovakia 7
Denmark 7
Finland 7
Ireland 7
Lithuania 7
Latvia 4
Slovenia 4
Estonia 4
Cyprus 4

Luxembourg 4
Malta 3

It may be observed that while the Treaty of Nice may generally be regarded as reinforcing the position of the large Member States, Spain and Poland in particular are favoured by this formula, and, for example, a combination of the Czech Republic, Hungary and Slovakia would have more votes than a large Member State with less than half the population.

Out of the total of 345 votes accorded under this formula, the Declaration envisages that acts of the Council should require for their adoption at least 258 votes in favour, subject to the same caveats as under the Protocol on Enlargement, including the requirement of verification that the Member States constituting the qualified majority represent at least 62 percent of the total population of the Union. The mathematics of this means that if all these States were to become Members of the EU, it would at last be possible for three large Member States to be outvoted, unless one of them was Germany, in which case the population threshold would not be met. This trend is further reinforced by a further Declaration on the Qualified Majority Threshold and the Number of Votes for a Blocking Minority in an Enlarged Union, which states that:

> Insofar as all the candidate countries listed in the Declaration on the enlargement of the European Union have not yet acceded to the Union when the new vote weightings take effect (1 January 2005), the threshold for a qualified majority will move, according to the pace of accessions, from a percentage below the current one to a maximum of 73.4 percent. When all the candidate countries mentioned above have acceded, the blocking minority, in a Union of 27, will be raised to 91 votes, and the qualified majority threshold resulting from the table given in the Declaration on enlargement of the European Union will be automatically adjusted accordingly.[2a]

This presumably means that the qualified majority will be reduced to 255, which in turn means that the population requirement is likely to play an increasingly important role.

On the other hand, it may be observed that while the current qualified majority represents about 71 percent of the weighted votes, in those areas where it was anticipated under the Maastricht Treaty that Community activity might involve less than all the Members of the Community, notably under the Social Protocol[3] and eventually under the third stage of Economic and Monetary Union,[4] a qualified majority was reduced to two-thirds of the available votes. This model has not been followed in the Treaty

---

[2a] Under the 2003 Treaty of Accession, a qualified majority is 232 out of 311 votes.
[3] Art 2.
[4] EC Treaty Art 122(5).

of Amsterdam: in the Title on free movement of persons, asylum and immigration, in which the United Kingdom, Ireland and Denmark do not in principle participate, a qualified majority is defined as 'the same proportion of the weighted votes of the members of the Council concerned as laid down in Article 205(2)', and the same formula is used in the provisions on Closer Cooperation and Flexibility. However, the Amsterdam Treaty did not amend the EMU provisions introduced at Maastricht, nor did the Nice Treaty, so that for the 12 participants in EMU a qualified majority remains two-thirds of the available votes. The question then arises as to whether this would be with or without the population requirement, a matter not envisaged in the texts. This depends on whether Article 122(5) should be construed as a derogation from the whole of Article 205 or simply as a derogation from the voting figures in Article 205. From its wording, it may be suggested that Article 122(5) appears to be a derogation from Article 205 as such, so it is at least arguable that the population requirement would not apply in this context.

Another consequence of the Amsterdam decision not to interfere with the EMU provisions is that the old cooperation procedure may still be used in EMU context. While the policy at Amsterdam was in other areas of the EC Treaty to replace cooperation procedure by co-decision, at the Nice IGC it would appear that the French presidency tabled proposals to replace cooperation with the Parliament in the EMU context with simple consultation of the Parliament. However, it would further appear that a number of Member States took the view that this would constitute an impermissible step backwards, with the result that the cooperation procedure remains in this part of the EC Treaty.

b.   Commission

While, under Article 213 of the EC Treaty, the members of the Commission must neither seek nor take instructions from any government or from any other body, only nationals of Member States may be members of the Commission, and the Commission must include at least one national of each of the Member States, but may not include more than two members having the nationality of the same State. Following the 1995 accessions, there are currently 20 Commissioners, two from each of the big countries (which for this purpose include Spain) and one from each of the other Member States. However, the second paragraph of Article 213 provides that the number of members of the Commission may be altered by the Council, acting unanimously. One of the matters long discussed in political circles is whether the number of Commissioners should be reduced to one per State, and there have been ideas floated of grouping some of the smaller countries together to have a rotating Commissioner between them, which essentially is the system used for selecting Advocates-General before the Court (other than those who come from the four big countries). This debate puts clearly into focus the question whether the Commission should be regarded as a representative body or simply in terms of its operational needs.

The Treaty of Amsterdam did not directly respond to any of these proposals, but as mentioned above, it contained a Protocol on the institutions with the prospect of enlargement of the European Union which linked the size of the Commission to the weighting of votes in the Council. Under this Protocol, at the date of entry into force of the first enlargement of the Union the Commission is to comprise one national of each of the Member States, provided that, by that date, the weighting of the votes in the Council has been modified, in a manner acceptable to all Member States, notably compensating those Member States which give up the possibility of nominating a second member of the Commission. Here, therefore, the Commission is clearly treated as part of the representative equation and not as a body whose composition is determined according to its operational needs.

This is reflected in the Nice Protocol on Enlargement, Article 4 of which provides that on 1 January 2005[4a] (the same date as the change in voting weights in the Council) and with effect from when the first Commission following that date takes up its duties, 'The Commission shall include one national of each of the Member States', although the amended Article 213 would still allow the number of Members of the Commission to be altered by the Council, acting unanimously. However, it is further provided in the Protocol that when the Union consists of 27 Member States, Article 213(1) of the EC Treaty shall be revised again and that the number of Members of the Commission shall be less than the number of Member States. Under this provision, 'The Members of the Commission shall be chosen according to a rotation system based on the principle of equality, the implementing arrangements for which shall be adopted by the Council, acting unanimously' and 'the number of Members of the Commission shall be set by the Council, acting unanimously'.

Unlike the amendments to voting weights in the Council, here there is on the face of it no special treatment of the bigger Member States, and the example of the Executive Board of the ECB, which has members from only six of the 12 participant Member States, springs to mind.

Article 4(3) of the Protocol adds that the Council, acting unanimously after signing the treaty of accession of the twenty-seventh Member State of the Union, must adopt:

— the number of Members of the Commission;
— the implementing arrangements for a rotation system based on the principle of equality containing all the criteria and rules

---

[4a] Changed to 1 November 2004 in the 2003 Treaty of Accession.

necessary for determining the composition of successive colleges automatically on the basis of the following principles:

(a)   Member States shall be treated on a strictly equal footing as regards determination of the sequence of, and the time spent by, their nationals as Members of the Commission; consequently, the difference between the total number of terms of office held by nationals of any given pair of Member States may never be more than one;

(b)   subject to point (a), each successive college shall be so composed as to reflect satisfactorily the demographic and geographical range of all the Member States of the Union.

Finally, Article 4(4) of the Protocol gives the reassurance that any State which accedes to the Union shall be entitled, at the time of its accession, to have one of its nationals as a Member of the Commission until the rules for the Community of 27 apply.

However, important as the changes in the composition of the Commission may be, the Nice Treaty also makes changes of equal if not greater importance with regard to the appointment of the Commission and with regard to the political responsibility of its members. The Maastricht and Amsterdam Treaties made important changes to the role of the Parliament in the appointment process, and the current version of Article 214(2) of the EC Treaty provides that the governments of the Member States are first to nominate by common accord the person they intend to appoint as President of the Commission, subject to the approval of the European Parliament. Then, by common accord with the nominee for President, they are to nominate the other persons whom they intend to appoint as members of the Commission. Next, the President and the other nominees for membership of the Commission are subject as a body to a vote of approval by the European Parliament, and it is only after that vote of approval by the European Parliament that the President and the other members of the Commission are finally appointed by common accord of the governments of the Member States. Thus, as in the system of co-decision in the legislative process, the Member States cannot override the Parliament and the Parliament cannot override the Member States.

The Nice Treaty makes two important changes to this procedure. In one sense it makes it more like real co-decision, in that the nomination for the Presidency is to be made by the Council, meeting in the composition of Heads of State or Government, and the other nominations are to be made by the Council, in both cases acting by a qualified majority. The move to a majority vote is clearly important in the context of a Commission with fewer members than there are Member States, since it prevents a disgruntled Member State from blocking the process (unlike the situation with regard to the appointment of the Executive Board of the ECB). On the other hand, while some might see it as expressly subordinating the Commission to the Council (though it is just as subordinate, if that is the appropriate term, to the Parliament), others might argue that it goes a long way to removing the appearance of intergovernmentalism from the appointment of the Commission—thus exposing as ever more fallacious the linkage between votes in the Council and the number of members of the Commission.

So far as political responsibility is concerned, the Nice Treaty amends Article 217 in particular so as to increase the powers of the President—and also so as to provide a mechanism for the removal of individual Commissioners. The revised Article 217 provides for the Commission to work under the political guidance of its President, who is to decide on its internal organisation in order to ensure that it acts consistently, efficiently and on the basis of collegiality. The responsibilities incumbent upon the Commission are to be structured and allocated among its Members by its President, who may reshuffle the allocation of those responsibilities during the Commission's term of office. The Members of the Commission will be required to carry out the duties devolved upon them by the President under his authority. Perhaps most important of all (and it may be recalled that President Prodi has taken a written undertaking from each Member of the Commission to resign if called upon so to do by the President), a revised Article 217(4) expressly requires a Member of the Commission to resign if the President so requests, after obtaining the approval of the College.

On the other hand, the Nice text did not take up the idea put forward by some delegations of enabling the President of the Commission to ask the European Parliament for a vote of confidence on the basis of a general policy statement.[5]

c.   European Parliament

Since 1979, the European Parliament has been elected directly by the citizens of the Community, albeit not by uniform methods. The seats are nevertheless allocated to each Member State in a way which is not directly proportionate to population but which gives the bigger Member States more seats than the smaller ones. Until German reunification, the range went from 6 seats for Luxembourg to 81 each for Germany, France, the UK and Italy. However, following the reunification of Germany, it was agreed to recognise the demographic consequences at least to some extent: the number of seats for Germany was raised to 99 (an increase of 18 seats), but the seats for the other three big states were raised by six each to 87, making a total of 18 additional seats between those States. The consequence overall therefore was to increase the relative representation of the big Member States as compared to the smaller ones, but also to ensure that the increase for Germany was balanced by an increase for the other big States, thus showing that the balancing of political weight was as important as (if not

[5] Presidency Note of 24 May 2000 (CONFER 4744/00).

more important than) the representation of additional population. Be that as it may, it may be wondered whether a possible way forward with regard to new small states would be not to eliminate their representation but to increase the representation of the bigger Member States.

The Treaty of Amsterdam did not in itself change the composition of the European Parliament, but it set a limit on its future expansion, by amending Article 189 of the EC Treaty to provide that 'the number of Members of the European Parliament shall not exceed seven hundred'. This limit has however proved to be very short-lived. The Treaty of Nice has amended Article 189 again to raise the limit to 732, which could be exceeded on a transitional basis following new accessions under Article 2 of the Protocol on Enlargement. The provisions relating to the European Parliament take effect from 1 January 2004 and with effect from the start of the 2004–2009 term, so that the Parliament elected in the summer of 2004 will take part in the appointment of the first Commission governed by the new rules, which will take office in January 2005.[5a] It is provided that the number of representatives elected in each Member State are to be as follows:

Belgium 22
Denmark 13
Germany 99
Greece 22
Spain 50
France 72
Ireland 12
Italy 72
Luxembourg 6
Netherlands 25
Austria 17
Portugal 22
Finland 13
Sweden 18
United Kingdom 72

The practical result is that there will be a reduction of representation for most existing Member States except Germany and Luxembourg. In the Declaration on the enlargement of the European Union the common position to be adopted by the Member States at the accession conferences, as regards the distribution of seats at the European Parliament, will be as follows:

Germany 99
United Kingdom 72
France 72

[5a] Changed to 1 November 2004 by the 2003 Treaty of Accession.

Italy 72
Spain 50
Poland 50
Romania 33
Netherlands 25
Greece 22
Czech Republic 20
Belgium 22
Hungary 20
Portugal 22
Sweden 18
Bulgaria 17
Austria 17
Slovakia 13
Denmark 13
Finland 13
Ireland 12
Lithuania 12
Latvia 8
Slovenia 7
Estonia 6
Cyprus 6
Luxembourg 6
Malta 5

This gives a total of 732 seats, but it may be suggested that some of the numbers are difficult to explain objectively: on a population basis there is no reason why the Czech Republic and Hungary should each elect two fewer MEPs than Greece, Belgium or Portugal.[5b]

While there is some provision for a limited increase in use of co-decision procedure, the other matter of legal interest with regard to the European Parliament under the Treaty of Nice is that it is at last given the same rights of action as other institutions with regard to action for annulment (Article 230) and requesting an opinion on an international agreement (Article 300) —which leads to consideration of the changes to the European Court of Justice effected by the Treaty of Nice.

d.   European Court/Court of First Instance

Unlike the Commission, no change has been made in the method of appointing the members of the ECJ and CFI. Judges continue to be

---

[5b] This was corrected in the 2003 Treaty of Accession, which also reallocated the seats provisionally alloted to Romania and Bulgaria.

appointed by common accord of the representatives of the governments of the Member States. Changes are however to be made to the membership of the Courts: traditionally the Treaties have provided for a fixed number of judges, sometimes the same number as the number of Member States (as in the Communities of 9 and of 15) and sometimes one more judge than the number of Member States (as in the Communities of 6 and 12). The Nice Treaty provides however for the ECJ to have one judge per Member State (Article 221), but the CFI is to have *at least* one judge per Member State (Article 224), the number of Judges of the CFI being determined by the Statute of the Court of Justice. It is therefore clear that if additional judicial personnel are to be provided, they will be at the level of the CFI which, as will be seen, may be given increased jurisdiction.

There are also major changes in the groupings of judges in the ECJ for the purposes of hearing and deciding cases. Under the new version of Article 221, the Court of Justice shall sit in chambers or in a 'Grand Chamber', in accordance with the rules laid down for that purpose in the Statute of the Court of Justice, and it is only when provided for in the Statute that the Court of Justice may also sit as a full Court. This may in effect be regarded as relating to the question of enlargement and the perceived problem of the Court becoming too big to operate effectively. Article 16 of the new Statute of the Court provides that the Grand Chamber shall consist of 11 Judges, which means that in a Community of 27, it would comprise less than half the judges. It is to be presided over by the President of the Court, and the Presidents of the chambers of five Judges and other Judges appointed in accordance with the conditions laid down in the Rules of Procedure shall also form part of the Grand Chamber. It is envisaged that the Court will sit in a Grand Chamber when a Member State or an institution of the Communities that is party to the proceedings so requests (the circumstance under which it must currently sit as a Full Court). On the other hand it is provided that the Court shall sit as a full Court where cases are brought before it pursuant to Article 195(2) (dismissal of the Ombudsman), Article 213(2) (breach of obligations by a member of the Commission), Article 216 (serious misconduct by a member of the Commission) or Article 247(7) of the EC Treaty (deprivation of office of a member of the Court of Auditors) or parallel provisions of the EAEC Treaty. It does however remain possible for the Court itself, where it considers that a case before it is of exceptional importance, to decide, after hearing the Advocate-General, to refer the case to the full Court.

A new tier of judicial activity is also envisaged in so far as Judicial Panels are to be attached to the CFI (Article 220) under the conditions laid down in Article 225a 'in order to exercise, in certain specific areas, the judicial competence laid down in the Treaty'. Under Article 225a, the Council, acting unanimously on a proposal from the Commission and after consulting the European Parliament and the Court of Justice or at the request of the Court of Justice and after consulting the European Parliament and the Commission, may create judicial panels to hear and determine at first instance certain classes of action or proceeding brought in specific areas. Many of the essentials are left to such decisions: it is provided that the decision establishing a judicial panel shall lay down the rules on the organisation of the panel and the extent of the jurisdiction conferred upon it.

The members of the judicial panels are to be chosen from persons whose independence is beyond doubt and who possess the ability required for appointment to judicial office. They are to be appointed by the Council, acting unanimously, and they themselves may establish their Rules of Procedure in agreement with the Court of Justice subject to the approval of the Council, acting by a qualified majority.

In a Declaration on Article 225a of the Treaty establishing the European Community adopted at Nice, the Conference asked the Court of Justice and the Commission to prepare as swiftly as possible a draft decision establishing a judicial panel with jurisdiction to deliver judgments at first instance on disputes between the Community and its servants.

So far as appeals are concerned, decisions given by judicial panels may be subject to a right of appeal on points of law only or, when provided for in the decision establishing the panel, a right of appeal also on matters of fact, before the Court of First Instance. A new Article 225(2) provides that the Court of First Instance is to have jurisdiction to hear and determine actions or proceedings brought against decisions of the judicial panels set up under Article 225a. Decisions given by the Court of First Instance under this paragraph may exceptionally be subject to review by the Court of Justice, under the conditions and within the limits laid down by the Statute, where there is a serious risk of the unity or consistency of Community law being affected.

The Treaty of Nice also includes a new Statute of the Court and new procedure for its amendment under a revised Article 245. This provides that the Council, acting unanimously at the request of the Court of Justice and after consulting the European Parliament and the Commission, or at the request of the Commission and after consulting the European Parliament and the Court of Justice, may amend the provisions of the Statute, with the exception of Title I (which is concerned with the duties and privileges of judges and advocates general). To the extent therefore that the Statute may govern the allocation of jurisdiction as between the ECJ and the CFI, this provision means that changes may be made without further Treaty amendment.

In this context, the current major limit on the jurisdiction of the CFI, the fact that it may not hear references from national courts, could be overturned. Under Article 225(3), the Statute could give the CFI power to hear references from national courts. The new Article 225(3) provides that the Court of First Instance is to have jurisdiction to hear and determine questions referred for a preliminary ruling under Article 234, in specific areas laid down by the Statute. On the other hand, where the Court of First Instance considers that the case requires a decision of principle likely to affect the unity or consistency of Community law, it in turn may refer the case to the Court of Justice for a ruling. Given that delays arising from appeals from judgments given on such references would make the system effectively unworkable, there is only a limited power of review. It is envisaged that decisions given by the Court of First Instance on questions referred for a preliminary ruling may *exceptionally* (emphasis added) be subject to review by the Court of Justice, under the conditions and within the limits laid down by the Statute, where there is a serious risk of the unity or consistency of Community law being affected.

This problem is also alluded to in a Declaration on Article 225(3) of the Treaty establishing the European Community. This states that the Conference considers that, in exceptional cases in which the Court of Justice decides to review a decision of the Court of First Instance on a question referred for a preliminary ruling, it should act under an emergency procedure.

However, the opportunity was not taken to make some other radical alterations which had been suggested in the context of references for preliminary rulings. The Reflection Group set up by the Commission on the future of the Community Judicial system[6] had suggested amending Article 234 so as to state expressly that national courts may decide points of Community law that come before them, and that in making references national courts should take account of the importance of the question for Community law, and of the existence of a reasonable doubt as to the answer to be given. However, while these suggestions might seem to have been intended to reduce the flow of references to the European Court, the Reflection Group also recommended an express statement of the duty of a national court to make a reference where it was minded not to a apply a Community act on the grounds of its invalidity, thus putting into Treaty form the case-law developed in Case 314/85 *Foto-Frost*,[7] where although only Article 41 of the ECSC Treaty gave the Court express *exclusive* jurisdiction to consider the validity of Community legislation at issue before national courts, Article 234 of the EC Treaty being silent on the point, it was held that under the EC Treaty also only the European Court may declare Community legislation invalid, since it must be valid or invalid for the Community as a whole, not just within one national jurisdiction.[8] In this context it may be observed that difficulties arise from the drafting of Article 68, introduced by the Treaty of Amsterdam, applying the system of references for preliminary rulings to Title IV on Visas, Asylum and Immigration. Under Article 68, there is only provision for references from 'a court or a tribunal of a Member State

[6] Report published in January 2000.
[7] [1987] ECR 4199.
[8] Case 314/85 *Foto Frost v HZA Lubeck-ost* [1987] ECR 4199.

against whose decisions there is no judicial remedy under national law', but that court or tribunal 'shall', if it considers that a decision on the question is necessary to enable it to give judgment, request the Court of Justice to give a ruling. If the European Court alone may pronounce on the validity of Community legislation, this both leaves the lower courts with some awkward questions and seems to indicate that all such cases will have to be appealed to the highest level.[9] A proposal was therefore put forward by the 'Friends of the Presidency'[10] to the effect that the normal rules of Article 234 should apply in the context of Title IV, subject to the Court continuing, as under the current Article 68(2), not to have any jurisdiction to rule on any measure or decision taken pursuant to Article 62(1) relating to the maintenance of law and order and the safeguarding of internal security. These suggestions were not however taken up in the texts adopted at Nice.

e.   Flexibility and Enhanced Cooperation

The general provisions introduced by the Treaty of Amsterdam have not yet been used, so one is tempted to ask why they have been revised. One answer may be that, quite apart from the fact that there was only a period of 18 months between the entry into force of the Treaty of Amsterdam and the negotiation of the Treaty of Nice, these provisions are intended to find their vocation in the context of an enlarged EU. However, although the Amsterdam provisions have not been used as such, it should nevertheless be remembered that under the terms of the Amsterdam Treaty itself there are situations where those provisions are deemed to have been used: under Article 1 of the Protocol Integrating the Schengen acquis into the Framework of the European Union, Belgium, Denmark, Germany, Greece, Spain, France, Italy, Luxembourg, the Netherlands, Austria, Portugal, Finland and Sweden, as signatories to the Schengen agreements, are 'authorised to establish closer cooperation among themselves' within the scope of those agreements and related provisions; furthermore, under Article 5 of that Protocol, where either Ireland or the United Kingdom or both have not notified the President of the Council in writing within a reasonable period that they wish to take part,

> the authorisation referred to in Article 11 of the Treaty establishing the European Community or Article 40 of the Treaty on European Union[11] shall be deemed to have been granted to the Members States referred to in Article 1 and

---

[9] Though it has been suggested that the *Foto-Frost* doctrine should not apply in the context of Art 68, see A Arnull *The European Union and its Court of Justice*, (Oxford, OUP, 1999) pp 70–71.

[10] Presidency Note of 31 May 2000 (CONFER 4747/00).

[11] Art 40 of the TEU sets the general framework for closer cooperation, and Art 11 of the EC Treaty applies the concept in the context of the EC.

to Ireland or the United Kingdom where either of them wishes to take part in
the areas of cooperation in question.

Whatever may be the reasons for the subsequent failure to use these
provisions, their revision or replacement was one of the substantive items
on the agenda of the Inter-Governmental Conference which culminated in
the Treaty of Nice. The Nice text does make a number of important
changes, and the extent to which they may make it more likely that the
closer cooperation provisions will be used in practice will be considered at
the end of this paper. On the other hand, there is already a growing number
of examples of the use of other forms of flexibility.

The Nice Treaty transfers all the detailed conditions relating to the use
of enhanced cooperation to Article 43 of the EU Treaty, the revised text of
which provides that Member States which intend to establish enhanced
cooperation between themselves may make use of the institutions,
procedures and mechanisms laid down by this Treaty and by the Treaty
establishing the European Community provided that the proposed
cooperation:

(a)   is aimed at furthering the objectives of the Union and of the
      Community, at protecting and serving their interests and at rein-
      forcing their process of integration;
(b)   respects the said Treaties and the single institutional framework
      of the Union;
(c)   respects the *acquis communautaire* and the measures adopted
      under the other provisions of the said Treaties;
(d)   remains within the limits of the powers of the Union or of the
      Community and does not concern the areas which fall within the
      exclusive competence of the Community;
(e)   does not undermine the internal market as defined in Article 14(2)
      of the Treaty establishing the European Community, or the eco-
      nomic and social cohesion established in accordance with Title
      XVII of that Treaty;
(f)   does not constitute a barrier to or discrimination in trade between
      the Member States and does not distort competition between them;
(g)   involves a minimum of eight Member States;
(h)   respects the competences, rights and obligations of those
      Member States which do not participate therein;
(i)   does not affect the provisions of the Protocol integrating the
      Schengen acquis into the framework of the European Union;
(j)   is open to all the Member States, in accordance with Article 43b.

It may be observed at the outset that while the Amsterdam provisions
required the participation of a majority of the Member States, the Nice

Treaty substitutes the figure of 8 Member States, which is currently a majority, but would be less than a third of the members of an EU of 27.

So far as the substantive conditions are concerned, the requirement that closer cooperation should not concern areas which fall within the exclusive competence of the Community continues to raise exactly the same question as arises in the context of subsidiarity under Article 5. Putting it very briefly, the common commercial policy[12] and common fisheries policy[13] have been held to be areas of exclusive Community competence, and it may be suggested that monetary policy has become so in the third stage of Economic and Monetary Union so far as the participants are concerned.[14] On the other hand, it would appear that in other areas of activity, Community competence only becomes exclusive once complete or comprehensive Community legislation has been enacted, even in the area of the common agricultural policy.[15] However, the list in the revised Article 43 of the EU Treaty no longer includes the requirement in the current Article 11(1)(b) that closer cooperation should not affect Community 'policies', which, if taken literally, would appear to preclude closer cooperation in the area of the common agricultural policy and in other areas where the Community is required to have a common policy, such as transport.[16] If however it is not meant literally, and means that closer cooperation should not be used in areas already subject to Community rules, it adds little to the requirement that it should not be used in areas which fall within the exclusive competence of the Community—which perhaps explains why it is not in the Nice text.

It may be suggested that problems may however arise from the requirement in the current Article 11(1)(e) of the EC Treaty, reproduced in the Nice text of Article 43(f) of the EU Treaty, that closer cooperation should not distort conditions of competition. Historically the use of Article 94 (and subsequently Article 95) of the EC Treaty to enact legislation in areas such as environmental protection or consumer protection was often claimed to be justified on the grounds that differences in national legislation amounted to distortions of competition[17]—yet the result of closer cooperation would appear to be that some Member States will have legislation which differs from that of other Member States; that was already clearly the result of the Maastricht Social Protocol. However, the view that differences in national

---

[12] *Opinion 1/75* [1975] ECR 1355.

[13] Case 804/79 *Commission v UK* [1981] ECR 1045.

[14] By virtue of Art 4(1) of the EC Treaty there is a single monetary policy at the single currency stage, and under Art 105(2) it is the task of the ESCB to define and implement this monetary policy.

[15] Case 222/82 *Apple and Pear Development Council* [1983] ECR 4083.

[16] EC Treaty Art 70.

[17] See eg the recitals to Council Directive 85/374 on liability for defective products (OJ 1985 L210/29).

legislation amount to distortions of competition has now been limited by the judgment of the Court in Case C–376/98 *Germany v EP and Council*[18] in relation to the tobacco advertising Directive.[19] The Court there stated that a measure adopted on the basis of Article 95 'must genuinely have as its object the improvement of the conditions for the establishment and functioning of the internal market' and that:

> if a mere finding of disparities between national rules and of the abstract risk of obstacles to the exercise of fundamental freedoms or of distortions of competition liable to result therefrom were sufficient to justify the choice of [Article 95] as a legal basis, judicial review of compliance with the proper legal basis might be rendered nugatory.

The Court then went on to assert that in order to justify legislation under Article 95, the distortion of competition must be 'appreciable'. It may therefore be argued from this that conversely, the differences in legislation resulting from closer cooperation would only breach Article 11 (and the new Article 43 of the EU Treaty) if they in turn were 'appreciable'.

On the other hand, it may be observed that the requirement in Article 11 of the EC Treaty that the proposed cooperation should not concern the citizenship of the Union or discriminate between nationals of Member States is not included in the provisions retained by the Treaty of Nice and transferred by that Treaty to the general provisions of the TEU.

Procedurally, the most important change resulting from the Treaty of Nice is that a veto on proposed enhanced cooperation will no longer be possible under Article 40a of TEU or Article 11 of EC Treaty (though assent of the European Parliament is required if it is a co-decision matter). In the terms of the new Article 40a of the EU Treaty, Member States which intend to establish enhanced cooperation between themselves under Article 40 (with the aim of enabling the Union to develop more rapidly into an area of freedom, security and justice) are to address a request to the Commission, which may submit a proposal to the Council to that effect. Those Member States may then submit an initiative to the Council designed to obtain authorisation for the enhanced cooperation concerned. Under Article 40a(2) this authorisation is to be granted, by the Council, acting by a qualified majority, on a proposal from the Commission or on the initiative of at least eight Member States, and after consulting the European Parliament. While a member of the Council may request that the matter be referred to the European Council, after that matter has been raised before the European Council, the Council may act 'in accordance with the first subparagraph of this paragraph', ie by qualified majority, unlike the present requirement for unanimity if the matter is referred to the European Council.

---

[18] 5 October 2000.
[19] EP and Council Directive 98/43 (OJ 1998 L213/9).

In the context of the EC Treaty, the revised Article 11 provides that Member States which intend to establish enhanced cooperation between themselves in one of the areas referred to in this Treaty shall address a request to the Commission, which may submit a proposal to the Council to that effect. Authorisation to establish such enhanced cooperation is again to be granted, in compliance with Articles 43 to 45 of the Treaty on European Union, by the Council, acting by a qualified majority on a proposal from the Commission and after consulting the European Parliament. However, when enhanced cooperation relates to an area covered by the co-decision procedure under Article 251, the *assent* of the European Parliament will be required. As under the EU procedure, a member of the Council may request that the matter be referred to the European Council,[20] but after that matter has been raised before the European Council, the Council may again act by qualified majority.

The Nice Treaty also extends enhanced cooperation to implementation of a joint action or common position under the second pillar (Article 27b of the EU Treaty) but subject to a possible veto (Article 27c and 23(2)). Under the new Article 27b of the EU Treaty, such enhanced cooperation must be aimed at safeguarding the values and serving the interests of the Union as a whole by asserting its identity as a coherent force on the international scene. In particular, it must respect:

— the principles, objectives, general guidelines and consistency of the common foreign and security policy and the decisions taken within the framework of that policy;
— the powers of the European Community, and
— consistency between all the Union's policies and its external activities.

Article 27b makes it clear that enhanced cooperation pursuant to this Title must relate to implementation of a joint action or a common position, and that it must not relate to matters having military or defence implications. The procedure is however subtly different from the first and third pillars: under Article 27c, Member States which intend to establish enhanced cooperation between themselves under Article 27b must address a request to the Council to that effect. The request is to be forwarded to the Commission and to the European Parliament *for information* (emphasis added). The Commission is to give its opinion particularly on whether the enhanced cooperation proposed is consistent with Union policies. Authorisation is however to be granted by the Council, acting in accordance with the second and third subparagraphs of Article 23(2), under which, if a member of the Council declares that for important and stated reasons of national policy,

---

[20] It may be wondered whether this should, as in the current Art 11, be a reference to the Council meeting in the composition of Heads of State or Government.

it intends to oppose the adoption of a decision taken by qualified majority, a vote shall not be taken; rather the Council may, acting by a qualified majority, request that the matter be referred to the European Council for decision by unanimity; compliance with Articles 43 to 45 of the EU Treaty is in any event required. Thus enhanced cooperation is extended to the second pillar subject to procedural rules similar to those which currently allow closer cooperation under the first and third pillars to be blocked by a dissentient State, but enhanced cooperation under the first and third pillars will no longer be subject to such a possibility of veto—and may well therefore become a much more practical proposition.

f.   Charter of Fundamental Rights

The Charter of Fundamental Rights may have a different genesis from the Treaty of Nice, but it coincides in time with the Nice IGC. Indeed it may be observed that the first substantive amendment printed in the Treaty of Nice does actually relate to fundamental rights, amending Article 7 of the TEU with regard to the determination of a 'clear risk' of serious breach by a Member State of principles mentioned in Article 6(1)—liberty, democracy, respect for human rights and fundamental freedoms, and the rule of law.

While the Charter of Fundamental Rights may have been 'proclaimed' rather than included in Treaty text, its status is on the agenda for the IGC in 2004, following initiatives to be agreed in December 2001 according to the Declaration on the Future of the Union annexed to the Treaty of Nice. In the meantime, its current status has been considered in the Opinion of AG Tizzano in Case C–173/99 *Broadcasting, Entertainment, Cinematographic and Theatre Union (BECTU) v Secretary of State for Trade and Industry*.[21] The case was concerned with the right to annual paid leave, and after considering other international instruments relevant to the concept, AG Tizzano stated that:

> Even more significant, it seems to me, is the fact that that right is now solemnly upheld in the Charter of Fundamental Rights of the European Union, published on 7 December 2000 by the European Parliament, the Council and the Commission after approval by the Heads of State and Government of the Member States, often on the basis of an express and specific mandate from the national parliaments. Article 31(2) of the Charter declares that: 'Every worker has the right to limitation of maximum working hours, to daily and weekly rest periods and to an annual period of paid leave. And that statement, as expressly declared by the Presidium of the Convention which drew up the Charter, is inspired precisely by Article 2 of the European

---

[21] [2001] ECR I–4881.

Social Charter and by paragraph 8 of the Community Charter of Workers' Rights, and also took due account 'of Directive 93/104/EC concerning certain aspects of the organisation of working time.

Admittedly, like some of the instruments cited above, the Charter of Fundamental Rights of the European Union has not been recognised as having genuine legislative scope in the strict sense. In other words, formally, it is not in itself binding. However, without wishing to participate here in the wide-ranging debate now going on as to the effects which, in other forms and by other means, the Charter may nevertheless produce, the fact remains that it includes statements which appear in large measure to reaffirm rights which are enshrined in other instruments. In its preamble, it is moreover stated that 'this Charter reaffirms, with due regard for the powers and tasks of the Community and the Union and the principle of subsidiarity, the rights as they result, in particular, from the constitutional traditions and international obligations common to the Member States, the Treaty on European Union, the Community Treaties, the European Convention for the Protection of Human Rights and Fundamental Freedoms, the Social Charters adopted by the Community and by the Council of Europe and the case-law of the Court of Justice of the European Communities and of the European Court of Human Rights.

I think therefore that, in proceedings concerned with the nature and scope of a fundamental right, the relevant statements of the Charter cannot be ignored; in particular, we cannot ignore its clear purpose of serving, where its provisions so allow, as a substantive point of reference for all those involved—Member States, institutions, natural and legal persons—in the Community context. Accordingly, I consider that the Charter provides us with the most reliable and definitive confirmation of the fact that the right to paid annual leave constitutes a fundamental right.

If it is indeed the case that the Charter may serve as a 'substantive point of reference for all those involved', then it may be suggested that its precise legal status becomes a matter of secondary importance. However, while the Court reached the same conclusion as the Advocate General, and did make express mention of the Community Charter of the Fundamental Social Rights of Workers,[22] it did not find it necessary to discuss, or even mention, the EU Charter of Fundamental Rights.

III.   CONCLUSIONS

While the Nice IGC may not have had a good press, and took two Irish referendums to approve it, it has nevertheless produced institutional solutions to the issues perceived as arising with the prospect of enlargement—whatever one may think of their merits. On the other hand, though hardly noticed by the headline writers, it has also effected serious and important

---

[22] Para 39.

institutional changes to the Commission, the EU judicial structure, and the procedure for enhanced cooperation. While these may have been triggered by the prospect of enlargement, they are not for the most part conditional upon it, and it may be suggested that they will have fundamental long-term consequences.

7

Enhancing Cooperation After Nice: Will the Treaty Do the Trick?

JO SHAW*

I. INTRODUCTION

THE CHANGES TO the enhanced cooperation provisions of the EC and EU Treaties which were introduced by the Treaty of Nice could be characterised at one level as largely technical in nature. They could be categorised as 'improvements' to a set of provisions introduced by the Treaty of Amsterdam which were widely thought to be unhelpfully drafted. Closer examination of the process and content of the Nice reform, however, quickly reveals a number of important points:

— reforming the enhanced cooperation provisions in the Treaties inevitably resuscitates the wider debate on flexibility as constitutive idea and practice for the EU;
— as neither flexibility in general nor enhanced cooperation in particular were on the original 2000 IGC agenda (the so-called Amsterdam triangle or Amsterdam leftovers), their subsequent inclusion on the agenda and their appearance in the final Treaty text provides a case study of political agenda management, especially on the part of successive Presidencies;
— while the amendments have clarified and simplified some of the most problematic and even dysfunctional aspects of the original Amsterdam provisions on 'closer cooperation',[1] it remains difficult to provide a precise interpretation of what the future

---

* Professor of European Law and Jean Monnet Chair of European Law at the University of Manchester; Senior Research Fellow at the Federal Trust. Correspondence address: School of Law, University of Manchester, Oxford Road, Manchester, M13 9PL, UK; jo.shaw@man.ac.uk. Previous versions of the paper were presented at a UKAEL Conference on the Treaty of Nice, London, May 2001, the UACES Annual Conference, Bristol, September 2001 and a Manchester Law School Work in Progress seminar, November 2001.
[1] For the purposes of this paper, nothing should be read into the shift in terminology from 'closer cooperation' (Treaty of Amsterdam) to 'enhanced cooperation' (Treaty of Nice); indeed,

significance and effects of post-Nice enhanced cooperation might be and in particular whether they are any more likely to be applied in practice than the dormant provisions which they have succeeded.

This paper seeks to bring out the issues and arguments raised by these three basic points. In order to put the changes introduced by the Treaty of Nice into context, the Treaty of Amsterdam is also examined in outline. The paper attempts to show how enhanced cooperation specifically, and flexibility more generally, remains a delicate equation to balance for the actors involved, both the Member States and the EU institutions. It proceeds on the clear assumption that the new provisions must, like their predecessors, be interpreted and continually re-interpreted in the light of their wider political context. They cannot be viewed in isolation, even before any attempts are made to use the opportunities they may in the future offer for the creation of multiple configurations of integration and dis- or non-integration across the Member States.

II.   ENHANCED COOPERATION IN CONTEXT: FLEXIBILITY AS IDEA AND PRACTICE

The enhanced cooperation provisions of the EC and EU Treaties, whether in their Amsterdam or Nice guises, represent a key manifestation of a pervasive phenomenon in the EU: flexible integration. Flexible integration has always been built into the foundations of the original European Communities, as well as being a more recent phenomenon of the European Union. Examples are legion, but include the EC Treaty's recognition of the regional Benelux union (Article 306 EC), the manifold possibilities for ongoing 'old fashioned flexibility'[2] in the form of international agreements between the Member States (perhaps most notoriously the Schengen Agreement on border controls which was intended to operate as a laboratory for integration), and the highly co mplex patterns of territorial differentiation which have always conditioned the geographical scope of application of EU law.[3] More recently, the famed examples of flexibility introduced by the Treaty of Maastricht, namely the framework for Economic and Monetary

the latter accords more closely with the French term: 'la cooperation renforcée'. The paper adopts the term 'closer cooperation' when discussing Amsterdam, and 'enhanced cooperation' in the context of Nice.

[2] B de Witte, 'Old-fashioned Flexibility: International Agreements between Member States of the European Union', in G de Búrca and J Scott (eds), *Constitutional Change in the European Union: From Uniformity to Flexibility?* (Oxford, Hart, 2000).

[3] J Ziller, 'Flexibility in the Geographical scope of EU Law: Diversity and Differentiation in the Application of Substantive Law on Member States' Territories', in de Búrca and Scott, above n 2.

Union providing for a variety of modes of being 'out', and what turned out to be the time-limited 'opt-out' from social policy-making for the United Kingdom, were by no means a break with the past, even if they did reinforce the impression of an emerging Europe of 'bits and pieces'.[4]

No discussion of flexibility in general or enhanced cooperation in particular can proceed without some attempt to delimit the subject and to define the terms in use. In very broad terms, we can define flexibility as varying levels, patterns and modes of membership in a compound political structure. Following the work of Alexander Stubb and Claus-Dieter Ehlermann, the variables of 'time', 'space' and 'matter' offer a useful means of ordering the terminology, predicting the effects and determining the correct conditions of differentiated or flexible integration.[5] Others have suggested that the crucial distinction is between flexible structures where the participants commit themselves to a common end, and those in which it is acknowledged that the participants in the overall integration project might have different ends. This might be termed the 'psychological dimension' of flexibility.

We can also usefully distinguish between uses of the term flexibility to connote a general political principle, to operate as a framing structure for different actors within the policy and socio-economic arenas, and to describe the establishment of a primary law framework for differentiation and/or the secondary output of such a primary framework.

Viewed as a general political principle, we find contestation rather than consensus shaping the use of the term flexibility. It can be argued that flexibility *ought* to be regarded as a constitutional shaping principle of the EU, co-existing in comfortable synergy with the general principles of democratic constitutionalism which can be said to underlie the general system of the treaties, especially Article 6 TEU.[6] According to Xenophon Yataganas,[7] closer cooperation could even be considered a materialisation of the constitutional tolerance principle enunciated by Joseph Weiler.[8] These types of normative position sit especially comfortably with the proposition that any

---

[4] D Curtin, 'The Constitutional Structure of the Union: a Europe of Bits and Pieces', (1993) 30 *Common Market Law Review* 1274; see also S Weatherill, 'Flexibility and Fragmentation: Trends in European Integration', in J Usher (ed), *The State of the European Union* (Harlow, Longman, 2000).

[5] A Stubb, 'A categorization of differentiated integration', (1996) 34 *Journal of Common Market Studies* 283; C-D. Ehlermann, 'Increased differentiation or stronger uniformity', in J Winter *et al* (eds), *Reforming the Treaty on European Union – The Legal Debate* (The Hague, Kluwer, 1996).

[6] J Shaw, 'Relating Constitutionalism and Flexibility in the European Union', in de Búrca and Scott, above n 2.

[7] X A Yataganas, 'The Treaty of Nice: The Sharing of Power and the Institutional Balance in the European Union – A Continental Perspective', *The Jean Monnet Chair Working Papers* 01/01 at p 49 (www.jeanmonnetprogram.org).

[8] J H H Weiler, 'Federalism and Constitutionalism: Europe's Sonderweg', *The Jean Monnet Chair Working Papers* 10/00 (www.jeanmonnetprogram.org).

constitution is to be seen as an evolving project rather than as the perfect and generally immutable rendering of a fixed moment involving the exercise of political will by a popular sovereign. That proposition in turn finds strong support, I would argue, in both normative theories of constitutions as dialogic and relational sets of practices,[9] and in the rich constitutional practices of many, if not indeed most, states. A very different thesis is articulated by Akos Toth when he argues that 'as a means of ensuring the future progress of the Union, no amount of opt-out, opt-in, derogation and flexibility can provide a credible alternative' to the reforms which he advocates, namely strengthening the current constitutional elements of the Treaties in particular by altering the procedure for Treaty amendment (ie ironically by making the whole system more flexible).[10] This type of argument thrives upon the generally implicit rider that EU constitutionalism is actually and immutably constitutionalism *for* integration, and is based upon a rather monocular perspective of the EU as the supplier of more integration, frequently in conjunction with the supply of law.[11] George Bermann views the provisions of enhanced cooperation—however skilfully drafted to protect the interests of both the 'ins' and the 'outs'—as missing the real challenge of managing diversity, and adapting the deliberative process in view of enlargement:[12]

> [This] lies in finding legislative solutions at the Community level that entail the political participation of all Member States and that bind all Member States, even while permitting differential solutions or otherwise responding to the diversity of circumstances and needs among the ... Member States.

On the other hand, all these differences in approach do reflect real contestations visible within more general political discourse, where politicians as

[9] See in particular the work of the Canadian political theorist James Tully: J Tully, *Strange Multiplicity. Constitutionalism in an Age of Diversity* (Cambridge, Cambridge University Press, 1995); J Tully, 'The Unfreedom of the Moderns in comparison to their ideals of Constitutional Democracy', ms October 2001. I have applied Tully's work in other writings on EU constitutionalism, including 'Relating Constitutionalism and Flexibility', above n 6; 'Postnational Constitutionalism in the European Union', (1999) 6 *Journal of European Public Policy* 579; most recently, 'Process, Responsibility and Inclusion in EU Constitutionalism', (2003) 9 *European Law Journal* 45.
[10] A Toth, 'The Legal Effects of the Protocols relating to the United Kingdom, Ireland and Denmark', in T Heukels, N Blokker and M Brus (eds), *The European Union after Amsterdam* (The Hague, Kluwer Law International, 1998).
[11] See in particular W Hallstein, *Europe in the Making* (London, Allen & Unwin, 1972), ch 2: 'Law in Place of Force', who described the EEC as a creation of the law, as a source of law and as a legal system.
[12] G Bermann, 'Law in an Enlarged European Union', (2001) 14 *European Union Studies Association Review* 1.

diverse as Joschka Fischer,[13] William Hague[14] and Jacques Chirac[15] all manage to use the language of flexibility or variable geometry as the basis for engaging in debates about the futures of the European Union. Helen Wallace evocatively describes flexibility as a 'new principle and a new tool for responding to differences in the enthusiasms and capabilities of the member states of the EU to take on new tasks of policy integration',[16] but one could extend beyond the rubric of 'enthusiasms and capabilities' to the realm of ideological differences about the nature of European integration.[17] As Alex Warleigh comments, a 'more normative issue' is hard to imagine, 'since flexibility calls into question isuses of solidarity, legitimacy and polity-building'.[18]

Interestingly, flexibility seems to share many commonalities with that other rather plastic concept, subsidiarity. Like subsidiarity, it can be made to mean most things to most people, depending upon the way in which it is understood and those aspects which are given most emphasis. Substantively, it offers a mechanism for choosing the appropriate frame of reference for political and legal arrangements. In that context, it seems to be a way of satisfying the varying expectations and needs of both the Member States and the EU institutions thereby balancing various 'public' interests, as well as other 'private' stakeholders such as citizens, businesses and organisations. These expectations arise at a number of different levels, including the supranational, the national and the subnational. Overall, it is a way of balancing the dynamism of an integration process against the diffusion effects which derive from the very success of an integration project which involves already a much larger number of participants than in its original conception of the 'Six'. Likewise, subsidiarity can be seen simultaneously as meaning both 'more' and 'less', as well as a stronger and weaker 'Europe', depending upon whether it is given the 'sovereignty' or the 'federalism' 'spin'. It has been used by different political actors to buy off

---

[13] Joschka Fischer's speech to the Humboldt University, Berlin, 12 May 2000.

[14] William Hague's speech as Leader to the UK Conservative Party Conference, 5 October 2000, reported in House of Commons Research Paper 00/83, *IGC 2000: from Feira to Biarritz*, 27 October 2000, at p23; see also his comments on UK Prime Minister Tony Blair's statement on the Feira European Council, June 21 2000, reported in House of Commons Research Paper 00/88, *IGC 2000: Enhanced Cooperation*, November 21 2000, at p 24.

[15] Jacques Chirac's address to the German *Bundestag*, 27 June 2000.

[16] H Wallace, 'Flexibility: A Tool of Integration or a Restraint on Disintegration?', in K-H Neunreither and A Wiener (eds), *European Integration after Amsterdam: Institutional Dynamics and Prospects for Democracy* (Oxford, Oxford University Press, 2000) at p 173.

[17] See, for this type of discussion, B Hall, *How flexible should Europe be?* (Centre for European Reform Working Paper, London, 2000). M Dewatripont *et al*, *Flexible Integration: Towards a More Effective and Democratic Europe* (London, CEPR, 1995) provides a slightly older review of positions on the desirability of flexibility, as does F de la Serre/H Wallace, *Flexibility and Enhanced Cooperation in the European Union: Placebo rather than panacea?*, Notre Europe Research and Policy Paper, no 2, September 1997.

[18] A Warleigh, 'After Nice: Making Flexibility Work', Paper to the UACES Research Conference, University of Bristol, 3–5 September 2001.

both the German *Länder* and the strongly Euro-sceptic wing of the British Conservative party, even though the two groups have markedly different perceptions of the interests which need to be protected.

Extending beyond the realm of politics alone, of course, flexibility also offers a fruitful framing structure for understanding the actions and decision-making processes of many different actors within integration and other socio-economic processes. For example, for economic actors, flexibility connotes the capacity to choose (different standards, laws and legal systems, and regulations), especially in view of the pursuit of competitiveness and perhaps the race for the bottom. For regulators themselves, flexibility implies the capacity for policy choice and discretion. Finally, for courts, flexibility is the interpretative space that all concepts of legal interpretation allow for judges.

Flexibility can be used as a term to describe a wide range of legal structures, of varying constitutional significance.[19] The primary rules of flexibility split into two categories: dispositive and enabling. Many are the examples of dispositive systems of flexibility under the EU Treaties, most notably in the context of the Treaty of Amsterdam the opt-out system for the United Kingdom, Ireland and—under different conditions—Denmark in relation to the incorporation of the Schengen extra-Treaty system into the EU and EC Treaties. Misleadingly, the Schengen Protocol describes itself as an applied case of the enabling framework of closer cooperation, a description which elides crucial constitutional differences and disregards the fact that the Schengen arrangements do not themselves conform to all the requirements which the Treaty of Amsterdam attached to the enabling of what it termed closer cooperation. It is these enabling rules which form the primary focus of this paper.

The secondary level of flexible rule-making likewise has multiple manifestations. It is difficult to equate the foundational regulations of Economic and Monetary Union putting into effect the enabling framework agreed at Maastricht for only a limited number of Member States to participate in the single currency, on the one hand, with the provisions of a directive offering longer time limits for implementation or special dispensations to particular Member States who have sought an exception, on the other. However, both fall within the general category of 'secondary flexibility' (as indeed would measures adopted under the enhanced cooperation provisions studied in this paper), so far as they comprise specific detailed rules instantiating variable effects, whatever the source of the authorisation given for that variation. Clearly some manifestations of secondary flexibility are of a systemic nature, comprising a package of measures such as EMU, while others should be

---

[19] A Arnull *et al, Wyatt and Dashwood's European Union Law* 4th edn (London, Sweet and Maxwell, 2000) p 168; see also the survey in F Tuytschaever, *Differentiation in European Union Law* (Oxford, Hart Publishing, 1999).

characterised instead as 'sub-systemic', in the sense that they are not as such part of a package of flexible measures, but are flexible in impact.

III.   THE TREATY OF AMSTERDAM: BACKGROUND AND TREATY PROVISIONS

Shifting the view away from the diverse meanings of flexibility within the history, politics and law of the integration process towards a more specific focus on recent EU developments, what is clear is that the last 10 years have seen a marked intensification of the role the concept has played in the EU arena. Flexibility in terms of institutional and legal structures and patterns of policy making has gradually emerged as a *de facto* tool for an increasingly diverse EU where some of the key objectives of the integration process have been heavily contested by some Member States (eg social policy, EMU and some aspects of the free movement of persons). It then came to dominate many of the debates which preceded and shaped the 1996–1997 IGC leading to the Treaty of Amsterdam, an IGC which was—it should be recalled—'battered for months by the obstructive strategy adopted by the UK Conservative government', in office up until May 1997.[20] According to Helen Wallace[21] specific to the debate about flexibility within and in the shadows of the 1996–97 IGC were five key factors:

— the well-defined plan to develop EMU which was 'the first flagship project in the EU which had deliberately envisaged the participation of only some of the EU members';
— previous successive enlargements had already brought within the EU 'more coutnries which were able, but not willing, to extend the shared agenda, as well as countries which lacked some of the capabilities to attain certain policy objectives;
— the expectation that 'two different projects of integration might be elided, namely the political economy project, developed through the EC, and the defence and security project, hitherto organized through NATO and the WEU';
— both the EU and NATO were contemplating and/or actively planning Eastern enlargement and 'the prospect of developing pan-European frames of reference'; and
— the salience of the issue of the 'permeability of borders', which brought the issue of the free movement of persons and controls on borders to the fore.

---

[20] E Philippart, 'The New Provisions on "Closer Cooperation": A Call for Prudent Politics', (2001) 14 *European Communitiy Studies Association Review* 6.
[21] Wallace, above n 16 at p 177.

Wallace argued that together these factors 'raised major questions about the recasting of the European integration model and its methodologies'.[22] They presented in addition a constant tension between freedom and discipline for the Member States, and between using flexible projects as a means of responding to both problems of management and efficiency in policy-making and the ongoing task of providing a legitimate foundation for the EU polity.[23] Accordingly, flexibility was taken up as a theme, even a *leitmotiv*,[24] in the Amsterdam Treaty.[25] Amsterdam added several new instances of Treaty-based flexibility to the previous ones, especially in relation to Schengen and the new Title IV of the EC Treaty on aspects of the free movement of persons (border controls, asylum, immigration), for the UK and Ireland. Denmark, too, was able to 'opt out' of the incorporation of Schengen (of which it is a member) into the EU legal order by being given permission to treat 'Schengen-law' as international law. Crucially, Amsterdam also 'constitutionalised' a notion of closer cooperation, by introducing the formalised possibility for the future development of flexible integration *under the Treaties*, subject to certain conditions.[26]

The framework used for the instrumentalisation of flexibility within the EC/EU Treaties after Amsterdam was in fact relatively straightforward in structural terms, in the form of an authorisation to be granted by the Council to participating states to implement closer cooperation and to use the institutions, procedures and mechanisms of the Treaties to that end. Strikingly, however, 'closer cooperation' is nowhere defined—hence the ideological issues raised about its multiple meanings have remained unresolved. Thus flexibility managed to be a *leitmotiv* of the Treaty without the normative implications ever being fully thrashed out.[27] Hence the concern that the issues of efficiency were more prominent in the drafters' minds than issues of legitimacy.[28] Furthermore, it was not given a mention in the preambles to any of the Treaties, introduced as an objective of the Union or the Community, or cited as a means to attain such objectives. In other words,

---

[22] Wallace, above n 16 at p 178.

[23] J Shaw, 'The Treaty of Amsterdam: Challenges of Flexibility and Legitimacy', (1998) 4 *European Law Journal* 63.

[24] Editorial, 'The Treaty of Amsterdam: Neither a bang nor a whimper', (1997) 34 *Common Market Law Review* 767.

[25] See generally A Stubb, *Flexible Integration and the Amsterdam Treaty: Negotiating Differentiation in the 1996-97 IGC*, PhD Dissertation, London School of Economics, 1998;

[26] For commentary see Shaw, above n 23; S Weatherill, '"If I Had Wanted You to Understand I Would Have Explained it Better": What is the purpose of the provisions on closer cooperation introduced by the Treaty of Amsterdam?', in D O'Keeffe and P Twomey (eds), *Legal Issues of the Amsterdam Treaty* (Oxford, Hart Publishing, 1999); Kortenberg, 'Closer Cooperation in the Treaty of Amsterdam', (1998) 35 *Common Market Law Review* 833; E Philippart and G Edwards, 'The Provisions on Closer Cooperation in the Treaty of Amsterdam: the Politics of Flexibility in the European Union', (1999) 37 *Journal of Common Market Studies* 670.

[27] Warleigh, above n 18.

[28] Shaw, above n 23 at p 85.

[29] Weatherill, above n 26 at p 27.

none of the normal techniques used by the drafters of the Treaties to ascribe formal foundational significance to a concept or principle were adopted, even though there is no doubting its 'unwritten' and implicit constitutional position within the system. Articles 43–45 TEU, introduced by the Treaty of Amsterdam, provide a set of general principles for 'closer cooperation', supplemented by specific principles applying to each pillar. These are to be found in Article 40 in respect of pillar three and in Article 11 EC in respect of pillar one. No general provision for closer cooperation was made within pillar two, where the possibilities of introducing flexibility are limited to 'constructive abstentionism' (Article 23). Articles 43–45 TEU offered an overarching frame for the development of 'closer cooperation', rather than a separate freestanding mechanism for such cooperation.

The technique used in the Treaty is for Articles 43–45 TEU to 'authorise' Member States wishing to engage in 'closer cooperation' to make use of 'the institutions, procedures and mechanisms laid down' in the TEU and the EC Treaty provided that the cooperation complies with certain guarantees relating to the objectives of the EU, the principles of the EC and EU Treaties, the protection of the *acquis communautaire* and the single institutional framework, and the commitment to use closer cooperation only as a 'last resort' mechanism. A specific authorisation by the Council is also required for each instance of closer cooperation, which must involve a majority of Member States but must be open to the participation of all Member States. The pre-determined and closed inner 'core' of states is thereby obviated as a possible outcome of using the closer cooperation technique.

Article 11 EC built on Articles 43 and 44 TEU by providing the specific conditions under which forms of secondary flexibility can be put in place within the framework of pillar one competences and the *méthode communautaire*. The areas in which closer cooperation might be engaged in were not predetermined, but neither were any specific areas expressly excluded. In other words, there were no negative or positive lists, as was mooted during the negotiating process for the Treaty of Amsterdam. Instead, Article 11 provided a set of five supplementary commandments, which in some ways replicate Article 43 TEU, but in other ways add extra and more precise conditions which closer cooperation must satisfy before it can validly be authorised. These comprise the principle of attributed powers, the exclusion of areas of 'exclusive' Community competence, the injunctions not to 'affect Community policies, actions or programmes' or to 'concern the citizenship of the Union or discriminate between nationals of Member States', and finally the exclusion of measures which 'constitute a discrimination or a restriction of trade between Member States' and 'distort the conditions of competition between the latter.'

Notwithstanding the innovatory character of the institutional dimension of these provisions their practical utility has been regularly doubted in view of the severity of the conditions which need to be satisfied. Weatherill comments that the stiff conditions of Article 11 combined with Article 43 TEU 'is doubtless indicative of nervousness that the legal order may be tipped towards indecipherable fragmentation'.[29] Together these provisions manage the remarkable feat of buttressing both the 'constitutionalising' and the 'conservatory' aspects of the EU system.[30]

The institutional arrangements for instances of secondary flexibility under pillar one can be derived from Article 11 EC, read in conjunction with Articles 43–45 TEU. *Authorisation* would be provided by the Council acting by a qualified majority, on a proposal by the Commission, after consulting the European Parliament. Article 11(2) provided an interesting and, some would say, worrying example of the importation of intergovernmental influences into pillar one, since it effectively brought a Luxembourg Accords type arrangement into play in the event that one of the non-participating Member States became unhappy about the move to closer cooperation by the majority. The reluctant non-participant must cite 'important and stated reasons of national policy' and no vote will be taken. In that case the Council may request, by a qualified majority, that the matter be referred to the European Council which will itself decide by unanimity. This was termed the 'emergency brake'. The Commission was from the beginning made central to the arrangements, both for drawing up proposals to initiate closer cooperation and to manage the arrangements for accession by non-participants. Not so the European Parliament, whose role in legitimising the initiation of new policy activities was significantly sidelined by the Amsterdam provisions.

IV.   AFTER AMSTERDAM

One point of clear agreement can be found in the post-Amsterdam commentary: the conclusion that the provisions were so restrictively drafted that it was difficult to conceive of the circumstances in which they could be used. Stephen Weatherill has shown how even in a field such as cultural policy, which is sparsely occupied by EU measures of a relatively unobtrusive type at present, the effect of the 'hemming in' of the policy field by other related measures in fields of single market law such as intellectual property or broadcasting services could be to reduce the possibility of 'closer cooperation' in effect to zero.[31] Whether this is seen as a good or a

---

[30] Weatherill, above n 26 at p 32, applying the terminology of Alan Dashwood, 'States in the European Union', (1998) 23 *European Law Review* 201.
[31] S Weatherill, 'Finding Space for Closer Cooperation in the Field of Culture', in de Búrca and Scott, above n 2.

bad thing will depend upon the orientation of the particular commentator towards the closer cooperation provisions, and towards the dynamics of 'flexible integration' more generally.[32] For example, Weatherill himself argues for a less restrictive interpretation of the provisions, and indeed for a 'flexible' approach to avoid the 'self-defeating' conclusion that the Amsterdam provisions are by their very nature unusable.[33]

The prediction made by many that the provisions would not be used also proved to be correct. Application of the provisions was mooted in a number of contexts, including the adoption of the Statute for the European Company, to institute a proper institutional structure for the Euro-12, for energy taxation,[34] and for a wider tax package. A combination of the restrictive provisions, the emergency brake (applied by Spain in the case of the Company Statute[35]), and the psychological barrier of using the provisions for the first time meant that discussions never went beyond the preliminary. Most recently, the idea of using Article 40 TEU (pillar three closer cooperation) was briefly mooted by Graham Watson, MEP, Chair of the European Parliament Committee on Citizens' Freedoms and Rights and author of an EP report on a European arrest warrant which came out shortly before 11 September 2001.[36] This came at the time when Italy was blocking the adoption by unanimity of what had come to be seen as an essential limb of the coordinated European response to the threat of international terrorism.[37] In any event, as several commentators have pointed out, with the entry into force of the Treaty of Amsterdam being delayed until May 1999, there was little opportunity for the provisions to be used before the topic was re-engaged at the 2000 IGC.[38]

After Amsterdam, the imminence of enlargement also gave a new edge to the debate. This was well captured in the Report of the House of Lords Select Committee on the European Union's Report on the 2000 IGC,[39]

---

[32] For a positive evaluation of the need for the provisions from an 'integrationist' perspective, see E. Philippart and M Sie Dhian Ho, *The Pros and Cons of 'Closer Cooperation' within the EU*, WRR Working Document, W104, The Hague, March 2000.

[33] Weatherill, above n 31 at p 256.

[34] 'EU vanguard may set pace on green tax – Commissioner', 9 February 2001, Reuters (http://forests.org/archive/europe/euvanmay.htm); Speech by Michaele Schreyer, European Budgets Commissioner on *Instruments for European Environmental Policy*, to the 2001 Environment Conference of the German Greens in the Bundestag, Berlin, February 4 2001 (Rapid: SPEECH/01/51).

[35] A difference of view between the Council Legal Service and the Spanish Government is reported by J M de Areilza, 'The Reform of Enhanced Cooperation Rules: Towards Less Flexibility?', Francisco Lucas Pires Working Papers Series on European Constitutionalism, Faculdade de Direito da Universidade Nova de Lisboa, Working Paper 2001/01 (http://www.fd.unl/).

[36] A5-0273/2001, approved by the European Parliament on 5 September 2001.

[37] Letter of the Financial Times, 8 December 2001, 'Go ahead on arrest warrant without Italy'.

[38] Philippart and Sie Dhian Ho, above n 32 at p 12.

[39] House of Lords Select Committee on the European Union, Eleventh Report, Session 1999–2000, *The 2000 Intergovernmental Conference*, at para 71 of the Report.

relating the import of evidence given by Helen Wallace on the question of the appearance of a 'pioneer group' or pre-selected core of states to take forward a closer integration agenda, which might at the same time undermine the very meaning 'membership' for some of the outer circle.

> Professor Wallace described the area as a 'poisoned chalice' and considered that, there was a danger that flexibility might become 'a vehicle for extensive opting out of collective regimes by one government after another. Thus a reform ostensibly designed to facilitate initiatives might turn out to be the driver of a large wedge between the real insiders and the rest'. She also warned that it could be used as a tool to deny the new member states a real voice in EU decision-making.

This was seen as a real risk attendant upon taking the flexibility agenda forward in the context of the 2000 IGC, given certain political pronouncements made during the course of 2000, notably by French President Jacques Chirac, about the possibilities for 'pioneer groups'. This is one important benchmark against which to assess the outcome of the Nice negotiations and the content of the new Treaty provisions.

Finally, it is vital to insist that the Treaty of Amsterdam, with its flexibility agenda, should be seen as an opening not a closure in terms of the development of the Treaty-based dimension of variable arrangements for integration. Eric Philippart describes the Amsterdam compromise as a 'first step', to be followed by a period of 'acclimatization'.[40] To view a Treaty amendment in this manner would likewise be an appropriate assessment of the steps taken in earlier amendments of the Treaties. For example, the single market flexibility instrument introduced by the Single European Act in what was then Article 100a(4) EC, in order to allow for variable national approaches to certain single market harmonisation issues, was rendered considerably more sophisticated when it was reworked as Articles 95(4)–(7) EC by the Treaty of Amsterdam. Moreover, the UK social policy opt-out appended to the Treaty of Maastricht could be seen as a laboratory for both the subsequent opt-outs from Schengen and the free movement of persons provisions introduced by the Treaty of Amsterdam and for the structural organisation of 'authorisations' to use the Treaties and the institutions adopted by the closer cooperation provisions. There is something of a paradox involved in the Treaty amendment process. The requirement of unanimity for Treaty amendment in Article 48 TEU makes it highly unlikely that certain provisions—such as the competition policy provisions of Articles 81–86 EC, in which a vast historical legacy of legal and policy development and entrenched and vested national interests are now invested—could ever be amended, however desirable or necessary that

---

[40] Philippart, above n 20.

might now seem. On the other hand, in the case of recently introduced provisions where there is less invested in the maintenance of the status quo or the avoidance of specific undesired outcomes, it seems that there are fewer obstacles and a lower political cost involved in amendment. This narrative owes much to the understanding of EU policy-making as a process of experimentation, involving stages of initiation, monitoring and reform and the story of the closer/enhanced cooperation provisions would appear to bear out this point.[41]

V.   THE IGC 2000 AND THE REVISION OF THE CLOSER COOPERATION PROVISIONS

A brief introduction to the 2000 IGC is necessary in order to understand the agenda established at the outset and the context, therefore, in which flexibility was subsequently taken onto the IGC agenda. The initial IGC agenda was determined by the earlier failures of the Treaty of Amsterdam to deal with the institutional issues associated with enlargement. Thus when the European Council meeting in Cologne originally resolved to open an IGC in 2000, it specified that[42]

> In accordance with the Amsterdam Protocol on the institutions with the prospect of enlargement of the European Union and the declarations made with regard to it, the brief of the Intergovernmental Conference will cover the following topics:
>
> — size and composition of the Commission;
> — weighting of votes in the Council (re-weighting, introduction of a dual majority and threshold for qualified-majority decision-making);
> — possible extension of qualified majority voting in the Council.

This is the so-called 'Amsterdam triangle' of issues, often unflatteringly termed the 'Amsterdam leftovers'; these were the matters relating to institutional reform which the Amsterdam IGC was unable to resolve, which were specifically reserved, in a protocol appended to the Treaty of Amsterdam, for *later* consideration but *before* enlargement. Preparation for the 2000 IGC began in earnest in 1999, after the Cologne European Council. The Report by the Finnish Presidency to the Helsinki European Council in December 1999 left open the possibility of adding new agenda items; it fell to the Portuguese Presidency, which chaired the initial stages of the negotiations in the first half of 2000 after the official opening of the IGC on 14 February 2001, to suggest the addition of further agenda items,

[41] Warleigh, above n 18.
[42] Conclusions of the Cologne European Council, 5 June 1999.

including a review of the closer cooperation provisions, in a Report for the Feira European Council of June 2000. That in turn determined some additional agenda items to be added, notably a review of the 'closer cooperation' (flexibility) provisions of the Treaty of Amsterdam. According to David Galloway, in the meantime the Portuguese Presidency allowed low key informal discussions to take place on the question of it being formally included on agendas during early 2001.[43] The Portuguese pressed for the inclusion of enhanced cooperation on the IGC agenda, as one of the major threatening prospects for the 2000 IGC in the middle of that year was that the agenda was too small, when restricted to the Amsterdam leftovers, to allow for effective negotiation, compromise and decision across 15 Member States with widely differing preferences and interests.[44] This strategy had risks, of course, because as Alexander Stubb and Mark Gray rightly point out, flexibility can be seen as 'the link between the IGC and the debate on the future of Europe'.[45] In that sense, enhanced cooperation was more than just 'another agenda item' included to oil the wheels of compromise. Potentially, it was a Pandora's Box which could have derailed the whole process by raising too many intensive points of disagreement amongst the negotiating parties; at the very least, the discussion of enhanced cooperation would serve to remind all of those involved in or observing the IGC that their work was indeed 'just one piece of a much larger puzzle'.[46]

In the event, flexibility was not available to oil the wheels of compromise throughout the later stages of the 2000 IGC, as political agreement on the main items was already reached by the stage of the Biarritz European Council meeting on 13/14 October 2000. The only exception to this early agreement was European security and defence policy, and that was eventually dropped and excluded at the final Nice European Council meeting in December 2000.[47] In other words, by the time the Member States did come to discuss the institutional reform issues about voting weights, QMV and the size and composition of the Commission, enhanced cooperation was effectively off the agenda and no longer available to act as an ingredient in the trade-offs essential to all EU decision-making. Although there was no reason in principle why the re-negotiation of flexibility could not encompass discussion of further instances of 'pre-determined' enhanced cooperation along the lines of those instituted at Maastricht and Amsterdam, the discussion of flexibility generally remained at a very abstract level.

---

[43] D Galloway, *The Treaty of Nice and Beyond* (Sheffield, Sheffield Academic Press (Contemporary European Studies Series), 2001) p 131.
[44] G Edwards and G Wiessala, 'Conscientious Resolve: The Portuguese Presidency of 2000', (2001) 39 *Journal of Common Market Studies, Annual Review 2000/2001* 43 at p 45.
[45] A Stubb and M Gray, 'Intergovernmental Conference 2000—the end of the beginning or the beginning of the end?', *Challenge Europe On Line Journal*, 12 September 2000.
[46] Stubb and Gray, above n 45.
[47] The insistence of the UK Government was crucial in this matter: Yataganas, above n 7 at p 47.

Consequently, the only detailed work was done on the reworking of the Amsterdam enabling clauses,[48] and focused on three main themes: the removal of the 'emergency brake' or veto, the reduction of the number of states required to initiate enhanced cooperation and a slight relaxation of the very strict conditions highlighted in the previous sections.[49] David Galloway describes the IGC as finding itself 'in the somewhat surreal position of considering amendments to treaty provisions which had never been used, to deal with situations which could not be clearly identified and for no clearly defined objective'.[50]

A number of submissions were made to the IGC by Member States on the question of enhanced cooperation, but these were consistently notable for their broadbrush approach rather than their commitment to detailed exposition of proposed reforms.[51] A number of smaller and medium-sized Member States were initially rather suspicious of an initiative emanating essentially from their larger counterparts, but none the less saw the discussions as an opportunity to consolidate their relative advantage over the applicant countries.[52] This suggests rather venial motives operating below the surface, but at least these were not evident in the public disucssion. The joint position paper issued by Germany and Italy in October 2000 very much set the tone of the debate:[53]

> Germany and Italy reject the notion of a 'Europe à la carte'. The instrument of enhanced cooperation must under all circumstances be used in a selective and politically responsible manner. Enhanced cooperation should not lead to uncoordinated and random parallel initiatives of divergent groups of Member States. In this sense, the goal is not so much 'enhanced cooperation' as 'enhanced integration'.

Furthermore, Presidency papers issued on this topic right up to the Biarritz European Council tended to be interrogatory rather than dispositive,[54] and while the issue was successfully 'packaged' at Biarritz on 13/14 October 2000, bizarrely no actual article drafts appeared on the table until

---

[48] Galloway, above n 43 at p 133.

[49] M Gray and A Stubb, 'Keynote Article: The Treaty of Nice – Negotiating a Poisoned Chalice?', (2001) 39 *Journal of Common Market Studies, Annual Review 2000/2001* 5 at p17.

[50] Galloway, above n 43 at p 133.

[51] See for example the Benelux Memorandum on the IGC and the future of the European Union, The Hague, 29 September 2000; Belgian delegation comments to the IGC Group of Representatives on closer cooperation, 28 August 2000, CONFER 4765/00.

[52] Yataganas, above n 7 at p 47.

[53] Joint submission by the German and Italian delegation to the IGC Group of Representatives, 4 October 2000, CONFER 4783/00.

[54] Typical is the Presidency Note on *Closer Cooperation*, 18 July 2000, CONFER 4761/00 issued after a discussion at the IGC Representatives' Group on 14 July 2000, consisting of a series of questions for delegations to consider about the conditions for enhanced cooperation and how it should operate in the future.

18 October 2000.[55] The final published version (17 November 2000) of what were then known as 'Clauses A-P', which were subsequently transmuted into the legal form of amendments to and substitutions for the relevant EC and EU Treaty provisions, is textually very close to that which was finally agreed in Nice.[56] The frequency of political discussion of flexibility eased the process of agreement. The lack of detailed discussion of the actual provisions points to the crucial role of the Council secretariat in shaping the final outputs. David Galloway judges the revision of the enhanced cooperation provisions to be an example of the IGC method working well, on the basis of effective and thorough preparation at various political and technical levels.[57]

VI.   THE NICE PROVISIONS

The broad lines of the Nice amendments are rather easy to state.[58] They concern the procedural conditions for engaging in flexibility and many of its substantive conditions. As to the procedural conditions, the new provisions provide that the number of participating states must be eight, even after the Union enlarges; thus the requirement of a participating majority will disappear in 2004. The emergency brake has largely been removed in pillars one and three, along with the language of 'important and stated reasons of national policy' which recalled the Luxembourg Accords of the 1960s and the dark days of stagnation for the pre-Single European Act European Communities. The substantive terms have also been changed, with the hurdles set by the cumulative conditions for EC Treaty flexibility of Article 43 TEU and Article 11 EC being lowered. At the same time, the essential protections both for the non-participating Member States, for the institutions, and for the character of the Community legal order and the Union *acquis* are in large measure retained. It is explicitly established, for example, that measures adopted under the closer cooperation provisions *do not* become part of that *acquis*. On the other hand, by way of illustration of the eased substantive conditions, the condition not to *affect* the *acquis communautaire* (which is a challenging negative injunction) becomes a positive injunction to *respect* it, which can presumably be fulfilled in a variety of more creative ways. The guarantee that enhanced cooperation cannot extend the existing range of EC/EU powers is made more explicit. Under the new provisions, there is an explicit and generally applicable statement

[55] Presidency Note, *Enhanced Cooperation*, 18 October 2000, CONFER 4786/00.
[56] Presidency Note, *IGC 2000: Enhanced Cooperation*, 17 November 2000, CONFER 4803/00.
[57] Galloway, above n 43 at p 142.
[58] They are not dissimilar to the recommendations contained in Philippart and Sie Dhian Ho, above n 32 at p 43 *et seq.*

in Article 43(d) TEU that the proposed cooperation [in any of the pillars] must remain 'within the limits of the powers of the Union or of the Community ...'. The role of the European Parliament under pillar one enhanced cooperation is marginally strengthened as it is given a veto under Article 11(2) EC over enhanced cooperation if it relates to an area where legislation is normally to be adopted by co-decision under Article 251 EC. This is intended to protect democratic legitimacy. The already strong role of the European Commission is preserved.

In addition to the formal legal language in which the Nice provisions are for the most part inevitably couched, there are continuous reiterations of the 'last resort' nature of flexibility, the openness of the approach which must be adopted by the participating states *vis-à-vis* the non-participating states, and the need for 'consistency', exhortations which are not always phrased in strict legal language and which are not necessarily technical legal necessities. On the contrary, such provisions are often rather about giving the right message on flexibility. As David Galloway comments, 'while lawyers may be critical of the fact that a number of the general conditions laid down in Article 40 are repetitive or redundant from a strictly legal point of view, sometimes provides the necessary reassurance for obtaining agreement ...'[59] For one thing, such 'legally unsatisfactory' provisions were included also as a political signal to the candidate countries about the EU having rejected the idea of a hard core from which the Central and Eastern Europe countries will forever be excluded.

However, since the Treaty provisions were quite substantially reshaped with shifts, for example, between the old Article 11 EC and the old Article 43 TEU, it is easiest to review the details of the changes to these provisions by reference to a set of tables setting out the old and the new provisions in parallel. Such tables bring out even the subtle changes instituted by the Treaty of Nice in a relatively user-friendly way.

Table 1 sets out the basic conditions for all forms of enhanced cooperation across the three pillars; these are now encompassed in Article 43 TEU, which in some respects supercedes or takes over the specific pillar one conditions contained in (old) Article 11 EC. The reference to the reinforcement of integration in Article 43(a) is extremely interesting. This comprises only the second explicit citation of the concept of 'integration' in the EC and EU Treaties, throughout their 50 years of existence.[60] Operating in the question-setting mode which marked the earlier stages of its management of the negotiation of flexibility, it was the French Presidency which set this ball rolling by asking the delegations in July 2000 whether it would be possible

---

[59] Galloway, above n 43 at p 139.
[60] This point is also emphasised by J V Louis, 'Le Traité de Nice', (2001) *Journal des Tribuneaux, Droit Européen* 25; see also K St C Bradley, 'Institutional Design in the Treaty of Nice', (2001) 38 *Common Market Law Review* 1095 at p 1121.

TABLE 1: Enhanced Cooperation: the basic conditions

New Provisions	New Texts	Old Provisions	Old Texts
Art 43	Member States which intend to establish enhanced cooperation between themselves may make use of the institutions, procedures and mechanisms laid down by this Treaty and by the Treaty establishing the European Community provided that the proposed cooperation…	Art 43(1)	Member States which intend to establish closer cooperation between themselves may make use of the institutions, procedures and mechanisms laid down by this Treaty and the Treaty establishing the European Community provided that the cooperation…
Art 43(a)	is aimed at furthering the objectives of the Union and of the Community, at protecting and serving their interests and at reinforcing their process of integration	Art 43(1)(a)	is aimed at furthering the objectives of the Union and at protecting and serving its interests;
Art 43(b)	respects the said Treaties and the single institutional framework of the Union	Art 43(1)(b)	respects the principles of the said Treaties and the single institutional framework of the Union
Art 43(c)	respects the *acquis communautaire* and the measures adopted under the other provisions of the said Treaties	Art 43(1)(e)	does not affect the 'acquis communautaire' and the measures adopted under the other provisions of the said Treaties
Art 43(d)	remains within the limits of the powers of the Union or of the Community and does not concern the areas which fall within the exclusive competence of the Community	Art 11(1)(d)	remains within the limits of the powers conferred upon the Community by this Treaty
		Art 11(1)(a)	does not concern areas which fall within the exclusive competence of the Community
Art 43(e)	does not undermine the internal market as defined in Article 14(2) of the Treaty establishing the European Community, or the economic and social cohesion established in accordance with Title XVII of that Treaty	Art 11(1)(b)	does not affect Community policies, actions or programmes
		Art 11(1)(c)	does not concern the citizenship of the Union or discriminate between nationals of Member States
Art 43(f)	does not constitute a barrier to or discrimination in trade between the Member States and does not distort competition between them	Art 11(1)(e)	does not constitute a discrimination or a restriction of trade between Member States and does not distort the conditions of competition between the latter

(continued)

Art 43(g)	involves a minimum of eight Member States	Art 43(1)(d)	concerns at least a majority of Member States
Art 43(h)	respects the competences, rights and obligations of those Member States which do not participate therein	Art 43(1)(f)	does not affect the competences, rights, obligations and interests of those Member States which do not participate therein
Art 43(i)	does not affect the provisions of the Protocol integrating the Schengen acquis into the framework of the European Union	Art 11(5)	...without prejudice to the provisions of the Protocol integrating the Schengen acquis into the framework of the European Union
Art 43(j)	is open to all the Member States, in accordance with Article 43b	Art 43(1)(g)	is open to all Member States and allows them to become parties to the cooperation at any time, provided that they comply with the basic decision and with the decisions taken within that framework
Art 43b	When enhanced cooperation is established, it shall be open to all Member States. It shall also be open to them at any time, in accordance with Articles 27e and 40b of this Treaty and with Article 11a of the Treaty establishing the European Community, subject to compliance with the basic decision and with the decisions taken within that framework. The Commission and the Member States parties to enhanced cooperation shall ensure that as many Member States as possible are encouraged to take part		
Art 43a	Enhanced cooperation may be engaged in only as a last resort, when it has been established within the Council that the objectives of such cooperation cannot be attained within a reasonable period by applying the relevant provisions of the Treaties.	Art 43(1)(c)	is only used as a last resort, where the objectives of the said Treaties could not be attained by applying the relevant procedures laid down therein
[...]	[no longer necessary]	Art 43(1)(h)	complies with the specific additional criteria laid down in Article 11 of the Treaty establishing the European Community and Article 40 of this Treaty, depending on the area concerned, and is authorised by the Council in accordance with the procedures laid down therein

to go further than stipulating merely that closer cooperation is a means of furthering the Union's objectives to provide that 'such cooperation constitutes a means of integration.'[61] Also interesting to note is that the drafters of the Treaty have reordered the basic substantive conditions regarding the compatibility of enhanced cooperation with the system of the EU Treaties (new Articles 43(d)–(f) TEU; old Articles 11(1)(a)–(e) EC) to bring the more general requirements to the head of the list.[62]

Two examples of the use of more open-textured language to make enhanced cooperation seem an open and inclusive project are included in this Table. First, the requirement that enhanced cooperation activities remain open to the non-participating states (old Article 43(1)(g) TEU) is elaborated through the exhortation to the Commission and the participating Member States to seek to encourage non-participating Member States to join in (new Article 43b TEU) and second, the requirement that enhanced cooperation be a last resort exercise (old Article 43(1)(c) TEU) is likewise elaborated through an injunction to establish within the Council that the objectives of such cooperation cannot be attained within a reasonable period by applying the relevant provisions of the Treaties (new Article 43a TEU). Since it cannot be known, scientifically speaking, what a 'reasonable' period of time might be, and since the Court of Justice would be very unlikely to be tempted to define such a period if it were to be brought into a dispute on this matter, this seems—in effect—an unenforceable injunction to the Council to behave reasonably.

Table 2 shows that there have been relatively few changes to the general institutional framework applying to all instances of enhanced cooperation, so far as that framework applies to all three pillars. These are the texts dealing with issues such as what constitutes a qualified majority in the context of a reduced number of participants in decision-making and the allocation of expenditure to the participating Member States. Changes include a requirement to consult the European Parliament before the Council takes a unanimous decision to decide that budgetary expenditure resulting from the implementation of enhanced cooperation will be borne other than simply by the participating Member States. The removal of the reference in old Article 45 TEU to the Council and the Commission informing the European Parliament of the development of closer cooperation under Title VII TEU constitutes the tidying up of a somewhat anomalous provision. Title VII was never a freestanding basis for closer cooperation; enhanced cooperation must be engaged according to these general requirements and the specific rules of each of the three pillars. These rules in turn provide for the degree of involvement of the European Parliament, involvement shaped

---

[61] CONFER 4761/00, above n 54 at p 1.
[62] Cf Shaw, above n 23 at pp 72–73, where I analysed the conditions of Art 11(1) in the order of (d), (a), (b), (c), (e) in which they now appear, in effect, in Art 43 TEU.

TABLE 2: Enhanced cooperation: the general institutional framework

New Provisions	New Texts	Old Provisions	Old Texts
Art 44(1)	For the purposes of the adoption of the acts and decisions necessary for the implementation of enhanced cooperation referred to in Article 43, the relevant institutional provisions of this Treaty and of the Treaty establishing the European Community shall apply. However, while all members of the Council shall be able to take part in the deliberations, only those representing participating Member States shall take part in the adoption of decisions. The qualified majority shall be defined as the same proportion of the weighted votes and the same proportion of the number of the members of the Council concerned as laid down in Article 205(2) of the Treaty establishing the European Community, and in the second and third subparagraphs of Article 23(2) of this Treaty as regards enhanced cooperation established on the basis of Article 27c. Unanimity shall be constituted by only those Council members concerned. Such acts and decisions shall not form part of the Union acquis.	Art 44(1)	For the purposes of the adoption of the acts and decisions necessary for the implementation of the cooperation referred to in Article 43, the relevant institutional provisions of this Treaty and of the Treaty establishing the European Community shall apply. However, while all members of the Council shall be able to take part in the deliberations, only those representing participating Member States shall take part in the adoption of decisions. The qualified majority shall be defined as the same proportion of the weighted votes of the members of the Council concerned as laid down in Article 205(2) of the Treaty establishing the European Community. Unanimity shall be constituted by only those Council members concerned.
Art 44a	Expenditure resulting from implementation of enhanced cooperation, other than administrative costs entailed for the institutions, shall be borne by the participating Member States, unless all members of the Council, acting unanimously after consulting the European Parliament, decide otherwise	Art 44(2)	Expenditure resulting from implementation of the cooperation, other than administrative costs entailed for the institutions, shall be borne by the participating Member States, unless the Council, acting unanimously, decides otherwise.
Art 44(2)	Member States shall apply, as far as they are concerned, the acts and decisions adopted for the implementation of the enhanced cooperation to which they are party. Such acts and decisions shall be binding only on those Member States which are party to such cooperation and shall be directly applicable only in those States. Member States which are not party to such cooperation shall not impede the implementation thereof by the participating Member States. [...]	Art 43(2)	Member States shall apply, as far as they are concerned, the acts and decisions adopted for the implementation of the cooperation in which they participate. Member States not participating in such cooperation shall not impede the implementation thereof by the participating Member States
Art 45	The Council and the Commission shall ensure the consistency of activities undertaken on the basis of this Title and the consistency of such activities with the policies of the Union and the Community, and shall cooperate to that end	Art 45	The Council and the Commission shall regularly inform the European Parliament of the development of closer cooperation established on the basis of this Title. [...]

essentially according to the precepts of each individual pillar. The addition of the duty on the Council and the Commission to ensure consistency within the activities undertaken on the basis of enchanced cooperation and with the wider frame of policies of the Union and the Community (new Article 45 TEU) forms part of the group of provisions couched in open-textured language which are included to ensure that enhanced cooperation does not have a divisive and fragmentary impact upon the legal and political order of the Union, but is able to operate—on the contrary—as a constructive tool of governance within diversity.

It is within this group of provisions that the drafters chose to locate the similarly conservatory statement that acts and decisions taken to implement the enhanced cooperation provisions *do not* become part of the Union *acquis*. Although the (laudable) intentions behind such a provision are undoubtedly to protect the interests of the non-participants, the attempt thus to restrict the development of European Community and European Union law—although beguilingly simple—is somewhat misleading. The development of important principles on judicial protection and the understanding of how concepts of representative and associative democracy can operate in the EU system[63] which can be seen in the ruling of the Court of First Instance on the challenge brought by UEAPME against its exclusion from the social partner negotiations which gave rise to the parental leave agreement[64] makes it clear that the boundaries of the *acquis* cannot so easily be sealed. This is especially so as regards the development of principles and concepts. Although now applicable to all Member States, the measure under challenge (the Parental Leave Directive) was originally adopted under the provisions of the post-Maastricht Social Policy Agreement from which the UK opted out. In every respect, the Court of First Instance's judgment treats the measure as an 'ordinary' measure of Community law by applying its general case law on judicial protection and in particular the standing of non-privileged applicants for judicial review, as indeed it would, under Article 11(3) EC, if the measure under scrutiny were one which had been adopted under enhanced cooperation. Inevitably, however, the application of the general provisions of the EC Treaty to the enhanced cooperation measure has the capacity—as it did in the *UEAPME* case—to contribute to the incremental development of a single and generally applicable case law on concepts of judicial protection and access to justice.[65] To that end, at least, the *acquis* will inevitably develop if the enabling clauses for enhanced cooperation are actually implemented, even if the specific policy measures

---

[63] For commentary, see N Bernard, 'Legitimising EU Law: Is the Social Dialogue the Way Forward? Some Reflections Around the UEAPME Case', in J Shaw (ed), *Social Law and Policy in an Evolving European Union* (Oxford, Hart Publishing, 2000).
[64] Case T–135/96 *UEAPME v Council* [1998] ECR II–2335.
[65] See generally the discussion of *UEAPME* in J Shaw, *Law of the European Union* 3rd edn (London, Palgrave, 2000) at pp 240, 342 and 517.

adopted are themselves excluded from the *acquis* and would not need to be transposed by a new Member State in the event of enlargement.[65a] EU lawyers cannot, therefore, in any circumstances ignore the concrete outputs from enhanced cooperation projects, any more than they could ignore the social policy measures adopted by the 'Fourteen' during the UK opt-out, or indeed the Justice and Home Affairs measures being adopted under the Tampere Framework for the development of the Area of Freedom, Security and Justice, from which the UK is in large measure opted out by virtue of the arrangements made at Amsterdam.

Table 3 sets out the specific arrangements for pillar one enhanced cooperation, under Articles 11 and 11a EC, which are somewhat truncated in comparison to the former Amsterdam versions, since many of the conditions of enhanced cooperation have now been rationalised in the general framework of Article 43 TEU. The procedure for setting about establishing an enhanced cooperation project is now slightly clearer and more rationally organised. Of considerable importance is the improvement in the position of the European Parliament under the authorisation process, as it now has the capacity to veto enhanced cooperation projects in fields where co-decision under Article 251 EC applies. This is a minimal response to the demands of the European Parliament, which had sought an across-the-board veto in its October 2000 Resolution on closer cooperation.[66] Of course, the European Parliament was never likely to succeed in obtaining a veto over enhanced cooperation activities in fields where it has no such veto over 'normal' policy-making. The European Parliament also supported the removal of the national veto or 'emergency brake' as it was termed, and that wish accorded with those of the Member States, who duly amended Article 11(2) second paragraph. A referral to the European Council can still be requested by a dissenting Member State, but even after such referral the Council *may* take a decision, under the same conditions of qualified majority voting as would normally apply. The possibility of resolving the matter by unanimity alone in the European Council—meeting as the Council—is removed.

Changes to the enhanced cooperation provisions under pillars two and three have also been instituted by the Treaty of Nice. The Treaty of Amsterdam established a framework for closer cooperation under Title VI of the Treaty on European Union (pillar three), in the form of Articles 40–41 TEU. This was instituted to enable the Union 'to develop more rapidly into an area of freedom, security and justice' (Article 40(1)(b) TEU), an interesting reference to enhanced cooperation operating in the service of the

---

[65a] This specific meaning of Art 44(1) TEU became clearer in the context of the deliberations of the Convention on the Future of the Union on whether enhanced cooperation should be included in the new (draft) Constitution. See CONV 723/03 of 14 May 2003, p 5.

[66] European Parliament Resolution on Closer Cooperation, 25 October 2000, 2000/2162, endorsing the Gil-Robles Gil-Delgado Report on Reinforced Cooperation drawn up for the Committee on Constitutional Affairs, 12 October 2000, A5–0288/2000.

TABLE 3: Enhanced cooperation in the first pillar

New Provisions	New Texts	Old Provisions	Old Texts
	[...]	Art 11(1)	Member States which intend to establish closer cooperation between themselves may be authorised, subject to Articles 43 and 44 of the Treaty on European Union, to make use of the institutions, procedures and mechanisms laid down by this Treaty, provided that...
Art 11(1)	Member States which intend to establish enhanced cooperation between themselves in one of the areas referred to in the Treaty establishing the European Community shall address a request to the Commission, which may submit a proposal to the Council to that effect. In the event of the Commission not submitting a proposal, it shall inform the Member States concerned of the reasons for not doing so.	Art 11(2) third para	Member States which intend to establish closer cooperation as referred to in paragraph 1 may address a request to the Commission, which may submit a proposal to the Council to that effect. In the event of the Commission not submitting a proposal, it shall inform the Member States concerned of the reasons for not doing so.
Art 11(2) first para	Authorisation to establish the enhanced cooperation referred to in paragraph 1 shall be granted, in compliance with Articles 43 to 45 of the Treaty on European Union, by the Council, acting by a qualified majority on a proposal from the Commission after consulting the European Parliament. When enhanced cooperation relates to an area covered by the procedure referred to in Article 251, the assent of the European Parliament shall be required	Art 11(2) first para	The authorisation referred to in paragraph 1 shall be granted by the Council, acting by a qualified majority on a proposal from the Commission and after consulting the European Parliament

(continued)

Art 11(2) second para	A member of the Council may request that the matter be referred to the European Council. After that referral, the Council may take a decision in accordance with the provisions of the first subparagraph.	Art 11(2) second para	If a member of the Council declares that, for important and stated reasons of national policy, it intends to oppose the granting of an authorisation by qualified majority, a vote shall not be taken. The Council may, acting by a qualified majority, request that the matter be referred to the Council, meeting in the composition of the Heads of State or Government, for decision by unanimity.
Art 11(3)	The acts and decisions necessary for the implementation of enhanced cooperation activities shall be subject to all the relevant provisions of the Treaty establishing the European Community, save as otherwise provided in this Article and in Articles 43 to 45 of the Treaty on European Union.	Art 11(4)	The acts and decisions necessary for the implementation of cooperation activities shall be subject to all the relevant provisions of this Treaty, save as otherwise provided for in this Article and in Articles 43 and 44 of the Treaty on European Union.
Art 11a	Any Member State which wishes to become a party to enhanced cooperation established in accordance with Article 11 shall notify its intention to the Council and to the Commission, which shall give an opinion to the Council within three months of receipt of that notification. Within four months of receipt of that notification, the Commission shall take a decision on it, and on such specific arrangements as it may deem necessary.	Art 11(3)	Any Member State which wishes to become a party to cooperation set up in accordance with this Article shall notify its intention to the Council and to the Commission, which shall give an opinion to the Council within three months of receipt of that notification. Within four months of the date of that notification, the Commission shall decide on it and on such specific arrangements as it may deem necessary.

speed of development of integration, which has no explicit parallel in the context of pillar one enhanced cooperation. Article 40 TEU has been replaced by new Articles 40–40b TEU. The objective of rapid development of the AFSJ is preserved (new Article 40(1) TEU). The most important changes comprise the removal of the emergency brake (new Article 40a(2) TEU) and the formal institution of the possibility for the Member States wishing to embark upon enhanced cooperation to request the necessary authorisation from the Council, in the event that the Commission decides not to take the necessary initiative upon their request (Article 40a(1) TEU).

After the Treaty of Amsterdam, no formal arrangements for enhanced cooperation under pillar two were in place3, with the exception of the possibility of constructive abstention under Article 23(1) TEU, to allow a dissenting Member State to avoid the outcome that its dissent stymies all Union policy development in the foreign and security policy fields. The Treaty of Nice provisions formally establish the possibility of enhanced cooperation under Title V of the TEU (Articles 27a–27e TEU), although after a failure to agree at Nice, Article 27b TEU explicitly excludes matters having military or defence implications from the range of matters on which enhanced cooperation may be engaged. Enhanced cooperation in this field is limited to the arrangements to be made for the implementation of a pre-existing joint action or common position, and hence it presupposes a degree of commonality in policy formulation prior to the engagement with variability in implementation. Pillar two enhanced cooperation must be aimed at 'safeguarding the values and serving the interests of the Union as a whole by asserting its identity as a coherent force on the international scene' (Article 27a(1) TEU). It must be seen, therefore, as a tool of governance aimed at efficiency rather than the promotion of closer integration. Unlike pillars one and three, the Commission does not have a role in initiating the Council's decision. Its role is limited to giving an opinion upon the request forwarded to it by the Council. Decision-making by qualified majority is foreseen, under the same conditions as applying generally to Title V TEU (Article 23 TEU). An emergency brake in the form of a reference to the European Council is provided for, as it was in the original Amsterdam versions of pillar one and pillar three enhanced cooperation. Given the intergovernmental nature of pillar two, this seems a consistent development, as is the role given to the High Representative for common foreign and security policy to ensure that the European Parliament and all Member States, including the non-participants, are kept fully informed of the implementation of enhanced cooperation in this field (Article 27d TEU). However laudable the intentions of the drafters of the new provisions, it is difficult to escape the preliminary conclusion that since the Treaty of Nice came into force the range of variants for enhanced cooperation have become needlessly complex.[67] In the interests of avoiding the proliferation of different systems, there is a case to be answered

[67] Warleigh, above n 18.

as to why the pillar two arrangements do not more closely resemble those for pillar three, rather than offering a third set of variables, as they do at present. Some reduction in this complexity is envisaged by the (draft) Constitutional Treaty agreed by the Convention on the Future of the Union in June 2003. [67a]

VII.   CONCLUSION

The subtitle of this paper is the question: 'will the Treaty do the trick?'. But what exactly is this 'trick'? In fact, the gist of this paper is that the questions to be asked and the answers to be given about enhanced cooperation after the Treaty of Nice are by no means simple. However, the trickery necessarily involved in balancing many apparently competing interests via a single set of Treaty provisions enabling future enhanced cooperation seems as challenging now as it was after the Treaty of Amsterdam. In the light of this basic question, the concluding section will consider the following three sets of subquestions before ending with a more general meditation on the outcomes of the Nice amendments:

— What summary evaluation of the new provisions should be given? Are they likely to be more functional than the previous Amsterdam versions? Will the new provisions be implemented in practice after they come into force, and if so in what areas?

— Will the new provisions reduce, increase or leave unchanged the likelihood that 'vanguard' Member States may have recourse to mechanisms outside the framework of the Treaties in order to pursue their objectives of closer integration?

— Do the new provisions change the balance of arguments or forces in relation to the wider debate about flexibility, especially in the view of ongoing discussions such as those on the Governance White Paper and the Convention established at the Laeken European Council to prepare the 2004 IGC?

a)   Summary Evaluation?

The commentators have generally welcomed the new post-Nice provisions on enhanced cooperation, as an improvement upon their predecessors, using phrases such as 'reasonably operational', 'fairly well balanced', and 'some progress on making the provisions easier to operate'.[68]

[67a] CONV 820 of 20 June 2003, Draft Treaty Establishing a Constitution for Europe, Article I–43 and CONV 802 of June 2003, Draft Constitution, Volume II, Articles III–318 – III–325. See, generally, J Shaw, 'Flexibility in a "Reorganized" and "Simplified" Treaty', (2003) 40 *Common Market Law Review* 279.

[68] Gray and Stubb, above n 49 at p 17.

For example, Eric Philippart is markedly upbeat about the future of enhanced cooperation:[69]

All in all, with the Treaty of Nice, the EU is now equipped with a reasonably operational mechanism for closer cooperation. Indeed, preliminary attempts to make use of closer cooperation have shown that many pre-conditions are less restrictive than expected. The services of the Council and the Commission have, for instance, adopted a rather liberal interpretation of the 'last resort' or the protection of the *acquis*. For a number of important areas such as the environment, justice and home affairs, taxation and other flanking measures of monetary policy, closer cooperation can now function as a 'laboratory' for the EU. The willing can 'experiment' with new policies and regimes which could eventually be of interest for the entire Union. The others can wait for the first result, before deciding to join the experiment or not. It offers the possibility to establish 'large sub-systemic' closer cooperation—ie by focusing on a topic interesting only to a sub-group of member states.

At the same time, however, he also cautions that:

combined with the persistent absence of catch-up mechanism, however, the lowering of the participation threshold could undermine the principle of the single institutional framework. Fragmentation induced by closer cooperation remains the main danger for the current EU model. Prudent politics should therefore preside over its use.

As part of a more general review of the Treaty of Nice, Xenophon Yataganas (whose perspective is that of an institutional insider) suggests that:[70]

In the end, the 'closer cooperation package' appears to be fairly well balanced. It ensures that the EU will not stagnate by, on the one hand, allowing Member States who so wish to advance, subject to certain conditions, while guaranteeing the others the right to be able to join the leading group. By preserving the Community framework and the cohesion effort, the closer cooperation mechanisms appear capable of keeping Europe on track towards ever-tighter integration, while allowing each country to go along this route according to its own rhythm and special needs.

In sum, the Treaty constitutes 'clear progress' over what had been achieved at Amsterdam. Meanwhile, for Kieran Bradley[71] the step from Amsterdam to Nice is between making enhanced cooperation 'respectable' (Amsterdam) and making it a 'practical proposition' (Nice). He believes that the credible 'threat' of enhanced cooperation could be enough to make

---

[68] Gray and Stubb, above n 49 at p 17.
[69] Philippart, above n 20.
[70] Yataganas, above n 7 at p 48.

Member States less likely to have recourse to their 'veto' in fields of decision-making by unanimity. As ever in the case of enhanced or closer cooperation, however, comments like this are longer on generalised exhortations about the increased user-friendliness of the provisions, and shorter on specifics as to individual fields in which they may be invoked.

b)   Enhanced Cooperation Inside or Outside the Treaties?

In contrast, there is no consensus amongst the commentators as to whether the new provisions will affect the likelihood that some of the Member States may in the future have recourse to enhanced cooperation mechanisms concluded outside the framework of the Treaty in circumstances where they wish to deepen the process of integration between them. This question goes to the most prominent challenge which enhanced cooperation is thought to face as an instrument of governance, namely that of affording flexibility without fragmentation. According to David Galloway, the new framework is 'a deterrent to states seeking solutions or constituting a 'core' group outside the Union's institutional future'; like any effective deterrent the provisions have to appear credible even if they are never actually used.[72] For him, it is part of an attempt to give an enlarged European Union a range of instruments to manage diversity—an 'insurance policy'. Mark Gray and Alexander Stubb back up this view.[73] They describe this as the 'real success' of the reworked provisions. Going even further, Xenophon Yataganas asserts that flexibility can be (inherently) integrative: opt outs can operate like 'a locomotive pulling the latecomers in the desired direction, and may be (sic) that closer cooperation will have the same effect'.[74] By way of contrast, Alex Warleigh thinks it is just as likely that the Member States will go outside the Treaty.[75] This is, of course, probably the most crucial question to which the advocates of enhanced cooperation must face up. From an integrationist perspective, the provisions can have little utility if they have not succeeded in attaining the publicly acknowledged goal of allowing vanguard Member States to proceed, by balancing the preservation of the *acquis* and the principles of EU law against the pursuit of integration.

c)   The Effects on the Wider Debate?

One of the symbolic impacts of the enhanced cooperation debate is that it serves as a general reminder to observers that deepening will not be sacrificed

---

[71] Bradley, above n 60 at p 1122.
[72] Galloway above n 43 at p 140.
[73] Gray and Stubb, above n 49 at p 17.
[74] Yataganas, above n 7.

to the project of widening. That conclusion is strengthened when one observes that the specific discussions over changes to the flexibility provisions were merely the foreground to a wider picture in which the backdrop was made up of high level exchanges of view between key political stakeholders in the EU Member States about the nature of the European 'finality' and whether there should be a 'vanguard' group going forward quickly to adopt a constitutive treaty and other aspects of a recognisably 'federal' Europe.[76]

There are two specific 'wider' debates to which it is essential to try to link the enhanced cooperation agenda. The first is the debate about the governance of the European Union, a debate managed in some measure by the European Commission, especially in the context of its presentation in July 2001 of a White Paper on European Governance.[77] This much criticised paper was soon picked up for its failure to discuss the possibilities offered for 'flexible' governance by the mechanisms of enhanced cooperation. According to Fritz Scharpf:

> It seems puzzling that the Commission is not actively promoting closer cooperation as an instrument that would accommodate a moderate degree of diversity without relaxing the controls of the 'Community method'.[78]

Puzzling too is the absence of any reference to flexibility, never mind enhanced cooperation in the recent Laeken Declaration of December 2001, a document which summarises in sweeping language many of the problems of a 'Europe' which finds itself at present at a crossroads, in terms of both its internal and external images and perspectives.[79] This rather grandly worded document established the Convention on the Future of the Union to prepare the 2004 IGC, chaired by ex French President Giscard d'Estaing. The fears that some Member States may prefer in the longer term to opt out of the European Union altogether, by developing a concept of 'centre of gravity' or 'pioneer group', a fear stemming in no small part from the pronouncements on these matters by Giscard d'Estaing's great proponent as Chair of the Convention, French President Jacques Chirac, inevitably circulated in and around the meeting rooms of the Convention. The question was not formally on the agenda, but the uses and abuses of enhanced

---

[75] Warleigh, above n 18.
[76] See House of Commons Research Paper 00/88, *IGC 2000: Enhanced Cooperation*, 21 November 2000, pp 10–14. See also more generally C Joerges, Y Mény and J H H Weiler (eds), *What Kind of Constitution for What Kind of Polity? Responses to Joschka Fischer*, Harvard Jean Monnet Working Paper 7/00 (www.jeanmonnetprogram.org).
[77] COM(2001) 428 of 25 July 2001.
[78] F Scharpf, 'European Governance: Common Concerns vs. the Challenge of Diversity', *The Jean Monnet Chair Working Papers 06/01*, Symposium on The Commission White Paper on Governance, at p 11 (www.jeanmonnetprogram.org).
[79] European Council Meeting in Laeken, 14 and 15 December 2001, Presidency Conclusions, Annex 1: Laeken Declaration on the Future of the European Union.

cooperation did receive a reasonable airing during the 16 months of the Convention's existence between March 2002 and June 2003, culminating in a modest simplification of the rules, with very little substantive change. This brings us back to the crucial question and general conclusion of this paper. We are no nearer, after the Treaty of Nice and indeed the Convention's draft Constitution, to finding a general consensus on what flexibility 'means' for the European Union. It is possible that after the Convention's discussions, the EU may be closer to fulfilling Alex Warleigh's wish that flexibility should be explicitly developed from being merely a *tool* of EU governance, to being a *principle* of governance. This can only be achieved if a clear model of flexibility is formulated and the knotty normative questions of what flexibility actually means for an evolving European Union are directly engaged rather than perpetually skirted around. In the meantime, it would appear that the capacity of the flexibility concept to contribute to the resolution of the EU's difficulties with legitimacy will continue to be sacrificed in favour of promoting its more limited capacity to offer efficient tools of governance in an ever more diverse Union.

8

The Treaty of Nice and the Treaty Structure: Repainting the Pillars?

STEVE PEERS*

I. INTRODUCTION

T HE COMPLEX AND unwieldy constitutional structure created by the negotiators of the original Treaty establishing the European Union (TEU) in 1991 is still with us 10 years later. Indeed, it is set to remain with us at least until the next Intergovernmental Conference (IGC) in 2004, because the Treaty of Nice (if ratified) will not abolish this structure. Although the new Treaty would not make any radical change to the structure of the Union, it would make a number of modest changes to that structure that would impact upon the relationship between the various 'pillars' of the Union and which may, following future IGCs, be seen as significant turning points.

This chapter will therefore consider three issues in turn. First, what would happen to the structure of the European Union with the ratification of the Treaty of Nice, including the impact of the EU Charter of Fundamental Rights on such structural issues? Second, in light of the first issue, can we draw any conclusions regarding the nature of the European Union from the perspective of legal theory? And third, what issues arise as regards the future of the Treaty structure?

II. BACKGROUND

The structure of the European Union should first be briefly recalled. From 1958, a central feature of the Community system has been the multiplicity of different Treaties governing it, when two separate Treaties establishing the European Economic Community (EEC, renamed the EC in 1993) and the European Atomic Energy Community (Euratom) joined the Treaty

---

* Professor in Law, University of Essex. This Chapter was written before entry into force of the Treaty of Nice, the expiry of the ECSC Treaty and the work of the EU constitutional convention.

establishing the European Coal and Steel Community (ECSC), which had entered into force in 1952 but which will expire in July 2002.[1] The institutions of the three Communities were subsequently fully merged by the Merger Treaty of 1967,[2] but the three Treaties still differ in certain respects.

Subsequently, the 'European Union' was created formally by the TEU (in force November 1993). While the regime governing the three Community Treaties (and the Merger Treaty) was complicated enough on its own, the adoption of the TEU further complicated matters. Moreover, there has been no simplification of the system since, because the Treaty of Amsterdam (in force May 1999) simply further amended all three Community Treaties and the TEU, and the Treaty of Nice, if it is ratified, would do the same.

The initial version of the TEU was an overarching treaty containing amendments to each of the three Community Treaties in its Articles G, H and I (now Articles 8, 9 and 10), constituting Titles II, III and IV. But it also contained free-standing provisions of its own: Title V (Articles J to J.11, now Articles 11 to 28) concerned Common Foreign and Security Policy (CFSP) matters (the 'second pillar'), while Title VI (Articles K to K.9, now Articles 29 to 42) concerned Justice and Home Affairs (JHA) issues (the 'third pillar').[3] In addition, Title I on 'common provisions' (Articles A to F, now Articles 1 to 7) and Title VII on 'general and final provisions' (Articles L to S, now Articles 46 to 53) both contained provisions that were relevant to all three pillars, including many express or implied links between them. The most significant points were that the Community institutions had different roles within the framework of the 'intergovernmental' EU Treaty,[4] and different instruments were used to adopt measures. Indeed, the EU Treaty, rather than the Community Treaties, defines the composition and role of the European Council.[5] But the Union is 'founded upon' the Communities,[6] pursues objectives under the EC *and* EU Treaties,[7] has a 'single institutional framework' requiring consistency between Union policies,[8] must observe founding principles across all pillars, including respect for human rights as 'general principles of Community law',[9] and has a single

---

[1] Its subject-matter will be dealt with pursuant to the EC Treaty after its expiry.

[2] Most provisions of the Merger Treaty were inserted into the Community Treaties by the TEU, and the Merger Treaty was then repealed by Art 9 of the Treaty of Amsterdam.

[3] These provisions formalised and to some extent amended pre-existing forms of intergovernmental cooperation.

[4] See particularly Art E (now 5) EU and, as regards the Court of Justice, Art L (now 46) EU. Many EC Treaty rules on the composition and functioning of the European Parliament, Council and Commission applied to the second and third pillars: see Arts J.11(1) and K.8(1) EU.

[5] Art D (now 4) EU.

[6] Art A (now 1) EU.

[7] Art B (now 2) EU, which also referred to the subsidiarity principle in Art 3b (now 5) EC and to maintaining 'the acquis communautaire'.

[8] Art C (now 3) EU.

[9] Art F (now 6) EU.

procedure to amend the EU Treaty and the three Community Treaties along with a single procedure to join the Union as a whole.[10] Finally, the integrity of the Community Treaties was protected by Article M (now Article 47), which specified that nothing in the EU Treaty was intended to amend the EC Treaties, except for the express amendments made by Articles G, H and I.

Furthermore, the detailed provisions of the EU Treaty governing the second and third pillars made further references to Community Treaties, providing, among other things,[11] for the possible use of the Community budget,[12] the potential transfer of some third pillar provisions to the first pillar;[13] and the application of certain EC Treaty provisions governing the composition and functioning of the Council, Commission and European Parliament (EP).[14] Conversely, the EC Treaty now contained references to the EU Treaty, in particular as regards using the EC budget for EU measures and the adoption of economic and financial sanctions following second pillar decisions.[15]

The structure of the Union attracted considerable comment and criticism, notably by Curtin,[16] whose well-known initial analysis of the TEU structure includes four major critiques:[17] the territorial fragmentation caused by opt-outs from common rules; the over-complexity of the Treaty system; the 'subversion' of the EC system by intergovernmental methods lacking judicial and democratic oversight and the qualities of Community law; and the risk of substantive fragmentation of policy through having such different methods of adopting measures on connected or overlapping issues. In practice, following entry into force of the TEU, the institutions managed to avoid substantive fragmentation.[18]

---

[10] Arts N and O (now 48 and 49) EU.

[11] See also the cross-references in Art J.3(2) (now 23(2)), J.6 (now 20), J.8(5) (now 25), K.1 (now 29), K.3(2)(c) (now deleted), K.4(1) (now 34(3)) and K.4(3) (now 36) EU.

[12] Arts J.11(2) and K.8(2) EU.

[13] Art K.9 EU; this provision was not used.

[14] Arts J.11(1) and K.8(1) EU.

[15] Arts 199 (now 268) EC and 73g and 228a (now 60 and 301) EC. The EC Treaty also contained detailed rules concerning the new concept of 'citizenship of the Union' in Arts 8 to 8e, 138a, 138d and 138e (now Arts 17 to 22, 191, 194 and 195) EC; see also the cross-references to the EU Treaty in former Arts 100c(6), 100d and 189b(8) EC (all since deleted).

[16] 'The Constitutional Structure of the Union: A Europe of Bits and Pieces' 30 *Common Market Law Review*. (1993) 17. For further discussion, see Weiler, 'Neither Unity nor Three Pillars: The Trinity Structure of the Treaty on European Union', in Monar, Ungerer and Wessels, eds, *The Maastricht Treaty on European Union* (European Interuniversity Press, 1994) 49; Demaret, 'The Treaty Framework', in O'Keeffe and Twomey, *Legal Issues of the Maastricht Treaty* (Chichester Wiley, 1994) 3; and Everling, 'Reflections on the Structure of the European Union', 29 *Common Market Law Review* (1994) 1053.

[17] I leave aside critiques not related to structure, such as the critique of the co-decision procedure.

[18] On the connections between different pillars in practice, see Curtin and Dekker, 'The EU as a 'Layered' International Organisation: Institutional Unity in Disguise' in Craig and de Burca, eds, *The Evolution of EU Law* (Oxford, 1999) 83 at 104–131.

Inevitably, there were disputes about the extent of the pillars before the courts and between and within the political institutions on several occasions before the Treaty of Amsterdam entered into force. In the *Airport Transit Visas* case, the Court of Justice ruled that it had jurisdiction to annul a third pillar (and presumably a second pillar) act of the Council if such an act 'encroached' upon first pillar powers.[19] The Court of First Instance ruled that the Council's rules on access to documents applied to third pillar documents, interpreting Article K.8(1) EU in the process.[20] Also, the Court of Justice ruled in several cases that certain matters with foreign policy impact fell within the scope of the EC's commercial policy,[21] and that EC development policy could to some extent address human rights and drug policy matters.[22] In practice, there were continued disputes over the use of the EC budget for EU measures,[23] even after the use of the EC budget became the norm;[24] the Council purported to redub itself the 'Council of the European Union';[25] and there was concern that the Council was overstepping the first/second pillar borderline by giving instructions to the Commission.[26] Furthermore, the institutions rechristened the Community budget as the budget of the 'European Union',[27] although this contradicted (and still contradicts) the express wording of the EU Treaty.[28]

The Treaty of Amsterdam made a single significant change to this structure, 'transferring' matters concerning visas, border controls, immigration, asylum and civil cooperation from the third pillar to the first pillar.[29]

---

[19] Case C–170/96 *Commission v Council* [1998] ECR I–2763. On the relationship between the 'Maastricht-era' first and third pillars, see Muller-Graff, 'The Legal Bases of the Third Pillar and its Position in the Framework of the Union Treaty' 31 *Common Market Law Review* (1994) 493.

[20] Case T–174/95 *Svenska Journalistforbundet* [1998] ECR II–2289.

[21] Case C–70/94 *Werner* [1995] ECR I–3189; Case C–83/94 *Leifer* [1995] ECR I–3231; Case C–124/95 *Centro-com* [1997] ECR I–81. See also Case C–162/96 *Racke* [1998] ECR I–3655, in which the Court interpreted the effect of a pre-TEU foreign policy measure upon the Community legal order, and Case C–120/94 R and C–120/94 *Commission v Greece* [1994] ECR I–3037 and [1996] ECR I–1513.

[22] Case C–268/94 *Portugal v Council* [1996] ECR I–6177.

[23] See Monar, 'The Finances of the Union's Intergovernmental Pillars: Tortuous Experiments with the Community Budget' 25 *Journal of Common Market Studies* (1997) 57.

[24] Peers, 'Common Foreign and Security Policy 1995–1996', 16 *Yearbook of European Law* (1996) 611 at 614.

[25] Decision 93/591 (OJ 1993 L 281/18); notwithstanding this Decision, all the Treaties refer (or would still refer) to it as the 'Council', even following the Treaties of Amsterdam and Nice.

[26] See Timmermans, 'The Uneasy Relationship Between the Communities and the Second Union Pillar: Back to the 'Plan Fouchet'?', *Legal Issues of European Integration* (1996/1) 61.

[27] This began with the budget for 1994 (OJ 1994 L 34/1).

[28] Using the current numbering, see Arts 28 and 41 EU; moreover, Arts 269–280 EC refer to the 'Community' throughout. See also Art 9(6) of the Treaty of Amsterdam.

[29] On the structure of the Union following the Treaty of Amsterdam, see De Witte,'The Pillar Structure and the Nature of the European Union: Greek Temple or French Gothic Cathedral', in Heukels, *et al* (eds), *The European Union after Amsterdam: A Legal Analysis* (Kluwer, 1998) 51, and Gormley, 'Reflections on the Architecture of the European Union after the Treaty of Amsterdam', in O'Keeffe and Twomey, (eds), *Legal Issues of the Treaty of Amsterdam* (Oxford Hart, 1999) 57.

However, it did this by means of creating an institutional 'ghetto' within the EC Treaty,[30] with unique institutional rules and territorial opt-outs for the United Kingdom (UK), Ireland and Denmark.[31] But links between these aspects of JHA law and the criminal and policing aspects remaining in the third pillar were retained by designating a single Union policy of creating an 'Area of Freedom, Security and Justice' which connected the EC and EU Treaties,[32] in parallel with allocating the 'Schengen acquis' between the two Treaties.[33] Also, a number of other amendments were made to the EU Treaty structure. The most important were:[34]

a)   the insertion of a new Article 7 EU, allowing for potential suspension of a Member States' rights in the event of a 'serious and persistent' breach of the principles in Article 6(1), possibly to be implemented by Community legislation;[35]

b)   the designation of the Secretary-General of the Council, appointed as before pursuant to the EC Treaty, as the 'High Representative' for the CFSP;[36]

c)   the switch to a presumption in favour of using the Community budget for second and third pillar operations, rather than a presumption against;[37]

d)   the extension of qualified majority voting into the second and third pillars, albeit with an 'emergency brake' for second pillar QMV;[38]

e)   the modification of the third pillar provisions so that the rules governing the Commission, the EP, the Court of Justice and the type of instruments used were closer to those in the first pillar;[39]

f)   the possibility of transferring the remaining provisions of the third pillar to the first pillar;[40]

g)   the introduction of a new Title VII of the EU Treaty,[41] setting out rules on 'enhanced cooperation' (flexibility) that would govern

---

[30] Title IV of Part Three of the Treaty (Arts 61–69).

[31] Arts 67 and 68 EC and the Protocols on Denmark, Schengen, internal border controls and the UK.

[32] See Arts 61 EC and 2 EU.

[33] See Protocol on Schengen.

[34] See also: the new Art 16 EC; the cross-references to Art 255 EC added to Arts 28(1) and 41(1) EU (previously Arts J.11(1) and K.8(1) EU); the cross-reference to Art 195 EC added to Art 28 EU, the new cross-references in Art 23(1) EU and Art 125 EC; and the Protocols attached to the EU Treaty *and* one or more Community Treaties, following the first example of this practice in the TEU (the Protocol on abortion).

[35] Arts 309 EC, 96 ECSC and 204 Euratom.

[36] Arts 207 EC and 18 and 26 EU.

[37] Arts 28(2) to (4) and 41(2) to (4) EU.

[38] Arts 23(2) and 34(2) EU.

[39] Arts 34, 35 and 39 EU.

[40] Art 42 EU.

[41] Arts 43–45 EU.

jointly the more specific provisions concerning first and third pillar closer cooperation;[42] and

h) the extension of the Court's jurisdiction not only within the context of the third pillar, but to the application of the Title VII provisions on flexibility and to the human rights provisions of Article 6(2) EU, 'with regard to action of the institutions, insofar as the Court has jurisdiction' under the Community and EU Treaties.[43]

Moreover, the Treaty of Amsterdam gave power to the Council to negotiate and conclude treaties within the framework of the second or third pillars,[44] although it was a matter of dispute as to whether such treaties would be concluded by the Member States or by the European Union, enjoying a legal personality distinct from them.[45]

Since entry into force of the Treaty of Amsterdam, the Court of First Instance has followed its *Svenska Journalistforbundet* ruling in its *Hautala* judgment as regards second pillar documents,[46] this time interpreting Article J.11(1) EU. Following this, the Council and Parliament agreed a Regulation on access to documents that applies to second and third pillar documents,[47] and which moreover clearly distinguishes between the Union and its Member States.[48] Also, the case law on second pillar documents not only refers to the Council's political discretion in the field of CFSP, but refers to the EU's 'diplomatic relations', 'positions' in negotiations and 'interests'; and the Court has also assumed jurisdiction to rule on the legal effect of Article 1 of the EU Treaty.[49]

In other case law, the Court of First Instance ruled that the Community was not liable for damage resulting from the bombing of Yugoslavia, despite the plaintiffs' argument that the EU's institutions were legally unified.[50]

---

[42] See Art 11 EC and Art 40 EU; there was no provision for second pillar closer cooperation in the Treaty. This chapter uses the phrase 'flexibility' to refer to *both* the 'closer cooperation' established by the Treaty of Amsterdam and the 'enhanced cooperation' referred to in the Treaty of Nice.

[43] Art 46(c) and (d) EU.

[44] Arts 24 and 38 EU.

[45] For arguments on legal personality, see Wessel, *The European Union's Foreign and Security Policy: A Legal Institutional Perspective* (Kluwer, 1999) and Blokker and Heukels, 'The European Union: Historical Origins and Institutional Challenges' in Heukels, n 29 above, 9 at 27–35, both with further references.

[46] Case T–14/98 [1999] ECR II–2489.

[47] Reg 1049/2001 (OJ 2001 L 145/43). This was legally necessary because Arts 28 and 41 of the EU Treaty were amended to refer to Art 255 EC (see n 34 above).

[48] Reg 1049/2001 (*ibid*), Arts 2(3) and 9(1). On the distinction between the Union and Member States, see earlier the Council's unilateral amendments to its access rules (Decision 2000/527/EC, OJ 2000 L 212/9), Arts 1(1), 1(2), 1(4), 2(1) and 2(2).

[49] See *Hautala*, n 46 above; Case T–188/98 *Kuijer* [2000] ECR II–1959; Case T–204/99 *Mattila* [2001] ECR II–2265; Case C–191/99 *Petrie* [2001] ECR II–2265; and Case T–211/00 *Kuijer II* [2002] ECR I–465.

[50] Case T–201/99 *Royal Olympic* [2000] ECR II–4005, appeal dismissed (Case C–49/01 P).

For its part, the Court of Justice has proved willing to interpret Article 6(2) EU, given its new license to do so.[51]

Within the political institutions, there have been disputes over the first and third pillar boundary as regards criminal law for the protection of the EC's interests,[52] criminal enforcement of environmental law;[53] illegal immigration;[54] and the allocation of the Schengen acquis between the pillars,[55] along with disputes as to whether passports and voluntary repatriation of third-country nationals fell within EC competence.[56] There has been no interest in transferring third pillar matters pursuant to Article 42 EU. The boundary between the first and second pillars has been less contested between the institutions, with the Council proving willing to adopt Regulations on funding the UN bodies in Kosovo and Bosnia-Herzegovina and establishing a Rapid Reaction facility and likely to agree a Regulation on funding for abolishing landmines,[57] all of which concern matters addressed by second pillar matters previously. Also, the Council has agreed a revised Regulation on dual-use goods, replacing a second-pillar measure on this subject in accordance with the Court's case law.[58] On the other hand, all three adopted Common Strategies have addressed matters from all the pillars, even though they are expressly confined to second pillar matters by Article 12 EU.[59]

Finally, there have been arguments as to whether the 'political dialogue' clauses in mixed agreements concluded between third states on the one hand and the Community and Member States on the other should have been concluded pursuant to Article 24 EU, rather than negotiated by the

---

[51] Order in Case C–17/98 *Emesa Sugar* [2000] ECR I–665; Case C–7/98 *Krombach* [2000] ECR I–1935; Case C–274/99 P *Connolly* [2001] ECR I–1661. See also the Court of First Instance ruling in Case T–82/99 *Cwik* [2000] ECR II–717.

[52] See proposed Directive on this issue, which would replace most of the relevant Convention and Protocols (COM (2001) 272, 22 May 2001).

[53] Compare proposed Directive (COM (2001) 139, 14 March 2001) to framework decision (OJ 2003 L 29/55), challenged in Case C–176/03, *Commission v Council*, pending.

[54] See Commission statement on adoption of the third pillar Decision on counterfeit documents (OJ 2000 L 81/1; Statement 22/00 in summary of Council acts for March 2000, Council doc 8080/00, 28 Apr 2000) and Commission working paper on the proposed framework decision on facilitating irregular migration (OJ 2000 C 253/6; SEC (2001) 727, 4 May 2001).

[55] Ultimately the legal bases of all of the provisions of the *acquis* to be allocated were agreed (see Council Decision, OJ 1999 L 176/17), except for those concerning the Schengen Information System, on which see now adopted Regulation and Decision (OJ 2001 L 238). See Peers, 'Caveat Emptor? Integrating the Schengen *Acquis* into the European Union adopted.

[56] The Member States argued that these matters could only be addressed by the Member States, rather than under any Union pillar. See House of Commons European Scrutiny Committee 29th Report 1998–1999 and 6th and 20th Reports, 1999–2000, and Member States' representatives' Resolution on passports and travel documents (OJ 2000 C 310/1).

[57] Respectively Reg 1080/2000 (OJ 2000 L 122/27); Reg 381/2001 (OJ 2001 L 57/5); and proposed Regs (COM (2000) 880, 20 Dec 2000).

[58] Reg 1334/2000 (OJ 2000 L 159/1); see *Werner* and *Leifer*, n 21 above.

[59] OJ 1999 L 157/1 (Russia); OJ 1999 L 331/1 (Ukraine); and OJ 2000 L 183/5 (Mediterranean).

Commission on behalf of the Member States.[60] By spring 2001, the Council had concluded the first agreement pursuant to Article 24 (or 38) EU, and concluded a further agreement that summer.[61] These agreements are expressly with the European Union, rather than with its Member States, and appear to treat the Union as a distinct entity from its Member States; so there is a strong argument that they constitute the first two formal acceptances that the Union has a distinct legal personality under the current Treaty provisions.[62]

III. THE TREATY OF NICE AND THE STRUCTURE OF THE UNION

a) Introduction

The first, most striking aspect of the Treaty of Nice is that the new Treaty would *not* make the structure of the EU any *more* complex. True, there are convoluted rules on specific issues like the Common Commercial Policy and the voting system in the Council after 2005, but these aspects of the new Treaty would not go to the *structure* of the Union system. In particular, the Treaty of Nice would not create any new 'pillars', or any new institutional 'ghettos' within a particular pillar (like Title IV EC). In itself, this would be progress, since the previous two treaties made the structure of the Union dramatically more complex. Instead, the new Treaty would affect the pillar structure fairly modestly.

b) Transfers Between Pillars

First of all, the Treaty of Nice does not *transfer* any substantive policy areas between pillars, despite the precedent of the Treaty of Amsterdam. In fact, the prospect of such a transfer was not even mentioned at any point in the negotiations on the new Treaty, and neither was the prospect of making transfers easier by amending Article 42 EU or providing a parallel possibility of transfers from the second to the first pillar. However, the Treaty of Nice would transfer a few *EC Treaty* provisions to the *EU Treaty*. This would result from the redrafting of the provisions on 'closer cooperation' (which the new Treaty would redub 'enhanced cooperation'), which would

---

[60] See the Council's legal opinions referred to in Council doc SN 1628/00, 16 Feb 2000.
[61] Decisions 2001/352/CFSP (OJ 2001 L 125/1) and 2001/682/CFSP (OJ 2001 L 241/1), with attached agreements. Further CFSP agreements have been concluded since, and in June 2003, the Council signed the first JHA agreements negotiated under Art 38.
[62] But see the argument of Wessels, n 45 above, that legal personality is not dependent on the Union's ability to sign treaties, but on its existence as a distinct entity from its Member States.

move certain clauses from Article 11 EC to Article 43 EU.[63] More particularly, the provisions in the current Article 11(1) EC precluding flexibility measures which concern areas within the EC's exclusive competence,[64] which are outside the powers of the Community,[65] or which discriminate or restrict trade between Member States or which distort competition between them,[66] would in future appear in Article 43 EU. Two other provisions in the current Article 11(1) EC otherwise limiting flexibility measures within the scope of Community law would be replaced by a more limited provision in Article 43 EU protecting the internal market and economic and social cohesion.[67]

But what appears to be a 'Unionisation' of EC Treaty provisions would in effect be the opposite. These amendments would actually *enhance* Community law because the new placement of these provisions in Title VII EU would also oblige second and third pillar flexibility measures to comply with conditions which previously governed only first pillar flexibility, and which solely concern protection of first pillar principles. Although it is true that these principles have been watered down during the transfer, this could have the effect of encouraging flexibility within the Union structure, rather than outside it. Furthermore the transfer would not diminish the jurisdiction of the Court of Justice, because the future Article 40(3) EU would still guarantee that the Court retains its first pillar jurisdiction as far as authorisation of third pillar flexibility is concerned.[68] Although the Court would not be granted any jurisdiction over authorisation of second pillar flexibility, this would not be a further restriction as compared to the present position because there is presently no possibility of second pillar flexibility.

The impact of these changes would be that measures authorising third pillar flexibility could be invalid not just for 'legal base encroachment' onto the first pillar in the sense of the *Airport Transit Visas* case,[69] but also for 'encroachment' of the EC law *principles* to be transferred to the future Article 43 EU. Arguably this would even apply to the subsequent measures implementing flexibility, since, like the basic decision authorising flexibility, they also would be subject to compliance with the substantive rules in the future Article 43 EU or its current equivalents. This is because, in contrast

---

[63] For a detailed analysis of the new flexibility provisions, see Shaw's chapter in this volume.
[64] Current Art 11(1)(a) EC and future Art 43(d) EU, second part.
[65] Current Art 11(1)(d) EC and future Art 43(d) EU, first part.
[66] Current Art 11(1)(e) EC and future Art 43(f) EU, although the future clause refers to a 'barrier' rather than a 'restriction' as at present.
[67] See current Art 11(1)(b) and (c) EC and future Art 43(e) EU; the latter would be the only provision of Art 43 to define its terms by a direct cross-reference to EC Treaty provisions. Specific first and third pillar provisions on the Schengen acquis would also be replaced by a general provision in Title VII EU (see current Arts 11(5) EC and 40(5) EU and future Art 43(i) EU).
[68] This jurisdiction is presently provided for by Art 40(4) EU, second sub-paragraph.
[69] N 19 above.

to the special procedural rules applying to the authorisation decision[70] and to the decision allowing 'party-crashing' Member States to join in,[71] the Treaties make no distinction between the authorisation decision and the implementing decisions as regards compliance with the substantive rules.[72]

At first sight, it is not possible to reach the same conclusion as regards second pillar flexibility, for the simple reason that the Court will have no jurisdiction over the authorisation or the implementing decisions in this area. So there will be a distinction between 'legal base encroachment' actions within the meaning of the *Airport Transit Visas* case, which could still be launched against second pillar flexibility measures pursuant to Article 47 EU, and 'encroachment' upon EC Treaty principles, which could not be attacked directly. While Member States objecting to a proposed authorisation of second pillar flexibility would of course have the power to use the 'emergency brake' to stop the authorisation, the Commission (which is rather more likely to be concerned about protection of Community principles) would have no power to do so. Later, when the Council adopted decisions implementing second pillar flexibility, neither the Commission nor the non-participating Member States would have the power to block them. However, the Court *would* arguably have jurisdiction in such cases pursuant to the EC Treaty, where the Commission or Member States wished to challenge a second pillar flexibility measure which allegedly undermined the internal market or economic and social cohesion in breach of the future Article 43(e) EU or which constituted a barrier to trade, a discriminatory trade rule, or a distortion of competition in breach of the future Article 43(f) EC.[73] Alternatively, in those circumstances, the Commission or Member States could arguably try to sue those Member States participating in such actions pursuant to the EC Treaty infringement procedure. In either case, Articles 296–298 EC might be relevant.

Finally, the last potential issue here is the temporal scope of the revised rules as regards first and third pillar flexibility. It might be argued that if any flexibility is authorised within the scope of the current provisions before the Treaty of Nice enters into force, then the current substantive grounds limiting flexibility measures will continue to govern the implementation of flexibility, rather than the future more generous grounds. This interpretation is supported by the Court's case law confirming that the subsidiarity principle, introduced by the TEU, only governs measures adopted after its entry into force.[74] Of course, this could be avoided simply be

---

[70] Present Arts 11(2) EC and 40(2) EU; future Arts 11(1) and (2) EC, 27c EU and 40a EU.
[71] Present Arts 11(3) EC and 40(3) EU; future Arts 11a EC, 27e EU and 40b EU.
[72] See further Peers, 'Who's Judging the Watchmen? The Judicial System of the Area of Freedom, Security and Justice', 18 *Yearbook of European Law* (1998) 337 at 390.
[73] The other provisions of the future Art 43 EU designed to protect the Community interest would be harder to invoke within the context of the Court's EC Treaty jurisdiction.
[74] Case C–114/96 *Kieffer* [1997] ECR I–3629.

arranging for fresh authorisation of such flexibility following entry into force of the Treaty of Nice.

c) Changes to the EU Treaty As Such

A number of the new (or amended) provisions of the EU Treaty would be relevant to the structure of the Union, firstly by modestly enhancing the 'Community method' to some extent within the EU Treaty and secondly by adding further indications that the Union is a distinct entity.

i) The Community Method

First of all, the jurisdiction of the Court of Justice would be enhanced modestly in three ways: by the extension of the grounds of review of third pillar flexibility discussed above;[75] by clarification that its jurisdiction extends to all the rules governing the authorisation of third pillar flexibility;[76] and by its new power to review the procedural aspects of the invocation of Article 7 EU,[77] which would in future include a power for the Council to issue Member States with a 'yellow card' for threatening human rights abuses, along with (at present) a 'red card' for actually breaching human rights.[78] Of course, these amendments would still leave the Court unable to interpret Title V and most of Title I of the EU Treaty. In one respect they are also unclearly drafted. Does the future Article 46(e), which refers expressly only to actions brought by Member States concerned by decisions pursuant to Article 7 EU, mean that *only* the Member State concerned can challenge decisions before the Court of Justice? Or does it mean that such decisions will be subject rather to the Court's ordinary first pillar jurisdiction allowing also for direct challenges from the EC institutions or Member States *not* subject to such measures,[79] and preliminary rulings on the invalidity of such measures from national courts, with the simple amendment that if a Member State concerned wishes to bring an action for annulment, it must do so more quickly? It is submitted that the second interpretation is correct,

---

[75] S 3(b).

[76] Future Art 40(3), granting the Court jurisdiction pursuant to the EC Treaty to interpret all of Arts 40, 40a and 40b. The present Art 40(4) EU, second sub-paragraph, only grants the Court jurisdiction over Arts 40(1), (2) and (3) EU, not 40(4) and (5) EU which contain three further rules, including the provisions on the Court's own jurisdiction. For criticism see Peers, 'Watchmen', n 72 above at 390–92.

[77] See the future Art 46(e) EU; the present Art 46(e) would become Art 46(f).

[78] See the future Art 7(1) EU.

[79] Although the vote to issue a 'red card' must be unanimous (current Art 7(1), future Art 7(2)), a vote to issue a 'yellow card' (future Art 7(1)) or to suspend rights of the Member State concerned or vary or revoke such sanctions need not be (current Art 7(2) and (3), future Art 7(3) and (4)).

because the 'chapeau' of Article 46 refers expressly to the Court's first pillar jurisdiction. If the drafters of the Treaty of Nice had wanted to limit the power to challenge Article 7 decisions only to those Member States affected, they could have used more precise wording,[80] or otherwise indicated the limits on the Court's jurisdiction.[81] In any event, there is nothing to limit the Court's jurisdiction over implementing measures taken pursuant to the Community treaties following an Article 7 decision.[82] Finally, another issue of temporal scope could potentially arise: could the Court of Justice exercise powers over Article 7 measures where the 'red card' was initially issued before the new Treaty entered into force?

Secondly, there would be changes as regards the Council. Any powers which the Council transfers to the Political and Security Committee would be subject to two limitations: they would have to be exercised '[w]ithin the scope of this Title' and 'without prejudice' to Article 47 EU.[83]

The prospect of qualified majority voting with an 'emergency brake' would be removed as far as the third pillar is concerned.[84] Since this prospect would also be removed from the EC Treaty,[85] the only possibility in future for QMV with an 'emergency brake' would be in the second pillar, pursuant to Article 23(2) EU. Indeed, this form of qualified majority voting, which presently applies to measures implementing a second pillar measure (subject also to a further exception for decisions having military or defence implications), has been used frequently since the Treaty of Amsterdam entered into force.[86] It would be extended further by the Treaty of Nice to three more situations: appointment of special envoys, second pillar treaties which implement a joint action or common position, and authorisation of 'enhanced cooperation'.[87] The new Treaty would also introduce 'normal' qualified majority voting to one aspect of the second pillar: the vote on whether a 'party-crashing' Member State could join second pillar flexibility in progress.[88] But it is striking that the more extended use of QMV with an emergency brake in the second pillar, and its exclusion to that pillar, would now parallel the lack of Court jurisdiction over that pillar.

---

[80] For example, 'the purely procedural stipulations in Article 7, solely at the request of the Member State concerned, on condition that it submits a request to the Court within one month ...'.

[81] Arts 46(b) and (c) refer to 'conditions' provided for in specific Arts of the Treaties, while Art 46(d) refers more generally to the extent of the Court's jurisdiction set out in Treaty provisions.

[82] See Arts cited in n 35 above.

[83] Future Art 25 EU; these provisions would be in addition to the protection for Coreper's role, by reference to the EC Treaty, found in the current version of Art 25.

[84] See present Art 40(2) EU and future Art 40a(2) EU.

[85] See present and future Art 11(2) EC.

[86] For details, see Peers, 'Common Foreign and Security Policy 1999–2000', 20 *Yearbook of European Law* (2000–2001) 531.

[87] See future amended Art 23(2) and 24(3) and new Art 27c EU.

[88] Future Art 27e EU, although note that it would take a qualified majority *against* the 'party-crasher' to prevent it from joining.

So following Nice, it could be argued that that the Union system provides for a system of *legal* control over qualified majority voting via the Court of Justice in the first and third pillars, and in the absence of the Court, *political* control over qualified majority voting via the emergency brake in the second pillar.

As for other extensions of QMV, the Portuguese Presidency at the outset of the IGC negotiations raised the question of whether there should be extended QMV on third pillar matters, but there was clearly no interest from other Member States.[89] Ultimately the only extension of QMV in the third pillar resulting from Nice, apart from the removal of the 'emergency brake' over flexibility decisions, would be its use to adopt third pillar treaties which implement third pillar decisions.[90]

However, for the other EC institutions, the Community method would be modestly enhanced by the Treaty of Nice as regards flexibility measures. This would result from the requirement to consult the European Parliament, *without* a time limit, on all third pillar flexibility authorisation measures,[91] and to give the Commission the first opportunity to propose a third pillar authorisation measure.[92] These amendments would not only enhance the role of those two institutions considerably as compared with the current third pillar flexibility rules,[93] but also as compared with the normal rules for adopting third pillar measures.[94] Taken with the requirement to inform the EP of second pillar flexibility proposals and the extension of EP assent to some first pillar flexibility proposals, flexibility decision-making rules would be more closely aligned with the 'regular' decision-making rules in each pillar, thereby reducing the proliferation of different decision-making rules across the pillars. Also, the changes made to third pillar flexibility and third pillar treaty-making would mean that the third pillar would again move (albeit incrementally) toward the Community method, following the Treaty of Amsterdam moves to greater similarity between first and third pillar rules on institutions and instruments.

ii)   Status of the Union

First of all, Article 24(6) EU, the preamble to the new Treaty and Declaration 23 refer for the first time to the Union's 'institutions'.[95]

---

[89] The issue was raised at an early date by the Portuguese Presidency (CONFER 4710/00, 22 Feb 2000), but not further considered.

[90] See the future Art 24(4) EU, referring to Art 34(3) EU (which would be unchanged).

[91] Future Art 40a(2) EU.

[92] Future Art 40a(1) EU.

[93] Presently, the EP need only be *informed* and the Commission lacks even a *shared* power of initiative with the Member States (current Art 40(2) EU).

[94] The EP can be required to give its opinion within three months (Art 39 EU) and the Commission simply shares the right of initiative with Member States, with no 'first dibs' rule (Art 34(2) EU).

[95] Point 6 of the Declaration. However, outside the main Treaty texts, the protocol on subsidiarity and proportionality already refers to 'the Union's institutions'.

Which institutions are these? Since the European Council, whatever its status, is only a singular body, and the preamble to the new Treaty assumes a process of institutional reform continuing from the Treaty of Amsterdam, the reference to multiple 'institutions' in the preamble can only be a reference to the *Community* institutions which have a role in the Union by virtue of Article 5 EU. Although Article 5 EU does not describe the Community bodies as 'institutions' within the framework of the TEU, it is obvious that the drafters of the Treaty of Nice consider them as such. Applying these references in practice, Article 24(6) EU would logically only bind the institutions within the framework of the EU Treaty, because the effect of the agreements in question is limited to Titles V or VI of the EU Treaty.[96] However, the preamble to the Treaty of Nice must logically be referring to the institutions within *every* pillar, as their composition could not be altered as regards the EU Treaty only.[97]

Secondly, the future Article 44(1) EU would refer to the Union 'acquis'. What is this? This would be the first reference to this concept, which would co-exist with the existing references to the *acquis communautaire* in Articles 2, 3 and 43 EU.[98] Since this reference is placed in Title VII EU, which governs all three pillars, it could be argued that it would govern flexibility in all three pillars, particularly since the first sub-paragraph of the future Article 44(1) refers to both the EC and EU Treaties (twice each). At any rate, the application of this clause to the second pillar would in any event be qualified, since second pillar flexibility could only extend to implementation of measures binding all Member States (unless one or more Member States have invoked 'constructive abstention' against a parent measure).[99]

Thirdly, there would in future be some general references to the 'Union's policies' in the EU Treaty. In particular, according to the future Article 27a(1) EU, second pillar flexibility would have to respect consistency between all the Union's policies and its external activities, and according to the future Article 27c EU, the Commission would have to give an opinion as to whether proposed flexibility was consistent with the Union's policies. The context of these references suggests that the 'Union policies' referred to encompass all three pillars, in light of Article 3 EU. However, in contrast, Article 45 EU would require the Council and Commission to ensure consistency between all flexibility measures and the policies of the 'Community and

---

[96] The Art 24 treaties would have to be 'in implementation of this Title', according to Art 24(1) EU; Art 24(4) would extend this to Title VI EU treaties. This wording also appears in the current Art 24 EU.

[97] See also the future protocol on enlargement, which would largely amend the Community Treaties but would also amend the EU Treaty (Art 3(1)(b) and (c)).

[98] The last of these references, as noted above, would be reshuffled from Art 43(1)(e) to 43(c) EU by the new Treaty.

[99] Future Art 27b EU.

the Union', clearly drawing a distinction between the two. The result is that the references to 'Union' policies have a different meaning in different provisions relating to the same subject.

Fourthly, the future Article 43(d) EU would expressly require flexibility measures to 'remain within the limits of the powers of the Union or of the Community', and 'not concern the areas which fall within the exclusive competence of the Community'. Again, the future flexibility provisions would distinguish between the EU and EC; but the most important feature of this clause is that it expressly assumes that *the Union's powers are limited*. This is hardly a surprise, but it would be the first formal recognition of this fact. However, unlike the principle of subsidiarity,[100] the concept of limited powers would not be further defined by the EU Treaty, although logically it is hard to imagine that is has a meaning significantly different from the equivalent rule in the first paragraph of Article 5 EC. Furthermore, the wording of the future Article 43(d) EU suggests by *a contrario* reasoning that there are *no* areas in which the Union, as distinct from the Community, has exclusive competence; thus, in accordance with Article 5 EC, the subsidiarity principle will apply to *all* acts of the Union. It should be observed that there is still no express reference anywhere in the EU Treaty to *proportionality*, the third principle found in Article 5 EC.[101]

Finally, the most striking change to the status of the EU could potentially be the amendments to Article 24 EU, which arguably affect the question of the Union's legal personality. As noted above, the future Article 24(6) EU would state that treaties concluded pursuant to Articles 24 and 38 EU are binding on the Union's institutions; moreover, the future Article 24(5) EU would simply permit provisional application of treaties, in place of provisional application to *some* Member States. There is no reference to an express legal personality of the Union, and neither of these changes necessarily leads to the conclusion that there is an implied legal personality. It could still be argued that the Union's institutions are simply acting as representatives of the Member States in the context of the EU Treaty, and that the future Article 24(5) would still implicitly confirm that only the Member States are parties to agreements. However, in light of the conclusion of the first agreement under the current Article 24, the revisions to Article 24 could be considered as simply confirming existing practice.[102] This is the view of the IGC Legal Adviser (the Council legal service), in its submissions on the draft revision of Article 24 during the IGC.[103]

---

[100] See the reference to Art 5 EC in Art 2 EU.

[101] It is arguable that the obligation to take the rights and obligations of persons into account pursuant to Art 7(2) (future Art 7(3)) EU would entail an application of the proportionality principle.

[102] See text at n 61 above.

[103] Council doc SN 5332/1/00, 24 Nov 2000; see also Council doc SN 1628/00, 16 Feb 2000.

The revised Article 24 would streamline the Union's external relations by borrowing its structure and several concepts from Article 300 EC,[104] which sets out the procedure for concluding treaties binding the EC.[105] However, there would still be distinctions between the two Articles, as regards negotiator, the signature phase, the role of the European Parliament,[106] the role of the Court of Justice, and the limited ability of treaties concluded by the Community to amend the EC Treaty, along with the vagueness about who is bound by the relevant treaties.

d)   EU Treaty Measures with Relevance to the Community Treaties

Certain amendments to the EU Treaty would have a knock-on effect on the Community Treaties. The transfer of certain provisions of Article 11 EC to Art 43 EU was discussed above,[107] but in addition, other amendments to the general flexibility provisions would affect EC Treaty flexibility. In particular, such measures would in future also have to protect and serve Community interests and objectives, assist Community and Union integration,[108] respect the EC and EU Treaties (rather than respect their principles),[109] and respect the acquis communautaire (rather than 'not affect' it).[110] The 'last resort' clause, the protection for non-participating Member States and the threshold for participation would also be changed.[111]

Another EU Treaty amendment with a direct impact on the EC Treaty would be the amendment to Article 7 EU. As a result of this amendment, the three Articles in the Community Treaties which permit the Council to back up the 'red card' by implementing sanctions within the scope of Community law would be amended to refer to the amended numbering of the paragraphs of Article 7, following the insertion of a 'yellow card' power in the future Article 7(1) EU.[112]

However, in the context of Article 7 EU, it is remarkable that the Treaty negotiators entirely failed to consider amendments to the Protocol on asylum for nationals of Member States, the so-called 'Spanish Protocol' added to the EC Treaty by the Treaty of Amsterdam. This Protocol purports to

---

[104] Compare the first line of the future Art 24(1) EU with the first-sub-paragraph of Art 300(1) EC; the future Arts 24(2) to (4) with the first-sub-paragraph of Art 300(2) EC; and the future Art 24(6) EU with Art 300(7) EC.

[105] But see Art 111(3) EC as regards monetary treaties.

[106] However, it is arguable that Art 21 and 39 EU apply to conclusion of treaties.

[107] S 3(b).

[108] Compare present Art 43(1)(a) EU and future Art 43(a) EU.

[109] Compare present Art 43(1)(b) EU and future Art 43(b) EU.

[110] Compare present Art 43(1)(e) EU and future Art 43(c) EU.

[111] Compare respectively present Arts 43(1)(c) EU, 43(1)(f) EU and 43(1)(e) EU with future Arts 43a EU, 43(h) EU and 43(g) EU.

[112] See future versions of Arts 309 EC, Art 96 ECSC and Art 204 Euratom.

rule that applications for recognition of refugee status made by nationals of Member States are entirely inadmissible, except in four situations. Two of these situations refer expressly to Article 7 EU: applications must still be examined if the procedure in Article 7(1) EU has been initiated and the Council has not yet acted, and if the Council has determined a breach of human rights by a Member State in accordance with Article 7(1) EU.[113] The latter provision could only, following the Treaty of Nice, refer to the future Article *7(2)* EU; but the former provision still could be taken to refer to the future Article *7(1)* EU. This would mean that the examination of a potential *threat* to human rights by a Member State, rather than the examination of an alleged *breach* of human rights, would in future trigger an obligation to consider asylum claims by nationals of that Member State. Is this what the Nice negotiators intended? In light of their failure to amend paragraph (c) of the Protocol, it is unlikely that they deliberately intended to leave paragraph (b) of the Protocol unamended so that it now refers to the possible issue of a 'yellow card' instead of the possible issue of a 'red card'. This interpretation is strengthened by the logic of the sequence of events that would apply: it would be odd if asylum claims had to be considered when the 'yellow card' was in prospect, but not after the 'yellow card' had been issued or when the 'red card' was in prospect. So the better view is that both references to Article 7(1) EU in the Protocol on asylum should be read as reference to Article 7(2) EU in future.

This clumsy approach to an important matter raises two issues. First of all, how did the negotiators (particularly the Spanish negotiators) and the IGC legal advisers miss it? This saga suggests that the Treaties have become so complex that even trained negotiators and legal advisers, many of whom likely negotiated or advised on the Treaty of Amsterdam negotiations only three years before, are losing track of events. The alternative possibility is that the negotiators were aware of the issue but deliberately chose to ignore it because of political differences about whether or how to amend the Protocol; but this seems unlikely as the issue was not raised in any of the preparatory documents made available during the IGC. Secondly, *should* the Protocol have been amended to oblige Member States to examine applications when a yellow card is in prospect or has been issued? It is strongly arguable that it should have been, given that the Protocol removes from EU citizens a fundamental right recognised by the EU Charter of Fundamental Rights,[114] and is also legally dubious from the perspective of refugee law.[115] If the situation in a Member State is serious enough that the possible threat of a breach to human rights is being examined or that such threat has been found, it is surely appropriate to require Member States to examine asylum

---

[113] Paras (b) and (c) of the sole Article of the Protocol.
[114] See Art 18 of the Charter (OJ 2000 C 364/1).
[115] See Lenaerts and de Smijter, 'The European Union as an Actor under International Law', 19 *Yearbook of European Law* (1999–2000) 95 at 116–117.

claims from nationals of that Member State. It is still open to Member States to examine individual claims in accordance with the Protocol,[116] and their refusal to do so in such circumstances could still be challenged pursuant to Community or national law. Also, it is not clear whether the Protocol prevents claims for recognition of 'subsidiary protection' status under Article 3 ECHR or other international or national rules as distinct from status as a refugee pursuant to the 1951 Geneva Convention on refugees; if not, then Member States would still be obliged to consider claims for subsidiary protection in any case.

e)   EC Treaty Measures with Relevance to EU Treaty

A number of amendments to the EC Treaty relate also to the EU Treaty. The first of these is the change from unanimity to QMV for appointing the Secretary-General of the Council, who is also the High Representative for the CFSP.[117] This means that the High Representative, despite holding a significant second pillar role, would in future be appointed by QMV without an 'emergency brake', and his or her appointment would be justiciable before the Court of Justice. This would contrast with the appointment of special envoys in the second pillar, who would in future be appointed pursuant to an 'emergency brake' without any potential Court involvement,[118] even though their appointment is surely less sensitive than the appointment of the High Representative.

The second significant change concerns the Statute of the Court of Justice.[119] At present there are actually three Statutes, one for each Community Treaty, and differing only slightly in accordance with the differences in the Court's jurisdiction pursuant to each Treaty. There is no Statute attached to the EU Treaty and the EU Treaty does not refer to any of the Community Statutes. Moreover, the EU Treaty does not refer to the Court's rules of procedure or to the EC Treaty provisions on the composition or functioning of the Court. Although Articles 5 and 46 EU could be taken to comprise such a reference, the Court's status as regards the EU Treaty is still rather vague in comparison with the Council, Commission and European Parliament, which are linked by detailed cross-references to the EC Treaty in Articles 28(1) and 41(1) EU.

---

[116] Para (c) of the sole Art of the Protocol; it is also possible, in accordance with paragraph (a), that there will be an obligation to consider the claim because the Member State in question has invoked the emergency derogation in Art 15 ECHR.

[117] Future amended Art 207(2) EC; for the High Representative's EU Treaty powers, see Arts 18 and 26 EU and future Art 27d EU.

[118] See future revision to Art 23(2) EU, discussed in s 3(c) above.

[119] On the Court's current status in the EU Treaty, see Peers, 'Watchmen', n 72 above at 365–412, particularly p 373 as regards the Statute of the Court.

This situation would be remedied by the Treaty of Nice, which would combine the two Statutes attached to the EC Treaty and the Euratom Treaty (adding certain additional amendments) and attach that single Statute also to the EU Treaty.[120] As a result, there would be a significantly strengthened link between the Court and the EU Treaty,[121] perhaps even prompting the Court to 'change' its 'name' from the 'Court of Justice of the European Communities' to the 'Court of Justice of the European Union'.[122] Moreover, in the absence of any procedure for amending the Statute in the EU Treaty, it could only be amended following the procedure set out in the EC Treaty (together with the Euratom Treaty);[123] this would be the first time that a Protocol attached to the EU Treaty could be amended pursuant to a Community law procedure. Finally, the drafting of this combined Statute required the insertion of several provisions specifically referring to the EU Treaty. In particular, Article 1 of the Statute would specify that the Court was constituted and functioned in accordance with the EU Treaty as well as the two Community Treaties and Article 23 of the Statute would refer to references for a preliminary ruling pursuant to Article 35 EU along with the two Community Treaties.

However, there are certain provisions of the Statute that would not refer to the EU Treaty. Article 21 would clearly assume that there can be no action for 'failure to act' pursuant to the EU Treaty; Articles 39, 57 and 60 would assume no EU Treaty jurisdiction to suspend measures or to issue interim rulings; Article 46 would assume that the Court has no jurisdiction over non-contractual liability pursuant to the EU Treaty; and Article 62 would assume that a review of a Court of First Instance decision could only be instituted pursuant to the Community Treaties. The assumptions on failure to act and non-contractual liability are surely correct in the absence of express wording in the EU Treaty on these issues, and the limitation of review of Court of First Instance judgments makes sense given that the judgments in question can only be given pursuant to the Community treaties. However, two of these issues raise further questions that should be addressed in future Treaty negotiations. First, since it is conceivable that the Court of Justice will one day attract a large number of third pillar cases which could then be transferred to the Court of First Instance but for the lack of provisions in the EU Treaty, it would be

---

[120] Protocol B to and Art 7 of the Treaty of Nice. This new Statute would also replace most (but not all) provisions of the Court Statute attached to the ECSC Treaty (Arts 8 and 9 of the Treaty of Nice). On the substantive provisions of the Statute, see Eeckhout's chapter in this volume.

[121] This will include a formal link to the two Courts' Rules of Procedure, by virtue of Art 63 of the revised Statute. In practice, it has already been assumed that the Rules of Procedure can apply to the EU Treaty: see amendments to the Rules in OJ 2000 L 122/43.

[122] Strictly speaking the Court's name is set out in the Community Treaties as the 'Court of Justice'; the longer title which it has used for many years can only be found in Art 46 EU.

[123] Future Arts 245 EC and 160 Euratom.

preferable to allow transfer of such cases.[124] Secondly, the absence of provisions concerning non-contractual liability of the Union raises a number of awkward issues.[125] As for the failure to provide for jurisdiction regarding interim measures or suspension of acts, it is arguable that the reference to the Court's first pillar jurisdiction in the 'chapeau' of Article 46 EU is sufficient to confer jurisdiction upon it as regards the EU Treaty measures listed in Articles 46(b) to (f), by reference to the relevant provisions in the Community Treaties.[126] By the same reasoning, the reference to preliminary rulings in the Statute as regards only Article 35 EU arguably could not prevent the Court receiving preliminary rulings on the EU Treaty or secondary EU Treaty measures to the extent referred to in Article 46 (c) to (f) EU. As for the effect of a challenge to an EU Treaty measure, it is arguable that it should be the same as the effect of a challenge to an EC Treaty measure pursuant to Article 242 EC, because this issue should be considered a matter relating to the 'exercise' of the Court's powers within the meaning of Article 46 EU. If a challenge had the effect of suspending an EU Treaty measure automatically, this would damage the consistency of Union activities and the single institutional framework as provided for in Article 3 EU, particularly where EU Treaty measures are linked to EC Treaty measures. If Member States were left to apply their own rules, there would be a patchwork application of Union law, similarly infringing the principles underlying Article 3 EU.

Finally, as regards Article 7 EU challenges in particular, it would be particularly incoherent if the Court had different powers over suspensory effect and interim measures as regards Article 7 EU decisions on the one hand and implementing measures adopted under the Community Treaties on the other, or if the legal effect of the different challenges were different.[127] If an implementing decision suspended a Member State's voting rights under the EU Treaty, it would be bizarre to imagine that the legal effect of a challenge to that decision was dependent upon different national laws, since the effect of a legal challenge in such circumstances should logically receive a single answer, otherwise almost all of the EU measures adopted in the meantime would be called into question.[128]

The third EC Treaty amendment relevant to the EU Treaty would be, in contrast, merely symbolic: the amendment to the name of the Official

---

[124] For the sake of coherence, the provisions on such transfer should be identical to those in the future Art 225 EC.

[125] See Peers, 'Watchmen', n 72 above at 413.

[126] See also the broader argument for interpreting the EU Treaty and the EC Treaty consistently 'as far as possible' in Peers, 'Watchmen' (n 72 above), 365–74.

[127] Logically one would expect a Member State challenging an Art 7 decision to challenge any EC or EU measures implementing it.

[128] The exception would be for measures adopted by a qualified majority, unless the Member States opposing a measure were just short of votes to block it; but all second pillar measures (except decisions on admitting latecomers to second pillar flexibility) could be considered potentially invalid regardless of QMV because the suspended Member State could have invoked the 'emergency brake'.

Journal to become the 'Official Journal of the European Union', rather than of the 'Communities'.[129] This amendment, entailing a 'collective' approach to the Union, would signify that all Union legislation has an equal status within its legislative journal. It would indicated that the Union has come a long way from the days when EU measures were published in *separate issues* of the Official Journal, without any EC legislation within that issue. The background to this practice, which apparently lasted from 1993 to 1999, is unknown, but it demonstrated a nearly hysterical fear of 'contamination' between the different pillars.

The fourth relevant measure is Declaration 3 to the Treaty, concerning Article 10 EC and Inter-Institutional Agreements. This Declaration only refers to the conclusion of such Agreements in the context of the EC Treaty, and thus assumes either that such agreements *cannot* be adopted in the context of the EU Treaty (or indeed the other Community treaties) or alternatively that there is no need to provide for them in that context. Presumably the Treaty negotiators took the latter view, since an inter-institutional agreement relating to the second pillar was negotiated in parallel to the Treaty of Amsterdam in 1997.[130]

f) The EU Charter of Fundamental Rights

Although not formally binding and not connected to the Treaty of Nice, the Charter could arguably shed some light on the distinctions between the Union and the Community.

According to its preamble, the Union is founded on 'values' and has a 'heritage'; it respects the diversity of cultures and traditions in Europe. The Charter is designed to reaffirm rights resulting from the EU Treaty and the 'Community Treaties', among other sources, and it is the Union which 'recognises' the rights, freedoms and principles in the entire Charter,[131] and certain rights in particular.[132] But the main text veers between references to the Union, references to the Community, and references to both.

Firstly, as regards the references to the 'Union': Article 12(2) refers to political parties at 'Union' level; Articles 15(2) and (3), 39(1), 40, 42, 43, 44, 45(1), 46(1) refer to 'citizens of the Union'; Articles 35, 37 and 38 require 'Union' policies to ensure or integrate health, environment and consumer protection;[133] Article 47 requires an effective remedy where a right or freedom

---

[129] Future Arts 248 and 254 EC, with corresponding ECSC and Euratom amendments.
[130] OJ 1997 C 286/80. This was later incorporated into an overall Inter-Institutional Agreement on the budgetary procedure (OJ 1999 C 172/1), Part II.H (paras 39 and 40).
[131] Preamble to the Charter.
[132] For example, see Arts 25 and 26 on the elderly and persons with disabilities.
[133] The first proviso was lifted directly from Art 152(1) *EC*; the second was apparently based on Arts 6 and 174(1) and (2) EC; and the third adapts Art 153(1) *EC*.

'guaranteed by the law of the Union' has been violated; a ban on double jeopardy applies within the 'Union';[134] the Charter is addressed to the 'institutions and bodies of the Union' and the Member States implementing 'Union law';[135] derogations can be based on 'objectives of general interest recognised by the Union';[136] 'Union law' can give more extensive protection than the Charter;[137] and existing rights recognised in 'Union law' are not adversely affected by the Charter.[138]

Secondly, freedom to conduct a business can be subject to 'Community' laws and practices; the right to asylum is guaranteed 'in accordance with' the EC Treaty; certain workers' rights are guaranteed 'under the conditions' set by or 'in accordance with' EC law; there is a reference to the non-contractual liability of the 'Community'; and EC Treaty provisions govern third country nationals' free movement rights.[139]

Thirdly, the references to both the Community and the Union appear in: Article 21(2) on non-discrimination; Article 34 on social security; Article 36 on services of general economic interest; Articles 41(1) and (4), which refer to good administration and language rights as regards 'institutions of the Union', with the latter right extending to the 'languages of the Treaties'; Article 43, on the 'Ombudsman of the Union', who can only review the Community institutions or bodies;[140] Article 51(2), which specifies that the Charter does not establish new powers or tasks for 'the Community or the Union' or modify those in 'the Treaties'; Article 52(2), which connects rights 'based on' the EC or EU Treaty to the original Treaty clauses; and Article 53, which refers to the Union or the Community as parties to international human rights treaties.

What conclusions can be drawn from these references? Some of the references to the 'Union' are unproblematic, since Article 12(1) of the Charter simply reflects the wording of Article 191 EC, the rights accruing to 'citizens of the Union' are already well-established and double jeopardy is essentially a third pillar issue. The other references solely to the Union appear to refer to the Union in the collective sense, comprising the Communities as well; for example, it cannot seriously be argued that the drafters wanted only *EU* Treaty measures to take account of environment, health or consumer concerns, or to protect existing rights only where *EU* Treaty measures recognise them. All the same, while this is the only plausible conclusion one can draw from the context of the Charter, it does not

---

[134] Art 50.
[135] Art 51(1).
[136] Art 52(1).
[137] Art 52(3).
[138] Art 53.
[139] Respectively, Arts 16 (employment); 18 (asylum); 27, 28 and 30 (workers); 41(3) (non-contractual liability); and 45(2) (third-country nationals).
[140] This is based on the wording of Art 195 (except for the Ombudsman's title), but note that the Ombudsman has competence over third pillar matters pursuant to Art 41(1) EU.

flow easily from the Charter's text, for why are there so many references to the EC Treaty alone and the Community alongside the Union?

Taken as a whole, the Charter appears to boost the status of the Union in several respects. The Union can sign not just any treaties separately from the Member State, but *human rights treaties*. There are only references to the Union institutions, not the Community institutions, in tune with the approach of the Treaty of Nice; and all references are to 'Union law', not 'Community law'. There are no references to the values or the principles of the Community; instead, all of the references to the Community are technical, often in the context of limiting or setting conditions upon the specific rights which the Union recognises. In fact, if someone first read the Charter without a broader knowledge of EU law,[141] he or she would gain the impression that the Union's activities were the rule and the Community's the exception, with the Union devoted to defining and guaranteeing rights and the Community waspishly and pedantically controlling their exercise. The Charter thus seems to come from a 'mirror universe' from that criticised by Curtin in 1993, in which the 'unique values' of *Union* law are threatened with subversion by the *Community*!

g) Other Structural Issues

First of all, the new Treaty fortunately would not introduce any substantial added complexity to the structure of the Union by means of new Protocols. While the original TEU added 17 Protocols to the various Treaties and the Treaty of Amsterdam added a further 13,[142] the Treaty of Nice would add only four Protocols. Of these, the Protocol on enlargement would replace the current Protocol on the institutions; the Protocol on the Statute of the Court would merely consolidate two existing Protocols and part of a third attached to the different Community Treaties; the Protocol on the ECSC facilitates the demise of that Treaty; and the Protocol on Article 67 EC relates to a single EC Treaty Article. So only the last of these is really an addition to the Treaties, although it is unfortunate and somewhat inexplicable that it was not simply integrated into Article 67.

Secondly, the new Treaty brings with it some 24 joint declarations and three unilateral declarations. One can at least welcome the drop in the number of declarations compared to the Treaty of Amsterdam. As with previous declarations attached to the Treaties and their amendments, they raise several issues. First, what legal effect do they have, particularly in light of the case

---

[141] Since the Charter may appear to the public as more accessible, relevant and appealing than the Treaties, this is surely a likely prospect in future.

[142] To be fair, it also rescinded two Protocols dating from the TEU and a number of Protocols dating from the original Treaty.

law on transparency, interpreting the access to documents rules by reference to the relevant TEU declaration,[143] and the recent judgment in *Kaur* referring to UK declarations on the definition of UK citizenship?[144] The first set of cases appears to suggest that a Treaty declaration is relevant for interpreting later secondary measures and the latter case, unless it is considered relevant only to accession treaties, suggests that declarations can alter the meaning of the Treaty itself, at least in some circumstances. Either way, a number of the declarations in the Final Act to the Treaty of Nice could be considered relevant.

The second issue concerning declarations is transparency. For anyone trying to determine what the European Union is doing, the proliferation of declarations makes the job unreasonably difficult, particularly as they are not often included in private publications of Treaty texts. It is submitted on these grounds that declarations should be avoided altogether or at least reduced to the absolute minimum. This could be achieved with modest effort, as those declarations related to the interpretation of Treaty Articles should be included in the Treaty; declarations calling on the institutions to act should appear instead in the Conclusions of the European Council meeting in parallel to the final Treaty negotiating session; and all other declarations should be avoided. As examples of each type, see respectively Declaration 3 on inter-institutional agreements, Declaration 12 on Article 225 EC and Declaration 2 on Article 31 EU. If the negotiators had paid greater respect to the issues of transparency and accountability, Declaration 3 in particular should have taken the form of a Treaty Article giving a proper legal base for such measures, within the Treaty provisions dealing with the different institutions,[145] fleshed out with rules on the legal effect and decision-making procedures relating to inter-institutional agreements. This is surely even more necessary since the future Article 161 EC would for the first time refer to inter-institutional agreements in the Treaty and attribute legal effect to them.

Third, if Nice is ratified, the institutional 'ghetto' of Title IV EC Treaty would become slightly less of a ghetto, with the immediate shift to QMV and co-decision for civil law measures with the exception of family law and agreement on later changes.[146]

Fourth, the Treaty of Nice would continue the gradual tendency to refer to the European Council in the EC Treaty, even though that entity is defined in the EU Treaty. In addition to the European Council's existing functions set out in Article 99 EC (economic policy), inserted by the TEU, and Article

---

[143] See particularly Case T–188/97 *Rothmans* [1999] ECR II–2463; *Hautala*, n 46 above; Case T–92/98 *Interporc II* [1999] ECR II–3217; Case T–123/99 *JT Corporation* [2000] ECR II–3269; and Case C–353/99 P *Hautala* [2001] ECR I–9565.
[144] Case C–192/99 [2001] ECR I–1237.
[145] Arts 249–256 EC.
[146] Future Article 67(5) EC, Protocol on Art 67 EC and Declaration 5 to the Final Act of the Treaty.

128(1) EC (employment policy), inserted by the Treaty of Amsterdam, it would now also have a role in Article 11 EC (flexibility), replacing the Council at head of state or government level.[147] Having said that, the role of the Council at head of state and government level within the EC Treaty would also increase,[148] since it would in future have a role pursuant not only to Articles 112(2)(b) and 122(2) EC, inserted by the TEU,[149] but also pursuant to Articles 214(2) and 215 EC (Commission appointments) as amended by the Treaty of Nice. The number of decisions to be taken by 'Member States' would drop, with the amendment to the Commission appointments procedure leaving just the appointments to the Court of Justice, Court of First Instance and European Central Bank and the decision on the seat of the institutions pursuant to Article 289 EC to be taken by Member States.[150] As a result, appointments to the Courts and Bank would look anomalous in future, since all other appointments called for in the Treaty would be made by the EC institutions.[151] Did it occur to the negotiators in either of the last two IGCs that since a Member State facing sanctions pursuant to Article 7 EU would lose its right to vote as a member of the *Council*, but not as a *Member State*, it could arguably, as a measure of retaliation, still block appointments to the Court or renewals of existing appointments, thereby escalating the legal and constitutional crisis facing the Union?

Fifth, the new Treaty would alter the Treaty structure by accelerating the gradual move toward more forms of simplified Treaty amendment.[152] In addition to the existing provisions for simplified amendment in Articles 22, 67, 104(14), 107(5), 133(5), 175, 213(1), 221, 222 and 245 EC, Article 42 EU, and Article 6 of the Protocol on convergence criteria,[153] the new Treaty would add further possibilities in Articles 137(2) and 266 EC and Article 10.6 of the Statute of the European Central Bank, and expand the scope of Article 245 EC in several respects.[154] However, it would limit the scope for use of Article 67 EC by amending certain aspects of Title IV EC by means

---

[147] Significantly, in none of these cases can the European Council take binding decisions.

[148] On this formulation of Council decision-making, see Dashwood, 'The Constitution of the European Union after Nice: Law-making procedures', 26 (2001) *European Law Review* 215 at 234–236.

[149] See also Arts 117(1) and 121(3) and (4) EC (now redundant).

[150] This is a distinct category from *Council* (or European Council) decisions which must be *ratified* by Member States.

[151] All of these appointments would be made by the Council, except for the Ombudsman, who is appointed by the EP.

[152] On this issue, see 'Reforming the Treaties' Amendment Procedures', Second Report on the reorganisation of the EU Treaties, submitted to the European Commission on 31 July 2000 (European University Institute).

[153] These concern respectively: additional citizens' rights; Title IV EC; the Protocol on excessive deficits; the Protocol on the European Central Bank; commercial policy; environmental law; the numbers of Commissioners, Court of Justice judges and Advocate-Generals; the Statute of the Court; transfers from the third to the first pillar; and the conditions for monetary union.

[154] The Council would in future be able to amend Title II of the Statute of the Court and the Statute would contain a number of provisions previously found in the EC Treaty and the Decision establishing the Court of First Instance.

of Treaty amendment, rather than Council decision, and would similarly expand the scope of Article 133 EC by Treaty amendment, leaving the narrower Article 133(7) EC in place of Article 133(5). The Council would also lose the power to alter the number of judges in the Court pursuant to Article 221 EC. These new provisions are welcome insofar as not all Treaty amendments are significant enough to warrant a full Treaty amendment procedure. In any event national interests are protected in that all such measures must be approved by unanimity in the Council; some moreover must be approved by national parliaments or electorates,[155] and in any event the prospect of a simplified amendment procedure has been or would be in each case approved by national parliaments or electorates first. The downside is that a multiplicity of Treaty amendment procedures adds to the complexity and lack of transparency of the Union's structure.

Sixth, while the Treaty negotiators' decision to facilitate the demise of the ECSC Treaty rather than prolong it is welcome in the interests of simplicity and transparency, it is unfortunate that the negotiators yet again did not take the occasion to replace the Euratom Treaty's institutional provisions by a cross-reference to the EC Treaty on the model of Articles 28 and 41 EU, or even replace the entire Euratom Treaty by a Protocol attached to the EC Treaty. Such amendments could easily have been prepared by experts in the period between IGCs, and the fear that rejection of such a Protocol would amount to denunciation of the existing Euratom Treaty could have been addressed by appropriate wording. Alternatively this prospect could have been circumvented by means of a Treaty amendment giving the Council, acting unanimously, the power to replace the Euratom Treaty by such a consolidating Protocol.[156]

Finally, it is notable that none of the cross-pillar disputes about the structure of the Treaties would be settled by the Treaty of Nice,[157] except to confirm that passports and identity cards cannot be harmonised pursuant to Article 18 EC. However, this still leaves the possibility that they could be harmonised pursuant to other provisions of the EC Treaty.

IV.   LEGAL THEORY OF THE UNION AND THE TREATY OF NICE

De Witte has aptly described three broad views about the nature of the European Union: it is simply a means for the Member States to act collectively; it is a new legal entity with legal personality which has formally merged with and subsumed the Communities; or it is an international

---

[155] This is the case for Art 42 EU and Art 10.2 of the Central Bank Statute.
[156] If the relevant Council act were subject to national ratification, it could be provided expressly in the relevant Treaty amendment that failure to ratify the new Protocol would not affect obligations under the existing Euratom Treaty.
[157] On these disputes, see s 2 above.

organisation, possibly with legal personality, which is intertwined with the Communities but which does not exist separately from them.[158] The first possibility takes no account of the express wording of the Maastricht version of the TEU, to say nothing of the Amsterdam or Nice versions, as regards the role of the Community institutions in the EU Treaty and the distinction between the Union and its Member States. The Treaty of Nice would further cement this conclusion, in particular with the amendments to Article 24 EU and the application of the 'conferred power' principle to the Union.

The second and third approaches have been defended in particular by von Bogdandy and by Curtin and Dekker,[159] and share many common assessments but reach different conclusions in some respects. How would the Treaty of Nice affect each approach? Curtin and Dekker's conclusion is that the Union is a 'layered' entity, with no full fusion of the Union and Communities but different organisations working together within a single framework organisation: a type of 'Russian doll' approach. The new Treaty clearly supports that thesis, by maintaining the current structure of the Union, by expanding Title VII EU to cover second pillar flexibility, by adding more rules governing all types of flexibility, and by amending Article 25 EU to protect the first pillar further from 'contamination' by the second. Also, as discussed above, several of the flexibility provisions and the Charter follow a similar approach, referring generally at several points to the activities of the Union as a whole but in certain cases expressly distinguishing between the Union and the Community.

In support of the 'fusion' thesis, one could point to the new references to the 'institutions of the Union', the 'limited power' principle and the 'Union acquis', as well as the 'Union-wide' possibility of issuing 'yellow cards' pursuant to Article 7 EU. However, the two central problems with this thesis would not be addressed by the Treaty of Nice. The first (and less important) of these is the issue of liability, where von Bogdandy appears to argue that the EU institutions would incur non-contractual liability pursuant to their second or third pillar activities and cites this as evidence for the 'unity' thesis.[160] In the *Royal Olympic* order, the Court of First Instance dismissed an argument for non-contractual liability expressly based on a version of the 'unity thesis', finding that there was no link between the plaintiffs' damage resulting from the bombing of Yugoslavia and the Community's acts within the first pillar.[161] I have elsewhere criticised aspects of this ruling,[162]

---

[158] 'The Pillar Structure', n 29 above.
[159] Respectively: 'Ex Pluribus Unum: Fusion of the European Communities into the European Union', 2 *European Law Journal* (1996) 267, continued in 'The Legal Case for Unity: the European Union as a single Organisation with a Single Legal System' 36 (1999) *Common Market Law Review* 887; and 'Institutional Unity', n 18 above.
[160] 'The Legal Case for Unity', *ibid*, at 906–907.
[161] N 50 above.
[162] Peers, 'CFSP 1999–2000', n 86 above.

but the underlying approach to jurisdiction and damages is correct: the Court only has jurisdiction to examine second and third pillar measures to the extent permitted by Article 46 EU, which means there must be a causal link between a *Community* act and the damages suffered. The Treaty of Nice would not amend this system, and indeed Article 41(3) of the Charter would confirm it. It is possible that the EC institutions acting within the framework of the Union could still be sued within other fora, such as national courts,[163] but this would raise such complex problems of choice of law, jurisdiction and enforceability that one could hardly speak of such a system as a 'fusion'.

The bigger problem is the continued legal distinction between the Community and the Union. Von Bogdandy argues that the drafters of the Treaty of Amsterdam simply omitted to note that they intended to merge the two organisations.[164] If so, as Saddam Hussein might say, this was the 'mother of all omissions', particularly as the Treaty negotiators considered texts which would expressly merge the two organisations and declined to adopt them.[165] Indeed, far from merging the EC and EU and forgetting to tell anyone, the negotiators revised various Treaty Articles referring to the distinction between the EC and the EU without eliminating that distinction,[166] and added new Treaty Articles referring to this distinction for good measure.[167] It is hard to see what more the negotiators could have done to emphasise that they had *not* merged the Community and the Union.

As for the Treaty of Nice, none of the *travaux preparatoires* suggest that the negotiators considered the issue of merging the Communities and the Union. As we have seen above, while the Treaty includes some new clauses which appear to refer to the Union as a merged entity, other new clauses do not, and most of the existing provisions that expressly distinguish between the different entities have not been amended. The evidence therefore overwhelmingly supports the 'institutional unity' thesis, not the 'fusion' thesis.

V.   THE FUTURE OF THE TREATY STRUCTURE

According to Declaration 23 to the Treaty of Nice, concerning the future of the Union, one of the four issues for the agenda of the IGC to be held in 2004 is the simplification of the Treaties 'with a view to making them clearer and better understood without changing their meaning'.[168]

---

[163] A case against the Union has been launched in the Irish courts: see Council doc SN 5332/1/00, n 103 above, p 4.

[164] N 160 above, at 891.

[165] For details, see Peers 'Common Foreign and Security Policy 1997', 17 (1997) *Yearbook of European Law* 539 at 561–562.

[166] Arts 2, 3, 5, 7, 20, 23, 25, 28, 29, 34, 36, 41 and 46 EU and 309 EC.

[167] Arts 40, 42, 43 and 44 EU.

[168] For a detailed analysis of prior attempts at Treaty simplification, see Schmid, 'Ways out of the Maquis Communautaire: On Simplification and Consolidation and the need for a

There would obviously be several possible ways to do this. In the Commission's view, there should be a 'Basic Treaty' containing the essential elements of European integration, governed by the current full Treaty amendment procedure, with an attached treaty or treaties setting out the detail and governed by a simplified amendment procedure.[169] To this end, the European University Institute has drawn up a 'Basic Treaty for the European Union' and a report on simplified amendment techniques.[170] The latter may fall outside the Declaration's mandate not to change the meaning of the existing Treaties, although it seems likely that the issues listed in Declaration 23 will not be an exhaustive list of the issues addressed by the next IGC.[171] However, the former suggests a dramatically simplified text of 95 Articles comprising the main substantive and institutional features of all the relevant Treaties, while keeping the legal distinctions between the pillars fully intact.

In my view, Declaration 23 to the Treaty of Nice rightly lays emphasis on the linked issues of the *clarity* and *comprehensibility* of the upcoming revisions. The main impediments to clarity and comprehensibility are the complexity of structure of the Union treaties, the complexity of the language used, and the sheer length of the relevant documents. To address the first point, it is essential to reduce the number of primary law provisions and to simplify the relationship between different primary law measures. While it would be preferable to have only one primary law document for the Union, to address the other two objectives it would unfortunately be necessary to have two—a basic and an extended document. But any more than two documents and the Treaties could not credibly be considered simplified.

How should the simplification be accomplished? First of all, with great respect to the excellent work of the EUI drafters, the 'Basic Treaty' should be considerably less than 100 Articles, ideally 30 to 50 at most. This should constitute a clear statement of the basic principles, objectives and institutional structure of the Union, which should be comprehensible to a large majority of potential readers among the general public and which more of them would be likely to peruse. The 'Extended Treaty', linked fully to the basic Treaty, should constitute a consolidated text of the Community Treaties and the EU Treaty. As suggested above, the Euratom Treaty could simply form a consolidated Protocol to this Treaty. This would also be an opportune time to cull the other Protocols that have accumulated over the

[169] Report to the Commission on 'The Institutional Implications of Enlargement' ('Dehaene report'), 18 Oct 1999, and Communication on a Basic Treaty for the European Union (COM (2000) 434, 12 July 2000).

[170] 'Basic Treaty of the European Union', May 2000 draft (European University Institute).

[171] See Swedish Presidency 'Report on the Debate on the Future of the European Union' (Council doc 9520/01, 8 June 2001), particularly para 40.

years, firstly deleting those which are now irrelevant,[172] and secondly consolidating those which exempt various Member States from various provisions of the Treaties either into Protocols containing all measures which are relevant to a particular Member State,[173] including any derogations set out in accession treaties which have unlimited effect, or (ideally) a *single* 'derogations Protocol' which contains all measures exempting various Member States from aspects of the Treaties. One advantage of the latter approach would be that any unlimited derogations deriving from future accessions could simply be added to the Protocol.

In any simplification, it is particularly important to ensure not only that the number of Treaties and annexed measures is reduced, but also that the Communities and Union are merged. The continued existence of legal distinctions between these entities would be difficult to maintain within a single treaty, or even within an approach consisting of a basic Treaty and an extended Protocol. More importantly, the system is legally unclear and is hardly comprehensible to the public. It would be easy to maintain the distinctions between the institutions and instruments found in the different Treaties at present in the framework of a single Treaty; Articles 67 and 68 EC already provide an example of such a distinction as regards the institutions.

Finally, what changes should be made to the Treaty amendment system? As argued above, there is a good case that Treaty rules of lesser importance need not be subject to a full Treaty amendment procedure. In the interests of transparency and clarity, the methods of simplified amendment procedure should be limited to the current two: Council amendments with and without the ratification of national parliaments or electorates, with the latter only used where an amendment is insufficiently important to require further democratic scrutiny.[174] It is surely doubtful that the possibility of changing the Council voting procedure from unanimity to qualified majority voting in any area meets this criterion, although it is notable that the relevant Treaty clauses permitting the Council to do this have never been invoked outside the context of a full Treaty amendment by means of an IGC.[175] It might be objected that a Council decision subject to national ratification does not really differ from an IGC, but quite apart from the distinction that the Court of Justice can annul a Council act, Treaty amendment

---

[172] For example, the TEU Protocols on the European Monetary Institute and the entry into force of monetary union and the Amsterdam Protocol on defence.

[173] For example, the TEU Protocols on Danish second homes and monetary union could be consolidated with the Treaty of Amsterdam Protocol containing sundry Danish exemptions from the Treaties.

[174] The Protocol on national parliaments will apply to such Council measures in any event.

[175] More particularly, in spite of Art 175 EC, it was the TEU which altered the environmental voting rules; in spite of Art K.9 EU, it was the Treaty of Amsterdam which made transfers between pillars; and the Treaty of Nice would give effect to Art 67 by amending the Art directly, adding a Protocol to it, and determining the content of the future Council decision pursuant to Art 67 by means of Declaration 5 to the new Treaty.

by means of a Council decision rather than an IGC would avoid the manic atmosphere present at Maastricht, Amsterdam and Nice, which proved conducive only to dodgy compromises and poor legal drafting.

As for the voting procedure on Treaty amendments, there is no convincing case for the Council voting by qualified majority or any other procedure short of unanimity, except perhaps for the 'emergency brake' procedure, which would still allow Member States to block Treaty amendments for 'important and stated reasons of national policy'. Of course, unanimity is less efficient than QMV, but amending the Treaty against the will of a Member State would raise huge problems of legitimacy for the European Union as long as its citizens feel greater attachment to their Member States than to the Union. If a given provision of the Treaty is so unimportant that it should be amended by a qualified majority, it might as well be removed from the Treaty altogether.

VI.   CONCLUSIONS

There are three paradoxes in the new Treaty regarding the structure of the Union. First, although the Treaty structure would not become more complex, there would nonetheless be an increased risk of substantive and territorial fragmentation following its entry into force, because the flexibility provisions would be more appealing. Secondly, although the new Treaty would modestly 'Unionise' the European Union's structure, by enhancing the TEU as compared to the TEC, it would nonetheless have the overall effect of modestly enhancing the 'Community method'. Thirdly, although the Treaty of Nice amendments are structurally simple, the existing treaties are so fiendishly complex that the negotiators actually overlooked a major amendment that they arguably should have made to an important primary law provision, with potentially significant consequences.

Although there is little evidence to suggest that the Nice negotiators wished to 'fuse' the Communities and the Union into a single legal entity, the Treaty of Nice does contain several incremental steps in that direction. This process is also supported by the Charter of Fundamental Rights, although at least one reference to the 'Union' in the preamble is surely really meant to refer to the Member States and generations past: hopefully the Charter's drafters do not seriously think that the EU Treaty and the secondary measures adopted since 1993 constitute a 'spiritual and moral heritage'! One can only hope that in the interests of transparency, the next Treaty will complete the process of merging the Communities and Union and will dramatically simplify the Treaty structure. Perhaps the only sure way to ensure simplification would be to oblige all the Treaty negotiators to explain the current Treaty structure to a cross-section of the general public, which would demonstrate to them just how detached the public has become from the convoluted structure established in their name.

9

The Treaty of Nice and Social Policy: The Amendments to Article 137 EC

HARIS KOUNTOUROS*

T HE ADOPTION OF the Nice Treaty came at a time of renewed interest in the European social model. It may be recalled that a few months earlier the Lisbon European Council proclaimed a 'new strategic goal' for the European Union in the new decade: '*to become the most competitive and dynamic knowledge-based economy in the world, capable of sustainable economic growth with more and better jobs and greater social cohesion*'.[1] In Nice, alongside the amended Treaty, the European Council also adopted the Commission's Social/ Policy Agenda (SPA),[2] which forms the roadmap for the modernisation of the European social model and the realisation of the ambitious new strategic goal.

The SPA seeks to align and promote the Union's economic, employment and social policies in a triadic model. Importantly, the SPA explicitly recognises the positive impact that social policies and sound industrial relations may have on economic competitiveness.[3] At the same time it acknowledges that the absence of social policies entails significant social and economic costs, including poverty, social exclusion, illness, loss of valuable human resources and considerable strains on public finances.[4] The promotion of quality in employment, social policy and industrial relations are, thus, placed at the heart of the effort to accomplish the Lisbon goal. The means employed towards the attainment of this aim include the open method of coordination (OMC), legislation, social dialogue, the European structural

---

* Visiting Lecturer in European Law, King's College London.
[1] European Council, *Presidency Conclusions of its Meeting in Lisbon*, 24 March 2000, para 5 (emphasis in the original).
[2] European Commission Communication: *Social Policy Agenda*, COM(2000) 379 final.
[3] *Ibid*, paras 1.2 and 4.3.
[4] *Ibid*, and see D Fourage, *Costs of Non-Social Policy: Towards an Economic Framework of Quality Social Policies – and the Costs of Not Having Them*. Report for the Employment and Social Affairs DG, 3 January 2003.

funds, programmes underpinning the development of policy initiatives, mainstreaming, policy analysis and research.[5]

Against this background, this chapter considers a number of issues relevant to the amendments made to Article 137 EC by the Treaty of Nice (TN).[6] As well known, Article 137 forms the principal legal basis for Community action in the field of social policy. Amendments to the Social Chapter are invariably controversial, not least because of the different approaches to social policy issues by Member States, and the Nice round of amendments is no exception. Its results deserve close scrutiny since the provisions of the Social Chapter form a key component of the Lisbon process.

The discussion is organised in four sections. The first section highlights the basic provisions of Article 137 prior to its amendment by the Treaty of Nice. The second section outlines the relevant amendments. The third section discusses in more detail the amendments to Article 137, focusing on three issues. Firstly, I look at the issue of financing job creation, hitherto included in Article 137 EC but deleted by the Nice Treaty. As an integral part in the effort to promote full employment, developments in that area provide concrete evidence of what is happening on the ground. Secondly, I consider the amendments to Article 137(5) (TA)—new Article 137(4) (TN)—which has been supplemented with a new rule requiring that Community measures adopted under Article 137 must respect the basic principles and financial equilibrium of national social security systems. Thirdly, I discuss the amendments to Article 137(2), third subparagraph, which hitherto provided for the adoption of measures designed to encourage cooperation between Member States in order to combat social exclusion. Poverty and social exclusion are issues which have been recently given a renewed attention by the Union, not least because of the Union's new strategic goal which, *inter alia*, aims to promote social cohesion. The final section forms the conclusion of the chapter.

I.   ARTICLE 137 EC PRIOR TO THE TREATY OF NICE

Article 137 EC was included in the Treaty of Amsterdam (TA) following the incorporation of the Social Policy Agreement into the body of the Treaty.[7] It provides the legal basis for Community action in the field of social policy which is directed towards achieving the objectives of

---

[5] COM(2000) 379 final, para 3.3.

[6] [2001] OJ C 80/1.

[7] The legal basis for the improvement of the working environment in order to protect workers' health and safety was, prior to the revision of the Treaty in Amsterdam, Art 118a (which was inserted in the Treaty by the Single European Act 1986). Before the Social Policy Agreement was incorporated into the EC Treaty, it formed the only express legal basis for the adoption of

Article 136 EC. These objectives include the promotion of employment, improved living and working conditions, proper social protection, dialogue between management and labour, the development of human resources with a view to lasting high employment, and the combating of exclusion. Community action in the field of social policy is not exclusive, but complementary and supportive. As such it must be deployed to the extent that it accords with the principle of subsidiarity as laid down in Article 5 EC.[8] Within the limits of its powers the Council is empowered to adopt, by means of directives, minimum requirements in the following fields:

— working conditions;
— improvement in particular of the working environment to protect workers' health and safety;
— the information and consultation of workers;
— the integration of persons excluded from the labour market, without prejudice to Article 150;[9]
— equality between men and women with regard to labour market opportunities and treatment at work.

Directives in the above fields may be adopted according to the procedure laid out in Article 251 EC (codecision) and must avoid imposing administrative, financial and legal constraints in a way which would hold back the creation and development of small and medium-sized undertakings.[10] Based on the same procedure the Council may also adopt measures designed to encourage cooperation between Member States through initiatives aimed at improving knowledge, developing exchanges of

---

social policy measures, other than those relating to issues of equality between men and women and those relating to action taken in the field of free movement of workers. Art 118a served as the legal basis for a plethora of Community measures in the relevant area, most controversially for the adoption of the Working Time Directive (Directive 93/104/EC). See J Kenner, *EU Employment Law. From Rome to Amsterdam and Beyond* (Hart Publishing, Oxford, 2003) pp 91–105. On the Social Policy Agreement generally see B Bercusson, 'Maastricht – A Fundamental Change in European Labour Law' (1992) 23 *IRJ* 177, and by the same author, 'The Dynamic of European Labour Law After Maastricht' (1994) *ILJ* 1. On the evolution of the Community's social policy from Maastricht to Amsterdam see, *inter alia*, C Barnard, 'EC "Social" Policy' in P Craig and G De Burca, *The Evolution of EU Law* (Oxford University Press, Oxford, 1999) pp 479–516 and E. Szyszczak, 'The New Parameters of European Labour Law' in D O'Keeffe and P M Twomey, *Legal Issues of the Amsterdam Treaty* (Hart Publishing, Oxford, 1999), pp 141–155; J Kenner, *ibid*, at 293–391.

[8] See also Protocol on the application of the principles of subsidiarity and proportionality, annexed to the EC Treaty.
[9] Art 150 EC provides for Community action in the field of vocational training. Adopted measures must respect the responsibility of the Member States for the content and organisation of vocational training, while harmonisation of relevant national laws and regulations is explicitly excluded.
[10] Art 137(2) EC, first and second indents.

information and best practices, promoting innovative approaches and evaluating experiences in order to combat social exclusion.[11]

According to Article 137(3) the Council may, furthermore, adopt measures in the areas of:

— social security and social protection of workers;
— protection of workers where their employment contract is terminated;
— representation and collective defence of the interests of workers and employers, including codetermination, subject to paragraph 6 of Article 137;
— conditions of employment for third-country nationals legally residing in Community territory;
— financial contributions for promotion of employment and job creation, without prejudice to the provisions relating to the Social Fund.[12]

For these measures unanimity is required and Parliament has only the right to be consulted. This procedure entails two obvious problems. The first relates to the significant difficulty to achieve unanimity on a proposed law. In a Community of twenty-five Member States this difficulty is bound to increase further, creating a real problem for the development of social policy at Community level. The second problem concerns the limited role of the European Parliament in this legislative procedure and the related issues of legitimacy and democratic deficit.

In line with the enhanced role envisaged for the social partners, Article 137(4) provides that a Member State may entrust management and labour, at their joint request, with the implementation of directives adopted pursuant to paragraphs two and three of the same Article. In such a case Member States are obliged to guarantee the results imposed by a directive.[13] Article 137(5) provides that Member States are not prevented by any provisions adopted pursuant to Article 137 from maintaining or introducing more stringent measures, but these have to be compatible with the Treaty. Finally, Article 137(6) excludes Community competence in relation to the approximation of the laws of the Member States concerning pay, the right of association, the right to strike and the right to impose lock-outs.[14]

---

[11] Art 137(2) EC, third indent.
[12] Art 137(3) TA.
[13] Note the criticisms expressed by the Committee on Employment and Social Affairs of the European Parliament in relation to the implementation of the Working Time Directive (A5–0010/2002 final, 18 January 2002), Explanatory Statement.
[14] Arguably, the provisions of Art 137(6) are restricted to the adoption of Directives and, moreover, do not apply in the case of social dialogue. See ESC Opinion on the Communication concerning the application of the Agreement on Social Policy presented by the Commission to the Council and to the Parliament (OJ [1994] C 397/40), paras 1.3.6 and 5.3.7–5.3.9. See also B Bercusson, *European Labour Law* (Butterworths, London, 1996), pp 546–548.

This anachronistic exclusion, particularly in relation to the rights of association and strike, has received severe criticism, not least from the European Parliament which has called for its repeal.[15]

II.   ARTICLE 137 AFTER THE TREATY OF NICE

In light of the renewed interest in the European social model and the improvement of living and working conditions, one would expect the Nice Treaty to strengthen the Social Chapter. Yet, from the outset it can be said that the amendments to Article 137 by the new Treaty are rather cosmetic and more worthy of note for what they did not accomplish than for what they did. The relevant amendments are outlined below.

First of all, a reorganisation of the fields of action has been made. Thus, all fields where the Community may adopt directives[16] are consolidated in the new Article 137(1) (TN). The field concerning financial contributions for the promotion of employment and job-creation has been deleted. On the other hand, two new fields have been added to new Article 137(1), that is:

— the combating of social exclusion; and
— the modernisation of social protection systems, without prejudice to social security and social protection of workers (ie without prejudice to point (f) above)

More specifically, new Article 137(1) reads as follows:

> With a view to achieving the objectives of Article 136, the Community shall support and complement the activities of the Member States in the following fields:
> (a) improvement in particular of the working environment to protect workers' health and safety;
> (b) working conditions;
> (c) social security and social protection of workers;
> (d) protection of workers where their employment contract is terminated;
> (e) the information and consultation of workers;
> (f) representation and collective defence of the interests of workers and employers, including codetermination, subject to paragraph 5;
> (g) conditions of employment for third-country nationals legally residing in Community territory;
> (h) the integration of persons excluded from the labour market, without prejudice to Article 150;

---

[15] European Parliament, *Resolution on transnational trade union rights in the European Union* ([1998] OJ C 226/64), point 13.
[16] That is, those provided by Art 137(1) and (3) EC (TA).

(i)   equality between men and women with regard to labour market opportunities and treatment at work;
(j)   the combating of social exclusion;
(k)   the modernisation of social protection systems without prejudice to point (c).

The requirement of unanimity remains for all the fields previously included in Article 137(3) EC (TA), that is, for the fields in (new) Article 137(1)(c), (d), (f) and (g). Nonetheless, new Article 137(2) EC (TN) provides that the Council, acting unanimously on a proposal from the Commission and after consulting the European Parliament (EP), may decide to apply to the fields in Article 137(1)(d), (f) and (g) the codecision procedure.

The two new fields concerning the combating of social exclusion and the modernisation of social protection systems are beyond the Council's competence to adopt directives. This is implied by new Article 137(2)(b) which exhaustively lists the fields in which the Council may adopt directives and which excludes the new fields. Any measures in respect of these new fields may be adopted only in order to encourage cooperation between Member States, but such measures *must exclude harmonisation* of the laws and regulations of the Member States.[17] To this end, the Council may also adopt measures in any of the other fields of Article 137(1).[18]

The exclusion of Community competence to enact directives in the areas mentioned in paragraph 6 (new para 5) also remains. Finally, a new paragraph 4 reiterates the provision of old Article 137(5) (TA), permitting Member States to maintain or introduce more stringent protective measures compatible with the Treaty and adds that provisions adopted pursuant to Article 137:

> shall not affect the right of Member States to define the fundamental principles of their social security systems and must not significantly affect the financial equilibrium thereof.

III.   ANALYSIS

In this section I focus on three issues: the deletion of financial contributions, the amendments to Article 137(5) (new 137(4)) and the changes to Article 137(2), third subparagraph (new Article 137(2)(a) EC), principally in relation to the inclusion of a legal basis for making use of the open method of coordination in the field of social policy.

---

[17] See new Art 137(2)(a) and the discussion that follows.
[18] See the discussion that follows.

A.   Financial Contributions

As mentioned above, the area of financial contributions for the promotion of employment and job creation has been deleted from Article 137. At first, this development appears rather innocuous. From one perspective it may be seen as being directed towards a clearer demarcation of the employment and social policy areas, particularly in light of Article 129 EC. Article 129 EC, which comes under the provisions of the Employment Title, empowers the Council to adopt incentive measures designed to encourage cooperation between Member States and to support their action in the field of employment.[19] Under Article 129, however, harmonisation of domestic laws and regulations is expressly forbidden. This stands in marked contrast to Article 137(3) (TA) which provided a clear legal basis for the adoption of Directives. Furthermore, unlike Article 137(3) which specifically addressed the objective of job creation, Article 129 is generally worded.

Relatedly, it should be pointed out that incentive measures which may be adopted on the basis of Article 129 must comply with three additional conditions which are laid down in a Declaration attached to that provision.[20] These are:

(1)   the grounds for taking them based on an objective assessment of their need and the existence of an added value at Community level;
(2)   their duration, which should not exceed five years;
(3)   the maximum amount for their financing, which should reflect the incentive nature of such measures.

Furthermore, two identical Declarations which are attached to the Treaty in respect of Articles 129 and 137 provide that any expenditure incurred under these Articles falls within Heading 3 of the Community's financial

---

[19] On the development of a Community employment policy see, *inter alia*, S Sciarra, The Employment Title in the Amsterdam Treaty. A Multi-language Legal Discourse', in D O'Keeffe and P Twomey, *Legal Issues of the Amsterdam Treaty* (Hart Publishing, Oxford, 1999) pp 157–170; J Goetschy, 'The European Employment Strategy: Genesis and Development' (1999) *EJIR* 117; E Szyszczak, 'The Evolving European Employment Strategy', in J Shaw (ed) *Social Law and Policy in an Evolving European Union* (Hart, Oxford, 2000) pp 197–220; M Freedland, 'Employment Policy' in P Davies *et al*, *European Community Labour Law: Principles and Perspectives. Liber Amicorum Lord Wedderburn of Charlton* (Clarendon Press, Oxford, 1996) pp 275–309.

[20] Declaration 23 on Art 109r (129) of the (Amsterdam) Treaty establishing the European Community (OJ [1997] C 340/135). This Declaration does not appear on the Final Act adopting the Nice Treaty, but given that the Article has not been amended the presumption must be that it still applies.

perspectives which covers internal policies.[21] The overall share allocated for these comprises a mere 6.46 per cent of the total Community budget regarding appropriations for commitments.[22] This compares with a staggering 45.78 per cent allocated to Agriculture (Heading 1), which even excluding expenditure for rural development and accompanying measures (therefore covering solely CAP expenditure), comprises 41.16 per cent of the entire budget. In light of this, the gap between the proclamations of the European Council and actual practice could not be more glaring. It is suggested that the real political priorities of the Union must, accordingly, be traced in its budgetary commitments and not in the often misleadingly upbeat rhetoric on the European social model. In the words of the European Commission itself:

> The classification of Community expenditure in the headings of the financial perspective reflects the various policy options. The breakdown of total expenditure between the various headings must therefore revolve around the main political priorities adopted for the period.[23]

B.   Amendments to Article 137(5) EC (new 137(4))

Article 137(5) EC (TA) states:

> The provisions adopted pursuant to this Article shall not prevent any Member State from maintaining or introducing more stringent protective measures compatible with this Treaty.

Article 137(5) becomes Article 137(4) and a new subparagraph has been added. This lays down that:

> [The provisions adopted pursuant to this Article] ... shall not affect the right of Member States to define the fundamental principles of their social security systems and must not significantly affect the financial equilibrium thereof.

---

[21] See Declarations 24 and 25 on Arts 109r (129) and 118 (137) of the Treaty establishing the European Community (OJ [1997] C 340/135) and Declaration No 8 on Art 137 of the Treaty establishing the European Community (OJ 2001 C/80/78). The repetition of the Declaration on Art 137 has been presumably considered necessary in view of the amendment of Art 137 EC by the Treaty of Nice. In respect of the Declaration on Art 129 the above (n 21) applies *mutatis mutandis*.

[22] Expenditure under the Employment Title also comes under this Heading. Figures refer to 2001. By 2006, Heading 3 on Internal Policies will represent 7.27 percent of the total budget. Source: European Commission, DG XIX, Budget.

[23] DG XIX, Budget, 'Financial Framework of the European Union', at http://europa.eu.int/comm/budget/en/cadrefinancier/index.htm

There is no doubt that one of the major long-term challenges for the Union concerns the viability of national social security systems.[24] Certainly, demographic changes can, and do, affect significantly the social security systems. It is well known that greater longevity combined with a declining working-age population will add considerable pressure to pension systems over the next 30–40 years.[25] Currently, the combined cost of old-age and survivors' benefits represents nearly 45 per cent of total social protection spending in the EU, that is around 12 per cent of GDP. In some Member States this expenditure may rise to 20 per cent by 2030.[26]

At the same time, however, it must be emphasised that, crucially, meeting the challenges from demographic trends lies primarily with raising the employment rate, in particular of women and older workers, reducing unemployment and eliminating poverty and social exclusion. This is something that has been stressed by the EU institutions and the ILO.[27] It is also well accepted that in the effort to promote employment and social inclusion, social measures, including Community legislation, play a decisive role. It would, in almost every conceivable case, be deeply paradoxical and manifestly wrong to use the need for viability of social security systems as a reason not to adopt measures in the fields of Article 137(1) (TN).[28] It is therefore important to guard against the (mis)use of the new subparagraph of Article 137(4) (TN) as a pretext for blocking labour legislation.

C. Article 137 and Social Exclusion

Particular issues are raised by the amendments made by the Nice Treaty to Article 137(2), third subparagraph, which in the Amsterdam Treaty read as follows:

> The Council, acting in accordance with the [procedure referred to in Article 251, after consulting the Economic and Social Committee and the Committee of the Regions], is also empowered to adopt measures designed to

---

[24] *Cf.* European Commission Communication: *The Future Evolution of Social Protection from a Long-term Point of View: Safe and Sustainable Pensions*, COM(2000) 622 final.
[25] *Ibid*, p 5.
[26] *Ibid*, pp 3–4. To this we should add the increased expenditure for health which inevitably follows the demographic trends.
[27] COM(2000) 376 final, para 2.3; ILO, *Report of the Committee on Social Security*. Conclusions (adopted by the Plenary on 21 June 2001, 89th Session). See also European Parliament, *Report on the Commission Communication 'Supporting National Strategies for Safe and Sustainable Pensions Through an Integrated Approach'*, A5–0071/2002 final.
[28] It is worth noting that the Commission had proposed that the relevant provision be accompanied by a declaration referring to the relevant part of the Edinburgh Declaration, by which Member States asserted their right to pursue their own policies with regard to the distribution of income, as well as to maintain or improve social welfare benefits. See CONFER 4784/00. In the end, no such declaration was adopted.

encourage cooperation between Member States through initiatives aimed at improving knowledge, developing exchanges of information and best practices, promoting innovative approaches and evaluating experiences *in order to combat social exclusion*.[29]

This provision has been amended by deleting the phrase 'in order to combat social exclusion', adding instead the phrase *'excluding any harmonisation of the laws and regulations of the Member States'*.[30] This is one of the most significant developments that have resulted from the amended Treaty in relation to the field of social policy. It is however one which comes with a range of problems.

Ignoring for a moment the reference to the prohibition of harmonising measures, new Article 137(2)(a) may be construed widely as to include measures aimed at combating social exclusion (in other words, the deletion should not imply exclusion of such an objective), but also measures aimed at *other objectives* in the field of social policy. Two possible interpretations follow from this reading.

Firstly, it is possible to construe these objectives to relate to the improvement of knowledge, development of exchanges of information and best practices, promotion of innovative approaches and evaluation of experiences, ie the fields of Article 137(2)(a) (TN). These become objectives *in se*, rather than intermediate objectives solely directed toward the combating of social exclusion, as used to be the case. On the other hand, one is left wondering as to what an objective like the promotion of innovative approaches means, or refers to, if it is not directed at a specific aim such as the combating of social exclusion. Accordingly, a real danger is that the lack of specific and clearly definable objectives to which interstate cooperation should be aimed at could cause ambivalence and abstraction to the extent that the provision might be rendered practically meaningless and inoperable.[31]

However, a second interpretation is more plausible and arguably more in line with the actual wording of the Article. The objectives which are to be promoted by the application of Article 137(2)(a) (TN) are the fields specified in Article 137(1) (TN) which includes the combating of social exclusion, the modernisation of social security systems and a whole range of other fields. The improvement of knowledge, exchange of information and promotion of innovative approaches are means with which the relevant

---

[29] Emphasis added.
[30] Art 137(2)(a) (TN). Emphasis added.
[31] The concern about rendering the provision meaningless through lack of specific direction is all the more serious, given the fact that Community powers in the social field are specific and enumerated, and that other provisions in the field of social policy refer specifically to which objectives Community action may be taken. For example, education and vocational training, which relate to the objective of knowledge, are covered by Arts 149 and 150, respectively.

objectives may be furthered. Is, then, the amendment to this provision a positive development? The express exclusion of harmonisation in respect of any measures that may be adopted on the basis of Article 137(2)(a) raises a series of issues.

In light of the launch of the strategy to combat poverty and social exclusion,[32] it is this, second, interpretation which reflects current practice. The strategy relies on the open method of coordination (OMC), itself developed within the context of the European Employment Strategy. The OMC includes a combination of soft-law measures, guidelines, reports, reviewing and benchmarking. While one of its main long-term aims is the convergence of national policies, it explicitly rejects the idea for their harmonisation.[33] At the same time it is an approach which portrays a marked lack of enthusiasm for (Community) legislative intervention.[34]

These developments indicate clearly that the Nice Treaty seeks to extend the OMC to the field of social policy by formally providing a legal basis for it. It is considered that while the OMC may be appropriate to some areas where legislation is not as yet appropriate or feasible, it cannot be a substitute for specific action in other areas, which require harmonising legislation. This is especially true in respect of minimum labour standards.[35] By codifying a basis for making use of the OMC in the areas covered by Article 137(1) (TN) as a substitute for more substantive harmonisation, the Nice Treaty threatens to legitimise legislative abstention.[36]

IV. CONCLUSION

The erosive impact of the process of neo-liberal economic globalisation, elements of which include deregulation, liberalisation and the proliferation of atypical and informal employment, is today manifest across the Union. Uneven as the effects of this process may be, they present a compound and common threat to the fundamental rights and core labour standards in

---

[32] European Parliament and Council Decision 50/2002/EC, [2002] OJ L 10/1.
[33] *Cf.* COM(2000) 379 final, para 1.2. See also, A Diamantopoulou, Address to the Conference on the *Mid-term Review of the Social Policy Agenda. Achievements and Perspectives*, Brussels, 19 March 2003.
[34] *Cf.* E Szyszczak, 'The New Parameters of European Labour Law', *op cit* n 7, and J Kenner, 'The EC Employment Title and the "Third Way": Making Soft Law Work?' (1999) 15 *IJCLLIR* 33. See also Opinion of the Committee on Economic and Monetary Affairs for the Committee on Employment and Social Affairs on the Commission's Communication on Supporting national Strategies for Safe and Sustainable Pensions Through and Integrated Approach, 22 January 2002, A5–0071/2002 final, Short Justification.
[35] ETUC, *Resolution on the Commission Communication on the Social Policy Agenda*, 26 October 2000, Analysis, paras 12–13.
[36] It has to be reiterated that new Art 137(2)(a) is not limited to the field relating to combating exclusion (and the modernisation of social security systems) but applies to all the fields of activity laid down in new Art 137(1).

every current and future Member State. Commenting on the promotion of core labour standards in the context of globalisation, an EP Committee Opinion considers that:

> The way to promote fundamental rights in non-member States is to start by upholding social rights in Europe. In fact, the attack that has been launched on all that the working class has achieved over the last 150 years is leading to non-observance of fundamental standards in non-member States, as it exacerbates unlimited competition.[37]

Against this background, Community action with respect to living and working conditions is not an option but a necessity. The Nice summit missed an opportunity to re-orientate the focal point of Union activity towards the modernisation of the European social model on the principles of social justice and equality. Moreover, far from improving a greater degree of complementarity between the various existing policies and processes, the Nice Treaty serves in many cases to complicate their relation. For instance, the link between the European Employment Strategy and the Social Chapter's provisions is still not clearly established.

Perhaps the most important aspect of the Nice round of amendments to Article 137 EC concerns the insertion of a legal basis for the use of the open method of coordination across the field of social policy. The OMC has already been employed with respect to employment, poverty and social exclusion and, more recently, in the area of pensions.[38] Significantly, the European Convention's Working Group XI 'Social Europe' has proposed that the inclusion of a legal basis for the OMC in the Social Chapter must be accompanied by a provision indicating clearly that it cannot be used to undermine existing Union competence. Hence it has been emphasised that this method can be implemented only where the Union does not have legislative competence, and where Union competence in the area of sectoral coordination is not enshrined in the Treaty (Articles 99, 104 and 128 EC), or where the Union has competence only for defining minimum rules, 'in order to go beyond these rules'.[39] According to the Group, the '[OMC] constitutes an instrument which supplements legislative action by the Union, but which can under no circumstances replace it'.[40]

---

[37] See European Parliament, *Report on the Commission Communication entitled 'Promoting Labour Standards and Improving Social governance in the context of globalisation'*, Opinion of the Committee on Industry, External Trade, Research and Energy (A5–0251/2002 final). Cf. ETUC, *Resolution on the Social Situation in Europe*, 6 June 2002.

[38] See Commission Communication, *Supporting National Strategies for Sage and Sustainable Pensions Through an Integrated Approach*, COM(2001) 362 final. Cf. European Council, *Presidency Conclusions of the Meeting in Göteborg*, 16 June 2001, para 43; European Council, *Presidency Conclusions of the Meeting in Laeken*, 14 December 2001, para 30. See also European Parliament, *op cit*, n 27.

[39] See Report of WG XI – Social Europe, CONV 516/1/03 REV 1, 4 February 2003, para 43.

[40] *Ibid.*

Likewise, in his address to the conference on the mid-term review of the SPA, Patrick Cox, President of the European Parliament, aptly remarked that 'we must not allow benchmarks and indicators to become surrogates for reform'. It may be argued that the Nice Treaty does exactly that. What emerges, therefore, is the prospect of greater use of the OMC, reflecting an apparent reluctance to work towards the setting of transnational labour standards. Sadly, this looming prospect is already becoming a reality, considering that the Social Policy Agenda contains virtually no concrete legislative proposals for action in the social field beyond the year 2002.[41] Relatedly, examining the Commission's proposals the Parliament criticised 'the regrettable lack of precise information about actions, players, the time-frame envisaged, the instruments selected and the reasons for selecting them'.[42]

It should also be noted that the OMC, as currently applied, allows for a very limited involvement of the European Parliament. In its Report on the implementation of the Social Policy Agenda the Parliament states that 'to date there has been no response to Parliament's requests to play an enhanced—and equal—role in the open coordination system, which is now applied to a whole range of social policy areas'.[43] Similarly, in the Opinion of the Committee on Economic and Monetary Affairs on the extension of the OMC to the area of pensions, the draftsman observes that:

> To a far greater extent than it is already the case with the majority of decision-making procedures at European level, it is hard to avoid the impression that the [open method of coordination] implies a number of experts determining behind closed doors the direction to be taken, without a political and public debate being held. There are inherent problems associated with this method from a democratic point of view.[44]

In light of the Union's legislative hibernation, the social dialogue may potentially provide an alternative. Yet the problems in relation to that process are considerable, not least because of the employers' continuing negative attitude towards regulation. What is more, the social dialogue process has been instituted in a framework which ignores the substantive imbalance between organised labour and capital and rests on a misconceived premise of industrial harmony devoid of industrial conflict.[45]

---

[41] Other than for the revision of the Directive on European Works Councils, which was supposed to have been revised already.
[42] European Parliament, Committee on Employment and Social Affairs, *Report on the Scoreboard on Implementing the Social Policy Agenda* (A5–0256/2002, 2001/2241(INI)), 10 July 2002, Explanatory Statement.
[43] *Ibid.*
[44] A5–0071/2002 final.
[45] See European Commission Green Paper: *Partnership for a New Organisation of Work*, COM(97) 128 final.

The continuing exclusion of the rights of association and strike from the Community legal system seems more and more at odds with the ever-increasing emphasis on the social dialogue.[46] Lord Wedderburn appositely observes that:

> There is, in truth, a contradiction at the core of Community labour law. It encourages 'dialogue', which is sometimes collective bargaining, sometimes not. But it averts its eyes from, or is blind to, freedom of association and the right to strike which are essential to that process for workers' interests.[47]

The adoption of the EU Charter of Fundamental Rights in Nice is a step in the right direction. Article 28 of the Charter provides that:

> Workers and employers, or their respective organisations, have, in accordance with Community law and national laws and practices, the right to negotiate and conclude collective agreements at the appropriate levels and, in cases of conflicts of interest, to take collective action to defend their interests, including strike action.

Should the outcome of the new European Constitution make the Charter legally binding, this will begin to build a much needed edifice of collective labour rights.[48] At the same time, given that the proposed Constitution preserves the exclusion of the Union competences with respect to these issues,[49] the prospect of affording the Charter legal enforceability reveals serious tensions in the new Constitution between the relevant rights and the Union's competences.[50] A related issue concerns the application of Article 28 of the Charter, where it is unclear whether this is subject to the conditions and limits defined in accordance with Community law and national law and practices, or whether it permits collective action at the EU level.[51]

---

[46] Likewise, the exclusion of pay prevents even the consideration of establishing Community rules ensuring a minimum standard of income, something which can be explored in the context of fighting poverty and social exclusion.

[47] Lord Wedderburn, 'Freedom and Frontiers of Labour Law', in Lord Wedderburn, *Labour Law and Freedom. Further Essays in Labour Law* (Lawrence and Wishart, London, 1995) pp 350–437, at 404.

[48] At present the Charter, though not legally binding, has been said to constitute a substantive point of reference which cannot be ignored in proceedings concerned with the nature and scope of a fundamental right which is protected under the Charter. See Opinion of A-G Tizzano in Case C–173/99, *R v Secretary of State for Trade and Industry, ex parte Broadcasting, Entertainment, Cinematographic and Theatre Union (BECTU)* [2001] ECR I–4881, paras 26–28. In the draft Constitution the Charter is included in Part II (text as at 20 June 2003 – CONV 820/03).

[49] See Art III–99(6) of the draft Constitution (text as at 12 June 2003), CONV 802/03, Volume II.

[50] *Cf.* draft Art II–52

[51] See Art 52 of the Charter (Art II–52 in the draft Constitution) and B Veneziani, 'Right of Collective Bargaining and Action', in B Bercusson (ed), *European Labour Law and the EU Charter of Fundamental Rights. Summary Version* (ETUI, Brussels, 2002) pp 53–61, at 59–60.

There is also a pertinent need to explore possibilities to provide a framework for conflict resolution at European level.[52] This issue was examined by a group of experts set up by the Commission in 2001.[53] Despite the significant diversities which exist at national level in respect of such practices, the study provides some indication that the establishment of extrajudicial collective dispute resolution systems (ECDRS) might offer some possibilities for fostering formulas that support and uphold collective bargaining itself.[54] Indeed, such systems may provide an operational impetus to the social dialogue (in particular Article 139), especially in respect of agreements which are not intended to be submitted to the Council for implementation through a decision (typically a directive).[55] However, as the ETUC rightly observes, 'European-level conciliation can only function if it is part of a European system of industrial relations which includes freedom of association, the right to collective bargaining and the right to cross-border action'.[56]

As indicated above, the more recent developments in relation to the European Constitution do not portray any change to the current exclusion of Community (now Union) competence in respect of Article 137(5). Notably, the relevant provisions in the proposed Constitution leave Article 137 (TN) practically unaffected. In the meantime, the apparent scarcity of legislative proposals and the increasing Community reliance on soft-law measures reveal not only the difficulties in achieving political consensus, but arguably a misguided approach to the issue of social regulation and, perhaps, a salient resignation in light of the ever-expanding forces of the global market. At a time when the emphasis should be on the promotion of transnational labour standards, not least because of the imminent enlargement of the Union, the Treaty of Nice, and now the new European Constitution, come as a disappointment for the field of social policy.

---

[52] This is especially the case since the signing of the Telework Agreement between the social partners which, for the first time in relation to agreements signed by the inter-sectoral social partners making use of the social dialogue process, is to be implemented in accordance with domestic laws and procedures.

[53] Visit http://europa.eu.int/comm/employment_social/news/2002/may/conciliation_en.html

[54] *Cf.* F Valdés Dal Ré, *Synthesis Report on Conciliation, Mediation and Arbitration in the European Union Countries*, March 2002, p 6 (accessible on the Internet, above n 53).

[55] This is particularly relevant in light of the current constraints surrounding this provision and which relate to the uncertainty concerning the legal status and implementation of agreements produced as a result of the social dialogue process. See Declaration no 27, on Art 118b(2) [139] of the Treaty establishing the European Community, attached to the Treaty of Amsterdam. *Cf.* B Hepple, *European Social Dialogue – Alibi or Opportunity?* (IER, London, 1993).

[56] See ETUC, *Anticipating and Managing Change: A Dynamic Approach to the Social Aspects of Corporate Restructuring*, Resolution on the First Phase Consultation, Annex: Position Paper, para 19, 11–12 March 2002.

10

Towards New Objectives for the Common Agricultural Policy

JOSEPH A MCMAHON*

I. INTRODUCTION

CONCERNED ABOUT THE erosion of the rights of the Länder the German Chancellor, Gerhard Schröder, persuaded other European Union (EU) leaders at Nice of the need for another Inter-Governmental Conference (IGC), to be convened in 2004, to discuss regional rights and responsibilities.[1] Two months later, Wolfgang Clement, premier of the Länder of North Rhine Westphalia, proposed radical changes in regional aid mechanisms and the Common Agricultural Policy (CAP). He commented that:

> We must take leave of guaranteed prices for agricultural goods. The future involves direct assistance to farmers, based among other things, on social and ecological criteria, and on structural policy instruments.[2]

A month earlier, the new German farm minister, Renate Kunast, had proposed the replacement of the existing mechanisms of the CAP with a mixture of organic farming, natural animal raising and greater consumer protection.[3] Support for this position emerged from Portugal but the Portuguese minister envisaged that these objectives would be realised

---

* Professor of International Trade Law, the Queen's University of Belfast. This Chapter was completed in October 2001.

[1] See Declaration 23 attached to the Treaty of Nice. Para 5 of this declaration on the future of the Union states that the debate to be launched in 2001 will, *inter alia*, address the question of how to establish and monitor a more precise delimitation of powers between the European Union and the Member States, reflecting the principle of subsidiarity.

[2] *Financial Times*, 12 February 2001.

[3] *Financial Times*, 21 May 2001. The previous German farm minister had resigned in the wake of the appearance of BSE cases in Germany. The opinions expressed by Kunast had originally been voiced by the German Chancellor in the previous November during parliamentary discussions of a bill to ban completely the use of meat-based animal feeds in Germany. *Financial Times*, 29 November 2000.

within a common EU agricultural and rural policy rather than, as Kunast had proposed, greater national (and regional) responsibility for farm policies.[4]

Opposition to the radical reform of the CAP emerged from France. President Chirac indicated that France would oppose the renegotiation of the deal reached at the 1999 Berlin Summit on the reform of the CAP.[5] That summit, which had agreed the reforms originally proposed in the Agenda 2000 document, had set 2006 as the date for further reform of the policy. Joining the fray, Lionel Jospin, the French Prime Minister, in his speech outlining his vision of the future development of the EU rejected 'the re-nationalisation of policies devised and conducted at the European level.' Although the CAP would remain at the European level, it would be redirected:[6]

> While preserving the competitiveness of our agriculture, we must help farmers to produce better to enable them to meet the demand for food quality and safety. The common agricultural policy must encourage more balanced development of rural areas, [and preserve] the diversity of our traditional rural life and agricultural practices.

The debate sketched above arose out of a concern for the future of European agriculture in the wake of the BSE crisis and more recently, the outbreak of foot and mouth in the United Kingdom. Other factors will influence this debate not the least of which are the possible renegotiation of the Uruguay Round Agreement on Agriculture and the probable enlargement of the EU to include the countries of Central and Eastern Europe. As for when further reform will occur many dates can be suggested. The mid-term review of the Agenda 2000 reforms will occur next year, the peace clause of the Agreement on Agriculture expires in 2003, the next Inter-Governmental Conference will be held in 2004, enlargement may become a reality by 2005 and the Berlin Summit set the end-date for the current reforms as 2006.

Irrespective of which date is chosen, the policy will be subject to further reform and, consequently the CAP may pursue different objectives. In all previous reforms, the objectives of the policy as enshrined in Article 33 of the Treaty of Rome have never been changed and these objectives have never been the subject of discussion at an IGC. This time it may be different as the next IGC has been specifically instructed 'to establish ... a more precise delimitation of powers between the European Union and the Member States, reflecting the principle of subsidiarity'. Two questions arise; firstly, why have past reforms not lead to a re-writing of the objectives on the policy?

---

[4] *Financial Times*, 22 May 2001.
[5] *Financial Times*, 18 February 2001.
[6] Available on the Europa website.

Secondly, if the objectives are to be re-written, what objectives will be pursued by the EU and the Member States in the area of agriculture and rural policy? This chapter will address these two questions, however, before doing so, it is necessary to examine the objectives set for the CAP, especially as interpreted by the European Court of Justice.

II. THE OBJECTIVES OF THE CAP

The objectives set for the CAP in Article 33 EC (ex Article 39) are:

1. (a) to increase agricultural productivity by promoting technical progress and by ensuring the rational development of agricultural production and the optimum utilisation of the factors of production, in particular labour;
    (b) thus to ensure a fair standard of living for the agricultural community, in particular by increasing the individual earnings of persons engaged in agriculture;
    (c) to stabilise markets;
    (d) to assure availability of supplies;
    (e) to ensure supplies reach consumers at reasonable prices.
2. In working out the common agricultural policy and the special methods of its application, account shall be taken of:
    (a) the particular nature of agricultural activity, which results from the social structure of agriculture and from structural and natural disparities between the various agricultural regions;
    (b) the need to effect the appropriate adjustments by degrees;
    (c) the fact that in the Member States agriculture constitutes a sector closely linked with the economy as a whole.

The objectives are a reflection of the three factors that have always been used to justify governmental intervention in the agricultural sectors.[7] Firstly, the politico-economic factor, to contribute to overall economic growth of the Member States, both individually and collectively, which is reflected in Article 3(e), Article 33(1)(a) and (c) and Article 33(2)(c). Secondly, the socio-political factor, a concern with the welfare of the rural population, reflected in Article 33 (1)(a) and, more significantly, (b) and in Article 33(2)(a) and (b). Thirdly, and finally, the socio-economic factor, a concern with adequate food supplies for consumers, which is reflected in Article 33(d) and (e).

---

[7] See El-Agraa, A *The Economics of the Common Market* 4th edn (London, Harvester Wheatsheaf, 1994) pp 211–12 and Marsh, J and Swanney, P *Agriculture and the European Community* (London, Allen & Unwin, 1980) pp 12–16.

Looking more closely at the objectives, the first objective to be pursued in Article 33(1), an increase in agricultural productivity, is to be pursued by promoting technical progress and a rational development and optimum use of agricultural production factors. This implies a type of regional structural policy; an implication which is given added weight by Article 33(2)(a) which requires the particular nature of agricultural activity to be taken into account in the working out of the policy. Using the word 'thus' in paragraph (b) it appears that both objectives are connected. Therefore, it could be argued that the regional structural policy must lead to an achievement of a fair standard of living for the agricultural community. However, some doubt can be cast on this interpretation because of the second part of paragraph (b), which sets as an objective, an increase in the individual earnings of persons engaged in agriculture. This may mean that the most important aspect of the objectives is to increase the earnings of agricultural producers so that they have a fair standard of living, thus making paragraph (b) a type of income guarantee. As such, it would have to be achieved over the longer term. In contrast, paragraph (c) is more interested in the short-term effects of fluctuations in prices, demand and supply. The policy must therefore include mechanisms designed to smooth out these fluctuations, thereby connecting paragraph (c) with paragraph (d) although no reference is made to techniques which would ensure such availability of supplies or to the scope of Community activity in this area. Finally, paragraph (e) confirms that the scope of the policy is not to be limited to producers and processors but is to extend to consumers. Prices for them are to be 'reasonable' as opposed to the standard of living of farmers, which is to be 'fair'.

Turning from the literal approach to Article 33(1) to the jurisprudence of the European Court of Justice on the separate objectives of the CAP, the range of possible approaches to the future development of the policy may be identified. For example in the *Danske Landboforeninger* case, the Court pointed out that:[8]

> ... the very wording of Article 39(1) shows that the increase in the individual earnings of persons engaged in agriculture is envisaged by being primarily the result of the structural measures described in sub-paragraph (a).

The Court has also declared that Article 33(1)(b) does not constitute an income guarantee for farmers.[9]

With respect to the remaining objectives of Article 33(1), the Court has held that a range of measures may be used to stabilise markets.[10] Measures to

---

[8] Case 297/82 [1983] ECR 3299, p 3317. See also cases 36 and 71/80 *Irish Creamery Milk Suppliers Association* [1981] ECR 735.
[9] See for example, case 2/75 *Mackprang* [1975] ECR 607 and case 281/84 *Bedburg* [1987] ECR 49.
[10] Case 250/84 *Eridania* [1986] ECR 117 and case 46/86 *Romkes* [1987] ECR 2687.

effect such stability which impact adversely on individuals do not give that individual the right to complain.[11] In relation to the safeguarding of supplies there are no fixed mechanisms to achieve this. Finally, with respect to paragraph (e), the Court made it clear in the case of *Germany v Commission* that reasonable prices did not mean the lowest possible prices but had to be considered in the light of the CAP.[12] In a later case, the Court would rule that Article 33 would only be breached if a measure led to consumer prices that were obviously unreasonable.[13]

No hierarchy of objectives is indicated in Article 33(1) but it is obvious that the CAP has a series of objectives that are both conflicting and not capable of reconciliation. As early as 1968, the Court recognised that the Community institutions would have to balance the competing demands of Article 33(1).[14] The classic formulation of this balancing act occurred in the case of *Balkan*, where the Court stated:[15]

> In pursuing these objectives the Community institutions must secure the permanent harmonisation made necessary by any conflict between these aims taken individually and, where necessary, allow one of them temporary priority in order to satisfy the demands of the economic factors or conditions in view of which their decisions are made.

The formulation has been repeated by the Court on several occasions with the Court limiting itself to an examination of whether the measure in question contains a manifest error, constitutes a misuse of power or whether the discretion enjoyed by the Community institutions has been exceeded.[16]

With respect to the *Balkan* formula it must be pointed out that it is in conflict with the Court's approach to the interpretation of Article 2 of Regulation 26/62 where an agreement hoping for exemption from the competition provisions must satisfy all the objectives of the CAP. This is demonstrated by the decision in *FRUBO*.[17] Secondly, the statement suggests that at some stage the Court may overrule a measure of the institutions if the situation of 'temporary priority' is continued for a substantial period,

---

[11] Cases 63–69/72 *Wehrhahn* [1973] ECR 1229.

[12] Case 34/62 [1963] ECR 131.

[13] Case 5/73 *Balkan* [1973] ECR 1091.

[14] Case 5/67 *Beus* [1968] ECR 83 where the Court stated that: 'As those objectives are for the protection of agricultural producers as well as of consumers, they cannot all be realised simultaneously and in full'.

[15] Above n 13, p 1112.

[16] See for example, case 29/77 *Roquette Frères* [1977] ECR 1835; case 203/86 *Spain v Council* [1988] ECR 4563 and case C–311/90 *Hierl* [1992] ECR I–206. See also the repetition of the *Balkan* formula by the Court of First Instance case T–489/93 *Unifruit Hellas* [1994] ECR II–1201.

[17] Case 71/74 [1975] ECR 563. See also case C–399/93 *Oude Luttikhuis* [1995] ECR I–4515.

thus jeopardising the achievement of the other objectives of the policy. The possibility that the Court could adopt such an approach was highlighted in its decision in *Behla-Mühle*.[18] The Court in this case declared a regulation on the compulsory purchase of skimmed milk powder, which was designed to reduce stocks of this product that had increased significantly, to be null and void. In doing so, the Court used the objectives in Article 33(1), the rule on non-discrimination contained in Article 34(3) and the general principle of proportionality to rule that the obligations imposed by the regulation were discriminatory and not necessary to attain the objectives of the CAP. One further interesting feature of the case, arising from the current reforms of the CAP, was the suggestion by Advocate General Capotorti that a strict interpretation of Article 33(1) might:[19]

> ... justify the conclusion that the whole of the market policy so far followed by the Community is illegal in view of the fact that ... its essential basis is the fixing of prices to suit agricultural products in order to assure farmers an adequate income, whereas the policy favouring the modernisation and structural improvements and, in consequence, the rational development of agricultural production has been late in gathering momentum and is now evolving slowly and with considerable difficulty.

Whilst the Community institutions enjoy considerable discretion in the implementation of a policy to achieve the objectives of Article 33(1), both individually and collectively, it is important to conclude that the discretion is not unlimited. Considerable latitude has been given to the institutions by the *Balkan* formula but as *Behla Mühle* indicated there are limits to that latitude. The limits were hinted at in *Crispoltoni II* where after repeating the *Balkan* formula the Court continued: 'That harmonisation must preclude the isolation of any one of those objectives in such a way as to render impossible the realisation of other objectives'.[20]

It must be acknowledged that Article 33 is not the only relevant provision when it comes to establishing the objectives of the CAP. According to Article 3(e), a common policy in the sphere of agriculture is one of the mechanisms available to the Community institutions for achieving the general objectives of the Treaty.[21] The Court has made it clear, for instance, that the objectives set by Article 33 cover all aspects of agricultural production

---

[18] Cases 114, 116 and 119–20/76 [1977] ECR 1211.
[19] *Ibid*, p 1229. See also case C–353/92 *Greece v Council* [1994] ECR I–3411 involving a challenge to Regulation 1765/92 (OJ 1992 L 181/12) where the Court accepted that stabilising markets can take precedence over a fair income for farmers in certain circumstances.
[20] Joined cases C–133/93, C–300/93 and C–362/93 [1994] ECR I–4863, p 4903. See also joined cases 197–200, 243, 245 and 247/80 *Ludwigshafner Walzmühle* [1981] ECR 3211 for a similar statement.
[21] See for examples, case 48/74 *Charmasson* [1974] ECR 1383, cases 80 and 81/77 *Ramel* [1978] ECR 927 and case 68/86 *UK v Council (Hormones)* [1988] ECR 855.

from public health and consumer protection to animal welfare issues.[22] Moreover, the interpretation advanced by the Court allows the scope of the CAP to expand to embrace new policy goals identified within the Treaty, such as environmental regulation in Article 174 or development cooperation in Article 177.[23] The only restrictions imposed by the Court are that the measures adopted must concern agricultural products as defined by Annex II of the Treaty and that the measure is intended to achieve one or more of the objectives of Article 33.[24]

III. PAST REFORMS OF THE CAP

In December 1960, the Council made their first substantive decision on the CAP, thus paving the way for the introduction of that policy. The significance of that decision rests with its establishment of the three basic principles of the common agricultural policy; common prices, common financing, and Community preference.[25] In the years that followed, common organisations were gradually introduced so that by the end of the transitional period common organisations existed for the bulk of the products listed in Annex II. A single Guidance and Guarantee Fund (known by its French acronym, FEOGA) was introduced in 1962 and split into two separate sections in 1964; a Guarantee section to finance the prices and markets policy and a Guidance section to finance structural operations. Only in the early 1970s did the Community institutions seriously address the need to reform the structure of European agriculture through a reappraisal of the structural policy. The original principles were designed to meet the situation where Europe was still a net importer of agricultural products. The support of farm incomes through internal price arrangements and the partial or total exclusion of imports of certain products because of increased protection at the frontiers of the Community ensured that the policy met the problems it was initially designed to deal with. However, once this situation had been reached, the instruments of the policy were not changed. Therefore surpluses

---

[22] On public health and consumer protection, see for example case 11/88 *Commission v Council (Pesticides)* [1989] ECR 379, case C–146/91 *KYDEP* [1994] ECR I–4199 and case C–180/96 *United Kingdom v Commission* [1998] ECR I–2265; on animal welfare see case 131/86 *UK v Council (Battery Hens)* [1988] ECR 905 and case C–27/95 *Woodspring* [1997] ECR I–1847.

[23] See case C–280/93 *Germany v Council* [1994] ECR I–4973 where the Court rejected the German argument that the regulation establishing the common organisation of the market in bananas was part of a development policy for the ACP and so could not be based on Art 37 (ex Art 43).

[24] See for example, case 68/86 *United Kingdom v Council*, above n 21 and case 11/88 *Commission v Council*, above n 22. On the interpretation of Annex II, see Cases 2 & 3/62 *Commission v Belgium and Luxembourg* [1962] ECR 425, case 185/73 *König* [1974] ECR 607, case 77/83 *CILFIT* [1984] ECR 1257 and case 123/83 *BNIC v Clair* [1985] ECR 391

[25] Bull CE 1/61, p 83.

appeared in a number of areas, with a consequent negative impact on prices, and trade relations with third countries deteriorated with increases in the level of Community subsidised exports and continuing restrictions on imports.

Reform of the policy was inevitable. Such reform, according to the Commission in 1980, would have to reconcile four main objectives:[26]

(1)   to maintain the positive aspects achieved, ie consumer security of supply, income of farmers, free trade and the contribution of farming to external trade;

(2)   to set up mechanisms whereby the budgetary consequences of production surpluses may be held in check. This could be achieved by adjustment of market organisations to introduce the principle of co-responsibility or producer participation;

(3)   to ensure better regional distribution of the benefits derived by farmers from the CAP; this would entail a radical readjustment of structural policy aimed at the reduction of regional disparities; and,

(4)   to organise the financing of the CAP on sound foundations which will not cause disputes in future between Member States.

Gradual reforms were introduced throughout the 1980s and, to a limited extent, they met the objectives set by the Commission in the above statement. For example, on the introduction of mechanisms to check the budgetary consequences of surplus production, it is possible to point to the introduction of milk quotas in 1984.[27] Further confirmation of the emergence of a fourth principle, producer responsibility, would emerge in 1986 and 1987 as limits were imposed on market support for cereals and milk products. In 1988 further stabilisation measures were introduced in all market organisations and also in 1988, the European Council agreed to place an overall ceiling on agricultural expenditure, linking it to trends in the Community's GDP. Reform of structural policy later in 1988 constituted an attempt to ensure a better regional distribution of the benefits derived from the CAP.

These reforms represented the beginning of a process of continuing reform of the CAP. Further reforms emerged in 1992 with the so-called 'MacSharry reforms'. In essence, these reforms were two-fold. Firstly, there was a three-year reduction in the level of prices in the arable crops and beef sectors. The purpose of such a reduction was to bring the level of Community prices closer to those on the world market, so improving the competitiveness of Community production. The negative impact of such prices reduction on

---

26 COM (80) 800 *Reflections on the Common Agricultural Policy.*
27 See Avery, G 'The Common Agricultural Policy: A Turning Point' (1984) 21 *Common Market Law Review* 481.

the income of farmers was mitigated by the introduction of compensatory payments which in the case of certain arable crops was based on the withdrawal of land from production—referred to as the set-aside premium; the premium being linked to past production. Likewise in the beef sector compensatory payments were introduced and were made payable based on a reduction of the stocking rate per hectare. The second set of reforms built on the compensatory payments by introducing a range of accompanying measures, such as the granting of aid to farmers to encourage the protection of the environment, the landscape and natural resources. These latter reforms would be built on as a consequence of the reference in the Maastricht Treaty to rural areas in the context of the economic and social cohesion of the Community. They would also allow the Community to build on the 1988 reforms of the structural funds that had encouraged integrated rural development.

As for an assessment of these reforms, it must be pointed out that they were limited to cereals, oilseeds and the dairy and beef sectors. These were areas where the budgetary and international trade problems had become most acute; other areas such as sugar were excluded, as such problems had not arisen. So the 1992 reforms were not a wholesale reform of the CAP rather a response to both internal and external problems thus raising some doubt as to what was likely to happen in other sectors of the policy in the years that would follow, where the problems were not so prominent. As was usual the Commission's reform proposals were more dramatic than the end result; the original proposals had called for a 40 per cent reduction in cereal prices but the final figure was 29 per cent. Having said this, agreement on such a large cut did represent a significant shift in the attitudes of the Member States and a symbol of the future direction of the CAP. As for the nature of the symbol, it was clear, especially concerning the conditions attached to the set-aside provisions, that the burden of financing agricultural expenditure was being shifted from the consumer to the taxpayer. One commentator concluded:[28]

> They have failed to address the fundamentally objectionable features of the CAP and they have introduced a new and unwelcome policy instrument into the CAP's operations. They have not addressed the distortions the CAP creates, they leave decision making capacity in the hands of institutions that have demonstrated their incapacity to make good decisions, and they even appear unlikely to have solved the budgetary problems that first put reform on the EC agenda.

Coupled with these reforms, agreement was reached in 1994 in the Uruguay Round of multilateral trade negotiations, including for the first time an

---

[28] Atkin, M *Snouts in the Trough* (Woodhead Publishing, 1993), p 146.

Agreement on Agriculture that would establish commitments in the areas of market access, domestic support and export subsidies. Parties to the Agreement would be expected to increase market access, through tariff reductions and the adoption of the process of tariffication for existing non-tariff barriers. The level of support offered by domestic agricultural policies would be calculated and reductions would have to be made in certain areas. Aspects of such policies were categorised in terms of boxes, with the MacSharry reforms being placed in the Blue Box. Finally, budgetary restraints and quantitative limitations would be placed on export subsidies. This Agreement also provided for the introduction of a further Agreement on Sanitary and Phytosanitary Measures and there would be stronger and more operationally effective GATT rules. The Uruguay Round Agreement and the new GATT rules would be policed by the newly created World Trade Organisation (WTO) which would enforce the rules through the newly effective dispute settlement process. The Agreement on Agriculture, the overall activities of the WTO and its Dispute Settlement Body would accentuate the impact of the 1992 reforms, and emphasised the need for further reform of the policy.

In its assessment of the MacSharry reforms the Agenda 2000 document noted a considerable improvement of market balances, continuing improvements in average agricultural incomes but the reforms had mixed effects on the environment and had led to increased budgetary expenditure in the sectors affected by the reforms. The reforms were characterised as insufficient to meet the new demands confronting the CAP in the years to come, of which the Commission identified three distinct, but inter-related, problems. The first problem was the adaptation of the existing policy to maintain the Community's position in world trade. An element of that adaptation would involve the re-negotiation of existing international commitments and the negotiation of new commitments and this was recognised as the second problem. The final problem was the adoption of the new policy (accompanied by consequential reforms) by the applicant countries of Central and Eastern Europe on their accession to the Community. Any one of these problems represented a significant challenge to the Community.

The initial Commission thinking on the nature of the reforms needed in the CAP was outlined in the Agenda 2000 document and it involved a 'deepening and extending' of past reforms through a further package that would convert the primary support mechanism of the CAP from price support to direct payments accompanied by a more aggressive rural policy. The latter was needed not only to implement a more coherent policy to tackle the social and economic problems of rural areas but also to reinforce and enhance the existing environmental aspects of these areas and the CAP. This particular aspect of rural policy was seen as increasingly demanded by the citizens of the Union, who at the same time, in their capacity as consumers, were also demanding greater food safety and products which are both 'environmentally-friendly' and 'culturally-significant'. In addition to these objectives, the new CAP would also demand the promotion of greater economic and social cohesion between the Member States.

In March 1998 more detailed proposals for the reform of the CAP were published by the Commission, which were intended to translate the above reforms into legal texts.[29] For arable crops, there would be a new regulation that would, in part, confirm the future role of intervention as a safety net for farmers rather than as a guarantee of price stability. To reinforce this change, the intervention price would be reduced by 20 per cent in one step. Beyond this the essential elements of the regime agreed in 1992 would continue. In the beef sector, the existing intervention scheme would be replaced with a private storage system, similar to that used in the pigmeat regime, to be introduced by 2002, by which stage the effective market support level for beef would have been reduced by 30 per cent. To ensure a fair standard of living for the farmers affected by these changes, the direct payments introduced in 1992 would be increased. In the dairy sector, internal prices were to be reduced by 15 per cent (in four stages), instead of the 10 per cent suggested in the Agenda 2000 document, whilst there would a 2 per cent increase in the total reference quantity for milk under the existing quota scheme. Young farmers in all Member States would benefit from a 1 per cent increase in the overall quota with the remaining 1 per cent to be allocated to farmers in mountainous areas, so not all Member States will benefit. Changes were also proposed to the premium paid to dairy farmers.

The proposals recognised the diverse nature of the agricultural situation in the Member States by promoting a new division of functions between the Community and the Member States. For example, in the area of direct payments to producers, compensation would be provided in the form of national envelopes by the Community, with the Member States being responsible for the allocation of this money, subject to agreed criteria, to its agricultural producers. As examples of the agreed criteria, a degressive ceiling was proposed on the amount of direct aid that a farm could receive and Member States would be able to adjust the direct aids awarded on criteria they defined relating to the number of workers employed on a farm. A similar decentralised approach was also to be taken in the area of rural development, where there would be a new legal framework as part of the process of the simplification of Community agricultural legislation.

The new framework provided for two groups of rural development measures, a kind of second pillar to the CAP. Those relating to less favoured areas and the measures in the 1992 reform package such as early retirement, and agri-environment measures would be co-financed by the Community through the FEOGA Guarantee section for all regions of the Community.

---

[29] COM (98) 158. This publication can also be found on the Directorate-general of Agriculture's website.

The second group of measures relating to modernisation and diversification would be financed as part of the Community's efforts to promote greater economic and social cohesion in the Community in the newly defined Objective 1 and Objective 2 areas. (Measures in Objective 1 areas would be financed through the Guidance section and measures in Objective 2 areas were to be financed through the Guarantee section.) Beyond these areas, rural development measures would be financed across the Community from the Guarantee section. As a further contribution to the simplification of existing agricultural legislation, a new Regulation on the financing of the CAP was proposed.

In the aftermath of the publication of the Commission proposals considerable discussion occurred between the Member States on the scope of the reform of the CAP. In preparation for the European Council in Berlin in March 1999, the Council eventually reached a political agreement on a compromise package of reforms.[30] As for the elements of the reform package, the intervention price for arable crops was to be cut by 20 per cent in two steps starting in 2000/2001. To compensate farmers for the loss of income, direct payments were to be increased. With the return of intervention to the role of providing a safety net, seasonal price corrections were to be abolished as would the reference price system for oilseeds. In recognition of the Blair House Accord, limitations on oilseeds production would begin in the marketing year 2002/2003. As for other measures, compulsory set aside was to be retained with the basic rate to be set at 10 per cent for the two marketing years beginning in 2000 but it would be reduced to 0 per cent as from 2002; the system of voluntary set aside was to be maintained and improved. In the beef sector, the price reduction was also set at 20 per cent to be achieved by three equal steps; when the final step is taken a basic price for private storage of beef will be established as will a 'safety-net' intervention system. Once again, as compensation for the price reductions payments under various premia would be increased subject to various regional ceilings. As a measure to promote flexibility, various national envelopes were established allowing Member States to compensate producers for regional variations in production practices and conditions.

The political agreement on reforms to the arable crops and beef sector followed the proposals advocated by the Commission with important changes, notably the price reduction in the arable crop sector was to be 20 per cent over two years rather than the one year proposed and price reduction in the beef sector was to be 20 per cent rather than the 30 per cent advocated. This pattern would be repeated in the reforms agreed in the milk sector. Although the intervention price was to be reduced by 15 per cent, as advocated by the Commission, the increase in quotas was

---

[30] See European Commission Directorate-general of Agriculture Newsletter 11 (Special Edition) *Agriculture Council: Political Agreement on CAP Reform* (Brussels, 1999).

set at 2.39 per cent rather than 2 per cent. The quotas for most Member States would be increased by 1.5 per cent in three steps as from 2003 with provision for special quota increases for some Member States as from 2000. As for the future of the regime beyond 2006, discussions would begin in 2003. Once again to compensate farmers for the price reductions a system of aids would be introduced that could be supplemented through agreed national envelopes.

As for measures applicable to all common organisations of the market, there was broad agreement within the Council on the proposals advanced by the Commission, although significantly the proposal to impose ceilings on direct payments was not endorsed. In relation to rural development policy, the Council endorsed the Commission's proposals for a more coherent and sustainable rural development policy which would create a stronger agricultural and forestry sector which would be more competitive and respectful of the environment and the rural heritage. Overall, although less ambitious than the original proposals of the Commission, the political agreement on reforms represented an attempt by the Council to continue with the reform process initiated by the MacSharry reforms. However, the agreement still had to be endorsed by the European Council, as it was only one part of the Agenda 2000 package of reforms. In welcoming the political agreement of the Council, the European Council commented that:[31]

> The content of this reform will ensure that agriculture is multifunctional, sustainable, competitive and spread throughout Europe, including regions with specific problems, that it is capable of maintaining the countryside, conserving nature and making a key contribution to the vitality of rural life, and that it responds to consumer concerns and demands as regards food quality and safety, environmental protection and the safeguarding of animal welfare.

Despite this welcome, various changes were made to the political agreement on reform.[32]

For example, the agreed changes to the dairy regime, save those on quotas, were not to enter into force until the marketing year 2005/2006 and the intervention price for cereals instead of being reduced by 20 per cent was to be reduced by 15 per cent with the base rate of compulsory set aside to be fixed at 10 per cent for all of the period 2000–2006. Beyond these changes the Council and the Commission were requested to pursue additional savings, except in the areas of rural development and veterinary measures, to ensure that average annual agricultural expenditure over the period 2000–2006 would not exceed 40.5 billion euros. It was considered by the European

---

[31] *Presidency Conclusions Berlin European Council*, Part I A. Heading 1 (Agriculture) 2 (available on europa website).
[32] See European Commission Directorate-general of Agriculture Newsletter 10 *Berlin European Council: Agenda 2000, Conclusions of the Presidency* (Brussels, 1999).

Council that the reform of the CAP over this period along the lines agreed by the Council, as amended by the European Council, would lead to a reduction in expenditure over the period thus contributing to the overall objective of achieving a more equitable financial framework. One aspect of the latter objective was agreement on another major aspect of the Agenda 2000 reform package—structural operations.

As part of improving the effectiveness of structural operations, thus promoting greater economic and social cohesion within the Community, the number of Objective Areas was reduced to three.[33] Objective 1 areas, which would be allocated 74 per cent of the available funds, would promote the development and structural adjustment of those regions whose *per capita* GDP fell below 75 per cent of the Community average. Just short of 13 per cent of available structural funds would be used to support the economic and social conversion of those areas facing structural difficulties, defined as Objective 2 areas, which includes declining rural areas. Finally, Objective 3 would lend support, in the form of just over 12 per cent of the available structural funds, to the adaptation and modernisation of policies and systems of education, employment and training outside Objective 1 areas. Furthermore, the number of Community initiatives in the field of structural policy would be reduced to three.[34] Additional funding for rural development would also be available under the agricultural aspect of the financial perspective, which indicates that financing for rural development and accompanying measures shall not exceed an average of 4340 million Euro over the period 2000–2006.

The overall agreement on the Agenda 2000 package reached at the Berlin European Council undoubtedly represented an important milestone for the CAP and for the Community. As for the nature of that milestone, several points may be made. Reform of the policy up to this time has concentrated on the three (or four) core principles established in 1960 for the policy. Although the MacSharry reforms added a more effective second pillar to the CAP, they did not fundamentally alter the fact that the CAP was a price support and production control policy. With the changes to the role of intervention, an increasing emphasis on direct payments and greater support for rural policy, the Agenda 2000 reforms signal a further realignment of the twin pillars of the CAP towards a situation of greater equilibrium. Although the objectives set for the policy in Article 33 can accommodate this realignment, just as all past extensions of the scope of the CAP have been accommodated, the Agenda 2000 reforms also signal a partial re-nationalisation of the policy. This will occur through the operation of the national envelopes, which promote a new division of functions between

---

[33] Above n 31, Heading 2 (Structural Operations)
[34] These include the INTERREG scheme on cross-border and inter-regional cooperation and the LEADER scheme on rural development.

the Community and the Member States. Likewise, a more decentralised approach will be adopted in the area of rural development, thus increasing regional rights and responsibilities.[35] This is one of the issues to be addressed at the 2004 IGC. Given the re-nationalisation of elements of the CAP, an increasing emphasis on decentralisation and the process of the simplification of agricultural legislation, it may be appropriate to address the objectives of the policy at that conference.

IV.   NEW OBJECTIVES?

The Commission has listed five particular objectives as motivating its proposals for reform of the CAP, these are:[36]

— to increase competitiveness;
— to assure food safety and food quality
— to maintain a fair standard of living for the agricultural community and stabilise farm incomes;
— to better integrate environmental goals into the CAP and
— to develop alternative job and income opportunities for farmers and their families.

For the Commission, such objectives would confirm the nature of the European model of agriculture as being multifunctional. How would such objectives be achieved?

In November 1995, the Directorate-General for Agriculture invited a group of experts to analyse the inconsistencies and problems inherent in the existing CAP and in this light to define a series of principles that would form the basis of a new integrated rural policy. The resulting report, known as the Buckwell report, proposed that the existing CAP should be transformed into a Common Agricultural and Rural Policy for Europe (CARPE) whose objective would be 'to ensure an economically efficient and environmentally sustainable agriculture and to stimulate the integrated development of the Union's rural areas'.[37] The three elements of the new policy, economic efficiency, the environment and rural development, would, unlike the CAP, be equally balanced. The report made it clear that the new policy, although revolutionary, would also be evolutionary, so allowing the policy to respond to new challenges as they emerge.

---

[35] See also in this respect, Regulation 1244/2001 (OJ 2001 L173/1) establishing a simplified scheme for small farmers, which is part of the ongoing process of the simplification of agricultural legislation. See also COM (2001) 48.
[36] These were suggested by the Commission as the five main objectives motivating its proposals for reform of the CAP, COM (99) 22 *Directions towards Sustainable Agriculture*, p 30.
[37] See europa.eu.int/en/comm/dg06/new/buck_en/index.htm, ch 6.1.

As for the first element of the new policy, economic efficiency, the goal would be to reduce the level of price support to world market levels and the role of the Community will be to provide a safety net in the form of intervention. There is no doubt that the MacSharry and the Agenda 2000 reforms have reduced the level of price support within the Community and the Agenda 2000 reforms, when fully implemented will begin the process of returning intervention to its proper role as a safety net. However, a number of problems remain. With respect to the probable enlargement of the Community, in relation to direct support there are no proposals for the abolition of this form of support or for their conversion into truly decoupled payments. This raises the prospect of the acceding countries receiving 'compensation' for losses that they have not suffered, this assumes they have the same rights and duties with respect to agriculture as the existing Member States. Second by agreeing to lesser price reduction than originally proposed and by delaying in some cases actual price reductions, the Agenda 2000 reforms add to the cost of enlargement. A more radical reduction in prices and the end to the use of existing direct support measures would have the advantage of opening the Community market to greater imports as the isolation of that market is ended. This would allow the Community to participate effectively in the next round of international trade negotiations on agriculture, as the support that it provides would be decoupled. There are two particular areas to be examined here, market access and domestic support

In relation to market access, the Agreement on Agriculture provided for the usual reduction in tariffs and the conversion of existing non-tariff barriers into tariffs, the process of tariffication. Although the agreement on tariffication was significant, the impact of that process has not been. One reason for this is the choice of base period, 1986–88, when the difference between world and domestic prices was particularly high. Another reason is that several WTO members have engaged in the process of 'dirty tariffication'—the setting of tariff equivalents in excess of the price differential for that period.[38] Consequently, many tariffs contain what is referred to as 'a good deal of water' allowing for their subsequent reduction without adversely affecting domestic prices. When combined with the Special Safeguard Provision in Article 5 of the Agreement on Agriculture, the net result is that there has not been a significant increase in market access for a number of WTO members. The Community has been one of the guilty parties here. Indeed, the Agenda 2000 reforms did not lower import tariffs thus increasing the amount of 'water' in its tariff.[39]

In recognition of the likely marginal impact of the market access commitments, the Agreement on Agriculture provides for a range of minimum

[38] See Ingco, 'Tariffication in the Uruguay Round: How much Liberalisation?' (1996) 19(4) *The World Economy* 425.
[39] See Swinbank 'CAP Reform and the WTO: Compatibility and Developments' (1999) 26(3) *European Review of Agricultural Economics* 389, pp 396–99.

access tariff quotas (5 per cent of 1986–88 consumption levels by 2000, if 1986–88 imports fell short of this amount). Such quotas have again proved problematic, not least because they lack transparency. It is no surprise, therefore, that major reform of such quotas is high on the agenda of the current discussions. Even the Community has proposed that a set of rules and disciplines should be defined to increase the transparency, the reliability and the security of the management of Tariff Rate Quotas, so that concessions granted should be fully realised.[40] Beyond this, it has proposed the retention of Article 5, the special safeguard clause, and measures:[41]

(a) to guarantee effective protection against usurpation of names for agricultural products and foodstuffs;
(b) to protect the right to use geographical indications or designations of origin; and
(c) to guarantee consumer protection and fair competition through regulation of labelling.

To enable the Community to achieve these non-trade concerns objectives may require additional concessions in the area of market access. At least the Community has provided itself with room for manoeuvre in this area.

The existing Community position on domestic support in the negotiations for a new Agreement on Agriculture does not envisage the abolition of the Blue Box, indeed such payments are seen as an important tool in further agricultural reform and so the concept of the Blue Box would be retained.[42] Most WTO members do not envisage the retention of this exceptional measure, and envisage changes in the nature of the Aggregate Measurement of Support (AMS). For example, it has been suggested that the new Agreement should introduce product-specific limits on support rather than having the AMS calculated for the entire agricultural sector. Such a change, effectively repealing the Blair House Accord, would generate significant problems for the Community.

More immediately, additional problems in the Blue Box may also be generated as a result of the Agenda 2000 reforms. Under Article 13 of the Agreement on Agriculture, during the implementation period, which ends in 2003, limited protection is provided to Blue Box measures that conform fully to the provisions of Article 6(5) and where no determination of injury or threat thereof is shown. According to Article 6(5)(a) direct payments under production-limiting programmes will be exempt from the domestic support reduction commitment if:

---

[40] See WTO documents G/AG/NG/W/90—EC Comprehensive Negotiating Proposal, paras 2–4.
[41] *Ibid*, paras 18–19. See also G/AG/NG/W/18—Food Quality: Improvement in Market Access Opportunities.
[42] See in particular, G/AG/NG/W/17—EC Proposal on Domestic Support.

(i) such payments are based on fixed areas and yields; or

(ii) such payments are made on 85 per cent or less of the base level of production; or

(iii) livestock payments are made on a fixed number of head.

In the Agenda 2000 document and the 18 March proposals, the Commission went to great lengths to create a 'virtual cow' as the basis for compensating farmers for the reduction in the level of support prices for milk. Such a payment could have come within Article 6(5)(a)(iii). However, the premium eventually agreed is based on the farmer's milk quota, and, as a result, is unlikely to come within the scope of Article 6(5). At least, the European Council set the base rate of compulsory set aside at 10 per cent for the period 2000–2006, rather than at 0 as recommended by the Commission, thus ensuring that the policy could appear to the production-limiting.

Rather than promote competitiveness, it seems clear that the Community is intent on maintaining the Blue Box as an integral element of the CAP. Such a policy will be dependent on the continuation of Article 13 of the Agreement on Agriculture. As for the future of this provision, some countries envisage a new Peace Clause that ensure that they would not be challenged so long as they comply with their commitments on export subsidies and domestic support under the Agreement. For others, the new Agreement would contain no new Peace Clause, as this would frustrate their overall objective of bringing agriculture under general WTO disciplines. Some countries have proposed variants.[43] The conclusion is that, given few WTO members actually use the Blue Box,[44] the Community may have to pay heavily for its retention and the protection provided by Article 13, even if it is prolonged, is very limited. An approach that would promote the objectives identified by the Commission as motivating the Agenda 2000 reforms and which would not be as problematic internationally merits consideration. Such an approach would eschew continued reliance on the Blue Box in favour of policy objectives that could be pursued legitimately under the Green Box of the Agreement on Agriculture.

One of the legitimate public policy objectives to qualify as a Green Box policy, the protection of the environment, formed the second aspect of the proposed CARPE. Environmental and Cultural Landscape Payments would be made for positive action taken by farmers. This was defined as the provision of services that impose an additional cost on farmers. The payments would be

---

[43] For example, Canada would like to see 'green box' domestic supports freed from the possibility of countervailing action under the Subsidies Agreement. (G/AG/NG/W/92) India proposes something like the peace clause should be retained but only for developing countries, so that some subsidies are free from the possibility of countervailing duty. (G/AG/NG/W/102)

[44] See the Memorandum of the Australian Government in *House of Commons, CAP Reform: Agenda 2000. Volume II. Second Report from the Agriculture Committee 1997–98 Session* HC 311–11 (London, HMSO, 1998).

regionally based and there would be two levels of payments. The first level would be directed to farming systems providing high nature value whilst the second level would concern specific environmental management practices, such as intensive action to preserve or create significant environmental effects. The distinction between the two levels rested in the fact that level one was directed at farming whereas level two was directed at the environment, although there would be some cross-fertilisation between the two levels.

With respect to the Green Box, the Community's negotiating position recognises the need to retain the Green Box, which is viewed as including measures that meet important societal goals such as the protection of the environment and the sustained vitality of rural areas.[45] However, the position advocates a re-assessment of the criteria used for Green Box measures so as to ensure that such measures are well-targeted, transparent and cause minimal trade distortion. One problem that has not yet surfaced in relation to the Green Box is the criterion that support provided by such policies should have a minimal impact on production. Again, it emerges from Article 13 of the Agreement on Agriculture which affords protection, during the implementation period, to Green Box measures that conform fully to the provisions of Annex 2. The protection is limited, as Annex 2 requires that Green Box measures must have a minimal impact on production. This raises two questions:[46]

(a) if payments are made whose primary aim or effect is to increase producer incomes, will these payments have a minimal impact on production?

(b) if payments are made to achieve other aims, eg environmental objectives, is it logical to require these to have a minimal impact on production?

Any payments made will increase the funds available to the producer for use in his/her business, so it will have an impact on production. It will also have an impact on the other less obvious outputs of agriculture—this is the multifunctionality argument. With respect to the generation of employment, it would be more rational to allocate resources to rural development as a means of generating rural employment. As for the protection of the rural landscape, the payment will necessarily have an impact on production— for example supporting particular production methods—and of necessity on trade. Clearer criteria, as the Community itself has recognised, are needed for all Green Box payments. The problem here for the Community is that existing policy measures under the second pillar of the CAP may not

---

[45] Above n 40, paras 13–16.
[46] See Blandford 'Are Disciplines Required on Domestic Support' (2001) 2(1) *The Estey Centre Journal of International Law and Trade Policy* 35, p 48.

fully conform to Annex 2. For example, there are no clear environmental criteria used in the payment of various premiums or they are limited to those farmers in the less-advantaged areas of the Community. The Environmental and Cultural Landscape Payments recommended by the Buckwell Report are much more in accordance with the existing criteria of Annex 2 of the Agreement on Agriculture.

These payments, according to the Buckwell Report, would form part of the third aspect of the proposed new CARPE, Rural Development Incentives. Rural development would remain wider than agricultural development and the approach would involve a continuation of the existing policy of promoting sustainable rural development. So the existing measures of assistance directed towards agricultural development would continue. Given the major changes involved in the transition from the CAP to the CARPE, the report recommended the transformation of the compensation payments introduced in the 1992 reform package into what is termed Transitional Adjustment Assistance. The three principles of such assistance are that it will be decoupled from production, be non-distorting of competition and that recipients should respect environmental conditions. It is worth noting that the proposed objectives of the Commission are met to a greater extent by the proposed CARPE than by the Agenda 2000 reforms. Market stabilisation measures would increase the competitiveness of European agriculture. Equally, the Environmental and Cultural Landscape Payments and the Rural Development Incentives would maintain a fair standard of living for the agricultural community and stabilise farm incomes, whilst better integrating environmental goals into the CAP and developing alternative job and income opportunities for farmers and their families.

The Commission's policy, supported by the Council and the European Council, is much more problematic. It involves continued reliance on an instrument whose future is uncertain, the Blue Box, and whose continued existence may require significant sacrifices to be made by the Community. Moreover, the Agenda 2000 reforms have actually increased the possibility of a WTO challenge to existing measures. Article 13 of the Agreement on Agriculture provides only limited immunity from such challenges. Existing policy with respect the environmental aspects of the CAP is also not immune from challenge in the WTO. The approach of the Community to the negotiations for a new Agreement on Agriculture has been to stress the balance between trade and non-trade concerns. In order to promote future liberalisation and expansion of international agricultural trade, which will contribute to economic growth in all countries, the Community claims that:[47]

> ... it is vital to muster strong public support, which can only be achieved if other concerns are met, in particular the multifunctional role of agriculture,

[47] Above n 40, para 1.

which covers the protection of the environment and the sustained vitality of rural communities, food safety and other consumer concerns including animal welfare.

The objective for the Community is WTO recognition of the multifunctional role of agriculture. The problem for the Community is that the objectives of the CAP do not afford recognition of that multifunctionality.

V.　CONCLUSION

One element of whether or not it is appropriate to re-write the objectives of the CAP at the 2004 IGC may be determined next year as the Commission assess the impact of the Agenda 2000 reforms. Speaking at a conference in Dublin, Franz Fischler, the Commissioner for Agriculture, suggested that the future of the CAP rested with consumers.[48] He continued by noting that the mid-term review of Agenda 2000 may be viewed as the 'ideal opportunity for all the stakeholders to contribute to the future orientation of a genuinely European agricultural policy'. At present, what is envisaged is a further strengthening of the second pillar of the CAP, the rural development policy. However, this may not be enough, after all the pursuit of the objectives of the CAP has led to mounting concerns about human health and safety, and the environmental and ethical aspects of agricultural production.

Opening a High Level Round Table on Food Quality in March this year, David Byrne, the Commissioner for Health and Consumer Protection noted that the goal of food security has been realised. He continued:[49]

> … general affluence and surplus in our food supply has resulted in a gradual change in public policy focus away from efficiency and productivity towards quality and diversity in agri-food production. Indeed modern food production methods themselves have raised matters of public concern beyond human health and safety in relation to environmental and ethical aspects of agri-food production, ….

He went on to suggest the need for a new food production/consumption model, which would be focused on food safety and food quality.[50] If the argument being advanced is that the objectives of the CAP have been realised, especially in the area of food security, then should the new food

---

[48] Speech 'Agriculture and Agri-Food: A clean green future' available on Rapid (DN: Speech/01/254), Dublin 31 May 2001.
[49] See http://www.europa.eu.int/comm/dgs/health_consumer/library/speeches/speech88_en.html.
[50] See COM (2000) 716 Proposal for a Regulation of the European Parliament and of the Council laying down the general principles and requirements of food law, establishing the European Food Authority, and laying down procedures in matters of food and COM (99) 719 White Paper on Food Safety.

production/consumption model have new objectives? Equally, if the Community is seeking WTO recognition of the multifunctional role of agriculture then should the objectives of the CAP not recognise that multifunctionality?

The key to this concept is the contribution that farming makes to a series of societal goals or non-trade concerns. Two points must be emphasised here. First, to be acceptable it must be shown that the net contribution made by agriculture is greater or more valued by society than the net contribution of equivalent sectors. Only when this can be shown will assistance to agriculture be seen as worthy of continued government assistance as opposed to other sectors that do not receive assistance, yet contribute to societal goals. It is here that evidence is particularly difficult to determine. For example, is there a difference between general product safety and food safety? Is there something culturally significant about food and farming which merit especial attention? The argument of the Community is that there is a difference with respect to food and that there is a European model of agriculture. The second point is that price support is not the appropriate mechanism to promote the multifunctionality of agriculture. There will have to be a re-balancing of the existing pillars of the CAP in favour of the second pillar. So, the protection of the environment would be a part of the broader Community environmental policy. The focus of the existing environmental aspect of the CAP needs to reflect concern with the environment rather than being used as a means to supplement farmers' income. Payments must become truly decoupled. The 'sustained vitality of rural communities' would be a part of the Community policy to promote economic and social cohesion. Farmers would be seen as part of the rural community but it must be acknowledged that the policy of price support is a blunt instrument to support that community. A more regionalised approach to rural development is needed.

The European model of agriculture, and the means to realise it, must be included within the Treaty. The existing objectives do not reflect what is being characterised as 'the European model of agriculture.' Moreover, it is unlikely that they can provide a sufficient basis for a new production/consumption model. To emphasise the nature of the changes to the existing objectives, the new objectives should place the consumer first through an emphasis on food safety and food quality. The means to achieve this objective include existing mechanisms promoting such areas as organic production, geographical indicators and animal welfare issues. Other existing areas would be re-focused, for example, greater use of instruments to support environmentally sound production methods. Such instruments would be environmentally based rather than producer based. Moving to the producer, payments would be made, sufficient to ensure a fair standard of living, on the basis of the contributions made to the societal goals recognised in the European model of agriculture, for example, the cultural landscape.

In addition, the farmer would be seen as part of the rural community and mechanisms would be devised to promote the economic and social cohesion of such communities.

The Buckwell report concluded:[51]

> From its origins, when the CAP was most definitely part of the big European political and cultural compromise—assistance for agriculture to adjust, in return for an open market for industrial products—it has descended into [a] purely commodity approach. In this process it lost its sense of purpose. A bold new start towards a more integrated rural policy could reassert a constructive role for this important aspect of the European Union.

Considerable political capital has been invested in the CAP throughout the history of the Community. However, a time has been reached when the objectives of the policy are no longer appropriate to the model of agriculture that consumers are demanding. Coupled with the concerns of consumers, the international environment in which the policy operates is fundamentally different from that of the 1950s. A new set of objectives must be drawn up, especially if the Community wish to defend successfully in international negotiations what it has labelled the 'European model of agriculture.' A debate on the future objectives of the policy should be launched as a result of the mid-term review of the Agenda 2000 reforms and the 2004 IGC offers an ideal opportunity to realise a new set of objectives for the policy. These objectives would be more regionally and environmentally oriented than the existing objectives and would place the consumer at the heart of an integrated agricultural and rural policy. A common policy at European level would continue to exist but, respecting the principle of subsidiarity, would increase regional rights and responsibilities, as direct assistance to farmers would be tailored to the needs of each region. Such new objectives would represent a bold new start for the CAP and re-establish its constructive role within the European Union.

[51] Above n 37, ch 8.5.

Part III

The European Courts

11

The European Courts after Nice

PIET EECKHOUT*

I. INTRODUCTION: LEFT OVERS OR HORS D'OEUVRE?

T HE AMSTERDAM TREATY was intended to address, in a comprehensive and fairly definitive manner, the institutional overhaul of the European Union required for enlargement. As the negotiators did not manage to find solutions for all outstanding issues, there were 'leftovers' which Nice was to deal with. In the mean time, as we know, there are further constitutional issues scheduled for debate, first in a convention, and later on in an IGC.[1] But that debate appears less connected with the institutional set-up of the EU, and it may well be that, with time, Amsterdam and Nice prove to contain a relatively long-lasting institutional settlement. Does that settlement include what is now commonly referred to as the judicial architecture of the European Union? At the Amsterdam negotiations, the Court of Justice (ECJ) appeared to be in the dock, rather than being the subject of any serious reflection on judicial architecture.[2] As regards the European Courts, therefore, Nice could hardly be said to deal with the Amsterdam leftovers. Nice did engage in such serious reflection, but the thesis of this contribution is that the results are little more than an hors d'oeuvre. There are many changes to the basic texts governing the functioning of the European Courts, in the various Treaties and in the Statute. There are significant modifications to the various heads of jurisdiction of the Courts, and to their mode of operating. But it is questionable whether any of this is in any way sufficient to enable the Courts to function effectively in an

* Professor of European Law and Director, Centre of European Law, King's College London. I am indebted to Luca Rubini for the excellent research assistance, funded by the Centre of European Law, as well as to Thomas Deisenhofer for comments. This chapter was finalised in February 2002.
[1] See the Presidency Conclusions of the Nice European Council and the Declaration of Laeken, annexed to the Presidency Conclusions of the Laeken European Council, both at http://ue.eu. int/en/Info/eurocouncil/ index.htm.
[2] A Arnull, 'Taming the Beast? The Treaty of Amsterdam and the Court of Justice', in D O'Keeffe and P Twomey (eds), *Legal Issues of the Amsterdam Treaty* (Oxford, Hart Publishing, 1999) 109–21.

enlarged European Union. In fact, the thesis of this contribution goes even further—or less far: the changes are insufficient even if there were no enlargement, for the state of the judicial architecture is such that the premises are unadapted to even the current demands made on the delivery of justice in the sphere of EU law.

Much has already been said over the last couple of years about judicial architecture, by reflection groups,[3] by the Court of Justice and Court of First Instance (CFI) themselves,[4] by the clients of the Courts,[5] and by academic commentators.[6] Most of this debate predates Nice, and one option for this contribution would be to provide a detailed analysis of the Nice changes. Yet much in those changes is prospective and needs colouring by implementing measures which cannot be adopted before the ratification process is completed. Moreover, there are at the time of writing already a couple of excellent detailed analyses of the Nice changes.[7]

The aim of this contribution is to take a somewhat more distanced look. As Nice did make a number of changes, it does not appear to make much sense to write a further academic piece geared towards making specific proposals for a revised judicial architecture. Nor am I convinced that making such proposals is as straightforward as is sometimes suggested. Arnull has

---

[3] British Institute of International and Comparative Law, *The Role and Future of the European Court of Justice* (1996); European Commission, *Report by the Working Party on the Future of the European Communities' Court System ('Due Report')*, January 2000, published in A Dashwood and A Johnston, *The Future of the Judicial System of the European Union* (Oxford, Hart Publishing, 2001) 145–204.

[4] *The Future of the Judicial System of the European Union (Proposals and Reflections)*, published in Dashwood and Johnston, cited above n 3, at 111–43.

[5] See the Submission of the CCBE (Council of the Bars and Law Societies of the European Union) to the Nice IGC, 18 May 2000, CONFER/VAR 3966/00 (http://ue.eu.int/cigdocs/EN/03966en.pdf).

[6] See eg J P Jacqué and J H H Weiler, 'On the Road to European Union - A New Judicial, Architecture: An Agenda for the Intergovernmental Conference', 27 *Common Market Law Review* (1990) 185–207; W Van Gerven, 'The Role and Structure of the European Judiciary Now and in the Future', 21 *European Law Review* (1996) 211–233; T Koopmans, 'The future of the Court of Justice of the European Communities', 11 *Yearbook of European Law* (1991) 15; D Edward, 'Reform of Article 234 Procedure: The Limits of the Possible', in D O'Keeffe (ed), *Judicial Review in European Union Law - Liber Amicorum Lord Slynn of Hadley - Vol. I* (Kluwer Law International 2000) 119–42; C Turner and R Muñoz, 'Revising the Judicial Architecture of the European Union', 19 *Yearbook of European Law* (1999–2000) 1–93; H Rasmussen, 'Remedying the crumbling EC judicial system', 37 *Common Market Law Review* (2000) 1071–112; various contributions to Dashwood and Johnston, cited above n 3; P Craig, 'The Jurisdiction of the Community Courts Reconsidered', in G de Búrca and J H H Weiler, The European Court of Justice (Oxford, Oxford University Press 2001) 177–214; J H H Weiler, 'Epilogue: The Judicial Après Nice', *ibid* 215–26; B De Witte, 'De hervorming van bevoegdheden en werkwijze van Europees Hof en Gerecht', 48 *Social-Economiscks Wetgeving* (2000) 354–362; P J G Kapteyn, 'Reflections on the Future of the Judicial System of the European Union after Nice', 20 *Yearbook of European Law* (2001) 173–90.

[7] A Johnston, 'Judicial Reform and the Treaty of Nice', 38 *Common Market Law Review* (2001) 499–523; A Dashwood and A Johnston, 'Part Two: The Outcome at Nice', in Dashwood and Johnston (eds), cited above n. 3, 217–268; J S van den Oosterkamp and S Terstal, 'De hervorming van de communautaire rechtspleging', 49 *Social-Economiscks Wetgeving* (2001) 166–72.

said that it is relatively easy to draw up a blueprint for reform of the Union's judicial system which looks fine on the back of an envelope.[8] Weiler, disagreeing, submits that the back of a postal stamp on that envelope could do the job just as well.[9] Both statements may be correct, provided the designers limit their blueprint to some basic contours, or use minute micro print. Neither of those options appears particularly attractive. Instead, this contribution aims to discuss a number of issues which are in my view foundational for the whole reform process. Indeed, I feel that, in spite of the intensity of the judicial architecture debate, quantitatively and qualitatively, there is still a lot of reflection to take place on the appropriate foundations for the judicial architecture. Reflection on what could and should be the functions of the European judiciary, in the concrete context of the way in which EU law and the European Courts currently operate, but also from a more general perspective on the role of the judiciary.

What follows is no more than a short attempt to engage in some of the type of reflection which may be needed. However, there are of course the Nice changes which triggered this contribution to begin with. The paper therefore sets out to offer a concise description and characterisation of the main changes, and then takes that as a base for the broader reflections which will hopefully convince the reader that Nice is indeed merely an hors d'oeuvre, and that, if no main course is to follow, the European Union runs the risk of gradual judicial starvation.

II. NICE, AN ENABLING FRAMEWORK

The changes which the Treaty of Nice makes to the current judicial architecture are clearly not inconsequential. Many of them are in the nature of enabling provisions, which as indicated will need to be implemented and which may be coloured in different ways. To mention just one example, the new Article 225a EC allows the Council to set up judicial panels, to hear and determine at first instance certain classes of action or proceeding. The provision, however, in no way determines how many of those panels will be set up, nor in what areas, and as long as there is no more clarity in this respect, it is difficult to gauge the impact and import of this modification. Thus, the Nice changes are an ongoing process, on which no definitive verdict can be reached before full implementation.

It is also clear that the Nice negotiations on judicial architecture were dominated by one overriding concern: the problem of case- or workload. Nearly all significant modifications can be explained as attempts to address

---

[8] A Arnull, 'Judicial Architecture or Judicial Folly? The Challenge Facing the EU', in Dashwood and Johnston, cited above n 3, at 41. I hasten to mention that the author immediately adds that it is much more difficult to devise a blueprint that works in practice.
[9] 'Epilogue: The Judicial Après Nice', cited above n 6, at 222.

this problem, which is indeed a very real and urgent one. The problem is well documented,[10] and there is no particular need for describing it again here. Whilst it cannot be denied that the mounting caseload and resulting delays and loss of quality are the most corrosive element for the European judicial architecture—one need only think of its effects on the proper functioning of the preliminary rulings system—there may be risk of myopism here. As will be argued below, there are other concerns too, some of which may be more profound and fundamental than the mere arithmetic of the caseload.[11] Or, to look at it somewhat differently, the caseload problem may itself be caused by features of the current judicial architecture which have become inadequate.

As will be seen, the most important common element in many of the Nice changes consists of a strengthening of the role of the CFI. There is the beginning of a tendency towards making the CFI the EU's general court, and towards limiting the role of the ECJ to that of a supreme court. This calls for some further comments, but let us first take a look at the main Nice changes.

1. First, one may mention that, independently of the Nice negotiations, changes were made to the Rules of Procedure of both the ECJ and CFI, with a view to permitting a swifter judicial process, in at least certain types of cases.[12] There will be fewer oral hearings,[13] reductions in the exchange of written pleadings,[14] scope for the expedition of urgent cases,[15] and scope for orders in clear cases.[16] Connected to these changes are the new rules on modifying the Rules of Procedure: ECJ and CFI may themselves establish those Rules, but approval of the Council is required, acting by a qualified majority (new Article 223–224 EC). Those provisions fall short of the Courts' own preference for full autonomy in the adoption of procedural rules.[17] Member State governments are apparently intent on continuing to play something of a stepmother's role towards the courts, as can also be seen in relation to the Courts' budget, over which the Courts have no control.[18]

---

[10] See, for a range of tables and statistics, Turner and Muñoz, cited above n 6, at 5–19.
[11] See also Weiler, cited above n 6, at 219–20.
[12] Amendments to the Rules of Procedure of the Court of Justice of 16 May 2000, OJ 2000 L 122/43 and Amendments to the Rules of Procedure of the Court of Justice of 28 November 2000, OJ 2000 L 322/1; Amendments to the Rules of Procedure of the Court of First Instance of 6 December 2000, OJ 2000 L 322/4.
[13] ECJ Rules of Procedure, Art 104(4).
[14] CFI Rules of Procedure, Art 47.
[15] ECJ Rules of Procedure, Arts 62a and 104a.
[16] ECJ Rules of Procedure, Art 104(3).
[17] See the Courts' report, cited above n 4, at 126–27.
[18] Edward, above n 6, at 138.

2.   The foundational and constitutional Article 220 EC, according to which the Court of Justice ensures that in the interpretation and application of the Treaty the law is observed, is amended so as to include the Court of First Instance. It also makes reference, 'in addition', to the judicial panels which may be attached to the CFI. This provision endorses the equal judicial status of the ECJ and CFI, and confirms the growing importance of the CFI, which is no longer simply a junior first instance court whose main task is to try facts.

3.   As mentioned, under Article 225a EC the Council may in future create judicial panels to hear and determine at first instance certain classes of action or proceeding brought in specific areas. The initiative needs to come from either the Commission ('proposal') or the Court of Justice ('request'). The Council acts unanimously, after consulting the European Parliament and either the Commission or the Court (depending on which institution took the initiative). Article 225a leaves open whether there is to be a right of appeal before the CFI on points of law only, or also on matters of fact. There is no further right of appeal before the ECJ, but appellate decisions by the CFI may exceptionally be subject to review by the ECJ, where there is a serious risk of the unity or consistency of Community law being affected (see new Article 225(2) EC). The procedure for such review is contained in the new Protocol on the Statute of the Court of Justice. According to Article 62 of the Statute, it is up to the First Advocate-General of the ECJ to propose review, within one month of delivery of the decision of the CFI. The ECJ shall then decide, within one month, whether or not the decision should be reviewed. No further particulars are given,[19] but it may be noted here that it will be possible in future for the Council to amend the Statute (except for Title I), under the same procedure as that for the establishment of judicial panels. That is an important achievement, as it will enable gradual modification of significant elements of the jurisdiction and operating modes of the European Courts, without having to go through the cumbersome IGC process. Up until now, the scope for extra-IGC amendment of the Statute was confined to Title III, on procedure.

Nice did not decide in which areas judicial panels are to be set up, but Declaration 16 of the IGC calls upon the ECJ and the Commission to prepare as swiftly as possible a draft decision

---

[19] See also Declarations 13 and 14 of the IGC on Art 225(2) and (3) EC, according to which the essential provisions of the review procedure should be defined in the Statute. They should in particular specify: the role of the parties in proceedings before the ECJ; the effect of the review procedure on the enforceability of the decision of the CFI; and the effect of the ECJ decision on the dispute between the parties.

establishing a judicial panel for staff cases. Commentators also say that certain types of intellectual property cases are another candidate.[20]

4.   As regards the latter, however, there is also a new Article 229a, which enables the Council to confer jurisdiction on the Court of Justice in disputes relating to the application of acts which create Community industrial property rights. The second sentence peculiarly adds that the Council shall recommend the relevant provisions to the Member States for adoption in accordance with their respective constitutional requirements.

If indeed there is undecisiveness as regards the location of intellectual property cases, the options appear rather extreme: either judicial panels, ie the lowest level of the EU's judicial architecture, or the Court of Justice, which is at the highest level.

5.   In relation to the judicial panels, the CFI will acquire appellate jurisdiction. Its role is further boasted by a major modification of the judicial architecture: the possibility for the CFI to deal with certain preliminary rulings cases. Up until some time ago, this was considered the 'chasse gardée' of the ECJ, as it was felt that the preliminary rulings procedure is so vital for the uniformity and proper application of EC law that only the ECJ should have jurisdiction. New Article 225(3) EC changes that. It provides that the CFI shall have jurisdiction to hear and determine questions referred for a preliminary ruling under Article 234, in specific areas laid down by the Statute. Those areas have not yet been identified, but the idea seems to be to transfer preliminary rulings jurisdiction in certain well-defined areas requiring considerable technical expertise.[21]

Although this is a major breakthrough, the fears for negative effects on the uniformity of EC law have not been laid to rest, as is evident from the second and third subparagraphs of new Article 225(3). They provide, first, that where the CFI considers that the case requires a decision of principle likely to affect the unity or consistency of Community law, it may refer the case to the ECJ; and second, that decisions given by the CFI may exceptionally be subject to review by the ECJ, where there is a serious risk of the unity or consistency of Community law being affected. As regards the latter, the Statute will lay down the relevant rules, as in the case of review of CFI appellate decisions in judicial panel cases.[22] In Declaration 15 the Conference considers that, in such

---

[20] Johnston, cited above n 7, at 514.
[21] Such was suggested by the Due Report, cited above n 3, at 172.
[22] Declarations 13 and 14, cited above n 19, also apply to this review procedure.

exceptional review proceedings, the ECJ should act under an emergency procedure.

6. New Article 225(1) further broadens the jurisdiction of the CFI, by enabling it to hear all direct actions in a number of types of proceedings, the most important of which are actions for annulment (Article 230 EC) and failure to act (Article 232 EC). Until now, the CFI only has jurisdiction over such actions if they are brought by private parties. The Statute will further provide over which actions the CFI will not have jurisdiction, because they will be assigned to judicial panels or to the ECJ.[23] Article 225(1) also adds that the Statute may provide for the CFI to have jurisdiction for other classes of action or proceeding. A possible candidate here, one assumes, are enforcement actions under Article 226 EC (Commission v Member State).

In Declaration 12 the Conference calls on the Court of Justice and the Commission to give overall consideration as soon as possible to the division of jurisdiction between the ECJ and the CFI, in particular in the area of direct actions, and to submit suitable proposals for examination by the competent bodies as soon as the Treaty of Nice enters into force. At the time of writing, the Court had issued a 'document de travail' (working document), proposing a division of jurisdiction which would enable the ECJ to continue to deal with the most significant challenges (actions for annulment and for failure to act). Transfer of enforcement actions is not recommended.[24]

The provisions on appeals from decisions of the CFI are moved to the new Statute, so that they may be more easily amended.

7. Further changes to the judicial architecture concern the European Courts' members, and their functions and ways of operating.

Under new Article 20 of the Statute the Court may decide, where it considers that a case raises no new point of law, and after hearing the Advocate-General, that the case shall be determined without a submission from the Advocate-General. New Article 222 EC fixes the number of Advocates-General on the current eight, which is a small number in light of enlargement. Should the ECJ so request, however, the Council, acting unanimously, may increase the number.

---

[23] New Art 51 of the Statute states that the ECJ shall have jurisdiction in actions brought by the Member States, by the institutions of the Communities and by the European Central Bank.
[24] The 'document de travail' is only available from the Council's register of public documents, with document number 10790/01.

Judges and Advocates-General of the ECJ will continue to be appointed by common accord of the governments of the Member States, for a term of six years. The Treaty now confirms that the ECJ shall consist of one judge per Member State, which means that with enlargement the EU will have at its disposal a much expanded ECJ. This raises issues as regards deliberations and decision-making within the Court. In their report for the IGC the Courts drew attention to the fact that too large an ECJ risks, when ruling in plenary composition, becoming an assembly rather than a court.[25] This concern has been met by the creation of a new type of composition, the Grand Chamber, consisting of 11 judges (new Article 221 EC). This Grand Chamber is intended to deal with the standard type important cases,[26] whereas the full Court will only deal with exceptionally important and unusual cases (such as compulsory retirement of Commissioners). Next to those types of composition, the Court will continue to deal with run-of-the-mill cases in chambers of 5 or 3 judges (new Article 16 Statute).

The judges of the CFI will also continue to be appointed by common accord of the governments of the Member States, for six years. New Article 224 EC now clarifies that there is to be *at least* one judge per Member State, which emphasizes the possibility of expanding the CFI beyond the number of Member States. As the CFI never decides cases in plenary session, this poses no particular problems for deliberations and decision-making. The CFI is thus the EU court which is easiest to expand with a view to facing the increasing caseload. It has been suggested for some time now that the CFI will soon be expanded, but at the time of writing no decision has been taken, apparently due to difficulties of nationality choice.

New Article 224 also enables the Statute to provide for the CFI to be assisted by Advocates-General. New Article 49 of the Statute maintains the current system—fallen into disuse—whereby members of the CFI may be called upon to perform the task of an Advocate-General.

Those are, briefly sketched, the main Nice changes. But what further reflections can be offered on the appropriate foundations for the judicial architecture? The first set of reflections relate to the Courts' role from a constitution-building perspective.

---

[25] Courts' report, cited above n 4, at 130–31.
[26] Ie those cases for which the Court itself considers the Grand Chamber to be appropriate, and when a Member State or an institution so requests (new Art 16 Statute).

III.   SHAPING THE NEW LEGAL ORDER

The ECJ has been instrumental in shaping the 'new legal order' on which the European Union is based.[27] It is difficult to over-emphasise the importance of the role of law—indeed, the rule of law—in the construction of European integration, both factually and normatively, the latter in the light of the issues of legitimacy specific to European integration.[28] The main hallmarks of the new legal order are well-known, and do not need much further analysis here. Direct effect, supremacy, implied powers, general principles of EC law, together make up what has been termed European constitutionalism.[29]

It is of course true that most of the construction of the general framework of the new legal order took place in previous decades. Yet we should not be deceived as to the completion of such construction. The often held view that the ECJ's major constitutional work lies in the past, and that its current role and task is generally confined to arbitrating rather than further developing EU law, is in my view erroneous. The construction of the new legal order is clearly an ongoing building site—one where old wings may need refurbishment; such as the approach towards horizontal direct effect, mixed agreements, standing in direct actions.[30] And, more importantly, one where new wings will need to be added. Here one may think of the concept of European citizenship, where the building work has started;[31] non-discrimination law, much expanded beyond sex and nationality discrimination through the two new directives,[32] and thus made much more important and sensitive; the legal dimension of good governance;[33] the interpretation and effect of the EU Charter of Fundamental Rights;[34] the legal dimensions of the Second and Third Pillar, on which the ECJ has not been able to say much at all yet.[35] All this is not to say that the constitutional building site

---

[27] Case 26/62 *Van Gend en Loos* [1963] ECR 1.

[28] But not confined to the EU, see E Stein, 'International Integration and Democracy: No Love at First Sight', 95 *American Journal of International Law* (2001) 489–534.

[29] J H H Weiler, *The Constitution of Europe - 'Do the new clothes have an emperor?' and other essays on European integration* (Cambridge, Cambridge University Press 1999) at 19–25.

[30] Those at least would be on my personal shopping list.

[31] Case C–85/96 *Martínez Sala v Freistaat Bayern* [1998] ECR I–2691; Case C–274/96 *Bickel and Franz* [1998] ECR I–7637; Case C–184/99 *Grzelczyk v Centre public d'aide sociale d'Ottignies-Louvain-la-Neuve*, judgment of 20 September 2001, not yet reported.

[32] Council Directive 2000/43 implementing the principle of equal treatment between persons irrespective of racial or ethnic origin, OJ 2000 L180/22 and Council Directive 2000/78 establishing a general framework for equal treatment in employment and occupation, OJ 2000 L303/16. For an analysis see L Waddington and M Bell, 'More Equal than Others: Distinguishing European Union Equality Directives', 38 *Common Market Law Review* (2001) 587–611.

[33] See in particular the case-law on access to documents. For an overview see A Tomkins, 'Transparency and the Emergence of a European Administrative Law', 19 *Yearbook of European Law* (1999–2000) 217–56.

[34] OJ 2000 C 364/1.

[35] Jurisdiction over Third Pillar matters was conferred by the Treaty of Amsterdam (Art 35 TEU).

could or should be in the hands of just a court. There is a healthily growing awareness of the limits to the ECJ's role, and any desire to go back to the good old days of *Van Gend en Loos*, *Costa*, and *Dassonville*, is purely nostalgic. But it is just as obvious that, without a supreme court being able to contribute to the construction works, through the incrementality, topicality, and strong legal dose of case-law, those works risk producing a much more defective European constitution.

The above has important implications for the proper organisation of the EU's judicial architecture. In particular, the quality of the ECJ's contribution to the ongoing constitution-building will partly depend on the availability of sufficient time and resources. In that respect, it is most revealing to contrast the ECJ's current set-up, in terms of caseload, jurisdiction, and type of work, with the organisation of the judiciary within nation States. Many States, including Member States, have a separate constitutional court which, by definition, is able to concentrate on constitution-building. That is not the case for the ECJ, and one may have considerable doubts as to whether the EU is actually in need of such a court.[36] In EU law, the interconnection between substantive—often highly technical—law and constitutional-type questions is too close for the model of a separate constitutional court to work well. For example, questions about the division of competence between the EU and its Member States may be entangled with the scope of the internal market freedoms; see the Tobacco Advertising Directive case.[37] Or the scope of European citizenship rights may have to be determined in a case involving the interpretation of a directive on student mobility.[38]

The EU judicial architecture bears more resemblance with legal systems where there is a general supreme court, such as in the United Kingdom. However, such general supreme courts typically have much more control over their judicial diary than does the ECJ, through systems of certiorari or leave to appeal. Moreover, they operate at an appellate level, which means that the legal issues they are dealing with are extensively debated and crystallised by the time the supreme court is required to decide them. The ECJ, by contrast, is faced on a daily basis with highly technical legal questions, particularly through the preliminary rulings procedure, which are often not crystallised at national level, let alone at pan-European level.[39] Add to that the inherent complexity of dealing, not just with EU law, but, unavoidably, also with national law, and the expanding reach of European law (see the next section), and one can only wonder how on earth

---

[36] See Weiler's suggestion for the creation of a European Constitutional Council, in *The Constitution of Europe*, cited above n 29, at 353–54.
[37] Case C–376/98 *Germany v European Parliament and Council* [2000] ECR I–8419.
[38] Grzelczyk, cited above n 31.
[39] This points towards a further problem of the EU legal order: the information deficit as regards national case-law on European law; see below.

the ECJ will still be able to cope and ensure high quality in its constitutional rulings, in the absence of some form of control over its own judicial diary.

IV.   LITIGATION BOOM AND STRUCTURAL MEASURES

Picking up on the latter points, it is worth considering a little further in what way the tasks of the European Courts, and particularly of the ECJ, are evolving, and are likely to evolve. The emphasis here is, again, on the growing workload. However, the analysis is not quantitative in character. There are other studies which have attempted, with merit, to quantify the growing caseload.[40] Yet it is not obvious as to how to go about that. Does one look at the number of cases? Or does one count the number of pages the judgments take up? Both of those are no doubt useful indications, but they clearly do not reveal the whole picture of the Courts' workload. One also needs to pierce the veil of the numbers and try to gauge the impact of the complexity of the work performed.

First, there is the fact that current societies are ever more litigation-oriented. There is no particular link here with the development of the European Union, but there is no doubt that this phenomenon reaches and affects the EU judicial system. And there appears to be no impending reversal of this trend.

Second, the jurisdiction of the European Courts is expanding, in a number of ways. The Amsterdam Treaty created jurisdiction over certain Third Pillar matters, as well as over matters covered by the new Title IV of the EC Treaty.[41] We are still to see the effects of that expansion, as the cases are only starting to reach the ECJ. Other extensions of jurisdiction may be more limited.[42] There is however also a hidden expansion of jurisdiction, caused by a number of phenomena. In many areas EU policies are ever developing, giving rise to legislation and other forms of action, with ensuing litigation. Clearly, one does not need to see new powers conferred upon the EU to witness a growth in case-law. Take, just as an example, environmental protection policies. The EC is competent to act in this field since the Single European Act, but there are many more environmental law cases before the European Courts than in the late 80's or early 90's. There is probably also some hidden expansion coming from the case-law itself. There are subjects of *contentieux*, which have a tendency of

---

[40] See Turner and Muñoz, above n 6.
[41] For analyses see S Peers, 'Who's Judging the Watchmen? The Judicial System of the "Area of Freedom Security and Justice"', 18 *Yearbook of European Law* (1998) 337–413; P Eeckhout, 'The European Court of Justice and the "Area of Freedom, Security and Justice": Challenges and Problems', in D O'Keeffe (ed), cited above n 6, 153–66.
[42] For an overview, see the Courts' Report, cited above n 4, at 117–19.

developing and mushrooming as well. Here, an example is the case-law on access to documents, which is fast growing.[43] Another example is Member State liability, even though growth in that type of case-law appears to have abated now.[44] A third example is case-law on the relationship between competition law and social policies.[45]

Third, but related, there are the further consequences of the increased use of legislation by the European Union: it does not merely give rise to more case-law, but also raises the level of complexity and specialisation. Important though it may be, developing the interpretation of the basic Treaties may be a more straightforward judicial task than making sense out of technical, diverse, and often vague EC legislative provisions.[46] In the process of doing the latter, the ECJ is watched, not by EU law generalists, but by specialists at national level. Often the legislation is in the nature of harmonisation of national law, raising delicate issues of interconnection with and embedding in different legal systems. One simply needs to browse through the ECJ's judicial diary to be appraised of the legal diversity and complexity of that diary.[47] And it is the diary, not of a general lower instance court, but of the supreme European court in the matters referred to it.

Those are just some of the causes of the litigation boom, and the resulting increase in judicial workload, both quantitatively and qualitatively. This boom shows no signs of being cyclical, it risks creating a major judicial deficit, and in light of this, structural measures are needed to address the deficit.

Contrary to what is sometimes suggested, such structural measures cannot come from the Courts' own case-law. Judicial rulings clearly should not be inspired by concerns over docket control, and if they are, they risk being highly ineffective. For example, in the context of the preliminary rulings procedure there appears to be some opinion that the case-law on (in)admissibility of references may serve to limit the caseload.[48] That opinion

---

[43] See above n 33.

[44] For a recent overview see T Tridimas, 'Liability for Breach of Community Law: Growing Up and Mellowing Down', 38 *Common Market Law Review* (2001) 301–32.

[45] Case C–67/96 *Albany v Stichting Bedrijfspensioenfonds Textielindustrie* [1999] ECR I–5751; Joined Cases C–180–184/98 *Pavlov and Others v Stichting Pensioenfonds Medische Specialisten* [2000] ECR I–6451; C–222/98 *van der Woude v Stichting Beatrixoord* [2000] ECR I–7111; Case C–218/00 *Cisal di Battistello Venanzio & C Sas v Istituto nazionale per l'assicurazione contro gli infortuni sul lavoro (INAIL)*, judgment of 22 January 2002, not yet reported.

[46] For further reflections see P Eeckhout, 'The European Court of Justice and the Legislature', 18 *Yearbook of European Law* (1998) 1–28.

[47] Thus, in the first three weeks of January 2002 the ECJ handed down judgments in the following areas: competition law and compulsory accident insurance; recognition of diplomas; the internal market in television; staff; accession and olive oil stocks; company accounts; company taxation; establishment and services; social security; sugar levies; admissibility in a coal and steel appeal; residues in foodstuffs; VAT; BSE and subsidies; and BSE and slaughtering.

[48] Craig, cited above n 6, at 186–87; C Barnard and E Sharpston, 'The Changing Face of Art 177 References', 34 *Common Market Law Review* (1997) at 1157–160.

is erroneous. It probably takes the ECJ about as much judicial energy to declare a reference inadmissible as it would take to reply to the questions referred, and the number of inadmissible references is so small that it cannot in any way affect the caseload. Similarly, the suggestion that the ECJ's preliminary rulings case law on validity of EC legislation, where the Court emphasises the political discretion of the EU legislature, has a limiting effect on the judicial workload,[49] seems to me unpersuasive. In any event, the effect clearly cannot be such as to amount to the structural measures required.

V.   DEMANDS ON THE DELIVERY OF JUSTICE

Current societies make increasing demands on the delivery of justice. Judicial institutions need to be oriented towards efficient, effective, speedy, and high quality settlement of disputes. In the framework of EU law, those demands put particular pressure on the preliminary rulings procedure, as it is only an 'incident' in the main action. There is general awareness that preliminary rulings need to be handed down within a reasonably short time period, preferably shorter than the current average of more than 20 months.[50] But preliminary rulings must also be effective in resolving a dispute. Where, after having received the ECJ's judgment, the referring court has to engage with complex further issues, because the judgment is too vague, indeterminate or optional,[51] the effectiveness of the preliminary rulings procedure will be further questioned. The consequences may be less visible than one might think, as the procedure is no doubt to some extent self-regulating: courts are less likely to refer cases to Luxemburg, if the procedure does not work fast enough, and thus the statistics may not reveal the full scale of the problem. However, the negative effects of such a scenario on the proper and uniform interpretation and enforcement of European law do not need much spelling out. By contrast, an effective and speedy preliminary rulings procedure is a marvellous tool for the efficient administration of justice, in that it permits resolution of often complex legal issues by a highly qualified court, at the instance of any domestic court or tribunal, so possibly and hopefully at an early stage of the settlement of a dispute.

It is not only the preliminary rulings procedure which needs to conform to standards of effectiveness and speed. Direct actions, too, in particular

---

[49] Craig, cited above n 6, at 187–88.
[50] Turner and Muñoz, cited above n 6, at 15.
[51] With respect, it is submitted that examples of such cases are: Case C–368/95 *Familiapress v Bauer* [1997] ECR I–3689 and Case C–405/98 *Konsumentsombudsmannen v Gourmet International Products*, judgment of 8 March 2001, not yet reported (see A Biondi, 'Advertising alcohol and the free movement principle: the *Gourmet* decision', 26 *European Law Review* (2001) 616.

actions for annulment and actions in damages must be decided upon within a reasonable period of time, including, where relevant, appeal.[52]

Beyond those obvious demands made on the delivery of justice in and by the EU, there are further requirements, which the ECJ has in fact been quite good in expressing in its case-law. Indeed, the ECJ often speaks of the need for a coherent system of remedies, which must be able to guarantee effective access to justice[53] and effective protection of rights.[54] The application of those principles, and the issues to which they give rise, cannot all be usefully summarised in a few sentences, as they entail intricate questions of remedy architecture which are linked to substantive legal issues such as supremacy, direct effect and general principles of EC law. There are none the less a couple of problems which stand out in this respect, and which Nice did not address.

The first are the intolerably restrictive EC Treaty provisions on the standing of private parties as regards actions for annulment (Article 230(4) EC). This is not the first paper making this claim,[55] nor doubtless the last. As is well-known, it is, with the odd and unpredictable exception,[56] impossible for private parties directly to challenge the legality of EU normative action. The classic defence of that approach consists of (a) emphasising the Treaty language of 'direct and individual concern' and (b) pointing to the fact that it is possible for private parties to challenge EC[57] normative action through the preliminary rulings procedure. Neither of those defences is convincing. The Treaty language can easily be interpreted in different ways, and the ECJ has not in the past refrained from adopting remarkable interpretations of other Treaty provisions on remedies,[58] or from overriding them altogether.[59] The preliminary rulings procedure argument may in fact be turned on its head. If it is indeed accepted that private parties can challenge the lawfulness of EC normative acts indirectly, in a case pending before a national court, what on earth then is the justification for not allowing those parties to do this directly before the competent European Courts? And there can be little doubt that it is indeed appropriate that private parties should have the right to challenge EU legislative action, even of the most general normative kind. Such is,

---

[52] Case C–185/95 P *Baustahlgewebe v Commission* [1998] ECR I–8417.
[53] See also Art 6 ECHR.
[54] See eg M Brealey and M Hoskins, *Remedies in EC Law* 2nd edn, (Sweet & Maxwell, 1998) 99–117; J Temple Lang, 'The Principle of Effective Protection of Community Law Rights', in D O'Keeffe, cited above n 6, 235–74.
[55] See recently A Ward, 'Amsterdam and Amendment to Art 230: an opportunity lost or simply deferred?', in Dashwood and Johnston (eds), cited above n 3, 37–40; A Arnull, 'Private Parties and the Action for Annulment since *Codorníu*', 38 *Common Market Law Review* (2001) 7–52.
[56] Case C–358/89 *Extramet Industrie v Council* [1991] ECR I–2501 and Case C–309/89 *Codorníu v Council* [1994] ECR I–1853.
[57] As well as Third Pillar action, one suspects, insofar as there is preliminary rulings jurisdiction under Art 35 TEU.
[58] Case 314/85 *Foto-Frost* [1987] ECR 4199.
[59] Case C–70/88 *European Parliament v Council (Chernobyl)* [1990] ECR I–2041.

in my view, indispensable in the particular EU setting, characterised as it is by the distance between the citizen and the institutions, and the ensuing legitimacy issues. Judicial review is no alternative to greater citizen involvement and democracy, but at least it permits the citizen to mount a legal challenge to European decisions, and it enables the European institutions to defend the legality of their actions, and to claim that justice can be seen to be done.

The current detour via the preliminary rulings procedure is clearly insufficient. In some cases, as has been observed, it may require that the party interested in challenging an EC act exposes itself to criminal prosecution for failing to observe national rules which implement an EC directive, for example.[60] That can hardly be said to be an effective remedy.

However, it is not difficult to see why there is resistance against removing the standing limitations, and why Nice did not manage to introduce any changes. The pragmatic objection has always been, and continues to be, that the European Courts would be flooded with cases. In a sense, therefore, current times are most unpropitious for a move towards liberalisation. Yet is this not putting the cart before the horse? Surely, if there are more instances in which judicial protection is called for, such protection should be given. And surely it must be possible to devise a swift procedure for claims which are clearly unmeritorious.[61] Moreover, relaxed standing rules would release much judicial energy which is now directed at determining the (in)admissibility of actions brought, and would entail some reduction in preliminary references on validity. Also, direct actions based on the alleged illegality of general normative acts do not require the current two-tier jurisdiction; I return to that in the concluding section.

In the setting of the Third Pillar, private parties cannot bring direct actions at all.[62] Here, private parties are able to challenge acts through the preliminary rulings procedure only, but that will depend on whether the Member State of litigation allows for the use of that procedure.[63] This means that, next to the lack of standing, there is inequality in the rights of individuals to challenge Third Pillar acts, along national borders. And in the context of Title IV EC, there is the further problem that lower courts are unable to send references to the ECJ (see Article 68(1) EC), again rendering it more difficult for private parties to challenge EC acts.[64]

However, issues of access to justice are not confined to the flagship standing restrictions, and their effect on the right to challenge EU measures. Intervention by private parties in direct actions before the European Courts

---

[60] K Lenaerts, 'The Legal Protection of Private Parties under the EC Treaty: A Coherent and Complete System of Judicial Review', in *Scritti in onore di G.F. Mancini - Vol II - Diritto dell'Unione europea* (Giuffrè, 1998) at 619–20.
[61] Inspiration can perhaps be drawn from the procedure before the ECtHR.
[62] See Art 35 TEU.
[63] Options chosen by Member States are listed in OJ 1999 L 114/56 and OJ 1999 C 120/24.
[64] For further discussion see Eeckhout, cited above n 41, at 157–59.

is also strictly regulated,[65] and there is no right of intervention in preliminary rulings cases.[66] The contrast with the right of Member State governments to participate in all such cases is rather too sharp. Even certain privileged participants of the European polity, such as the social partners, are unable to present their views, either by way of intervention or through *amicus curiae* briefs. Nor is there any particular role for civil society. In times of emphasis on good governance, it is hard to defend such treatment of what are clearly also stakeholders in European integration.

The Commission's White Paper on European governance speaks of participation as one of the principles of good governance. It pleads for ensuring wide participation throughout the policy chain, from conception to implementation. The White Paper also emphasises the role of civil society, which 'plays an important role in giving voice to the concerns of citizens'.[67] Whilst the recommendations of the White Paper are geared towards policy-making as such, it is clear that the judicial process must be an important element in any system of good governance, given the crucial role it plays in the implementation and, through legal interpretations, in the more detailed formulation of adopted policies. We are all aware that courts may take decisions which are central to the development of certain policies. If then, indeed, civil society is to play a greater role, should it not also have a greater say in certain types of litigation? In the EU context, one may think particularly of preliminary rulings, through which the ECJ may adopt important interpretations of Treaty provisions or of EU legislation.

VI. UNIFORMITY AND COHERENCE

A well-functioning judicial system also requires that certain standards of uniformity and coherence are met (or unity in the language of the Courts' report).[68] In the EU system, the ECJ is seen as the great guarantor of such uniformity and coherence, through the preliminary rulings procedure, which is concentrated in its hands, and through appeals against CFI decisions. The CFI is structurally less concerned with these requirements, as it allocates all cases to chambers.

The Nice changes display some anxiety as to their effects on uniformity and coherence: see the scope for ECJ review of both CFI appellate decisions

---

[65] Such parties must show an interest in the result of the ruling, which is strictly interpreted, and they cannot intervene in cases between Member States, between institutions, or between Member States and institutions. See Brealey and Hoskins, cited above n 54, at 403–06.

[66] See eg Case C–181/95 *Biogen v Smithkline Beecham Biologicals* [1996] ECR I–717. The only route through which private parties may have their say in a preliminary rulings case is by participating in the proceedings at national level. It must be said that in Case C–the ECJ accepted that such intervention could take place after the reference had been made.

[67] European Governance - A White Paper, COM(2001) 428 final, at 10 and 14.

[68] Cited above n 4 at 129.

and CFI preliminary rulings. That anxiety may be a little exaggerated, however, and there are other reflections to be made concerning uniformity and coherence. The starting-point of such reflections, it is submitted, must be that in a mature legal system there is scope, in the case-law, for some lack of uniformity and coherence. Indeed, too much coherence and uniformity may have an atrophying effect on the law. Conversely, interjudicial disagreements stimulate debate and discussion, and may create new judicial discourses. Obviously, a balance needs to be struck so as not to jeopardise satisfactory standards of equality before the law and of legal certainty.

Returning to EU law, views may differ as to the level of maturity it has reached, but we should surely be past the days when the ECJ's overriding preoccupation was to ensure the enforcement of EC law at national level—a preoccupation which obviously required a high level of uniformity and coherence.

But let us look a little closer at the various forms of action before the EU Courts. As regards direct actions, one may actually wonder whether there should be much concern at all with uniformity and coherence. What we are looking at here is a two-tier judicial system, with a limited number of courts, the two main ones[69] operating next to each other, within the same institution. Of course there may always be arguments as to whether, in a particular case, the CFI operated on the basis of a correct understanding of the ECJ's case-law on the matter. Such arguments are unavoidable, but they do not necessarily express major concerns over uniformity and coherence. In fact, similar arguments as to lack of consistency can often be made with respect to the case-law of just one court, too.[70]

However, uniformity and coherence are a wholly different game in the context of the preliminary rulings procedure. The division of jurisdiction between the ECJ and national courts, whereby the ECJ interprets and national courts apply, gives much more scope for discrepancies. Add to that the fact that many (indeed, one should hope the majority of) national cases turning on a point of EU law never reach the ECJ, as well as the fact that such EU law needs to be applied in the context of different legal systems, and one may perhaps wonder whether uniformity and coherence are not most relative notions as regards the domestic application of EU law. From that perspective, the Nice anxiety over the transfer of some types of preliminary rulings cases to the CFI may seem justified. Yet, is it really? The above problems and concerns are not resolved through concentrating all preliminary rulings in one court. They rather concern the relationship between the European court and national courts, and indeed between national courts themselves. As regards the former, for example, achieving high standards of uniformity and coherence may require well-considered

---

[69] Ie ECJ and CFI, which will no longer be the only ones after creation of the judicial panels.
[70] Consider for example the twists and turns of the ECJ's case-law on Art 28 EC.

and sometimes restrained interpretations of the relevant EU law rules by the European court. Indeed, from the perspective of uniformity national courts are ill-served with legal interpretations which are too detailed and specific.[71] It may also require much more information about national case-law. Is it not utterly remarkable that there is no central reporting system of national decisions concerning EU law, and that there is no accessible central database of such decisions? Most of the time we all study the case-law of the European Courts as if it were the only case-law on European law. To my mind this is a major defect of the EU judicial system, and it can easily be overcome through the use of information technology.

VII.   QUALITY

The last set of (short) reflections on the proper foundations for the reform of the judicial architecture relate to the quality of the case-law. Obviously, the concern for maintaining quality permeates all considerations and reflections on judicial achitecture. It is moreover a notion which is difficult to capture and translate in specific recommendations. I shall therefore mention here only one aspect of judicial architecture which has a close connection with maintaining quality, namely the procedure for appointment of the Members of the European Courts. The quality of every institution's work depends to some extent on the quality of its personnel, and judicial institutions are no different in that respect. None the less, in this context too, quality is an elusive concept, which cannot be measured, and is sensitive to discuss.

There can in my view be no doubt that the European Courts have, throughout their existence, consisted of excellent Members. From that angle, one may feel that nothing particular needs to be changed. However, much as justice must not only be done, but must also be seen to be done, there may be a need for a procedure of appointment which is more open than the current one, which is purely in the secret hands of Member State governments. Various alternatives have been suggested, but Nice did not make any changes. This paper does not aim to discuss the matter any further, with one exception. As it is now clear that there will continue to be one judge per Member State (in the case of the CFI, at least one judge), there would be scope here for some form of action at national level. Indeed, there may even be no particular need for further regulation of the appointment procedure at European level, provided within the Member States more transparent and open procedures are used for appointment. As the Members do have some function of representation of national legal

---

[71] See for further reflections the Opinion of Advocate General Jacobs in Case C–338/95 *Wiener v Hauptzollamt Emmerich* [1997] ECR I–6495.

systems within the Courts, there would be merit in national organisation of appointment.

VIII.   RETURN TO NICE

After this dicussion of what I see as some of the foundations for the reform process, not without emphasising again that those are personal reflections and that a lot more can and perhaps should be said, it may now be possible to provide some further assessment of the Nice changes, and to make just a couple of further suggestions for reform.

As was mentioned, it is clear that the problem of the Courts' workload dominated the Nice negotiations, and that much less attention was paid to some of the other concerns identified above. Even so, it is questionable whether, in the middle to longer term, Nice will be sufficient to keep the workload problem manageable. To some extent this will of course depend upon the further colouring of the changes. For example, the revised EC Treaty in principle allows a very substantial transfer of preliminary rulings cases from the ECJ to an expanded CFI. Yet in practice that does not seem to be in the offing, nor does it sit easily with the notion of transfer 'in specific areas' (new Article 225(3) EC). The advantage of Nice is, none the less, that it provides a fairly open-ended enabling framework, which can serve as a basis for gradual modification. But whether it is sufficient for the adoption of the structural measures alluded to, remains to be seen.

In relation to workload, it is perhaps possible to consider the preliminary rulings procedure a little further, as it is at the same time the main cause and the greatest victim of the increasing workload. Over the last few years, many proposals have been made for revision or even abolition of this procedure. Abolition, however, seems an odd cure for an illness which is largely caused by an overdose of success. Would it not be marvellous for the EU law edifice if it were possible to maintain this system, in one form or other, a system which is perhaps as much a hallmark of EU law as direct effect and supremacy?

There is, in my view, an attractive solution which is not sufficiently considered. It consists of the complete transfer in principle of all references to the CFI, associated with a particular method or procedure for enabling the most important references to be decided by the ECJ, the Supreme Court of the European Union.[72] As the CFI can easily be expanded so as to cope with its caseload, such a transfer would allow the maintenance of the

---

[72] See also Weiler, cited above n 6, at 222–24. It is however questionable whether his suggested ECJ appellate jurisdiction for preliminary rulings is workable. It is not particularly attractive for parties to litigate a case up to the highest court for the purpose of questioning a CFI ruling; nor are highest courts always the most appropriate ones for engaging in such questioning.

current system, in which any court or tribunal can make a reference, without any need for filters, stricter admissibility requirements or some form of appellate system. The transfer would be justified from the perspective that the majority of references concern technical legal issues, and increasingly so with the growth of EU legislation in many different spheres. Chambers in the CFI could develop some measure of specialisation, enabling better communication with the specialised *clientèle* of the relevant litigation. However, the success of such a transfer would crucially depend upon finding the right method for sending the more important references to the ECJ.[73] It would be wholly premature to suggest such a method here, but it is difficult to see why it could not be found, provided serious further reflection on the issues involved takes place. Such reflection may in any event be required, as Nice enables the transfer of some of the preliminary rulings jurisdiction.

The system would, with time, work even better if there were more information about national case-law applying EU law, as suggested above. Intervention by the ECJ could then really work in a supreme-court-like manner, ie such intervention could occur in a context where important legal issues have crystallised in the case-law of the CFI and/or national courts, and require decision by the supreme court. Thus, the ECJ could continue to shape the EU legal order, and play its full constitutional role.

Leaving the issue of workload, Nice makes no progress whatsoever as regards access to justice. Article 230(4) EC is not amended, nor is there any change in the limited jurisdiction as regards Title IV EC and the Third Pillar. Much as the EU proclaims to be doing its utmost to connect with the citizen, it continues to be unwilling to allow the citizen directly to challenge EU normative action in the Courts.

If ever this was changed, and the standing requirements were relaxed, the following approach as regards division of jurisdiction with respect to actions for annulment could be considered. Where indeed general normative, or legislative, action is challenged, on the basis, for example, of breach of the Treaty or of general principles of EC law, there appears to be no particular reason for applying a two-tier judicial system. Such challenges are constitutional in character, and it should be for the supreme court, the ECJ, to decide them. In the great majority of such challenges, there are no difficult questions of fact, requiring the intervention of the CFI, which is the EU's general trier of facts. There is not much new in this, as already today the ECJ often hears such cases, brought by Member States or one of the EU institutions. Why not open this up to private parties? The effect on workload is not a valid objection. To the extent that this liberalisation gives rise to frivolous and unwarranted litigation, it must surely be possible to devise

---

[73] To some extent, though, the importance of cases depends on the quality and content of the judicial decision to which they give rise.

procedural methods for dealing with that. The judicial energy which is now directed towards identifying those which are directly and individually concerned could be used for weeding out unmeritorious claims.

Challenges to forms of EU action which are not of a legislative kind could continue to be brought before the CFI, again with relaxed standing requirements, limited to some level of affected interest, and with a weeding-out method. Here it is appropriate for the CFI to be involved, as a general first instance court, since many such cases do involve issues of fact. And one does not see why, with respect to such cases, the CFI's jurisdiction should not extend to cases brought by Member States or EU institutions. As to the objection that it is difficult, if not impossible, to distinguish in EU law between legislative and non-legislative action, it seems to me that there is a workable criterion (although no doubt not wholly perfect): what could be considered legislative action are all general legal instruments (regulations, directives, framework decisions, decisions concluding international agreements, etc) which are based directly on the founding treaties. One would see that this approach would capture quite neatly the difference between constitutional-type challenges and administrative-type challenges.

Beyond the issue of standing, there are other concerns over access to justice, referred to above. Rights of intervention and similar devices for a more broadly-based and participatory litigation system, involving civil society, can be created via the Statute and the Rules of Procedure, and therefore can be usefully explored as from today. I find it remarkable, for example, to see that in the WTO, an organisation infinitely more inter statal than the EU, the dispute settlement organs have been compelled to set up a procedure for *amicus curiae* briefs,[74] whereas the EU judicial system does not allow for such briefs in any form. One is left with the impression that the good governance project, however fractured and imperfect it may be, still has not reached the judicial system. Let us hope that Nice is indeed only an *hors d'oeuvre*.

---

[74] P Mavroidis, '*Amicus curiae* briefs before the WTO: Much ado about nothing', Jean Monnet Working Paper No 2/01, at http://www.jeanmonnetprogram.org/papers/papers01.html.

12

Effective Judicial Protection of Individuals in the European Union, Now and in the Future

FRANCIS G JACOBS*

A LEADING THEME, a leitmotif, of the case-law throughout the past 50 years has been the theme of effective judicial review. The Court of Justice, and recently the Court of First Instance, have in general shown themselves resolute to review measures taken by the Institutions and the Member States, to uphold the rights of individuals, and thus ensure observance of the rule of law.

In a series of striking judgments the Court of Justice has, over the years, given preference to those values even over the text of the founding Treaties.

Most notably, in 1963,[1] it proclaimed the principle of the direct effect of the EEC Treaty, and held that it conferred rights on individuals, enforceable in the courts of the Member States; it did so in the absence of any clear indication to that effect in the Treaty itself, and notwithstanding the opposition of the Member States.

Many other striking illustrations could be given. In the *ERTA* case,[2] it held that although the Treaty appeared to give it jurisdiction, under Article 173, only to review regulations, directives and decisions of the Council and Commission, nevertheless it could review the legality of innominate Council proceedings regarding the negotiation and conclusion by Member States of an international agreement. In *Les Verts*,[3] it held that it could review measures adopted by the European Parliament, which was not mentioned in Article 173. In the *Chernobyl*[4] case, it held that it could review measures

---

* Advocate General, Court of Justice to the European Communitites. Talk given at a conference of référendaires and former référendaires at the Court of Justice, Luxembourg on 5 October 2002; published in Il Diritto dell' Unione Europea 2002, p 203.
[1] Case 26/62 *Van Gend en Loos* [1963] ECR 1.
[2] Case 22/70 *Commission v Council* [1971] ECR 263.
[3] Case 294/83 *Les Verts v Parliament* [1986] ECR 1339.
[4] Case C–70/88 *Parliament v Council* [1990] ECR I–2041.

at the suit of the European Parliament, although once again Article 173 contained no mention of the right of the Parliament to sue. In *Francovich*,[5] the Court held that an individual has, under certain conditions, a right to claim damages in the national courts against Member States who infringe their Community obligations, again in the absence of any Treaty provision to that effect.

Although these remarkable decisions could be and have been criticised as going beyond the proper interpretative role of a court, they can be justified by the special nature of the Treaty and the special role assigned to the Court as having the duty (under Article 164, now Article 220) to ensure that 'the law is observed', perhaps better rendered 'the rule of law is observed'. As the Court stated in *Les Verts*, the Community is a Community based on the rule of law, inasmuch as neither its Member States nor its institutions can avoid a review of the question whether the measures adopted by them are in conformity with the basic constitutional charter, the Treaty.

The Court even expressed the view, in *Les Verts*, that the Treaty had established a complete system of legal remedies and procedures designed to ensure judicial review of the legality of acts of the institutions.

There is however a question which has arisen constantly over the past 40 years: the question of standing for individuals to challenge general measures, since the Court has generally interpreted restrictively the requirement in Article 173, paragraph 2 of the Treaty (now Article 230, paragraph 4) that the measure challenged should be of direct *and individual* concern to the applicant. In response to the criticism that the Court's case-law on standing, first laid down in *Plaumann*[6] in 1963, made it difficult, or insome cases even impossible, for the individual to obtain a remedy where he was affected by a general measure, the Court has relied on two main arguments: first the language of the Treaty; although that is an argument which elsewhere, as we have seen, has not been prominent in the field of judicial remedies. Second, it has said that the individual can go to his national court and seek a reference to the Court of Justice on the validity of the measure.

But what if he cannot get such relief via the national court? The issue arose in *Greenpeace*[7] in 1998. There the applicants—a number of individuals and environmental or\ganisations—sought to challenge a Commission decision granting Community funding for the construction of two power plants in the Canary Islands. They argued that they had no means of challenging the measure in the national courts, and should therefore be

---

[5] Case C–6/90 *Francovich and Bonifaci v Italy* [1991] ECR I–5357.
[6] Case 25/62 [1963] ECR 199.
[7] Case C–321/95 *Greenpeace and others v Commission* [1998] ECR I–1651.

entitled to challenge it directly before the Community courts. Their action was nonetheless rejected as inadmissible by the Court of First Instance. On appeal the Court of Justice also held the action inadmissible; but it pointed out that Greenpeace had in fact brought proceedings before the national courts. Was that a relevant factor in its decision? If so, then it could be argued that an individual must be granted standing to challenge a Community measure where it was not possible to challenge the measure in proceedings before the national courts, so that there would otherwise be a denial of effective judicial protection, a denial of justice.

The next step was the case of *Unión de Pequeños Agricultores (UPA)*,[8] a challenge by a trade association which represents small Spanish agricultural businesses to a Council regulation on the market in olive oil. The Court of First Instance, applying the traditional case-law on individual concern, dismissed the application by order as manifestly inadmissible. On appeal, the Court of Justice decided to hear the case in plenary formation, partly perhaps in response to the uncertainty created by the *Greenpeace* judgment, partly perhaps by a desire to review more generally its case-law on standing.

The decision by the Court to reconsider its case-law made it necessary for me as Advocate General to look at the overall picture on standing for individuals to challenge Community measures.

There were for me several striking features in that overall picture.

First, there seemed much force in the long-standing criticisms of the case-law. It appeared hard to reconcile with emerging fundamental rights of access to a court, of effective judicial protection, and to an effective remedy. It was out of line, as we have seen, with the Court's general case-law on remedies, and also, as it seemed to me, with developments in public law in some of the Member States.[9]

Second, the alternative remedy of a reference from national courts seemed in certain cases less satisfactory than a direct action. References for preliminary rulings are in my view the keystone of the Community legal system and the rulings of the Court on the interpretation of Community law (although not generally rulings on validity) have of course played an immensely important part in the development of that system. But our appreciation of the value of preliminary rulings should not lead us to

[8] Case C–50/00 P *Unión de Pequeños Agricultores v Council*, judgment of 25 July 2002.
[9] Standing for individuals has been significantly widened in several systems of national law. It is true that only some national legal systems recognise the right to challenge legislative (as distinct from regulatory) measures. But there is as yet no such "hierarchy of norms" in Community law. On the contrary, the Treaty allows the Court to review all measures adopted by the institutions, at any rate within the "Community pillar". Moreover the Court can do so even at the instance of individuals, although only *indirectly*: by way of a reference on validity under Art 234 EC; in an action for damages before the Court of First Instance under Art 235 EC; and by a plea of illegality under Art 241 EC.

assume that a reference on validity is necessarily a means of challenge preferable to a direct action.[10]

There may be cases where questions of validity arise incidentally in national proceedings, and should be referred. But it is quite another thing to hold that where the sole object of the proceedings is judicial review—a challenge to the validity of the measure—then the individual must go via the national court, simply because the measure is a general one.

In fact, that involves a double dislocation. First, he must go to the national court, which ex hypothesi has no jurisdiction to grant the remedy he seeks—it cannot find the measure invalid. Secondly, it requires the national court to send the case to what may now be regarded as the wrong Community court, since the Court of First Instance was established precisely to hear actions brought by individuals challenging Community measures and thus to improve the judicial protection of the individual. Moreover it is contrary to the idea of access to a court competent to grant a remedy.

In my Opinion, delivered on 21 March 2002, I advanced a number of arguments for revising the case-law. I concluded that a broader test of standing could be adopted without departing from the notion of individual concern: an applicant could be regarded, in my view, as individually concerned by a Community measure where the measure has, or is likely to have, a substantial adverse effect on his interests.

The *UPA* Opinion had several consequences, some perhaps predictable, others less so.

First, it had a very favourable reception from legal scholars. That was not perhaps surprising since many of them had long been critical of what they saw as the Court's restrictive case-law, and had regularly urged the Court to adopt a more liberal approach. Indeed the case-law had been criticised by several members of the Court, writing in their individual capacities.

Secondly, the Opinion seems to have encouraged a far wider debate on the issue of standing. Indeed I was informed by an eminent source, shortly after the Opinion was delivered, that several Member States had taken an interest in the issue and were interested in particular in the idea of amending the Treaty to enlarge standing for individuals. I understand that there is now a majority of Member States in favour of enlarging standing.

Thirdly, as you will know, the Court of First Instance took up the cause in the *Jégo-Quéré* case.[11] Relying in particular on the Charter of Fundamental Rights, and referring also to my Opinion in *UPA*, it adopted a

---

[10] However, if individuals are given standing to challenge a general measure by way of a direct action in the Court of First Instance, the absence of such a challenge would plainly not exclude a subsequent reference by a national court on the validity of that general measure: the *TWD* line of case-law (Case C–188/92 [1994] ECR I–833) clearly cannot be applied to general measures.

[11] Case T–177/01 *Jégo-Quéré*, judgment of the Court of First Instance of 3 May 2002.

much broader view of standing than it had previously done. That might have seemed surprising, given that it had not previously sought to take a broader view by an incremental expansion of standing, and also in that it seemed to jump the gun without awaiting the judgment of the ECJ in *UPA*. The Court of First Instance can however be seen to have made a valuable contribution. Its support for enlarging standing is very significant, not least as it is the court which will be the court of first resort for individual applicants. Since one of the main concerns among those who resist wider standing is the so-called 'floodgates' argument, it is significant that the court most directly and individually concerned has not been deterred by that argument.[12] But more importantly, the support of the Court of First Instance for a wider test of standing as a matter of principle must also carry great weight.

Ultimately, as you know, the ECJ in its judgment of 25 July 2002 felt compelled to maintain its existing case-law.

I can very well understand that the Court should have found it difficult to depart from a body of case-law going back nearly 40 years, even though there were, in my view, a number of exceptional reasons why that particular aspect of the case-law was now ripe for reconsideration and a departure from the case-law would have been, in all the circumstances, fully justified.[13] Nonetheless, the reluctance of the Court to take that step is perfectly understandable.

The judgment essentially recapitulates the previous case-law. One point of interest is on the *Greenpeace* issue: the question whether standing might depend on whether the individual can bring an action in the national courts. The Court holds that standing cannot depend on whether or not there is such a possibility. The judgment explicitly follows my Opinion on that point.

What then if there is no remedy? The Court puts the onus on the national courts to do all they can to create one:

> National courts are required, so far as possible, to interpret and apply national procedural rules governing the exercise of rights of action in a way that enables natural and legal persons to challenge before the courts the legality of any decision or other national measure relative to the application to them of a Community act of general application, by pleading the invalidity of such an act.[14]

---

[12] On that argument, I would only add here that the requirement of direct concern, if retained, will provide an effective check, as will the time-limit of two months; and that the Court of First Instance will certainly be able to find ways of dealing with, for example, multiple claims, as well as cases which are manifestly ill-founded. If however claims are genuine and well-founded, then ways must be found to hear them, if necessary by enlarging the membership or staff of the Court of First Instance.

[13] Paras 82 to 99 of my Opinion.

[14] Para 42 of the judgment.

That approach, I think, leaves a number of questions unresolved.

Can for example national courts be expected to stretch the contours of their own systems merely in order to construct a path to the Court of Justice, when the Court is apparently not prepared to open a direct route? And what is the solution where, as may often be the case (and was one of the concerns of the Court of First Instance in *Jégo-Quéré*), the only route available to challenge a regulation is to infringe it so as to provoke prosecution in the national courts, with a view to getting a reference from them? Can this be regarded as a proper way of securing judicial review?

But perhaps the most striking point in the judgment is the last point, where the Court points to the possibility of Treaty amendment 'to reform the system currently in force'. This is a weighty indication, especially coming as it does in the context of the ongoing Convention on the Future of Europe. Moreover I think there may well be advantages in going down the route of Treaty amendment rather than developing the case-law—provided of course that the Treaty amendment is fully adequate. So I turn to Treaty amendment and the Convention.

I would make some preliminary comments on the Convention. First, it seems clear that several Governments are determined, at the highest level, to ensure that the constitutional foundations of the European Union are given a firm anchorage in a new constitutional Treaty. On a personal note: earlier this year I had the privilege of being invited to take part in a conference organised to that end by the Government of Finland, hosted by the Prime Minister with the active participation of the Ministers of Justice of Finland and Germany and, from the United Kingdom, the Attorney-General. There can be no doubt of the resolve (no doubt shared by the other Member States) to establish the European Union on a new constitutional basis, with fundamental rights at the top of the agenda. So there seem to be good prospects for the outcome of the Convention on these matters to be accepted in a new constitutional Treaty.

Secondly, it seems to be increasingly recognised that there is likely to be agreement in the Convention both on giving some form of legal effect or recognition to the EU Charter of Fundamental Rights and on accession by the EU to the European Convention on Human Rights, leading to acceptance by the EU of the jurisdiction of the European Court of Human Rights. It seems clear that these developments will reinforce the need for changes in the system of judicial remedies.

Working Group II of the Convention, 'Incorporation of the Charter/accession to the ECHR', is at this moment turning its attention to this subject. As a paper[15] dated 1 October 2002 from Mr Vitorino, Chairman of the Working Group, explains in its opening sentence,

---

[15] WD 021

> One remaining subject for examination by the Working Group is the question whether the current system of judicial remedies of individuals against acts of the institutions needs to be reformed in the light of the fundamental right to effective judicial protection as recognised by case-law of the Court of Justice and restated in Article 47 of the Charter.

The working paper goes on to mention three main options for possible further action at Treaty level.

Option A is a special remedy based on alleged violations of fundamental rights, ie a new action enabling the individual to challenge any Community act, including those of general application, directly before the Court of Justice where an infringement of fundamental rights is alleged.

The working paper rightly mentions, however, the criticisms of that proposal that can be advanced. It would be difficult to distinguish alleged violations of fundamental rights from other violations of the law serving as causes of action under Article 230 EC; experience in Germany with the *Verfassungsbeschwerde*, which goes direct to the Federal Constitutional Court, suggests that it is almost always possible to express an alleged illegality in terms of an infringement of fundamental rights, given the broad scope of many fundamental rights in modern constitutional law; and the relationship between such a special 'constitutional' action and the ordinary system of remedies would be difficult to establish, especially if the constitutional action were to be introduced before the Court of Justice while 'ordinary' actions continued to be brought before the Court of First Instance.

Those objections, recorded (but not evaluated) in the working paper, show conclusively in my view that the proposal is unnecessary, would largely duplicate the ordinary system of judicial remedies, and would cause the greatest confusion between the role of the Court of Justice and that of the Court of First Instance. It would be infinitely preferable to make the necessary reforms in the ordinary system of judicial remedies.

One such reform is of course the amendment to Article 230, paragraph 4, which is indeed Option B in the working paper. Here the paper considers a number of possibilities, including, perhaps most simply and most attractively, deleting from the expression 'direct and individual concern' the words 'and individual'.

Option C is entitled 'Enshrining an obligation of Member States to provide for effective rights of action before their courts'. I would only comment that this seems no substitute for providing for effective rights of action before the Community Courts.

I would suggest that there are essentially three sets of reform which are necessary if an up-to-date judicial system is to be put in place, consonant with proper constitutional foundations of the EU and full observance of the rule of law, and all the more necessary in the light of the Charter and of accession to the ECHR.

1.   **Standing of individuals to challenge general measures**

First is the adoption of a broader test of standing, of which enough has been said, and on which the principle seems to have been widely accepted (although there will be need for further discussion on its implementation).

2.   **Extension of the scope of judicial review to measures taken by all institutions and bodies of the Union**

The Treaty allows challenges by individuals only to measures taken by the Institutions. The Charter is however (rightly) addressed to the 'institutions and bodies' of the Union (Article 51(1)). Since many of the bodies set up to implement Union policies will exercise powers affecting individuals, it seems clear that an action must be available to individuals against measures adopted by all institutions and bodies of the Union.

A further question which will arise if remedies are to be available against all measures adopted by the institutions and bodies of the Union is whether the existing forms of action as provided for by the Treaties against the Community institutions can simply be transposed to the 'bodies' of the Union. It seems clear that they cannot, if only because the current text of Article 230 still refers to reviewing 'the legality of acts' of the institutions, appearing to involve an action for annulment of a decision or other measure. It cannot be assumed, however, that an unlawful measure by a Union body will necessarily, or even normally, be a decision liable to annulment.

The inadequacy of this formula is well illustrated by the cases recently brought by the Commission against the European Central Bank and the European Investment Bank in which the Commission essentially submits that both Banks have acted unlawfully in failing to cooperate with OLAF, the European Office for the prevention of fraud.

The cases gave rise to much debate on admissibility since it appeared necessary to identify a decision taken by the Banks which could be the subject of an action for annulment. Whatever the outcome of those cases, it seems clear that the present formula does not provide a model which should be transposed to all other Union bodies.

One suggestion which I should like to advance would be to provide instead for an action for a declaration, which would lead the Court to declare (where an action succeeded) that the body had acted (or failed to act) unlawfully,[16] and in addition

---

[16] The action for a declaration can already be found in the Treaty in a different context, eg (although the term "declaration" is not used) where the Commission (or another Member State) takes infringement proceedings against a Member State (Art 226 EC).

(where necessary) to grant any appropriate remedy. This would have the following advantages:

(1)   It would avoid the need to identify a measure which has to be annulled, which may often be an inappropriate requirement.

(2)   It would avoid the chronic problems which have arisen over the years with the action under the Treaty for failure to act (Article 175, now Article 232), which has proved an ineffective form of action.

(3)   It would enable the Court to grant (as well as a declaration) whatever remedy was appropriate in the circumstances, which might be annulment; or damages; or an injunction; or some combination of these remedies.

3.   **Extension of the scope of judicial review to measures across the whole range of Union activities**

Under the current system the Community Courts' jurisdiction is severely limited or even excluded as regards the Union's activities in certain fields, as a result of the three-pillar structure introduced by the Maastricht Treaty and refined—but made far more complex—by the Treaty of Amsterdam. In consequence the jurisdiction of the Community Courts has become a complex patchwork, especially as regards the jurisdiction of the Court of Justice to give preliminary rulings, and there is even uncertainty in some respects whether the Court has jurisdiction or not. Legal certainty is threatened in an area where it is of paramount importance, and the availability of judicial review seems at some points almost random.

The need for reform will be intensified if the Charter and accession to the ECHR are taken seriously. In particular the limitations on the jurisdiction of the Court under Article 68 EC and under Title VI of the Treaty on European Union—areas where the need for an effective protection of fundamental rights is of special importance—raise serious questions about the compatibility of the current state of the law with the Charter and the ECHR. It will therefore be important to ensure that the Community Courts have jurisdiction to review all measures across the whole range of Union activities. Since those measures will in any event be subject to review by the European Court of Human Rights in the event of accession to the ECHR,[17] any argument for excluding them from review by the Community Courts seems to have little force.

---

[17] Moreover, where the measures are adopted by Member States pursuant to activities of the Union, they are already subject to review by the European Court of Human Rights.

The working paper refers to this issue (under the rubric of Justice and Home Affairs) but states that it goes beyond questions of fundamental rights and will be treated in the newly constituted Working Group X (Area of liberty, security and justice). It also seems likely that the Convention will accept a proposal to abolish the much-criticised three-pillar structure and reintroduce a unitary scheme for all Union activities. If that is done, it will be important to ensure that the jurisdiction of the Community Courts is at the same time extended to all Union activities.

CONCLUSION

If these reforms are introduced, we may be in sight of achieving the goal of a Union based on the rule of law, in which, to paraphrase the *Les Verts* judgment, all measures of its Member States, institutions and bodies are subject to judicial review, and the Treaty establishes a complete system of remedies.

13

The Past and Future of the Preliminary Rulings Procedure

ANTHONY ARNULL*

ARTICLE 234 (EX 177) EC has remained essentially unchanged since the Treaty of Rome was signed, but the way it is applied by the Court of Justice has evolved, primarily in response to the increasing volume of cases referred by national courts. The Treaty of Nice and changes to the Court's Rules of Procedure take that process of evolution further. This is essential if the preliminary rulings procedure is to continue to fulfil its role as a fundamental guarantor of the proper functioning of the Community legal order.[1]

The discussion which follows is divided into two main sections. The first section deals with what the Court of Justice now expects of national courts when they ask for a preliminary ruling under Article 234. The second section examines some of the changes to the preliminary rulings procedure which were suggested at the 2000 IGC and the effect on that procedure of the Treaty of Nice, agreed by the Member States in December 2000.[2]

I. THE DISCRETION CONFERRED ON INFERIOR NATIONAL COURTS

As every law student knows, lower national courts enjoy a discretion in deciding whether or not to ask the Court of Justice for a preliminary ruling.[3] It is well established that the national court is in principle the sole judge of whether a preliminary ruling is necessary and of the relevance of the questions referred. Notwithstanding the breadth of the discretion

* Professor of European Law and Director of the Institute of European Law, University of Birmingham. This chapter was completed in September 2001.
[1] See generally Anderson, *References to the European Court* (1995); Arnull, Dashwood, Ross and Wyatt, *Wyatt & Dashwood's European Union Law* 4th edn, (2000), ch 11.
[2] See OJ 2001 C 80/1.
[3] See Arnull, *The European Union and its Court of Justice* (1999), pp 56–60.

enjoyed by lower national courts, a reference will be rejected by the Court of Justice where it is plain that the questions referred are entirely irrelevant. However, for many years the Court refused in other circumstances to go behind the decision of the national court to make a reference.

A fundamental assault on the discretion previously enjoyed by the national courts was mounted in the notorious *Foglia v Novello* cases in the early 1980s.[4] There the Court refused to entertain a reference made in the context of a collusive action brought in one Member State, by parties who were not really in dispute, with the intention of challenging the compatibility with the Treaty of the law of another Member State. The Court's judgments in those cases were the subject of heavy criticism[5] and they were subsequently applied with considerable restraint.[6] However, they were given a new lease of life in *Meilicke v ADV/ORGA*,[7] a case which shows that practitioners can be even more eccentric than academics. Meilicke was a German lawyer who had contrived the case to test a theory advanced in a book he had written. He persuaded a German court to ask for a preliminary ruling, but the Court of Justice declined to answer, taking the view that the questions referred were hypothetical in nature and that the legal and factual background had in any event not been adequately explained.

Notwithstanding the curious nature of the case, *Meilicke* proved to be the harbinger of a new enthusiasm on the part of the Court of Justice for reviewing the circumstances in which references were made. The Court's new approach was underlined in *Telemarsicabruzzo v Circostel*,[8] where the Court refused to answer questions referred by an Italian court because the orders for reference contained very little information about the factual background to the cases or the relevant provisions of Italian law. As a result, the Court did not feel able to give a useful ruling. The judgment in *Telemarsicabruzzo* was delivered by the *grand plenum* and was clearly intended to give a clear message to national judges contemplating a reference: if the background to the case was not clearly set out, the Court might simply decline to give a ruling. That message was subsequently driven home in a series of cases in which inadequately-explained references were dismissed as manifestly inadmissible under the truncated procedure for which

---

[4] Case 104/79 [1980] ECR 745; Case 244/80 [1981] ECR 3045.
[5] See eg Barav, 'Preliminary censorship? The judgment of the European Court in *Foglia v Novello*' (1980) 5 *European Law Review* 443; Bebr, 'The existence of a genuine dispute: an indispensable precondition for the jurisdiction of the Court under Art 177 EEC Treaty?' (1980) 17 *Common Market Law Review* 525 and 'The possible implications of *Foglia v Novello II*' (1982) 19 *Common Market Law Review* 421.
[6] Cf Case 261/81 *Rau v De Smedt* [1982] ECR 3961; Case C–150/88 *Parfümerie-Fabrik 4711 v Provide* [1989] ECR 3891.
[7] Case C–83/91 [1992] ECR I–4871. See Kennedy, 'First steps towards a European certiorari?' (1993) 18 *European Law Review* 121; Arnull (1993) 30 *Common Market Law Review* 613.
[8] Joined Cases C–320/90, C–321/90 and C–322/90 [1993] ECR I–393. See Arnull (1994) 31 *Common Market Law Review* 377.

provision is made in Article 92 of the Court's Rules of Procedure.[9] In one case[10] the Court went further, declining to give a ruling where it considered that a reference, although admissible at the time it was made, should have been withdrawn in the light of later developments.

The overall effect of this line of case law was to place greater emphasis on the circumstances in which references should *not* be made. Was this a welcome development?[11] The Court's new approach was clearly influenced by its heavy workload. Cases in which the background has not been properly set out are particularly time-consuming for the Court and it is entitled to expect national judges to play their part in identifying the issues on which preliminary rulings may properly be sought. However, the *Telemarsicabruzzo* line of authority posed two dangers.

The first was that it could lead the Court to refuse to address a question which the national court needed to resolve in order to give judgment. In those circumstances, the national court would be faced with the choice of making a further reference to the Court[12] or deciding the question itself.

Where it chose the latter option, the very risk against which Article 234 is intended to guard—that of divergences in the application of Community law—would be heightened. The second danger was that national courts might be discouraged from using the preliminary rulings procedure. For many national judges, even in States which have been members of the Union for some time, a reference to the Court of Justice remains an exceptional event. It is not always easy for a judge who is unfamiliar with Community law, and who may not have the benefit of experienced counsel, to identify and formulate relevant questions and to set out the background to a case clearly and concisely. This is especially true of judges in new Member States, who face a particularly steep learning curve. It is vital to the healthy development of the Treaty system that such judges should not be discouraged from making references where the guidance of the Court of Justice is genuinely needed.

That said, the limits of the *Telemarsicabruzzo* line of authority should be acknowledged. There were a number of factors which might have been said to mitigate the rigour of the Court's new approach. First, it did not exclude the possibility of pursuing before the Court test cases, that is to say,

---

[9] See eg Case C–157/92 *Banchero* [1993] ECR I–1085; Case C–386/92 *Monin Automobiles* [1993] ECR I–2049; Joined Cases C–128/97 and C–137/97 *Testa and Modesti* [1998] ECR I–2181; Case C–361/97 *Nour v Burgenländische Gebietskrankenkasse* [1998] ECR I–3101.

[10] Joined Cases C–422/93, C–423/93 and C–424/93 *Zabala Erasun and Others* [1995] ECR I–1567.

[11] See further Anderson, 'The admissibility of preliminary references' (1994) 14 *Yearbook of European Law* 179; Barnard and Sharpston, 'The changing face of Art 177 references' (1997) 34 *Common Market Law Review* 1113; O'Keeffe, 'Is the spirit of Art 177 under attack? Preliminary references and admissibility' (1998) 23 *European Law Review* 509.

[12] See eg Case C–428/93 *Monin Automobiles* [1994] ECR I–1707; Case C–387/93 *Banchero* [1995] ECR I–4663.

real disputes which have implications for large numbers of people who find themselves in a similar position and which are therefore conducted with special vigour. Cases of this nature have made an important contribution to the development of Community law, notably in the area of equal treatment for men and women, and the Court has never shown any reluctance to deal with them.[13] Secondly, the Court continued to deal with some references which might have been thought to fall within the *Telemarsicabruzzo* doctrine. In *Vaneetveld*,[14] for example, the order for reference contained no information about the facts of the case. Nonetheless, Advocate General Jacobs thought that they were clear from the case-file and the written observations. Moreover, the issue was in his view a straightforward one and there was no doubt that the answer to the questions would be helpful to the referring court. He did not therefore think it would be appropriate to decline to answer or to reject the reference as inadmissible. The Court agreed:[15]

> It is true that the Court has held that the need to arrive at an interpretation of Community law which is useful for the national court requires that court to define the factual and legislative context of the questions, or at least to explain the factual hypotheses on which they are based ... None the less, that requirement is less pressing where the questions relate to specific technical points and enable the Court to give a useful reply even where the national court has not given an exhaustive description of the legal and factual situation.

The Court concluded that it had enough information to enable it to give a useful answer. The result appeared to be that, where the referring court set out clearly what the case was about and gave a plausible explanation of why it needed an answer to the questions it had referred, the Court would normally proceed to answer them.[16]

II.   REFORMING THE PRELIMINARY RULINGS PROCEDURE

The stricter approach to the admissibility of references which developed in the 1990s did not offer a long-term solution to the burden imposed on the

---

[13] See eg Case 69/80 *Worringham and Humphreys v Lloyds Bank* [1981] ECR 767; Case 96/80 *Jenkins v Kingsgate* [1981] ECR 911; Case C–9/91 *Equal Opportunities Commission* [1992] ECR I–4297.

[14] Case C–316/93 [1994] ECR I–763. See also Case C–412/93 *Leclerc-Siplec v TF1 Publicité and M6 Publicité* [1995] ECR I–179; Case C–415/93 *URBSFA and Others v Bosman and Others* [1995] ECR I–4921.

[15] Para 13.

[16] A suggestion by AG Jacobs in Case C–338/95 *Wiener v Hauptzollamt Emmerich* [1997] ECR I–6495 that national courts should be encouraged to exercise a greater measure of self-restraint before asking for preliminary rulings was not taken up by the Court in that case.

Court by the preliminary rulings procedure. The number of references made in 1999 was roughly 80 per cent higher than the number made in 1990 and the number can be expected to carry on growing over the coming years. References now take on average over 22 months for the Court to deal with. This led to examination, within the framework of the 2000 IGC, of ways in which the procedure might be reformed.[17]

One of the leading contributions to the debate was made by the Reflection Group set up by the Commission. The Group was chaired by the former President of the Court, Mr Ole Due. In its report published in January 2000, the Group suggested that the objective should be to return to the situation in 1983, when references were on average dealt with within one year. One way of achieving that end would be to give national courts greater encouragement to apply Community law for themselves. With that aim in mind, the Reflection Group proposed three amendments to the text of Article 234. The first would make it clear that lower national courts are entitled to decide questions of Community law for themselves. The second would be designed to discourage national courts from referring cases systematically and would say that, in deciding whether to make a reference, a national court should take account of the importance of the question for Community law and whether there is reasonable doubt about the answer. Thirdly, the Reflection Group suggested that national courts of last resort should only be required to refer questions which are of sufficient importance for Community law and where there is reasonable doubt about the answer.

In a submission to the IGC, the CCBE expressed strong opposition to amending Article 234, particularly in a way which would:

> discourage national courts from referring questions of interpretation of Community law to the Community courts or which would take away explicitly or as a matter of practice the obligation for national courts of final instance to refer questions of Community law raised before them.

The CCBE noted that

> [i]n the majority of Member States, it is practising lawyers' experience before national courts in cases raising EC law issues that it is already today extremely difficult to obtain references to the European Court of Justice and that in the rare cases where references are made, they often relate to the wrong questions. It shows also that very often, national courts take decisions which are questionable from an EC law perspective, arguing that they are *acte clair*. The CCBE wonders, in these circumstances whether it is wise to encourage them to do so even more frequently.

---

[17] This part of the discussion draws on Arnull, 'Modernising the Community Courts' (2000) 3 *Cambridge Yearbook of European Legal Studies* 37, which contains a more comprehensive examination of the effect of the Treaty of Nice on the Community Courts.

The Commission also rejected the idea of relaxing the obligation to refer imposed on top courts, observing 'that the advantages of such flexibility are very slight and that there are real dangers for the uniform application of Community law, especially with enlargement on the horizon'. In the event, no amendments to Article 234 were made at Nice. The Member States also declined to follow up a Commission suggestion that the preliminary rulings procedure applicable under Title IV of the EC Treaty,[18] which makes no provision for inferior national courts to refer,[19] should be aligned with the classic procedure applicable under the rest of of the Treaty.

It is submitted that it is a matter for satisfaction that the obligation imposed on top courts by Article 234 is to remain unchanged, though there may be some who would disagree.[20] There are many examples of cases in which top national courts have failed to make references in circumstances where that step ought probably to have been taken.[21] In some of them,[22] the famous *CILFIT* criteria[23] were used to give a cloak of legitimacy to the decision not to send the case to Luxembourg. It cannot therefore be said with complete confidence (to borrow a phrase)[24] that all top national courts invariably apply Community law conscientiously and pay due regard to their obligations under the third paragraph of Article 234. Moreover, the periodic arrival of new Member States brings into the Community system national courts of last resort who have no experience whatsoever of dealing with points of Community law. The Member States need to be wary of giving the impression that the obligation laid down in the third paragraph of Article 234 is not something to be taken seriously.

If the object of enabling references to be turned round more quickly was to be achieved, the focus therefore had to be on the way they were handled in Luxembourg. On 1 July 2000, several changes to the Court's Rules of Procedure took effect[25] with a view (among other things) to streamlining the process of dealing with references from national courts. Three of the

---

[18] Which is concerned with visas, asylum, immigration and other policies related to free movement of persons.

[19] See Art 68 EC, introduced at Amsterdam.

[20] See eg Rasmussen, 'Remedying the crumbling EC judicial system' (2000) 37 *Common Market Law Review* 1071, 1107–10; Vaughan and Randolph, 'The interface between Community law and national law: the United Kingdom experience' in Curtin and O'Keeffe (eds), *Constitutional Adjudication in European Community and National Law* (1992), ch 20, p 228; British Institute of International and Comparative Law, *The Role and Future of the European Court of Justice* (1996), pp 75–7. For a short general discussion, see Anderson, above n 11, pp 170–1.

[21] See Anderson, above n 11, pp 167–70.

[22] See AG Tesauro in Case C–83/91 *Meilicke v ADV/ORGA* [1992] ECR I–4871, 4917 (n 23); Arnull, 'The use and abuse of Art 177 EEC' (1989) 52 *Modern Law Review* 622.

[23] See Case 283/81 *CILFIT v Ministry of Health* [1982] ECR 3415.

[24] See *R v Stock Exchange, ex parte Else (1982) Ltd* [1993] 2 WLR 70 at 76, *per* Sir Thomas Bingham MR.

[25] See OJ 2000 L 122/43.

changes are worth mentioning here. One of them[26] enables references of exceptional urgency to be dealt with under an accelerated procedure adapted to the circumstances of the individual case. This might involve derogating from the procedure normally applicable (something which was not previously permitted) and in particular reducing the period within which written observations may be submitted from two months to 15 days. The Advocate General must be heard, but is not required to deliver an Opinion. Another change[27] enables the Court to ask the national court to clarify its order for reference. This should reduce the need for the Court to dismiss inadequately explained references, a step which has sometimes led to cases being referred back to it. A third change[28] is that the Court may now give its decision by reasoned order where the answer to a question which has been referred to it 'may be clearly deduced from existing case-law or where the answer to the question admits of no reasonable doubt'. Previously that possibility was only available where the question referred was 'manifestly identical' to one on which the Court had already ruled.

More radical suggestions about the treatment of references were made by the Reflection Group. One was that there was a number of special situations where the CFI should be given a preliminary rulings jurisdiction. One of the situations envisaged was references made in the course of national proceedings concerning infringements of Community trade marks. The thinking of the Reflection Group was that, since the CFI already deals with direct actions concerning the registration of such marks, jurisdiction to deal with all cases arising out of the Community trade mark regulation[29] should be consolidated. Another important category of proceeding in which the Reflection Group suggested the CFI might be given a preliminary rulings jurisdiction was cases concerning private international law instruments adopted in accordance with Article 65 EC.[30] The Group's thinking here was that these cases are only indirectly connected with Community law in the strict sense and that they require specialised judges to deal with them.

At Nice agreement was reached on a new version of Article 225 EC. Paragraph 3 of the revised text takes up the suggestion in the Due Report. It provides as follows:

> The Court of First Instance shall have jurisdiction to hear and determine questions referred for a preliminary ruling under Article 234, in specific areas laid down by the Statute.

---

[26] See Art 104a.
[27] Art 104(5).
[28] Art 104(3).
[29] Council Regulation 40/94, OJ 1994 L 11/1.
[30] See eg Council Regulation 44/2001 on jurisdiction and the recognition and enforcement of judgments in civil and commercial matters, OJ 2001 L 12/1, which largely superseded the Brussels Convention with effect from 1 March 2002.

Where the Court of First Instance considers that the case requires a decision of principle likely to affect the unity or consistency of Community law, it may refer the case to the Court of Justice for a ruling.

Decisions given by the Court of First Instance on questions referred for a preliminary ruling may exceptionally be subject to review by the Court of Justice, under the conditions and within the limits laid down by the Statute, where there is a serious risk of the unity or consistency of Community law being affected.

The Member States made four declarations at Nice touching on that provision. One calls on the Court of Justice and the Commission to give overall consideration as soon as possible to the division of jurisdiction between the Court and the CFI. Another envisages that the essential features of the review procedure contemplated by the new Article 225(3) will be defined in the Statute, which will specify in particular:

— the role of the parties in proceedings before the Court of Justice, in order to safeguard their rights;
— the effect of the review procedure on the enforceability of the decision of the Court of First Instance;
— the effect of the Court of Justice decision on the dispute between the parties.

A third declaration contemplates that the Council will make provision for the practical operation of the new provisions to be evaluated three years after their entry into force. A fourth declares that:

in exceptional cases in which the Court of Justice decides to review a decision of the Court of First Instance on a question referred for a preliminary ruling, it should act under an emergency procedure.

Under Article 62 of the Statute agreed at Nice, which replaced the three pre-existing Statutes, it will be the task of the First Advocate General to propose that the Court review a preliminary ruling given by the CFI where the conditions set out in the third subparagraph of the new Article 225(3) are met. The proposal of the First Advocate General will have to be made within one month of the CFI's decision. The Court will have a further month in which to decide whether to act on the proposal.

The Statute agreed at Nice does not lay down any areas in which the CFI is to have a preliminary rulings jurisdiction. However, the Council, acting unanimously, will be able to amend the relevant provisions.[31] Indeed, there never seems to have been serious opposition among the Member

---

[31] See the new Art 245 EC. The Council will not be able to amend Title I of the Statute ('Judges and Advocates-General').

States to the idea of giving the CFI a preliminary rulings jurisdiction, although they were reluctant to do so without providing for oversight by the Court of Justice. Finding an acceptable mechanism for enabling the Court to have the final say on important questions proved difficult. One possibility might have been to provide for 'referral in the interests of the law' by a body like the Commission to enable the Court to give an authoritative ruling for the future independently of any specific case. Such a mechanism applied under Article 4 of the Protocol on the interpretation by the Court of Justice of the Brussels Convention[32] and forms part of the modified preliminary rulings procedure applicable since Amsterdam under Title IV of the EC Treaty.[33]

However, there were misgivings about employing such a mechanism to secure oversight of the exercise by the CFI of its preliminary rulings jurisdiction. Essentially the worry was that it might undermine the credibility of the CFI and the authority of its decisions. Moreover, as the French Government observed in a contribution to the IGC, if such a referral were made shortly after the decision of the CFI had been delivered, the effect might be to prolong suspension of the national proceedings, thereby lengthening the overall procedure.

It must be said, however, that the solution chosen by the Member States is open to similar objections. If reviews by the Court of preliminary rulings given by the CFI were to become at all frequent, the confidence of national Judges in the CFI, and their willingness to refer questions to it, would be shaken. In any event, there is a serious risk that national courts will not feel able to apply a preliminary ruling given by the CFI until they know whether the First Advocate General has decided to propose that it should be reviewed by the Court of Justice. Once such a proposal has been made, the ruling will clearly not be applied by the referring court until the Court of Justice has decided whether to act on the proposal and, if it decides to review the decision, until the review is complete. The suspension of the national proceedings will therefore last at least until the First Advocate General has decided what to do, which will mean a further delay of up to a month. Although the Statute will deal with the effect of the review procedure on the enforceability of the CFI's decision and on the dispute between the parties, it is hard to see how a national court can be expected to apply a ruling which has been reversed by the Court, whatever the Statute may say. The advantage of a mechanism for referral in the interests of the law along the lines of Article 68(3) is that it would allow the Court to address a question outside the confines of a particular case.

---

[32] See OJ 1998 C 27/28.
[33] See Art 68(3) EC, which applies to Reg 44/2001, above, which has now largely superseded the Brussels Convention.

III.   CONCLUSION

National judges are clearly going to have to accustom themselves to important changes in the reference procedure. Changes to the Court's Rules of Procedure mean that they may be asked to clarify their order for reference and that the answer is more likely to be given by reasoned order. The Treaty of Nice will permit the Court to decide a case without an Advocate General's Opinion where it does not think any new point of law is raised.[34] National judges may also, in due course, find themselves dealing not with the Court itself but with the CFI. The relationship between the national courts and Luxembourg could undoubtedly be affected by these changes. Whether the preliminary rulings procedure is thereby undermined may depend on whether they enable references to be dealt with more promptly while at the same time maintaining—or even improving—the quality of the guidance given to national courts. Strong reservations about the most significant of the reforms envisaged—the conferral of a preliminary rulings jurisdiction on the CFI—were expressed by Advocate General Colomer in *François de Coster v Collège des Bourgmestres et Echevins de Watermael-Boitsfort*,[35] but the die may have been cast.

---

[34] See the new Art 222 EC and Art 20 of the Nice Statute.
[35] Case C–17/00, Opinion of 28 June 2001, paras 73 and 74.

14

A European Certiorari Revisited

LIZ HEFFERNAN*

I. INTRODUCTION

IN DECEMBER 2000, the European heads of government, gathered at
Nice, took several important steps in the constitutional development of
the European Union. Chief among them are the various provisions in
the Treaty of Nice[1] disposing of the so-called 'Amsterdam leftovers', ie
those issues of institutional reform left unresolved by the Treaty of
Amsterdam. The central focus of IGC 2000, and of the publicity surrounding
its negotiations, was reform of the political institutions, notably the
Commission and the Council, in preparation for enlargement. Reform of
the Community courts was a less conspicuous but, ultimately, no less
important item on the agenda. In the case of the judicial branch, the new
provisions are inspired in large part by the well publicised need to remedy
overburdened dockets and the attendant inefficiencies in the administration
of justice in Luxembourg.[2]

This article revisits an issue in the debate over judicial reform first
raised several years ago, namely, whether the time is ripe to attribute to the
Court of Justice a discretion to filter its caseload along the lines of
the United States Supreme Court's *certiorari* jurisdiction. It begins,
however, with an overview of the projected reforms contained in the Treaty
of Nice.

* LLB, LLM, JSD, BL, Lecturer in Law, University College Dublin. This article appears in
2003 52 ICLQ. It was written prior to the entry into force of the Treaty of Nice.
[1] Treaty of Nice Amending the Treaty on European Union, the Treaties Establishing the
European Communities and Certain Related Acts, [2001] OJ C80/1.
[2] For recent statistics in relation to judicial activity at the Community courts, *see*
http://www.curia.eu.int/en/pei/rapan.htm; and C Turner & R Munoz, 'Revisiting the Judicial
Architecture of the European Union', (1999-2000) 19 *Year book of European Law* 1. See
generally: A Dashwood & A Johnson, (eds), *The Future of the Judicial System of the European
Union* (2001); G de Burca & JHH Weiler, (eds), *The European Court of Justice* (2001);
A Johnson, 'Judicial Reform and the Treaty of Nice', (2001) 38 *Common Market Law Review*.
499; H Rasmussen, 'Remedying the Crumbling Judicial System'. (2000) 37 *Common Market
Law Review* 1071.

II.   THE TREATY OF NICE

(i)   IGC 2000

An eclectic range of judicial reforms was mooted in advance of IGC 2000.[3] Proposals ranged from modest tinkering with current practice and procedure to radical ideas for restructuring the system. The conference deliberations focused primarily on the submissions of the Community courts, the Commission and the individual member states.[4] Two official reports proved particularly influential in shaping the reforms ultimately adopted, as well as those rejected, at Nice. The Community Courts published their views on the workload dilemma in a May 1999 paper.[5] Cast as a springboard for debate on the future of the judicial system, the paper is reflective rather than directive in tone, the courts discussing the pros and cons of various reforms without endorsing any one, much less presenting a vision of where they see themselves 10 or 20 years down the line. The Commission took up the reins by setting up an independent working party under the chairmanship of former president of the Court of Justice, Ole Due. The Due Report, published in January 2000, contains a more comprehensive and rigorous analysis but, ultimately, settles for a relatively conservative approach to reform.[6]

There are several drawbacks to the intergovernmental conference as a vehicle for reform of the judicial branch. Participation is limited to the member states and issues are tabled and ultimately decided through barter and compromise among the national delegations. The mood is 'make or break': the participants must broker a deal within a designated time-frame or live with the *status quo*. The proceedings are less open and transparent than national parliamentary proceedings and lack the democratic credentials of procedures for the amendment of national constitutions. In addition, IGC 2000 followed a tradition of prioritising reform of the political institutions over reform of the courts. Notwithstanding the extent of the workload crisis, judicial reform was not tackled at Amsterdam nor included

---

[3] *See generally:* C Costello, 'Preliminary Reference Procedure and the 2000 Intergovernmental Conference', (1999) 21 40; A Arnull, 'Judicial Architecture or Judicial Folly? The Challenge Facing the European Union', (1999) 24 *European Law Review* 516; W van Gerven, 'The Role and Future Structure of the European Judiciary Now and in the Future', (1996) 21 *European Law Review* 211.

[4] The Friends of the Presidency Group was intimately involved in all stages of IGC 2000. See, eg, *IGC 2000: Interim Report on Amendments to be Made to the Treaties With Regard to the Court of Justice and the Court of First Instance,* CONFER 4747/00 (March 2000). The European Bar was represented in the guise of a report by the Council of the Bars and Law Societies of the European Union (CCBE) which shed some welcome light on the perspective of litigant and practitioner. *See Contribution from the CCBE to the Intergovernmental Conference,* CONFER/VAR 3966 (18 May 2000).

[5] Court of Justice and Court of First Instance, *The Future of the Judicial System of the European Union (Proposals and Reflections)* (1999).

[6] Commission, *Report by the Working Party on the Future of the European Communities' Court System* (2000).

in the initial agenda of IGC 2000. Eventually, it was added to the miscellany of secondary items tackled at the Conference, but only after the judiciary publicised the issue, both officially and extra-judicially,[7] and the President of the Court took the unprecedented step of airing his concerns in the press.[8] Throughout the Conference, the future of the Community courts was overshadowed by controversy surrounding the fate of the Commission and Council. It is fair to say that, given the sum of tasks to be completed, the Conference was neither able nor disposed to give reform of the judicial system the attention it deserved.

Influenced in all likelihood by the cautious tenor of the Courts' Paper and the Due Report, the Conference eschewed radical reform. Indeed, a dramatic overhaul of the judicial system was rejected, virtually from the outset. The reticence to grasp the proverbial nettle is also explained in part by the procedural labyrinth of reform methodology. At issue for the Conference was not only the nature and extent of reform but also the means and the timing. At the end of the day, the Conference opted to renovate rather than redesign the judicial architecture and, at the same time, to make the system more adaptable to change in the future. Thus, it adopted some proposals, rejected many others, left to the Council the resolution of many of the details and, finally, declared the debate on-going.

(ii) The Nice Reforms

The following is a brief summary of the more significant changes to the judicial system contained in the Treaty of Nice.[9]

(a) Flexibility

The reform philosophy underpinning the Treaty's provisions relating to the judicial system is aptly encapsulated by the term 'flexibility'. The changes crafted at Nice are not offered as an end in themselves but rather as a first, but by no means insubstantial, step. For example, the Treaty re-organises various provisions in the EC Treaty, the Statute of the Court of Justice[10] and the Rules of Procedure in a sensible bid to rationalise the judicial code. In the first place, certain provisions will be transferred from the Statute to the Rules and vice versa, to ensure a proper hierarchy. Secondly, the method

---

[7] See, eg, J Cooke, 'European Judicial Architecture: Back to the Drawing Board', (1999) 5 *Bar Review* 14.

[8] Statement of the President of the Court of Justice, *The EC Court of Justice and Institutional Reform of the European Union* (April 2000).

[9] For a more detailed discussion see L Heffernan, 'The Treaty of Nice: Arming the Courts to Defend a European Bill of Rights?' (2002) 65 *Law & Contemporary Problems* 189; and 'Judicial Reform Under the Treaty of Nice' in MC Lucey & C Keville (eds), *Irish Perspectives on European Community Law* (2003) 51.

[10] The Statute is contained in a protocol attached to the Treaty.

of amending the Statute and Rules will be modified to facilitate future changes to the judicial code. An opportunity to give the Courts autonomy over their Rules was sadly lost: the Council will continue to have the final say over amendments, although its approval will be based on a qualified majority rather than unanimity.[11] Given the eclecticism of Community jurisdiction, it is in the Rules that flexibility is needed most. This lament aside, these changes to the judicial texts will facilitate the introduction of substantial amendments to the judicial system in the future without recourse to the cumbersome process of treaty amendment.

(b)   The Composition of the Court of Justice

The most controversial of the issues debated at IGC 2000 was the size of the Court of Justice in an enlarged Union. As the Court warned at the last enlargement, an increase in its current membership of 15 could transform the plenary session from a collegiate court to a deliberative assembly, while extensive recourse to decision-making by chambers could pose a threat to the consistency of Community law.[12] Of course, the problem is not merely one of numbers. The composition of the Court is defined by the unwritten nationality requirement—one judge per member state. With the prospect of enlargement to a Union of 20 or even 30 member states, the possibility of abandoning the requirement—in favour, for example, of a system of rotational appointments—had been mooted.

The issue of national representation in Community government is uniquely delicate and dominated negotiations on reform of each of the Community institutions at IGC 2000.[13] In deciding the future size of the courts, the Conference applied a model of automatic national representation. The new version of Article 221 entrenches the principle that the Court of Justice shall consist of 'one judge per Member State', but tempers its effect by providing that the Court shall sit in chambers and, only exceptionally, in plenary session.

The wisdom of this move is open to question on several grounds. Whatever the merits of automatic representation for a political institution, the administration of justice has its own special concerns, such as the quality

---

[11] Some delegations were in favour of the change (or, at least, did not come out against it). See, eg, *Contribution from the Dutch Government – An Agenda for Internal Reforms in the European Union*, CONFER 4720/00 (6 March 2000); *Information Note from the Italian Delegation, 2000 IGC: Italy's Position*, CONFER 4717/00 (3 March 2000).

[12] *Report of the Court of Justice on Certain Aspects of the Application of the Treaty on European Union* (May 1995) at 16.

[13] All but a couple of the delegations were unwilling to relinquish the nationality requirement. *See Friends of the Presidency, Interim Report at 10.*

and impartiality of judicial adjudication, which place a higher premium on size than national interest. In a fully enlarged Union, the benefit of a full panoply of nationalities must be balanced against the cost in terms of functional capacity and jurisprudential integrity. At the very least, the Conference could have settled on a compromise: including the advocates general in the distribution of judicial posts at the Court of Justice. The role and stature of the office is such that the periodic substitution of an advocate general for a judge should not be too bitter a pill for the member states to swallow.[14] It would certainly make a difference to the numbers: the current arrangement of 15 judges and nine advocates general could accommodate a membership of 23 states and, in all likelihood, the number of advocates general will increase at some point in the future.

To allay concerns over the Court's functional cohesion, the Conference established a new structure, designed to accommodate a uniquely large and potentially unwieldy bench. Under the new arrangement, the Court will sit in chambers of three and five judges, in a new *grand* chamber and in plenary session.[15] This is not a tremendous leap from the current structure but it involves two important modifications. In the first place, the *grand* chamber will serve as the storm centre in the new regime, handling cases currently heard in *petit* and *grand* plenum. Whereas privileged parties—a member state or Community institution—will no longer have automatic access to the full court, they will be entitled to have their cases heard by the *grand* chamber. If the real judicial power is wielded in the *grand* chamber, one can expect that its composition will prove controversial.[16] Presided over by the President of the Court, it will comprise the presidents of the chambers of five judges and will function with a quorum of nine. Both the President of the Court and the presidents of the five-judge chambers will hold their offices for three-year renewable terms and, aside from their tenure on the *grand* chamber, will carry out important tasks within their respective spheres of influence. Thus, there is a danger that the new arrangement will create a sense of judicial hierarchy at the Court.

The second significant development is that the plenary session will become very much the exception. The new version of the Statute provides that the Court will sit as a 'full court' in certain specified proceedings or where,

---

[14] Advocates general are generally regarded as 'members' of the Court, even though they lack ultimate decision-making authority. See FG Jacobs, 'Advocates General and Judges in the European Court of Justice: Some Personal Reflections' in D O'Keefe and A Bavasso, (eds), *Judicial Review in European Union Law: Liber Americorum in Honour of Lord Slynn of Hadley* (vol I) (2000) 17 at 18.

[15] New version of the Statute, Art 16.

[16] The Conference sensed as much and whereas the *petit* plenum is currently constituted on an informal, *ad hoc* basis, the membership of the *grand* chamber will be imprinted in the Statute.

after hearing the views of the advocate general, the Court considers that a case is 'of exceptional importance'.[17] Precisely how the full court will function is an open question. A packed plenary session is curiously at odds with the Court's valued tradition of collegiate decision-making. At the same time, adjudication of these exceptional cases by a number less than the full compliment may raise doubts about the unity of the bench and the equality of national representation. Looking at the overall structure, a more serious concern is whether the Court, sitting in its various satellite formations, will be able to maintain the jurisprudential integrity that is central to its constitutional mandate.[18]

(c)   Direct Actions

One of the more attractive features of the Treaty of Nice is an enhanced role for the CFI. The jurisdiction of the CFI over direct actions has gradually increased over the years. At the current time, the CFI hears actions brought by private parties (individuals or corporations) and the Court actions brought by privileged parties (member states or Community institutions). The new version of Article 225 states that the CFI shall have jurisdiction over most classes of direct action 'with the exception of those assigned to a judicial panel and those reserved in the Statute for the Court of Justice'. Although it falls short of declaring the CFI the first or primary judicial forum for all direct actions, the provision embodies an important change in emphasis: trial and adjudication by the CFI will become the rule rather than the exception. It is natural and desirable that, as the legal system matures, the CFI and the Court pursue their respective primary vocations, the former as a general trial court and the latter as an appellate court of final resort.

What does this reform mean in practical terms? The Treaty of Nice changes nothing in itself; the details will be thrashed out in the Council and implemented by way of amendment to the Statute. Thus, this is one of the important reforms sketched only in principle. When the CFI's jurisdiction is broadened, the change will affect its personal, as opposed to subject matter, jurisdiction. Thus, the CFI will continue to hear the same categories of cases but its competence will extend to at least some of the suits involving privileged parties, which are currently heard by the Court. The extent of the

---

[17] New version of the Statute, Art 16.

[18] The composition of the CFI is far less controversial. Increasing its ranks is a less risky proposition, not least because any threat to the consistency of Community law can be tackled on appeal by the Court of Justice. Thus, the new version of Art 225 provides that the CFI will comprise 'at least one judge per member state'. Apparently, the Council has given the nod to an increase of six judges at the CFI, although a system for rotating the additional appointments has yet to be settled. See Commission, *Memorandum to the Members of the Commission: Summary of the Treaty of Nice* (Brussels, 18 Jan 2001) SEC (2001) 99 at 5.

Court's residual jurisdiction over direct actions and the manner in which that jurisdiction will be defined are as yet unclear. A meaningful improvement in the working conditions at the Court will require a marked decrease in its responsibilities.[19]

(d) Judicial Panels

The most innovative change to the current system is the introduction of a new form of judicial institution, the specialised judicial panel. Under a new treaty provision, Article 225a, the Council 'may create judicial panels to hear and determine at first instance certain classes of action or proceeding brought in specific areas'. The judicial panels will be attached to the CFI and their jurisdiction and *modus operandi* determined at a later date by a decision of the Council.

The concept of specialised judicial panels was inspired in part by the burden of staff cases which has dogged case management in Luxembourg over the years. Another likely candidate is trademark cases, currently adjudicated by the Alicante Boards of Appeals.[20] Specialisation within the judicial system is an attractive development and one familiar to continental lawyers. However, it should not be given free rein; most cases are not amenable to simple categorisation and it may be naïve to assume that the factors that lend staff and intellectual property cases to specialised treatment apply to other, wide-ranging areas of Community law.[21]

(e) Appeals

The Treaty of Nice is conspicuously silent on the subject of appeals from the CFI's decisions relating to direct actions, so presumably the current system, whereby the parties and privileged interveners are automatically entitled to appeal any point of law, will continue unchanged. The introduction of a discretionary jurisdiction for the Court of Justice (a European *certiorari*) is a promising idea, sadly overlooked at IGC 2000. The Community should also consider limiting the right of privileged parties to lodge appeals. While it is appropriate that the member states and the institutions retain the right to intervene in the first instance, it is questionable whether they should enjoy the right to appeal where they have made no such prior intervention.

---

[19] The Court of Justice has made an initial proposal on the issue in its *Working Document relating to the re-allocation of jrisdiction between the Court of Justice and the Court of First Instance in respect of direct actions*, posted on the Court's website.

[20] See Council Regulation 40/94 on the Community Trademark [1994] OJ L11/1.

[21] See, eg, *Due Report at* 29–35 (canvassing the possibility of specialised regimes in fields such as private international law, judicial cooperation and competition).

The contribution of judicial panels to reform will depend in large measure on appellate procedures. Article 225a states that:

> decisions given by judicial panels may be subject to a right of appeal on points of law only, or, when provided for in the decision establishing the panel, a right of appeal also on matters of fact, before the Court of First Instance.

This wording is somewhat ambiguous; it is not clear whether the Council, in establishing a panel, may opt to limit appeals altogether, for example, through a filer or leave to appeal mechanism.

Further uncertainty surrounds the possibility of subsequent review by the Court of Justice. The new version of Article 225(2) provides that decisions by the CFI on appeal from judicial panels may 'exceptionally' be subject to review by the Court 'where there is a serious risk of the unity or consistency of Community law being affected'. The assessment of this serious risk is made by the First Advocate General and the ultimate decision in favour or against review lies with the Court.[22] The gatekeeping role of the First Advocate General departs from the principle of party autonomy and places a uniquely judicial function in the hands of an official without ultimate decision-making authority. For example, it is somewhat incongruous that appellate options should end at the CFI in the case of a complex intellectual property dispute, but extend to the Court in any other commercial case. Notwithstanding these anomalies, the limitation will have the welcome benefit of forestalling lengthy appellate proceedings.

(f)   Preliminary Rulings

Appropriately enough, the preliminary reference procedure dominated negotiations on judicial reform at IGC 2000. The strategic importance of the procedure can scarcely be overstated. In terms of caseload, preliminary references occupy half of the Court's docket and, on average, proceedings take over 21 months to complete.[23] Even within this protracted time-frame, the Court is in danger of ruling with undue dispatch, placing in jeopardy the quality of judicial discourse, the integrity of the institution and, ultimately, the rule of law within the Community. Yet, if preliminary rulings are the key to reform, the results of IGC 2000 are disappointing; given the range and depth of the various proposals mooted in advance of the Conference, the modesty of the projected changes is striking.

---

[22] See new version of the Statute, Art 62.

[23] See statistics on judicial activity at the Court of Justice for 2000, http://www.curia.eu.int/en/pei/rapan.htm.

The significant step taken at Nice was to remove the exclusivity of the Court's jurisdiction. Under the new Article 225(3), the CFI 'shall have jurisdiction to hear and determine questions referred for a preliminary ruling under Article 234, in specific areas laid down by the Statute'. The envisioned role for the CFI marks a profound shift in traditional thinking which associates preliminary references with the Court's uniquely constitutional function. The Court itself had previously opposed the move, principally on the ground that it would threaten its special relationship with the national courts.[24]

It is too early to say whether the Treaty of Nice will lead to any demonstrable change in practice. It creates no more than a potential jurisdiction for the CFI; actual reform will follow later, if at all, in the form of an amendment to the Statute, which must be carried by a qualified majority vote in the Council. Thus, the future of the preliminary reference procedure remains very much on the drawing board. Assuming that the CFI is conferred with *de facto* competence, there is every reason to believe that its contribution will be limited. For a start, the CFI's functional capacity will already be stretched to meet its additional responsibilities over direct actions and appeals from judicial panels. In addition, staking out a distinct preliminary reference jurisdiction for the CFI is a testing conceptual puzzle. Article 235(3) speaks of 'specific areas laid down in the Statute', which suggests a substantive definition. The specific areas might include the more technical fields, such as competition, that the CFI routinely tackles under the rubric of direct actions or, indeed, the specialised fields that will comprise its appellate jurisdiction over judicial panels, such as trademarks. However, drawing jurisdictional boundaries through a system of subject matter categorisation may prove a double-edged sword. It would be difficult to devise a clear delineation of competence over hybrid requests, involving two or more subject areas. Moreover, subject matter categorisation could subvert the natural judicial hierarchy insofar as an issue of primary importance—ideally destined for the Court—may lurk in a case of any stripe or hue.

The nub of the challenge is to devise an effective and efficient means of delegating the more routine requests for preliminary rulings to the CFI while retaining the defining controversies of the day for the Court. A possible solution is to identify the cases of primary importance *a priori*, at the time of filing, and assign them directly to the Court. Judge John Cooke has offered an interesting suggestion, grounded in Article 234's distinction between references emanating from lower national courts and those from national courts of last resort: give the CFI jurisdiction over the former and the Court jurisdiction over the latter.[25] Some such structural allocation may

---

[24] See *Courts' Discussion Paper at* 25–26 (noting its previous objections but suggesting that the idea should not be dismissed out of hand).
[25] See Cooke at 18.

be as close as one can get to a workable formula of general application. The downside would be a potential double reference—first to the CFI and later to the Court—during the course of a single case with the consequent increase in the length and cost of proceedings. The possibility of a single preliminary reference to the CFI, copperfastened by an immediate right of appeal to the Court, would be only marginally more palatable.

The introduction of a centralised system for the allocation of preliminary references might prove a more pragmatic and effective solution. Under such a system, all requests for preliminary rulings would be filed at the Court of Justice and subjected to an expedited screening process. The Court would allocate the requests on a case-by-case basis, retaining for itself the cases it considers of primary importance and referring all others to the CFI.[26] Unlike the US Supreme Court's *certiorari* jurisdiction, the system would not operate as a discretionary filter; the mandatory character of the preliminary reference jurisdiction would remain unchanged and, consequently, any preliminary reference that crossed the current admissibility threshold would lead to a ruling, whether from the Court or the CFI.

Admittedly, there are drawbacks to this approach. *A priori* allocation might increase the margin of error. The importance of a case may be difficult to gauge from the face of the national court reference and may emerge only through its *denouement* before the Court of Justice or the national court. A further concern is the time-frame for the putative screening process. Speed and efficiency would be essential but not at the expense of a judicial, as opposed to purely administrative, allocation of preliminary references. At the end of the day, the additional cost in terms of time would have to be weighed against the overall savings of a more efficient system. In particular, if the burden of preliminary references were shared with the CFI, the Court might be free to issue its substantive rulings with greater care and dispatch. Finally, an allocation system would rule out a two-tiered review of preliminary references in Luxembourg—the Court reviewing the rulings of the CFI—and the attendant delay in the underlying national court proceedings.

Regardless of how cases reach the CFI or, indeed, how many cases, it will be important to determine the circumstances in which they progress to the Court. The issue of supervising the CFI's jurisdiction over preliminary references is framed by competing concerns: the need to preserve a role for the Court versus the need to reduce the length of proceedings. The Treaty of Nice confronts the issue in two ways. In the first place, under the new version of Article 225, the CFI may refer a case to the Court for a ruling where the CFI considers that the case requires 'a decision of principle likely

---

[26] See Costello at 53 (defending *ad hoc* allocation against the objection that it offends the principle of *judge legal* or *gesetzlicher richter* whereby the judge in a particular case must be pre-ordained in advance by law).

to affect the unity or consistency of Community law'.[27] This preview mechanism is reminiscent of the proposal for a system of allocating preliminary references, just discussed, with two important distinctions: it is intended as an exceptional safeguard rather than a routine allocation procedure and, in addition, the screening function will be conducted by the CFI rather than the Court.

Secondly, in exceptional circumstances, 'where there is a serious risk of the unity or consistency of Community law being affected', a decision of the CFI in response to a preliminary reference may be reviewed by the Court, under the same conditions as a decision of the CFI in response to an appeal from a judicial panel. The assessment that such a risk exists will be made by the First Advocate General within a month of the CFI's decision; within a further month, the Court will determine whether or not the decision will be reviewed.[28] Thus, here also, the parties lack standing to challenge the CFI's ruling before the Court.[29] In a declaration attached to the Treaty of Nice, the Conference expressed the view that where the Court of Justice reviews a CFI decision in response to a preliminary reference, it should act under an emergency procedure.[30]

These preview and review mechanisms share similar flaws. The initial decision whether the Court of Justice should decide a case is essentially subjective[31] and it is made by an entity other than the Court itself. It is highly unusual in modern legal systems that a court should lack control over its own jurisdiction and, in this instance, that the jurisdictional gatekeeper should be a subordinate court or an officer that lacks ultimate judicial decision-making authority.[32] At the risk of overstating the point, leaving the decision in the hands of the CFI and the First Advocate General could in its own way threaten the uniformity, consistency and, indeed, objectivity of Community law. A further and more serious concern is that referral to the Court will become routine rather than exceptional and will increase the length and cost of proceedings. It will be important to ensure that the participation of the CFI does not simply add an additional tier of review, all the more so since the preliminary reference procedure stays national court proceedings.

The headaches do not necessarily end there. The finality of the CFI's decision will be crucial, and not merely as a matter of form. To hypothesise,

---

[27] This provision was influenced, in particular, by a proposal from the Dutch Government. See *Contribution from the Dutch Government at 15.*

[28] See new version of the Statute, Art 62.

[29] A change recommended by the CCBE. See *Contribution from the CCBE at 9.*

[30] See *Declaration on Article 225,* [2001] OJ C80/79.

[31] The First Advocate General, at least, will have the benefit of the CFI's decision on which to base her assessment of a serious risk to the unity or consistency of Community law.

[32] Indeed, there is an inherent contradiction between the Conference's willingness to attribute this authority to the First Advocate General and its refusal to count advocates general in the judicial tally for the composition of the Court.

where the CFI has delivered a preliminary ruling in response to a request from a lower national court, would it be possible for a national supreme court to effectively appeal the CFI's ruling by seeking a preliminary reference from the Court itself? The spectre of two distinct preliminary references during the course of a single action is equally apposite in this context. Thus, the success of the procedure will turn in no small measure on the CFI's ability to exercise a firm and decisive hand in responding to national court requests.

Regrettably, the Treaty of Nice makes no attempt to address the problem at source, namely by reducing the volume of requests for preliminary rulings emanating from the national courts. Notwithstanding the many and varied proposals of the Due Report and others, the Conference decided against altering the mechanics of the preliminary reference procedure. Thus, the role of the national courts and the terms and conditions under which cases are currently referred will remain unchanged.[33] Retention of the *status quo* will assuage the concerns of many, anxious to preserve automatic access to the Community courts but it will not lead to any significant reduction in the length and cost of proceedings. For the time being at least, we can assume that preliminary references will continue to be an enormous drain on resources at the Court.

(iii)   Future Reform

While the Treaty of Nice does not alter the essential structure of the judicial system, comprising the Court of Justice, the CFI and the national courts, it does presage two related structural developments: increased responsibility for the CFI and the creation of specialised judicial panels. Both initiatives are welcome and should lead to a more equitable division of judicial labour within a strengthened system. Potentially, the CFI will become the primary forum for direct actions, a secondary forum for preliminary references and an appellate forum with respect to decisions from judicial panels. The CFI will no longer be simply 'attached' to the Court;[34] rather, ensuring that the law is observed will be the task of both courts, each within its own jurisdiction.

The problem with the Treaty of Nice is not the emphasis on the CFI, nor the addition of judicial panels, *per se*. Rather the Conference's legacy turns on the questionable assumption that modifying the role of the CFI will cure the ills of the entire system. Thus, quantitative change at the CFI is designed to produce a qualitative change at the Court of Justice. The promise will hold true, if at all, only if two conditions are met: the transfer of jurisdiction

---

[33] See AWH Meij, 'Guest Editorial: Architects or Judges? Some Comments in Relation to the Current Debate', (2000) 37 *Common Market Law Review* 1039 at 1043 (noting that the national courts were not associated with the reform negotiations in any way).
[34] In the words of the current version of EC Treaty, Art 220 (ex Art 164).

from the Court to the CFI must be real and substantial; and the CFI must be provided with adequate budgetary and administrative resources to equip it for the task. The fulfillment of either condition does not seem fanciful when applied to direct actions. The Council could make the CFI the *de facto* first judicial forum for direct actions and, presumably, marshal the necessary resources. Direct actions, however, account for far less of the judicial workload than preliminary references[35] and the gains for the Court must be counterbalanced against a projected increase in appeals.[36]

The fallacy of the Conference's reform strategy is revealed in its treatment of preliminary references. The Conference seised on the CFI as the key to reducing the length of preliminary reference proceedings and made no effort to attack the problem at source, namely, by taking steps to stem the flow of preliminary references from the national courts. Nor did the Conference offer a framework for the potential sharing of the preliminary reference burden between the Community courts. These fundamental deficiencies in the Treaty of Nice underscore a continuing need to discuss alternative reform measures *post* Nice. If the central objective is to render the legal system more efficient and to equip the Court of Justice to perform as a supreme court, (as the reformists, including the Courts and the Commission's Working Group contend), the Treaty falls short of the mark. The Nice reforms will undoubtedly improve the system but not to the extent necessary to remedy the workload crisis, much less prepare the courts for enlargement. Moreover, assuming that the member states ultimately copperfasten the Charter of Fundamental Rights with judicial protection, the implications for the workload of the Community courts will be enormous.[37]

III.   THE CERTIORARI OPTION

(i)   Introduction

The Treaty of Nice extends the appellate jurisdiction of the Court of Justice in three important respects. In the first place, the projected increase in the

---

[35] For example, of the 503 cases filed at the Court in 2000, 197 were direct actions as opposed to 224 preliminary references. See statistics on judicial activity at the Court of Justice for 2000, http://www.curia.eu.int/en/pei/rapan.htm.

[36] *Ibid* Appeals accounted for 79 of the 503 cases filed at the Court in 2000.

[37] [2000] OJ C364/1. The status of the Charter is tabled for discussion at IGC 2004. See *Declaration on the Future of the Union* [2001] OJ C80/85. A further potential source of work for the Community courts is the suggested liberalisation of the rules on standing for private applicants in judicial review proceedings embodied in the recent Opinion of Advocate General Jacobs in Case C–500 P, *Unión de Pequeños Agricultores v Council* [2002] 3 *Common Market Law Reports* 1 and the decision of the Court of First Instance in Case T–177/01, *Jégo-Quéré v Commission* [2002] 2 *Common Market Law Reports* 44. However, in its subsequent decision in *Unión de Pequeños Agricultores*, the Court of Justice reaffirmed the strictures of the

CFI's responsibilities over direct actions should lead to a corresponding increase in appeals to the Court. Secondly, the Court will hear a limited range of 'appeals' (for want of a better term) from the CFI's preliminary rulings in response to national court requests. Finally, in certain circumstances, the CFI's decision in relation to appeals from judicial panels will be examined by the Court. One of the most important issues left unresolved is the procedure whereby the Court of Justice will review these various decisions of the CFI. Presumably, it is one aspect of the division of labour between the Court and the CFI with respect to which the Conference has solicited the views of the Court of Justice and the Commission.[38] The occasion provides an opportunity for the Community to consider replacing the current system of mandatory appeals with a filter mechanism that would give the Court of Justice the freedom to choose a limited and select number of cases for review.

A system for filtering the caseload of the Court of Justice could also contribute to reform of the preliminary reference procedure. In theory, a European *certiorari*—a discretion to accept some references and to decline others—could enable the Court to prioritise its agenda and maximise the use of its time and resources. Free from the burden of an excessive caseload, the Court could devote adequate time and attention to the pressing constitutional and legal issues of the day. As we shall see, however, filtering preliminary references is a far more problematic prospect, both in principle and in practice. Whether in the context of appeals or preliminary references, the US Supreme Court's *certiorari* practice provides a potentially insightful model for the Community courts.[39]

(ii)   The United States

Article III of the US Constitution declares that '[t]he judicial power of the United States shall be vested in one supreme Court, and in such inferior Courts as Congress may from time to time ordain and establish.'[40] There are two tiers of lower Article III courts: federal district courts[41] and

---

Plaumann test of individual and direct concern. Given the opposition of the Council and the Commission, an amendment to the EC Treaty (which is, in the Court's view, a prerequisite to reform), seems a remote possibility. See Editorial, '1952-2002: plus ça change ...' (2002) 27 *European Law Review* 509.

[38] See *Declaration on Article 225 of the Treaty Establishing the European Community*, [2001] OJ C80/79.

[39] For an earlier view, including a discussion of the propriety of comparing the EC and US systems, see L Heffernan, 'A Discretionary Jurisdiction for the Court of Justice?' (1999) 34 *Irish Jurist* (ns) 148.

[40] Congress has also established a number of specialised courts and tribunals pursuant to its Article I powers.

[41] There are approximately 100 district courts of general jurisdiction in the territories comprising the United States and Puerto Rico. District judges are assisted by magistrate and bankruptcy judges.

federal courts of appeals.[42] An appeal lies from a final order or judgment of the district court to the federal court of appeals for the circuit in which the district court is located.[43] Subsequently, the unsuccessful party may seek Supreme Court review of the decision of the court of appeals. Mixed cases, involving issues of federal and state law, may be litigated in federal or state court. Where the parties have opted to proceed in state court, the determination by the state supreme court of any federal question may be appealed to the US Supreme Court.[44]

Of the various procedural routes to the Supreme Court, *certiorari* is the most significant from a practical standpoint.[45] The procedure formally dates back to 1925 when Congress enacted a law giving the Court discretion to determine which cases it should hear and decide.[46] The development was made possible in part by previous initiatives, principally the introduction of the federal courts of appeals. *Certiorari,* in turn, has facilitated a gradual accommodation of the Supreme Court's burgeoning docket, thereby obviating the need for dramatic institutional reform. It allows the Court to select from among the vast number of petitions submitted annually for review those cases that most clearly invoke the Court's essential functions. Thus, in theory at least, it enables the Court to map out the parameters of the legal landscape, identifying the important issues of the day and resolving conflicts among the lower courts over the application of federal law.[47]

The Supreme Court has the capacity to decide only a small percentage of the cases it receives and, consequently, some form of filter mechanism is an operational necessity. This reality is underscored by the demanding standards and rigorous decision-making associated with Supreme Court practice. In contrast to the preliminary reference procedure, review takes the form of full-blown appeal, the Court resolving actual cases rather than hypothetical questions, either by disposing of a case in its entirety or remanding it to a lower court for proceedings consistent with its opinion. Unlike the Court of Justice, which functions increasingly through the use of

---

[42] There are 11 courts of appeals for numbered, geographically-defined circuits and one court of appeals for the District of Columbia. In addition, a court of appeals for the federal circuit exercises appellate jurisdiction over customs and patent cases and claims against the US government.

[43] 28 USC s 1291.

[44] The Supremacy Clause, Art VI(2) of the US Constitution, provides an indirect basis for appellate jurisdiction.

[45] The other procedural routes are: original jurisdiction, appeal, certification and extraordinary writ. See 28 US ss 1251, 1254, 1651 & 2241.

[46] Judiciary Act of 13 February 1925, ch 229, 43 Stat 936. See *Dick v New York Life Ins Co,* 359 US 437, 48–63 (Justice Frankfurter dissenting).

[47] See generally: RL Stern *et al, Supreme Court Practice* 7th edn, (1993); HW Perry, *Deciding to Decide: Agenda Setting in the United States Supreme Court* (1991); Stephen M Shapiro, 'Certiorari Practice: The Supreme Court's Shrinking Docket', (1998) 24 *Litigation* 25; RK Willard, 'Strategies for Case Preparation and Argument Before the Supreme Court', (1992) 5 91; SA Baker, 'A Practical Guide to Certiorari', (1984) 33 611.

chambers, the Supreme Court hears and decides cases as a plenary body of six or, more usually, nine justices.[48] The persona of the individual justice, noticeably absent in Luxembourg, is a defining feature of Supreme Court culture. Individual justices can and, frequently, do write individual opinions, either concurring with or dissenting from the collective decision of the Court. Whether this practice acts as a spur or a rein on collective judicial deliberation is an open question but, in either event, (and notwithstanding the practical advantages of operating in one rather than a multiplicity of languages), the drafting of judicial opinions is a time-consuming process and, generally speaking, Supreme Court judgments are considerably longer and more detailed than the judgments of the Court of Justice.[49] Thus, *certiorari* enthusiasts maintain that, by allowing the Court to maintain its workload, the system balances these competing concerns, ensuring uniformity in the application of federal law and, ultimately, preserves the integrity and efficiency of judicial decision-making as well as the quality of the Court's opinions.

The *certiorari* procedure is relatively straightforward.[50] A party who has lost her case in the lower court (generally a federal court of appeals or a state supreme court) brings a petition requesting the Court to hear and decide the case. The Court will grant *certiorari* and proceed to a decision on the merits if, after a summary consideration of the case, at least four justices are in favour of so doing.[51] Supreme Court Rule 10 explains that a petition will be granted only for 'compelling reasons', which include, but are not limited to, a conflict among the lower courts, an unwarranted departure from judicial protocol or Supreme Court precedent, and an unsettled but important question of federal law. Rule 10 itself sheds no further light on the meaning or relative importance of these conditions and the unpredictability of the exercise is underscored by a telling caveat that the Rule neither controls nor fully measures the Court's discretion.

The Supreme Court's *certiorari* practice is only moderately more enlightening. The Court generally refrains from indicating the reasons for denying review, although occasionally an individual justice will break ranks to explain why she would have heard the case.[52] When review is granted, the stated reasons tend to be conclusory at best. While it behoves the hopeful

---

[48] See R Posner, *The Federal Courts: Challenge and Reform* (1996) at 82 (arguing that nine justices is the maximum viable number if the Court is to sit as a single panel).

[49] At the same time, the importance of prompt consideration is reflected in the Court's practice of disposing of the vast majority of cases within each annual term (which officially begins on the first Monday in October and closes at the end of June) rather than carrying them over to the next term.

[50] See 28 USC ss 1254(1) & 1257 and Supreme Court Rules 10 to 14.

[51] This is a derogation from the Court's general practice of operating by majority rule.

[52] See, eg, *Voinovich v Women's Medical Professional Corp*, 118 SCt 1347 (1998) (Justice Thomas, joined by Chief Justice Rehnquist and Justice Scalia, dissenting from the denial of cert in a challenge to the constitutionality of an Ohio abortion statute).

petitioner to study the general history of grants and denials in a particular type of case, the precedential value of *certiorari* denials is limited; justices frequently emphasise that a denial should not be interpreted as an official endorsement of the decision below.[53] Thus, the Court has been accused of defining 'certworthiness' tautologically.[54] Indeed, Chief Justice Rehnquist has conceded '[w]hether or not to grant *certiorari* strikes me as a rather subjective decision, made up in part of intuition and in part of legal judgment'.[55]

Nevertheless, certain ground rules have emerged in practice. Great emphasis is placed on the relatively objective ground of the existence of a conflict among the lower courts.[56] The conflict in question must relate to the same matter of law or fact and must be current and real, some would say even 'intolerable'.[57] Conflicts which are narrowly defined or which are likely to be resolved through future litigation in the lower courts may escape review. By the same token, the importance of the issue and the extent of the conflict's recurrence are significant, if not, decisive factors. A conflict between federal courts is essentially limited to a conflict between two, or usually more, federal courts of appeals. In the case of conflicts between decisions of courts of appeals and those of state courts of last resort, Supreme Court review is necessarily limited to disputes over substantial federal questions. In other words, federal jurisdiction can and, indeed, must be avoided when the strategic interests of a case are essentially more state than federal.

A more subjective and elusive but, nonetheless, significant, consideration is the so-called 'importance' of the case. The Court is concerned primarily with public or societal importance than with results in specific cases and, consequently, accepts cases, for example, involving significant constitutional questions or decisions invalidating general legislation or substantial government programmes. Even so, not infrequently, the Court declines jurisdiction in the face of a seemingly pressing federal issue on the premise that a particular case is an unsuitable vehicle for review.[58]

While the Supreme Court's *certiorari* jurisdiction is well entrenched, its operation in practice has generated some controversy over the years. Given the physical demands of screening thousands of petitions annually, it has been suggested that the Court spends as much time setting its agenda

---

[53] See, eg, *Brown v Allen*, 344 US 443, 542–43 (1953).
[54] Perry at 34 & 221.
[55] WH Rehnquist, *The Supreme Court, How it Was, How it is* (1987) at 165.
[56] See *Braxton v United States*, 500 US 342, 247–48 (1991), Stern *et al* at 167–84.
[57] Baker at 617.
[58] A noticeable omission from Rule 10's lists of grounds for review is the correction of lower court error. The function of supervising the lower courts in their application of federal law is primarily a matter for the federal courts of appeals and state supreme courts. Since the Community judicial system lacks comparable institutional safeguards, the task of overseeing national court interpretation of Community law falls squarely on the shoulders of the Court of Justice.

(deciding which cases to decide) as it does carrying it out. The loudest criticisms are less institutional in focus and emanate from the Bar where much ink has been spilled schooling practitioners in the quixotic art of drafting 'certworthy' petitions. Controversy also surrounds the role of law clerks (*referendaires* in Community parlance) who generally assume responsibility for screening petitions in the first instance. Chief Justice Rehnquist has defended the practice on the ground that the decision whether or not to grant *certiorari* is a much more channeled decision than a decision on the merits of a case.[59] That may be so, but it is hard to reconcile this justification for a surprising measure of delegation with the Chief Justice's previously cited recognition of the inherent subjectivity of the *certiorari* decision.[60]

(iii)   A European Certiorari?

The notion of filtering the caseload of the Court of Justice is not new. It was first floated in advance of the Intergovernmental Conference that culminated in the Maastricht Treaty on European Union. In presenting an agenda for discussion and debate, Jean Paul Jacqué and Joseph Weiler proposed a new architecture for the judicial system which included four Community Regional Courts with jurisdiction over direct actions, actions for non-contractual liability and preliminary references from the national courts.[61] Under the proposed scheme, the Court of Justice, renamed the 'European High Court of Justice', would have discretion whether or not to admit an appeal from a decision or preliminary ruling of a Regional Court. While Jacqué and Weiler did not specify a procedure to govern the scheme, they suggested that the Court should admit an appeal in the following circumstances: (i) the Court itself or the Regional Court considered that the decision raised a major issue of Community law; (ii) a divergence had developed between the jurisprudence of one or more of the Regional Courts; or (iii) the record revealed that the Regional Court had committed a manifest error.[62]

The issue was raised anew in a comprehensive report on the role and future of the Court of Justice completed in 1996 by a study group established by the British Institute of International and Comparative Law and chaired

---

[59] Rehnquist at 264–66 arguing that a significant number of petitions, perhaps as many as half, are patently without merit and do not even reach the stage of being discussed at a conference of the justices).

[60] A further criticism, leveled at the current Court from time to time, and the converse of the complaint in Luxembourg, is that the current Court is not deciding enough cases or, specifically, enough important cases. If the Court of Justice has too little flexibility, the Supreme Court is said to have too much.

[61] JP Jacqué & JHH Weiler, 'On the Road to European Union—A New Judicial Architecture: An Agenda for the Intergovernmental Conference' (1990) 27 *Common Market Law Review.* 185 at 192–95.

[62] *Ibid,* at 193.

by Lord Slynn of Hadley.[63] Among a range of innovative reform proposals, the Slynn Report canvassed, but ultimately rejected, both the creation of distinct Community courts along the lines of the US federal system and the introduction of a filter or *certiorari* mechanism. In relation to the latter, the Report noted that at the heart of the arguments for and against a power of selection[64] lies a question about the way a supreme court should function: 'should it work through selected cases of importance or should it ensure that all errors are corrected?'[65] It observed that:

> in those jurisdictions which have introduced the principle of selection, the global results have been found to be satisfactory and, whatever particular criticisms there are, do not call into question the principle of selection.[66]

Nevertheless, filters pose unique problems in the Community context: Community law is a relatively immature system; cases which raise new points of law are not always easy to identify; and preliminary references represent a very special case.[67] Thus, the Report concluded that:

> at the present stage of development of the Community legal system, the intro-duction of filters or selection mechanisms for the Court of Justice would be undesirable and difficult to achieve.[68]

More recently, the possibility of a European *certiorari* was canvassed in the context of the intergovernmental negotiations that led to the Treaty of Nice. In their 1999 Discussion Paper, the Community Courts alluded to the intro-duction of a filtering system as one of a number of radical solutions to the workload dilemma. While highlighting the potential merits of such a system, the Courts shrewdly observed:

> [t]he effectiveness of such a power of selection would depend on its scope and on the conditions governing its exercise. In order effectively to stem the inflow of references for preliminary rulings, there would be a need for selection criteria capable of being applied in a flexible and prudent manner.[69]

---

[63] *The Role and Future of the European Court of Justice* (1996) ('Slynn Report').
[64] A power of selection is broader than the concept of a filter. Selective mechanisms may be exercised by a supreme court or a lower court and the criteria of selection may be very wide. Filters are one form of case selection and tend to be applied by a supreme court on the basis of clearly defined criteria. See also Turner & Munoz at 89–90.
[65] *Slynn Report* at 117.
[66] *Ibid.*
[67] *Ibid*, at 117–18.
[68] *Ibid*, at 118–19.
[69] *Courts' Discussion Paper*, at 23.

The Courts then revisited the drawbacks identified by the Slynn Report, concluding that:

> a system of filtering references for preliminary rulings … would not be easy to reconcile with the principle of mutual cooperation between the national courts and the Court of Justice which is a feature of the preliminary ruling procedure and which, by ensuring uniformity and consistency in the interpretation of Community law, has made such a major contribution to the proper working of the internal market.[70]

The overall conclusion was fittingly ambivalent: a filtering mechanism would constitute a possible solution to an excessive caseload and, from that point of view, 'there is much to be said for a more thorough examination of such a mechanism and the ways of implementing it'.[71] A year later, having refined its proposals for the consideration of the intergovernmental conference, the Courts took a more conservative line and recommended the introduction of a limited form of filter for a select range of appeals from the CFI to the Court. The recommendation was aimed, in particular, at cases where a matter had already been considered by an appellate body, such as a judicial panel, before coming to the CFI. The proposed amendment to Article 225(1) of the EC Treaty would have enabled the Council to determine, by way of amendment to the Statute, the appropriate classes of cases.[72]

The Commission's Working Party tendered a far more robust proposal for filtering appeals in its submission to IGC 2000. The Due Report envisioned that all appeals from the CFI to the Court should be subject to a uniform 'leave to appeal' requirement. On the basis of a swift, written procedure, a chamber of three judges at the Court of Justice would issue a reasoned opinion, on the basis of which the President of the Court would ultimately decide whether to grant or withhold authorisation to appeal. In addition to Article 225(1)'s requirement that appeals to the Court must be limited to points of law, the proposed leave to appeal mechanism introduced a second criterion, namely, that the appeal has major importance either for the development of Community law or the protection of individual rights.[73]

In contrast, the concept of filtering preliminary references was rejected by the Working Party on the premise that a *certiorari* arrangement 'cannot be transposed at present to a system of courts which is radically different from that of the United States'.[74] Indeed, this was one of several reforms (including the proposal, ultimately adopted at Nice, to confer a preliminary

---

[70] *Ibid*, at 25.
[71] *Ibid*.
[72] *Contribution by the Court of Justice and the Court of First Instance to the Intergovernmental Conference* (April 2000) at 3.
[73] *Due Report*, at 28–29.
[74] *Ibid*, at 21.

rulings jurisdiction on the CFI) discounted by the Working Party in deference to a series of alternative proposals designed to encourage a more assertive Community persona on the part of the national courts.[75]

(iv) Filtering Appeals

It is important to emphasise, as a preliminary matter, that the potential application of a European *certiorari* is limited to two forms of judicial jurisdiction: appeals from direct actions and preliminary rulings. It has never been suggested, for example, that the Court of Justice should exercise a discretionary first instance jurisdiction over direct actions filed by the privileged applicants or enforcement actions brought by the Commission—and rightly so. Even within the realm of a potential *certiorari*, a firm distinction must be drawn between the Court's respective jurisdictions over appeals and preliminary references. The differences between the two, in terms of function and operation, cannot be overstated for purposes of the present discussion.

In the appellate context, a European *certiorari* would target appeals from decisions of the CFI, whether in the context of direct actions, preliminary rulings or appeals from judicial panels. The prospect of an enhanced appellate jurisdiction, generated by the CFI's extended responsibilities under the Treaty of Nice, underscores the need for some method of case selection. From a pragmatic standpoint, a filtering mechanism would ensure that the burden of the Court's original jurisdiction does not resurface in appellate form.[76]

In terms of procedural mechanics, the discretionary jurisdiction might operate along the following lines. In keeping with current practice, the party or parties that has lost its case in the CFI would petition the Court for review of the CFI's decision, within a limited time-frame. The right to petition would be confined to the parties that had intervened below. The parties and any interveners would each be entitled to make a single submission, again within a specified period. The original petition and any such submission would be required to conform to a generally prescribed format and word or page limitation. On the basis of these submissions, and without convening an oral hearing, the Court would decide whether to hear

---

[75] The essential purpose of the Working Party's proposed reforms was that 'the national courts themselves should be better placed to give informed decisions on a growing number of questions of Community law which they meet in the exercise of their national jurisdiction'. *Ibid* at 18. The proposals included: limiting references from courts of last resort to questions which are 'sufficiently important' for EC law; weeding out 'irrelevant, premature or poorly-prepared references'; and increasing recourse to preliminary ruling by reasoned order. *Ibid*, at pp15–18.
[76] The Commission's Working Party highlighted that the failure rate of the approximately 30 per cent of appeals that are brought against the decisions of the CFI runs as high as 75–93 per cent. *Due Report* at 28.

the appeal. Where leave to appeal was denied, the judgment of the CFI would become final.

The underlying objective would be to facilitate quick, thorough and decisive action on a petition. There are several potential ways in which this might be achieved. Feasibly, appeals could be assigned in the usual way and the decision to accept or decline jurisdiction made *ad hoc*, for example, after the *juge-rapporteur* issues her preliminary report. A centralised screening system would be preferable, whether carried out by one or more chambers, through the offices of the advocates general or otherwise. The Due Report proposed that a chamber of three judges deliver a reasoned opinion which would form the basis of a decision on the part of the President of the Court in favour or against allowing the appeal.[77] Presumably, the President's guiding hand would ensure consistency in the operation of the procedure. Possibly and exceptionally, the initial decision could be subject to some form of summary ratification or veto by the *grand* chamber or plenary court. Alternatively, these decisions could be taken by the *grand* chamber in a manner akin to that of the US Supreme Court: the judges could analyse the petitions, assisted by their *referendaires,* whether acting individually or as a pool, and then vote in favour or against review. Review would be granted where a petition met or exceeded a set minimum (eg, four votes at the Supreme Court).[78] This style of approach would have the benefit of regular and direct participation of the broad membership of the Court in the screening process.

It would be essential to specify the criteria that the Court would use to review requests for leave to appeal. The most likely contenders would be the importance of the case (assessed, for example, in terms of the development of Community law and the need to protect individual rights[79]) and the existence of a threat to the uniformity or consistency of Community law. Both criteria are essentially subjective, although a threat to uniformity or consistency could operate as an indirect barometer of conflicts within the system. A further criterion, suggested by Jacqué and Weiler in the context of their alternative judicial architecture, would be the commission of a manifest error on the part of the CFI.[80] Although it would be important for the Court to explain its reasons for accepting or declining jurisdiction, American experience signals caution: the practice might involve a counterproductive expenditure of time and resources and there is a danger that the Court would be lured into reviewing the merits through the backdoor. Again, a clearly defined set of criteria for review would guard against an

---

[77] *Ibid*, at 29.
[78] The *en banc* procedure in the US courts of appeals might serve as an alternative model. See Fed R App Proc 35.
[79] A definition suggested by the *Due Report* at 29.
[80] Jacqué and Weiler at 193. Presumably, this criterion would be limited to errors of law, given that the Court's appellate jurisdiction does not extend to points of fact.

open-ended power of selection and would provide the Court with a point of reference in explaining its decisions.

A filter of this kind would operate principally in relation to the current source of appellate jurisdiction, namely, appeals from the CFI's decisions over direct actions. The Treaty of Nice, however, paves the way for important changes in the CFI's mandate: the Council will be empowered to make the CFI the primary forum for direct actions and, in addition, to endow it with a preliminary rulings jurisdiction and an appellate jurisdiction over any judicial panels that are created. At least in principle, a European *certiorari* could extend to the full breadth of the Court of Justice's appellate docket, comprising appeals from the CFI's decisions in response to preliminary references and appeals from judicial panels, as well as direct actions. However, the Treaty of Nice has designated a new procedure (an alternative filtering mechanism) that effectively forecloses such a possibility: acting on a proposal from the First Advocate General, the Court of Justice will review the CFI's decisions on preliminary references and appeals from judicial panels where there is a serious risk to the unity or consistency of Community law. Only time will tell whether the premise that such cases will reach the Court only in the most exceptional of circumstances will hold true, particularly in relation to preliminary rulings. A more serious objection is that this procedural distinction (between direct actions, on the one hand, and preliminary rulings and appeals from judicial panels, on the other) has no bearing on whether the substantive issues in a particular case merit adjudication by the Court of Justice.[81] Certainly, if the current levels of congestion continue unabated, future reformists may wish to revisit the possibility of a unified appellate procedure.

(v) Filtering Preliminary References

The Supreme Court's *certiorari* practice also provides a potential model for reform of the preliminary reference procedure, the 'hard core of Community litigation'[82] where the rationale for streamlining the Court's docket applies with even greater force.[83] The jurisdiction is broad and eclectic, 'an open valve, with few regulators to control the volume or content of cases'.[84] Save for a technical flaw or a patently redundant question, each national court request forms the basis of a ruling by the Court, regardless of its novelty,

---

[81] In the case of preliminary rulings, at least, the Treaty of Nice prescribes an additional safeguard, namely, the possibility that the CFI will decline jurisdiction in favour of the Court.

[82] T Koopmans, 'The Future of the Court of Justice of the European Communities' (1991) 11 *Yearbook of European Law* 15 at 29.

[83] The present discussion refers to the original version of the preliminary reference contained in Art 234 of the EC Treaty, although in principle any solution could potentially embrace the variants contained in Art 68 of the EC Treaty and Art 35 of the EU Treaty.

[84] Costello at 58.

complexity or importance.[85] If, as is commonly believed, most references concern issues of secondary importance, there is ample scope to reduce the Court's caseload. IGC 2000 concluded that this was best achieved by sharing the preliminary reference burden with the CFI. However, as noted above, the Conference left unresolved the crucial question of precisely how the jurisdiction might be divided between the two courts.

One possible solution would be to give the Court a discretion to select certain cases for adjudication and to assign all others to the CFI. This would be a halfway house between the current regime and a full-blown discretionary jurisdiction. Every national court would retain an entitlement to receive a preliminary ruling on the interpretation of Community law but the Court of Justice would enjoy a discretion to determine which of the two Community courts would deliver the ruling. A caveat might be entered in deference to the principle that the Court of Justice alone has the authority to annul Community acts.[86]

A distinct but related issue is whether it would be feasible and, if so, desirable to give the Court of Justice a radical, full-blown discretion in relation to preliminary references, along the lines of the US Supreme Court's *certiorari* jurisdiction. Under such a regime, some or potentially all of the national courts would lose their automatic entitlement to a preliminary ruling; instead, the Court would decide, on a case-by-case basis, by reference to a specified set of criteria, whether or not to adjudicate on the merits of national court requests. The Court's admissibility jurisprudence reflects a growing consensus that mandatory review is no longer necessary nor desirable and, consequently, points in the general direction of, but stops far short of, a European *certiorari*.[87]

Reservations over any form of filtering system for preliminary references have emerged from virtually every quarter of the Community. The member states fear a loss of prestige for the national courts[88] and the Bar a loss of

---

[85] See Advocate General Jacobs's opinion in Case C–338/95, *Wiener v Hauptzollamt Emmerich* [1997] ECR I–6495.

[86] Case 314/85, *Foto-Frost* [1987] ECR 4199. But see the recent Opinion of Advocate General Jacobs in Case C–500 P, *Unión de Pequeños Agricultores v Council* [2002] 3 *Common Market Law Reports* 1.

[87] The Court has declined to respond to requests for preliminary rulings for a number of reasons. See, eg, Case 104/79, *Foglia* [1980] ECR 745 (the main action does not involve a genuine dispute); Case C–342/90, *Dias* [1991] ECR I–4673 (the questions are not unconnected to the main action); Case C–83/91, *Meilicke* [1992] ECR I–4673 (the questions posed are purely hypothetical); Case C–167/94, *Grau* Gromis [1995] ECR I–1023 (requests for interpretation of provisions of the TWU over which the Court has no jurisdiction); Case C–307/95, *Max Mara* [1995] ECR I–5083 (the questions are unrelated to the interpretation of Community law). See also, the opinion of Advocate General Jacobs in Case C–338/95, *Wiener v Hamptzollamt Emmerich* [1997] ECR I–6495 at 6502 (foreshadowing the current admissibility test). See generally, T Kennedy, 'First Steps Towards a European Certiorari?' (1993) 18 *European Law Review* 121; C Barnard & E Sharpston, 'The Changing Face of Art 177 References' (1997) 34 *Common Market Law Review* 1113.

[88] See some member state submissions to IGC 2000, eg, above n 11.

indirect access to Luxembourg for their clients.[89] For its part, the Court of Justice is anxious not to disturb Article 234's climate of judicial co-operation.[90] A variation on this theme is the lament that *certiorari* could stimulate a judicial tendency to 'take things easy' by dodging 'perilous questions'.[91] These are legitimate concerns, albeit at times overstated. Would a filtering system actually augment Community jurisdiction at the expense of national jurisdiction or, in the final analysis, rewrite the adage that the Court of Justice has the final say on Community matters and the national court on national matters? Arguably, the role of the national court would be enhanced rather than reduced if it were forced to exercise greater responsibility in interpreting and applying Community law.[92]

There would be at least three significant stumbling blocks on the road to this potential reform. In the first place, *certiorari* is a creature of a conventional appellate system and, by design, ill-fitted for the preliminary reference procedure. In the United States, litigants trigger Supreme Court review by appealing the final decision of the court below. The Supreme Court alone decides whether to accept or decline the case and, in either eventuality, the Court's ultimate decision generally represents a definitive resolution of the matter. In contrast, a preliminary ruling is essentially an advisory opinion in relation to pending proceedings. It is the national court that seeks the intervention of the Court of Justice, decides whether a ruling is necessary and, ultimately, resolves the case. (One might quibble over the accuracy of these generalisations but hardly with the recognition that the procedure has its own unique characteristics). One obvious drawback is that the Court of Justice would decline jurisdiction without knowing how the national court would ultimately play its hand.[93]

The most promising way around this dilemma would be the commencement of a practice whereby the national court would include in its request a proposed interpretation of the Community law issue. The Court could then expediently endorse as much of the reasoning and result as it deemed appropriate. This 'green light' approach is used in Germany where a reference to the constitutional court contains a reasoned argument, penned by the referring judge, in favour of the unconstitutionality of the measure.

---

[89] See, eg, *Contribution from the CCBE to the Intergovernmental Conference*, CONFER/VAR 3966 (18 May 2000).

[90] The Court's explanation of the threat is cast in vague and less than compelling terms. See also Arnull at 519 (arguing that a filtering system is 'unattractive' because it could damage the spirit of cooperation on which Art 234 rests).

[91] Koopmans at 30.

[92] This enhanced role for the national courts was the imperative behind the proposals of the Commission's Working Party. See Due Report at 18.

[93] Jacqué and Weiler's filter proposal did not suffer from this deficiency; in their alternative judicial system, the European High Court of Justice would exercise discretionary jurisdiction over appeals from decisions and preliminary rulings of intermediate Community Regional Courts.

In addition to promoting judicial economy at the Court of Justice, this practice would nurture a more proactive role on the part of the national courts. It was for this latter reason that the Commission's Working Party promoted it at IGC 2000 as one of several laudable reforms to the preliminary reference procedure.[94] At the same time, it must be conceded that a green light approach would not necessarily guarantee major savings in the Court's time and resources. The quality of the national courts' proposed answers would be expected to vary and, in extreme cases, could counterproductively complicate the Court's task.[95] This limitation aside, the suggestion has much to recommend it. Arguably, the seeds have already been sown in the Court of Justice's current practice of re-writing, or seeking clarification of, the questions posed.[96]

A second concern is that the filtering of preliminary references would undermine the prevailing, co-operative relationship between the Court of Justice and the national courts. Traditionalists argue that the Court's rejection of a request for a preliminary ruling would be viewed as a slight and even a breach of trust.[97] After all, for most national courts the decision to refer is discretionary and therefore already presupposes some element of selection on the part of the national judge or judges. Precisely how the national courts would react to a *certiorari* system is anyone's guess; some courts might react by referring cases with excessive zeal, others with undue caution.[98] Certainly, there is a danger that national judges might eschew the risk of a denial from the Court of Justice by referring only the most imponderable of cases, a practice that could undermine the uniformity of Community law if taken to an extreme. On the other hand, the system might have the beneficial effect of encouraging national courts to engage the procedure more seriously and exercise greater care in the formulation of requests. Finally, one might predict that once a filtering system became entrenched, a rebuff from the Court of Justice might be seen less as a personal slight than an institutional reality.

One possible safeguard against leaving the national courts entirely without guidance would be to retain the obligation currently resting on the Court under Article 234, paragraph 3, to deliver a preliminary ruling in response to a request from a national court of last resort.[99] This would effectively

---

[94] *Due Report* at 18. In addition, the *Courts' Discussion Paper* at 24 cited a green light system as a beneficial means of mitigating the drawbacks of a filtering system.

[95] An objection noted by the *Slynn Report* at 82. The Report also predicted that this approach would add to the burden of translation.

[96] See, eg, Case 19/81, *Burton v British Railways Board* [1982] ECR 555; Joined Cases C–171 & 172/94, *Mercks & Neuhuys* v Ford Motors [1996] ECR I–1253. See generally, Court of Justice, *Note for Guidance on References by National Courts for Preliminary Rulings* (1997).

[97] See, eg, *Courts' Discussion Paper* at 24; *Slynn Report* at 118.

[98] See, eg, Turner & Munoz at 66 speculating that national courts may choose not to refer through fear of their reference being rejected.

[99] A suggestion offered by Koopmans at 29–30.

give the Court a discretionary jurisdiction over preliminary references from the lower national courts and a mandatory jurisdiction over references from national courts of last resort. Under this approach, however, the Court's ability to define its agenda—the very essence of *certiorari*—would be partially lost and its caseload only partially reduced. A further objection is the lack of political appetite, manifest at IGC 2000, for the drawing of distinctions between national courts of first and last resort.[100] A distinct but related concern is that the national courts in the candidate countries should not be deprived of the Court of Justice' guiding hand in developing their Community credentials. Given the spectre of on-going enlargement, it might be prudent to establish transitional arrangements that would allow new judicial entrants full and automatic access to the Court of Justice for an initial period following accession.

The third concern is the risk that filtering preliminary references would bring some measure of uncertainty to the legal system. Uncertainty might surface in a number of guises, whether practical or doctrinal. Even assuming that the Community courts were ready to take the plunge, the success of a European *certiorari* would depend on several practical imperatives, such as efficiency in the screening of petitions, consistency and transparency in the exercise of the Court's discretion, and diligence and care in the formulation of requests by the national courts. The need to preserve the unique features of the Community system would also give cause for concern. *Certiorari* might alter the judicial dynamic insofar as it would allow judges to bring their personal and policy preferences to bear on the shaping of the Court's docket; the persona of the individual justice, so a much a feature of the Supreme Court culture, is markedly absent on the collegiate Kirchberg. In addition, some accommodation would be required to safeguard the Community's formidable linguistic regime.

The most ominous cloud of uncertainty, however, is the potential threat a European *certiorari* could pose to the consistent application of Community law throughout the member states. Whereas consistency is also a basic principle in the application of federal law in the United States, that judicial system has safeguards that the Community lacks, notably, lower and intermediate federal courts. *Certiorari* enthusiasts would respond that close supervision of the national courts is no longer a necessity and that a discretionary jurisdiction would strengthen rather than weaken the Court's ability to steer the course of Community law. Arguably, increased flexibility and decentralisation in the judicial system would facilitate the percolation of legal discourse through the national courts (both within the member states and, eventually, between the member states) and leave to the Court of Justice the resolution of fresh and defining Community controversies.

---

[100] One proposal that made little headway at IGC 2000 was to limit, or remove altogether, the right of lower national courts to refer.

But whether the Community system is sufficiently mature to reap these benefits remains an open question. Writing in 1991, former Judge Koopmans commented:

> When compared to Community law, American constitutional law is a traditional and stabilized system; it was so, at any rate, when *certiorari* was introduced. In comparison, the very foundations of Community law are still being established. Consequently, it is not always easy to predict whether a certain case can ultimately contribute to the further growth of the Community legal system. Judgments which, taken in isolation, may look somewhat innocuous, sometimes turn out to constitute the basis for a completely new chapter of the Court's case-law. Under a *certiorari* system, there would be every possibility that cases of this kind would not, at first sight, look interesting enough to be taken by the Court.[101]

The maturing of the Community judicial system during the intervening decade has softened but by no means muted this concern. At the end of the day, the success of a European *certiorari* would turn, not on its application in limited cases (or even categories of cases) but rather on the benefits it would bring to the judicial system overall. In the United States, *certiorari* operates as an efficient and cost-effective means of handling the Supreme Court's docket given the enormous number of cases referred annually for review. Whether the business of the Community courts has reached a stage where the benefits would outweigh the burdens is an open question. But if that day is not here, it cannot be too far hence, a reality recognised by Judge Koopmans.[102] The Court of Justice may not yet be the magnet for the range and depth of legal controversies drawn to the Supreme Court but it exercises a comparable degree of centripetal force within its own sphere of influence.

IV. CONCLUDING REMARKS

On the basis of the foregoing, a strong case may be made in favour of the introduction of a *certiorari* or leave to appeal mechanism in relation to appeals from the CFI to the Court. The need for some such mechanism, while perhaps not yet pressing, will grow exponentially with the projected increases in Community litigation.

Far greater caution is required in relation to preliminary references where the benefits of filtration are balanced, if not outweighed, by credible

---

[101] Koopmans at 30 (citations ommited).
[102] *Ibid*, at 31: '[I]t may be necessary to have a second look at the problem after some time, [in particular when delays for getting an answer to questions for preliminary rulings will again begin to increase. The moment may come that the disadvantages inherent in *certiorari* systems are less important than those resulting from the existing situation'.

objections in terms of policy and procedure. Although the complexity of the task gives reason for pause, it does not justify dismissing the concept out of hand. In truth, at this stage of Community development, there are no easy answers to the preliminary reference conundrum. The theoretical benefits of a European *certiorari* justify a closer look, particularly in relation to the practical steps that might be taken to facilitate and optimise such a procedure within the Community framework. Much will depend, however, on whether the Treaty of Nice's promised preliminary reference jurisdiction for the CFI is realised in practice and, if so, how the jurisdiction is shared between the two courts. An extensive or even respectable command of preliminary references by the CFI would effectively render redundant any proposal to filter the preliminary reference caseload of the Court of Justice.[103]

The results of IGC 2000 make plain the lack of political appetite for a European *certiorari* or, indeed, for dramatic reform. It cannot be gainsaid, however, that the Nice reforms, standing alone, are too modest to guarantee effective, lasting solutions to the present workload crisis, much less to equip the courts for future challenges, including enlargement and, potentially, the defence of the Charter of Fundamental Rights. Only time will tell whether the Treaty of Nice will pave the way for the lasting administration of justice or condemn courts and litigants alike to continued gridlock. In either event, the pressure for further reform must be maintained.

---

[103] A reduced preliminary reference caseload for the Court of Justice would in itself remove the need for a filter. Depending on the nature of preliminary references over which the CFI exercises jurisdiction, it might be incongruous to provide the national courts with automatic access to the CFI but limited access to the Court of Justice. Nevertheless, a discretionary jurisdiction for the CFI would be a non-starter for several reasons, not least because *certiorari* is feted as a boon to the Court of Justice's uniquely constitutional mandate.

Part IV

The Human Rights Charter

15

A Charter of Rights, Freedoms and Principles

LORD GOLDSMITH QC, HM ATTORNEY GENERAL*

I. INTRODUCTION

THE INVITATION TO write this chapter suggested that I might discuss the origins and the legal nature of the EU Charter of Fundamental Rights. I feel reasonably well placed to attempt the first of those topics. I was privileged to have participated, before my current Government appointment, as the Prime Minister's personal representative in the drafting Convention which produced the Charter. So I can certainly give you the view of one participant on how we got to where we are today.

The second topic, the legal nature of the Charter, is less straightforward. I can and will give an account of the contents of the Charter and offer some observations about their status and value. But I shall do so from an historical perspective, because the legal status of the Charter is, you might say, a moot point. The issue is currently being debated within the Convention on the Future of Europe. It will be for the Convention to propose what part the Charter should play in the vision of Europe they are working to create. And then, at the Intergovernmental Conference in 2004, the Member States will decide. The Charter, and its constitutional relationship with the Treaties and the Future of Europe, may well, I suspect, turn out to be one of the most interesting legal and political debates of them all.

II. ORIGINS

I would like to start in 1999, which is where the immediate history begins: the decision of the Cologne European Council

> "that at the present stage of the development of the European Union, the fundamental rights applicable at Union level should be consolidated in a Charter and thereby made more evident."

* Speech to the British Institute of International and Comparative Law: 10 October 2002.

Three questions arise at once. First, *why*: what was it that caused the Council to believe that such an undertaking was needed at this stage of the Union's development? Second, *what*: precisely which fundamental rights are applicable at Union level? And third, perhaps illuminating the answers to the first two questions, *what is meant by 'evident'* in this context: is this simply an exercise in visibility and transparency for the citizen or is more intended?

To tackle the first question, about the rationale, I think we need to take a step back from the detail and notice that for most of the last 50 years, European human rights, and the Community, have been largely separate legal developments. The Treaty founding the European Economic Community made no mention of fundamental rights and the European Court of Justice was, in the early days, reluctant to accept that the decisions of, for example, the High Authority of the Coal and Steel Community were bound to respect fundamental rights.[1] But, as the Community began to develop its areas of activity, so have human rights appeared increasingly relevant to the acceptable exercise of its new competences.

And so it was, in a 1969 case about an apparent conflict between a social welfare scheme and the right to privacy,[2] the Luxembourg Court first developed the concept that fundamental rights existed as general principles of Community law and would be protected as such by the Court. The primary sources of inspiration for the content of these rights at Community level were found to be in the constitutional traditions common to the member States and international human rights instruments, most particularly the European Convention on Human Rights.[3]

The jurisprudence in this area was consolidated by the 1992 Maastricht Treaty which introduced what is now Article 6 of the Treaty on European Union.[4] This takes the form of an explicit recognition of the concept of fundamental rights as part of the Community legal order and imposes an obligation on the Union to respect as general principles of Community law those rights which are guaranteed by the ECHR and which result from the common constitutional traditions of the Member States.

III.   WHY 'AT THIS STAGE'?

What Article 6(2) of the TEU does not do is to provide a detailed catalogue of the rights which are to be respected at Union level. Apart from the reference

---

[1] Case 1/58 *Stork v High Authority* [1959] ECR 17.
[2] Case C29/69 *Stauder v City of Ulm* [1969] ECR 419.
[3] See Case 4/73 *Nold KG v Commission* [1974] 2 CMLR 338.
[4] TEU Art 6(2): 'The Union shall respect fundamental rights, as guaranteed by the European Convention for the Protection of Human Rights and Fundamental Freedoms signed in Rome on 4 November 1950 and as they result from the constitutional traditions common to the Member States, as general principles of Community law.'

to rights guaranteed by the ECHR, there is no indication in the Treaties of what are the fundamental rights which the Union institutions are to respect. It was therefore very difficult for the citizen to see what rights are protected at Union level and enforceable by the ECJ. This lack of visibility of rights caused concern, particularly in the European Parliament.

In addition, Article 6(2) of the TEU does not set out any rights which the Union might itself claim to have established. The sources are all outside the Union's own legal order, namely the constitutional traditions of the Member States and the ECHR, adopted within the framework of the Council of Europe. The casual reader of the Union Treaty—if such an animal exists—might be forgiven for concluding that fundamental rights are something that the Union respects; but that the Union has not itself formulated any rights itself which its institutions are bound to respect.

For some that is not a satisfactory position, particularly if he or she is from a member State which has a strong written national constitution. How, they ask, how can it be proper for my country to participate in ever closer cooperation within the European Union, particularly in areas such as Justice and Home Affairs in which the Union's activities engage basic civil and political rights, if the Union is not clearly bound by at least the same safeguards which exist in relation to the exercise of those powers in my own country?

This then is the background against which the European Council decided in December 1999 that the time had come to embark on a project to make existing rights more visible to the citizen. And the history, I think, gives something of a clue to the answer to the first question posed earlier, namely why at this stage was it necessary for the Union to embark on this project. The EU's objectives were, as I saw it, to strengthen the culture of rights and responsibilities within the EU by producing a document which would reinforce in the minds of administrators, governments and legislators the need to respect fundamental rights and to remedy the lack of clarity in the content of the rights protected at EU level.

IV.   WHAT RIGHTS?

So what precisely are the rights to be respected at Union level? There are two aspects to this question. First, what did the European Council mean when it referred to rights 'applicable at EU level'? It should be clear from my description of the underlying purpose of the Charter that it was intended to describe the limits on the powers of the Union. The principal addressees of the Charter were therefore intended to be the EU institutions, as it is they who legislate at EU level. I will come back later to how this understanding was eventually reflected in the Charter text.

The second issue is how the content of the rights applicable at EU level was to be determined. As I mentioned earlier, Article 6(2) of the TEU refers to two sources of fundamental rights which the Union should respect: the ECHR and the constitutional traditions common to the Member States. But we have to recognise that the Member States have different constitutional traditions and approaches to the protection of rights. Certainly, there are elements in common—commitment to the ECHR for instance—but there are dissimilarities too.

Social and economic rights is one obvious area. Some Member States, for example, recognise certain aspects of labour law as constitutional rights. Others, no less developed or enlightened in their practice on the ground, do not. Still others recognise some such rights as guiding principles which inform the legislator but are not binding in a court of law. We should not be surprised, still less alarmed, about this lack of uniformity. Pooling sovereignty within the EU does not mean tearing up one's own constitutional traditions.

We find a similar position, if less marked, when we come to look at the ECHR. Yes, all the Member States have ratified the Convention as adopted in 1950. But not all have accepted all the subsequent Protocols. For example, five Member States[5] have yet to ratify Protocol No 7 which adds a number of new additional rights to those already protected by the Convention. Moreover, many Member States have entered reservations in respect of various rights conferred either by the Convention or Protocols, which seek to impose limitations on the extent to which those States are prepared to be bound by the rights in question. Germany, Ireland, and the United Kingdom have all been unable to accept the right to education contained in Article 2 of Protocol 1 to the Convention without qualification or explanation. A number of Member States have entered reservations to Articles 5 and 6 of the Convention (the rights to liberty and security and to a fair trial). And others have made reservations to Article 1 of Protocol 1 (the right to the peaceful enjoyment of property). The position is even more diffuse when we come to consider other international human rights instruments, such as those adopted under the auspices of the United Nations.

I think we can regard such variety, if that is *le mot juste*, as part of the margin of flexibility which is necessary if you are to bring nation states together under a system of international supervision. I make the point here simply to note that defining the detailed content of the rights which are common to the Member States is not at all straightforward, since the approach of the Member States to the recognition and protection of rights is by no means uniform.

V.   AN EXERCISE IN VISIBILITY AND TRANSPARENCY?

Despite the wording of the Cologne conclusions, not all of us saw the task as consolidating *existing* rights, which the Union ought to respect, and making

---

[5] The Member States who have not ratified are: Germany, Netherlands, Portugal, Spain and the UK.

them more visible to the citizen. Many non-governmental organisations made contributions and sought inclusions on the basis that we were in the business of minting new rights. Still others pressed for the inclusion of rights which were part of the legal traditions of some, but plainly not all, the Member States. A further number, though broadly satisfied with a Charter based clearly on existing rights, believed that the Charter should seek to modernise the language and the content of the rights, taking account for example, of bio-technology[6] or the development of the media.[7]

The arguments went back and forth over the 29 or so negotiating meetings I attended on the Charter as we struggled to find compromise and consensus. Ultimately the view that the European Council had not mandated the development of new rights prevailed, although not without some opposition. But most representatives came to accept that the Charter was not the correct legal vehicle to establish new rights, since there is already an established procedure for the creation of legal rights at EU level through the adoption of legislation in accordance with the procedures laid down by the Treaties in which each of the institutions plays its role.

One other important issue, on which happily we reached agreement early on, was that the Charter should be written with the citizen primarily in mind and should thus be drafted in the clearest and simplest terms possible. Provided we could find a way of reconciling that aim without sacrificing legal certainty, here at least was one agreed element of the approach.

In the end I think the drafting body did succeed in covering most of the ground the various groups wanted and in producing a Charter which was, for the most part, composed in admirably succinct terms. It also found a way of preserving legal certainty and the position of the Member States, at least for the purposes of the Charter as a political declaration. I will return later to the Charter's so-called 'horizontal articles', that is Articles 51 to 54, and the Praesidium Commentary, which contain the bulk of the solution. But let us look first at the substantive, rights-bearing, content of the Charter.

VI. CONTENTS OF THE CHARTER

The Charter has six chapters: Dignity, Freedoms, Equality, Solidarity, Citizens' Rights and Justice. It is exceptionally broad—unprecedented I think—in the scope of its coverage. Excluding the Protocols, the ECHR has just 14 substantive articles; the Charter has 50. The difference in number is indicative of the wider coverage. The Charter covers the classic rights and freedoms: the right to life and liberty, to freedom of thought and expression and association, privacy and family life, the right to a fair trial etc. But it

[6] See Charter Art 3.
[7] See Charter Art 11.

also includes economic freedoms to seek employment, to conduct a business and to property. And it includes citizenship provisions deriving from the EC Treaty itself: participation in elections, access to documents of the EU institutions and to the European ombudsman, the right to petition the European Parliament, the right of freedom of movement and residence within the EU etc. Finally, and most controversially, the Charter includes a raft of social and economic rights and principles, such as workers' rights to information, to collective bargaining and to take strike action.

I would like to make a few remarks first about the relationship with the ECHR. To my mind, it was of paramount importance to avoid creating an apparently competing version of fundamental human rights and I argued strongly against this within the Convention. That applied in my view as much to the jurisprudence on those rights, developed by the Strasbourg institutions over 50 years, as it did to the expression of those rights in the text of the Convention and its Protocols.

Some disagreed. The ECHR, 50 years old, was out of date they said, both in language and content. I felt that this misunderstood the nature of the ECHR as a 'living document', whose interpretation has been developed over time by the Strasbourg Court in the light of contemporary social and political standards. Thus, the Court has, over the years, expanded the reach of the Convention to cover issues such as environmental protection, the rights of non-traditional families and protection from discrimination on grounds of sexual orientation in private life. That dynamic process should not be underestimated or discarded.

In the end, the argument that the relevant rights should have the same meaning and scope as the ECHR prevailed. We achieved this by the use of a general clause, one of those all important 'horizontal articles' I referred to earlier. Thus, whilst leaving the Union the right to legislate for more extensive protection in the future—the ECHR is a floor not a ceiling—Article 52(3) provides that:

> Insofar as this Charter contains rights which correspond to rights guaranteed by [the ECHR] the meaning and scope of those rights shall be the same as those laid down by the said Convention.

A similar solution was found for the Charter articles which are based on provisions of the EU Treaties. Another of the horizontal provisions, Article 52(2), provides that Charter rights deriving from EU law are to be exercised under the conditions and within the limits defined by the EU Treaties.

So far so good, but legal clarity also demands identification of the corresponding provisions being referred to. Fortunately, there is a Commentary to the Charter by the Praesidium (the secretariat to the Charter drafting body). The Commentary amounts to a diluted version of a proposal I made for a Charter in two parts: a Part A containing a clear declaration of rights and a Part B which provided a more detailed definition, particularly by reference across to the existing source of law. The Praesidium Commentary goes some way to achieving the objective of my proposal, which was to resolve the inherent tension between the Charter as a clear statement of citizens' rights and the need for legal precision.

The aim of the horizontal articles is to tie the substantive provisions of the Charter to the existing sources of fundamental rights, particularly the ECHR and the EU Treaties. The Commentary makes it clearer what the link is. For example, it explains that 12 Charter articles, or parts of them, are intended, despite different wording, to correspond exactly with specified articles in the ECHR. In view of the difference in language and, in some cases, the absence of express limitations on the exercise of the rights which appear in the corresponding provisions of the ECHR, these articles could be interpreted in a wholly different way from the provisions on which they are based, were it not for the link provided by the horizontal articles and the explanation given by the Commentary. The same is true of other articles of the Charter which are based on provisions of the EU Treaties.

Let me give just two examples.

First, take Article 6 of the Charter which provides simply that 'Everyone has the right to liberty and security of person'. Those of you familiar with the ECHR will realise that this Charter text corresponds exactly with the first sentence of Article 5 of the Convention. But of course Article 5 of the ECHR goes on to specify particular aspects of the right to liberty and also to provide for circumstances in which individuals may lawfully be deprived of their liberty. The Commentary to Charter Article 6 makes it clear that 'the rights in Article 6 are the rights guaranteed by Article 5 ECHR and, in accordance with Article 52(3) of the Charter, they have the same meaning and scope'. It then sets out the full text of Article 5 ECHR.

Secondly, compare the wording of Articles 39(1) and 40 of the Charter (the right to vote in EP and municipal elections) with Article 19 of the EC Treaty. The Charter articles appear to confer on citizens of the Union residing in another Member State an absolute right to vote in these elections under the same conditions as nationals of the State of residence. But, the EC Treaty provisions provide that these rights are to be exercised in accordance with detailed arrangements to be laid down by the Council, which may provide for derogations from the right 'where warranted by problems specific to a Member State'. The Commentary to Articles 39 and 40 makes clear that the rights in these Charter articles correspond to the rights guaranteed by Article 19 of the EC Treaty and, in accordance with Article 52(4) of the Charter, are to apply under the conditions laid down by the Treaty.

So it is clear, the Charter by itself *identifies*, but does not *define* the rights which are applicable at EU level. This approach to the drafting of the Charter becomes explicable when it is understood that the drafting body was simply trying to capture in a clear way, comprehensible to the citizen, the fundamental essence of the rights. To find out the full content of the rights, you have to look back at the underlying source of each provision of the Charter as the horizontal articles and the Commentary make clear.

The other main issue addressed by the horizontal articles is the question of the scope of the Charter: to whom are its provisions addressed and in what circumstances. As I explained earlier, the remit of the Cologne European Council was to consolidate in a single text the rights applicable 'at EU level', which meant that the Charter was directed, principally, to the EU institutions. This was made clear in Article 51 of the Charter, which reads:

> The provisions of this Charter are addressed to the institutions and bodies of the Union with due regard for the principle of subsidiarity and to the Member States only when they are implementing EU law.

The Member States are already bound to respect rights arising from the ECHR, the EU Treaties or from their own constitutions. The Charter, by contrast, is intended to demonstrate the limits on the powers of the *Union* and to list the rights and principles which the institutions should have in mind when exercising their *existing* competences under the EU Treaties. (Article 51 also makes clear that the Charter does not extend or modify the scope of competence of the European Community or European Union.) For the most part, therefore, the Charter does not affect the member States, or the constitutional safeguards they give to their citizens, except when they are implementing Union law. When they are acting in that capacity they are, in effect, acting as agents of the Community or Union in implementing legislation adopted by the institutions. It therefore makes sense for them to be subject to the same constraints as are applicable at EU level to the institutions. But it is critical to a proper understanding of the Charter to realise that it is not intended to affect the Member States when they are acting within areas of national competence.

VII.   SOCIAL AND ECONOMIC RIGHTS

I turn now to what I regard as the other area of greatest difficulty the drafting body faced in drawing up the Charter, namely the proper treatment of social and economic rights. The Cologne Conclusions required that in drawing up the Charter account should be taken of economic and social rights as contained in the European Social Charter and the Community Charter of the Fundamental Social Rights of Workers, insofar as they do not merely establish objectives for action by the Union. Unfortunately, the European Council gave no guidance on how the Union should take such rights into account. Were they, for example, to be placed alongside, and on the same footing as, the classic civil and political rights? This was an issue which generated considerable debate.

There are important differences between social and economic rights and the classic civil and political rights. First, social and economic rights are not usually justiciable individually in the same way as other rights. Rather, they inform policy making by the legislature. They require judgments to be made about the allocation of scarce national resources, which are decisions to be made by governments, not judges. Secondly, they are 'rights' which are recognised and given effect in different ways in the Member States. Each national government decides in accordance with its own priorities how to give effect to such 'rights'.

The debate was long and difficult. The ultimate solution to this problem emerged as a notion—new I believe to Community law, but familiar to some constitutional traditions—that such rights might best be regarded as guiding principles, which, while common to the Member States, are implemented differently in their national law and practices. Such principles would give rise to rights to the extent that they are implemented by national law, or, where there is such competence, by Community law. This novel distinction is reflected in the final preambular paragraph of the Charter which states 'the Union recognises the rights, freedoms *and* principles set out hereafter'.

The Charter texts use a variety of techniques to signal this special status. They need to be understood if the Charter is to be interpreted properly. Sometimes the word 'principle' is used explicitly.[8] Also not infrequently an expression is used which captures the concept of non-interference by the Union with a right accorded by national law. For example, Charter Article 34 says 'the Union recognises and respects the entitlement to social security benefits and social services ...'. This does not mean that the Union has competence to legislate in this area. Nor does this impose any requirement on Member States. It means that the Union should not violate the principle of entitlement to benefits and social services by a side-wind in some other legislation within its competence.

The Charter also contains frequent references to rights being exercised in accordance with 'national law and practice'.[9] Article 28, which covers among other things the right to strike is an example of this type of provision. The article expressly states that the rights conferred by the article take effect 'in accordance with national law and practices'. The Commentary makes this limitation even more explicit. These references to national law indicate that the Charter is not interfering with national legislation in these

---

[8] Charter Art 23 (equality between men and women), 49 (principles of legality and proportionality of criminal offences and penalties).
[9] Charter Art 9 (right to marry), 10(2) (right to conscientious objection), 14 (right to education), 16 (freedom to conduct a business), 27 (workers' right to information and consultation), 28 (right of collective bargaining and action), 30 (protection in the event of unjustified dismissal), 34 (social security), 35 (health care), 36 (access to services of general economic interest).

sensitive fields. On the contrary it emphasises the need to respect national differences and that it is not for the Union to impose rights in this area except through recognised Treaty procedures.

It will be apparent from my description of the content of the Charter that the nature and status of some of the Charter's provisions is not immediately obvious from a cursory inspection of the texts. The reader needs to study the subtle drafting closely and make a number of inferences, aided by the Praesidium Commentary mentioned earlier, and the general provisions in the last few articles of the Charter. Ideally she or he needs to know something of the background too. I believe that, generally, this task is most difficult in relation to the social and economic provisions.

The result was in my view very satisfactory for the purposes of a political declaration. It achieved the twin objectives of *identifying* key fundamental values and *increasing the visibility* of these rights for the citizen. Indeed the UK warmly welcomed the Charter to serve precisely that role. I was glad—and proud—that it did so. But British lawyers are trained hard in the drafting schools of legal precision and clarity. It was clear to me that some adjustments to the text would be needed if the Charter were to become law.

VIII.   FUTURE OF THE CHARTER

The proclamation of the Charter by the EU institutions as a political, non-binding declaration in December 2000 was not, of course, the end of the story. The Cologne European Council conclusions had stated that, once it had been drawn up, consideration would be given as to whether, and if so, how the Charter should be integrated into the Treaties. In parallel with the proclamation of the Charter, the Nice European Council decided that the question of the Charter's force would be considered later. Then in June 2001 at its meeting at Laeken in Belgium, the European Council convened a Convention on the Future of Europe. Among the issues to be considered by the Convention is whether the Charter should be included in the Treaties. As I mentioned at the start of this paper, this work is now underway.

President Herzog, the Chairman of the drafting body expressed the wish that the Charter should be drafted 'as if' we were drafting a legally binding document in case the Union should determine that to be the fate of the Charter. But in this respect I do not believe the drafting body succeeded in its aims. The compromises struck during negotiations on issues where there were strong differences of opinion, such as those I have described, led to a text which, as it stands, lacks the precision necessary for law. The Convention on the Future of Europe is examining the options for incorporation. But I do not believe that this issue can be tackled without being very clear about the strengths and weaknesses of the Charter and the purposes for which it was created.

In particular, I believe there is a need to face the facts to which I have referred:

— First, the wording of the articles departs in many places from the corresponding ECHR and EU treaty rights, often not setting out vitally important qualifications and conditions. Without clear links to the underlying legal base, there would in my view be an inadequate and dangerous restatement of fundamental rights, risking creating two competing and contradictory sets of basic rights;

— Second, there are important limitations of the meaning and scope of the Charter. The horizontal articles I referred to earlier provide for some of these limitations. But these articles were designed for inclusion in a political declaration. There is a serious question as to whether they could bear the weight that would be placed upon them in the event of Charter incorporation;

— Third, there is also a need to be clearer about when the Charter is talking about rights, when about freedoms and when about principles, so as to respect national competences and the principles of subsidiarity and not create by a side-wind a competence for the Community which was expressly not intended.

In view of these concerns, I was therefore pleased to hear that the Convention Working Group on the Charter has accepted the need to clarify and strengthen the "horizontal" articles in the event that the Member States decide to make the Charter legally binding.[10] The Working Group has in particular recommended that new horizontal provisions should be added to clarify the meaning and scope of those Charter provisions which do not derive from the ECHR or EU Treaties, or which do not contain substantive rights at all, and to recognise the importance of the references in the Charter to national law and practices. It has also endorsed the significance of the Praesidium Commentary as an essential tool for properly interpreting the Charter.

It is my view that these elements of a possible solution already exist in the Charter and its Preamble: it could well be a question of drawing them together and clarifying the interrelationship.

I shall continue to follow the debate with great interest. I believe and have always believed that the Charter is needed to give the people of Europe a firm guarantee of the Union's respect for their rights at EU level. I am hopeful that, if the Community pursues greater integration of the Charter, this can be done in a way that maintains the Union's roots in the democracies

[10]See Final Report of Convention Working Group II, 22 October 2002.

of the Member States. Acceptance of that principle was, I believe, the secret of the consensus we reached in 2000. I believe that it will be the key to success in the future.

16

The EU Charter of Rights: A Poor Attempt to Strengthen Democracy and Citizenship?

SIONAIDH DOUGLAS SCOTT*

I. INTRODUCTION

O N 7 DECEMBER 2000, the EU Charter of Fundamental Rights was proclaimed by the respective presidents of the EU Institutions. It was not a high-profile occasion, overshadowed by the wrangling over the forthcoming Treaty of Nice. The Charter's apparent lack of importance seemed to be underlined by the fact that the Institutional presidents were not even given the time to complete their speeches.[1]

The Charter was proclaimed by the EU Institutions, rather then by the member states, but this should not undermine the fact that this Charter was a Member State initiative, first suggested by the German Presidency in the first part of 1999, its operational structure detailed in the Presidency conclusions of the Cologne and Tampere European Councils of June and December 1999, and finally agreed by the European Council in Nice 2000. Although it was proclaimed in Nice, it is not yet legally enforceable, and, if it is to have any future legal effect, this too will be a decision for the Member States.

This lack of solemnity on the proclamation of something designed at the very least to be a 'showcase'[2] of fundamental rights, directed at EU citizens in order to secure greater popular legitimacy for the EU legal order, and on more ambitious accounts, a key step in the building of a European constitution,[3] as well as continuing uncertainty as to essential aspects of the Charter

---

* Senior Lecturer, King's College London. This paper was originally prepared for the UACES conference on the Treaty of Nice in May 2001 and it has not been possible to update it substantially. An updated and reworked version of this paper appears in chapter 13 of Sionaidh Douglas Scott, *Constitutional Law of the European Union* (Longman 2002).
[1] Editorial (2001) 38 *Common Market Law Review* at 1.
[2] Keith Vaz, Minister for Europe, reported in the HL Select Committee report on the EU Charter of Fundamental Rights, 24 May 2000, HL 67 ISBN 004067004.
[3] See accounts given below in the section on the legal effect of the Charter.

(was the Charter to be legally binding, what were its drafting body's terms of reference to be?) illustrates the ambiguities and tensions inherent in the EU constitution building process. Such ambiguities have been apparent at least since Maastricht, when grand designs for political union were watered down into a sprawling and inconsistent 3 pillar structure, and also at Amsterdam, in which designs for an area of freedom, security and justice resulted in mostly minor and insignificant treaty changes. However, in the course of EU history, seemingly small, unrecognised as important at the time, changes have sometimes provoked unexpected evolutions within the European polity, as did the extension of qualified majority voting of the 1986 Single European Act, which made possible the relatively speedy completion of the Internal Market. Might the EU Charter in fact turn out to be such a step, if not the Trojan horse which Euro sceptic UK Tory MPs[4] have sometimes insisted on portraying it?

This paper aims to show that the European Charter of Fundamental Rights does not yet herald a new European dawn, although it is just possible that it might, in time, come to do so. On the positive side, the Charter might be seen as a significant exercise in constitution building—a swift agreement, a common consensus, reached on the notoriously controversial and conflictual issues of human rights which form part of the European heritage. As such, it might be seen as an example of what the liberal philosopher John Rawls has termed 'public reason'[5]—namely, shared principles within the public domain in a society in which there is no comprehensive underpinning, no shared moral outlook.

On the negative side, 3 major fault lines have straddled the creation of this new document. The first is that the document is not yet binding, at present a mere proclamation, which in itself sends out a negative message to the beleaguered European citizen. Second, of the long list of rights which it contains, many still derive from the old model of 'market citizen', the possessive individual. The type of citizenship created is that of the informed, empowered, isolated but complaining and litigious being (nothing wrong with most of these except in what is missing—a strong, complementary, social and political sense). Although chapter IV of the Charter adds a long list of social rights, many of these are opaquely drafted,[6] and, as the Charter avoids the creation of new rights and competences (Article 51) it cannot add much to existing social protection. The fact that the model of citizenship it contains owes very little to a sense of participatory democracy is underlined by the very personnel and organisation of the Convention which drafted it. A large proportion of the Convention was made of

---

[4] Eg *Daily Mail* 12 Oct 2000, 'Blair to sign away rights in Charter'.
[5] For a further discussion of this see below at p 412.
[6] For example, what is meant in Art 29 by the right of access to a 'free placement service'? For a discussion of these, and similar issues, see the section of this paper on the rights protected by the Charter.

governmental representatives, with little input from civil society at large, nor by experts on human rights (nor from women and ethnic minorities). (On the other hand, it must be acknowledged that in some ways, the Convention was new and path breaking—in the amount of transparency of its proceedings, and in the processes it employed, which might profitably be taken up by future IGCs—another example of the current ambiguities and tensions inherent in the present state of EU constitutionalism). Thirdly, the Charter raises problems of scope. Although according to Article 51, it is 'addressed to the institutions and bodies of the Union ... and to the member States only when they are implementing Community law', the extent to which Member States will be bound by the Charter raises some serious legal problems.

These three fault lines—current lack of legal enforceability; underdeveloped notion of citizenship; problems of scope, will be examined in this paper. But their analysis is preceded by a short consideration of the necessity of an EU Charter of Rights, and examination of the processes by which the current Charter was drafted—with the aim of showing the Charter as another (confused?) step in the development of an EU constitution.

II.　NECESSITY FOR THE CHARTER

The President of the European Commission, Romano Prodi, introducing the Charter in the welcome page of the Commission's Charter website,[7] stated that the objective of the Charter is, 'to make more visible and explicit to EU citizens the fundamental rights they already enjoy at European level'. Thus it brings together in a concise text, rights scattered throughout many different sources. This echoes the Presidency Conclusions of the Cologne European Council of June 1999, which, in paragraph 44, stated that fundamental rights applicable at Union level should be consolidated in a Charter and 'thereby made more evident'. Greater visibility and coherence for EU fundamental rights is by no means the only justification for the drafting of the Charter, but it is an important, although contested one,[8] and so I shall examine it first.

To date, protection of fundamental rights in the EU has been executed in an ad hoc, incremental way, making a comprehensive overview very difficult to generate. As the Treaty of Rome contained no Bill of Rights, the ECJ has played an important role in the development of a fundamental rights jurisprudence for the EC. Although in early cases (the so-called 'sins of youth'[9]) the

---

[7] At http://europa.eu.int/comm/justice_home/unit/charte/en/welcome.html.

[8] Weiler JHH, Editorial: 'Does the European Union Truly Need a Charter of Rights?' (2000) 6 *European Law Journal* 95.

[9] See eg case 1/58 *Stork v High Authority* [1959] ECR 17; cases 36,37,38 and 40/59 *Geitling v High Authority* [1960] ECR 423; and case 40/64 *Sgarlata v Commission* [1965] ECR 215, in which the Court refused to allow the Treaty to be overridden by a plea based on fundamental rights.

European Court of Justice rejected any applications based on alleged breach of fundamental rights by the EEC Institutions, by the late 1960's and early 1970's it was forced to acknowledge such claims, and to offer protection to individuals who asserted that the EEC was infringing their fundamental rights.[10] But it did so, the popular history goes, not because of any great love for the noble ideas of human rights, but rather because the European Court feared that if it did not, some Member State courts, particularly the constitutional courts of Germany and Italy, would refuse to accord supremacy to EEC law if they found it violated fundamental rights in their own constitutions. Anything was preferable to that, so the European Court identified a respect for fundamental rights within the Community legal order itself. These fundamental rights have taken the form of *general principles of law*.

In addition to that, the European Court also named specific treaty items as fundamental rights—namely, non-discrimination on grounds of nationality in Article 12 EC and the four fundamental freedoms of goods, services, persons and capital.[11] They have also referred to equal pay (Article 141) and equal treatment as fundamental rights.[12] The new legal basis introduced by Article 13 of the TEU for non-discrimination legislation has also had its impact on fundamental rights legislation.[13] Some provisions named as fundamental rights exist as secondary legislation rather than treaty provisions—the equal treatment directive is a good example.[14]

There are yet other aspects of EU law which have most definite relevance for human rights, without providing remedies for rights violations. The new Title IV of the EC treaty concerns immigration and asylum, with the aim of establishing 'an area of freedom security and justice'. This is a highly complex area, including transitional arrangements, but rules on immigration and asylum are clearly capable of affecting individual rights. The third pillar (or what is left of it following the transfer of immigration and asylum to Title IV) concerns police and judicial cooperation in the EU, another area with a potential impact on human rights. And yet control by

---

[10] Eg case 29/69 *Stauder v City of Ulm* [1969] ECR 419.
[11] See case 240/83 *Procureur de la Republique v ADBHU* [1985] ECR 520, 531 where the Court stated 'It should be born in mind that the principles of free movement of goods and freedom of competition, together with freedom of trade as a fundamental right …' This 'elevation' is regretted by Coppell and O'Neill in 'The European Court of Justice: Taking Rights Seriously?' 29 *Common Market Law Review* (1992) at 689.
[12] Case 149/78 *Defrenne II* [1978] ECR 1365 at para 27.
[13] Art 13 reads as follows: 'the Council … may take appropriate action to combat discrimination based on sex, racial or ethnic origin, religion or belief, disability, age or sexual orientation.' The Council has now taken action under Art 13 EC—see, for example, Council Directive 2000/78/EC establishing a general framework for equal treatment in employment and occupation (27/11/00), and Council Directive 2000/43/EC implementing the principle of equal treatment between persons irrespective of racial or ethnic origin (29/06/00).
[14] Dir 76/207.

any court (ie whether national or Community courts) of these provisions is very limited.[15] And finally, the EU's external relations—presently divided between the EC treaty provisions, (such as those on development cooperation) and the second pillar of the EU, that of the Common Foreign and Security Policy, also sometimes address human rights issues.

The lack of an EU Bill of Rights for over 40 years meant that there was no definite statement within EU law of the sort to be found in the concisely worded US Bill of Rights, or even the hazier contours of the European Convention on Human Rights. For some, this may not necessarily be a disadvantage. The Victorian jurist, Dicey, stressed what he perceived to be a great advantage of the British Constitution—that individual rights had arisen by way of judge-made law, by an inductive process, rather than by the general declamations of continental charters, which left their remedies to be developed. He thus found the British system to be more stable.[16] However, the British Constitution has not always proved so satisfactory in its protection of rights (at least up until the adoption of the UK Human Rights Act) and it is suggested that, in the field of rights, it has not provided the best model for the EU.[17]

There is no clear, conceptual underpinning to the rights protected under EU law prior to the introduction of the Charter—probably because they have been developed in such an *ad hoc* way. The rights protected under EU law also take all forms—to use the terminology of the American jurist, Wesley Hohfeld, they exist as claim rights, imposing positive duties on others (ie social rights) as well as liberty rights, such as freedom of expression, powers and immunities.[18] So many things have been called 'fundamental rights' in the EU context that we seem to have an *embarrass du choix* and a choice to suit any fantasy, in the guise of what might be called, in psychoanalytic terms, a floating signifier, namely a concept which can mean whatever its interpreters wish it to.[19] As has been suggested,[20] one may have to employ some sort of definitional refinement, otherwise the fishing rights claimed by the Spanish fishermen in *Factortame* will be jurisprudentially indistinct from 'cruel and unusual punishment'. It is however, difficult to find such a refinement within the *acquis communautaire*, or more particularly, within the case law of the ECJ, a fact which has surely made the creation of an EU Charter of Rights all the more necessary.

---

[15] See Art 68 TEC and Art 35 TEU for the limited preliminary reference procedures applicable.
[16] Dicey AV, *Introduction to the Study of the Law of the Constitution* (first pub in 1885).
[17] Ewing K and Gearty C, *Freedom under Thatcher* (Oxford, 1990) for a general critique of rights protection in the UK.
[18] Hohfeld, *Fundamental Legal Conceptions* (New Haven, Yale University Press).
[19] See Barthes R, *Myth Today* (1957) for one of the first uses of the term 'empty signifier'. See also Lacan J, *Ecrits* (London, Tavistock, 1977).
[20] Ward I, *A Critical Introduction to European Law* (Butterworths, 1996) at 139.

Some would dispute that this is so. Joseph Weiler has suggested that 'the citizens of Europe appear to "suffer" from a surfeit, rather than a deficit, of judicial protection of their fundamental rights'[21] and that:

> The real problem of the Community is the absence of a human rights policy with everything this entails: a Commission, a Directorate-General, a budget and a horizontal action plan for making those rights already granted by the treaties and judicially protected ... effective.[22]

In this, both the Bar Council of England and Wales and the Law Society agreed, in the submissions which they made to the Convention.[23]

However, although the EU may lack a human rights policy,[24] surely this does not mean that it may not also have a Charter. There is a great deal to be said for a Charter of Rights as a 'road map' to human rights protection in the EU, and the several pages already spent in this paper merely introducing in a very summary form, human rights protection in the EU up to the introduction of the Charter, surely illustrates this need.

Therefore, previous incoherence regarding human rights would, I argue, be sufficient to justify the EU introducing its own Charter, although it must not to be used to divert from other essential work which needs to be done—the creation of a human rights policy and essential Commission reforms.[25] In Jonathan Swift's *Tale of a Tub* of 1704, Swift describes how sailors, encountering a whale which threatened to damage their ship, flung it an empty tub by way of amusement to divert it. In the context of the drafting of the US Bill of Rights, this passage was used as a metaphor for the situation in which Madison had proposed rights amendments rather than those designed to change the structure or essence of the new government—in this way, it was said, Leviathan was diverted and the ship of state sailed away intact.[26] Likewise in the EU we should beware of being diverted by the prospect of a Charter of Rights from the need for other urgent reforms.

---

[21] Weiler J, 'Editorial: Does the European Union Truly Need a Charter of Rights?' (2000) 6 *European Law Journal* at 95.

[22] *Ibid*, at 96.

[23] Submission by the General Council of the Bar of England and Wales, Brussels, 2 May 2000 CHARTE 4234/00 CONTRIB. 108; a contribution submitted by the Law Society of England and Wales, Brussels, 22 June 2000 (26.06) CHARTE 4380/00 CONTRIB.

[24] Although there is now a Commissioner with responsibility for human rights, and also a new Human Rights unit responsible for human rights and democracy in the DG for External relations. See also the references made by Commissioner Chris Patten at the *Human Rights Discussion Forum* in recognition that the Commission lacks a coherent strategy regarding human rights. (Report available on http://europa.eu.int/comm/dg1a/human_rights/intro.)

[25] Information about the Commission reforms is available at http://europa.eu.int/comm/reform/index.

[26] Swift J, The prose of Jonathan Swift, vol 1: *A Tale of a Tub and other early works*, Herbert Davies (ed) (Oxford, Blackwell, 1965); mentioned in *Creating the Bill of Rights: The Documentary Record for the First Federal Congress* Veit, Bowling, Bickford (eds) (Baltimore, Johns Hopkins, 1991).

There are also other reasons why a Charter might be thought necessary, and I shall deal with these briefly. First, notwithstanding Joseph Weiler's remarks regarding 'human rights saturation' in the EU, there are in fact, currently, areas in which human rights protection is not satisfactory. For example, the near absence of judicial control over the third pillar matters (PJCC) and little control over Title IV EC regarding asylum and immigration.[27] There is also the fact of continuing opaque decision-making in the EU and lack of access to information, notwithstanding continuing initiatives such as the proposed White Paper on Governance.[28] The Charter is likely to bring about improvements in both of these areas. Secondly, the ECHR, drafted over 50 years ago, although a 'dynamic'[29] instrument, is unsuitable for dealing with certain contemporary developments. In this respect, the introduction into the Charter, for example, of provisions concerning protection of personal data (Article 8) or particular rights regarding the integrity of the person in the fields of medicine and biology (Article 2) are to be welcomed.

There is also another way in which the Charter might be innovation, rather than mere confirmation. A reason given by the Commission[30] supporting the need for a Charter was that 'the European Union has entered a new and more resolutely political stage of integration'. The European Parliament, in its draft Resolution on the drawing up of the Charter in January 2000[31] described the Charter as providing the basis of an EU constitution. Such a reason might strike fear into the hearts of Eurosceptics, especially those who fear the German urge for a truly 'constitutional' IGC in 2004. But it cannot be ignored. Although the ECJ has on some occasions[32] described the treaties as a constitution of the EU, they do not look really very constitutional in nature. With a Charter of Rights incorporated, they might begin to appear more so—especially if this were done in the context of a redrafting of the treaties at an IGC in 2004, following the work of the Convention on the Future of Europe.

III.   THE CONVENTION

The name is significant. 'Convention' was the term used by those delegates who gathered in Philadelphia to draft the American Constitution. It was

---

[27] See Art 68 EC and 35 TEU regarding ability of ECJ to give preliminary rulings on these matters.

[28] Information about this is available at: http://europa.en.int/comm/governance/index.

[29] See Jacobs F, and White R, *The European Convention on Human Rights* (Oxford, Clarendon, 1996) who state (at 31): '... the interpretation of the Convention must be "dynamic" in the sense that it must be interpreted in the light of developments in social and political attitudes.'

[30] At http://europa.eu.int/comm/justice_home/unit/charte/en/FAQ.html.

[31] B5–0110/1999 OJ C54 25.02.2000 at 93.

[32] Eg in Case 249/83 *Parti Ecologiste 'Les Verts' v European Parliament* [1986] ECR 1339.

also used by gatherings during the French Revolution. The less evocative IGC is the body/structure which is used to bring about significant changes in EU law, and which has altogether a different sort of resonance—that of international law, in which sovereign states negotiate through their representatives. The term 'Convention' makes the EU Charter sound like more of a constitutional initiative.[33] Just how significant was the structure and organisation of the body which drafted the EU Charter?

There is no doubt that in some respects it was new and radical. Its parameters had been set out (but not in very great detail) in the Cologne Presidency Conclusions in June 1999 and in the Presidential Conclusions of the Tampere Council in October 1999, with regard to its composition, practical arrangements, methods and time limits. The time limit was very short—only 9 months in which to produce a Charter. According to Tampere, it was to have 62 members, drawn from 4 areas—member state governments (15), the Commission (1), the European Parliament (16) and national parliaments (30). There were also two representatives from the Court of Justice and Council of Europe (one from the Court of Human Rights) who had observer status.[34] It first convened in December 1999 and met thereafter every week.

Notably, it operated in an atmosphere of transparency, according to the principle of openness—both its hearings and documents submitted for hearings were public,[35] and the latter available on its website. Such openness was encouraging, and certainly not the case in the context of the IGC[36]— nor was it the case in the drafting of the ECHR, which proceeded by way of a committee on administrative questions which reported to the Committee of Ministers. On the other hand, the US Bill of Rights[37] was engendered in public. The press were admitted to the US House of Representatives, in which it was debated, from its first session. However, they did not have the advantage of those who follow our contemporary Charter's proceedings, having to proceed in dim light, with quill pens and poor acoustics, rather than the relative ease of web site.

The Convention's methods were unorthodox. The Praesidium (namely, the President, the Commission representative and the three Vice Presidents representing the Council, European Parliament and national parliaments)

---

[33] It is also of course the term used by the more recent body drafting a constitutional treaty for the EU. Even so, it may also bring confusion in sounding as if it refers to a human rights instrument, such as the ECHR, rather than a drafting body.

[34] The Convention's detailed membership is to be found on the European Parliament's Charter website: http://europarl.en.int/charter/composition_en.htm.

[35] Available at the Convention website, http://db.consilium.eu.int/df, which contains a large number of documents, both the Convention's working papers, and observations of various groups.

[36] Or certainly not until recently. Secrecy was one of the charges made against the 1996 IGC which preceded the Treaty of Amsterdam.

[37] Unlike the Philadelphia Convention, which drafted the US Constitution of 1787, which proceeded without publicity, reports of which were not even published until considerably later.

would put forward a proposal which would be extensively debated in the Convention itself, with the aim of reaching consensus without a formal vote. It succeeded in producing a final text in 9 months. In both its transparency and working methods it set a fine example to the 2000 ongoing IGC.

However, other aspects of the Convention's processes might have seemed less encouraging. As already stated, its terms of reference were not particularly clear or precise—being simply those set out by the European Councils at Cologne and Tampere.[38] Therefore it is not surprising that members of the Convention had different ideas about what they were doing. For its President, Roman Herzog,[39] the Charter was not of constitutional importance—rather its significance lay in raising rights awareness in Europe. Others such as Inigo Mendes de Vigo, the chairman of the European Parliament's delegation, saw it as an important constitutional step towards a federal Europe.[40]

Furthermore, the Convention provided an institutional (if we are to count national governments, which were well-represented) response to the need for a Charter.

However, even if national and the European Parliaments were well represented, civil society had no place on the Convention itself. Neither NGOs nor human rights experts had a place on it. This did not, however, mean that civil society had no voice. For example, 70 associations representing various interests (Churches, trade unions, asylum, gays and others) took part in a hearing on 27 April 2000, and then most of these produced a written submission. But there was no requirement for the Convention actually to heed their views, although it did apparently do so in at least some cases—for example, that of the European trade unions.[41] On the other hand, there was no parliamentary selection process (in the UK at least) for the governmental and parliamentary representatives on the Convention.[42] The Charter was not debated in the UK Parliament and the average person knew very little, if anything, of it. One commentator[43] has remarked on the irony of Lord Goldsmith, selected by the Government, telling us what our

---

[38] The relevant provisions of which are set out as an annex to this conference paper.

[39] Former German President from 1994–1999, and President of the German Constitutional Court 1987–94.

[40] As cited in House of Commons Research Paper 00/32 20 Mar 2000, 'Human Rights in the EC: the Charter of Fundamental Rights' at p 24.

[41] *Ibid.*

[42] The UK's representatives were Lord Goldsmith (for the Government) Lord Bowness (for the House of Lords) and Wyn Griffiths (for the House of Commons). Andrew Duff MEP commented that the representative of national parliaments on the Convention were somewhat of a 'curiosity'—unlike the EP representatives (whose Constitutional Affairs committee had prepared them for it) they had no mandate, simply putting forward their own views. See HL select committee on EU affairs 67 24 May 2000, 'The EU Charter of Fundamental Rights'.

[43] Professor Conor Gearty, at the Conference on the Charter at King's College London, October 2000, also was referring to 'some sort of Platonic guardianship' at work.

rights are. Some[44] saw the 9 month time span as far too short both for adequate preparation and consultation. However, it was a much longer time than was taken for the drafting of the US Constitution in Philadelphia—only from June–September 1787, although half as long as the time taken for the drafting of the European Convention on Human Rights (which however was volleyed back and forward through debate in the Council of Europe Parliamentary Assembly, as well as its Committee of Ministers).

The Convention was provided with administrative assistance—this was mainly provided by the General Secretariat of the Council of Ministers, and headed by JP Jacqué, a senior legal adviser to the Council. Jacqué had produced an earlier, conservatively worded legal opinion, concerning the EU's lack of competence to legislate in the field of human rights, and this may have influenced the views of the Convention regarding the potential of the Charter to create new rights.[45]

Nonetheless, innovative though its methods were, the Charter cannot be said to have been a generally participatory document, being the preserve of the institutions, and so it is not surprising that it failed to produce a strong sense of the citizen, grounded in participatory democracy. In this respect it may be contrasted with the South African Constitution, which given the participatory way in which it was drafted, brought about a wider-felt ownership.[46]

IV.   THE LEGAL EFFECT OF THE CHARTER

The Charter is not currently legally binding, although it may become so. According to Declaration 23 on the Future of the Union attached to the Treaty of Nice:

4.   Following a report to be drawn up for the European Council in Göteborg in June 2001, the European Council, at its meeting in Laeken/Brussels in December 2001, will agree on a declaration containing appropriate initiatives for the continuation of this process.

5.   The process should address, inter alia, the following questions:
   —   how to establish and monitor a more precise delimitation of powers between the European Union and the Member States, reflecting the principle of subsidiarity;

---

[44] For example, the British Institute of Human Rights, cited in HL select committee on EU affairs 67 24 May 2000, 'The EU Charter of Fundamental Rights.'
[45] See discussion in Weiler and Fries 'A human rights policy for the European Community and Union: the Question of Competencies' in Alston (ed) *The EU and Human Rights* (Oxford, OUP, 1999). See also G de Burca, 'The Drafting of the European Union Charter of Fundamental Rights' (2001) 26 *European Law Review* 126 at 135.
[46] *Human Rights Discussion Forum* paper at p 22.

— the status of the Charter of Fundamental Rights of the European Union, proclaimed in Nice, in accordance with the conclusions of the European Council in Cologne;

There has been a clear division of opinion between those who wish to see the Charter binding and those who do not. Among the former we may cite the Commission[47] which has stated its belief that the Charter 'is destined to be incorporated sooner or later into the treaties,' and among the latter, the UK government—Tony Blair, for example, stating in November 2000, 'The Charter is simply a statement of policy and the UK is not the only member state to oppose something of a binding legal nature'. (Surely there is something somewhat ironic about this pronouncement—support being given by the UK government for the Charter only if it had no effect).

There is also a link to be drawn between the legal status of the Charter and the future issue of the reorganisation of the treaties and the move toward a formal EU constitution. The Convention on the Future of the EU, chaired by Giscard d'Estaing, incorporated the Charter into its constitutional treaty and recommended that it be legally binding.[48] The Commission also posited a very close link between the reorganisation of the treaties and the inclusion of the Charter in them.[49] So it might seem that the issue of the Charter's legal status might be divided up—pre-2004 and post 2004, although the debate referred to in the Declaration attached to the Nice treaty has already commenced, with the contributions about the future of EU made by Gerhard Schroeder in late April 2001.[50]

In any case, the Charter was drafted from the outset 'as if' incorporated into the treaties, drafted in a formal way, as a document suitable for incorporation into the Treaties, even although the Convention did not know what the final outcome would be—they left the choice to the European Council.

Regardless of its legal status, the Charter has already begun to have a legal impact. In Case C–173/99 *BECTU v Secretary of State for Trade and Industry*, AG Tizzano spoke of the Charter as a 'substantive point of reference' and in Case C–270/99 P *Z v European Parliament* AG Jacobs stated of the Charter, 'whilst itself not legally binding, [it] proclaims a generally recognized principle ...' Therefore, although both AG's recognised that it was not legally binding, they stated that this did not mean that it could not have legal consequences. They saw it at the very least as enumerating in a systematic way those rights which are part of the Community *acquis*.

---

[47] Commission communication on 'The legal nature of the Charter', Brussels 11.10.2000 COM (2000) 644 Final.
[48] See convention website at: http://european-convention.en.int.
[49] 'The legal nature of the Charter', Brussels 11.10.2000 COM (2000) 644 Final.
[50] Eg 'Germany wants EC to be Government', *The Guardian* 1/05/01.

The Charter has since been referred to on a number of occasions, including by the Court of Justice in the *British American Tobacco* case in December 2002.

The European Parliament has also made its contribution concerning the effect of the Charter. In a report on 'The Treaty of Nice and the future of the EU', the Parliament has stated:

> The fact that it is not incorporated into the treaty does not in any way mean that the Charter will not have an effect: a political effect as demonstrated by the references to the Charter in the report ... on the situation in Austria; a legislative effect stemming from the firm commitment given by the Parliament and the Commission to regard the Charter as an essential reference point to be included in all the legislation; or jurisdictional effects as evidenced by the first judgments delivered by the German and Spanish constitutional courts, which use the Charter as a reference point.

This is all very well. It indicates that the Charter will have, for the next couple of years at least a fairly high status of soft law. Its affect will not be negligible. However, as a public statement, the message presented is not optimal. The Charter will subsist, in some sort of legal twilight, albeit as a reference point for the citizen, a clearer statement than previously existed, but with its status as a proclamation revealing a lack of confidence on the part of the EU and its Member States about citizens' rights, and the relationship between the individual and authorities in the European legal space. There are already enough such Solemn Declarations on human rights by EU institutions. On a symbolic level this says much. It carries forward the ambiguities and ambivalence which has characterised the very sui generis process of European constitutionalism over the past 15 years or so. If we wish to know why the European public still makes so little of its status as a European citizenry, we need look no further than the status of the Charter proclaimed in December 2000.

V.   THE CONTENT OF THE CHARTER

There are plenty of rights here. The Charter has for example at least twice as many rights as the Declaration of Fundamental Rights adopted by the European Parliament in 1989.[51] The 50 rights in the Charter are set out in six Chapters, with the headings Dignity, Freedoms, Equality, Solidarity, Citizens'

---

[51] EP Resolution adopting the Declaration of Fundamental Rights and Freedoms Doc A2–3/89 OJ C 120/51. See also the Draft Constitution of the European Union adopted by the European Parliament in 1994 which contained a section on human rights largely based on its earlier 1989 Declaration—A3–0064/94 OJ C 61/166.

rights and Justice—names that are 'meaningful and easy to remember.'[52] Each of the Charter's 50 rights are taken from a 'precursor' text—such as the ECHR, the European Social Charter, the Community Charter of Social Rights of Workers, common constitutional traditions, rulings of the ECJ and Court of Human Rights, as well as international conventions of the Council of Europe, UN and ILO. Some of the rights are specifically introduced to deal with contemporary problems—such as protection of personal data, given the proliferation of information about persons in the more barrier-free Europe[53] or new innovations in bioethics.

However, the Charter is innovative in containing, in the same instrument, both economic and social rights along with the more traditional civil and political rights, which has never been done before in an international human rights instrument. In this way the Charter presents in sharpest relief the *indivisibility* of human rights.[54]

At a first glance, the Charter might seem to present a series of rights founded on an agreeable view of society, and of the worth of human beings. For too long it has been possible to charge EU law with being over-preoccupied with commercial interests and with rights of the 'market citizens'. Norbert Reich has suggested that:

> The economic rights of market citizens are certainly the nucleus of any rights granted by the European Community or Union ... the European Constitution might thus be said to resemble a Russian doll which at its core contains a basic (economic) structure, but which has several layers of dress around it which show us the true shape of the figure.[55]

Therefore, it is encouraging to see that economic and social rights have been included in the Charter, even against the wishes of industry and employers' groups.[56] It also counters the views of those who believe that economic and social rights are of a singular nature and difficult to incorporate into human rights documents because of the positive action which they require of governments.[57] Such rights address the concerns of everyday people and the inclusion of rights recognising the fundamental status of workers rights in the Community Charter is important. The rights of solidarity set out in Chapter IV have an impressive breadth and scope.

---

[52] Editorial, (2001) *Common Market Law Review*.
[53] Eg Schengen Information System, Europol data bases.
[54] Commission Communication in the Nature of the Charter 'The legal nature of the Charter', Brussels 11.10.2000 COM (2000) 644 Final.
[55] Reich N *A European Constitution for Citizens* (1997) European Law Journal 131–64.
[56] Eg CBI submission to the Convention on the Charter—12 April 2000, CHARTE 4226/00 CONTRIB 101.
[57] See eg the views of Schermers in giving evidence to the House of Lords select committee, noted in their report no 67 2000. Also submissions of the CBI CHARTE 4226/00 CONTRIB 101.

John Rawls has in his later works, expounded a theory based on 'public reason'. According to Rawls, the 'burdens of judgement' (namely, causes and sources of disagreement) ensure that there will be reasonable disagreement in society.[58] In such circumstances, Rawls suggests that the citizen will accept the value of reaching agreement based on public principles of justice, thereby forming an 'overlapping consensus', in spite of lacking a shared comprehensive account of the good. Rawls therefore defines political liberalism as a 'public culture as a shared fund of implicitly recognised basic ideas and principles.'[59] And because such an overlapping consensus lacks a comprehensive foundation, it may escape charges levelled at other liberal doctrine, such as Rawls' own earlier theory of justice, or some rights-based political theories, such as those of Nozick, of being too universalising and thus unsuitable for a culturally plural society such as the EU.

Such an overlapping consensus might be identified in the context of the EU. Principles such as citizenship, human rights (Article 6 TEU refers to the 'common constitutional traditions of the member states') respect for democracy and the rule of law, suggest some sort of existing, public, normative consensus in the EU which goes beyond the desirability of economic efficiency and free markets. The Charter seems to be a further such example, taking what is perceived as best from the common European heritage of human rights. Such shared principles operate perhaps only as a bare minimum but might be, as La Torre suggests, suitable for what in MacCormick's terms is the 'mixed commonwealth' of the EU.[60]

Specific Problems

However, there are significant problems which indicate that the Charter might promise more than it can return. The first of these is the often opaque language in which its provisions are drafted—although opaque language is nothing new in EU law. Article 29 states that 'Everyone has a right of access to a free placement service'. In the Explanatory note for the Praesidium,[61] this provision is stated to be based on Article 1(3) of the European Social Charter and point 13 of the Community Charter of the Fundamental Social Rights of Workers. It relates to a practice apparently used in Scandinavia but hardly transparent to Anglo-Saxons, and of sweeping generality in any case.

---

[58] Rawls J, *Political Liberalism* 55.
[59] Rawls above n 58 at 8.
[60] See La Torre Massimo, 'Legal Pluralism as an evolutionary achievement of Community law', Ratio Juris June 1999 and MacCormick N, 'Sovereignty, Democracy and Subsidiarity' in *Questioning Sovereignty* (Oxford 1999).
[61] CHARTE 4473/00 Text of the Explanations relating to the complete text of the Charter as set out in CHARTE 4487/00 and CONVENT 50, of 11/10/00.

Another opaquely drafted provision is Article 36, concerning 'Access to services of general economic interest' which states that:

> The Union recognizes and respects access to services of general economic interest as provided for in national laws and practices, in accordance with the Treaty establishing the European Community, in order to promote the social and territorial cohesion of the Union.

Once again, the explanatory notes of the Presidium are not illuminating, merely stating:

> This Article fully respects Article 16 of the Treaty establishing the European Community and does not create any new right. It merely sets out the principle of respect by the Union for the access to services of general economic interest as provided for by national provisions, when those provisions are compatible with Community legislation.

Likewise Article 38—'Union policies shall ensure a high level of protection'. Again vague in the extreme and not drafted in terms of rights at all.

A second problem pertaining to the provisions on rights of solidarity concerns the way in which some of them are highly qualified. Article 27 for example, provides for a 'Workers' right to information and consultation within the undertaking' but this is only to be 'in the cases and under the conditions provided for by Community law and national laws and practices'. Similarly for Articles 28, 34, 35 and 36. A general limitations clause set out in Article 52[62] applies to the rights in chapter 4 (as it does to the rights in the other chapters).

Another fundamental problem stems from the history of the Community courts' interpretation of fundamental rights, rather than from the drafting of the Charter. As the Charter contains no new rights and is not yet legally binding, there is no reason to believe that, for the time being, the Community courts will make a radical departure from their past approach to the issue of fundamental rights. The most highly developed aspect of EU rights protection is the right to economic activity, closely linked with 'market' citizenship[63]—political and social rights have been far less developed. The Community courts sometimes seem quite uncertain about the status of

---

[62] Any limitation on the exercise of the rights and freedoms recognised by this Charter must be provided for by law and respect the essence of those rights and freedoms. Subject to the principle of proportionality, limitations may be made only if they are necessary and genuinely meet objectives of general interest recognised by the Union or the need to protect the rights and freedoms of others.

[63] See Sionaidh Douglas-Scott 'In Search of European Union Citizenship' (1998) *Yearbook of European Law*. Although the ECJ has recently been willing to derive rights based on a very distant link to market activity—see case C–60/00 *Carpenter* [2002] ECR I–6279.

[64] Case T–96/92 *Comité Centrale d'Entreprise de la Societé Generale des Grands Sources v Commission* [1995] ECR II–1727.

social rights—in *Comité Centrale*[64] the CFI was less sure of its handling of the rights of workers to keep their jobs, and of their representatives to be consulted, than in the case of its usual more confident handling of property rights. The *Comité des Sages* were appointed by the Commission to look into civic and social rights in 1995. In their report they argued that if the EU was to become:

> an original political entity, it must have a clear statement of the citizenship it is offering to its members. Inclusion of civil and social rights in the treaty would help to nurture that citizenship and prevent the EU being perceived as a bureaucracy assembled by technocratic elites far removed from daily concerns.[65]

A stress on free market rights and interests can sit uneasily with fundamental rights protection—in most constitutions and international rights documents greater priority is given to civil and political rights. They make no appearance in the US Bill of Rights, and little more in the ECHR, where the right to property in protocol 1 has just recently come to the awareness of the rights bearing public. Coppell and O'Neill, in a now famous article, commented:

> It would seem, then that there is no distinction and hence no hierarchical relationship being posited by the European Court between the basic human rights outlined, for example, in the European Convention on Human Rights and the free market rights arising out of the treaties of the European Community.[66]

The basis of the EU Single Market was that of an ordoliberal economic theory of the market—but one in which market freedoms are seen as intrinsic to the notion of human dignity, as well as upholding the theory of contract and private property rights.[67] Thus, rather than uplifting the economic rights to the same status as a right to human dignity, it might be said that, under this vision, human dignity is achieved by the functioning of a free and equal market society. Under ordoliberalism, which is closely related to

---

[65] Report of the Comité des Sages, *For a Europe of Civic and Social Rights*, chaired by Maria Lourdes Pintasilgo, Brussels 95–96.

[66] Coppell and O'Neill 'The European Court of Justice: Taking Rights Seriously?' *Common Market Law Review* at 669. See also see also EJ Mestmacker, 'On the Legitimacy of European Law' (1994) 58 RabelsZ 615, and EU Petersmann, 'Proposals for a new Constitution of the European Union: Building Blocks for a Constitutional Theory and Constitutional Law of the EU' (1995) 32 *Common Market Law Review* 1123.

[67] See Petersmann 'National Constitutions, Foreign trade policy and European Community law' 5 *European Journal of International Law* 1992 1; see also Chalmers D, 'The Single Market: from prima donna to journeyman' in Shaw and more (eds) *New Legal Dynamics of the European Union in Shaw and More* (1996) who suggests that the European Court is now less influenced by ordoliberal theory than in its early days.

[68] Hayek, *The Road to Serfdom* (London, ARK).

the neoliberalism of Hayek[68] the protection of a free and equal society ensures prevention of the atrocities of Nazi Germany and the like. Economic rights are secured in return for our surrender of our natural state, in the belief (or perhaps, 'fantasy') that society can be unified and rationally organised—a promise which may remain undelivered. And it is questionable whether it is sufficient for a 21st century EU which has moved beyond a common market. The EU must avoid the danger of what Terry Eagleton has termed 'commercial humanism', by which the citizen is defined not by political virtue but by rights to and in things.[69] This is easily done in the EU if there is too great a focus on market rights and market citizenship. It is to be hoped that the Community courts will develop greater confidence in their handling of social rights if the Charter is to make any impact.

On the other hand, one might point to some more positive aspects of the Charter. First, Article 53 which states that:

Nothing in this Charter shall be interpreted as restricting or adversely affecting human rights and fundamental freedoms as recognized, in their respective fields of application, by Union law and international law and by international agreements to which the Union, the Community or all the Member States are party, including the European Convention for the Protection of Human Rights and Fundamental Freedoms, and by the Member States' constitutions.

What does this provision amount to? Does it mean that Charter rights must meet as a minimum the rights referred to in the texts included in Article 53? Are those texts then incorporated into the Charter by reference? Is this not suggested by the wording of the Preamble, which refers not only to the need to 'strengthen the protection of fundamental rights' but also 'reaffirms' the 'rights as they result' from a number of international obligations common to the Member States including the Social Charters adopted by the Community and by the Council of Europe?[70]

Additionally, Article 51 requires EU institutions to 'respect the rights, observe the principles and promote the application thereof in accordance with their respective powers'—this apparently placing on them a positive obligation to promote these rights—a rather bizarre requirement, given that the Charter is not supposed to introduce any new tasks for the EU in the human rights field.

---

[69] Eagleton T, *Marx* (Routledge 1999).
[70] The international agreements referred to in Art 53 'to which ... all the member States are party' are:
    ILO Convention 87 (Freedom of Association and Protection of the Right to Organise)
    ILO Convention 98 (Right to Organise and Collective Bargaining Convention)
    ILO Declaration on Fundamental Principles and Rights at Work 1998
    Council of Europe Social Charter of 1961 (ratified by all EU member states, though not all have accepted all of its provisions).

All in all, a short scrutiny of the rights contained in the Charter raises a mixed response—some reasons to be cheerful, for example the inclusion of social rights. However, this author has reservations as to what might be accomplished by their inclusion—there are still opportunities for the Court to continue with its past, market focused appreciation of fundamental rights.

VI.   SCOPE

Article 51 raises difficult questions. It reads as follows:

> The provisions of this Charter are addressed to the institutions and bodies of the Union with due regard for the principle of subsidiarity and to the Member States only when they are implementing Union law...

But what exactly is covered by Member States in the act of implementing EU law? As Laws J commented in *First City Trading*[71] 'This is a deep question. It concerns the depth of the Community's bite.'[72] In the *ERT*[73] case the ECJ stated that: 'as soon as any such legislation enters *the field of application* of Community law this Court is sole arbiter in this matter'. Therefore is it the case that the only actions which the ECJ might decline to vet would be those falling within the Member States' exclusive jurisdiction? This had seemed to be the interpretation of Advocate General van Gerven in the *Grogan* case who stated:

> Once a national rule is involved which has effects in an area covered by Community law ... then the appraisal of that rule no longer falls within the exclusive jurisdiction of the national legislator.

This is a very wide interpretation indeed. Given the scope and width of Community law it may conceivably come into contact with just about any area of national law.

Laws J in *First City Trading*, was unwilling to extend the scope of Community competence this far, preferring to stick to situations in which the national authorities were implementing or derogating from Community law:

> The fact that a legal problem has arisen as a result of the adoption of Community rules is in my view, not in itself sufficient to entail that the

---

[71] *R v Min. of Agriculture ex parte First City Trading* [1997] 1 CMLR 250.
[72] At para 24.
[73] Case 260/89 *ERT* [1991] ECR 2925.

solution adopted for that problem by the national authorities must necessarily respect fundamental rights applying in the Community legal order.[74]

However, he added significantly that there was additionally, a 'fundamentally different kind of legal obligation ... the duty to apply the Treaty.'(para 40). This would cover provisions like the prohibition on discrimination on grounds of nationality which would apply whatever the context.[75] However, this is a decision of the English court, rather than of the ECJ.

There are other questions regarding the scope of the Charter. The following are some examples. Title IV of the EC treaty refers to 'Visas, Asylum, Immigration and Other Policies related to the Free Movement of Persons'. Asylum is an area which potentially raises many fundamental rights issues. Does the fact that there is now some EC competence in this area mean that the Charter may apply to all asylum issues? Will any asylum law case become a case of EC law? Secondly, the reasonably extensive provisions in the Charter regarding economic and social rights would seem to be superfluous if they apply only in the context of staff employed by the European Union? Surely they must apply in the context of employment situations throughout the EU (in the same way as for example Article 141 EC) otherwise they can hardly be said to be really fundamental?

There are also some other questions regarding *scope*. Beyond the issue of Member State liability there is that of *which* EU and Member State bodies are covered by the Charter. In the context of Member States there is the question of how to define public authorities. It is suggested that the existing case law of the ECJ in the context of horizontal/ vertical direct effect might be applied in this context—ie *Foster v British Gas*.[76] Related issues might apply in the EU context. Will the Charter apply not only to formal EU institutions but to entities established within the framework of the EU context, such as Europol? Surely it must do so?

Secondly, should individuals be bound by the Charter? It is not usual for international human rights documents to bind individuals, although the issue of *drittwirkung* is complex. The appropriate course here might be that followed in the UK's Human Rights Act, namely to impose obligations on Public Authorities and to leave it up to the courts themselves as public authorities to decide whether and how to give horizontal effect.[77] Also, The South African Constitution of 1996 and its concept of *mittelbaredrittwirkung* might be cited here, namely that human rights have an indirect impact on the

---

[74] At para 35.
[75] See Case C–274/96 *Bickel* [1998] ECR I–7637.
[76] Case C–188/89 [1990] ECR I 3313. The test was set out by the ECJ para 20 of this judgement, in which it stayed that a public body was '... a body, whatever its legal form, which has been made responsible, pursuant to a measure adopted by the State, for providing a public service under the control of the State and has for that purpose special powers beyond those which result from the normal rules applicable in relations between individuals, is included in any event ...'
[77] Cf the decisions of the ECJ as indirect effect eg Case 14/83 *von Colson* [1984] ECR 1891.

development of all jurisprudence by means of a constitutional requirement that 'when developing the common law ... every court must promote the spirit, purport and objectives of the Bill of Rights'.[78]

VII.   CONCLUSIONS

The last issues border on the arcane. There will be time enough to deal with them if and when the Charter becomes binding. However, the main thrust of this paper has been concerned not so much with specific legal issues of scope as with more general, constitutional issues of the Charter's effect. It must become more than a showcase, and the protection of rights contained in it more comprehensive than the past focus on market rights if fundamental rights in the EU are not to be allowed to become the phenomena of 'smoke and mirrors' derided by Karl Marx.[79]

---

[78] Ref made by the General Council of the Bar (in CHARTE 4234/00) to a plea, made by Sidney Kentridge QC in Kentridge 'Lessons from South Africa' in Markesinis (ed) *The Impact of the Human Rights Bill on English Law* (Oxford, OUP, 1999).
[79] 'On the Jewish Question', republished in Waldron J (ed) *Nonsense on Stilts* (London, Methuen 1987).

ANNEX

Cologne: Conclusions of the Presidency June 1999

Protection of fundamental rights is a founding principle of the Union and an indispensable prerequisite for her legitimacy. The obligation of the Union to respect fundamental rights has been confirmed and defined by the jurisprudence of the European Court of Justice. There appears to be a need, at the present stage of the Union's development, to establish a Charter of fundamental rights in order to make their overriding importance and relevance more visible to the Union's citizens.

The European Council believes that this Charter should contain the fundamental rights and freedoms as well as basic procedural rights guaranteed by the European Convention for the Protection of Human Rights and Fundamental Freedoms and derived from the constitutional traditions common to the Member States, as general principles of Community law. The Charter should also include the fundamental rights that pertain only to the Union's citizens. In drawing up such a Charter account should furthermore be taken of economic and social rights as contained in the European Social Charter and the Community Charter of the Fundamental Social Rights of Workers (Article 136 TEC), insofar as they do not merely establish objectives for action by the Union.

In the view of the European Council, a draft of such a Charter of Fundamental Rights of the European Union should be elaborated by a body composed of representatives of the Heads of State and Government and of the President of the Commission as well as of members of the European Parliament and national parliaments. Representatives of the European Court of Justice should participate as observers. Representatives of the Economic and Social Committee, the Committee of the Regions and social groups as well as experts should be invited to give their views. Secretariat services should be provided by the General Secretariat of the Council.

This body should present a draft document in advance of the European Council in December 2000. The European Council will propose to the European Parliament and the Commission that, together with the Council, they should solemnly proclaim on the basis of the draft document a European Charter of Fundamental Rights. It will then have to be considered whether and, if so, how the Charter should be integrated into the treaties. The European Council mandates the General Affairs Council to take the necessary steps prior to the Tampere European Council.

Tampere Conclusions of the Presidency October 1999

ANNEX
B.   WORKING METHODS OF THE BODY

i)   Preparation
The Chairperson of the Body shall, in close concertation with the Vice-Chairpersons, propose a work plan for the Body and perform other appropriate preparatory work.

ii)   Transparency of the proceedings
In principle, hearings held by the Body and documents submitted at such hearings should be public.

iii)   Working groups
The Body may establish ad hoc working groups, which shall be open to all members of the Body.

iv)   Drafting
On the basis of the work plan agreed by the Body, a Drafting Committee composed of the Chairperson, the Vice-Chairpersons and the representative of the Commission and assisted by the General Secretariat of the Council, shall elaborate a preliminary Draft Charter, taking account of drafting proposals submitted by any member of the Body. Each of the three Vice-Chairpersons shall regularly consult with the respective component part of the Body from which he or she emanates.

v)   Elaboration of the Draft Charter by the Body
When the Chairperson, in close concertation with the Vice-Chairpersons, deems that the text of the draft Charter elaborated by the Body can eventually be subscribed to by all the parties, it shall be forwarded to the European Council through the normal preparatory procedure.

C.   PRACTICAL ARRANGEMENTS

The Body shall hold its meetings in Brussels, alternately in the Council and the European Parliament buildings.

A complete language regime shall be applicable for sessions of the Body.

17

A German View on the Charter: The Effect on the Bundesverfassungsgericht[1]

JÜRGEN SCHWARZE*

I. INTRODUCTION

T HE TITLE OF my chapter states that I will present *a* German view on the Charter. In Germany, like almost everywhere else, the views of lawyers hardly ever coincide – at least not completely. This is also true concerning a matter which has often been regarded as a typical German problem or to use the less diplomatic French expression: *une querelle allemande*: the need for a proper dogmatic concept of the protection of human rights in EC law.

In the first part, I will follow the title of my statement to the letter and illustrate the legal effect of the Charter of Fundamental Rights of the EU in the German Constitutional Court (*Bundesverfassungsgericht*) in a narrow sense. In the second part, I would like to extend my report, if I may, and talk about the general acceptance of the Charter in Germany in a broader sense. Finally, in the third part, I will conclude with a personal statement on the Charter.

II. EFFECT OF THE CHARTER ON THE *BUNDESVERFASSUNGSGERICHT*

The effect of the Charter on the *Bundesverfassungsgericht* evidently depends on its legal status (1) and its scope (2). Those are the main legal

---

* Professor, University of Freiburg.
[1] This article was already completed in June 2001. Nevertheless a few remarks concerning the later developments until June 2003 have been included (see fn 10a, 13a and 47a).

factors that determine the influence of the Charter on the jurisdiction of the *Bundesverfassungsgericht* (3).

1.   Legal Status of the Charter

The legal status of the Charter and the question of its force were deliberately left unresolved at its solemn proclamation during the European Council meeting in Nice from 7 to 9 December 2000.[1a] According to the Presidency Conclusions of the Nice summit, the question of the Charter's force, as well as the topics concerning a better delimitation and division of competences, better transparency of the Treaty's system and the increased role of the national parliaments in the European integration process, make up the four so-called 'post-Nice' questions. Their solution has been left on the agenda for the next intergovernmental conference in 2004.[2]

When starting the project of a Charter of Fundamental Rights of the European Union at Cologne in June 1999, the European Council already made it clear, that this Charter would not be part of the *acquis communautaire*.[3] According to the Presidency Conclusions of Cologne, the drawing up of the Charter should be facilitated by the fact that it was not to be established as a legally binding part of the Treaties right from the beginning. The question of the Charter's legal effect was intended to be considered later. Hence, the Convent, the body that elaborated the draft of the Charter, was not supposed to create something completely new or innovative. Its task was rather to sum up the existing rules and ideas about fundamental rights in the EU. This marks a major benefit of the Charter: the concentration of the Member States' human rights' traditions in one document.

However, from the outset the Convent tried to draft the Charter in a way which would make possible the Charter's integration into the Treaties or its conversion into other forms of a legally binding force.[4] Thus, the Convent in a way followed Kant's categorical imperative, acting on the maxim that the result could serve as a general rule.

Hence, from the beginning the Charter of Fundamental Rights was intended merely to be solemnly proclaimed.[5] If the European Council had intended to provide the Charter with a legally binding force, it would have stated that explicitly in the drawing up of such a charter. However, it deliberately did not do so.

[1a] Presidency Conclusions, Nice European Council Meeting, I. 2.; SN 400/00.
See also J Schwarze, 'The birth of a European constitutional order – Résumé', in J Schwarze (ed), *The birth of a European constitutional order*, (Baden-Baden/London 2001), pp 562 *et seq.*
[2] K H Fischer, *Der Vertrag von Nizza*, (Baden-Baden, 2001), pp 77, 269.
[3] K H Fischer, *Der Vertrag von Nizza*, (Baden-Baden, 2001), p 263.
[4] R Herzog, Interview in *Spiegel* 25 / 2000, p 42 at p 46.
[5] Annex IV to the Presidency Conclusions of the Cologne European Council, SN 150/99.

Therefore, it is uncontested that the Charter does not have a legally binding force at the present time. Additionally, the European Council in Nice has not adopted a resolution to add a reference to the Charter into the existing Article 6 paragraph 2 EU as another point of orientation for the standard of human rights' protection in the EU besides the rules of the ECHR and the inherent common constitutional principles of the Member States.

Furthermore, even by interpreting the proclamation of the Charter as a self-obligation for the institutions and bodies of the Union, one could hardly come to a different conclusion. In my view, no form of self-imposed commitment in Community law could lead to the result that the Charter would have legal effect in contradiction to the express original intention.

However, in the future the European Court of Justice might well refer to the Charter at least in order to confirm the legal conclusions which it found to exist on the basis of Article 6 paragraph 2 EU.[6]

In this context one could think of the *Hauer*[7] decision as a precedent. In this case which is—as you all know—of major importance for the development of human rights' protection in the Community, the European Court of Justice referred to the Common Declaration of 1977[8] in its reasoning. This Common Declaration was established by the European Parliament, the Council and the Commission of the EC to underline the importance of fundamental rights in the EC, shortly before the decision of the European Court of Justice was reached.

However, one should bear in mind that the Charter has specific features which ought to be distinguished from the Common Declaration of 1977: its legal status has deliberately been left unresolved. Therefore, the extent to which the European Court of Justice may refer to it in its future judgments is questionable.

In my view this may only be the case insofar as the Charter can be seen as one source amongst others for the existing standard of human rights' protection in the EU.[9]

Meanwhile, the Court of First Instance in a first reference to the Charter in February 2001 refused to apply it in an antitrust case.[10] The case dealt with the extent to which a company is entitled to refuse the disclosure of information because of the risk of self-incrimination. The Court of First Instance explained the refusal of application of the Charter by the fact that the Charter was proclaimed on 7 December 2000 whereas the contested measure, the Commission's request for information, had been taken earlier.

[6] See C Grabenwarter, 'Die Charta der Grundrechte für die Europäische Union', *DVBL* 2001, p 1 at p 11.
[7] Case C–44/79 *Hauer* [1979] ECR 3727, para 15.
[8] OJ EC, C 103/1 of 27 April 1977.
[9] See also Case C–340/99 *TNT Traco SpA v Poste Italiane SpA*, conclusions by Advocate General Alber of 1 February 2001, n 95. AG Alber referred to the Charter as one source for fundamental values and principles of the EC.
[10] Case T–112/98 *Mannesmannröhren-Werke AG* [2001] ECR II–729, para 76.

Thus, by deliberately leaving open the question as to what the result would have been if the Commission's request had taken place after 7 December 2000, the Court may again face the question of the Charter's relevance to current Community law.[10a]

2. Scope of the Charter

According to its wording in Article 51 paragraph 1, 'the provisions of this Charter are addressed to the institutions and bodies of the Union ... and to the Member States only when they are implementing Union law'. Hence, the Charter does not create a standard of control for Member States acting in the field of their own national competences.[11]

As stated in Article 51 paragraph 2, it 'does not establish any new power or task for the Community or the Union, or modify powers and tasks defined by the Treaties'. This specific regulation has deliberately been included in the Charter to increase its chances of acceptance, in particular in Germany.

Therefore, one can say that the intention of the Charter is to commit the law of the European Union, which is of growing importance for the citizens, to a catalogue of fundamental rights, rather than to extend the scope of European law.[12]

3. Jurisdiction of the *Bundesverfassungsgericht*

In summing up this account so far one can draw the following conclusion: because of the lack of legally binding force and because of its limited scope the proclaimed Charter of Fundamental Rights of the European Union does not directly affect the jurisdiction of the *Bundesverfassungsgericht*. On the contrary, the Court stays fully and solely responsible for defining and applying the standard of fundamental rights stated in the German Basic Law for the control of the exercise of public power in Germany.

Up until now, one can only speculate as to whether the *Bundesverfassungsgericht* will refer to the Charter when the next opportunity to make

[10a] In fact, since that time both the ECJ and the CFI have pointed out that the Charter of Fundamental Rights of the European Union does confirm general principles of Community law, such as the right to an effective remedy or the principle of good administration (Case C–232/02 P (R) *Commission v Technische Glaswerke Ilmenau GmbH* [2002] ECR I–8977, para 85; Case T–54/99 *max.mobil Telekommunikation Service GmbH v Commission* [2002] ECR II–313, para 48; Case T–177/01 *Jégo-Quéré et Cie SA v Commission* [2002] ECR II–2365, para 42; Case T–211/02 *Tideland Signal Limited v Commission* [2002] ECR II–3781, para 37; Joined cases T–377/00, T–379/00, T–380/00, T–260/01 and T–272/01 *Philip Morris International Inc. et al v Commission* [2003] not yet reported, para 122).
[11] C Engel, *The European Charter of Fundamental Rights*, (Bonn, 2001), p 13.
[12] R Herzog, Interview in *Spiegel* 25 / 2000, p 42 at p 42.

a statement on the standard of human rights' protection on Community level presents itself. This might be the case if an additional protection of fundamental rights from acts of Community institutions and bodies were questioned once again.[13]

Furthermore, according to the jurisdiction of the *Bundesverfassungsgericht*, the Community act of a proclamation may not only have an internal effect in Community law but also affect the legal relation between the Community and its Member States. With reference to the Common Declaration of 1977, the *Bundesverfassungsgericht* declared such a proclamation to be 'a clear affirmation of the institutions' intention to apply the Treaties'; therefore it attributed the Declaration with at least 'soft' legal effect at that time.[14]

Ultimately, however, we will have to wait for and observe the further development of the relevant jurisdiction of the *Bundesverfassungsgericht*.[13a]

4. Conclusion

Hence, I can sum up the first part of my intervention with the interim result that the Charter of Fundamental Rights of the European Union has, at least at the present time, had no direct legal effect on the jurisprudence of the *Bundesverfassungsgericht*.

III. GENERAL ACCEPTANCE OF THE CHARTER IN GERMANY

However, the set of questions of this conference has a wider scope, of course. The topic of my intervention evidently includes the broader aspects of the Charter's acceptance in Germany. Hence, I will try to exemplify the extent to which the Charter meets German expectations, especially those of the *Bundesverfassungsgericht* in terms of the general protection of human rights in the EU.

---

[13] See C Grabenwarter, 'Die Charta der Grundrechte für die Europäische Union', *DVBL* 2001, p 1 at p 11.

[13a] In the meantime the *Bundesverfassungsgericht* has mentioned the Charter of Fundamental Rights of the EU twice in its jurisdiction. In an order of 30 April 2003, concerning a mere national matter, it referred to Art 47 para 2 of the Charter to underline the importance of the right to be heard as a principle of judicial procedure under the rule of law (BVerfG 1 PBvU 1/02, para 38 *et seq.*). In an order of 22 November 2001 the *Bundesverfassungsgericht* refused to request the European Court of Justice to give a preliminary ruling because it found the European Union Law not applicable. It underlined its view that the Member States are only bound by EU law when implementing it by referring to Art 51 of the Charter (BVerfG 2 BvB 1/01, para 19).

[14] BVerfGE 73, 339 at 383 *et seq.*

1.   Political Acceptance

In the political sphere the Charter has wide support in Germany. This is impressively shown by the unanimous backing and appreciation of the Charter by the German *Bundestag*.[15] Beforehand, at the European Council meeting in Cologne, the German Minister of justice, Herta Däubler-Gmelin, had strongly supported the idea of drafting a Charter of Fundamental Rights of the European Union.[16] The Convent's president, the former German president and former president of the *Bundesverfassungsgericht*, Roman Herzog, may also have facilitated the wide acceptance of the Charter in Germany.

2.   Legal Acceptance

At first glance, the Charter is also accepted in principle in the legal sphere in Germany. The more so since the absence of a written catalogue of human rights at Community level has for a long time resulted in considerable distrust in Germany as to the standard of protection of human rights at Community level.[17]

The Charter follows the *Bundesverfassungsgericht*'s line that any public power has to be limited by fundamental rights. This means that judicial review in the field of human rights' protection must necessarily be available in the context of the new form of public power, the power of the Community.[18]

In this context, the *Bundesverfassungsgericht* has—as you will know— already in its *Solange I* decision of 1974[19] argued for a catalogue of fundamental rights at Community level. Strictly speaking, the tenor of the decision is limited to the extent of the *Bundesverfassungsgericht*'s right of judicial review in matters of human rights' protection—being, according to the decision, a right of additional judicial review of Community acts provided there is no catalogue of fundamental rights at Community level, passed by the European Parliament and comparable to the German Basic Law. However, this decision can be interpreted in the way that a Charter of fundamental rights is in principle welcomed from the perspective of German constitutional law.[20]

---

[15] This happened during a debate on the Charter in the Bundestag on 20 October 2000. All parliamentary parties welcomed the Charter in principle.

[16] See H Däubler-Gmelin, 'Eine europäische Charta der Grundrechte', *EuZW* 2000, p 1; H Däubler-Gmelin, Vom Marktbürger zum EU-Bürger, *FAZ*, 10 January 2000, p 11.

[17] J Schwarze, 'The birth of a European constitutional order – Résumé', in J Schwarze (ed), *The birth of a European constitutional order*, (Baden-Baden/London, 2001), p 533.

[18] J Limbach, 'Die Kooperation der Gerichte in der zukünftigen europäischen Grundrechtsarchitektur', *EuGRZ* 2000, p 417 at p 419; R Herzog, Interview in *Spiegel* 25 / 2000, p 42 at p 42.

[19] BVerfGE 37, 271.

[20] See also J Limbach, 'Die Kooperation der Gerichte in der zukünftigen europäischen Grundrechtsarchitektur', *EuGRZ* 2000, p 417 at p 417.

Incidentally, shortly after the *Bundesverfassungsgericht*'s *Solange I* decision, there were initial calls for a European catalogue of fundamental rights in the political arena.

The European Court of Justice has faced the challenge of the *Solange I* decision and has also criticised the existing standard of human right's protection in EC law. It has developed and extended the standard of human right's protection in EC law in a multitude of decisions.[21] This jurisdiction is, as you know, based on the common constitutional principles of the Member States and on the ECHR. This line of orientation has been acknowledged by the wording of the current Article 6, paragraph 2 EU.

Twelve years later, in its *Solange II* decision of 1986[22], the *Bundesverfassungsgericht* took into account the considerable progress concerning human rights' protection at Community level, and declared that it would no longer exercise its formal right of additional judicial review over Community acts as long as the established general standard of human rights' protection was maintained in the European Communities. The Court thus gave up its earlier position as it had been laid down in the *Solange I* decision of 1974.[23]

Another 7 years later one could observe a certain renunciation or at least a remarkable modification in emphasis of the *Solange II* jurisdiction. In its rather well-known *Maastricht* decision[24] the *Bundesverfassungsgericht* reserved its right of judicial review not only insofar as it claimed to be in a position to judge whether a Community act would remain within the limits of the Community's competences or be *ultra vires* but also in the area of human rights' protection: whereas the European Court of Justice was said to be responsible for the exercise of judicial control in actual cases, the *Bundesverfassungsgericht* expressly conferred upon itself the right of control as far as the general standard of human rights' protection in the Community is concerned. Thus, it has defined the relationship between itself and the European Court of Justice as one of 'cooperation'.[25]

These conclusions have been at the centre of a heated debate not only in German legal circles,[26] and the exact relationship between Community law and German constitutional law has been unclear for a while. However,

---

[21] As actual guarantees of fundamental rights as well as unwritten general principles of administrative law. For further details see J Schwarze, *European Administrative Law* (Baden-Baden/London, 1992).
[22] BVerfGE 73, 339.
[23] BVerfGE 37, 271.
[24] BVerfGE 89, 155 at 188.
[25] BVerfGE 89,155 at 175; BVerfGE 73, 339 at 387.
[26] See U Everling, 'Bundesverfassungsgericht und Gerichtshof der Europäischen Gemeinschaften nach dem Maastricht-Urteil', in Randelzhofer, Scholz and Wilke (eds), *Gedächtnisschrift für Eberhard Grabitz*, (München, 1995) p 57; J A Frowein, 'Das Maastricht-Urteil und die Grenzen der Verfassungsgerichtsbarkeit', *ZaöRV*, 54 (1994), p 1; C Tomuschat, 'Die Europäische Union unter Aufsicht des Bundesverfassungsgerichtes', *EuGRZ* 1993, p 489.

it would seem now that the *Bundesverfassungsgericht* and the European Court of Justice are gradually coming together in a way that may illustrate what the *Bundesverfassungsgericht* meant by 'cooperation'.[27] Or, to quote Günter Hirsch, the former judge of the European Court of Justice and now President of the German *Bundesgerichtshof*, the highest court in matters of civil and criminal law:

> I am convinced that the two courts are not in a dangerous collision course like two huge tankers, but that they—with the full knowledge of and with respect for their respective constitutional structures—will exercise their jurisdiction in a constructive way in their respective areas of competence.[28]

The first example of this development is the *Alcan* decision[29] of the *Bundesverfassungsgericht* of 17 February 2000 where the court had to consider an action for infringement of the German Constitution brought by a company against the decision of the highest administrative Court in Germany (*Bundesverwaltungsgericht*) declaring that the company had to pay back state aids which infringed Community law.[30] In the administrative proceedings, the company had argued that the demand for the return of the money violated the principle of legitimate expectation as guaranteed by the German statute governing the return of unlawful state aids and that under the same statute, the time limit for the demand had expired. Therefore, the act of demanding the return of the money should be declared void. The *Bundesverwaltungsgericht* asked for a preliminary ruling from the European Court of Justice[31] and finally dismissed the action for annulment in accordance with the answers given by the European Court of Justice.[32]

The *Bundesverfassungsgericht* upheld the decision of the administrative court confirming that Community law overruled German law at least below constitutional level. Moreover, it declared that the decision challenged by the European Court of Justice could unquestionably not be considered *ultra vires*.

---

[27] See J Limbach, 'Die Kooperation der Gerichte in der zukünftigen europäischen Grundrechtsarchitektur', *EuGRZ* 2000, p 417 at p 419; G Nicolaysen and C Nowak, 'Teilrückzug des BVerfG aus der Kontrolle der Rechtmäßigkeit gemeinschaflicher Rechtsakte: Neuere Entwicklungen und Perspektiven', *NJW* 2001, p 1233.

[28] G Hirsch, 'Gemeinschaftsgrundrechte: Rechtsprechung des EuGH, Verhältnis zum Grundgesetz, EU-Charta', in Vertretung der Europäischen Kommission in der Bundesrepublik Deutschland (ed), *Europäische Gespräche*, Heft 2/1999, *Eine europäische Charta der Grundrechte, Beitrag zur gemeinsamen Identität*, (Berlin, 1999), p 43 at p 48.

[29] BVerfG, 2 BvR 1210/98 of 17 February 2000, *EuZW* 2000, p 445.

[30] BVerwGE 106, 328.

[31] Case C–24/95 *Land Rheinland-Pfalz/Alcan Deutschland* [1997] ECR I–1591.

[32] For more details on the question of the extent to which national constitutional law has been influence by EC law see J Schwarze, 'Synoptic evaluation of the national reports and comparative legal prospects', in J Schwarze (ed), *Administrative Law under European Influence* (Baden-Baden/London, 1996).

Without expressly renouncing its right to control Community acts touching on German fundamental principles, the Court has thus effectively shown its willingness to accept the supremacy of EC law over national law below constitutional level. It has made clear that the doctrine of supremacy of EC law does not infringe the German constitution even where it overrules statute law incorporating important fundamental principles such as the protection of legitimate expectation. Thus, the Court has taken a cautious approach towards the exercise of its self-imputed right of control.

The *Bundesverfassungsgericht* has continued this line in its decision of 7 June 2000 on the organisation of the market for bananas.[33] This decision—which, it might be interesting to note, was a unanimous decision of the Court—shows that neither the European Court of Justice nor the *Bundesverfassungsgericht* have slipped on bananas up to now.[34] This decision is of far-reaching importance in the area of additional or subsidiary judicial review of Community acts by the *Bundesverfassungsgericht*.

In this case, the *Bundesverfassungsgericht* rejected as inadmissible a request for a preliminary ruling as to the constitutionality of the regulation of the market for bananas by the administrative tribunal of Frankfurt. The *Bundesverfassungsgericht* held that a complaint or review procedure, which claims the contradiction of secondary Community law with fundamental rights as protected by the German Basic Law, has to show by way of detailed reasoning that the necessary standard of human rights' protection at Community level has generally declined since the *Solange II* decision of the *Bundesverfassungsgericht*.

Meanwhile, the new Article 23, paragraph 1, section 1 of the German Basic Law, governing the delegation of competences to the EU, expressly states that the protection of fundamental rights at Community level only has to be 'comparable in principle'. Hence, there has to be a correspondence of the level of human rights' protection in EC law and German constitutional law only in principle terms. The *Bundesverfassungsgericht* has clarified and emphasised this relation once again with its 'bananas' decision.[35] According to the provisions of the German Basic Law, the standard of human rights' protection in EC law may, to a certain extent, fall short of the national level.[36]

If we assume that there will be no intention on the part of the European Court of Justice to decrease or weaken the general standard of human rights' protection in the future, the bananas judgment of the *Bundesverfassungsgericht* of June 2000 has established such high barriers

---

[33] BVerfG, 2 BvL 1/97 of 7 June 2000, *NJW* 2000, pp 3124 *et seq.*
[34] U Everling, Will Europe slip on Bananas? The Bananas Judgement of the Court of Justice and national Courts, (1996) 33 *Common Market Law Review*, p 401.
[35] *NJW* 2000, p 3124 at p 3125; J Limbach, 'Die Kooperation der Gerichte in der zukünftigen europäischen Grundrechtsarchitektur', *EuGRZ* 2000, p 417 at p 420.
[36] R Scholz in Maunz/Dürig, *GG-Kommentar*, (München, 1994), Art 23, n 61.

for further judicial review of Community acts by means of national constitutional law as will rarely be overcome.

Although the bananas decision claims that only a 'misunderstanding'[37] of the *Maastricht* judgment could have led the referring administrative tribunal in Frankfurt to the assumption that the *Bundesverfassungsgericht* would actually exercise its jurisdiction, the judgment really deviates from the more demanding and critical *Maastricht* line and turns back to the *Solange II* judgment of 1986. This judgment had been regarded as a definitely Community-minded synthesis and conciliation of the demands of Community law and the requirements of national constitutional law.

The third decision of the *Bundesverfassungsgericht* which I refer to continues this line. In a decision of 9 January 2001[38] the Constitutional Court rendered void a decision of the *Bundesverwaltungsgericht*—so far known as being definitely Community minded—for not having requested a preliminary ruling of the European Court of Justice.

The case dealt with the equal treatment of men and women in professional life. A woman working part-time as a physician requested, in the course of her medical education, the acknowledgement of the title 'practical physician' although a European directive provides that full-time employment is a condition of this part of the training. The plaintiff regarded this provision as indirect sexual discrimination.

The *Bundesverfassungsgericht* ruled that the *Bundesverwaltungsgericht* was at fault not to request a preliminary ruling from the European Court of Justice as to whether the condition in this directive was compatible with fundamental rights granted by Community Law.

Furthermore, the *Bundesverfassungsgericht* expressly followed the new line of the bananas judgment. It confirmed that in these cases the protection of fundamental rights—here the equal treatment of men and women—has to be sought in the first place at Community level. It also affirmed its favourable position towards Community Law, that further judicial review by the *Bundesverfassungsgericht* in the form of constitutional complaints or preliminary reviews is only admissible if it could be established by detailed reasoning that the general standard of human rights' protection in the European Community had declined below the level of 1986, the year of the *Solange II* decision.

Therefore, the guarantees of fundamental rights in the jurisdiction of the European Court of Justice are the basis for the *Bundesverfassungsgericht*'s assumption of an effective protection of fundamental rights against the Community's public power. It has 'insofar relinquished its additional right to control' according to the explicit wording of the *Bundesverfassungsgericht* in this case.[39]

---

[37] BVerfG, 2 BvL 1/97 of 7 June 2000, 64; *NJW* 2000, p 3124 at p 3125.
[38] BVerfG, 1 BvR 1036/99 of 9 January 2001, 1, *NJW* 2001, p 1267.
[39] BVerfG, 1 BvR 1036/99 of 9 January 2001, 23, *NJW* 2001, p 1267 at p 1268.

This latest decision also shows that the *Bundesverfassungsgericht* is ready to criticise national courts of last instance in its jurisdiction for a lack of willingness to request preliminary rulings of the European Court of Justice. This time the criticism was aimed at the so far definitely Community minded *Bundesverwaltungsgericht* but this jurisdiction clearly shows how the relationship of 'cooperation' may look according to the *Bundesverfassungsgericht*.

Let me make one more remark in this context. This jurisdiction of the *Bundesverfassungsgericht* mentions the principle that problems occurring due to the intertwining of national and European law should be solved by using the instruments of the Treaties provided for such cases, in particular the procedure of seeking a preliminary ruling. However, this principle should also be followed by the *Bundesverfassungsgericht* itself. So far, like most of the other national constitutional courts in Europe,[40] it has not demanded a preliminary ruling of the European Court of Justice. A notable exception is the House of Lords, which has been exemplary in asking the European Courts of Justice for preliminary rulings, as shown for instance in the case *Factortame*.[41] It would undoubtedly further cooperation between national and European Courts if the *Bundesverfassungsgericht* as well as other continental European constitutional courts overcame their reluctance to make a reference for a preliminary ruling where appropriate, in particular with regard to the fact that under Article 234 paragraph 4 EC, the courts of last instance—to which constitutional courts belong—are under an obligation to initiate reference procedures in cases where the interpretation of Community law seems relevant.[42]

Nevertheless, all three quoted decisions of the *Bundesverfassungsgericht* since the *Maastricht* judgment mark decisive steps towards a true and genuine cooperation between the European Court of Justice and the *Bundesverfassungsgericht* in a field where common efforts should prevail: the protection of human rights by means of an effective system of judicial review.

The President of the *Bundesverfassungsgericht*, Jutta Limbach, has stated in a recently published scientific article that she personally appreciats the Charter and has emphasised that the *Bundesverfassungsgericht* would surely be the last to oppose the further development of the standard of human right's protection.[43] Such endeavour concurred with the

---

[40] With the recent exception of the Austrian Constitutional Court (österreichischer Verfassungsgerichtshof) in the *Adria Pipelines* case (Case C–143/99 *Adria Pipelines v Finanzlandesdirektion für Kärnten* [2001] ECR I–8365) and the regional Hessian State Court (Staatsgerichtshof des Landes Hessen) in the *Badeck* case (Case C–158/97, *Georg Badeck et al* [2000] ECR I–1875).

[41] Case C–48/93, *Factortame* [1996] ECR I–1029.

[42] See J Schwarze, 'The birth of a European constitutional order – Résumé', in J Schwarze (ed), *The birth of a European constitutional order*, (Baden-Baden/London, 2001), pp 538 *et seq.*

[43] See J Limbach, 'Die Kooperation der Gerichte in der zukünftigen europäischen Grundrechtsarchitektur', *EuGRZ* 2000, p 417 at p 420.

Bundesverfassungsgericht's principle that the supremacy of EC law over national law is dependent on the standard of human right's protection in Community law.[44]

However the legal implementation of the Charter will appear in the future, it already proclaims the limitations of the exercise of public powers by the Community in accordance with the *Bundesverfassungsgericht*'s opinion.[45]

3. Criticism Concerning the Charter

In spite of the wide political and legal approval of the Charter in Germany, there is a debate amongst constitutional lawyers about the deeper sense of such a Charter. A point of criticism often raised is the fact that the EU is no state or state-like unit, from which the citizens need to be protected by fundamental rights.[46] Moreover, the Charter's genesis has been criticised occasionally because of the absence of a public debate and because of the absence of a European public opinion in general.[47] Because of its nature as a mere declaration of intent some critics find the Charter to be of no real additional value or substantial gain as it does not extend the standard of human rights' protection but may lead to further problems in limiting and delineating competences.

This criticism has in turn provoked prominent foreign legal experts to ask—as was the case at a colloquium in Freiburg—how the German attitude is to be understood: on the one hand, it was in Germany where the demand for a charter of fundamental rights had been raised, not least under the influence of the *Bundesverfassungsgericht*, on the other hand it is in Germany where the Charter encounters criticism.

It is clear, however, that in spite of some criticism concerning the basis as well as certain particular provisions, the Charter is generally approved of in Germany.

---

[44] J Limbach, 'Die Kooperation der Gerichte in der zukünftigen europäischen Grundrechtsarchitektur', *EuGRZ* 2000, p 417 at p 420.

In this context the recent proposition of a judge at the *Bundesverfassungsgericht* Di Fabio should be mentioned. He suggested establishing alongside the European Court of Justice a common European constitutional court, consisting of judges from the national constitutional courts of the Member States. This way the balance between Member States and the EU should also be symbolised in the jurisprudence. See U Di Fabio, 'Ist die Staatswerdung Europas unausweichlich?', *FAZ*, 2 February 2001, p 8 and his contribution to this book (ch 3).

[45] G Hirsch, 'Ein Bekenntnis zu den Grundwerten', *FAZ* 12 October 2000, p 11.

[46] For more details see C Dorau and P Jacobi, 'The debate over a "European Constitution": Is it Solely a German Concern?', [2000] *European Public Law*, p 413 at pp 416 *et seq*.

[47] A Schachtschneider, 'Jeder Widerspruch gegen die Charta ist angezeigt', *Zeit-Fragen* Sonderbeilage October 2000, pp 1 *et seq*.

IV. PERSONAL STATEMENT ON THE CHARTER

1. General Approval

Speaking for myself, I can envisage the Charter as a fundamental part of a future European Constitutional Treaty. With regard to the next intergovernmental conference scheduled for the year 2004, in Germany questions concerning the Charter and questions concerning a better limitation of competences between the different political levels in the Community system have been linked.

Both elements could be the nucleus for what might be called a 'Constitutional Treaty'. This term expresses two constituents: on the one hand the reflection that the EU has reached a stage in its development that demands a constitutional debate, on the other hand it mirrors the more pragmatic approach by referring to the traditional form of international consent, the treaty.[47a]

This idea has recently been expressed by the German *Bundespräsident* Johannes Rau in a speech before the European Parliament on 4 April of this year. Rau underlined that apart from a better limitation of competences and the basic principles of the institutional order of the Community, the Charter of Fundamental Rights of the EU should be a substantial part of a future European constitution.[48]

I know that this view will at least not find unanimous approval in the UK. Some of the scepticism in this country seems very understandable to me in view of the fact that another catalogue of fundamental rights, the ECHR, has been integrated into UK law only last autumn. To me, however, a Charter of fundamental rights for the EU seems to be a better option than the adhesion of the EU to the ECHR. Such a purpose-built Charter may reflect the particular needs of the EU more accurately. The Community needs an autonomous codification of fundamental rights that, in conformity with the principles of the ECHR, corresponds to the Community's stage of integration and its requirements.[49]

From my point of view it is also sensible to strengthen the common standard of fundamental rights in a European Charter of fundamental rights.[50]

[47a] In the meantime a Draft Treaty establishing a Constitution for Europe, designed by the European Convention, has been presented to the European Council in Thessaloniki on 20 June 2003. The Charter of Fundamental Rights of the European Union forms the second part of the Draft Treaty.

[48] *FAZ*, 05 April 2001, p 8.

[49] See G Hirsch, 'Ein Bekenntnis zu den Grundwerten', *FAZ* 12 October 2000, p 11.

[50] See E Benda, 'Europa als Grundrechtsgemeinschaft', in *FS für F Schäfer*, (1980) p 12 at pp 22 *et seq*; B Beutler, '1996 - auf dem Weg zu einer europäischen Verfassung?', *Kritische Justiz* 1996, p 52 at pp 62 *et seq*, see also the opposing opinion J A Frowein, 'Die Verfassung der Europäischen Union aus der Sicht der Mitgliedstaaten', *Europarecht* 1995, p 315 at pp 326 *et seq*, preferring to revert to the ECHR; also F Cromme, 'Der Verfassungsentwurf des institutionellen Ausschusses des Europäischen Parlaments', *ZG* 1995, p 256 at p 261.

Although the standard of human rights' protection granted so far by the European Court of Justice's jurisdiction can be regarded as sufficient in practice,[51] one will have to bear in mind that a written catalogue of fundamental rights creates more transparency and predictability.

Hence, the need for legal certainty and transparency justifies, apart from its symbolic effect, therefore the Charter of Fundamental Rights of the European Union, as for instance the President of the Bundesverfassungsgericht, Jutta Limbach, has rightly emphasised in her recent Article.[52]

The Charter symbolises that the EU regards itself as a community expressly acknowledging the legal and practical value of fundamental rights. This has a legitimating effect on the whole system of the Union, which should not be underestimated.[53] In its relatively short and comprehensive text, Europe's rich heritage of values and ideals becomes apparent. In a speech at the Freiburg University the former Bundespräsident Roman Herzog stated:

> A Charter of fundamental rights is able to strengthen the emotional ties to the community of values of Europe as a liberal community that supports the building up of freedom, human rights and social justice all over the world. It will help the citizens to view the EU not only as an economic community but also as a legal community that grants rights to the individual and the opportunity to exercise them.[54]

All in all, I believe that the Charter is a good compromise. On the one hand it takes into account the constitutional traditions of the Member States, on the other hand it aims for the highest possible clarity and individual effectiveness, although it certainly needs some more precision and shape in some of its rights.[55]

---

[51] See J Schwarze, Art 220 EGV, n 17 in J Schwarze (ed), *EU-Kommentar*.

[52] J Limbach, 'Die Kooperation der Gerichte in der zukünftigen europäischen Grundrechtsarchitektur', *EuGRZ* 2000, p 417 at p 417.

[53] See the article of the German Minister of Justice H Däubler-Gmelin, 'Eine europäische Charta der Grundrechte – Beitrag zur gemeinsamen Identität', *EuZW* 2000, p 1; H Däubler-Gmelin, 'Vom Marktbürger zum EU-Bürger', *FAZ* 10 January 2000, p 11; as well as J Schwarze, 'Probleme des europäischen Grundrechtsschutzes', in *FS für A Deringer*, (1993), p 160 at p 174; U Everling, 'Weiterentwicklung des Grundrechtsschutzes durch den Europäischen Gerichtshof' in W Weidenfeld (ed), *Der Schutz der Grundrechte in der Europäischen Gemeinschaft*, (1992), p 73 at p 77.

[54] R Herzog, 'Demokratische Legitimation in Europa, in den Nationalstaaten, in den Regionen: Ansprache von Bundespräsident Roman Herzog zur Eröffnung des Symposiums an der Universität Freiburg am 28 April 1999', p 17.

[55] See also C Tomuschat, 'Manche Rechte bedürfen der Konkretisierung', *FAZ* 7 August 2000, p 13.

2. Objections to the Charter

One objection to the Charter is the fear that it will lead to a complicated situation in matters of human rights' protection, especially with regard to a splitting of courses of law. If the Charter were transformed into binding law, human rights' protection would be granted not only by the Charter itself, but also by the ECHR and national constitutional law. This could lead to problems particularly with overlapping guarantees. From a German point of view, one could imagine a 'Bermuda-Triangle' in matters of human rights' protection within the EU between Karlsruhe, Luxembourg and Strasbourg.[56]

Against this objection one might ask why we should not allow a certain competition between different systems of human rights' protection, competing for the best possible solution. In Germany, apart from the fundamental rights granted in the Basic Law at federal level, the constitutions of the *Länder* also know fundamental rights. Hence, there is already a co-existence of constitutionally granted fundamental rights and courses of law. So far, this co-existence has had no negative effects on human rights' protection in Germany. On the contrary, the citizen may gain from these different systems.[57]

In my view, it is also no ground for objection that the Charter mentions certain fundamental rights which are not actually relevant in the context of the European Community, given its still restricted competences, for example the prohibition of the death penalty (Article 2 paragraph 2). I can see no decisive argument against a European Charter of fundamental rights enriched by certain general principles and values, even if they have no actual effect under the present system of limited powers of the Community.[58]

It seems important to me, though, that prior to incorporation of the Charter into the Treaties certain rights still need to be made clearer and more distinct.[59] In particular, there are some uncertainties concerning their material content and their delimitation from the mere political goals of the Union.

This is for example the case with the protection of a worker in the event of an unjustified dismissal (Article 30) and the right to working conditions which respect the worker's health, safety and dignity (Article 31 paragraph 1). The exact scope of these provisions still needs to be clarified. It is questionable whether these articles will create subjective rights for the citizen or whether they are mere general provisions, that are to be implemented in a further

---

[56] See Chr Lenz, note to the Gibraltar-judgment, ECHR, judgment of 18 February 1999, *Denise Matthews v UK*, *EuZW* 1999, p 311 at p 312.
[57] J Limbach, 'Die Kooperation der Gerichte in der zukünftigen europäischen Grundrechtsarchitektur', *EuGRZ* 2000, p 417 at p 420.
[58] See also M Zuleeg, 'Zum Verhältnis nationaler und europäischer Grundrechte', *EuGRZ* 2000, p 511 at p 516.
[59] See also S Alber and U Widmaier, 'Die EU-Charta der Grundrechte und ihre Auswirkung auf die Rechtsprechung', 2000 *EuGRZ*, p 497, at p 500; C Tomuschat, 'Manche Rechte bedürfen der Konkretisierung', *FAZ* 7 August 2000, p 13.

lawmaking process.[60] According to the Presidency Conclusions of the Cologne summit of 1999, however, the Charter was supposed to be kept clear of mere statements about general goals and intentions.[61]

Further precise legal work is therefore needed particularly in order to clarify the modalities of application of some fundamental economic and social rights.

Professor Jochen Frowein's assessment is definitely correct that the success of a European Charter of fundamental rights should mainly be measured in terms of the precision for which the legal text of the Charter provides.[62]

In conclusion, I would like to emphasise one aspect concerning the chances for the realisation of a catalogue of human rights.

In order to lay the legal foundations for the incorporation into the Treaties, it seems fair to say that the necessary consensus between the Member States can more easily be achieved if it is guaranteed that such a catalogue of human rights cannot be used by Community institutions with a view to extending the Community's competence any further. Such a clause stating that the Charter can under no circumstances be used as the basis for an expansion of Community competences has therefore rightly been enshrined in Article 51 paragraph 2.

This clarification is also helpful with regard to the recent jurisdiction of the European Court of Justice.

The current tendency in the jurisdiction of the European Court of Justice which has most recently been expressed in the cases *Angela Maria Sirdar*,[63] concerning the armed forces in the UK, and *Tanja Kreil*,[64] concerning the armed forces in Germany, is not unproblematic in terms of delimiting the respective competences of the Community. The Court ruled that fundamental principles of Community law—such as equal treatment of men and women—also have to be respected in areas that are not part of the Community competences like the internal organisation of the national military forces.

The European Court of Justice's decision had serious repercussions in terms of national sovereignty.[65] German constitutional law, for instance, stipulated that women could only join the hospital service and the military music service of the armed forces; in the light of the prevailing

[60] C Tomuschat,'Manche Rechte bedürfen der Konkretisierung', *FAZ* 7 August 2000, p 13.
[61] Annex IV to the Presidency Conclusions of the Cologne European Council, SN 150/99.
[62] J A Frowein, 'Durchsetzung und Bindung der Grundrechte', in *Eine Charta der Grundrechte - Beitrag zur gemeinsamen Identität, Dokumentation einer Tagung in Köln am 27 April 1999*, ed by the Vertretung der Europäischen Kommission in der Bundesrepublik Deutschland, (Bonn, 1999), p 96 at pp 98 *et seq*.
[63] Case C–273/97 *Angela Maria Sirdar and The Army Board* [1999] ECR I–7403.
[64] Case C–285/98 *Tanja Kreil and Germany* [2000] ECR I–0069.
[65] In greater detail J Schwarze, 'German report', in J Schwarze (ed), *The birth of a European constitutional order* (Baden-Baden/London, 2001), pp 152 *et seq*.

traditional interpretation of Article 12 a section 1, paragraph 2 Basic Law[66] women were under no circumstances allowed to serve in the armed military service.

Most likely due to the fact that equal treatment of men and women is politically highly regarded and generally agreed upon in public opinion and as no political party seriously wanted to question this consensus, the result of the *Tanja Kreil* decision was politically welcomed on the whole in Germany.

However, in the field of constitutional law, this decision of the European Court was not unproblematic[67] and led to clarifying changes in German constitutional law—the present Article 12a paragraph 4 of the Basic Law. The Constitution now expressly states that women can under no circumstances be forced to do armed military service, which means on the contrary that nowadays, women are allowed to apply voluntarily for any kind of employment in the military forces, including the armed military forces. This corresponds with the *Tanja Kreil* decision of the European Court of Justice.

Because of this new legal situation, women have served in the armed forces of the German military since 1 January 2001.

As far as Community law in general is concerned, the concept of the European Court of Justice which has become evident in the *Tanja Kreil* case and in other similar cases, that is to apply fundamental principles of Community law in areas where there is no Community competence, leads at least in my view to problems where the Court's decisions do not contain a clear material justification and do not describe the possible limits of this doctrine. Clearly, there is a certain dilemma in so far as the jurisdiction, on the one hand, has to protect the important fundamental principles of EC law in the framework of the Community whilst, on the other hand, respecting the limits of the competence of the Community as a whole. If one does not intend to leave the process of finding solutions for such constellations of conflicting legal principles—on the one hand, the necessary protection for fundamental freedoms and human rights within Community law and, on the other hand, the due respect for the competences of the Member States in the political fields still left to them—exclusively to the jurisdiction, it might indeed be best to introduce rules into the treaties that provide for a

---

[66] Art 12 a s 4 GG states that in a case of defence women can, under certain circumstances and by law or on the basis of a law, be drafted into service in the civil hospital sector. Art 12 a s 4, para 2 GG states that 'under no circumstances' they can do 'armed service'. The question whether para 2 only applies to the scenario of conscription in a case of defence or whether it also deals voluntary service is answered by J Schwarze, 'German report', in J Schwarze (ed), *The birth of a European constitutional order* (Baden-Baden/London, 2001), pp 153 with further references.

[67] See J Schwarze, 'German Report', in J Schwarze (ed), *The birth of a European constitutional order*, (Baden-Baden/London, 2001), p 43; R *Scholz*, 'Nicht durch einen Federstrich des einfachen Gesetzgebers,' *FAZ* 24 August 2000, p 10.

clearer differentiation between the European and the Member States' level.[68]

In this respect, one could follow the idea expressed in Article 51 paragraph 2 of the Charter in a broader context and try to come to a better system of defining the competences of the Community and the Member States in the future. This could be done—from a German perspective—in particular within the framework of a so-called European Constitutional Treaty to be concluded in the future. It could have three main elements: the Charter of Fundamental Rights, a clearer division of competences of the main actors—the Community institutions and Member States, including their regions or *Länder*—and the main principles of the institutional order of the European Union.

V.   CONCLUSIONS

I would like to conclude my intervention by summing up some essential points:

1. In Germany, the Charter of Fundamental Rights of the European Union generally encounters wide acceptance.
2. It concurs with the line of the *Bundesverfassungsgericht* shown in its recent jurisdiction.
3. Overlapping competences between national constitutions (eg the Basic Law), the ECHR and the Charter are not real objections to the Charter in my view. On the contrary, competition concerning human rights' protection may produce a positive effect for the citizens.
4. Prior to an incorporation of the Charter into the Treaties certain rights still need to be made clearer and more distinct.
5. The principle stated in Article 51 paragraph 2 of the Charter, that it shall not establish any new power or task for the Community, should at present lead to reflection and possibly limiting clarifications in the future case law of the European Court of Justice.
6. The Charter is part of a constitutional process in the EU. The next step, besides the discussion of the Charter's legally binding force, should lead to better ways of delimiting the competences of the Community and the Member States.[69]

---

[68] For a recent example of the ECJ's emphasis on the importance of the distribution of competences, see case C–376/98, judgment of 5 October 2000, *EuZW* 2000, pp 694 *et seq.*
[69] See J Schwarze, 'The birth of a European constitutional order - Résumé', in J Schwarze (ed), *The birth of a European constitutional order*, (Baden-Baden/London, 2001), pp 564 *et seq.*